A HISTORY OF BOOK ILLUSTRATION
29 Points of View

Edited by
BILL KATZ

The History of the Book, No. 1

The Scarecrow Press, Inc.
Metuchen, N.J., & London
1994

British Library Cataloguing-in-Publication data available

Library of Congress Cataloging-in-Publication Data

A History of book illustration : 29 points of view / edited by Bill Katz.
     p.   cm. — (The History of the book ; no. 1)
    Includes bibliographical references.
    ISBN 0-8108-2742-5 (alk. paper)
    1. Illustration of books—History. I. Katz, William A., 1924– .
II. Series.
NC960.H56   1994
741.6′4′09—dc20   93-47581

CONTENTS

Contents

PREFACE

In this collection of scholarly articles, book illustration is traced from its first notion in cave art to the early 20th century. The purpose is to offer laypersons and students a sampling of not only the best writing in the field, but, equally important, an overview of a fascinating aspect of human endeavor.

As the bibliography indicates, there are many histories of illustration, and even specialized collections, but this, to be the best knowledge of the editor, is the only work to draw upon numerous points of view.

Contributors are distinguished art historians as well as well-known anthropologists and members of Classics and English departments. There are one or two librarians and educators. They share an involvement with the individual and the world as reflected in art and illustration. Their enthusiasm is matched only by their scholarship. The articles add up to a rewarding reading experience.

The present collection is a type of back-fill operation to support, not to replace, the histories of illustration. Major topics and periods are considered, as are several minor, yet fascinating aspects of illustration.

It is hoped that one or more of the articles will spark an interest in the reader to carry on with reading in the particular area. To this end most of the reprinted pieces boast detailed bibliographies. See, too, the bibliography at the end of this collection. All will lead to additional delights and discoveries.

FROM CAVE TO CHILD

This collection's organization is chronological, and it is divided into five distinct sections. The first covers the beginnings of illustration; the second moves from the illuminated manuscript to the advent of printing; and the third and fourth takes the reader from the earliest woodcut illustrations to the beginning of the 20th century. The final part is concerned with children's books. This is followed by an annotated bibliography.

The gathering begins with articles which, for most histories of illustration, are avoided or quickly skipped over. The reason is that cave art, much of Egyptian art and certainly traces of Greek painting are rarely connected by general histories to the development of book illustration. This art should be, particularly as it covers over 3,000 years, and, if only by implication, as many potential years of illustration.

In general surveys, as for example the otherwise basic *A History of Book Illustration* (David Bland), the beginnings of illustration in Egypt and Greece are dismissed in less than ten pages. In this collection there are five detailed articles on these periods, with particular focus on what Nicholas Horsfall calls, ''The origins of the illustrated book.'' Here, more than in other sections, an effort is made to show the relationship of illustration to art, e.g. Margaret Conkey's ''A Century of Palaeolithic Cave Art,'' and Sarah Morris's ''A Tale of Two Cities: The Miniature Frescoes from Thera and the Origins of Greek Poetry.''

For those who might question the place of papers on cave and Egyptian art in a history of book illustration, turn to the Morris article where, if only by deduction on the part of the reader, one may see the possible forms of illustrations of the Homeric epic poems in now lost rolls. It is only these and fragments of other wall paintings that hint at the possible glory of the Greek illustrated book. The pros and cons of whether such illustration existed are still being argued in scholarly papers. Morris's article is a good example, too, of the glories of iconography and how one discipline draws upon and strengthens others. Also, but not least, the article makes fascinating reading.

While early artists were not involved directly with illustrating the yet to be realized book, it is the beginning of that close relationship between artist and the intellectual concept. The wedding itself takes place in Egypt and possibly Mesopotamia; and later probably in Greek literature. The interdependence of art and illustration is such that even without examples of Greek illustrated rolls, we can assume that they existed from extant bits of painting and the black and red figure vases.

Moving to the by now well-documented and explored area of the illuminated manuscript, the second section is a reflection of illustration grounded in Greece, Egypt and Rome. Beginning with the Lindisfarne Gospels and ending with an imaginative discussion of northern European contributions, this part touches on major points of interest to anyone who has an appreciation of the contribution of the illustrator/artist before printing. Here the problem, unlike the opening section, is not finding material suitable for consideration, but discovering the most representative and the best in a well-researched, ever-developing area.

The late Philip Hofer opens the third part with an excellent overview of illustration after the advent of printing and before the industrial revolution. The variations in types and scope of illustrations for the critical period are highlighted in the other pieces which examine the finer points of scientific and literary illustration, culminating with Diderot's *Encyclopédie*.

William Blake is the single great genius who foresaw the meaning of the Industrial Revolution and, suitably enough, was born in the century of Diderot and died as the 19th century began to take its shape. Then comes the greatest age of all for popular illustration and illustrators, from Thackeray and Dickens to Rossetti and Du Maurier. As in the case of illuminated manuscripts, this period in illustration is covered in great depth. Here only an indication of what can be found in the riches of illustration history is given.

The three final pieces in this section indicate other possibilities, from the imaginative discussion of graphics to the unique contributions of Americans who took pride in leading multiple professional lives. Finally, a footnote on the private press which introduced the world to the 20th century and, paradoxically, both the birth and the death of illustration—the birth of the artist book and the death of popular illustration of novels, to be replaced by magazine illustrators.

Although there are articles that reflect the modern artist's involvement with illustration, this aspect was purposefully avoided because it is well covered elsewhere; see the bibliography, for example.

Today, as for most of the 20th century, the real home of illustrators is in children's tales. The history of children's illustration is a thing apart, and here only an indication is given of possibilities. At the same time, the final part is required because all too often scholars seem to dismiss, forget or simply overlook the role of the children's illustrator in the history of the subject.

Given the nature of the book's organization and the types of articles, this collection may be read in almost any order, and the reader may skip from the first or second article to the last without any loss of continuity. At the same time, the articles are arranged in such a way that the beginner, the student, may, with the help of a more general history, follow the pieces consecutively. That student will end with a suggestion of what true scholarship and research means in a field which draws upon, and at the same time contributes so much to, our understanding of the world and both the nature of people and the place of the individual.

SELECTION PRINCIPLES

Selection first and foremost has been made to meet a need, the need for detailed coverage of an area, point or idea that is not covered generally in the basic histories of illustration. And even where coverage is impressive, as for example in the case of the medieval illuminated manuscript, the particular articles selected represent a new point of view, an original idea based on equally original reflection and research.

Other factors that determine a place in this collection include: (1) An impression by the editor that the article is as readable as it is pleasing in style; (2) And, a difficult, but necessary choice—the articles must be in English; (3) The author should afford a new insight into the subject and/or offer an overview which is not found in general works; (4) Finally, the material should be relatively current, although here and there articles of an earlier period are included because of their basic interest and relationship to the goals of this book.

The annotated bibliography follows the collected articles. This is both descriptive and evaluative and is an effort to point out the better books available for the non-specialist.

A word about the illustrations. Both the necessary limitations on cost and availability dictate black and white reproductions of what appeared in the original articles. These, one must admit, are not always as bright as the original, but at least they do satisfy the primary requirement of supporting the authors' arguments and points.

The editor wishes to acknowledge and thank the numerous teachers of the history of the book for their assistance in making suggestions as to need. Thanks to the authors and publishers of the articles who so generously gave permission to reprint their works and to the various institutions that permitted the reprinting of illustrations. And none of this would have been possible without the thorough attention to detail given by my able student assistant, Christa Burns.

BK

PART I

FROM THE CAVES TO THE GREEKS

A CENTURY OF PALAEOLITHIC CAVE ART
Margaret W. Conkey

Just over a century ago, in 1879, a small girl whose father had taken an interest in a cave on the north coast of Spain made a spectacular discovery: the ceiling of the cave was covered with vivid polychrome paintings of bison and other animals. The little girl obviously had a better perspective than her father, Marcelino Sanz de Sautuola; he had overlooked the ceiling, even though he had explored the cave and had already carried out preliminary excavations in its vestibule. These were the first Palaeolithic cave paintings to be recognized for what they were—many millennia after they had been drawn. Almost 200 painted caves have been discovered since Altamira, but its decorated ceiling remains among the most magnificent examples of cave art. Although the cave of Altamira is closed to the public and the paintings are threatened by deterioration, the room which contains them still deserves to be called the "Sistine Chapel" of prehistoric art.

The field of prehistory was young in 1879 but Sautuola appreciated what these paintings might be. He could not anticipate, however, that it would take the scholarly world so long to accept the age of these works. The fact that they were the products of peoples who had lived during the late Ice Age some 15,000 years ago was a conclusion neither easy to reach nor accept. In 1879 only 20 years had passed since the publication of Darwin's *Origin of Species,* and another 20 would pass before sufficient evidence was gathered to confirm the Ice Age antiquity of this cave art.

Now, a hundred years later, the study of Palaeolithic art is still a challenging and exciting field. Ironically, however, this century of scholarship remains less well known than the tales of discovery about the great caves like Altamira and Lascaux, discovered in

Reprinted with the permission of *Archaeology* Magazine, Vol. 34, no. 4 (Copyright the Archaeological Institute of America, 1981).

The famous cave of Altamira lies somewhat to the east of the Cantabrian coast of northern Spain, a region known for its abundant Upper Palaeolithic sites.

Montignac in the Dordogne region of France in 1940. With both of these magnificent painted sanctuaries now closed to the public because of the rapidly deteriorating condition of the paintings, it is timely that a century of inquiry and research be reviewed. Just as it still ranks among the most magnificent of the Palaeolithic painted sites, Altamira's artforms provide excellent examples for a review of Palaeolithic art studies up to the present.

The past century can be divided into three broad periods of study and research. The dates for each period are somewhat arbitrary, but they can nonetheless serve as convenient markers. The first period lasted from 1879–1902; the second from 1902–1960; the third from 1960 until the present. The first was a period of intellectual ferment and exploration, and it encompassed the pioneering discovery of many caves and the first formulation of hypotheses concerning the antiquity and meaning of cave art. In 1902, the French prehistorian Emile Cartailhac published his landmark document "Confessions of a Skeptic," in which he admitted that he had finally been convinced of the Ice Age antiquity of the paintings at Altamira and other newly-found sites such as Font de Gaume in southwestern France. A number of factors contributed to the triumph of an early date for these paintings. One was the geological antiquity of the painted wall surfaces—which were sometimes covered over and sealed with ancient layers of calcite. Another was the identification of regionally long-extinct species such as reindeer and wooly mammoth as the subject of much of the cave art. Yet another factor was the stylistic affinities between some wall art and decorated portable artforms that were often found in dateable archaeological contexts. The portable artforms had been known since before the discovery of cave paintings and included objects of bone and antler incised with geometric or animal designs. A final factor was the occasional painted wall found covered by archaeological deposits of considerable antiquity—deposits that had been laid down after the wall was decorated and even obscured the artworks, such as at Cap Blanc (Dordogne, France) where a covered over bas-relief frieze of nearly life-sized horses was partially destroyed by the unwitting excavators.

Even today questions remain about the authenticity of certain prehistoric caves and portable artforms, and an adequate way of

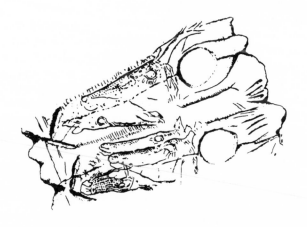

A perforated antler from El Pendo in Spain. Length, about 17 centimeters.

dating the paintings that does not depend on relative stylistic and geological grounds remains to be found. But there is no longer any doubt that most of the cave paintings were the work of *Homo sapiens* during the Upper Palaeolithic (ca. 35,000–10,000 years ago), nor that these peoples were capable of considerable cognitive, cultural and artistic achievements.

Once Cartailhac had published his "Confessions," the way was cleared for the second and longest period in the century-long study of Palaeolithic art. The usual tasks of a new field of study characterize this second phase; it was one of further exploration, discovery, ordering, and classifying which have long been the primary methods and goals of prehistorians. Caves and rock shelters were carefully explored as scholars searched for new paintings and engravings, which were even more difficult to observe than the paintings. In the days before flashlights and cameras with flash attachments, most exploration was conducted by torchlight and documentation took the form of drawings and paintings.

The greatest pioneer in documentation was also responsible for the single most influential chronology of cave art until 1965. He was the Abbé Henri Breuil, a French priest who devoted his time and skills to making a series of magnificent line and chalk drawings of the paintings in many caves, among them Altamira. Much of the succeeding interpretive work would be largely based on secondary observations and these drawings. When the Abbé's chronology of Palaeolithic art was finally published in its entirety in 1952 in *Four Hundred Centuries of Cave Art,* it was a milestone that had been adopted by most scholars. Although based on assumptions about how art ought to evolve, primitive art and magic, and lifeways of hunter-gatherers, a number of serious questions have since been raised about these assumptions and the Abbé's conclusions. He argued for two cycles of artistic production, each consisting of a development from simple to complex forms defined by the use of color, perspective and line technique. The first cycle began with negative hand-prints, simple one-color outlines, and animals presented in a twisted perspective with the head facing forward from a body done in side view. The second of these cycles was said to culminate in the most complex wall art of the Palaeolithic period—the polychrome paintings of the later Magdalenian period (ca. 13,000–10,000 B.P.), which were often enhanced by engraving or sculpting.

According to Breuil's scheme, the Altamira ceiling would have been the product of later Magdalenian artists, although it is now known that the roof over the cave entrance probably collapsed about this time, effectively sealing the entrance to no more than a crevice. The archaeological deposits, however, found in the vestibule area adjacent to the "Great Hall of Paintings" were attributed to the Solutrean period (ca. 19,000–17,000 B.P.) and the Early Magdalenian period (ca. 16,500–14,000 B.P.), based first on excavations carried out in 1904 and confirmed in 1924–25. Altamira has not been excavated since then and despite some changes in our understanding of the various Upper Palaeolithic toolmaking traditions that serve as the basis for identifying certain periods, it is still generally accepted that the archaeological remains derive from at least these two archaeological levels—the Solutrean and Early Magdalenian.

Despite this, however, the relationship between the painted ceiling, the many other less well-known paintings in the cave, and the archaeological deposits is still far from clear. In this respect, the state of affairs at Altamira is representative of the field of Palaeolithic art study: it has always been an easier and more straightforward task to chart the spatial distributions of the art and to describe the variations than to establish a chronology or temporal framework within which the artworks could be ordered. Because we lack secure means for dating most wall art, the chronology of Palaeolithic art remains incomplete even today. By attributing the paintings to the later Magdalenian, although the evidence for human occupation dates to earlier periods, Breuil reinforced a prevalent interpretation. According to this view, most paintings were thought to be situated in sacred locales—in areas of the caves that were not normally inhabited— and perhaps visited only by certain persons for ritual or religious purposes.

The "sacred cave" interpretation was further strengthened by the fact that many painted walls bore superimposed layers of paintings, while other seemingly suitable wall surfaces remained undecorated. Since Breuil saw no order or patterning among the many depictions on a wall, only the "sanctity" of the locale could explain the accumulated depictions. Drawing direct analogies from prevalent early twentieth-century enthnographic interpretations, he argued that the motives underlying the production of cave art were rooted in the life of the hunter. Anxiety over the search for food, the dynamism of the chase, and the confrontation between hunter and prey—only these factors could account for artforms so forceful and vital to modern observers and so naturalistic. It was an art that was central to sympathetic magic— magic that would ensure the fertility of the prey and the success of the hunter. The dynamic portrayals of bison on the Altamira ceiling were to be seen from the hunter's perspective as dying or charging bulls.

The hunting way of life, then, "explained" both the origins of the cave art—the early hand outlines were imitations of animal footprints, for example—and its demise. The retreat of the glaciers and the once-abundant herbivores could account for the disappearance of big-game hunting and the subsequent abandonment of the cave painting tradition. Even the "signs" or geometric, non-naturalistic depictions conformed to the hunting-magic hypothesis. Tectiforms, for example, represented traps; certain signs on animals could be interpreted as wounds.

The theory that cave art functioned as hunting magic and Breuil's two-cycle stylistic chronology dominated the literature well into the second half of this century. Throughout this period, moreover, the study of wall art predominated to such an extent that the exact relationship between wall art and portable art forms was never explicitly pursued despite the more reliable stratigraphic proveniences of much portable art. The two media were finally comprehensively considered together in the book by the Italian prehistorian Paolo Graziosi, *Paleolithic Art,* first published in 1956, although even this work clearly remained within the interpretative framework set forth by Breuil. But by 1960, exciting new currents of thought were in the air that were destined to have dramatic effects on the entire study of Palaeolithic art.

Three major trends since the 1960's have contributed to the challenge of Breuil's monolithic interpretations. The rise of structuralism; a revitalization of the anthropological study of primitive art and symbolic behaviors; and the reinterpretation of hunter-gatherer lifeways have all broadened the perspectives on Palaeolithic art. The resulting scholarship has stimulated inquiry into the *contexts* in which Palaeolithic art appears, and it has

An incised antler point from the Upper Magdalenian level of La Paloma in Asturias, Spain. Length, 9 centimeters.

broadened the current understanding of the complex relationship between wall art and portable art forms.

The most significant researcher who initiated the contemporary period of study has been André Leroi-Gourhan, a French prehistorian. His major work, *Treasures of Prehistoric Art,* was published in 1965. This volume, some earlier articles and the independent but related work of a French colleague, Annette Laming-Emperaire, were the first serious challenges to Breuil's interpretations. Leroi-Gourhan was also the first to propose a serious alternative chronology to that of Breuil, although to do so was not the primary goal of his book. And although this stylistically-based chronology has practically replaced Breuil's, Leroi-Gourhan's work is most significant because he proposes that the depictions are not random; they are part of a system of meanings. He argues that Palaeolithic art was part of an expression of a world-view, a cosmology, or a system of thought that organized the central elements of Upper Palaeolithic life. To Leroi-Gourhan, this system was based on the division of the world into male and female components, and accordingly, certain parts of the caves as well as certain groups or kinds of animals and signs assumed a masculine or feminine identity. The way depictions were arranged on a panel and where they were placed in a cave and in relation to each other, all derived from—and could be accounted for—by this organizational structure.

By counting how frequently certain subjects recurred and by seeing how subjects tend to cluster in various locales, Leroi-Gourhan also repudiated the long-held notion that most cave art appeared in the deep, dark inaccessible reaches of presumably sacred caves. Instead, certain themes and types of art tend to be in rock shelters or daylit locales, such as many depictions of females. Among the portable art, some themes or depictions were significantly correlated with certain artifact forms or types: the horse is a most usual figure in *art mobilier,* except on harpoons and half-rounded rods, whereas the bison do not occur on spears, are unusual on pierced staffs, but predominate on plaques. Additionally, the frequency of certain animal depictions often contrasted sharply with the availability of those animals as well as how often they are found among excavated food debris. One conclusion, also suggested by Patricia Vinnicombe's *People of the Eland,* an elegant study of the rock art of the !Kung of South Africa, might be the same as Lévi-Strauss' observation that certain natural species were selected—in these cases as the subject of rock art—not because they were ''good to eat'' but because they were ''good to think.''

Leroi-Gourhan's attention to context and the associations which exist among various artforms has brought into focus new facets of Palaeolithic art. Although the exact relationship between wall art and portable art has not yet been established, it is at least now possible to quantify what may be significant differences in subject matter and context. Bison, for example, tend to dominate on cave walls in Cantabrian Spain, including Altamira. But they are rarely depicted on portable art objects. Differences in distribution may occur even within the same site as they do at Altamira, where deer and not bison are often carved on scapulae or other bone or antler objects. For many reasons, this contextual approach to Palaeolithic art reinforces the belief that the social audiences as well as the uses of wall art may have been different from those of portable art.

Since Leroi-Gourhan, others have pursued the idea that there are systems of meaning that underlie Palaeolithic art. Alexander Marshack, a former science journalist, has carried out meticulous microphotographic studies of Palaeolithic art that have drawn attention to the fact that many of the visual forms are seasonally and ecologically related. One of Marshack's most striking inter-

pretations has been that certain artforms may have functioned as calendars, and that the multiple markings on many incised bones and antlers were notational in intent. Marshack has suggested how ecological information may have been encoded—how, for example, certain distinctive features of a season, like a plant in bud, or a part of a salmon, were selected for depiction.

In general, scholars have recently come to appreciate how many human groups employ ritual and art in synchrony with relevant and important ecological and seasonal changes. It should not be surprising that the successful hunter-gatherers of the last glacial period were ecologically sophisticated, nor that they were creating and manipulating visual forms to structure and give meaning to their existence. Ethnographic studies have shown how structuring principles, including different types of symmetry, may underlie the designs of many primitive artforms and characterize other aspects of daily life from social relations to village planning. Thus, there may be a redundancy or resonance of these principles in many domains of life that provides a structural congruence or coherence.

Redundancy and ambiguity are often characteristic of visual forms created in non- or preliterate societies. Ambiguity allows a great deal of potential information to be stored in very few symbols; often, it is the particular *context* in which the symbols are used that may determine their relevant meanings. In such cases, objects and artforms constitute the social process and are not merely reflective of it. In Palaeolithic art there are, for example, certain artforms that may be viewed as ambiguous, particularly those that are human or animal, depending upon how one looks at them. Some depictions have attributes of several animals and humans—a ''sorcerer'' with deer antlers, bison hooves, and a human penis. Since it is plausible to suppose that for Upper Palaeolithic peoples, continuities existed between human and animal life, and social world, such ambiguous depictions— which are so common in most cultures—may not represent a human or an animal exclusively, but indicate these continuities.

If one is willing to accept that continuities may have provided a potential source of meaning—a belief that also underlies Leroi-Gourhan's male-female system—a purely speculative but plausible reinterpretation of the Altamira ceiling can be put forth. It is with this painted ceiling, if any, that one could challenge Breuil's longstanding assumption that Palaeolithic depictions were random in nature. The Altamira ceiling may well be the closest thing to an arranged composition that has yet been identified. Here is a core group of dynamic polychrome bison, many of which are three-dimensional because the bulging natural wall surfaces were used as rumps or other body parts. This "core" group is more or less surrounded by a variety of other animals, often executed in a very different manner: one hind or red deer, one horse, two wild boars, and some standing bison. Scholars who championed the hunting-magic hypothesis saw these bison as dying or charging bulls. But it has been argued to the contrary by one rock art student, Nancy Olsen, that many of the dynamically depicted core bison are more in the posture of females giving birth. Although this is based on comparative studies of modern bison behavior, previous interpreters did not have the advantage of photographs of bison charging or birthing. That these are female bison may be significant since the social organization of bison is known to be essentially martrifocal: groups of females and their young form the central grouping to be joined by males only for breeding and calving. Many ethnographically known hunter-gatherers are organized in a similar fashion: cores of women and their children hunt or gather foodstuffs, while the men may be gone from the camp area for some time, especially when hunting or tracking certain animals. Even within the camp area, women and children are sometimes separated from the men.

The analogous social organization of bison could have had several levels of relevance for the painters at Altamira and for the prehistoric visitors or occupants of the site. On the most restricted level, the painted group on the ceiling could be as it appears—an arrangement of animals. But it could also serve as a model for the human social group. The core animals, especially if they were intended to represent female bison, could refer to the females of a single extended family group; each of the distinctive "surrounding" animals—such as the boar and the hind—could refer to one of the males associated with the matrifocal core. On the third and broadest level of meaning, the assembly could symbolize an aggregate of separate social groups which came to the cave, with the "core" animals as the host and each of the different animals as another group who joined them. There is reason to believe that Altamira may have been a seasonal aggregation site for groups

Three "sorcerers" or composite creatures sharing the attributes of deer, horses, humans and bison, from the cave of Les Trois Frères in the Ariège region of France.

that were otherwise more dispersed throughout the region. Although this interpretation of the Altamira ceiling cannot be tested easily, it does offer an example of how new insights into primitive art and the sources of meaning might be applied to the study of Palaeolithic art. When one considers the recent observations and scholarship, it becomes quite clear that a monolithic explanation for at least 20,000 years of artistic activity is no longer satisfactory. Not only has the range of subject matter of Palaeolithic art widened greatly, but there are many new methodologies and discoveries. The corpus and diversity of portable objects alone is so great in fact that it is plausible to expect that some incised pieces may constitute notational systems—as Marshack suggests—some may even be gaming pieces and yet others may simply be doodles!

Rejected now, too, is a single generalized view of Palaeolithic hunter-gatherers upon which Breuil had drawn. In the case of the Magdalenians, for example, there is little evidence from archaeology or the ethnography of most hunter-gatherers to support the view that they had been hard-pressed and anxiety-ridden in their search for food. The reverse might be argued; some of the hunting-gathering populations of the Upper Palaeolithic may have adapted so well that population increases were supported. Nor is an approach stressing the representational depictions of animals always considered appropriate in contemporary studies of Palaeolithic art. Although the naturalistic forms have always seemed the most spectacular, there is much more to Palaeolithic art than carved or painted animals. Among 1,200 engraved bones and antlers that come from 26 Cantabrian Magdalenian sites including Altamira, no more than 70 animal depictions were identifiable.

One of the newer approaches to decorative forms involves the analysis of the structure or internal organization of the designs themselves. This "design structural approach" focuses on the basic invariant units of decorative systems—whether ceramics, totem poles or engraved bones—usually called "design elements," and on their structural interrelations. Some of these analyses have even elucidated a set of rules or a "grammar" for the generation of certain artforms or styles. Given a set of such principles, the highly structured nature of the styles or traditions that archaeologists so often recognize can be made explicit. In the case of the 1,200 engraved Cantabrian Magdalenian pieces, it is

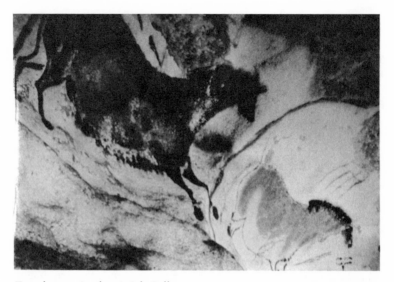

Two horses in the Axial Gallery at
Lascaux. Known as the "Chinese"
horse, the animal on the right displays
a tectiform above it; the cave wall
above the horse on the left has
chipped off, attesting to the deterioration of the cave in recent years.

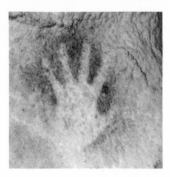

One of about 50 negative handprints
found on a cave wall at El Castillo in
Cantabrian Spain. Presumably an
adult hand, this lifesize print was
probably made by blowing or spitting
red ochre or manganese paint around
a hand held against the wall.

possible to derive a set of more than 200 distinct design elements. These geometric forms were then organized into 57 design element classes, and their use and arrangement on the engraved pieces could be studied quantitatively.

A recent analysis of the use of design elements at 15 sites, during each of the three different phases of the Magdalenian (ca. 15,000–11,000 years ago)—the Early, Middle and Late Magdalenian—has generated some interesting observations about engraving activities within the Cantabrian region of northcoastal Spain. When information on the choice of design elements is combined with other relevant aspects of design structure, such as the types of implements selected for engraving, the ways in which a design field may be defined, and the manner in which certain structural principles or different kinds of symmetry are used, they can provide the foundation for a comparative study of the decorative repertoire and design structure within the entire range of Palaeolithic art. Such a foundation can clearly allow for interpretations at a more refined level than initiated by Leroi-Gourhan, and it does not depend on assigning interpretive values like masculinity and femininity to the structural components in order to explain their interrelationships.

Such an analysis has, for example, identified a core set of 15 basic design elements in use throughout Magdalenian times and widespread in Cantabria. Many of these, such as the chevron or lunate, are also characteristic of engraved pieces found in sites outside of Cantabria. Attempts to identify intra-regional stylistic variability, which may be related to activities of different social groups, will have to focus on aspects of design that fall *outside* of these core and widespread design elements. In addition to identifying what many be called the basic Magdalenian engraving repertoire, the analysis revealed that most design elements were in use from the Early Magdalenian onward. Despite a threefold increase in the number of decorated objects from the Early to Late Magdalenian, the repertoire itself does not notably increase. Only 13 of the 57 classes are not found on pieces from Early Magdalenian levels. In other words, the engraving tradition seems to have been firmly set by at least 15,000 years ago.

At Altamira, this type of analysis reveals a rather striking diversity of engravings. Further, the recent reanalyses of the faunal remains from the site suggest that in addition to the

"L'unicorne" or "figure fantastique" in the Rotunda at Lascaux in the Dordogne region of France is one of the rare Palaeolithic depictions that does not represent any known Ice Age animal.

diversity of animal and shellfish remains, some specialized activities were taking place. Altamira could very likely have been a seasonal site to which Magdalenian peoples in the area traveled. Otherwise scattered populations may have convened at coastal Altamira in the fall to take large numbers of red deer and collect great numbers of limpets, a shellfish.

When the diversity of engravings at Altamira is compared with the kind of engravings at other Early Magdalenian sites, there is additional support for the hypothesis that a pooling of peoples may have taken place. In terms of design elements and other organizing principles, the comparative diversity of the Altamira repertoire is quite striking. This diversity is instructive on two counts: on the one hand, it is somewhat unique inasmuch as many of the Altamira design elements and principles for organizing the design elements are not found at any of the other Early Magdalenian sites that have been studied. On the other hand, there is at Altamira a unique *combination* of design elements and principles that may be found among other Early Magdalenian sites, although at no other site do they occur in these combinations.

This design structure approach also highlights some of the

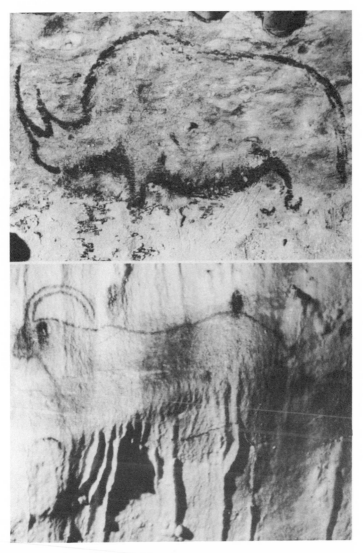

(Top) A rare little rhinoceros probably drawn in black manganese on the cave wall at Rouffignac in the Dordogne region of France. Many of the paintings in this deep cave including this rhinoceros have had their Ice Age authenticity challenged. *(Below)* An ibex on the cave wall of Cougnac in the Lot region of France is a good example of how ancient artists used existing natural cave formations—in this case stalagmites—to help define and outline their paintings.

general conceptual principles that may underlie much of Palaeo-lithic art. The lack of an explicit design field, for example, is striking in most portable and wall art. The space to be engraved or painted is almost never bounded or defined and explicit ground lines are rare. If parameters are set for the designs at all it is usually by the shape of the natural bone, the artifact or the morphology of the cave wall. This principle is evident not only in the bison rumps at Altamira, which conform to natural protruber-ances in the cave ceiling, but also in the head of a hind on a scapula found in the archaeological deposits. Here the edge of the bone ''stands for'' and in effect creates the hind's snout. This kind of artistic expression may be called ''iconic congruence.'' It remains to be seen to what degree this and other conceptual principles evident at Altamira are also characteristic of artforms outside Cantabria. Even so, it is clear that these structural perspectives may significantly augment the understanding of the cognitive processes of Palaeolithic artists.

Since the initial discovery of Palaeolithic cave art in 1879, more than 150 painted caves have been identified in southwestern Europe. Although the complete documentation of these remains a serious challenge, there is much that can be known and presently

A schematic drawing showing the relative placement of the various animals on the Altamira ceiling including at least four "curled" bison, a single deer, a boar, and numerous "standing" bison.

is known about this prehistoric art, the adaptive systems of the people who produced it, and the fundamentals of human symbolism that can be inferred from its study. Works of art that transform a piece of raw material, such as an antler, are forms of communication. Palaeolithic artists did not just select any bone, antler or cave wall; nor did they select just any animal or geometric form to depict. Their selections were deliberate and are significant clues to the meaning of Palaeolithic art.

The cave and portable art from Altamira provide a rich source both for scientific study and aesthetic appreciation. Although the portable art collection has not yet been augmented by recent excavations and the ceiling composition has been well known for a century, the perspectives on this important art have changed considerably. New methods and theories in archaeology as well as the study of the artforms themselves have influenced the understanding of prehistoric life at Altamira. Yet it is ironic and even tragic that after being preserved for 10,000 years, the decorated walls of Altamira have barely survived 100 years of study and inquiry. It would be even more ironic if our own interest in humanity were the cause of the destruction of these irreplaceable human achievements. The next century of research will be a challenge to archaeologists, but in ways that Sautuola and his daughter could not possibly have imagined.

FURTHER READING

On Altamira and Cantabrian prehistory: I. Barandiaran-Maestu, *El Paleomesolitico del Pireneo Occidental* (Zaragoza, Spain, 1967); Henri Breuil and Hugo Obermaier, *The Cave of Altamira at Santillana del Mar* (Madrid, 1935); L. G. Freeman, "The significance of mammalian faunas from Paleolithic occupations in Cantabrian Spain," *American Antiquity* 38 (1973): 3–44; L.G. Straus, "The Upper Palaeolithic Cave Site of Altamira (Santander, Spain)," *Quaternaria* XIX (1975–76): 135–48; "Of deerslayers and mountain men: Paleolithic faunal exploitation in Cantabrian Spain" in L. R. Binford, editor, *For Theory Building in Archaeology* (Academic Press, New York, 1977).

On interpretations of Palaeolithic art: I. Barandiaran-Maestu, *Arte Mueble del Paleolitico Cantabrico* (Zaragoza, Spain, 1973);

Henri Breuil, *Four Hundred Centuries of Cave Art* (Centre d'études et de documentation préhistorique, Montignac, 1952); Margaret W. Conkey, "Context, Structure, and Efficacy in Paleolithic Art and Design" in M. L. Foster and S. Brandes, editors, *Symbol as Sense* (Academic Press, New York, 1980); Paolo Graziosi, *Paleolithic Art* (McGraw-Hill, New York, 1960); André Leroi-Gourhan, *Treasures of Prehistoric Art* (Abrams, New York, 1965); Alexander Marshack, "The Baton of Montgaudier," *Natural History* 79 (1970): 56–63; "Cognitive Aspects of Upper Paleolithic Engravings," *Current Anthropology* 13 (1972): 445–72; *The Roots of Civilization* (McGraw-Hill, New York, 1972); "Exploring the Mind of Ice Age Man," *National Geographic* (1975): 62–89.

Two syntheses of Palaeolithic art: Ann Sieveking, *The Cave Artists* (Thames and Hudson, London, 1979); Peter Ucko and Andrée Rosenfeld, *Paleolithic Cave Art* (McGraw-Hill, New York, 1967), which is primarily a critique of Leroi-Gourhan.

On structuralism and design structural analyses: Terence Hawkes, *Structuralism and Semiotics* (University of California Press, Berkeley, 1977) and Jean Piaget, *Structuralism* (Basic Books, New York, 1970), both provide general backgrounds to a very extensive field. The following are good examples of the analysis of art forms from a structural perspective: M. J. Adams, "Structural Aspects of a Village Art," *American Anthropologist* 75 (1973): 265–79; Margaret Hardin Friedrich, "Design Structure and Social Interaction: Archeological Implications of an Ethnographic Analysis," *American Antiquity* 38 (1970): 3–44; Bill Holm, *Northwest Coast Art: An Analysis of Form* (University of Washington Press, Seattle, 1965); William C. Sturtevant, "Seminole Men's Clothing" in J. Helm, editor, *Essays on the Verbal and Visual Arts* (University of Washington Press, Seattle, 1967): 160–74; Patricia Vinnicombe, *People of the Eland* (Natal University Press, Pietermartizburg, 1976); Dorothy K. Washburn, *A Symmetry Analysis of Upper Gila Area Ceramics Design* (Harvard University Press, Cambridge, Massachusetts, 1977).

Papyrus and Ancient Writing: The First Hundred Years of Papyrology

by NAPHTALI LEWIS

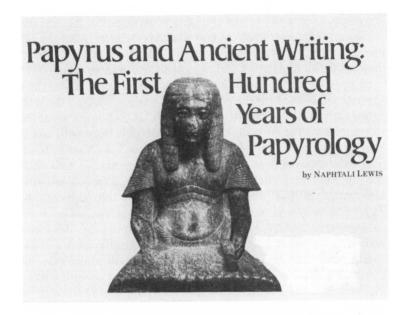

The Egyptians discovered a different use for their ubiquitous papyrus plant sometime before 3000 B.C. The papyrus roll held by General Haremhab exemplifies this new form of communication.

For the first four-fifths of its history, the material on which Western civilization did most of its writing was not paper but papyrus. Rag paper was invented by the Chinese. The Arabs learned the manufacturing process from the Chinese, and introduced the product to the Mediterranean world, where it came into common use after A.D. 1000. Paper therefore tells us nothing about writing in antiquity. For this, one has to turn to the rush-like plant that gives papyrus its name—*Cyperus papyrus* in Linnaeus's taxonomy—a versatile plant still growing in many parts of the world.

It is the papyrus of ancient Egypt that concerns us here: all through ancient times, it grew luxuriantly in the marshes along the Nile, its stalks sometimes as high as 15 feet; these are the Vulgate's "bulrushes" in which the infant Moses was found. The

Reprinted with the permission of *Archaeology* Magazine, Vol. 36, no. 4. (Copyright the Archaeological Institute of America, 1983).

Egyptians exploited every part of this valuable plant; they burned its woody rhizome as fuel, and also used the rhizome in the manufacture of furniture and utensils. With its feathery crown they made floral offerings and ornaments. Even more vitally, they used its stalk as food—in the words of one ancient writer, as a "refuge from want for the poor." They boiled or baked the stalk as we do vegetables, and they also ate it raw, chewing it for the sweet juice and spitting out the pulp, much as is done with young bamboo shoots. Stalks of papyrus were lashed together to make boats, the seaworthiness of which was demonstrated a few years ago by Thor Heyerdahl's transatlantic "Ra" expeditions. And with strips of the tough, fibrous cortex of the papyrus, the Egyptians wove plaited products—mats, baskets, sails, rope, candlewicks, and even sandals, examples of which, decorated with brightly colored beads, have been found in Egyptian tombs.

But most important in the history of civilization was the Egyptian's discovery, sometime prior to 3000 B.C., that a writing material could be readily manufactured from papyrus. Thin strips were cut from the pith of the stalk and laid side by side in two transverse layers; these layers, pressed together, adhered to form a surface eminently suitable for writing. Soot mixed with water, served as early ink, and the earliest pens were reeds sharpened to a point.

Before he died in the eruption of Vesuvius in A.D. 79, Pliny the Elder had compiled a voluminous *Natural History,* a work which has happily survived *in toto.* Though no great stylist—unlike his adopted son—the elder Pliny was a voracious reader and as a result his *Natural History* (in 37 books) is full of information about the animal, vegetable and mineral kingdoms as they were then understood. At one point Pliny devoted two pages to describing the manufacture and properties of ancient papyrus, which the Romans, borrowing the Greek word, called *charta.*

Pliny's is not an eyewitness account, for he never visited Egypt. His text, in Latin, combines details which he apparently did not understand with corruptions introduced by successive copyists. On several points, he has been the despair of scholars ever since the Renaissance. Fortunately, he was clearer about papyrus as a commodity routinely supplied by Egypt to Rome and the rest of the Mediterranean world. Commercial papyrus was assembled in the factories in standard rolls of 20 sheets pasted edge to edge; the user would then cut off pieces or paste on extensions as needed. One huge role of papyrus at the University of Michigan, for instance, runs to over 80 feet or about 25 meters in length, and appears to be made up of four standard rolls and part of a fifth glued together in series. It contains the tax register of a large village, and includes over 6,200 lines of writing.

Pliny also tells us about the different sizes and grades of papyrus. Six principal varieties were sold in the Roman market in his day, ranging from the superfine "Augustan," made up of sheets 13 digits wide (roughly ten inches), to the cheap coarse type of only six digits (four inches). The grades were determined by how fine, firm, white, and smooth the writing surface was. Anything poorer in quality than the six-digit was known as "commercial" papyrus, and was used only for wrapping.

It is a common misconception that papyrus is a naturally brittle and fragile material. This idea has given impetus to the notion that parchment replaced papyrus as the principal writing material in late antiquity because parchment was stronger and suppler. It is true that parchment came into increasingly frequent use for valuable texts and books, especially if they were to be illuminated or otherwise decorated. But parchment is expensive. It is processed from animal skins; and it is simply not the case that it is superior to papyrus for its general durability. In the years before World War II, for example, the curator of papyri in the Egyptian Museum at Berlin used to elicit astonishment and delight from visitors by cavalierly unrolling and rerolling a papyrus roll that was 3,000 years old. The *recto* (front) of another roll, now in London, was initially used for administrative records in A.D. 144. Years later when the records were no longer needed, the roll was discarded from the archives and presumably sold as waste paper, for in A.D. 259—115 years later—an estate manager used the *verso* (back) of the roll for one of his accounts.

Still, the idea that papyrus is brittle is an understandable fallacy: it is rare for a roll, or even a sheet, to be unearthed whole. Most examples of papyrus emerge from their centuries-long burial showing one or more kinds and degrees of damage. They are encrusted with dirt, crumpled, fragmented, abraded by the action of desert sands, and riddled with holes large and small chewed by

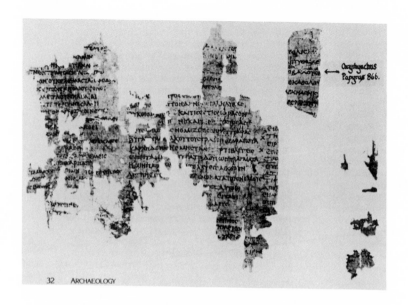

Oxyrhynchus
Papyrus 866.

32   ARCHAEOLOGY

These fragments from Menander's lost play, *The Man from Carthage,* are from *The Oxyrhynchus Papyri* (no. 2654, published in 1968). The "pages" of ancient books, as seen here, were columns of writing; the reader moved from column to column by rolling up with his left hand while unrolling from the right. These columns have 23 lines of writing—a relatively small format.

The style of the handwriting suggests that this copy of the play was made early in the first century A.D., some 300 years after Menander's death; in fact, other papyri show that his plays were still being copied and enjoyed as late as the fifth or sixth century. Visible in the second and third columns are the horizontal lines (called *paragraphoi* in Greek, whence our "paragraph") which indicated changes of speaker. Together, 16 x 17 centimeters.

worms and insects. Most recovered papyri are browned and desiccated, and some resemble delicate pieces of lace. Naturally, they have to be handled with great care.

The flexibility of ancient papyri can be temporarily enhanced by the process known as "damping out"—slowly feeding the papyrus fibers tolerable doses of moisture. This is usually done by gently tamping the papyrus with moist blotting paper or by suspending it for a period—overnight or even longer—over a miniature Turkish bath. Once a papyrus has been cleaned, smoothed and restored to whatever extent is possible, the papyrol-

A papyrus fragment now in the Egyptian Museum of West Berlin, crumpled when it was discovered, was "damped out" flat. The bits of writing visible on the crumpled papyrus *(right)* show that the document dates from the sixth century A.D. After cleaning and flattening *(left)*, the papyrus was revealed as the bottom part of a contract bearing the signatures of the parties in different hands. One of the signatories states, "I wrote for him because he does not know his letters." Length when flattened, 32.5 centimeters.

ogist can set about the business of studying it. But serious problems persist: the writing may be faded, the hand difficult to decipher, and overlapping messages may impinge on one another.

Even more seriously, the interior of a roll may be simply inaccessible. The earliest great find was also one of the most frustrating: a trial excavation conducted at Herculaneum back in 1752 yielded some 800 papyrus rolls. But the eruption of Vesuvius that had buried Herculaneum had carbonized these rolls, and the subsequent hardening of the tufa had turned them, effectively, into so many lumps of rock. Not even present-day technical processes have succeeded in unrolling them—although a few score have been broken open, revealing that they belonged to a library of philosophical works, preponderantly those of the Epicurean Philodemos, whose chief claim to fame is that he numbered Vergil among his pupils.

Papyri are, of course, of interest to any papyrologist; but "papyrology" is a term which, strictly speaking, is used inaccurately. By common consent it designates a branch of Classical studies: the study of papyri written in Greek and Latin. The study of papyri written in the Egyptian language remains a branch of Egyptology. Greek became the *lingua franca* of the eastern Mediterranean area after its conquest by Alexander the Great, and remained such even after those regions became Roman provinces. So Latin shows up infrequently in the papyri, mostly in records of the occupying Roman armies, and Greek remains the predominant language until after the Arab conquest of Egypt in A.D. 641.

Although Egypt is the land from which almost all papyri have been recovered, papyri have in fact been found in other parts of the ancient world. Papyri have also been found written in other languages—Coptic and Arabic as well as Latin and Greek, Hebrew, Syriac, and Persian. In recent years, small finds of Greek and Latin papyri have been made at the Roman military outpost at Dura-Europos on the Euphrates River, in the Negev, in a Dead Sea cave, and in Nubia (present-day Sudan). A single roll was found in Macedonia, preserved in a tomb which had become hermetically sealed against the elements. And in the spring of 1981 came the sensational news of the discovery of a small papyrus roll in a tomb in Athens which archaeologists date *circa* 450–400 B.C. Badly damaged and caked with mud when it was found, the roll is now in the hands of museum conservators. Its contents have not yet been announced, but whatever the text turns out to be, it will be older by a hundred years than the oldest Greek writing previously known.

What all of these finds have in common with Egypt is a preservative environment. Two conditions—protection from the open air and the absence of moisture—are the most conducive to the survival of papyrus. Today, Egypt bans the exportation of antiquities; but the restrictions now in force are of relatively recent date, and prior to their imposition the volume of papyri which left the country was enormous.

Indeed, the story of papyrology as we know it today begins on Egyptian soil just over a hundred years ago. Finds in Egypt as well as at Herculaneum had been made earlier, but in the winter of 1877–78 the antiquities market in Cairo was suddenly flooded with literally thousands of papyri written in various languages. These papyri had been found by peasants digging for compost in mounds that turned out to be the garbage dumps of ancient villages. The consuls in Cairo from Britain, France and Germany were quick to buy up portions of the great find for their home institutions. But the lion's share of it—and of the major finds made in the next few years—went to the Imperial Library in Vienna (now the National Library), where by the end of the nineteenth century the papyrus collection totaled close to a staggering 100,000 pieces, about a fourth of them written in Greek, about half in Arabic. The Archduke Rainer provided the funds for these acquisitions, and the collection, which still bears his name today, celebrated its centenary in 1982. So did the Egypt Exploration Society in London, which has remained the most consistent sponsor of archaeological work in Egypt over the century of its existence.

The manner in which the Society acquired its great papyrus collection is an exciting story. In the winter of 1895, two young Classics dons of Queen's College, Oxford, were commissioned to undertake a series of excavations aimed specifically at the recovery of papyri. The young men in question were B. P. Grenfell and A. S. Hunt, and they were destined to become the Damon and Pythias of modern papyrology. Together they explored a whole series of Hellenistic and Roman sites, and in most of these their diligence was rewarded with spectacular finds, especially of Greek (and some Latin) papyri, which they shipped back to Oxford by the thousands.

The most prolific site they excavated was at Behneseh, about 125 miles upstream from—which is to say, south of—Cairo (the Nile, of course, flows north). For three weeks, the pair dug in an ancient cemetery with disappointing results. Then they moved on to the ancient town itself. There, with almost the first spadeful of earth, they struck a bonanza in what proved to be the ruins of the capital of one of the districts (known as "nomes") of Ptolemaic and Roman times—the Oxyrhynchite nome.

In Grenfell's first report to the Egypt Exploration Society we can still sense the excitement of those heady days: "The ancient rubbish mounds are low, nowhere rising to more than thirty-five feet in height. Some of them are isolated, others connected by ridges into irregular groups. . . . We started to work upon the town on January 11th by setting some seventy men and boys to dig trenches. . . . The choice proved to be a fortunate one, for papyrus scraps at once began to come to light in considerable quantities, varied by uncial fragments and occasional complete or nearly complete official and private documents. . . .

"Since this rubbish mound had proved so fruitful I proceeded to increase the number of workers gradually up to 110, and, as we moved northwards over other parts of the site, the flow of papyri soon became a torrent which it was difficult to cope with. . . . We engaged two men to make tin boxes for storing the papyri, but for the next ten weeks they could hardly keep pace with us. . . .

"It was not infrequent to find large quantities of papyri together, especially in three mounds, where the mass was so great that these finds probably represent part of the local archives thrown away at different periods. . . . The third and by far the greatest find, that of the Byzantine archives, took place on March 18th and 19th, and was, I suppose, a 'record' in point of quantity. On the first of these two days we came upon a mound which had a thick layer consisting almost entirely of papyrus rolls. There was room for six pairs of men and boys to be working simultaneously at this storehouse, and the difficulty was to find enough baskets in all Behneseh to contain the papyri. At the end of the first day's work no less than thirty-six good-sized baskets were brought in from this place, several of them stuffed with fine rolls three to ten feet long, including some of the longest Greek rolls I have ever seen. As the baskets were required for the next day's work, Mr. Hunt and I started at 9 p.m. after dinner to stow away the papyri in some empty packing-cases which we fortunately had at hand. The task was only finished at three in the morning, and on the following night we had a repetition of it, for twenty-five more baskets were filled before the place was exhausted." In truth, the site was not exhausted of papyrus, and other excavators would follow in Grenfell and Hunt's footsteps.

This flood of Greek papyri presented the Classical scholars of the late nineteenth century with an exhilarating challenge. Previously limited mainly to Mediaeval manuscripts, Greek palaeography was abruptly extended a thousand years back and simultaneously broadened from the study of neat "book" hands to include the cursives of everyday affairs. In the very years when they were excavating, Grenfell and Hunt began publishing hundreds of texts from their finds, both literary and documentary; and yet despite the almost febrile pace of their productivity, they worked with a consummate skill that few have matched since. Together with F. G. Kenyon at the British Museum and U.

Wilcken and his associates in Berlin, they founded the discipline known today as papyrology.

In those years, as it brought to light long-lost works of Greek literature, papyrology made the headlines. In 1891, Kenyon published Aristotle's *Constitution of Athens,* which had been copied on the *versos,* or reverse sides, of four rolls; the *recto* or front side of these rolls had been used in A.D. 79 for someone's agricultural accounts. In the same year came the lively, sometimes bawdy *Mimes* of the Hellenistic poet Herondas. Yet another roll, published six years later in 1897, contains the *Odes* and *Dithyrambs* of Bakchylides, whose poetry had until then been completely lost; Bakchylides, as it turned out, was seen to have been a workmanlike successor who imitated Pindar but lacked his inspiration.

As the twentieth century proceeded, the rate of literary discoveries began to taper off. But just when some were thinking that all the surprises had been exhausted, others appeared. In 1958, for

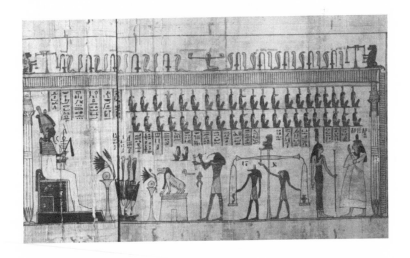

Thousands of papyri written in various languages—including the numerous Greek papyri from the Oxyrhynchite nome—survived in Egypt due to the wonderfully preservative environment. This attractive fragment, the Judgment Scene from the *Book of the Dead,* with its carefully rendered writing and vignettes, remains in good condition.

instance, the first entire play of Menander's known to us was published. This was an especially important discovery, because the ancient world regarded Menander as the greatest writer of comedy after Aristophanes. Theological literature has also been greatly enriched in this century, especially by the series of biblical works published in the 1930s. These include the earliest copy of the Gospels, a papyrus manuscript dating from about A.D. 100. That is just about the time when the composition of the Gospels was completed.

In addition to these and other complete works, the papyrus finds have brought us fragments of hundreds of other works of literature, most of them previously unknown. Homer, whom the Greeks referred to as ''The Poet'' throughout antiquity, is revealed—not surprisingly—to have been the all-time favorite not only in the schoolroom, where he comprised the basic text, but among the adult reading public as well. To date there have been published some 700 papyri and ostraca bearing Homeric texts, ranging from single or several verses quoted in one context or another to whole books, especially the *Iliad.* Next in frequency, but at a far cry from Homer, are Demosthenes, Euripides and Hesiod, whose works survive in about a hundred fragments each.

Literature, however, constitutes but a small portion of the total contents of extant ostraca and papyri. The bulk consists of documents—letters and accounts; notices of births and deaths; contracts of marriage, divorce, apprenticeship; contracts of sale and lease, tax receipts and census records; official communications of all kinds; and glimpses of religious and magical practices. The documentary papyri introduce us directly and without mediation to every facet of human existence. They show us people in high and low places—mostly low. We see an emperor visiting the province, and the governor performing his official duties; we see honest and dishonest functionaries; and most of all we meet ordinary people in every aspect of their daily lives from the cradle to the grave. Especially in the areas of government, economy, social structure, and law, the documentary papyri have added immeasurably to our knowledge of Classical antiquity.

Thus it comes as no surprise that town and village dumps have been the richest source of ancient papyri, since they are the repository of every kind of discarded paper, from tiny scraps of no importance to whole books and official documents. Cemeteries, too, have yielded papyri in part because of a custom in vogue for several centuries, especially just southwest of Cairo in the Arsinoite nome: mummies—both of human beings and of the nome's sacred crocodiles—were covered or wrapped in a cartonnage made of papyrus instead of the traditional linen (see ARCHAEOLOGY, March/April 1982, pages 18–25). Several layers of papyrus were stuck together and then plastered over to stiffen the whole into the desired shape; the plaster also served as a surface for painted decoration. These layers can now be taken apart by fairly simple chemical processes, without destroying the writing on the component sheets of papyrus.

Great quantities of ostraca have also been found in conjunction with papyri at many sites, mainly in Upper Egypt which was generally the poorer part of the country. While papyrus was inexpensive for all but the poorest consumers, it still had to be paid for, whereas potsherds—as dumps like Rome's Monte Testaccio vividly attest—were available for the taking and cost

Three columns of writing from a papyrus roll containing Menander's lost play, *The Man from Sikyon,* were recovered from a section of cartonnage shaped to cover the head or chest of a mummy. The style of the writing combines with the archaeological evidence to show that this copy was made in the latter part of the third century B.C., a mere 60 years or so after the poet's lifetime. This text thus claims pride of place as the oldest Menander manuscript in existence. Length, 29.3 centimeters; height, 16 centimeters.

nothing. The same pen and ink were used on ostraca as on papyri. The texts found on ostraca are almost always brief: school exercises, personal messages, lists, and, above all, tax receipts. Presumably the payer had to provide the material on which the collector wrote the receipt. Hence the use of ostraca, which cost nothing.

The non-literary ostraca and papyri almost never come to the attention of the general public, and even the Classical profession as a whole is content to leave their interpretation and decipherment to a few specialists. Including a mere handful in this country, the total number of scholars, worldwide, who make documentary papyri one of their principal concerns is less than a hundred. They are, however, a very active group, and the literature of papyrology's first hundred years encompasses thousands of published papyri and ostraca, not to mention a voluminous library of comment and interpretation. Otto Neugebauer described the situation with justice some 25 years ago in his acclaimed short book, *The Exact Sciences in Antiquity*: ''It can be said without exaggeration that the relatively young field of papyrology has truly revolutionized classical studies—even if by natural inertia this has not always become evident in the standard curricula.''

Many institutions and private individuals in Europe and the United States acquired collections of papyri before Egypt imposed its ban on the export of antiquities. Most of these collections—large and small alike—were purchased, although some are the result of archaeological expeditions conducted by institutions. The pace of publication has varied with the conditions of the several countries and institutions. The most extensive series is *The Oxyrhynchus Papyri,* whose first volume was published by Grenfell and Hunt in 1898; volume 49, which appeared in 1982, brings the number of published texts to 3,521, with at least as many more housed in the Ashmolean Museum awaiting future publication.

These documents instruct us—not the least of their many facets— in how Greek was spoken in ancient times; their writers display the colloquialisms of everyday usage and spell words phonetically, just as they pronounced them. They also introduce us to the characteristics of penmanship, and to the ancient differences between a ''book'' hand and cursive script. The book hand was used almost exclusively in copying works of literature; hence, it is relatively

Facsimile of the famous Ebers Papyrus, an important Egyptian document on the use of herbal medicine and magic.

stable. With two or three exceptions, its letters have the shapes that continued through the centuries, and still form the capital letters of today's Greek alphabet. Naturally, changing fashions in the course of the centuries dictated stylistic variations—a preference for an austere hand in one text, for more embellishments (such as serifs) in another; narrower or vertical letters in vogue at one time, slanting letters or broad-faced ones at another. But at all times the letters of the book hand are set down individually, without ligatures, and also without separation of words.

Cursives—"running" hands—comprise a more complex study, since their aim is writing speed, which gives rise to a great variety of forms and practices. The pioneers in papyrology had to teach first themselves and then their students to recognize the many different cursive letter forms and their evolution through the centuries—no mean task. In contrast to the standardized letters of the book hand, cursives tend to round points and angles in letter forms, and they introduce ligatures in order to string letters together without removing the pen from the page. Cursive is, in fact, the source of today's lower-case Greek alphabet. Its evolution, which we can trace in the papyri from the third century B.C. to the eighth century after Christ, shows how A became α, Δ became δ, and so forth.

The task of deciphering cursives is complicated by additional factors, such as the skill and idiosyncrasies of the individual writer, who might be a professional scribe displaying his calligraphy, or one scribbling quickly, abbreviating a great deal and letting mere squiggles stand as hints for certain letters. At the other extreme, the writer might be an illiterate peasant, barely able to sign his name in clumsy letters traced with great effort. Even the most experienced of papyrologists will find it difficult to read certain hands. The work gets easier, however, when the reader recognizes one or another of the many clichés, stereotypes and conventional formulations which characterized the language of business and government, then as now. But some scrawls have steadfastly defied all efforts to unravel them.

The more readable book hands can become difficult, too, when the papyrus is so damaged that the ink is hard to see—or, for that matter, to find. But identification is usually quick and easy when the text is from a known work of literature. Even tiny fragments can be easy to identify if they offer one or more key words. There is a small scrap of papyrus, not much bigger than a decorative postage stamp, which contains a total of 65 letters in nine lines of writing. These were found to contain the word "Achaians." A Homeric dictionary quickly identified the fragment as containing a remnant of verses 188–196 of Book 3 of the *Iliad.*

But where such obvious clues are lacking, recognition may occur belatedly, many years after publication. In 1936, a fragment was published not three inches high and less than an inch wide, and containing a mere two to seven letters on a line; it was finally identified in 1977 as coming from a copy of Demosthenes' speech *On the Crown*. Chance and serendipity play a large part in such identifications, but papyrological scholars pursuing tenuous leads have often shown remarkable powers of detection. Often pieces of the same papyrus are found in different collections. This is not surprising, since clandestine diggers commonly divide their finds to share the profits, and more than one papyrus displays a straight edge that was obviously made quite recently with a sharp knife or a pair of scissors. Five fragments from a roll that contained Aeschines' speech *Against Timarchos* are now located in Geneva; they were published in 1909. Three fragments from the same speech in Halle, published in 1913, were long assumed to be from another manuscript. In 1966, a Belgian scholar demonstrated where these two portions of the same manuscript had originally joined. Examples, literary and non-literary, can be multiplied: a Strasbourg fragment fits neatly across the top of a papyrus in Moscow; one half of a papyrus turns up in Florence, the other half in Cairo; and so on. The most remarkable instance of matching involves a fragment published in Cairo in 1925 and another in New York in 1940. A British scholar saw that both of these belonged with a third he was publishing in 1974; and in 1980, a Dutch scholar discerned that they all belonged with still another fragment located in New York.

Such vignettes, however, engaging as they are, are only the piquant caviar of the papyrologist's work. The solid substance of papyrology's first hundred years as a classical discipline lies in all the new knowledge it has given us about Greece and Rome—about Greek language and literature, and about private and public life in Classical antiquity.

COMMUNICATION AND DISPLAY: THE INTEGRATION OF EARLY EGYPTIAN ART AND WRITING
John Baines

Our contemporary world is literate, alphabetical, and controlled by texts. Written texts are formally more important
than images, and the separation of words and pictures is
sharp. When writing is pictographic, the distinction is not
always so sharp, and in early civilizations both texts and
pictures were rather scarce things. Here, the places of texts
and images in Egypt, and their relative standing, are explored.

Among systems of writing and representation, the ancient
Egyptian is the most closely fused, with the possible exception of
those of Mesoamerica (e.g. Marcus 1976; Schele & Miller 1986).
Whereas most scripts have moved away more or less quickly from
being clearly representational, Egyptian hieroglyphs continued to
depict identifiable objects until they ceased to be used in the 4th
century AD (te Velde 1988). Egyptian art should also be distinguished from Far Eastern systems, where an awareness of the
representational origins of characters is retained even though their
calligraphic form is not immediately representational. There, too,
writing is very common in pictures, but, if anything, the influence
is from writing to pictorial style and convention rather than the
other way round. Nearer to Egypt, there is a strong contrast with
Mesopotamia, where cuneiform writing very soon lost its representational character and there is little comparable interplay
between writing and representation, even though many pictures

Reprinted by permission of the publisher and author from *Antiquity* 63 (1989), pp.
471–482.

bear inscriptions; there, the public and monumental use of writing seems to be a rather later development (Larsen 1988).

The principal reason why Egyptian writing was able to stay so close to representation is probably that the script existed virtually from the beginning in two forms, the cursive signs used for administrative purposes, which developed into the "hieratic" script, and hieroglyphs, which were the vehicle of public writing, and more generally of written display (which mostly had a pictorial element). Although the two remained closely linked for 2000 or more years hieroglyphs, which were not used in everyday contexts, were able to retain their original organization and sign forms fundamentally unchanged. Because of the close links between the scripts, hieroglyphs probably moderated the development of hieratic. The connection between hieroglyphic and cursive was maintained until the appearance of demotic cursive in the 7th century BC. (On early Near Eastern writing see *Naissance* 1982; introduction to Egyptian writing: Davies 1987.)

This integration of writing and representation and separation of forms of writing relates to issues of literacy, which I have explored partially for the 3rd millennium BC (Baines 1988). Here, I discuss the integration itself for the beginning of that period and relate the system to its creators, the élite of a large, monarchically organized state, and their display (cf. Baines in press).

THE SETTING

The Political Context

Egypt was politically centralized in most periods, as was its artistic production and style. The system of writing and representation originated in late predynastic times, at the end of the 4th millennium BC. On present evidence, writing may have been invented and used for extended marks of ownership, especially royal names, slightly earlier than representational and iconographic conventions stabilized (e.g., Kaiser & Dreyer 1982). This distinction is suggested particularly by brief but detailed annotations of the delivery of goods that date several reigns before the beginning of the 1st dynasty (Kaiser & Dreyer 1982: 235), as well as being earlier than the principal monuments considered in the past to belong to the "unification" of Egypt. This period of definition of representation and invention of writing postdates slightly the creation of a large, centralized state with borders similar to those of later Egypt.

The system was thus probably created by the new state as an instrument of control, directed in the cursive forms of writing toward administration—about which little is known—and in the monumental, hieroglyphic and representational form toward display (a problematic category), prestige, and the articulation and affirmation of values. Egyptologists have mostly, and probably correctly, assumed that writing was invented for administration, which was its predominant use in later times. In such a view hieroglyphs are secondary, but for the early élite they should be considered as important as cursive administrative uses of writing. The inner élite were literate, probably in both cursive and hieroglyphs, and their artistic monuments, which included hieroglyphic writing, were central preoccupations. In addition, writing and representation were crucial for the formulation and presentation of royal and religious ideology. Egypt is thus a mixed case, whereas on present evidence Mesoamerica used writing exclusively for monumental purposes for many centuries (Marcus 1976).

Representation and Style

The instantly recognizable Egyptian rendering of nature and artistic style, which was analysed in the classic work of Heinrich Schäfer (1986), is oriented toward the "accurate" representation of figures and objects and lacks the stylistic exuberance of many artistic traditions. What is true of the rendering of nature by itself applies also to the fusion of the pictorial and linguistically-based representational systems—the latter being hieroglyphs—which come together in a complex that was organized to a great extent for clarity and "semantic" expression, rather than for emotional or sensuous impact, or for technical and compositional virtuosity. It is as if the originators of the mixed Egyptian system were the first semioticians: the system seems to be designed with the maximum emphasis on differentiation and meaning. Among other issues, this emphasis raises the question of why such clarity was sought, that is in part, whom it addressed. It is possible to speak of the system's having been designed, because of its contemporaneous integration of representation and writing, and because it was the product of a ruling group in a centralized state and was created in quite a short span of time, probably no more than a century leading up to the Narmer Palette (Figures 1-2), which exhibits all its features completely formed.

A vital feature of representation is its use of the human figure as the organizing principle of scale and composition. This can be seen emerging in late predynastic monuments, of which the earlier ones show more animals than humans (e.g. Asselberghs 1961: plates 65–7, 70–4, 76–9), and continues throughout dynastic times. Its definitive form is the "canon of proportion", a set of rules for the ideal proportioning of the human figure which can be extended to the design of whole compositions (summary e.g. Robins 1986; to be distinguished from "canonical" representation, often confusingly so termed by Davis, e.g. 1984). It is uncertain when this was introduced. Attempts to see its application in major early monuments have been methodologically circular (e.g. Iversen 1975: 60–6; Meyer 1974), but the compositional principles of these pieces are nonetheless comparable with later ones; other evidence is restricted to an empty, possibly canonical grid on a practice piece from a probable early dynastic context (Emery 1958: 84 no. 1, plate 97; Spencer 1980: 16 no. 16).

This central significance of the human figure is a powerful cultural statement, which has been variously interpreted, often as showing that whereas earlier Egyptians had conceived of divinity in animal form and felt their power inferior to that of animals, those of the early state viewed human form as the measure of things (e.g. Hornung 1982: esp. 100–8; for counter-arguments see Baines 1985; 72–5; Williams 1988: 35–46, 58–9). The principal meaning of the human figure is, however, probably not humanity in general, but the ideal representative or protagonist of "human" action—the king—as well as the gods, whose only "direct" iconography is human (see Williams 1988 for early human statues of gods). What seems a "humanistic" and levelling feature is a complex, hierarchical one that should be understood in terms of its relations with alternative representational forms, such as the animal and emblematic (discussed below), rather than in terms of its apparent content.

FIGURES 1–2. The Narmer Palette, from Hierakonpolis, main temple deposit. Cairo Museum CG 14716, h. 64 cm. (Photos courtesy Hirmer Fotoarchiv München.)

Between Representation and Writing

Early cursive and hieroglyphic writing was a limited instrument. Continuous language was not recorded; no more than a few words were written consecutively and they did not use linguistic syntax. Writing was adequate for some administrative purposes but not for encoding discourse or for any more than a few abstractions. Thus, representation and writing were not separate media; there was much that could be expressed only by the linked use of both. Writing needed representation to fill out the detail of ideology and specific statement, while representation did not seek to convey through iconography matters that were better notated in writing. The partial bias toward the visual in presenting complex matters results in there being few textual sources for early Egyptian ideology, "monumental" forms of which were in the mixed visual/verbal mode. There must have been a marked separation between oral discourse about ideology and these formulations. In addition, systematic constraints of decorum, which limited what could be represented and in what context (Baines 1985a: 277–305)—and later what was recorded in texts—result in there being no evidence for many central social and religious concerns.

Even though there is relatively little stylistic disjunction between representation and writing, direct interplay between writing and representation, in which figures act as hieroglyphs or hieroglyphs as figures (Fischer 1973; 1986), is less common than is sometimes implied: conventions of scale and other details almost always keep the two separate, and no one confuses picture with script (as is true also in Mesoamerica). There is an emblematic mode of representation (or textual encoding) that stands between normal representation and writing (Baines 1985a: 277–305); if the two other genres were not separate, such a bridging type could hardly exist. In its simplest form, in which its intermediate position is clearest, the emblematic mode consists of partly representational figures, such as hieroglyphs or symbols to which arms are attached to indicate actions (Figure 3). Extensions show that depictions of cult images of deities, or of the king in animal

FIGURE 3. Emblematic details on late predynastic palettes. (After Baines 1985a: 43, figure 12.)
a 'Cities' palette. Cairo Museum CG 14238, h. c. 19 cm.
b 'Battlefield' palette (detail). Oxford, Ashmolean Museum 1892.1171, h. of detail c. 12 cm.
c 'Bull' palette (detail). Paris, Louvre E 11255, h. of detail c. 15 cm.

form, belong in the same mode, which is fully integrated in the system of decorum.

The essential early sources for representation and writing are a few monuments with relief decoration from the turn of the 4th millennium BC. These are schist ''palettes'' of a design originally used for grinding cosmetics (Figures 1–2; Asselberghs 1961: plates 44–96 [full series]), mace heads (Figure 4), and various ivory objects (e.g. Quibell 1900: plates 5–16), as well as ivory tags of the 1st–2nd dynasties (c. 2950–2650 BC; Petrie 1900: plates 10–17; 1901: plates 2–12). Sculpture in the round was relatively rare and not so advanced stylistically as relief (cf. Williams 1988), or as comparable representational features of elaborate stone vases (e.g. Fischer 1972), but some ivory pieces are of very high quality. Most representations are relatively small and were either dedicated in temples (Dreyer 1986: 11–58) or placed in tombs. Their style and composition is very close to that of later large-scale or colossal works—it is easy to mistake the size of Egyptian works—and they are conventionally called monuments (as I do here). ''Memorial'' might be an apt term, because many pieces ostensibly commemorate events, and the making of ''memorials'' is one of the chief activities of the Egyptian king recorded when suitable textual contexts become available in the 4th dynasty (c. 2550 BC: Tawfik 1985), but the

FIGURE 4. The Narmer mace head from Hierakonpolis, main temple deposit. Oxford, Ashmolean Museum E 3631, height 19.8 cm. (Drawing from original by Pat Jacobs. Courtesy Ashmolean Museum.)

pieces are monumental also in the sense that they ignore scale and create compositions that are both meaningful and impressive. "Monuments" need not, however, be public, and the earliest known public pictorial compositions were set up outside Egypt (Williams 1986: 171–2 [conceivably a Nubian inscription]; Gardiner *et al.* 1952: plates 1–4). Within Egypt, decorum may have been one of the constraints that led to their absence.

RESTRICTIONS TO THE SPREAD OF WRITING AND REPRESENTATION

There are two essential restrictions to the spread of a system like the Egyptian, whose complexity and incorporation of the élite technique of writing placed it outside the reach of most people. These restrictions are the values it incorporates, which relate it almost exclusively to the élite, the king and the gods, and are manifested in detail in the system of decorum; and the connected use of other means of élite and royal display toward society as a whole and removal of access to art from all but the inner élite. Both of these are peremptory manifestations of the general reservation of works of art in complex societies for central concerns—a reservation that renders the definition of what counts as art and the status of art as "art" less problematic than has often been thought (e.g. Wolf 1957: 66–8), provided that an excessively narrow westernizing conception of art is not adopted.

Values in Representation

The representational and iconographic system depicts and comments on the society's cosmos (so far as evidence goes, only the élite's cosmos). On the best known early monument, the Narmer Palette (Figures 1–2), the mixed human/cows' heads at the top and the absence of a falcon above the patterned rectangle or *serekh* enclosing the king's name demonstrate that the main relief areas show the "world", above which is the sky, where the principal god Horus—the falcon—has his being, while the areas at the bottom present what is outside and "beneath" the ordered cosmos. This outside realm is not beyond royal intervention; the figure of a bull butting an enemy and an enclosure wall on one

FIGURE 5. Ivory cylinder seal of Narmer from Hierakonpolis, main temple deposit. Oxford, Ashmolean Museum E 3915, height c. 4.7 cm. (Drawing from original by Michele Germon Riley.)

side represents the king, who for reasons of decorum is not shown in his human form in this context. He both pervades the ordered cosmos and influences the realm beyond. A contemporaneous ceremonial cylinder seal presents similar distinctions in a highly sophisticated form (Figure 5). The king is shown as a catfish, a powerful and ambivalent being also incorporated in his principal title, his Horus name, which means something like "Mean Catfish". His human arms wield a long baton to smite enemies who are arranged in several registers and identified by a caption as Libyans. Above the king, a falcon facing in the opposite direction hovers in protection and holds out the hieroglyph for life. This falcon may be compared with the one in the main register of the Narmer Palette, which perches on a rebus for defeated countries and holds a rope securing the emblematic prisoner's head with a human arm. As is clearest in the rebus, both the falcons are indirect, emblematic representations of the god Horus, whose "full" iconography is not attested from this period. The benefits of victory and life that they proffer to the king are those which the divine world gives to him and, through him, to humanity. In return, the king presents the fruits of his actions in the world, and the order and prosperity they bring, to the gods.

On most of these monuments the king is the only being shown at full scale in human form, and in some contexts he too is shown emblematically, as in the base area of the Narmer Palette and on the seal. In later reliefs from the inner areas of temples—the earliest extensive material is of the 5th dynasty (Borchardt *et al.* 1913)—gods in human form interact directly with the king; this is the core idiom in which exchanges between human and divine are shown. Some emblematic figures (e.g. Figures 3a–c) probably antedate the Narmer Palette. Thus, the emblematic mode came into being about the same time as the script, when pictorial representation was being reformed and defined as the third, and ideologically the most important, member of the interdependent set (much later, writing became relatively more significant when its potential had increased). Discriminations of decorum in iconography, of which the emblematic mode forms an essential part, were therefore designed into the system from the beginning. In comparison with the conventions of slightly earlier palettes (e.g. Asselberghs 1961: plates 65–7) and decorated pottery (Petrie 1921; Vandier 1952: 329–65; Asselberghs 1961: plates 13–19), they leave little place on important monuments for humanity, whose radical exclusion has a later correlate in royal dominance and in the overpowering monuments of the pyramid age. Royal destiny and the destiny of society were identified. The force that made the élite espouse such a limited presentation was probably religious. The later Egyptians lived in a divine and human cosmos, surrounded and threatened by disorder, and championed by the king (e.g. Hornung 1982: 172–85). If this conception existed earlier, its urgency may have legitimized the restriction and focus on the king.

The system of decorum should not be reduced to a narrowly religious phenomenon; it is the society's definition of what central concerns may be represented, and has general ideological and political meaning. Because much in religion was not depicted— such as most royal rituals and all temple rituals—one concomitant feature of this system was that a great deal was retained in the oral sphere, where the restricted parts may have been safe from unwanted dissemination. (This continued to be the case in later times when continuous texts were written.) The exclusiveness of art is part of a wider exclusiveness. The limited cosmos that is depicted focuses on the king and emphasizes aggression. Centuries were to pass before any significant number of non-royal people had major works of representational art among their monuments, and when they did, the subject matter of these works was quite separate from that of royal monuments.

Art and Élite

The second restriction on the impact of representation and writing on society is the use of other types of symbol by those in authority. The creation of the monumental style and context in late "predynastic" times was accompanied by other crucial changes in material culture. The Naqada II–III period (c. 3400– 3000 BC), during which Egypt became culturally uniform, saw both the greatest development of predynastic prestige objects and the beginnings of their eclipse. The chief types were cosmetic palettes (typologically the same as the Narmer Palette; Petrie 1921; Asselberghs 1961: plates 42–96), mace heads (e.g. Adams 1974: plates 5–6), stone vases (el-Khouli 1978), and decorated pottery. Of these, only stone vases survived into dynastic times. The decorated pottery is important here, because its themes, which centre on boats and religious motifs, seem to go beyond what is known from later: many people, probably members of élites, had access to representations which may be of rituals, possibly mortuary ones (the scenes have not been successfully interpreted). The later disappearance of cosmetic palettes might relate to religious meanings of the cosmetics, which were made of valuable ores from the Eastern Desert and could have been restricted to certain groups of people or gods, but such an idea is problematic, because cosmetics continued to be used even though the objects on which they had originally been prepared ceased to be made. Maces, as symbols of individual martial values, are inappropriate to a centralized power; the king possessed and dedicated in temples the finest and largest mace heads ever made (Figure 4; Asselberghs 1961: plates 97–8; Adams 1974: plates 1–4). But these, too, ceased to be made, and although the king holds a mace in countless dynastic reliefs, maces were not significant objects (6th dynasty examples Quibell 1908: plate 5; 1909: 19–20).

Thus, traditional symbols of independence and status were appropriated by the king, and most of them subsequently disappeared. No representational materials were buried in normal graves, still less written ones. Members of the royal entourage of the 1st dynasty, who were buried around the royal tombs and mortuary cult areas at Abydos, might have crude stelae decorated with their names and a large sign representing a human being (Petrie 1900: plates 30–6; 1901: plates 26–30a), but elsewhere such an object is not known from before the end of the dynasty, in one of the grandest non-royal tombs at Saqqara (Kemp 1967: 27 figure 2). This is inferior in execution to royal works, although it is sophisticated in design and meaning. As in later times, the location of a monument was almost as significant as its scale and quality; people of high status buried close to the king might have quite poor tombs and memorials.

This impoverishment of the non-royal record was accompanied by standardization. Most dynastic Egyptian pottery is uniform and almost devoid of aesthetic significance. Early dynastic prestige materials included stone vases, which were developed in virtuoso designs both before and after the beginning of the 1st dynasty; metal (e.g. Petrie 1901: plate 9a; Emery 1949: plates 4–10); ivory, from which many temple offerings were made; and, less impressive as works of art, faïence (e.g. Quibell 1900: plates 21–2; for these materials Williams' dating, 1988, is too rigid, cf. Whitehouse 1987). By the 1st dynasty copper was used for many prestige containers, and for this purpose metal eventually ousted stone, whose use declined by the 3rd dynasty. Gold may have been relatively common but, as is to be expected, hardly any is preserved (for the 4th dynasty see e.g. Reisner & Smith 1955).

The differentiation and privileging of certain forms and materials deprived most people of artistic expression of any kind to which the élite accorded significance; here, representation was almost irrelevant. It is difficult to think ourselves into a world in which few people often see pictures, but the restriction of normative artistic expression and luxury objects to élites is common in many societies (and still applies in "major" art outside museums). Those who used representation also used writing, although there must have been many literate people who had no access to representations. Display which was addressed beyond the élite could not always be couched in the system of writing and representation, whose chief message for others would have been that they could not understand it in more than general terms—a point whose significance the élite would naturally have seen and the rest may also have taken. The content of much early writing is the recording of taxation and other levies, which are hardly ever welcome, even if the symbol justifying the exaction is respected; writing is an instrument of symbolic and executive authority rather than persuasion (cf. Larsen 1988). Apart from strictly written documents, the scale of almost all early representations, including such pieces as royal tomb stelae (e.g. Asselberghs 1961: plate 1; Petrie 1900: frontispiece; 1901: plate 31) is small and not suitable for addressing the people, who would not have had access to the places where they were sited.

Architecture

Instead of writing and representation, the chief form of more general display was therefore architecture. Royal names show an enclosure that is the juncture between the world of the gods and the human world through the descent of the sky god Horus to "inhabit" the king, who manifested Horus within the enclosure (Baines in press; classic example Asselberghs 1961: plate 1; early cases: Kaiser & Dreyer 1982: 263, figure 14). This image focuses on an architectural feature, the enclosure wall, which conveys its message to humanity through exclusion and dominates the landscape in which it is set. Enclosures themselves seem to have been uninscribed until more than a millennium later, and even then it was an inner enclosure which was decorated (Arnold 1988: 58–63, plates 30–6). The earliest royal names may be the first preserved examples of writing, and these enclosures must have been among the first major structures in Egypt. At the beginning they may have been constructed of perishable materials, as has been suggested for their formal counterparts in Mesopotamia (Heinrich 1982: 4–14, figures 1–43). Later they were of mud brick, plastered and painted white or perhaps with polychrome decoration; the largest structures standing from the early dynastic period, which are impressive by any standards, are the mortuary cult enclosures of 1st–2nd dynasty kings (O'Connor in press). In addition, the new capital Memphis was named "White Wall" or "Wall" (Zibelius 1978: 39–43) and seems to have had such an enclosure or defining element.

The dominance of architecture conveyed in positive terms the same message of exclusion as did the inward-turning character of the system of writing and representation. Architecture was, however, slightly less value-laden than representation, for non-royal tombs could be large and impressive, more so than the kings' own tombs (Kemp 1967). It is not known how they compared for size with palaces or temple enclosures. This relative freedom probably relates to the exclusive use of hallowed forms, materials and sites for royal tombs, while allowing the inner élite a medium of display away from the king that was not so tightly restricted as monumental representation (see also Kaiser 1985).

A SELF-SUSTAINING SYSTEM?

The communication and display of early works of art was virtually an internal matter for the gods, the king, and the élite. Until the Old Kingdom some centuries later, the élite appear to have been excluded from the most significant parts of the system. I consider at the end further aspects of this restricted system's place in its

social context. First I review the positions of pictorial representation and writing, and of the fusion and mediation of the two,
within the system. An essential question is how specific the
representations are, that is, do they record actual events or are they
generic? If the generic has a ritual function, it may fulfill it
without particular reference and without relating to anyone beyond the king and the gods. In this respect, there is an apparent
tension between pictorial records, which tend more toward the
generic than the specific, and other material such as ceremonial
labels with year names, which apparently record events. Records
similar to these probably formed the basis of royal "annals"
which both preserved an ideal record of mainly ritual and royal
events and acted as the point of reference when old documents
were consulted in administration (Redford 1986). They had
practical as well as ideological meaning, although all extant
examples are probably grand, non-utilitarian pieces.

The palettes and mace heads, which are the main early reliefs,
are slightly earlier than the annals. They too appear at first sight to
record specific events. The Narmer mace head (Figure 4) fuses
two possibilities by showing the royal *sed*-festival, a ritual of
renewal celebrated after 30 years of reign, with the enumeration of
vast numbers of captives and a representation of offerings and a
temple, in which the god to whom the fruits of royal success were
to be dedicated would be worshipped (early evidence: Williams &
Logan 1987). The figures for captives are, however, suspect, and
many depicted *sed*-festivals could not have occurred (Hornung *et
al.* 1974). Thus, what is shown is a ritual of conquest allied to a
prospective ritual that will bring benefits to the king, perhaps in
the next life, and hence indirectly to society. For reasons of
decorum, parts of the ritual which took place in a temple could not
be shown pictorially, any more than the god could appear within
the scenes, which include human beings and captives together
with the king.

The same general point applies to the "record" aspect of a
monument like the Narmer Palette. There have been numerous
attempts to identify the events it ostensibly shows, and one of
these may have the correct answer, yet the chief purpose of the
piece is not to record an event but to assert that the king dominates
the ordered world in the name of the gods and has defeated
internal, and especially external, forces of disorder. Whatever

events were the ultimate model for the composition, they were probably far back in time from the piece itself (the same probably applies to the seal, Figure 5); they were tokens of royal achievement. Ritual incorporated events and thus gave them full meaning, so that there was no necessary distinction between them and the celebration of the achieved order of the world. Rule was ritual and representation fused the two in recording them. Similarly, ritual and repetitive occurrences dominated the year names and "annals" assimilating transitory happenings to enduring meanings. Only in later times were there at all extensive written records of individual exploits. These events were themselves ritualized, but more weakly.

Until later times, the near-total integration of representation and writing with ritual favoured a cyclical, non-specific position of records and display, in which rulers participated in order to fulfill their rôle. This does not exhaust the functions of records, but affects strongly those likely to be excavated. Between the palettes and mace heads and the later early dynastic period, the only real evidence for kings' having projected their ritual rôle is in year labels, and this gap in the record needs further investigation, but the appearance of a fuller royal/divine iconography toward the end of that time (e.g. Quibell 1900: plate 2) implies the existence of lost monuments in which the tradition matured. The virtual separation of "record" and iconography from particular events rendered the system self-sustaining so long as there was no great change in the potential of other media, which there came gradually to be with the spread of continuous texts, and in a more limited way with extended records in the annals of the 4th–5th dynasties. Until that time, the fusion of writing and representation allowed the representational, and in a sense performative, aspect of the works of art to predominate.

CONCLUSION

Further aspects of communication and audience relate to the self-sustaining character of the system of writing and representation. This material also has implications for broader issues in the archaeological analysis of complex societies.

Although the communicative structure of early Egyptian writ-

ing and representation is not in doubt, and writing served important administrative functions, how far works of art meaningfully
communicated with anyone beyond the gods is less clear. At every
point, the apparent significance of works as statements that could
be available to many was subverted by scale and accessibility, by
the audience they were addressed to, and by the omissions and
formalizations in subject matter, which were such that what was
not recorded was more central to the functioning of king and cult
than what was. This leaves the identity of the non-divine audience
of the works unidentified, and this gap is acute because of the
system's semiotic clarity.

The essential human audience must be the small élite involved
in commissioning and producing the works, on which great
resources were expended, and among them must be sought an
explanation for the system's "realism" (Baines 1985b). No
adequate solution has been proposed for this problem, which has
cross-cultural dimensions because of the evolution of numerous
artistic traditions toward realism. This group's concern for a
system that excluded them is also problematic, and forms part of a
wider problem of social access to knowledge, whose dimensions
are beginning to be appreciated (cf. Baines forthcoming). Such
restrictions are common in small-scale societies, so that their
existence in Egypt is not surprising, but they are at variance with
some other aspects of ideology. A later religious analogy that may
suggest how these conflicting aspects could be integrated ideologically while excluding much of the élite is the solar cult, whose
central texts and institutions appear to have been kept "secret"
until relatively late times, perhaps in part because the matter was
too portentous to be "publicly" revealed (see Assmann 1983:
22–53, who ascribes great antiquity to some of these conceptions).

Similar questions of audience apply to display. In earlier
discussions (e.g. Baines 1983) I wrongly assumed that the display
of the early élite and their appropriation of writing and representation could be taken for granted once the identity of élite and
bureaucracy was appreciated. The essential form of display was
architecture, and it took centuries for the élite to supplement it to
any extent with representation or writing (cf. Larsen 1988). Even
royal reliefs were seldom placed in a public position, and here
they could have followed rather than led non-royal monuments. In
addition, luxury aspects of material culture were probably impor-

tant among the living, but hardly any evidence for them is preserved except from tombs. The crucial means—and to some extent the message—of display and differentiation was exclusion, as is fitting in a culture where representation and writing were very scarce resources.

Much of the core of high culture was in oral forms and in ritual. So long as continuous language was not written down, these retained their ideological precedence and escape the archaeological record, while representation only ever presented small excerpts from ritual. Writing and representation report minimally on the concerns of society as a whole and only partially on those of the élite. They say hardly anything about social cohesion, a topic that is often absent from the Egyptian record, but their character and distribution make them the wrong place to look for such a concern; in this period relevant conceptions were probably confined to oral contexts. Here as in so many spheres, the distribution of evidence and evaluation of restrictions on it and gaps in it are vital to interpreting what remains. But, although I suggest that the ultimate focus of ideology was oral, this devalues the significance of the recovered record only marginally. Architecture was visible, costly and enduring, while the fused form of writing and representation created something of fundamental importance that could not have a close oral counterpart.

This material has more general implications for the evaluation of archaeological evidence. The Egyptian construction of a system of writing and monumental representation occurred in a short period some time after the state was formed. Although state formation was the ultimate stimulus to this surge of creativity, the two cannot be linked immediately; such a time lag should not be taken to imply a lack of connection. The high-cultural system that formed was in some measure tangential to the wider social context. Its values, symbolism and functions cannot be derived simply from its position in society, but in their inward-turning character are typical of the exclusivism of small groups that are not directly answerable to an audience. The legitimation I have suggested, of maintaining the cosmos against disintegration, need not have been thought about or accepted by all.

In such a context, it could be misleading to read the broader archaeological record as showing the effects of these esoteric and artistically and semiotically ambitious products. For Egypt, such caution turns out to be unnecessary, because the restricted system has a negative counterpart in the deprivation and uniformity of the wider material culture. In other societies there might not be such a neat correspondence. Whether high culture sits easily within the record or not, archaeology cannot ignore something that absorbs so much of a society's resources and is the focus of so much of its prestige, even if the methods used for analysing the material may belong primarily to other disciplines.

Acknowledgments. This paper was delivered to a section on archaeology and art at the Theoretical Archaeology Group meeting, Bradford 1987. I am grateful to Tim Taylor in particular for inviting me to participate in a most interesting session, and to Richard Parkinson, Michele Germon Riley, Helen Whitehouse and Norman Yoffee. The final version was prepared during a Humboldt-Stiftung fellowship at the University of Münster.

REFERENCES

There is a large literature on many of the materials discussed; the references are selective.

Adams, B. 1974. *Ancient Hierakonpolis* and *Ancient Hierakonpolis: supplement.* Warminster: Aris & Phillips.

Arnold, D. 1988. *The pyramid of Senwosret I.* New York: Metropolitan Museum of Art. The Metropolitan Museum of Art Egyptian Expedition: The South Cemeteries of Lisht 1.

Asselberghs, H. 1961. *Chaos en Beheersing: documenten uit het aeneolitisch Egypte.* Leiden: E. J. Brill. Documenta et Monumenta Orientis Antiqui 8.

Assmann, J. 1983. *Re und Amun: die Krise des polytheistischen Weltbilds im Ägypten der 18–20. Dynastie.* Fribourg: Universitätsverlag; Gottingen: Vandenhoeck & Ruprecht. Orbis Biblicus et Orientalis 51.

Baines, J. 1983. Literacy and ancient Egyptian society, *Man* (NS) 18: 572–99.

    1985a. *Fecundity figures: Egyptian personification and the iconology of a genre.* Warminster: Aris & Phillips; Chicago: Bolchazy Carducci.

1985b. Theories and universals of representation: Heinrich Schäfer and Egyptian art, *Art History* 8: 1–25.

1988. Literacy, social organization and the archaeological record: the case of early Egypt, in B. Bender, J. Gledhill & M. T. Larsen (ed.), *State and society: the emergence of and development of social hierarchy and political centralization:* 192–214. London: Unwin Hyman.

In press. The origins of kingship in Egypt, in D. O'Connor & D. Silverman (ed.), Symposium volume on Egyptian kingship.

Forthcoming. Restriction of knowledge and hierarchy: modern perceptions and ancient institutions, *Journal of the American Research Center in Egypt* 27.

Borchardt, L. *et al.* 1913. *Das Grabdenkmal des Königs Śahu-Re 2: Die Wandbilder.* Ausgrabungen der Deutschen Orient-Gesellschaft in Abusir 1902–1908 7. Leipzig: J. C. Hinrichs.

Davies, W. V. 1987. *Egyptian hieroglyphs.* London: British Museum Publications.

Davis, W. M. 1984. Canonical representation in Egyptian art, *Res* 4: 20–46.

Dreyer, G. 1896. *Elephantine VIII. Der Tempel der Satet: Die Funde der Frühzeit und des Alten Reiches.* Mainz: Philipp von Zabern. Archäologische Veröffentlichungen des Deutschen Archäologischen Instituts, Abteilung Kairo 39.

Emery, W. B. 1949. *Great tombs of the first dynasty* 1. Cairo: Government Press. Service des Antiquités de l'Egypte, Excavations at Saqqara.

1958. *Great tombs of the first dynasty* 3. London: Egypt Exploration Society. Service des Antiquités de l'Egypte, Excavations at Saqqara.

Fischer, H. G. 1972. Some emblematic uses of hieroglyphs with particular reference to an archaic ritual vessel, *Metropolitan Museum Journal* 5: 5–23.

1973. Redundant determinatives in the Old Kingdom, *Metropolitan Museum Journal* 8: 7–25.

1986. *L'écriture et l'art de l'Egypte ancienne: quatre leçons sur la paléographie et l'épigraphie pharaoniques.* Paris: Presses Universitaires de France. College de France, Essais et conférences.

Gardiner, A. H., T. E. Peet & J. Cerny. 1952. *The inscriptions of Sinai* 1: *Introduction and figures.* London: Egypt Exploration Society.

Heinrich, E. 1982. *Die Tempel im alten Mesopotamien: Typologie, Morphologie und Geschichte.* Berlin: Walter de Gruyter. Deutsches Archäologisches Institut, Denkmäler Antiker Architektur 14.

Hornung, E. 1982 [1971]. *Conceptions of god in ancient Egypt: the one and the many.* Trans. J. Baines. Ithaca (NY): Cornell University Press.

Hornung, E., E. Staehelin *et al.* 1974. *Studien zum Sedfest.* Geneva: Editions de Belles-Lettres. Aegyptiaca Helvetica 1.

Iversen, E. with Y. Shibata. 1975. *Canon and proportions in Egyptian art.* 2nd edition. Warminster: Aris & Phillips.

Kaiser, W. 1985. Zur Entwicklung und Vorformen der frühzeitlichen Gräber mit reich gegliederter Oberbaufassade, in Posener-Kriéger (ed.): 25–38.

Kaiser, W. & G. Dreyer. 1982. Umm el-Qaab: Nachuntersuchungen im frühzeitlichen Königsfriedhof 2: Vorbericht, *Mitteilungen des Deutschen Archäologischen Instituts, Abteilung Kairo* 38: 211–69.

Kemp, B. 1967. The Egyptian 1st dynasty royal cemetery. *Antiquity* 41: 22–32.

Khouli, Ali A. H. el- 1978. *Egyptian stone vessels, predynastic period to dynasty III: typology and analysis.* Mainz: Philipp von Zabern.

Larsen, M.T. 1988. Literacy and social complexity, in B. Bender, J. Gledhill & M. T. Larsen (ed.), *State and society: the emergence of and development of social hierarchy and political centralization:* London: Unwin Hyman.

Marcus, J. 1976. The origins of Mesoamerican writing, *Annual Review of Anthroplogy* 5: 35–67.

Meyer, K.-H. 1974. Kanon, Komposition und 'Metrik' der Narmer-Palette, *Studien zur altägyptischen Kultur* 1: 247–65.

Naissance 1982. *Naissance de l'écriture, cunéiformes et hiéroglyphes.* Paris: Ministère de la Culture, Editions de la Réunion des Musées nationaux. Galeries nationales du Grand Palais, exhibition catalogue.

O'Connor, D. In press. [Preliminary report on Pennsylvania-Yale excavations at Abydos North], *Journal of the American Research Center in Egypt* 26.

Petrie, W. M. F. 1900. *The royal tombs of the first dynasty 1900* 1. London: various publishers. Memoir of the Egypt Exploration Fund 18.

  1901. *The royal tombs of the earliest dynasties 1901* 2. London: various publishers. Memoir of the Egypt Exploration Fund 21.

  1921. *Corpus of prehistoric pottery and palettes.* London: various publishers. British School of Archaeology in Egypt and Egyptian Research Account, 23rd year, 1917.

Posener-Kriéger, P. (ed.). 1985. *Mélanges Gamal eddin Mokhtar* 2. Cairo: Institut Français d'Archéologie orientale. Bibliothèque d'Etude 97.

Quibell, J. E. 1900. *Hierakonpolis* 1. London: Bernard Quaritch. Egyptian Research Account 4.

1908. *Excavations at Saqqara (1906–1907)*. Cairo: Institute Français d'Archéologie orientale. Service des Antiquités de l'Egypte.

1909. *Excavations at Saqqara (1907–1908)*. Cairo: Institut Français d'Archéologie orientale. Service des Antiquités de l'Egypte.

Redford, D. B. 1986. *Pharaonic king-lists, annals and day-books: a contribution to the study of the Egyptian sense of history*. Mississauga, Ontario: Benben Publications. SSEA Publication 4.

Reisner, G. A. & W. S. Smith. 1955. *A history of the Giza necropolis 2: the tomb of Hetep-heres the mother of Cheops*. Cambridge (MA): Harvard University Press.

Robins, G. 1986. *Egyptian painting and relief*. Princes Risborough: Shire Publications.

Schäfer, H. 1986 [1919–1963]. *Principles of Egyptian art*. Ed. E. Brunner-Traut, trans. & ed. J. Baines. Revised reprint. Oxford: Griffith Institute.

Schele, L. & M. E. Miller. 1986. *The blood of kings: dynasty and ritual in Maya art*. Fort Worth (TX): Kimbell Art Museum.

Spencer, A. J. 1980. *Early dynastic objects*. London: British Museum Publications. Catalogue of Egyptian Antiquities in the British Museum 5.

Tawfik, S. 1985. Der Palermostein als frühester Beleg fur die Weihformel, in Posener-Kriéger (ed.): 309–13.

Te Velde, H. 1988. Egyptian hieroglyphs as linguistic signs and metalinguistic informants. *Visible Religion* 6: 169–79.

Vandier, J. 1952. *Manuel d'archéologie égyptienne, 1, 1: Les époques de formation, la préhistoire*. Paris: Picard.

Whitehouse, H. 1987. King Den in Oxford, *Oxford Journal of Archaeology* 6: 257–67.

Williams, B. 1986. *Excavations between Abu Simbel and the Sudan frontier 1: The A-Group royal cemetary at Qustul: Cemetery L*. Chicago: University of Chicago Press. Oriental Institute Nubian Expedition 3.

1988. Narmer and the Coptos colossi, *Journal of the American Research Center in Egypt* 25: 35–59.

Williams, B. & T. J. Logan. 1987. The Metropolitan Museum knife handle and aspects of pharaonic imagery before Narmer, *Journal of Near Eastern Studies* 46: 245–85.

Wolf, W. 1957. *Die Kunst Ägyptens: Gestalt und Geschichte*. Stuttgart: W. Kohlhammer.

Zibelius, K. 1972. *Ägyptische Siedlungen nach Texten des Alten Reiches*. Wiesbaden: Dr. Ludwig Reichert. Beihefte zum Tübinger Atlas des Vorderen Orients B 19.

THE ORIGINS OF THE ILLUSTRATED BOOK[1]
Nicholas Horsfall

Eric Turner *in memoriam*

This paper does not offer any new evidence for the pre-history or proto-history of the illustrated book, nor does it claim to explore the genesis of such books in any original manner. No single theory of development will be proposed; rather, taking a somewhat wider view of the evidence than was done in certain recent studies and incorporating certain pieces of evidence which have come to light only recently, I shall argue that the only sort of account of the illustrated book's early history which will meet the facts is of a complex nature, involving several distinct and simultaneous channels of development. It will of course be recognised at once by specialists that such an approach represents a protest against the polarisation of attitudes in studies in this field. Thus, to quote K. Schefold:[2] "müssen wir also die These ablehnen, dass es bie den Griechen illustrierten Dichtungen gab, so kennt man doch seit langem illustrierte wissenschaftliche Texte." To pursue this argument to its logical conclusion is positively unnerving: it must, I think, mean that we are asked to suppose that Greeks of the classical and Hellenistic periods, who illustrated their myths by such works as—for example—the François vase and the N.Y. Euphronios-krater, the Laocoon group and the now-lost mythological frescoes of the Lesche of the Cnidians at Delphi could not or would not produce an illustrated edition of Homer and Euripides, but could and did illustrate works on astronomy or botany. On the other hand, Kurt Weitzmann, in a remarkable series of books and articles[3] has argued with eloquence and elegance that *Iliads* with up to seven hundred and twenty pictures and *Odysseys* not much less copiously illustrated did exist in the Hellenistic and

Reprinted by permission of the publisher from *Aegyptus* No. LXIII, 1983, pp. 199–216.

Roman worlds—as indeed, on his arguments, did equally lavish editions of the Epic cycle, Aeschylus, Sophocles, Euripides, etcetera.[4]

Let me begin with some technical considerations:

It has of course often been observed that numerous examples of the illustrated book survive from ancient Egypt, whereas Greek archaeological contexts provide little or nothing comparable. This fact in isolation provides no basis whatsoever for any argument regarding the diffusion of illustrated books, or attitudes towards such books. Conditions of survival provide an entirely sufficient explanation for this disparity: "the Egyptians, the inhabitants of the country where papyrus was manufactured and of which it had more or less a monopoly, used to place illustrated rolls as offerings in the tombs of the deceased."[5] Where of course they were discovered in large numbers by archaeologists. Not all the physical evidence on which my arguments rest is of Egyptian origin, but most is; after all, any ancient literary text of non-Egyptian origin is exceptional enough, and an illustrated text would be astonishing. Thus the state of affairs in Athens, Pergamum or Rome has inevitably to be reconstructed: we have no reason to expect directly applicable evidence. Just as significant is the fact that most surviving papyri were recovered from the rubbish heaps of the Egyptian *chora:* not a notably wealthy or cultured environment in antiquity, and certainly not one where one might expect a great deal of money to be lavished on the illustration of books, or, for that matter, upon the refinements of calligraphy.[6] It should also be borne in mind that there were many grades of finished papyrus and that in general the quality of that which survives declines steadily throughout its known history.[7] Prior to the successful application of pigments, the surface of a papyrus roll or book will have required prolonged and careful treatment;[8] pen-and-ink drawings, on which we will touch, are another matter. With the development of illustration on parchment this paper will not be concerned; parchment did not of course even begin to be used for literary texts till the late c. 1 A.D., which is too late a date to have much bearing upon the development of this argument.

Just enough illustrated texts have in fact survived from Egypt (and there is no reason to suppose that more will not be published, though one can hardly hope for many) to permit of a few general observations.[9] It is no accident that perhaps the finest of all the pictures which survive on papyrus, of not earlier than 450 A.D., showing six charioteers, from a page of circa 25 by 33 cm., and illustrating an unknown text comes not from a roll but from a codex.[10] The distinction is crucial: the roll does not represent a very satisfactory format for an illustrated literary text, awkward as it is to manage, extremely uneconomical in comparison with the codex in its ratio of text contained to space occupied and above all, necessarily holding the pictures wound tight in a continuous curve, with their fibres wound hard up against the fibres of the next column. Little wonder then that the admirable Antinoe charioteers belong to a codex. Down, then, to the c. 2 A.D., when the codex begins to take over from the roll as the chief repository of classical literature, the high likelihood of damage to the pigments during reading might be calculated to discourage coloured book illustration; note the number of our earliest illustrated literary papyri which contain only pen and ink drawings (P.Oxy. XXXII, 2652, 2653, PSI VII, 847 (roll), VIII, 919, Pap. München 128), or outline-and-wash illustrations (P.Oxy. XIII, 3001) or paintings from which a good deal of the colour has been worn (P.Oxy. XXII, 2331).

The exceptions to the outline (one that is probably over-schematic but should prove essentially correct in outline) are largely scientific in character. The earliest Greek illustrated literary papyrus (Pap. Louvre 1; TAV. 1)[11] is a remarkable document in a number of ways; it was probably executed just before 190 BC and is illustrated copiously with diagrams (in colour) of zodiac and constellations. The text is of no importance, purporting falsely to be by the astronomer Eudoxus,[12] but the pictures are on a lavish scale and show clear Egyptian influence, as, for example, in the use of the scarab to symbolise the sun (WEITZMANN, *IRC,* 49). This is not the only reason to make us think that there may have been an unbroken tradition of book-illustration between Pharaonic and Greco-Roman Egypt (WEITZMANN, *IRC* 7ff. et passim). Greek scientific illustration is not central to this paper, but a few striking examples require discussion; not least because the evidence is more copious and less controversial, such illustrations may serve as models for the sort of arguments that historians of the origins of book-illustration have been compelled to use.

Scientific illustration begins in the lecture-room (maps, which were never necessarily linked to an explanatory text, are quite another matter) and an early "visual aid" is clearly to be presupposed when Aristotle exhorts his readers.[13] "Observe the sexual organs of the cuttlefish; let A represent the ovum, B and C the eyes." Drawings are actually found in the eleventh-century A.D. commentaries by Michael of Ephesus on the *de partibus animalium* and the *de animalium incessu*[14] and it may be that they derive ultimately from the master's school. On the walls of the Lyceum, it seems likely that there were charts of anatomy and of species of bird and animal. Perhaps the clearest confirmation is to be drawn from the Vienna Dioscorides (Cod. Vindob. Med. Gr. 1); a later part of the volume contains a text on birds, itself of no importance,[15] but still reflecting, however dimly, the techniques of scientific research and taxonomic analysis practised in the school of Aristotle. The remarkable chart of birds on fol. 484 v (TAV. 2), likewise reveals that it is the product of a long development; it contains birds which are not mentioned in the texts and the birds cannot originally have belonged within a grid such as now encloses them; both the ostrich and the bustard are too large for their boxes and it is therefore likely that they come from a source where they had been given more room. The first three pictures of the second row are all water birds, the first three of both the third and the fourth rows are various members of the order *passeriformes.* The relics of a regular system of scientific ornithological illustration are therefore visible.[16] Moreover, the two ducks, first and third in the second row, are so clearly and specifically defined that a further step can be taken. We find *anas platyrrhyncha* and *tadorna tadorna* quite unmistakable and in close proximity in a mosaic from the Casa del Fauno at Pompeii.[17] It is not, of course to be suggested that the artist of the mosaic himself consulted directly an illustrated edition of a work of Aristotle on birds, but it seems clear enough that the first-century and sixth-century pictures have a common visual source which looks very likely to have been some sort of ornithological chart attached to a birdbook deriving from the school of Aristotle.

The argument from botanical texts is just as persuasive:[18] the elder Pliny writes[19] in complaint against the authors of Crateuas, Dionysius and Metrodorus "they painted likenesses of the plants and then wrote under them their properties,[20] but not only is a picture misleading when the colours are so many, particularly as the aim is to copy nature, but besides this much imperfection arises from the manifold hazards in the accuracy of copyists. In addition, it is not enough for each plant to be painted at one period only of its life since it alters its appearance with the fourfold changes of the year.'' That is clearly a fair and just criticism and it is surely in itself significant that Pliny writes as one to whom botanical illustration is thoroughly familiar. Dioscorides' survey of materia medica is roughly contemporary[21] and there is really no room for doubt that the magnificent illustrated manuscripts of this author go back to an original on papyrus, in which not only text but pictures must have been the author's responsibility.[22] It is perhaps worth adding the other instance—that is, in the field of entomology—where a reference in an ancient author adds weight to iconographical arguments. Tertullian refers to the scorpion, *tot venena quot et genera, tot pernicies quot et species, tot dolores quot et colores Nicander scribit et pingit.*[23] Nicander indeed describes scorpions in the *Theriaca* (770 ff.) and numerous species are illustrated in the c. 10 Cod. Par. Suppl. Gr. 247: similar conclusions regarding the pictures' origins are imposed.[24] It is as well to note that we have found illustrations both in prose quasi-scientific texts such as Dioscorides' and in versified popular abridged accounts such as Nicander's.

Ancient traditions of illustration in works on ichthyology, surveying, military science, anatomy and notably astronomy have been surveyed with comparable results (WEITZMANN, *ABI* 5 ff); indeed we are told that the *Phaenomena* of Aratus so attracted painters that there was no convention of iconographical uniformity and each one did as he pleased.[25]

However, when we turn to the illustration of literary texts, the evidence proves to be far more shaky. The case of literary works is indeed intrinsically different. Ancient critics spoke of a great virtue in authors called *enargeia,*[26] the capacity to conjure up a picture in the mind of the reader. In scientific works, pictures were necessary, in literary ones, arguably, superfluous, if the author was truly a master of his craft. It is therefore perhaps not altogether surprising that from the very earliest mythological scenes in Greek art (about 700 B.C.) for the next two hundred years, the artists do not consciously exhibit dependence on a specific scene in *Iliad* or *Odyssey*[27] and indeed it takes as long again before artists at all regularly specify explicitly which literary work they are following.[28] The place and function of literary texts in the development of Greek art have not been charted systematically and here only a few outlines and indications will be given. Verse inscriptions on black-figure and red-figure vases are rare; verse inscriptions relevant to the scene depicted very rare indeed, and relevant verse inscriptions citing a known text do not, so far as I know, exist. Scenes of reading on Attic vases are no more help: of the 45-odd in Immerwahr's 1964 and 1973 lists, 9 contain legible inscriptions, and only one, of two words from an Homeric hymn, is identifiable.[29] The Cleophrades painter characterises a rhapsode with the bombastic half line ὧδέ ποτ' ἐν Τίρυνθι, "so once upon a time in Tiryns";[30] Odysseus, passing the Sirens on a black-figure oenochoe, cries λῦσον,[31] "let me go" and Sophilos obligingly labels a scene on a dinos "Games of Patroclos."[32] Most of the figures in the vast and complex narrative scenes on the François vase are labelled. But the medium of the vase may reasonably have been felt to be restricting: thus on the chest of Cypselos, of cedar, and of ca. 550 B.C., as described by Pausanias, most of the figures were labelled[33] and there were several verse inscriptions describing the action.[34] When, a century and a half later, Polygnotos executed his large-scale painting of the Sack of Troy in the Lesche of the Cnidians at Delphi, it is clear from Pausanias' account that most of the figures were labelled, but though Pausanias does think at one point that he knows what the artist's literary source actually was,[35] the implication of that statement is clear—it had not been specified by the artist himself. Nor were the labels identifying figures and scenes felt to be really necessary; Pausanias says of one figure "you might guess it to be Helenus son of Priam, even before reading the inscription."[36] Similarly, Pausanias' contemporary Aelian comments on the unnecessary triviality of the labelling on some early paintings.[37] We are, after all, dealing with a common store of generally known heroes and heroines, stories, gestures and episodes. Just as authors were expected to conjure up pictures without illustrations, so artists represented scenes from great literature and familiar myth without resort to pedantically specific labels.

The evidence is comparable if we turn from epic to drama; it is generally true to say that artists were inspired more by stage performances than by the written text of plays, and it seems certain, to take an extreme case, that a vase which carries the name of poet, flute-player, lyre-player and chorus was produced to commemorate a specific performance of a satyr-play[38] (TAV 4). The first vases to be produced under the direct influence of the Attic dramatists probably appeared within ten years of Aeschylus' death; once again, the artists count upon the specificity of their depictions and their customers' love of the stage; figures are for the most part ungenerously labelled and identifications are often in doubt because the literary tradition is so lacunose. One solitary Apulian vase quotes a line and a half of comic verse which seems to belong to the scene portrayed.[39] Yet we know neither author nor play, for it is quite exceptional that either should be specified.

We have to turn to an altogether humbler art-form before we can trace the growth of a more integral link between literary texts and works of art. The so-called Megarian bowls are roughly hemispherical moulded ceramic bowls, often bearing mythological scenes and holding about half a litre; they date from the later c. 3 B.C. to Sulla's sack of Athens in 86.[40] Such bowls are essentially a pisaller, a poor man's substitute, for we hear repeatedly of fine bowls bearing mythological scenes in silver: Trimalchio is represented as an owner and indeed in a triumph of mythological confusion and artistic incomprehension he thinks that one depicts Daedalus who shuts Niobe inside the Trojan Horse.[41] Nero, moreover, dashed two favourite cups, which he called "Homeric" upon the ground when he heard of the mutiny of his armies in 68.[42] A Bactrian imitation from South Russia, probably bearing Euripidean scenes, may give a fair idea of such luxury cups.[43] Some sixty different moulds, deriving with fair certainty from literary texts have by now been identified;[44] the majority are Homeric, but some represent scenes from the Epic cycle and Euripides, and a very few are Sophoclean or Aeschylean. Some bowls merely label the figures, others add helpful remarks[45] such as "Agamemnon swears to satisfy Achilles with a view to the battle"; not infrequently the poet is specified: "according to the poet Lesches from the Little Iliad" and sometimes there are even long, though barely legible quotations (TAV. 5) from the original text.[46] It has long been wondered what relationship there may have been between pictures and text before they appeared on the bowls. The scenes are selected in several distinct ways and the whole process of selection is highly suggestive; we have, for example, two bowls which show scenes from *Odyssey* xxii, three scenes on each bowl, and each bowl illustrates only seventy or eighty lines of the book. These sequences look remarkably like sections taken from an immense cycle and there is a powerful temptation to infer that there were once seven bowls to illustrate the whole of *Odyssey* xxii and some 170 for the whole *Odyssey*.[47] On the other hand, there are bowls which select one scene only from three successive books of the *Iliad* and have been described as "epitomes of a cycle"; we might compare the Bactrian silver bowl, which displays two scenes from the *Alcestis* and two from the *Ion* of Euripides, and one each from the *Alope* and the *Bacchae* (cfr. WEITZMANN, *IRC* 27).

The Megarian bowls do not stand quite alone; until very recently, their only artistic analogue was the *"Tabulae Iliacae"* (see below); now K. Weitzmann and E. G. Turner[48] have published a glass, probably of the c. 1 B.C., bearing a comic scene and barely decipherable apparently from the dramatic original. The combination of text and scene (cfr. WEITZMANN (n. 48), 45 f.) is clearly very close to that on the Megarian bowls and it is of the greatest interest that such a combination has now been discovered in a new artistic medium: unlike the Megarian bowls, however, the painted glass was not mass-produced.

The *"Tabulae Iliacae"* appear to have been the product of even more prolonged and expensive labour: there are twenty-one often known to us.[49] The earliest is mid-Augustan (TAV. 6), the latest probably late Antonine. Materials vary widely, though most are marble. None was originally larger than 25 cm. by 40, though not one survives intact. They are called "Iliacae" since twelve out of the 21 portray scenes from the *Iliad.* When the provenance is known, it is always Rome or the Roman Campagna—indeed it is almost certain that they were made in Rome by Egyptian craftsmen.[50] A combination of low reliefs in miniature and inscriptions in Greek, often extensive and, curiously enough, not always explanatory of the reliefs they accompany, is what distinguishes the *Tabulae.*

They also represent a positive treasure house of misapplied ingenuity:

4N (TAV. 7) for example carries

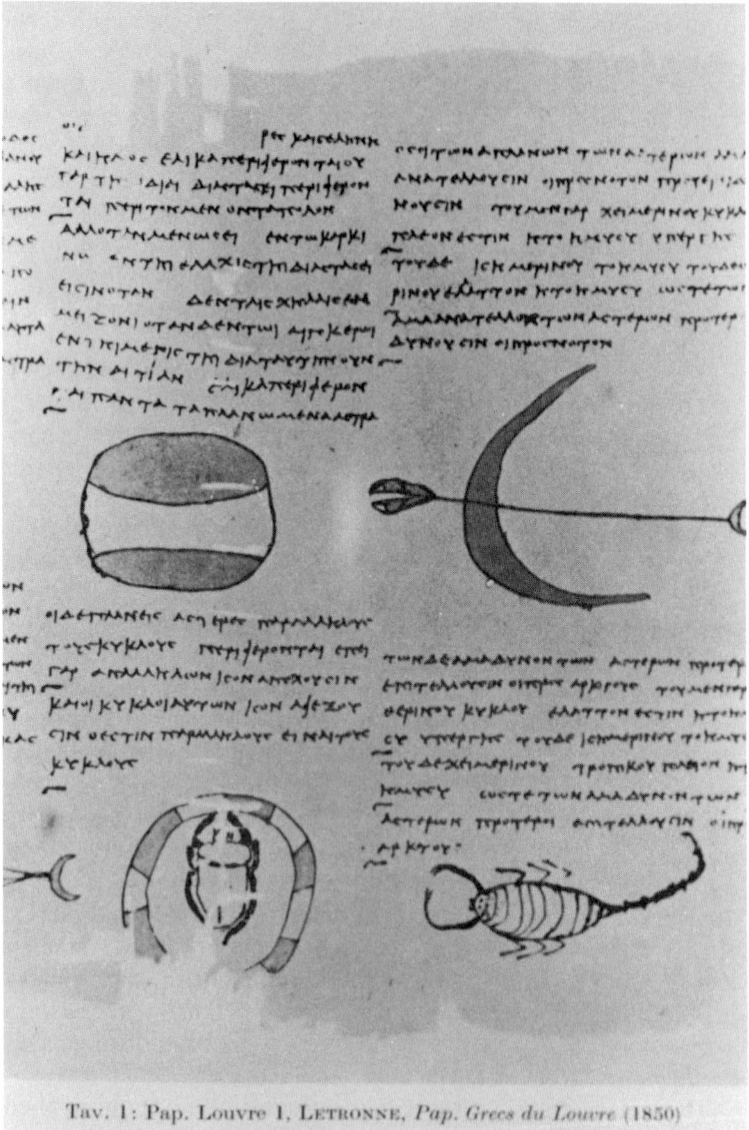

Tav. 1: Pap. Louvre 1, Letronne, *Pap. Grecs du Louvre* (1850)

Tav. 2: Cod. Vindob. Med.Gr. 1 fol. 484v, after the facsimile,
PREMERSTEIN, Leiden 1906

Tav. 3: C. Singer, «JHS» XLVII (1927), pl. 1, with thanks to Dr. W. E. H. Cockle.

Tav. 4: Napoli, Mus. Naz. 81673, bibliography, TRENDALL and WEBSTER, 29.

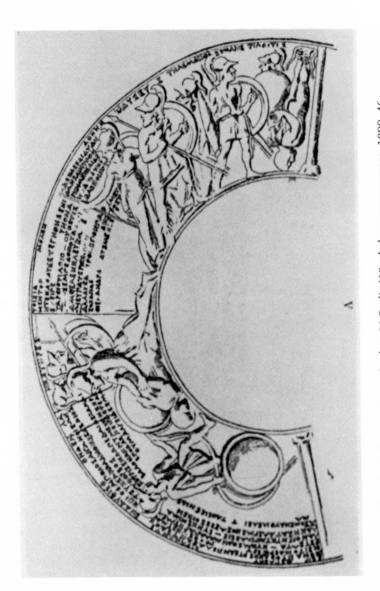

Tav. 5: C. ROBERT, *Hom. Becher*, 58 Berlin Winckelmannsprogramm, 1890, 46.

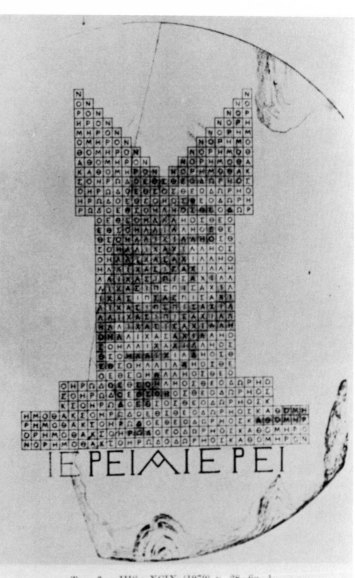

Tav. 7: «JHS» XCIX (1979) p. 28, fig. 1

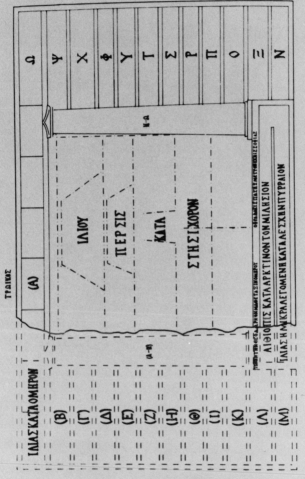

Tav. 8: «JHS» XCIX (1979) p. 36, fig. 3

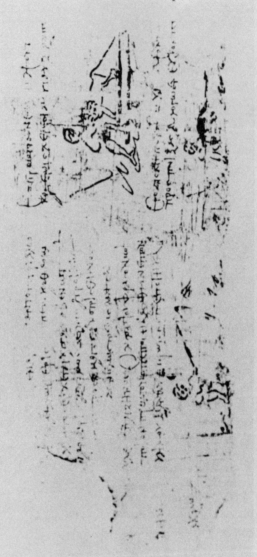

Tav. 9: P.Oxy. 22.2331; thanks to the Egypt Exploration Society

Tav. 10: P.München 128, ed. HEISENBERG and WENGER, 1914

2652

Tav. II: P.Oxy. 32.2652; thanks to the Egypt Exploration Society

(i) what appears to be the only palindromic Greek inscription (? humorously intended by association with the shape of (ii)), "from the priestess to the priest."

(ii) above it a grid of letters designed to resemble schematically an altar, reminiscent of the figure-poems of Dosiadas, Besantinus and Publilius Optatianus Porphyrius.

(iii) The squares of the grid within the altarconta in the "labelling" of the recto, and the artist's signature,[51] ἀσπὶς Ἀχιλλῆος Θεοδώρηος χαθ' "Ομηρον "The Shield of Achilles, the work of Theodoros, according to Homer." Starting from the centre of the grid, the reader may proceed upwards, downwards, or sideways, turning 90° where he will; he will ultimately reach the side, having read the complete message. Word-squares of this type are best attested in Egypt[52] and that is the strongest argument for the suggestion regarding the nationality of the craftsmen.

(iv) Written round the rim (4N is 18 cm. in diameter and 4 cm. thick) were originally ten columns giving the Homeric text describing the Shield of Achilles; five of the columns survive. The lettering is a remarkable tour de force.

The inscriptions on the *Tabulae Iliacae* are a strange mixture: intermittently they convey scraps of high erudition—for example, the number of lines in the lost poems of the Epic cycle[53] or the chronology of the events narrated in *Iliad*.[54] But the summaries of the poems, like that running down the pilaster on the *Tabula Iliaca Capitolina*[55] are appallingly jejeune and sometimes quite simply wrong, which is indeed what have come to expect in the Vulgarerzählung of ancient mythology.[56] The socio-economic context of such curious works, miniaturised, elegant, attractive, yet profoundly trivial, is a tempting matter for speculation. On the *Tabula Iliaca Capitolina,* by way of example, the figures and scenes are labelled, pretty thoroughly, though not comprehensively, and poems and authors are also specified, as often on the Megarian bowls:[57] "Iliad according to Homer," "Sack of Troy according to Stesichorus."[58] The serious lover of Greek literature would surely have been appalled by such a combination of the obvious, the trivial and the false. Likewise, the serious lover of art cannot have derived much pleasure from pictures so tiny that the sculptor could add little if anything of his own interpretations and emotions. On the other hand, the *Tabulae* must have taken much skill and a long time to produce. This was the reason behind my own proposal in 1979 that this expensive rubbish belonged in the homes of the nouveaux riches ("JHS" xcix, 35)—of men such as Calvisius Sabinus, who forgot the names of Achilles, Priam and Ulysses and Trimalchio himself, whom Petronius portrays as having Homeric cups, Homeric scenes on the walls and readings of Homer at dinner[59] and yet as utterly ignorant of myth; he thinks that Ulysses twisted the Cyclops' thumb,[60] he confuses Orpheus and Mopsus (cfr. supra, p. 9)—and it is therefore very tempting to imagine a Trimalchio explaining the palindrome and word-square with laborious pride.[61]

The *Tabulae* at the same time occupy a crucial place in the history of book-illustration.[62] Thus, for example, the band across the top of the *Tabula Iliaca Capitolina* (cfr. Horsfall, 36) (TAV. 8) contains seven scenes; the first four illustrate only lines 22–84 of *Iliad* i, in roughly the ratio to be expected of an artist who inserted one or two illustration per column in a papyrus roll. The remaining three were widely dispersed as though the artist of the Tabula were selecting from a wide range (WEITZMANN, *IRC* 41, Horsfall, 45). Other *Tabulae* illustrate both these techniques: on 16Sa, the Odyssean scenes illustrate consistently episodes taken from an early part of each book.[63] The ratios of pictures to text suggested by the principles of selection in the *Tabulae* were applied by Weitzmann to the Homeric epics as a whole (*ABI*, 37), and he reached the remarkable figure of some 720 pictures for the *Iliad* and not far fewer for the *Odyssey*. But it is also perhaps worth pointing out that the artistic traditions of the *Tabulae* and the Megarian bowls are altogether independent. If therefore (and a word of caution is still in place) both derive from illustrated editions, then there cannot have been a single standard sequence of *Iliad* or *Odyssey* pictures. The scale of illustration may appear implausibly large, and yet we are told quite specifically by the elder Pliny (xxxv, 11) that this gigantic task of illustration was not beyond the powers of the book-trade at least in the first century B.C., for after all Varro collected in his *Imagines* 700 portraits of great men in many fields and copies of the work were sent "to all lands."[64] These portraits were not, so far as we can tell, mere outline sketches; that of Aeneas copied a statute at Alba Longa (so the provenance of the original might be given) and appears to have been in colour, for his black boots are specified (Lyd. *Mag.* i. 12). Varro described each figure in a short epigram, of which two survive (NON. p. 528L, GELL. iii. 10), and it is clear that his work influenced both Virgil's parade of heroes in *Aen.* vi. and the great rows of statues which adorned the Forum of Augustus. Here it should be clear that we are talking about taste, money, time and culture; at the other end of the scale, many of the illustrations to literary texts on papyrus which survive are of the very poorest quality; perhaps the worst are illustrations of the deeds of Heracles, interesting though they are as showing the way in which pictures may have been laid out in a papyrus roll (P.Oxy, xxii, 2331) (TAV. 9). The reluctance of some scholars to accept that in the late Hellenistic world readers may have welcomed pictures in their books arises partly from a failure to distinguish between the artistic and financial resources available in the Egyptian country-side and those which a wealthy Roman connoisseur may have had at his disposal. Thus the younger Seneca, criticising the accumulators of vast libraries, whose very titles the collector would hardly have time to read, comments: "I would not mind if the error arose from an excess of zeal for learning: as it is, these works of sacred genius, copied pictures and all, are sought out to ornament and decorate the walls."[65]

It should, however, be observed that expenditure on illustrated books is not a regular element in the moralists' censures; it would appear that such books were not widely circulated or generally collected even in the wealthy milieu of Rome—yet the testimony that such books existed is impeccable.

The argument that massively illustrated *Iliads* and *Odysseys*— and it should be noted that the argument is not as yet concerned with any other genres—existed in the late Hellenistic world does not, fortunately, rest solely upon the evidence of the Megarian bowls and *Tabulae Iliacae.* Our one illustrated Homer-papyrus (P. München 128, c. 4 A.D.) (TAV. 10) shows Briseis in *Il.* i. led away by the heralds Talthybius and Eurybates and a striking correspondence exists between it and the corresponding scene in the *Ilias Ambrosiana.*[66] Other significant parallels in choice of scene and in iconographical detail exist between it and the *Tabulae Iliacae.*[67] The most striking is a scene from *Iliad* xxii; Hector stands in the Scaean gate, leaning on his spear and holding his shield in closely similar manner on the *Tabula Iliaca Capitolina* and in miniature no. 54 in the ms. But it would be gravely misleading if the impression were to be given that illustrated editions of the *Iliad*

were a simple and unarguable fact of artistic life in the Hellenistic
and Roman worlds. Not only, as has been observed, are the artistic
traditions of the *Tabulae Iliacae* and the Megarian bowls sharply
independent, but different *Tabulae* vary strikingly in their portrayal of the same scene;[68] the text on the *Tabulae* shows, often,
no direct knowledge of the poem (Horsfall, 34), whereas that on
the Megarian bowls, and, it must be said, on 4N ("Shield of
Achilles") quotes from the hexameters of Homer. Tempting
though it is to accept that the *Tabulae* are influenced by an
illustrated edition of Homer, their general ignorance of the text
constitutes a major difficulty.

At the same time, other cycles of pictures, quite different and on
a far larger scale were being produced; they were not only popular
on account of the unique fame of the story, but as a result of the
growing emphasis placed in the c. 1 B.C. and thereafter on the
mythological links between Troy and Rome[69] Trimalchio, as has
been noted, had a Homeric cycle on his walls (29.4); there was
another in the portico built by Augustus' stepfather, Lucius
Marcius Philippus, round the *aedes Herculis Musarum, plurimis
tabulis.*[70] When Virgil describes the Trojan scenes in the temple of
Juno at Carthage in *Aeneid* i,[71] he will have been describing not so
much an actual cycle but rather a familiar type or category.
Vitruvius comments[72] on *troianas pugnas seu Ulixis errationes
per topia* as a conventional cycle of pictures to have on the walls.
This popularity we find, predictably, reflected on the walls. This
popularity we find, predictably, reflected on the walls of Pompeii.
There is no need to attempt to duplicate Karl Schefold's admirable
Die Trojasage in Pompeii;[73] there are three main cycles, two
painted and one in stucco. Much the grandest is in the "Casa del
Criptoportico" of between 40 and 30 B.C. (HORSFALL, 42, n.
122). Three scenes lead into the *Iliad,* 72 illustrate the poem, and
another eight cover the events after the end of *Iliad* xxiv. Many of
the figures are labelled, yet there is no sign of extensive quotation
from the text of Homer, though it was common enough practice at
Pompeii to link paintings with epigrams.[74] Students of the "Casa
del Criptoportico" cycle are agreed that what lies behind it is an
artistic original of the late c. 4 B.C., independent of any text
(SCHEFOLD, *Trojasage,* 129), which was presumably transmitted
to Campania through the medium of some form of artist's
pattern-book. The relationship between the "Casa del Criptopor-

tico'' and the *Tabulae* is complex and delicate. We find both close
iconographical similarities, as in the case of *Iliad* xxi, which is
illustrated in both sequences by Achilles grasping Lycaon's arm,
though the spatial relationship of slayer and victim is not the
same. On the other hand, the two cycles illustrate Aeneas carrying
Anchises at their departure from Troy in strikingly different ways:
on the *Tabula Iliaca Capitolina,* Anchises sits on Aeneas' left
shoulder, in the manner of archaic Greek art, and as in all Roman
representations; at Pompeii, on the other hand, Anchises perches
pick-a-back behind his son, exactly in the classical Greek schema
(HORSFALL, 41). And yet, in both, Mercury serves as their guide,
which is a role we find portrayed nowhere else in the whole of
Greek and Roman art (*ib.,* 42). We are therefore, I would suggest,
compelled to infer the existence of a large number of cycles,
iconographically in part independent, yet regularly contaminating
each other. Some may have come from illustrated editions, some
certainly did not.

By way of contrast, we may turn very briefly[75] to consider New
Comedy, if only to demonstrate that there is excellent justification
for a refusal to come to any very definite conclusions regarding
the origins of the illustrated book. We may at least begin by saying
that there was a time when illustrated texts of new comedy were
regularly produced-particularly,[76] that is, of Menander. On P.Oxy.
xxxii, 2652 (TAV. 11) the name Agnoia, Ignorance, may be
discerned over an allegorical figure; she is the semi-divine
personage who speaks the prologue of Menander's *Perikeirom-
ene.* It is, moreover, possible that the soldier in the drawing on
P.Oxy. xxxii, 2653 belongs to another illustration of the same
play. Both these texts date from the second or third century A.D.
Earlier by a century or so is an unimpressive scrap now at
Florence[77] which does at least show that pictures stood not merely
at the head of a play, but were found, as we have seen elsewhere
(p. 13) in mid-column. The real problem is to determine whether
comic scenes in other art-forms—one thinks particularly of
mosaics and wall-paintings—derive from a tradition of illustrated
texts or have instead a direct link with stage performances—as
was the case on the Apulian vase carrying the cast-list of a
satyr-play (supra, p. 8)—and therefore serve rather as evidence for
continuing live performances of Menander.

Recent excavations have unearthed a villa at Mitylene[78] with seven mosaics from Menander plays and a house at Ephesus with wall-paintings[79] in which Euripidean and Menandrean scenes alternate.[80] In the scene from Mitylene which derives from the *Epitrepontes* of Menander, both the play and the act are named. Yet we know that Anthrakeus, the charcoal burner, is called Syriskos in the text of the play, that Syros ought to be called Daos and that Smeikrines ought to be written Smikrines. It looks therefore as though the mosaic artist here, even supposing he did have an illustrated manuscript in front of him, did not take the trouble to consult it too carefully. Many therefore have preferred to conclude that there was a tradition of illustration independent of any manuscript illustration. Moreover, the costumes and masks are quite specifically dated to the c. 3 A.D., at the end of which the mosaics were executed. We are back again vary close to the idea of illustrations of stage performances.[81] But because we know that illustrated editions of Menander did in fact exist, it emerges that there will have been a twofold tradition of illustration, part linked to the text, part independent. That is just what, *mutatis mutandis,* we found to have occurred in the case of Homer.

It is possible that there were fine illustrated papyri of Menander in the Hellenistic world, but that is more than we know. In the case of Homer, one would like to believe that such editions existed, and certainly they would provide a good, neat explanation of certain features of the Megarian bowls and *Tabulae Iliacae.* They were, moreover, not—so it would appear—beyond the capacities of the book-trade. But no more positive—or negative—conclusion is permitted by the present state of the evidence.

REFERENCES

[1]This paper has grown slowly and my debts are heavy: for their assistance with an earlier, trilingual version, to my mother, to Giovanna Vitelli, Luigi Enrico Rossi and to Rosemary Fleck (with the help of Orfeo Pagnani); for their energetic and valuable criticism, to audiences in England, Europe (notably at Zürich) and in Australia; for detailed discussion, above all to Hugo Buchthal (Warburg Institute) and Margaret Beattie (Macquarie University)

and lastly to Prof. G. Cavallo, who kindly proposed in late 1979 that this paper be published in Italy.

[2]*Wort und Bild* (Basel 1975), 127; see first *Orient Hellas u. Rom* (1949), 213 ff.

[3]«AJA» XLV (1941), 166 ff., to «AK» XXIV (1981), 39 f.; notably *Illustrations in Roll and Codex* (Princeton 1947) (hereafter *IRC*), *Ancient Book Illumination* (Harvard 1959) (hereafter *ABI*) and *Late Antique and Early Christian Book Illumination* (London 1977).

[4]But Prof. H. BUCHTHAL points out to me that in 7 *Kongr. für christ. Archäologie* 260 f. Weitzmann argues that antique and mediaeval techniques of book-illustration are in some sense discontinuous. 720 pictures: *ABI*, 37, 41.

[5]WEITZMANN, *IRC* 57.

[6]Cfr. E. G. TURNER, *Greek Papyri. An introduction* (Oxford 1968), 50.

[7]TURNER (n. 6), 2; but see N. LEWIS, *Papyrus in classical antiquity* (Oxford 1974) 58 f.; ib., 35 ff. for grades of finished papyrus.

[8]Cfr. above all PLIN. xiii. 81, LEWIS (n. 7), 62 f.; *PSI* xiii, p. 235; were the physical qualities of a fine writing papyrus equally advantageous for the application of pigment?

[9]LISTS in (e.g.) «EAA» s.v. *Papiro* (V. BARTOLETTI), O. MONTEVECCHI, *La Papirologia* (Torino 1973), 61.

[10]«JHS» xciii (1973), 192 ff.

[11]Cfr. «JHS» xcix (1979), 29 f., for bibliography.

[12]See P. W. s.v. *Eudoxos* § 24.

[13]Hist. An. v. 18, 550a 25.

[14]*C.A.G.* xxii; Z. KADAR, *Survivals of Greek Zoological Illuminations* (Budapest 1978), 30 ff.

[15]H. JACKSON, «Journ. Phil.» xxxv (1920), 193: lexture rooms. For the paraphrase of the *Ornithiaca* of Dionysius Poietes, see Z. KADAR (n. 14), 77, Kl. P. s.v. Dionysios No. 14.

[16]Z. KADAR (n. 14), 77 ff.

[17]K. SCHEFOLD, *Die Wände Pompejis* (Berlin 1957), 128.30; R. BIANCHI BANDINELLI, *Storicità dell'arte classica.* (Firenze 1950), tav. 95.

[18]WEITZMANN, *ABI*, 11 ff.

[19]PLIN. xxv. 8; references to illustrated books in ancient authors are not common; it is probably legitimate to infer that such books were rare; lavishly illustrated literary texts can only have been executed in small numbers for a luxury market; see below.

[20]This arrangement on P.Tebt. 679 (cfr. WEITZMANN, *ABI* pl. v., figs. 10 -b) and then far more impressively on both sides of a c. 4 fragment, of a codex, not a roll, significantly: C. SINGER, «JHS» xlvii (1927) pls. 1–2 and 1 ff. (TAV.3).

[21]For interesting remarks on his career, see R. W. DAVIES, *Epigr. Stud.* viii. 93 f. «Saalb. Jhb.» xxvii (1970), 88.

[22]It would be exceptionally interesting to know—and a careful survey of all illustrated texts on papyrus is required—whether scribe and illustrator can be differentiated.

[23]TERT. *Scorpiace* 1.

[24]Cfr. Z. KADAR (n. 14), 37 ff. for detailed arguments.

[25]*Comm. in Arat.* 80.24 ff., cfr. WEITZMANN *ABI,* 5 ff.

[26]Cfr. RUSSELL on Longinus 15.1.

[27]Cfr. K. F. JOHANSEN, *The Iliad in Early Greek Art,* 225 ff. (rather speculative), O. TOUCHEFEU-MEYNIER, *Thèmes odysséens dans l'art antique,* 284 ff.

[28]Cfr. too J. CARTER, «*ABSA*» lxvii (1972), 50 ff., M. WIENCKE, «AJA» lviii (1954) 289 ff.

[29]H. R. IMMERWAHR, *Studies in honor in B. L. Ullmann* I (Roma 1964) - 29, n. 5 for the Hom. Hymn (on which see too J. D. BEAZLEY, «AJA» lii (1948), 336 ff.); «AK» xvi (1973).

[30]*ARV*$_2$ 183.15 and 1632, JOHANSEN (n. 27), tav. 95.

[31]*Paralip.* 183.22 bis, J. BOARDMAN, *Black-Figure Vase Painting* tav. 286.

[32]*ABV* 39.6.

[33]PAUS. v. 17.3.

[34]PAUS. v. 18.2,3,4, 19.3,4.

[35]V. 25.3

[36]PAUS. *ibid.*

[37]AEL. *V.H.* x. 10.

[38]A. D. TRENDALL and T. B. L. WEBSTER, *Illustrations of Greek Drama* (London 1971) 29.

[39]*Ibid.,* 130.

[40]S. I. ROTROFF, *Megarian Bowls,* diss. Princeton 1976, U. SINN, *Die hom. Becher* (Berlin 1979) favours an earlier date.

[41]PETRON. 52.2.

[42]SUET. *Ner.* 47.1, cfr. PLIN. xxxvii. 29, WEITZMANN, *AK* 1981, 45.

[43]WEITZMANN, *ABI,* 69, «Art. Bulletin» xxv (1943), 289 f.

[44]SINN's 1979 collection has significantly increased the number, and it may be expected to rise further.

[45]C. ROBERT, «J.d.I.» lxxi (1919) 71, T. B. L. WEBSTER *Hellenistic Poetry and Art* (London 1964) 1 49.

[46]Lesches: F. COURBY, *Vases grecs à relief* (Paris 1922), 286; quotations (e.g.) SINN (n. 40) 89 f. (MB 21 = COURBY, 290.

[47]WESTZMANN, *IRC* 26,37 f.

[48]«AK» xxiv (1981), 39ff.

[49]Full bibliography, «JHS», xcix (1979), 26; the twenty-first I shall publish in «JHS» 1983.

[50]Cfr. M. T. BUA, «Mon. Lincei» 1971, I, 17ff.; M. GUARDUCCI, *Epigrafia Greca* (Roma 1974) iii, 425ff.

[51]«JHS» 1979, 27ff. (with full bibliography).

[52]Cfr., particularly, *S.E.G.* viii, 464.

[53]10K; A. SADURSKA, *Les Tables Iliaques* (Warsaw 1964), 59f.

[54]8E, SADURSKA (n. 53), 53f.

[55]SADURSKA (n. 53), 30f.

[56]«JHS» 1979, 33f., after WILAMOWITZ, *Kl. Schr.* vi-497–501.

[57]E.g. nn. 31, 32, 36 in SINN's catalogue.

[58]I hope to have renewed the challenge to the accuracy of this statement: «JHS» 1979, 35ff.; contra, LLOYD-JONES, *Magna Grecia* xvi, 2 (1980), 7.

[59]Petr. 29.9, 52.2, 59.3.

[60]M. COCCIA, «RCCM», xx (1978), 799.

[61]Cfr. Petr. 55.4, «JHS» 1979, 34f.

[62]WEIZMANN, *A.B.I.* 31ff, *IRC* 36ff., but see «JHS» 1979, 43–8.

[63]Roma, «Bibl. Vat. Mus. Sacro», Inv. 0066, SADURSKA (n. 53), 72ff.

[64]PLIN. xxxv 11; H. GERSTINGER «Jhb. Öst. Byz. Gesell.» 1968, 269ff.; «Prudentia» 1976, 83; «Ancient Society» x, 1 (1980) 20ff. (MACQUARIE).

[65]*Tranq. An.* 9.7.

[66]WEIZMANN, *ABI*, 32ff., R. BIANCHI BANDINELLI, *Hellenistic-Byzantine Miniatures of the Iliad* (Olten 1955), 37ff.

[67]BIANCHI BANDINELLI (n. 66), 26 et passim, SADURSKA (n. 53), 96ff.

[68]SADURSKA (n. 53), 10f, «JHS», 1979, 44.

[69]G. KARL GALINSKY, *Aeneas Sicity and Rome* (Princeton 1969), E. NORDEN, *Kl. Schr.* 358ff.

[70]PLIN xxxv, 144.

[71]*Aen*, i. 446ff.

[72]VITR. vii, 5.2.

[73](n. 2), 129ff. = *Netherlands Year Book for the History of Art*, 1954, 211ff.

[74]Cfr. M. GIGANTE *Civiltà delle forme letterarie nell'antica Pompei* (Napoli 1979) 223ff.

[75]Cfr. TRENDALL and WEBSTER (n. 37), *AK* Beiheft 6 (1970), T. B. L. WEBSTER *Hellenistic Art* (London 1967), 129ff, *Hellenistic Poetry and Art* (London 1964), 268ff.; for example.

[76]Cfr. Further now *AK* 1981, 47.

[77]P.S.I. vii, 847 (traces of colour).

[78]*AK*. Beiheft (n. 75), L. KAHIL, «Entr. Hardt» xvi (1969) 231ff.

[79]V. M. STROCKA «Gymn.», xxx (1973), 362ff.

[80]Cfr. the controversial scenes from the «Casa del Centenario»; further bibliography, WEITZMANN *AK* 1981, 48.

[81]Cfr. the iconographic analysis of the Theophoroumene mosaic of Mitylene (*AK* Beiheft 6, 48f.): an artistic tradition which goes back to stage performances of a period not long after the poet's lifetime; WEBSTER, *HPA* (n. 75), 185.

A TALE OF TWO CITIES: THE MINIATURE FRESCOES FROM THERA AND THE ORIGINS OF GREEK POETRY*

Sarah P. Morris

For Emily T. Vermeule

"The contemporary archaeologist is handicapped when dealing with poetry. Poetry, and art, offer selected myths and isolated heroic

*Reprinted by permission of the author and publisher from *American Journal of Archaeology,* October 1989, Vol. 93, no. 4, pp. 511–535.

*The author is more than usually grateful to the many contributors to this article: to her students at Yale, to her audiences at Columbia, Johns Hopkins, Chapel Hill, and UCLA, and to the two anonymous reviewers of the manuscript for *AJA.* In addition, the final result benefited beyond measure from the critical eye of Geoffrey Kirk, the kindness of Christos Doumas, and from the company of John Geanakoplos on a trip to Troy in May 1988. The article is dedicated to a teacher and scholar whose support and inspiration cannot be adequately honored.

The following abbreviations are used below:

N. Marinatos, *Art and Religion*	N. Marinatos, *Art and Religion in Thera. Reconstructing a Bronze Age Society* (Athens 1984).
Doumas, *Thera*	C. Doumas, *Thera. Pompeii of the ancient Aegean* (London 1983).
Fourth Cretological Congress	Πεπραγμένα τοῦ Δ Διεθνοῦς Κρητολογικοῦ Συνεδρίου (Athens 1981).
L'iconographie minoenne	P. Darcque and J.-C. Poursat, *L'iconographie minoenne* (*BCH* Suppl. XI, 1985).
Minoan Thalassocracy	R. Hägg and N. Marinatos eds., *The Minoan Thalassocracy. Myth and Reality. Proceedings of the Third International Symposium at the Swedish Institute in Athens, 31 May-5 June, 1982* (Stockholm 1984).
Morgan, *Miniature Wall Paintings*	L. Morgan, *The Miniature Wall Paintings of Akrotiri, Thera. A Study in Aegean Culture and Iconography* (Cambridge 1988).
TAW	C. Doumas ed., *Thera and the Aegean World* 1 (Athens 1978
Thera I–VII	S. Marinatos, *Excavations at Thera* I–VII (Athens 1968–1976).
Warren, "Miniature Fresco"	P. Warren, "The Miniature Fresco from the West House at Akrotiri, Thera, and its Aegean Setting," *JHS* 109 (1979) 115–29.

89

individuals, two elements archaeologists have been trained to ignore, perhaps abhor. An archaeologist is permitted by his colleagues to deal only with quantified, anonymous people, estimated consumers of barley, occupants of graves graphed on computers for place and time. He is not permitted to deal with individual yellow-haired chiefs of the Argives. He must subdue his private fictions to evidence photographable in the dirt, and should ideally publish his results as mathematical formulae. There is a clash of principle between archaeological reconstructions of the Bronze Age and Greek literary reconstructions of the same scene. Yet sometimes the two sides may offer mutual assistance.''[1]

One hundred years after the first Bronze Age frescoes were discovered on Thera, excavations at Akrotiri uncovered painted fragments "destined to open a new chapter in the history of the Aegean.''[2] The frescoes from Akrotiri afford an opportunity, rare in the Aegean Bronze Age, to examine wall paintings in their archaeological context instead of as burned or discarded fragments far from their original locale. The houses they decorated belong to a prosperous settlement of spacious, multistoried, freestanding structures comparable to smaller Minoan villas. Their architectural features conform closely to Minoan standards and techniques, including ashlar masonry reinforced with wood, pier-and-door arrangements, lustral basins and light-wells, and indoor plumbing.[3] Their size, elegance and *Minoitas* make the discovery of frescoes in quantity no surprise. In a town abandoned by its population, who cleared out valuable property and portable furnishings, painted wall plaster survives as eloquent as well as elegant evidence of the life and imagination of the inhabitants. For example, the frescoes and their distribution help illustrate the function of different spaces. The ground floor rooms open onto the street for commercial and industrial activity exposed to public life, while residential quarters and areas for leisure and family life were secluded upstairs.[4] This separation of public and private spheres suggests the segregation of male and female, and casts frescoes as decoration suitable for the latter sphere. Wall paintings are primarily found upstairs, and many represent women in activity involving costume, cosmetics, and ceremonies. The "House of the Ladies," for example, is named for a pair of frescoes where two women in Minoan ceremonial dress—the flounced skirt with bodice exposing the breasts—apply a similar costume to a third woman, presumably in preparation for a ritual where these garments are worn.[5] In the largest and most impressive single dwelling house excavated, Xeste 3, two stories of paintings surround Thera's only lustral basin with an elaborate panorama of women gathering saffron and offering it to a goddess, in a ceremony linked to rituals of initiation.[6]

On the basis of such frescoes, some scholars have imagined elaborate ceremonies in every house and called many dwellings "shrines," although more practical observers, including the director of current excavations at Akrotiri, see few or none.[7] In some cases, the utilitarian contents of a room and its architectural history argue for a more purely decorative purpose for Theran wall painting, as with the Lilies Fresco in Room Delta 2. An exception to the usual location of Theran paintings, Delta 2 was one of the few ground-floor rooms decorated with frescoes, when areas of the town were repaired after the initial catastrophe and before the final destruction.[8] The walls present a brilliant panorama of rocky formations crowned by lilies in bloom and swallows in flight. Once linked with the excavated contents of the room in a religious scenario celebrating spring, the landscape now appears as deliberate compensation for its small and confined space.[9] This more decorative interpretation for this attractive landscape liberates related scenes at Thera from a presumed relationship to ritual. They imply an aesthetic taste for interior decoration inspired by the natural world, appropriate to a culture which first applied engineering to the natural environment for the purposes of human comfort—indoor plumbing, light- and air wells, rooms that can be adjusted for climate. As an elegant and prosperous town, Akrotiri included attractive interiors much as in Greek and Roman houses at Delos or Pompeii, where natural landscapes decorated the walls of private homes. Social pretensions may have inspired the Cycladic population of Akrotiri to emulate Minoan culture in private interiors, including scenes of Minoan religious practices, much as Romans and Campanians affected Hellenic tastes in cult as in art.[10] Current perspectives on Roman painted walls in domestic settings may be more relevant to context than Egyptian or Minoan iconography commonly invoked in religious interpretations of the Thera frescoes.[11] It seems timely to heed Renfrew's recent reservations on identifying ancient cult evidence, and to acknowledge the same ambiguities in Aegean cult contexts recently acknowledged by archaeologists in the Near East.[12]

These preliminary observations on context serve to introduce the wall paintings from the West House as a decorative complex in a private home, without the assumption that it represents a cult center.[13] Compared to Xeste 3, the West House is modest in the number of its rooms and the absence of such Minoan features as a lustral basin or generous ashlar masonry. But it contained fine, imported Minoan pottery, much of it found in fragments with the miniature fresco, plus Minoan luxuries such as a lavatory, in addition to its fresco decoration.[14] The ground floor rooms face the Triangular Square, and a doorway which leads directly to a stairwell for access to the upper story (or stories). The street-level quarters are typically devoted to 'service' functions, while the upper floor has more spacious rooms, two of which (4 and 5, on the west side) were decorated with frescoes during the town's latest phase of repair. Room 4 is a bathroom complete with a latrine connected to the town's sewer system, as well as a clay bathtub and bronze vessels for heating and washing water.[15] A partition wall separated the bathroom area, the lower walls of which were protected with a ''splash'' coating of plaster painted yellow ochre, from the rest of Room 4 and its frescoes. Bowls of red pigment suggest the room was still being repainted in the period after the earthquake and before the final eruption.[16] Its window was attractively painted to imitate inlaid marble on the sill and marble jars with lilies against the jambs, resembling illusions for decorative effect in Roman painted interiors.[17] Around the walls of Room 4, a set of eight painted panels were found: above a dado of imitation marble is an oxhide stretched across a frame of three vertical posts topped with elaborate finials, and hung with festoons. The ship frieze next door explains these panels as a sort of open cabin or portable shield for an important figure on board each ship, presumably the captain.[18] The use of oxhides as temporary reinforcement of a wall under siege is attested by Homer (*Il.* 12.263; below, n. 73) in a passage which suggests that a freestanding shield of the type depicted here would be more useful. The isolation and abbreviation in painting of this nautical or military equipment resemble the style of panels depicting figure-eight shields found at Mycenae, Tiryns, Thebes, and Knossos.[19] When first excavated, these *ikria* encouraged a biographical explanation of the paintings in the West House, making it the home of a sea-captain, the "House of the Admiral." This initial reading of the frescoes treated them as scenes derived from personal experience, with the Nilotic frieze setting the maritime adventure in Libya, hence the miniature fresco's early sobriquet, the "Libyan Fresco."[20] While these panels do link Rooms 4 and 5 with a nautical theme, they contribute more to the general maritime decor of the West House rather than to any specific explanation of Room 4 as shrine or bedroom.

The only figural decoration associated with Room 4 is a large panel of a young woman now restored on the jamb of the doorway leading to Room 5.[21] Her hairstyle, pose, and garment instantly dubbed her a young "priestess," one of those identifications that has been retained since discovery and encouraged religious interpretations.[22] She carries what is probably a brazier (resembling clay ones found at Thera) with red, glowing coals, on which she is sprinkling some substance as if to release its fragrance when burned. The ritual explanation connects this figure with preparations, in Room 4, for a ceremony enacted in Room 5.[23] Context suggests a more practical explanation: she could be fumigating rooms near the lavatory, or applying cosmetics, rather than performing a ceremony.[24] Admitting these rooms their domestic function in the life of Thera allows the "priestess" a more ordinary place in the daily life of the Theran household, in a genre scene related to the home. Suspending ritual associations between the frescoes of Rooms 4 and 5 allows an examination of the miniature frescoes without a more programmatic link to the Room 4 paintings than a nautical theme.

The most famous room in the Aegean is a corner room ca. 4 × 4 m, found full of pottery but without much evidence for its function. The window sills were stacked with vessels, probably as a precaution in the final days of seismic unrest rather than in connection with any ritual.[25] The tripod table found on one of the north sills is a type often identified for offerings, but could as easily have served a more domestic function or could have been placed in the window for safety or to dry.[26] Imitation marble panels below the windows continue the decorative theme applied to the window in Room 4. Two large figural panels—two naked boys carrying fish—are restored at the outside ends of the two outer walls, flanking the windows. This theme is an Aegean favorite, familiar from the Middle Cycladic jar from Melos with a fisherman and his catch, and needs no assistance from ritual to account for its appearance on the walls of Thera.[27] Like the *ikria* panels from ships' cabins, these boys carrying fish abbreviate moments of island and seafaring life and bring the Cycladic world indoors. With its numerous windows, permanent paving of schist slabs, and imaginative painted decoration, Room 5 offered a comfortable attractive environment for daily and frequent occupation, the closest to a "living room" of the many excavated at Thera.[28]

Three sides of this room, on the north, east and south walls, carry miniature frescoes as an upper border ca. 40–43 cm high, of which a length of ca. 7.50 m is preserved. The fourth (missing) wall on the west probably once bore a similar frieze, implied by a fragment found in the excavations.[29] This placement of friezes is traditional inside Minoan villas and elsewhere on Thera, but is also common for other ancient decorative painting inside private homes, most significantly in the house of the Odyssey Landscapes in Rome.[30]

The three preserved walls present a landscape of ships and cities on the south facing military episodes on the north, linked by a Nilotic landscape on the east wall. As reviewed above (n. 20), Marinatos's original interpretation linked all three landscapes to the biography of the owner of the West House—an "Admiral" and veteran of a Libyan campaign. Both biographical interpretation and "Libyan" setting have ceded, in the last 10 years, to a more generic scenario within the Aegean.[31] Minoan and Cycladic archaeologists continue to seek specific correlations to Aegean realities in the prosopography and topography of these frescoes. The landscapes have been compared to many a mainland coast and island in the Aegean, beginning with Thera itself, to find a setting in the contemporary Bronze Age world. Its costumes and physiognomies have similarly been identified with Minoan, Mycenaean, Cycladic, and non-Aegean peoples in the reconstruction of plausible scenarios of the Late Bronze Age. The alternative to this historical approach invokes ritual as the source for the frieze's pictorial program. Morgan's identification of the scene as a seasonal ceremony has gained such wide acceptance that the scene is often labeled "procession of ships" or "nautical festival."[32]

I would like to reopen the debate on these frescoes and their pictorial relatives in Aegean art by examining their elements as part of a connected narrative transforming history into art, a visual counterpart to early epic poetry. The frieze is narrative in the most literal meaning, "erzählend" or story-telling. No claim can be made to specific names or places in these paintings, just as there are few identifiable Greek myths illustrated in the Bronze Age. But the classification as "genre" dilutes the impact of these frescoes as an expression of the kind of narrative developed in epic poetry.[33] Its images are cognates of epic motifs, without being illustrations of particular episodes. Nor does image defer to text, a view no longer popular in the study of art, where visual narrative is now accepted as independent of the text and even capable of generating stories derived from images.[34] The rich repertoire of visual formulae and motifs mirrors their proliferation not only in other visual arts but in poetic narratives now believed to be in circulation in the early Mycenaean age.

THE SOUTH FRIEZE

The Ship Fresco on the south wall (figs. 1–3) is the best preserved and most debated picture in Aegean art, particularly enlightening for nautical archaeology.[35] A fleet of ships amidst dolphins spans a single narrative perspective between two towns on separate landmasses which frame the fleet and whose figures focus on it. The town on the left (fig. 2) is more modest in size, architecture, population, and landmass, perhaps a small island, in comparison to the extensive promontory with many harbors and peaks which shelters the larger "city" on the right (fig. 3). The first town is encircled by a river which rises in a mountainous landscape and joins the sea abruptly, without a harbor. The rugged skyline beyond the town, made ferocious with a lion chasing deer, also runs above the pastoral world across the river from the town, on the viewer's left. A shepherd sits near a cluster of shelters, perhaps for flocks and their keepers, and seems in contact with the town through his conversation (?) across the stream with a standing townsman, in a similar long shaggy garment.

This environment is far too typical of the Aegean to claim a specific identity: it illustrates universal patterns rather than a

Fig. 2. South frieze, detail: first town. (From *Thera* VI, pl. 9)

Fig. 3. South frieze, detail: fleet and second town. (Photo: S. Morris)

single locale. The detailed hierarchy of settlements represented throughout these frescoes—from pastoral shelter to small island town, larger city or palace, peak tower/sanctuary, animal enclosures, and stone springhouse—provides a contemporary witness to Bronze Age sites retrieved by archaeological surface surveys. For example, any Greek rural setting features tiny farmsteads or overnight shelters (θημονιὲς, καθοίκια or καθέδρες in modern Greek) for animals and farmers commuting to fragmented farm holdings.[36] Without reviewing all the proposed and possible locales in the Aegean, an anonymous identity suits this town, in keeping with current consensus that this environment represents a generic Aegean setting.

It can be safely said and is generally accepted that the landscapes of the miniature frescoes are informed by a combination of Aegean reality and Minoan artistic conventions. But the impulse to represent such a town arose from more than environment alone. A story links this setting to the larger town across the water, to the episodes on the opposite wall, and possibly to the earliest Greek epic poetry. A counterpart to this town is an island like Ithaka in the *Odyssey,* home to a town and palace but also to outlying farmsteads like that of Eumaios or the more prosperous farm of Laertes (*Od.* 14.1–15; 15.555–57; 24.205–10). The two figures in the Theran landscape, separated by a stream, interact in the way that characters from different worlds, rural and urban, participate in the story on Ithaka. Animals and humans indicate a similar poetic interaction: in the landscape above the town, a lion chases deer in the manner of epic similes juxtaposing lions and heroes. Confrontations of warriors and lions in Mycenaean art have been familiar since the Shaft Graves were opened; a single dagger from Grave IV, for example, shows a lion pursuing deer on one side, and another hunted by men on the other side.[37] In this fresco, the world of nature forms not just the background but a metaphorical landscape for the world of heroes, as it does later in the imagery of poets. Similarly, the conventions of marine landscape, the dolphins cavorting in the sea (fig. 1), ultimately a Minoan theme, punctuate poetic descriptions of seascapes, as in the ἔκφρασις of the *Shield of Herakles* where dolphins define a harbor (207–15). The river encircles the town as Okeanos borders the shield of Achilles, or the world of Odysseus, an image always applied to circular shields or reconstructions of archaic cosmology (infra ns.

84–85). This prehistoric fresco suggests an alternative way to visualize this description from *Iliad* 18, a new source of poetic imagery that survives in Homer. Pictorial equivalents of Homeric formulae may have survived as vividly in the Greek visual imagination as in poetic memory, such that the description of the Shield of Achilles in *Iliad* 18 represents not so much an imaginary shield or a sophisticated cosmogony as a compound of narratives depicting nature and culture.

The inhabitants of the smaller town face right: all eyes are on the stretch of open water with its ships, the primary focus of the fresco and its narrative action. In a maritime culture, the iconography of departure and arrival by sea dominates daily life as it does art, transcending the "seasonal" specificity argued by Morgan. The "fleet" consists of seven ships which float, almost leisurely, toward a second larger town whose occupants hail them in a friendly way (fig. 3). Only one ship is under sail, while the others are being rowed or paddled, hardly methods of propulsion for rapid travel. Together with their festive appearance, their pace has encouraged the view that they are not warships or a true military "fleet" under sail, but participate in a seaborne ceremony.[38] But every ship contains warriors, or at least their helmets, and each is commanded by a captain perched in one of the "cabins."[39] These military details make the fleet one of the most "Mycenaean" elements of the fresco, as argued by proponents of "Mycenaeans at Thera."[40] This fleet is either departing on a military expedition or returning from one, arriving at a friendly port if not at its home.

Whatever the specific scenario, this image of a fleet corresponds to the poetic tradition of a catalogue of ships, each vessel differentiated in passengers and emblems, just as leaders and cities characterize each entry in a poet's catalogue. The variety in locomotion and decoration could indicate heroic ranking according to lineage or privilege, the way shield emblems in Archaic art distinguish individuals without identifying them. Greek poetry offers epithets embellishing ships with flowers and visual decoration as a literary device, not a ceremonial one. In a context where poetry recalls its own function, Pindar challenges anyone who claims greater κτεάνά τε καὶ τίμη among heroes who lived before Hieron (*Pyth.* 2.62–63): εὐ-ανθέα δ' ἀναβάσομαι στόλον ἀμφ' ἀρετᾷ | κελαδέων. Odysseus fetches Neoptolemos to Troy, after the death of Achilles, in a ποικιλοστόλῳνηὶ (Soph. *Phil.* 343), a ship whose gay decoration belied its grim mission, like the winning words of Odysseus himself. These epithets, and others, suggest that the decoration of ships represents an ornamental, narrative device, not a ceremonial function, in the fresco of the fleet.[41] What survives in the Homeric muster of ships (*Il.* 2.494–877), roster of heroes in battle (seen from the walls: 3.161–242), or in Hades (*Od.* 11.385–567) may be as old as panoramas like this one.[42] The thousands of vessels which sailed from Aulis far exceed the modest number on this fresco. But a fleet this small sufficed for the earlier expedition Herakles made to Troy, recalled in *Iliad* 5 (640–43, Lattimore trans.):

> he came here on a time for the sake of Laomedon's horses,
> with six vessels only and the few men needed to man them,
> and widowed the streets of Ilion and sacked the city . . .

The pictorial details of arrival at the larger town (fig. 3) belong to the world of Aegean topography but also recall the poetic description of that world in Homer. The long rocky promontory running up to a hill with buildings, and the two small harbors sheltering ships suit several epic descriptions, beginning with Ithaka (*Od.* 13.96–101):

> There is a harbor of the Old Man of the Sea, Phorkys,
> in the countryside of Ithaka. There two precipitous
> promontories opposed jut out, to close in the harbor
> and shelter it from the big waves made by the winds blowing
> so hard on the outside; inside, the well-benched vessels
> can lie without being tied up, once they have found their
> anchorage.

This description of a harbor is typical of Homeric arrival scenes and not intended to identify Homeric places in the fresco, as made clear in the fresco's similar correspondence to other Homeric harbors. When Odysseus arrives at the land of the Laistrygonians, it is also enclosed by towering cliffs and by two projecting promontories, protecting ships from the sea swell, but the hero proceeds cautiously, as he does on Aiaia (*Od.* 10.95–97; cf. 10.148):

> I myself, however, kept my black ship on the outside,
> at the very end, making her fast to the cliff with a cable.
> and climbed to a rocky point of observation and stood there.

The rocky promontory, small bays sheltering ships, and even the lookout point or σκοπιή are all suggested in this fresco (fig. 3), the last in three small buildings, one with a small figure before its doorway. Three men race up this hill (from town?) toward the peak, while two run back toward the settlement: news of the fleet's arrival, in other words, travels from lookout point to town, in details which unite ships and town in a single, coordinated narrative. Both poetry and geography provide parallels for this kind of landmark and its relationship to urban settlements. Near Homeric Troy, the fleet-footed scout and son of Priam, Polites, kept watch on the Achaeans from the hill called the burial mound of Aisyetes (*Il.* 2.790–94). This multiple function for a conspicuous topographic feature should assist the classification of sites in Aegean archaeology. For example, the landscape of prehistoric Kea is one of many to complement this fresco. The deep bay of Vourkari protects ships and the town of Agia Irini, while the peak of Troullos probably served as both watchtower and sacred peak, as suggested by Caskey with a reference to the mound of Aisyetes.[43] The mound of another hero at Troy also functioned in more than one way: the σῆμα 'Ίλου serves as sacred point and gathering place (*Il.* 10.415; 11.166–67), to be considered below in connection with the north frieze.

No single Aegean landscape can or should claim exclusive identity with the large town in the fresco (fig. 3), which has been called Cretan, Cycladic, and Mycenaean, if not Akrotiri itself.[44] Poem and painting may simply share the same inspiration in Aegean life, but epic as well as frescoes could derive from Bronze Age settings. The closest relatives of this town belong to the geography of the imagination, as in Nausikaa's description of Scheria (*Od.* 6.262–69):

> But when we come to the city, and around this is a towering
> wall, and a handsome harbor either side of the city,
> and a narrow causeway, and along the road there are
>   oarswept
> ships drawn up, for they all have slips, one for each vessel;

and there is a place of assembly, put together with quarried
stone, and built around a fine precinct of Poseidon,
and there they tend to all that gear that goes with the black
 ships,
the hawsers and the sails, and there they fine down their
 oarblades;
for the Phaiakians have no concern with the bow or the
 quiver,
but it is all masts and the oars of ships and the balanced
 vessels
themselves, in which they delight in crossing over the gray
sea; . . .

Painting and poetry agree on the image of a culture more
inclined to seafare than warfare, and a city offering ὅρμοδ,
κέρδος, and ξεινία, those vital signs of civilization sorely
missed on Lemnos (Soph. *Phil.* 302–303). Two figures carrying
sacks on poles across their shoulders stride on the tongue of land
between the σκοπίη and the second harbor, where two ships
smaller than those in the fleet look like transport vessels. Poet and
painter draw on Aegean life to depict an imaginary town, familiar
in the fresco without a specific name.

The town itself is nearly a city in comparison with the modest
one across the water (fig. 3). Its impressive facade of blue
masonry (ashlar limestone?) with a central gateway, and multistoried houses with windows and balconies punctuated by horns of
consecration resembles those seen in Minoan compositions. The
Cretan parallel most commonly invoked is the architectural
landscape represented in the so-called ''Town Mosaic'' of Knossos, a set of faience plaques that once formed an inlaid composition of houses, landscape, animals, and figures.[45] But several
features distinguish the Cycladic frescoes in style and subject
from the faience fragments, the military elements of which were
largely restored by Evans. The ''archers'' are reconstructed from
possibly bow-shaped objects on some fragments and figures on
others, the ''spearmen'' are probably shepherds.[46] The curious
spread-eagled figures may be drowners but could be swimmers,
and the recent rejection of a ship's prow as another ''dubious''
restoration eliminates the vessel present in mainland and Cycladic
shipwreck and sea-battle scenes.[47] The original restorations by

Evans were heavily influenced by his conviction that the silver siege rhyton from Mycenae (see below, fig. 8), the mosaic's closest analogy at the time, was itself Minoan rather than Mycenaean, as is generally accepted today.[48] To demonstrate a Minoan precedent for a mainland epic tradition, he restored military attributes, poses, and episodes, extracted from the silver siege rhyton, on the faience plaques, an important link in his argument. In fact, Evans restored those very features which would provide a city under siege to match the Homeric passage, and certify a Minoan contribution to the prehistory of the Greek epic tradition.[49] In reality, the plaques do not preserve more than a city at peace, and the Town Mosaic appears more pastoral than military. Its images of daily rural and town life could well belong to a Minoan narrative cycle, and scholars of philology as well as archaeology have postulated the existence of such cycles in poetry as well as art.[50] Such a narrative "cycle" is difficult to discern in the Town Mosaic, isolated panels originally set into another medium (wood?) as discrete units whose narrative connection has to be supplied by the viewer.[51] The frescoes from Tylissos, discovered and discussed before the Akrotiri excavations, allow the best impression of Cretan narrative painting, but like their companion miniature frescoes from Knossos, they cannot be securely dated before the frieze from Akrotiri.[52]

Despite these Minoan parallels, the miniature frieze from Thera belongs to a more Mycenaean world of hunting and battle as primary subjects for art.[53] Some of these subtleties were anticipated by the Kea frescoes, the closest analogy to those from Thera but published before the latter were discovered. Coleman's remarks on the Kea frescoes, with their scenes of towns in a maritime setting with figures engaged with chariots, hunting and feasting, could be applied to the frescoes from Thera: "The emphasis on narrative and a certain amount of drama rather than natural detail seem mainland in spirit."[54] The contrast between Cretan and Cycladic narrative is made vivid in comparing the spectacular new sealing from Chania with the Thera frescoes.[55] The seal impression frames a single dominant and symbolic figure—priest or king?—against a town designed to fit the lentoid shape. This image, however rich in its details of architecture, landscape, and symbolism, tells no familiar, heroic tale. Instead, it speaks a language idiomatic to Minoan iconography, one we may not be able to understand, and subordinates its landscape to a symbolic hierarchy dominated by this figure in a ritual or royal pose.

Here the pursuit of narrative collides with the standard pursuit of style in Aegean prehistory, at a critical period in antiquity (the 15th century B.C.) and in modern scholarship (the last decade) focused on the distinction of Minoan from Mycenaean art. Ever since Matz, we have accepted, abused, and revised certain well-worn stylistic formulas about torsional, flowing Minoan art and the schematic, ''emblematic'' style of the Mycenaean artist.[56] The Thera excavations offered a new challenge to these conventions, for the chronology of the eruption coincides with the emergence of Mycenaean art, in a context dominated by Minoan imports and influence.[57] In conventional scholarship, Minoan style would be demonstrated in an artifact from the West House at Thera: a limestone tripod-table with a painted marine landscape, where the dolphins leap in a freely improvised setting of rocks and plants.[58] A typical Mycenaean comparison would invoke the *ikria* from the same house, where a single motif has been extracted and repeated for a symbolic value of its own (above, n. 19). Although these critical stylistic features in fact help distinguish the Mycenaean component of the miniature frescoes, they may have exaggerated Minoan images as mobile action, Mycenaean as arrested symbols.[59]

One of the dangers of these definitions, even under recent modifications, is that they obscure the role of narrative. A more useful assumption might be that Mycenaean art tells a story familiar from Greek literature, while Minoan art accompanies a tradition whose language and meaning are lost. The miniature frescoes may be Minoan in their individual images, but these motifs contribute to a Mycenaean theme, as recognized by numerous scholars.[60] One would expect a narrative of the 15th century B.C. to be represented in Minoan images, if not composed by Minoan artists. But their story could well belong to a Mycenaean, even Greek epic tradition, much as a Mediaeval illustration of the Trojan War might include a cathedral facade without converting epic heroes to Catholicism. This makes, for example, the horns of consecration in the large town an architectural

convention, not necessarily an index of Minoan religion.[61] Greek
artists experimented in a similar manner in the early Archaic
period, incorporating Oriental motifs into mythological scenes.[62]
the emergence of Mycenaean art with the participation of Minoan
artists, or even as a later phase of Minoan art, presents problems
similar to the study of Greek art and artists in the production of
early Roman art.[63] Once Minoan motifs and Mycenaean stylistic
features have been identified in the Thera frescoes, their content
deserves the same attention earned by Roman art once generations
of scholars had exhausted its Greek elements. In the domain of
religion, archaeologists are now careful to distinguish between
Minoan motifs in circulation as early as the time of the Shaft
Graves and Mycenaean beliefs.[64] The same care should be applied
to Bronze Age narrative, in order to separate Minoan and Mycenaean spheres of symbol and meaning.

   These observations suggest how the Theran frieze might be
perceived as a chapter in the history of Aegean narrative, beyond
its generic panorama of Aegean life. The south frieze is, if not an
actual νόστος or story of return, a journey from one town to
another, one or both foreign, or an adventure which included two
towns, neither of them necessarily ''home'' to the fleet. Specific
coordination with Homeric episodes is unnecessary, since the
extant *Iliad* and *Odyssey* are a late survival of what may have been
extant in song in the 15th-century Aegean. Certain details support
a sea crossing like the one made by Telemachos from Ithaka to a
larger palatial town like Pylos, in the opening episodes of the
Odyssey. A line of young men below the town's facade march
toward the shore leading an animal, perhaps for a feast of
welcome for the arriving fleet. They recall the ceremony in
progress when Telemachos arrives at Pylos in the *Odyssey*
(3.5–6):

> ἷξον· τοὶ δ' ἐπὶ θινὶ θαλάσσης ἱερὰ ῥέζον,
> ταύρους παμμέλανας, ἐνοσίχθονι κυανοχαίτῃ.

Whether returning in triumph from an expedition abroad, visiting
guest-friends along the way, or departing on an expedition like the
one pictured on the north wall, the theme of travel enshrined in the
Odyssey has a rich prehistory of versions like this fresco.

THE NORTH FRIEZE

It is no surprise to find the complementary theme of war on the opposite wall, in a far more fragmentary state (fig. 4). The fragments cluster in two groups: the first, from the left, depicts a meeting of men in different kinds of garments on a hill (fig. 5). Minoan archaeologists attribute garments, gestures, and grouping to a ritual assembly at a peak sanctuary.[65] But the same scene allows a more military moment, a council between allies or enemies in different costume.[66] By applying a poetic scenario to this group, one could identify the tall figures wearing long robes as elders or chieftains rather than "priests," in council with younger figures (shorter, and in kilts). A gathering of the type is held frequently in the first few books of the *Iliad*. Distinctions in height and dress seem to emphasize the contrast between old and young men, ἠμὲν νέοι ἠδὲ γέροντες, that is formulaic to Homeric assemblies, as in *Iliad* 2.789–90:

> They were holding assembly in front of the doors of Priam
> gathered together in one place, the elders and the young men.

In any case, the figures on the hill wear the same garments— kilts and cloaks—worn by men in the fleet, and thus they could belong to the "invaders" as plausibly as to the "defenders." In the siege of an imaginary city on the Shield of Achilles, the invading army is divided in council whether to destroy the city or divide its contents (*Il.* 18.510–12), a disagreement to be solved with a council outside the walls. The two groups of figures on the hill could represent such a divided army, δίχα δέ σφισιν ἥνδανε βουλή (*Il.* 18.510). The surprise attack on their own herds catches them unprepared (18.531), εἰράων προπάροι-θε καθήμενοι, "sitting before [the city?] at their meeting places," the first word one of several *hapax legomena* which invite solutions from this painting. To complete the epic associations, the early scenario of the *Iliad* provides a landmark near Troy appropriate to the topography and iconography of this scene: ἔνθα τότε Τρῶές τε διέκριθεν ἠδ ἐπίκουροι (*Il.* 2.811–15):

> Near the city but apart from it there is a steep hill
> in the plain by itself, so you pass one side or the other;

Fig. 4. North frieze, military landing, Room 5, West House, Akrotiri (Thera). (Courtesy T.A.P. and National Museum, Athens)

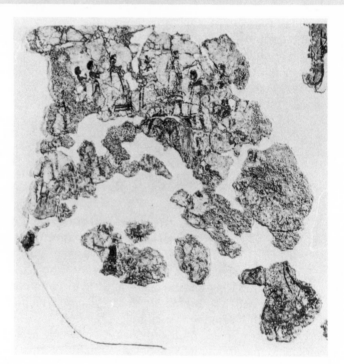

Fig. 5. North frieze, detail: meeting on hill. (From *Thera* VI, pl. 7)

The men call the Hill of the Thicket, but the immortal
gods have named it the burial mound of dancing Myrina.
There the Trojans and their allies were marshalled in order.

Other sacred hills where Trojans withdraw in times of council
include the mound of Ilos, where Hektor meets with ὅσοι
βουληφόροι εἰσίν, βουλὰς βουλεύει θείου παρὰ σήματι
'Ίλου, νόσφιν ἀπὸ φλοίσβου (*Il.* 10.414–16). Like the mound
of Aisyetes (*Il.* 2.790–94), ''Batieia'' commands both a sacred
and a strategic function in the landscape of Troy. Its pictorial
equivalent could well be the grave of a hero/ine and serve as a
gathering place for warriors.

Somewhere below this scene belongs a fragment with a single
figure in rustic garment raising arm and staff, as a herald might
call men to council, or a βασιλεύς raise the σκῆπτρον in a
claim to speech or bid for silence, if viewed in a Homeric rather
than a Minoan framework. Although it was originally restored
below the group on the hill, two independent observers recommend placement of the figure between the hill and the pastoral
group near the sheep.[67] They both connect the raised arm with
ceremonial gestures in Minoan scenes, to which one should now
add the Chania sealing (above, n. 45). But this figure, whatever his
relationship to the group, could be raising his staff in a claim to
speech (*Il.* 1.245, 2.45–46, 100–109, 278–82), or as a herald
keeping order in a discussion (18.503–505, 556–57). The first
scene preserved in the north frieze could illustrate an episode
traditional in epic narrative: the council of war with allies of
different costume, or even an embassy from one army to another.
The Greek expedition to Troy, in particular, began with an
embassy, a formal request for the return of Helen and her property,
before the siege of the city and the raids on the countryside which
occupied 10 years.[68]

This potential agreement between epic episodes and painted
fragments continues across the rest of the frieze, where the
landing of a military expedition makes plausible the need for such
a conference with allies. The maritime phase runs along the lower
border of the entire north frieze, according to the fragments of
more ships and drowning figures farther to the right, where the
shore runs below the land (fig. 4). Meanwhile, a contingent of
warriors in Mycenaean armor has landed: at least eight figures

march onward and upward across the frieze in oxhide body shields, boar's tusk helmets, and armed with swords and long spears (fig. 6). This coordinated attack—a sea-battle before a landing on shore—suggests the pattern of Greek campaigns remembered by Achilles, when he recalls the "twelve cities of men I sacked with ships and the eleven I attacked on land, throughout the fertile Troad" (Il. 9.328–29). The Greek landing at Troy narrated in the Kypria engaged the enemy in battle at once, according to the summary of the epic preserved by Proclus.[69] This synoptic view of the two forms of campaign, in a fresco painted around 1500 B.C., suggests how long their combination determined patterns of warfare in Aegean history and in human memory. A fragmentary stone rhyton from Epidauros illustrates a similar invasion, where ships with warriors in shields land at a rocky shore while others march toward the city (fig. 7).[70] In both landing scenes, men on board brandish long pikes which have been identified with Homeric ναύμαχα, a hapax legomenon in the only Homeric passage which describes a sea-battle.[71] The pictorial battle has its casualties, on the fresco as on the related vessels in stone and metal. At least one ship has damaged its bowsprit and three near-naked men clad in animal skins have lost their short shields and are drowning, upside down like the companions lost by Odysseus to Scylla (Od. 12.248–49): πόδας καὶ χεῖρας ὕπερθεν | ὑψόσ' ἀειρομένων. After the affront to Helios on Thrinakia, Odysseus loses more men to a storm from Zeus (Od. 12.417–19):

> My men were thrown in the water,
> and bobbing like sea crows they were washed away on the
>   running
> waves all around the black ship, and the god took away their
>   homecoming.

In Homer's phrase, λίπε δ' ὀστέα θυμὸς ἀγήνωρ (Od. 12.414); in paint, the bodies tumble and float helplessly, their hands limp in death. Later Greek art visualizes death in much the same manner, in the limp hands of fallen figures like the giants from the north frieze of the Siphnian treasury at Delphi. The image is as vivid in art as in words: these frescoes force us to

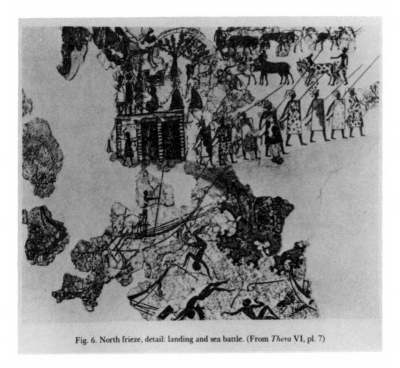

Fig. 6. North frieze, detail: landing and sea battle. (From *Thera* VI, pl. 7)

confront the origin of such imagery, and consider whether art could have anticipated, if not inspired, poetry.

The focus of the Theran battle may have involved not only the ships but a wall which protected them, in the tradition of the *Iliad*. Just before the fragment of coast ends, below the marching warriors and above the ships, a short stretch of wall, painted white with divisions like brick or stone masonry and black triangular crenellations along the left side, runs vertically, then turns right at an angle, as if seen in bird's-eye perspective (fig. 6).[72] Rarely discussed, this scrap of wall presumably lies too far from the missing city to fortify it, but it could protect the ships of an invading party, like the one built by the Greeks near Troy. The remains of such walls, or even of Early Bronze Age fortifications along the coast of Asia Minor, inspired legends about heroes invading, like the τεῖχος ʽΗρακλῆος remembered in the *Iliad*.[73] The wall built by the Greeks in the *Iliad* is most elaborately

Fig. 7. Stone rhyton from sanctuary of Apollo Maleatas, Epidauros. (From
A. Sakellariou, *RA* 1971, fig. 3)

described in the moment of its destruction, like a warrior at the
moment of death in epic poetry. Homer's wall features mysterious
κρόσσαι, πύργοι, στῆλαι and ἐπάλξεις (12.36, 258, 263, 444),
one of which may correspond to the triangular crenellations
visible in the fresco, perhaps the tops of pointed wooden posts
which form the stockade of a brick wall. It is in the same passage,
the destruction of that wall, that the ναύμαχα are invoked in the
Iliad (15.345–89), so that the painting juxtaposes two motifs—
seawall and sea-pikes—also found directly and exclusively near
each other in epic poetry.

The wall of Achaeans in the *Iliad* is not the only wall traditional
to the Trojan cycle. Thucydides indicates that there was another
wall (τὸ γὰρ ἔρυμα τῷ στρατοπέδῳ: 1.11.1) built earlier by the
Greeks. The testimony of Thucydides contradicts Homer's account of a wall built in the 10th year, but agrees with that of
Herodotus, who suggests a substantial structure built by the
Greeks shortly after landing (2.118: ἐκβᾶσαν δὲ ἐς τὴν γῆν καὶ
ἱδρυσθεῖσαν τὴν στρατιὴν). Aristotle solved this
conflict by assuming Homer invented the "second" wall, the one
built in the 10th year rather than the first year, in order to destroy
it (fr. 162 Rose: ὁ πλάστας ποιητὴς ἠφάνισε). The problem of
the wall(s) has plagued modern scholarship as well. The most

recent analysis suggests sensibly that Aristotle could be right: Homer could have invented the wall in *Iliad* 7 and 12 "for the purpose of supplying the *Iliad* with a *teichomachia,* a type of battle narrative that would otherwise be missing from the *Iliad.*"[74] The evidence of the Thera frieze suggests the historicity of an early wall, but also supports the importance of a τειχομαχία as an essential and early component of a story of campaigns abroad. In Proclus's account of the *Kypria,* for example, the embassy requesting the return of Helen is followed by a Greek assault on the walls of Troy, and the same sequence is narrated in the Thera fresco, if one reads the "meeting on the hill" as an embassy, the marching warriors as the inception of an assault on the missing city. Whether one subscribes to an "early" or a "late" wall from the testimonia, the painted fragment of wall belongs to this philological dispute.

In the landward side of this campaign, a pastoral background forms a study in contrast to its military tone. On the same level as the marching warriors, a squarish building represents the most substantial, architecture in this frieze to survive fragmentation. In elevation, one would describe the openings between ashlar trabeate shapes as doorways, one with a young boy standing in front, and possibly a second figure in the next "compartment" to the left. If so, this structure has a roof, on or above which four male figures, one seated, stare left, without visible narrative connections to other figures. Although they resemble the animal herders at their backs (to the right), these figures on or above the roof ignore the pastoral scene "behind" them and seem to concentrate on the hillside gathering. One could fancy them a juvenile version of the Τειχοσκοπίη in *Iliad* 3 (145–245), not a king and his elders but a youthful group of shepherds(?) excluded from battle, gaze riveted on the military assembly to the left. Their outfits resemble Athena's disguise (*Od.* 13.221–24):

> as a young man, a herdsman of sheep,
> a delicate boy, such as the children of kings are,
> and wearing a well-made shawl in a double fold over his
> shoulders.

They may be figures too young to fight, whose duties lie with the flocks which nourish the city and tempt invaders, yet their longing for battle makes them vulnerable, as future heroes. The painting juxtaposes their youth to heroes in battle with a poignancy one could imagine in poetry.

Above them, we can identify a well next to a tree surrounded by an enclosing wooden (?) or brush-work fence, often compared to a modern *mandri* or sheepfold. Spring, trees, and animals contribute to the topography of Homeric cities, as in the description of Odysseus's arrival in Ithaka (*Od.* 17.204–15). In this fresco, two women walk away from the spring/well carrying water jars in the direction taken by the warriors, parallel to them but without engagement. Poetry juxtaposes arriving warriors and female water-carriers in a similar manner, as when Odysseus and his men arrive at the land of the Laistrygonians (*Od.* 10.105–108): "and there in front of the town they met a girl drawing water. This was the powerful daughter of the Laistrygonian Antiphates, who had gone down to the sweet-running well-spring, Artakie, whence they would to carry their water back to the city."

The ἄστυ missing from this frieze probably lies to the right, the goal of both arriving warriors and water-fetching maidens, and perhaps the locale of a missing τειχομαχίη. Poetry also clarifies how a series of images from rural life are intrinsic to a military narrative, in verse as in art, and the juxtaposition is no coincidence. In this fresco, the women carrying water participate in a pastoral defined by well, tree, and two rows of animals—sheep, cattle, and goat—driven in two rows, one toward the water and the fold, the other toward the city or the hills. Two directions for animal traffic are formulaic in epic poetry: when Polyphemus addresses his favorite ram, he recalls how this prince of the flock used to be first in the stampede for pasture and river, and first to head home for the fold in the evening (*Od.* 9.450–51).[75] More specifically, these two lines of animals passing each other in opposite directions, each driven by a shepherd, provide a curious gloss on the Homeric description of Lamos, the city of the Laistrygonians (*Od.* 10.80–86), "where shepherd hails shepherd driving in [his flocks], and the one driving [his] answers back."

These fragments compose a larger picture of the topography of an epic city, comparable to the description of Troy in the *Iliad.* The conjunction of tree, spring, and hill, for example, appears in the same hexameter lines in the description of Achilles chasing

Hektor around the walls of Troy, τεῖχος ὑπὸ Τρώων (*Il.* 22.145–55);

> They raced along by the watching point and the windy
>   fig-tree
> always away from under the wall and the wagon-way
> and came to the two sweet-running well springs . . .
>   Beside these
> in this place, and close to them, are the washing-hollows
> of stone, and magnificent, where the wives of the Trojans
>   and their lovely
> daughters washed the clothes to shining, in the old days
> when there was peace, before the coming of the sons of the
>   Achaeans.

In the *Iliad,* it is this contrast between life at peace and death in battle which animates the narrative tension of a poem of war: not the bloody corpse of Hektor later dragged without mercy around the same race-course, but the memory of peaceful days filled with everyday domestic duties, the work of women and shepherds rather than the destruction of men. Even the enemy shares this image of Troy: Achilles remembers the prosperity of Troy τὸ πρὶν ἐπ' εἰρήνης, in a line which duplicates this one (9.403). Eventually, Achilles carries images of both cities, at war and in peace, into battle on his shield (*Il.* 18.490–608). This contrast is traditional to the imagery of city sieges in other epic poetry of the Late Bronze Age, as in the Canaanite epic of Keret, when El prescribes a siege:[76]

> Then, at sunset on the seventh day,
> you will arrive at Udm the great, Udm the well-watered;
> and attack the cities, raid the towns;
> drive the woodcutters from the fields, the gatherers of straw
>   from the threshing-floors;
> drive the water-carriers from the well,
> the women filling their jars from the spring.

The miniature fresco from Thera fulfills a Late Bronze Age vision of such an urban setting, with its σκοπιή or lookout-hill, spreading tree, spring for water, and citizens at work. Such a tree also marks a vulnerable point for attackers in Homer's Troy, a landmark in Andromache's futile advice to Hektor (*Il.* 6.433–35):

> draw up your people by the fig tree, there where the city
> is openest to attack, and where the wall may be mounted.

The missing portion of the painting could pursue this link between pastoral and polemic action, with the help of epic episodes. Most of the rest of the north frieze is missing, except for two (?) figures of bulls or cows midway down the upper part of the wall, presumably part of a herd of cattle completing the sheep and goats to the west (fig. 4).[77] If so, they become the goal of those marching warriors, who are perhaps a subdivision of the invading army sent to capture booty on the hoof. An important theme ancillary to the siege of a city in epic poetry is the cattle raid, which accompanies, even justifies, plenty of epic expeditions and heroic adventures. Cattle and city are captured together, as in Achilles' raid on the district of Aeneas (*Il.* 20.89–93), ὅτε βουσὶν ἐπήλυθεν ἡμετέρῃσι, |πέρσε δὲ Λυρνησσὸν καὶ Πήδασον (below, n. 104). Andromache lost all seven of her brothers to Achilles in such an ambush (*Il.* 6.421–24):

> for swift-footed brilliant Achilleus slaughtered all of them
> as they were tending their white sheep and lumbering
> oxen; . . .

One epic passage describes in detail how such an ambush can be integral to the siege of a city, even in the strategy of the besieged (*Il.* 18.508–40). Around the city the besiegers sit divided in council (58.510) while the besieged sally forth to seize the enemy's cattle and sheep, guarded by two herdsmen. The two herdsmen and their flocks in the painting could figure in such a cattle raid as they do in the poet's vision, where they are ambushed on their way to the river. The narrative is hard to follow, as if the poet stitched together a series of formulaic episodes from cattle-rustling stories, and commentators have long assumed that the poet imagined a work of art like the silver siege rhyton (fig. 8; infra n. 84). In its fragmentary condition this fresco requires assistance from Homer. To the right of the converging lines of figures, a clash between shepherds and warriors may have been painted a skirmish under the walls of the missing city. The lost portion of the frieze must have presented a substantial architectural vista to rival those on the south wall and in contemporary art. The silver siege rhyton from Shaft Grave IV at Mycenae provides a complete panorama of the missing city under siege, with women and children on the walls, differently armed allies defending the city, and a seaborne party arriving (fig. 8).[78]

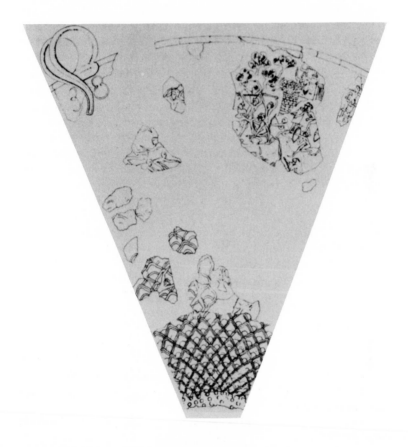

Fig. 8. Silver siege rhyton, Mycenae, Shaft Grave IV. (From drawing by Suzanne Chapman in E. Vermeule, *Greece in the Bronze Age*, pl. XIV)

The scene depicted in relief on this rhyton brings to life the ekphrasis of Achilles' shield (*Il.* 18.513; cf. *Aspis* 242–44): "But the city's people were not giving way, and armed for an ambush. Their beloved wives and their little children stood on the rampart to hold it, and with them the men with age upon them, but meanwhile the others went out."

On the conical rhyton, the battle near the walls dominates the rim area, but below unfolds a battle at sea, whose swimming figures and coastal setting approximate the north frieze at Akrotiri. Like the stone rhyton from Epidauros (fig. 7), the silver relief vase abbreviates scenes from a longer, sustained narrative represented more fully on the Thera frescoes and ultimately derived from a larger narrative tradition.

The important message of this north frieze is that it offers a predictable counterpart to the story of return on the opposite wall.The Siege Fresco tells a tale of war, of heroic encounters that comprise the theme of κλέος: the dangerous adventures abroad, at sea and on land, that make a safe return, a νόστος like the happy scene on the south wall, a reward worth celebrating in gesture and song. Greeks abroad on adventure pray for both, as in the opening of the *Iliad* (1.19) where Kalchas requests ἐκπέρσαι Πριάμοιο πόλιν, εὖ δ᾽ οἴκαδ᾽ ἰκέσθαι. Those who return home successfully, or hope to, might well adorn their finest room with this prayer. The juxtaposition between cities of war and of peace is emphatic in this confrontation on facing walls of a single room. They initiate a traditional contrast of themes in Greek literature, whether in ἔκφρασις on the shields of Achilles and Herakles or in the coexistence of two poems like the *Iliad* and the *Odyssey,* devoted to war and peace, respectively. In the history of ancient interior decoration, the juxtaposition of episodes from the two poetic traditions is repeated in Classical Greek painting, as on the walls of the Lesche of the Knidians (Paus. 10.25–32) and in Roman private settings like the villa of Tiberius at Sperlonga.[79] In the Bronze Age, art may even anticipate or encourage a configuration in literature. The tendency to confront scenes of peace and violence in prehistoric art is appropriate to the historical convergence of Minoan and Mycenaean traditions in art. The juxtaposition of peaceful and violent scenes on the pair of cups from the Vapheio tomb has even been attributed to different craftsmen, Minoan and Mycenaean.[80] The historical encounter of these two cultures in the Late Bronze Age may have contributed to the contrast between action and repose, if not war and peace, in the history of Classical and European literature.

THE EAST FRIEZE

The third frieze preserved in Room 5 of the West House participates in a literary tradition as well (fig. 9). Along the east wall runs a landscape reminiscent of Egypt, defined by a winding river bordered by exotic flora and fauna: palm trees, marshy plants, papyrus; duck chased by griffins and felines. This panorama is an enlargement of abbreviated scenes in contemporary Mycenaean art, most obviously the dagger from Mycenae's Shaft Grave V where a feline captures a duck amidst a papyrus thicket.[81] The ultimate source for such scenes is not so much the Nile itself, but Aegean fantasies of Egypt. This was a constant theme in antiquity, from improbable Homeric tales set in Egypt, and Herodotus's fascination with its flora, fauna, and culture, to Hellenistic novels and Roman seductions associated with the land of the Nile. The portrait of Egypt as an image of fertility and fantasy begins in Homeric hexameter, whose formulaic expressions correspond to

Fig. 9. East frieze, "Nilotic" landscape, Room 5, West House, Akrotiri (Thera). (From *Thera* VI, pl. 8)

these painted images of its lush landscape. In the *Odyssey,* Egypt is well-watered (εὐρρείτην: 14.257), with beautiful fields (4.229, 263), and a source of χρήματα for men. Homeric Egypt provides Helen with bewitching drugs, Odysseus with plausible wealth as well as with conveniently distant and dangerous setting for his tall tales (14.257; 17.430). Egypt lies between Troy and home for more than one hero in the *Odyssey,* whether in Menelaos's detour including Phoenicia (4.351–484, 615–19), or in the imaginary adventures of Odysseus (14.257–91; 17.423–44), and such Homeric fictions contributed to the Greek genre of the romance or novel. By the Hellenistic period, Egypt still exerted this fascination over Greeks, even after the foundation of Alexandria: Αἰγύπτιον γὰρ ἄκουμα καὶ διήγημα πᾶν Ἑλληνικῆς ἀκοῆς ἐπαγωγότατον (Heliodoros *Aethiopica* 2.27).[82]

In other words, visions of Egypt in poetry are a narrative device introducing an element of fantasy into familiar tales, just as this Nilotic landscape bridges two spheres in Aegean geography, injecting the exotic into heroic adventures.[83] We see here in painting an early version of a *topos* in Classical art and literature, not just a complement to contemporary imports. Its placement and narrative purpose suggest it was expressed in poetry, as well as in art, in the 15th century B.C.

PAINTING AND POETRY

These associations between epic poetry and Bronze Age paintings are intended to encourage further comparisons between visual and verbal configurations, between the epic tradition and narrative art of the Late Bronze Age. Ever since the first discoveries of Mycenaean art, 100 years ago, scholars familiar with Greek literature recognized in fragments of pictorial scenes the imagery of Homeric formulae.[84] Particularly striking among new discoveries were images recalling Homeric similes. The dagger from Shaft Grave V invoked above, for example, pairs a military scene on one side of the blade with a lion-hunt on the other; it complements in *Metallmalerei* what a Homeric simile does for a warrior.[85] Battle compositions correspond closely to typical combat scenes in epic poetry, according to Sakellariou's analysis of the silver krater from Mycenae.[86] When images like the silver rhyton first appeared 100 years ago, their associations with Homeric scenes benefited from ignorance of Cretan culture. Since the excitement of discoveries at Knossos and of related "Minoanizing" sites around the Aegean, the Homeric corpus has receded from the imagination of archaeologists. The Thera frescoes should have brought it back, had not philology and archaeology parted their specialized ways in recent decades.

The miniature frescoes from Thera synthesize as a coherent tradition, for the first time, scraps of narrative scenes in early Mycenaean art which also recall epic poetry. We can identify half a dozen thematic groups—arrival and departure by sea, council and battle, ambush and defense, the peaceful outskirts of a city, warriors landing and sailors drowning—that correspond to epic traditions. Stylistic analyses of the Thera frescoes imply similar technical similarities between poetic and pictorial compositions, such as "the tendency to string the figures out paratactically."[87] This is particularly vivid in the north frieze, whose episodic clusters of images do not imply strict dictates for narrative in art, but may express a poetic account of simultaneous events arranged in a linear sequence in time, translated here into two-dimensional space. The paratactic arrangement of episodes and images required for digressions in storytelling permits the painter simultaneous juxtapositions, where the poet would be dependent on ring composition. There is a rich world of such instructive comparisons between painting and poetry, of the kind more frequently derived from Greek and Roman painting (supra ns. 30, 34) than in Bronze Age archaeology. The Pylos frescoes, which benefit from their context in a palace identified with a Homeric place, have inspired a recent exception to this neglect, and the Thera frescoes deserve to be included in this Homeric environment.[88]

Although Homeric poetry deserves more frequent consultation as a source of narrative in prehistoric art, certain reservations should be repeated. Frequent convergence between formulae or lines with visual images cannot confirm that poems in circulation by 1500 B.C. were necessarily composed in dactylic hexameter, any more than the presence of Mycenaean realia in Homeric poetry makes these poems earlier than their latest element.[89] For other technical reasons, philologists have posited precursors of Homeric poetry in the Bronze Age. For some scholars, archaisms in Homer already eliminated in the stage of the Greek language represented in the Linear B tablets support this conclusion.[90] Others have argued for Mycenaean poetry from the antiquity of thematic and comparative material in Oriental and epigraphic sources.[91] Most recently, scholars have reaffirmed the existence of epic poetry, and even of hexameter, in the Mycenaean period.[92] But one philologist has even found support for pre-Homeric hexameter from the evidence of art, including these very frescoes. Hoekstra identifies the Late Mycenaean period as a *terminus ante quem* for the existence of epic poetry, with the following argument:[93] " . . . I find it difficult to believe that [narrative poetry] did not yet exist at the cultural stage represented by the Theraean frieze . . . In this respect I would not in the first place refer to the marching soldiers with their Mycenaean armour and weapons, but to the formal aspect of their representation. Whatever the interpretation of the scenes in question, there is little doubt that they tell some tale and that their form is the opposite of primitive. Is it probable that this type of art had no parallel in contemporary poetry?"

This is exactly what most Aegean archaeologists have missed, the forest that is hidden by the trees, by the excitement of armor and ships. I would add that not only the form but the content of these frescoes is difficult to imagine without a contemporary narrative tradition in poetry. Few would deny that the formative period of the *Iliad* and the *Odyssey,* as we know them, lies centuries later; but their source in older tales is as least as early as 1500 B.C. Since these frescoes and other early Mycenaean art were unknown to later Greeks, the very survival of Bronze Age history presumes a narrative tradition inherited from Bronze Age poetry.[94]

PAINTING AND HISTORY

If a poetic narrative is to be imagined behind these frescoes, what historical events inspired poetry in the 15th century B.C.? The first historical interpretations of these frescoes arranged Minoans and Mycenaeans in plausible Aegean scenarios, participating in joint expeditions, with Mycenaean warriors on Minoan ships, or assisting and attacking each other in various campaigns of conquest.[95] Most scholars now agree that the miniature frescoes represent a generalized picture of seaborne expeditions, "a kind of symbolic narrative conditions in the Aegean in the early fifteenth century."[96] But behind every general picture lies transformed experience, and the fact that scenes of seafaring and siege were repeated as popular themes implies that they happened in history. Evidence outside the frescoes is more useful than their contents alone, which are expressed in Aegean imagery but reflect more distant experience.

Archaeology and epigraphy animate the Thera frescoes with the record of Mycenaean involvement in Anatolia. As early as 1911, the name "Ahhiyawa" in Hittite texts for a people in conflict with the Hittites in western Anatolia was associated with Homeric Achaeans.[97] Individual names and places suggested tantalizing ties to Homer: Piyamaradas (Priam?); Alaksandos (Alexandros, or Paris?); Tawagalawas (Teucer?); Taruisa (Truiya > Τροίη?); and Wilusiya ("Ίλιος?). None of these words can be read without controversy and generous dose of faith, as admitted in learned circles. But recent and persuasive interpretations of these texts indicate sustained and repeated Aegean adventures on the western coast of Asia Minor beginning in the 15th century. The most intriguing of these documents is the Indictment of Madduwattas, which describes an Achaean based in southwest Anatolia (named Attarissiyas: Atreus?) who engages 100 chariots against a Hittite king, in an account where the death of a leader on each side sounds more Homeric than Hittite.[98] Relationships are complex when a vassal of the Hittites with a Lydian name is rescued by Hittites but then joins their enemies, the Arzawa, or even joins "Atreus" for raids on Cyprus. In an equally complicated text, the Tawagalawa letter, a protégé of the Hittites, "Piyamaradas," also attacks his protectors, while the Lukka turn to both parties for help. These shifting patterns of alliance, rivalry, and opportunism are what one would expect from Bronze Age warfare, when booty and glory counted for more than loyalty and allegiance. The redating of texts containing place-names like Wilusiya and Taruisa to the 15th century places them within a generation of early Mycenaean pictures of expeditions by sea and battles on land.[99]

Anatolian art and perhaps even poetry from the Hittite capital of Boghazköy enliven these texts. Five years ago, Calvert Watkins offered the Classical world a snatch of Luwian song from the Hittite archives which begins "They came from steep Wilusa," bestowing an exciting adventure on those names from the Trojan area.[100] More intriguing (and persuasive) for the archaeologist is the fragment of an incised bowl from the Hittite capital with a warrior in garb alien to Anatolian military (and visual) traditions (fig. 10).[101] His helmet with zones and crest looks vaguely Aegean, as does his spiral-covered cuirass and sword with round pommel, but he could come from southwest Anatolia, or be a descendant of a Mycenaean settler wearing an inherited or captured suit of armor, like Glaukos of Lycia (*Il.* 6.230–36). In other words, his attributes and identity are as colorful as the ethnic and political affiliations of Anatolian correspondents with the Hittites. Stratum and ceramic context date this bowl's burial to around 1400 B.C., in the period when the Ahhiwaya are long a significant presence on the western borders of the Hittite empire. Yet image and technique have no parallels in Hittite art, perhaps

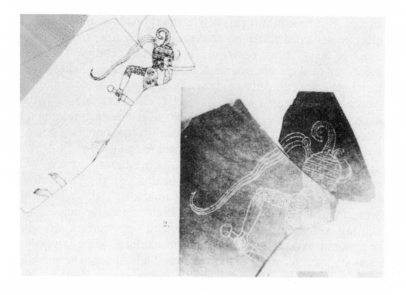

Fig. 10. Incised stone bowl from Bogazköy (Hattusas), Turkey. (From K. Bittel, *RA* 1976, 11, fig. 3)

because Luvian poems and real warriors both inspired an artist for the first time, with an improvised result not unlike what appears in the Thera frescoes. But a Mycenaean complement to this Anatolian portrait appears on a sherd from Miletos (Millawanda, home to many an Ahhiyawan?) in a picture of Hittite headgear.[102] In Anatolian as in Aegean art, images of warriors, foreign and native, suggest the intermediary of poetry or some heroic narrative version of history.

Closer to the Aegean, the coast of western Asia was explored by Minoans, later by Mycenaeans, throughout the second millennium.[103] Recent discoveries have intensified the number and raised the date of those raids remembered by Achilles as the storming of 12 cities by sea and 11 by land, in the Troad alone (*Il.* 9.328–29).[104] The piratical nature of these coastal raids, with their emphasis on portable booty like women, livestock and metal, closely resembles that of the skirmishes reported in Hittite accounts by independent ship-owning potentates like Madduwattas and Attarissiyas who attacked cities in Cyprus and Caria (above, ns. 97–98). The newly discovered cemetery at Menemen (Panaz Tepe), with is mixture of Anatolian and Mycenaean pottery and weapons in Aegean tholos tombs, suggests a settlement postdating such an expedition, as early as the LH IIIA period.[105] Finally, the Troad itself has produced the most exciting new evidence in new excavations of Beşik Tepe. This coastal site southwest of the mound of Hissarlik was almost certainly the landing place for Mycenaean Greeks bound for Troy, for topographic reasons alone.[106] A substantial cemetery of the late Troy VI period, contemporary with LH IIIB and containing Mycenaean sherds, includes burials of men, women and children, not just warriors. This suggests communities of families, perhaps men who married and settled in the Troad in the 13th century, in generations following military expeditions as at Panaztepe. Hittite and Mycenaean texts agree, for once, on similar consequences in bride barter and traffic in women. The household of the Pylos palace included women, captives or slaves, from Knidos and Miletos, a complement to the fate of the Hittite lady banished by her royal husband to the land of the Ahhiyawa.[107]

All this excitement has refocused attention on Hisarlik itself, and on the largest and most impressive of its prehistoric cities,

Troy VI. A major break at the end of the 14th century was attributed to natural causes by Blegen's team, but many have doubted his earthquake theory and associated the splendor of the city with Priam's Troy.[108] New ceramic evidence and analysis associate Troy VIIa with the Mycenaean IIIC era, and Troy VIIb now appears "Submycenaean," eliminating phases of the citadel later than Troy VI from the Homeric experience.[109] But the destruction of the Trojan citadel by the Greeks as a single, heroic event took place primarily in poetry. It may never be conveniently confirmed by an excavated destruction level, and the expectation of such "proof" ignores the power of poetry. In particular, the heroic tradition may represent that "motley series of miniwars" which "could have originated in the tensions generated in West Anatolia by the rival claims there of Hittites and Ahhiyawa."[110] As one scholar of Homer puts it: "The Trojan expedition, as it is presented in its ultimate form in the *Iliad,* is a grand theme which, by converging on the one main goal of Troy, unites on the level of content of the heroic and material resources of the various cultural centers that may each once have had their own epic traditions about conquering various territories."[111]

The great era of Mycenaean expansion into coastal Anatolia took place earlier in the Bronze Age than most of the "historical" dates for the destruction of Troy. It was that time remembered as the Heroic Age, in poetry and art, even as the first age of Greek colonization in Anatolia, to which the "historical" colonies of Ionia formed a modest and predictable sequel, under less heroic but more civilized conditions. The *Iliad* itself commemorates earlier expeditions undertaken by Herakles and the generation which fathered Homeric heroes like Diomedes (5.640–43), famous in the "first" Trojan War. The Thera frescoes hint as such historical expeditions translated into poetry, then into art, and not because the South Fresco fleet has the number of ships Herakles did, or because topography and landscape indicate Anatolia. These paintings contribute to a coincidence of evidence—from Hittite records, Luwian poems, Anatolian and Mycenaean pottery, and pre-Homeric patterns in epic poetry—which points to an earlier date for the first expeditions to Asia and the Troad and to a poetic, even heroic account of these expeditions, on both sides of the Aegean.

POETRY AND PERFORMANCE

These detours through philology and archaeology return to the context of these heroic paintings and their implications for the social dimensions of prehistoric poetry. At Delos or Pompeii, the stage or the library would help explain the selection of mythological themes on domestic walls, but no clues such as masks and poets accompany the narratives in the West House. The "audience" of the Thera frescoes belonged to a private room in an island town, not a royal palace with a patron for poets. A fresh restoration of the Pylos throne-room frescoes provides the latter scenario, with a poet entertaining a banquet of men seated in pairs at small tables, raising cups as if in tribute to Homer's praise of the lyre, δαιτὶ ἑταίρην (*Od.* 17.270–71).[112] If the silver siege rhyton and other luxury vessels (figs. 7–8) were for drinking, their epic decoration points to the same association between poetry and drink preserved in Homeric performance and in the earliest Greek inscriptions like the cup of Nestor. The Pylos arrangement allows the fragments of other narrative frescoes from the palace a closer comparison with Homeric poetry, supported by performances in the *Odyssey*.[113] But the Thera frescoes come from a private home, perhaps even a dining and drinking room, in a town without a palace; they suggest other locales for prehistoric poetry. It may only be a coincidence that Greece's earliest musicians appear in the Cyclades, as marble figurines of the Early Bronze Age. It would be equally tempting to invoke the Cycladic ancestry of Simonides and Bacchylides, natives of Kea, especially since it was Simonides who called painting "silent poetry" (ποίησιν σιωπῶσαν) and poetry itself "painting *with a voice*" (ζωγραφίαν λαλοῦσαν: fr. 53D = Plut. *De Glor. Ath.* 3). But the Kea frescoes, closest to the Thera miniatures in their narrative content, help establish the Cyclades as one home of Bronze Age narrative cycles.[114] The Kea fragments indicate an architectural landscape with figures, including singing and dancing, a hunt and a feast, and a seascape with dolphins and boats; their epic potential is rich, although the scene is already being classified as a "festival."[115] The frescoes from Thera suggest a Cycladic contribution to early epic poetry, just as discoveries from Lefkandi and other Iron Age sites have prompted a recent attribution of the *Odyssey* to Euboea.[116]

CONCLUSIONS

The "new chapter" opened by the Thera frescoes is written in several languages, few of which all can read. Hittite and Luwian cuneiform, Mycenaean and Homeric Greek, Bronze Age ceramic chronology, Minoan fresco technique, Semitic languages and Canaanite poetry, and Indo-European linguistics and metrics are minimum requirements. The paintings are a sobering as well as inspiring reminder that an understanding of Aegean prehistory needs both statistics and style, pottery and poetry, and that we exclude any dimension at our peril. In philology, some training and research have recognized modern critical theory at the expense of visual evidence, with the danger that contemporary techniques of analysis can seem more essential than ancient realities. The plight of the miniature frescoes in modern scholarship illustrates a divergence in disciplines but also recommends a reunion.

REFERENCES

[1] E. Vermeule, "Baby Aigisthos and the Bronze Age," *PCPS* 12 (1987) 145–46.

[2] *Thera* VI, 38. F. Fouqué, *Santorin et ses éruptions* (Paris 1879) 110–11 on the first frescoes; Doumas, *Thera* for a summary of excavations to date. Morgan, *Miniature Wall Paintings* for the most complete current analysis and documentation of these frescoes.

[3] C. Doumas, "Περὶ τῆς μινωικῆς ἀρχιτεκτονικῆς ἐν Θήρα," *ArchEph* 1974, 199–219; J. Shaw, "Consideration of the Site of Akrotiri as a Minoan Settlement," *TAW* 429–36; C. Palyvou, "Notes on the Town Plan of Late Cycladic Akrotiri, Thera," *BSA* 77 (1986) 179–94 and Ἀκρωτήρι Θήρας. Οἰκοδομικὴ Τέχνη καὶ μορφωλογικὰ στοιχεῖα στὴν Ὑστεροκυκλαδικὴ Ἀρχιτεκτονική (Diss. Athens Polytechneion 1988); R.L.N. Barber, *The Cyclades in the Bronze Age* (Iowa City 1987) 46–52, 201–21.

[4] Barber (supra n. 3) 50–51, 216; cf. Doumas, *Thera* 117. A. Michaelidou, "The Settlement of Akrotiri (Thera): A Theoretical Approach to the Function of the Upper Storey," forthcoming in P. Darcque and R. Treuil eds. *L'habitat égéen préhistorique (BCH*

Suppl. XVI). I am very grateful to Ms. Michaelidou for allowing me to read and cite her manuscript, and for criticizing my own text.

[5]*Thera* VI, 38–41; S. Petersen, "A Costuming Scene from the Room of the Ladies on Thera," *AJA* 85 (1981) 211. Less certain is whether this painting makes the room, the adjacent alcove with a papyrus fresco, and the entire architectural unit a "shrine" where such a ceremony was actually performed, as argued by N. Marinatos in *Art and Religion* 97–105, fig. 1, p. 9.

[6]*Thera* VII, 32–38, pls. A–L, 58–66; N. Marinatos, *Art and Religion* 73–84; *L'iconographie minoenne* 222–29; E. Davis, "Youth and Age in the Thera Frescoes," *AJA* 90 (1986) 399–406; C. Doumas, "Ἡ Ξέστη 3 καὶ οἱ κυανοκέφαλοι στὴν τέχνη τῆς Θήρας," in A. Kastrinaki, G. Orphanas, N. Giannagakis eds. ΕΙΛΑΠΙΝΗ, τόμος τιμητικός γιὰ Καθηγητὴ ΝΙΚΟΛΑΟ ΠΛΑΤΩΝΑ (Heraklion 1987) 151–59.

[7]N. Marinatos, *Art and Religion* 31–33 with a map of "shrines" (p. 9 fig. 1) and 219–30; cf. Doumas, *Thera* 54: "There is no direct or convincing evidence that specific rooms were used as shrines or sanctuaries."

[8]*Thera* IV, 20–25, 49–51, color pls. A–C; *Thera* VI, 11–13 on the remodeling that reduced the size of Delta 2 and its access.

[9]N. Marinatos, *Art and Religion* 93–94 for the religious interpretation; M. B. Hollinshead, "Room D2 and the Swallows of Akrotiri, Thera," *AJA* 92 (1988) 253–54 and "The Swallows and Artists of Room Delta 2 at Akrotiri, Thera," *AJA* 93 (1989) 339–54, for a new explanation. Hollinshead identifies the season as summer, not spring, and attributes the room's decoration and its contents (*Thera* IV, 42–43: storage jars, cooking pots, grills, sickles) to a late phase of occupation, not an early shrine.

[10]F. Schachermeyr, "Akrotiri—First Maritime Republic?" *TAW* 423–28 on the social dimensions of the Akrotiri settlement and their implications for private art and tastes; M. Wiener, "Crete and the Cyclades in LM I: The Tale of the Conical Cups," *Minoan Thalassocracy* 17–25, dubbed the influence of Minoan culture abroad the "Versailles effect." Cf. E. Leach, "Landscape and the Prosperous Life: The Discrimination of Genre in Augustan Literature and Painting," in R. Winkes ed., *The Age of Augustus* (Louvain/Providence 1985) 189–95, esp. 191 on the "prosperous emulation of plutocratic style" and the "aggrandizement of social status" through a deliberate variety of megalography; "Patrons, Painters and Patterns: The Anonymity of Romano-Campanian Painting and the Transition from the Second to the Third Style," in B. Gold, ed., *Literary and Artistic Patronage in Ancient Rome*

(Austin 1982) 135–73, esp. on Hellenizing wall decoration during the Augustan period as an expression of middle-class "fantasies of identification with a fabled stratum of society" (p. 153).

[11]E.g., by A. Sakellariou, "The West House Miniature Frescoes," *TAW* 147–53 (Isidis Navigium); K. Foster, "Snakes and Lions: A New Reading of the West House Frescoes from Thera," *AJA* 92 (1988) 253 and *Expedition* 30:2 (1988) 10–20, argues for influence from the Egyptian Jubilee Festival on the miniature frescoes.

[12]C. Renfrew, *The Archaeology of Cult* (London 1985) 11–26, 393–444. For a valuable survey of religion in Aegean archaeology, see J. Muhly's review of N. Marinatos, *Art and Religion* in *Gnomon* 59 (1987) 329–34. Near East: H. Shanks, "Two Israelite Cult Sites Now Questioned," *Biblical Archaeology Review* 14 (1988) 48–52.

[13]As argued, *inter alia,* by N. Marinatos, "The West House at Akrotiri as Cult Center," *AM* 98 (1983) 1–19; *Art and Religion; L'iconographie minoenne* 219–30; Foster (supra n. 11).

[14]*Thera* V, 17–20, 41–44; *Thera* VI, 19–34; Doumas, *Thera* 48–50. Michaelidou (supra n. 4) on the "clear preference for imported ware" indicated in Room 5, in contrast to the other rooms of the same house; Sakellariou, *Fourth Cretological Congress* 534, adduces the imported pottery as additional evidence for the Minoan style of the frescoes, while N. Marinatos sees the Minoan imports as one of the room's ritual qualities.

[15]The latrine was first called a "kitchen sink" (by S. Marinatos, *Thera* VI, 20, 24–29, figs. 2–3, pls. 58–63); more reasonably, Doumas, *ArchEph* 1974, 209–210, pl. 65b and *Thera* 54; Palyvou (supra n. 3) 184, 187 fig. 6; Barber (supra n. 3) 212–13. Inevitably, the toilet has been interpreted as an opening for ritual libations, and nearby objects, such as a clay rhyton in the shape of a lion's head, have been identified as "offerings" in support of a religious explanation: N. Marinatos, *AM* 98 (1983) 14 and *Art and Religion* 48–49; contra R.L.N. Barber, *JHS* 107 (1987) 243.

[16]*Thera* VI, 24–27, pls. 52–53, 58b and 59 (bowl of pigment still in situ; identified by N. Marinatos, *Art and Religion* 46, 49 as "body paint").

[17]Leach 1985 (supra n. 10) 190–91 on painted marble at Oplontis as an imitation of extravagant interiors.

[18]*Thera* V, 41–42, fig. 6, pl. I; *Thera* VI, 20, 25–26, 34–35, 43, 49, 54.

[19]L. Morgan, "The Ship Procession in the Miniature Fresco," *TAW* 639–40; M. Shaw, "Painted Ikria at Mycenae," *AJA* 84 (1980) 167–79, and "Ship-Cabins of the Bronze Age Aegean," *IJNA* 11 (1982) 53–58; I. Kritseli-Providi, Τοιχογραφίες τοῦ Θηρσκευ–τικοῦ Κέντρου τῶν Μυκήνων, (Athens 1982) 54–63, 103,

pls. 12–18; E. Davis, "The Iconography of the Ship Fresco from Thera," in W. Moon ed., *Ancient Greek Art and Iconography* (Madison 1983) 7; N. Marinatos, *Art and Religion* 46–47; Foster (supra n. 11).

[20]S. Marinatos, "The Libyan Fresco from Thera," *AAA* 7 (1974) 87–94; Thera VI, 34–60, called Room 4 the admiral's bedroom, with his portrait on board the largest ship on the south frieze of Room 5; cf. D. Page, "The Miniature Frescoes from Akrotiri, Thera," *Prakt-AkAth* 51 (1976) 135–52 and S. Stucchi, "Il Giardino delle Esperidi e le tappe della conoscenza greca della costa cirenaica," *QAL* 8 (1976) 19–73. P. Haider, "Grundsätzliches und Sachliches zur historischen Auswertung des bronzezeitlichen Miniaturfrieses auf Thera," *Klio* 61 (1979) 285–307 and Morgan, *Miniature Wall Paintings* 88–92 for critique of the "Libyan" theories.

[21]Doumas, *Thera* 84; N. Marinatos, *Art and Religion* 46.

[22]*Thera* V, 43, pls. J–K 100–101; N. Marinatos, *Art and Religion* 46, figs. 26–27. C. Televantou, " Ἡ γυναικεῖα ἐνδυμασία στὴν προϊστορικὴ Θήρα," *ArchEph* (1982, 124 n. 2, rejects parallels for the garment from Minoan glyptic; Davis and Doumas (supra n. 6) on hairstyle.

[23]Morgan (supra n. 19) 629, 640 identifies an "Egyptian offering gesture" made by the priestess in a ritual of blessing the ships by burning incense. N. Marinatos, *AM* 98 (1983) 7, 13; *Art and Religion* 46.

[24]Thus Doumas, *Thera* 84; N. Marinatos, *AM* 1983, 7, 13 identifies the red "coals" as cosmetic pigment.

[25]*Thera* V, 43–44; Hollinshead (supra n. 9).

[26]P. Muhly, *Minoan Libation Tables* (Diss. Bryn Mawr College, 1981) 278; N. Polychronakou-Sgouritsa, "Μυκηναϊκὲς τριποδικὲς τράπεζες προσφορῶν," *ArchEph* 1982, 20–33, cautions (p. 31) that such tables are not exclusively ritual.

[27]Melos jar: Atkinson et al., *Excavations at Phylakopi in Melos* (London 1904) pl. XXII; *Greek Art of the Aegean Islands. An Exhibition* (New York 1979) 69 no. 23, pl. 27; Barber (supra n. 3) fig. 13. N. Marinatos, *Art and Religion* 35–38 and *L'iconographie minoenne* 219–20 calls them "adorants" making a perpetual offering.

[28]*Thera* VI, 20, 28; Warren, "Miniature Fresco," 115; Page (supra n. 20) 136 called the frescoes "the wall-paper of a sitting-room in a private house"; Michaelidou (supra n. 4) suggests this room may have been "the gathering point for the occupants of the house" or even a dining-room.

[29]*Thera* VI, 24, 34–38; Warren, "Miniature Fresco," 116–18; Davis (supra n. 19) 3–5 begins the narrative on the south wall. Morgan,

Miniature Wall Paintings 162–63 attributes a fragment with a "processional ship" to the west wall.

[30]Davis (supra n. 19) 5 n. 10 for parallels from Crete and Thera; *Odyssey Landscapes*: P. von Blankenhagen, "The Odyssey Frieze," *RM* 70 (1963) 100–46; J. J. Pollitt, *The Art of the Hellenistic Age* (Cambridge 1986) 185–209; E. W. Leach, *The Rhetoric of Space. Literary and Artistic Representations of Landscape in Republican and Augustan Rome* (Princeton 1988) ch. 1.

[31]S. Immerwahr, "Mycenaeans at Thera: Some Reflections on the Paintings from the West House," *Greece and the Eastern Mediterranean in Ancient History and Prehistory. Studies Presented to Fritz Schachermeyr* (Berlin 1977) 173–91; Warren, "Miniature Fresco"; Morgan, *Miniature Wall Paintings* 88–92, 146–54.

[32]As in Barber (supra n. 3) 173 fig. 126, pp. 174–75; first argued by Morgan (supra n. 19) 629–44.

[33]Warren, "Miniature Fresco," 120–21; L. Morgan, "Theme in the West House Paintings at Thera," *ArchEph* 1983, 85–105 and *Miniature Wall Paintings* 146–54.

[34]See the essays in H. Kessler and M. S. Simpson eds., *Pictorial Narrative in Antiquity and the Middle Ages* (Washington, D.C. 1983).

[35]L. Basch, *Le musée imaginaire de la marine antique* (Athens 1987) 117–32. S. Marinatos, "Das Schiffsfresko von Akrotiri, Thera," in D. Gray ed., *Archaeologia Homerica G. Seewesen* (Göttingen 1974) 141–51. O. Hockmann, *Die Schiffe des Minos. Schiffbau und Seefahrt im alten Kreta.* RGZ Arbeitsbericht (1982) 8–12; Morgan, *Miniature Wall Paintings* 121–42; infra ns. 38–39.

[36]S. Marinatos himself illustrates such structures on nearby Anaphe: *Thera* V, 47 pl. 103; Warren, "Miniature Fresco," 119; C. Renfrew and M. Wagstaff eds., *An Island Polity. The Archaeology of Exploitation on Melos* (Cambridge 1982) 34–43, 108–110; R. Osborne, *Classical Landscape with Figures. The Ancient Greek City and Its Countryside* (London 1987) 37–40, 47–52; cf. review by V. Hanson in *AJA* 92 (1988) 296.

[37]E. Vermeule, *The Art of the Shaft Graves at Mycenae* (Cincinnati 1975) 41–42, 65 on lions and warriors; N. Marinatos, *AM* 98 (1983) 9–10; Morgan 1983 (supra n. 33) 85–87 reviews the dagger and related scenes, without Homeric analogies. The first warrior in the *Iliad* introduced with a simile is Menelaos, who is compared to just such a lion: *Iliad* 3.21–26. On Homeric similes and Mycenaean art, infra n. 85.

[38]As argued by L. Casson, "Bronze Age Ships. The Evidence of the Thera Wall Paintings," *IJNA* 4 (1975) 3–10; cf. Sakellariou, *TAW* 149–52; Morgan (supra n. 19); S. Wachsmann, "The Thera Water-

borne Procession Re-considered,'' *IJNA* 9 (1980) 287–95; A. Raban, ''The Thera Ships: Another Interpretation,'' *IJNA* 13 (1984) 11–19; Foster (supra n. 11).

[39]A. Tilley and P. Johnstone, ''A Minoan Naval Triumph,'' *IJNA* 5 (1976) 285–92; Warren, ''Miniature Fresco'' 121 n. 18; M. G. Prytulak, ''Weapons on the Thera Ships?'' *IJNA* 11 (1982) 3–6; Davis (supra n. 19) 9; J. Ernstson, ''The Ship Procession Fresco— The Pilots,'' *IJNA* 14 (1985) 315–20.

[40]S. Iakovidis, ''Thera and Mycenaean Greece,'' *AJA* 83 (1979) 101– 102; Immerwahr (supra n. 31); R. Laffineur, ''Mycenaeans at Thera: Further Evidence?'' in *Minoan Thalassocracy* 133–39, Contra: J. Davis, ''Mycenaeans at Thera: Another Look,'' *AJA* 85 (1981) 69–70, but see J. Crowley, ''More on Mycenaeans at Thera,'' *AJA* 87 (1983) 83–85; J. Vanschoonwinckel, ''Théra et la civilisation mycénienne,'' *AntCl* 55 (1986) 5–41.

[41]As suggested by R. Laffineur 1983 (infra n. 57) 113, who invokes Homeric similes and adjectives endowing warriors and their weapons with magical powers, as a parallel for the decorated ships.

[42]M. Edwards, ''The Structure of Homeric Catalogues,'' *TAPA* 110 (1980) 81–105, esp. 101–103 on catalogue form and narrative.

[43]J. Caskey, *Hesperia* 40 (1971) 392–95; map (fig. 1) and plan (fig. 3), with two small squarish structures adjoining each other, closely resembling the features on the hill in the Town Fresco from Thera. Morgan, *Miniature Wall Paintings* 85. The debate over Troullos (peak shrine vs. tower) was revived by Jack Davis in ''Cultural Innovation and the Minoan Thalassocracy at Ayia Irini,'' *Minoan Thalassocracy* 164 and debated by several experts (Peatfield Bikakis, etc.: p. 166). On Minoan peak sanctuaries, see A. Peatfield, ''The Topography of Minoan Peak Sanctuaries,'' *BSA* 78 (1983) 273–79. Page (supra n. 20) 144 suggests ''watchtowers'' for these buildings, citing parallels near Akrotiri.

[44]Akrotiri: Page (supra n. 20) 144; N. Marinatos, *AM* 98 (1983) 8; Crete: G. Gesell, ''The Town Fresco of Thera: A Reflection of Cretan Topography,'' *Fourth Cretological Congress* 197–204; Immerwahr (supra n. 31) 174–75; Davis (supra n. 19) 8 identifies the smaller town on the left as Akrotiri; Morgan, *Miniature Wall Paintings* 88–92.

[45]*PM* I, 301–14; A. Sakellariou, '' Ἡ κρητικὴ καταγωγὴ ἑνὸς μυκηναϊκοῦ εἰκονογραφικοῦ κύκλου,'' 532–38 in *Fourth Cretological Congress* and *L'iconographie minoenne* 294; K. Foster, *Aegean Faience of the Bronze Age* (New Haven 1978) 99–115. E. Hallager, *The Master Impression* (Göteborg 1985) 31–33, 38, pl. 1. Morgan, *Miniature Wall Paintings* 68–70.

[46]*PM* I, fig. 228p, q ("archer"), and t ("spearman"), more likely a figure with a shepherd's staff. Sakellariou, *Fouth Cretological Congress* 535–37 pl. 182 disputes "spearmen" and "archers" whose weapons are entirely restored and the martial nature of Evans's reconstruction, as does Foster (supra n. 45) 101–103 (e.g. Evans's "helmet-plumes" have now been recognized as animals' tails); Morgan 1983 (supra n. 33) 92 indicates some reservations by calling these figures "probably warriors."

[47]Sakellariou (supra n. 45) fig. 183; Foster (supra n. 45) 101–102, fig. 32 notes its lack of parallels and ambiguous identity; Morgan 1983 (supra n. 33) 92 n. 2 doubts the "prow."

[48]*PM* I, 311–14 and III, 89–106, esp. 101–106, where Evans emphasizes the Minoan identity of the silver rhyton and its kinship with epic city sieges, citing the Shields of Achilles and Herakles described by Homer and Hesiod, respectively. On the rehabilitation of the silver rhyton as a Mycenaean composition or at least commission, see W. S. Smith, *Interconnections in the Ancient Near East* (New Haven 1965) 63–95; E. Vermeule, *Greece in the Bronze Age* (Chicago 1964) 100–105. E. Davis, *The Vapheio Cups and Aegean Gold and Silver Ware* (New York 1976) 227–30, no. 87, maintains Evans's argument for a Minoan craftsman but allows for a Mycenaean patron; however, she classifies silver vessels as Cretan, gold ones as Mycenaean (pp. 328–33).

[49]The inverse of his method has also been practiced: thus Sakellariou "de-militarizes" the Thera scenes, denying the drowners and warriors in order to make the frescoes more "Minoan": *Fourth Cretological Congress* 534–35.

[50]As Vermeule put it (supra n. 48) 102–103; "No one is fighting, but all one needs for a good siege is present," Cf. fragments of Minoan stone vases representing a bearded archer, a man stealing (?) a goat, a boar and a helmet: Warren, "Miniature Fresco," 126–28 and *Minoan Stone Vases* (Cambridge 1969) 473, 488c. Sakellariou, *Fourth Cretological Congress* 532–38 on the Minoan derivation of Mycenaean narrative cycles; C. J. Ruijgh, "Le mycénien et Homère," in A. Morpurgo Davies and Y. Duhoux, eds., *Linear B. A 1984 Survey* (Louvain 1985) 150–51, 166–67 on the Minoan origins of Greek hexameter poetry. It should be noted, however, that Ruijgh's argument is largely based on the analogy of material culture, where Mycenaean civilization demonstrates a vivid debt to Crete, rather than on specific linguistic arguments. Cf. M. Lang's "A Protean Proto-Odysseus?," *Bryn Mawr Now. Supplement* (Fall 1988) 7–11 on possible Cretan forerunners of the *Odyssey*.

[51]S. Immerwahr, "A Possible Influence of Egyptian Art in the Creation

of Minoan Wall Painting," *L'iconographie minoenne* 41–50 emphasizes the mosaic's formal and paratactic composition, closer to Egyptian conventions.

[52]M. C. Shaw, "The Miniature Frescoes of Tylissos Reconsidered," *AA* 1972, 171–88 for fragments which suggest a performance or games by male figures; Warren, "Miniature Fresco," 127–28.

[53]Davis (supra n. 19) 11 on Theran adoption of Minoan imagery, lacking scenes of "direct conflict," but she presumes lost military scenes. A. Sakellariou, "Identité minoenne et identité travers à les compositions figuratives," *L'iconographie minoenne* 292–309, stresses (pp. 302–308) the un-Minoan nature of themes of conflict (hunt, battle).

[54]K. Coleman, *A Study of Painted Wall Plaster Fragments from the Bronze Age Site of Ayia Irini in the Island of Kea* (Diss. Columbia Univ. 1970) 200; see esp. 200–205 on the kinship of the Kea frescoes with mainland rather than Cretan art. Cf. Sakellariou, *TAW* 148–49.

[55]Hallager (supra n. 45); E. Davis, "The Political Use of Art in the Aegean," *AJA* 90 (1986) 216.

[56]Vermeule (supra n. 37; the Semple Lectures were delivered in 1971, before the discovery of the miniature frieze); J. Hurwit, "The Dendra Octopus Cup and the Problem of Style in the Fifteenth-Century Aegean," *AJA* 83 (1979) 413–26; G. Walberg, *Tradition and Innovation in Minoan Art* (Mainz 1986).

[57]As Immerwahr recognized (supra n. 31) 191 in calling the miniature frescoes "the pictorial equivalent of the early Mycenaean art of the Shaft Graves"; O. Negbi, "The 'Miniature Fresco' from Thera and the Emergence of Mycenaean Art," *TAW* 645–55; R. Laffineur, "Early Mycenaean Art: Some Evidence from the West House in Thera," *BICS* 30 (1983) 111–22 and "Iconographie minoenne et iconographie mycénienne à l'époque des tombes à fosse," in *L'iconographie minoenne* 245–66.

[58]*Thera* V, 43–44, pls. 24b–25, C; *Thera* VI, 27; *Greek Art* (supra n. 27) 31, 79, no. 35.

[59]E.g., in the work of Laffineur (supra n. 57) with his emphasis on the emblematic and symbolic value of Mycenaean images.

[60]E.g., by Immerwahr (supra n. 31) 180: "a real narrative style, that might be termed Mycenaean"; Warren, "Miniature Fresco," 129: "From Thera to Homer we may not need the aid of the clew of thread"; Sakellariou (supra n. 45); Vermeule 1983 (infra n. 98) 142.

[61]Thus Morgan's subtle analysis (supra n. 33) assumes that the arms of the woman depicted near the horns are lifted in a "votive gesture," according to Minoan convention, rather than in a gesture of

greeting, appropriate to a story of arrival or return, as maintained by Warren, "Miniature Fresco," 119, Davis (supra n. 19) 8, and others.

[62]As observed by Davis (supra n. 19) 6 who compares the artists of the Thera frescoes and their exploration of the Minoan pictorial repertoire to early Archaic vase-painters.

[63]As observed by Hurwit (supra n. 56) 426 n. 2; cf. Pollitt (supra n. 30) 150–63. In the Aemilius Paullus monument at Delphi, for example, style, subject and probably artist are Greek, but the message and occasion are historical and Roman, such that one could perform the following substitutions for "Greek" and "Roman," respectively (Pollitt 155–58): "In style, the frieze is [Minoan]: in subject, intention and function it is [Mycenaean]" (157).

[64]R. Hägg, "Mycenaean Religion: The Helladic and Minoan Components," in Davies and Duhoux (supra n. 50) 203–25; C. Renfrew, "Questions of Minoan and Mycenaean Cult," in R. Hägg and N. Marinatos eds., *Sanctuaries and Cults of the Aegean Bronze Age* (Stockholm 1981) 30–33.

[65]S. Iakovidis, "A Peak Sanctuary at Thera," in A. Biran ed., *Temples and High Places in Biblical Times* (Jerusalem 1981) 54–60; cf. Page (supra n. 20) 139; B. Rutkowski, "Kykladen und Kreta: Bemerkungen über die bronzezeitliche Religion," *AAA* 9 (1976) 231–32, fig. 2; Morgan (supra n. 33) 88–89, and Morgan, *Miniature Wall Paintings* 156–58.

[66]S. Marinatos, *Thera VI*, 40 simply calls it a "Meeting on a Hill," in which he detects "a moment of crisis"; Immerwahr (supra n. 31) 183 suggests a conference or truce between Minoans and Mycenaeans; Davis (supra n. 19) 10 identifies a conference called in response to an invasion by the Theran fleet, claiming "no parallel in Aegean art" without help from Homer.

[67]Iakovidis (supra n. 65) 57; L. Morgan, "The West House Paintings, Thera," *BICS* 28 (1981) 166 and (supra n. 33) 89 n. 3, pl. 32; Morgan, *Miniature Wall Paintings*, pl. 1.

[68]According to Herodotus's version of the Greek expedition (2.118): ἐκβᾶσαν δὲ ἐς τὴν γῆν καὶ ἱδρυθεῖσαν τὴν στρατιὴν πέμπειν ἐς τὸ Ἴλιον ἀγγέλους and to Proclus's summary of the *Kypria*, where the Greeks sent envoys (διαπρεσβεύοντα) to the Trojans after landing and the first battle. See below, n. 74, for modern discussion of the Greek landing.

[69]ἔπειτα ἀποβαίνοντας αὐτοὺς εἰς Ἴλιον εἴργουσιν οἱ Τρῶες, καὶ θνήσκει Πρωτεσίλαος ὑφ' Ἕκτορος.

[70]A. Sakellariou, "Scène de bataille sur un vase mycénien en pierre?," *RA* 1971, 3–14; *Fourth Cretological Congress* 532–38; Page (supra

n. 20) 148, n. 1; Warren, "Miniature Fresco," 127 fig. 5. For an additional fragment showing a swimming or drowning figure over a stylized marine background like that on the silver siege rhyton, see V. Lambrinoudakis, *Prakt* 1975, 172–73, pl. 149a; *Miniature Wall Paintings,* figs. 193–94.

[71]S. Marinatos, in *Thera* VI, 41 (*Il.* 15.387–89): the Achaeans defend their ships with ξυστὰ ναύμαχα ("long pikes that lay among the hulls for sea-fighting").

[72]S. Marinatos, *Thera* VI, 45 identifies the crenellations as wooden projections in half-timbering; Page (supra n. 20) 137 suggests a vertical pillar with lintel and calls the building a "portico" but cannot explain the "jagged edge"; Warren, "Miniature Fresco" 118; Sakellariou, *TAW* 148; Davis (supra n. 19) 12 n. 79 classifies them as "foreign"; Morgan, *Miniature Wall Paintings* 85 concludes that the projecting triangles are either lifting devices or for decorative effect. Comparable crenellations on the Kea frescoes are "without parallels in Aegean art" (Abramowitz [infra n. 114] 60, adducing Near Eastern and Anatolian parallels); cf. Assyrian fortifications: J. Reade, *Assyrian Sculpture* (London 1983) figs. 11, 28, 48, 96.

[73]20.145–46; cf. 7.433–64; 12.1–40, 257–64; 15.352–66 for the wall built by the Greeks: R. Scodel, "The Achaean Wall and the Myth of Destruction," *HSCP* 86 (1982) 33–50.

[74]E. Dolin, "Thucydides on the Trojan War: A Critique of the Text of 1.11.1," *HSCP* 87 (1983) 130, with summary of earlier bibliography by P. Girard, D. S. Robertson, R. M. Cook, J. de Romilly, J. A. Davison, etc.

[75]As observed by S. Marinatos in *Thera* VI, 41.

[76]M. Coogan, *Stories from Ancient Canaan* (Philadelphia 1978) 60 (El's instructions are repeated, verbatim, by the poet at a later point in the narrative: p. 63).

[77]*Thera* VI, pls. 6–7, fig. 7; *TAW* color pl. K; Warren, "Miniature Fresco," 118; Morgan 1983 (supra n. 33) 90, n. 1.

[78]Vermeule, Smith, and Davis (supra n. 48); A. Sakellariou, "La scène du siège sur le rhyton d'argent de Mycénes d'après une nouvelle reconstitution," *RA* 1975, 197–208; *Fourth Cretological Congress* 532–38.

[79]The latest reconstruction of the Polygnotan paintings, by Mark Stansbury-O'Donnell (*AJA* 93 [1989] 203–15) arranges the Nekyia and Ilioupersis scenes facing each other on the two short walls of the building. Sperlonga: R. Hampe, *Sperlonga und Virgil* (Mainz 1972); Pollitt (supra n. 30) 122–26.

[80]Davis (supra n. 48) 1–50; cf. *ArtB* 56:4 (1974) 474–87.

136

A History of Book Illustration

81Vermeule (supra n. 48) 21–22, figs. 18–19.

82H. Whitehouse, "Shipwreck on the Nile: A Greek Novel on a 'Lost' Roman Mosaic," *AJA* 89 (1985) 129–34, esp. 132 n. 18; B. Kytzler, "Zum utopischen Roman der klassischen Antike," 7–16 and M. Fusillo, "Textual Patterns and Narrative Situations in the Greek Novel," 17–31 in H. Hofman ed., *Groningen Colloquia on the Novel* 1 (Groningen 1988) on the Homeric origins of the Greek novel and of Greek fascination with Egypt.

83Immerwahr (supra n. 31) 174 on how this fresco "serve[s] the artistic function of removing the shipwreck and sheepfold scenes to a more distant land." Davis (supra n. 19) 5–6 on its deliberately foreign, exotic element.

84W. Helbig, *Das homerische Epos aus den Denkmälern erläutert* (Leipzig 1884) 291–310; C. Tsountas, *ArchEph* 1891, 14–22; H. Kluge, "Der Schild des Achilleus und die mykenischen Funde," *NJbb* 149 (1894) 81–90. The new Mycenaean finds were immediately incorporated into commentaries and texts of Homer, as in Leaf and Bayfield's *Iliad* (1895) pl. II. For a summary, see K. Fittschen, *Der Schild des Achilleus* (1973).

85The traditional scholarship includes W. Schadewaldt, "Die Homerischen Gleichnisse und die kretisch-mykenische Kunst," *Festschrift für O. Regenbogen* (1952) 9–27; Laffineur (supra n. 57) on Homeric similes and such images. Morgan 1983 (supra n. 33) 85–87 and *Miniature Wall Paintings* 44–49 explores this visual juxtaposition between warriors and lions without reference to Homeric similes (but see *L'iconographie minoenne* 34); C. Baurain, "Recherche sur l'iconographie créto-mycénienne du lion iliadique," in J. Serrais, T. Hackens, and B. Serrais-Soyez eds., *Mélanges . . . offerts à Jules Labarbe* (Liège 1987) 339–67.

86A. Sakellariou, "Un cratère d'argent avec scène de bataille provenant de la IVe tombe de l'acropole de Mycènes," *AntK* 17 (1974) 3–20; Vermeule (supra n. 37) 29–30; cf. Davis (supra n. 48) 222–27, no. 86; B. Fenik, *Typical Battle Scenes in the Iliad* (Wiesbaden 1968).

87As observed by Immerwahr (supra n. 31) 179–80; Davis (supra n. 19) 11.

88M. Lang, "Pylos Polytropos," *Minos* 20–22 (1987) 333–41 juxtaposes poetry, frescoes, and epigraphy in the pursuit of similar "descriptive techniques" and "recurrent themes": cf. McCallum (infra n. 112).

89G. S. Kirk, "Dark Age and Oral Poet," *PCPS* 7 (1961) 34–48; M. L. West, "Greek Poetry 2000–700 B.C.," *CQ* 67 (1973) 179–92; O. T. P. Dickinson, "Homer, the Poet of the Dark Age," *Greece and Rome* 33 (1986) 20–37; but see now West (infra n. 92).

[90]G. C. Horrocks, "The Antiquity of the Greek Epic Traditions: Some New Evidence," *PCPS* 26 (1980) 1–11; *Space and Time in Homer: Prepositional and Adverbial Particles in the Greek Epic* (New York 1980). F. Adrados, "Towards a New Stratigraphy of the Homeric Dialect," *Glotta* 59 (1981) 13–27; J. T. Hooker, "The Homeric Dialect," *Concilium Eirene* XVI (Prague 1983) 75–79.

[91]M. Durante, *Sulla preistoria della tradizione poetica greca* (Rome 1971); L. Stella, *Tradizione micenea e poesia dell' Iliade* (Rome 1978); Hooker (infra n. 108) 7–8; C. O. Pavese, "L'origine micenea della tradizione epica, rapsodica," *SMEA* 21 (1980) 341–52. W. Calder, "Gold for Bronze: *Iliad*. 6.116–118," *Studies Presented to Sterling Dow* (*GRBS* Suppl., 1984) 31–35.

[92]See Ruijgh (supra n. 50); J. R. Green, "A Chariot-Krater from Sydney: Some Notes on Mycenaean Vase-Painting and Poetry," 43–49, and J. T. Hooker, "From Mycenae to Homer," 57–64 in J. Betts and J. T. Hooker eds., *Studies in Honor of T.B.L. Webster* 1 (Bristol 1986); Baurain (supra n. 85) 366–67; M. L. West, "The Rise of the Greek Epic," *JHS* 108 (1988) 151–72 now defends not only a 14th-century epic but the existence of hexameter in the 15th century.

[93]A. E. Hoekstra, *Epic Verse before Homer* (New York 1981) 34–35.

[94]As argued by Vermeule (supra n. 1) 122–52.

[95]*Thera* VI, 38–57 and Page (supra n. 20) for the biographical version of the frieze, as the story of the life of the West House "Admiral"; Warren, Gesell, Ruijgh, and West (supra ns. 44, 50, 92) 197–204 argue for a Cretan setting. Cf. the essays and discussion in *Minoan Thalassocracy*.

[96]Immerwahr (supra n. 31) 183.

[97]H. Güterbock, "Troy in Hittite Texts? Wilusa, Ahhiyawa and Hittite History," in M. Mellink ed., *Troy and the Trojan War* (Bryn Mawr 1986) 133 n. 1 traces the history of these associations, which begin with Luckenbill's equation of Alaksandus and Alexandros (*CP* 6 [1911] 85–86), even earlier than Kretschmer (*Glotta* 13 [1924] 205–13) and Forrer, *MDOG* 16 [1924] 1–22).

[98]According to Güterbock, "The Hittites and the Aegean World: 1. The Ahhiyawa Problem Reconsidered," *AJA* 87 (1983) 133–38 and "Hittites and Achaeans: A New Look," *ProcPhilSoc* 128 (1984) 114–22; cf. E. Vermeule, "The Hittites and the Aegean World. 3. Response to Hans Güterbock," *AJA* 87 (1983) 141–43; "Priam's Castle Blazing," in Mellink (supra n. 97) 85; cf. L. A. Gindin and V. L. Tsymbursky, "The Ancient Greek Version of the Historical Event Reflected in a Hittite Text," *VDI* 176 (1986) 81–87 on KUB XXIII.13 and the *Kypria*.

[99]Güterbock 1983 (supra n. 98) 133–35 and 1984; H. Otten, *Sprachliche Stellung und Datierung des Madduwatta-Textes. Studien zu den Bogazköy-Texten* 11 (Wiesbaden 1969).

[100]"The Language of the Trojans," in Mellink (supra n. 97) 58–62; cf. *Hethitica* 8 (1987) 423–26.

[101]K. Bittel, "Tonschale mit Ritzzeichunung von Bogazköy," *RA* 1976, 9–14, figs. 2–3; D. Rittig, *Orientalia* 52 (1983) 156–60; Vermeule (supra n. 1) 143–44 fig. 5; Güterbock 1984 (supra n. 98) 115 fig. 6.

[102]Güterbock 1984 (supra n. 98) 115, figs 4–5.

[103]*Minoan Thalassocracy,* esp. essays by Benzi, Laviosa and Schiering; M. Wood, *In Search of the Trojan War* (London 1985) 161–64. I am grateful to Iris Love for the opportunity to supervise the first trench at Knidos which produced Minoan and Mycenaean pottery (in 1977), an experience which has maintained my faith and enthusiasm for Aegean involvement in Anatolia. M. Mellink, *AJA* 82 (1978) 321, 324 and *AJA* 87 (1983) 139 n. 3; I. Love, "From Crete to Knidos—A Minoan Sea Route via the Dodekanese," *AJA* 88 (1984) 251; see also T. R. Bryce, "The Nature of Mycenaean Involvement in Western Anatolia," *Historia* 38 (1989) 1–21.

[104]O. Taplin, "Homer's Use of Achilles' Earlier Campaigns in the Iliad," in J. Boardman and C. E. Vaphopoulou-Richardson eds., *Chios* (Oxford 1986) 15–19 reviews the campaigns of Achilles at Lyrnessos, Pedasos, Tenedos (11.624–25), etc.

[105]M. Mellink, *AJA* 89 (1985) 558; 91 (1987) 13; 93 (1989) 117; *AnatSt* 16 (1986) 207; Vermeule (supra n. 1) 143.

[106]M. Korfmann, "Besik Tepe: New Evidence for the Troy Sixth and Seventh Settlements," in Mellink (supra n. 97) 17–28; cf. his reports in *AA* 1984, 165–95; *AA* 1985, 157–94; *AA* 1986, 303–63; *AA* 1988, 391–404; *AnatSt* 36 (1986) 181–82.

[107]Güterbock 1983 (supra n. 98) 134 n. 11 (KUB 14.2; AU 298–306); Vermeule 1983 (supra n. 98) 142.

[108]Vermeule (supra n. 48) 275–78; supra n. 98, 1983, and 1984, 87–92; Wood (supra n. 103) 112–18; J. T. Hooker, "Ilios and the Iliad," *WS* 13 (1979) 5–21, summarizing earlier arguments including C. Nylander, *Antiquity* 37 (1963) 6–11; Page, *Antiquity* 33 (1959) 25; etc.

[109]D. Easton, "Has the Trojan War Been Found?" *Antiquity* 59 (1985) 188–95; E. Bloedow, "The Trojan War and Late Helladic III C," *PZ* 63 (1988) 23–52; cf. Dickinson (supra n. 89) 23 n. 11, and M. Jacob-Felsch, *GGA* 237 (1985) 47.

[110]Easton (supra n. 109) 189–90.

[111]G. Nagy, *The Best of Achaeans* (Baltimore 1979) 140; cf. Hooker (supra n. 108) 7 and M. Jameson's portrayal, recalled by Vermeule

1983 (supra n. 98) 142, of " 'the *Iliad* as the record of all the Mycenaean adventures overseas', telescoping and combining memorable episodes in epic song."

[112]L. McCallum, "Frescoes from the Throne Room at Pylos: A New Interpretation," *AJA* 91 (1987) 296.

[113]M. Lang. *Minos* 20–22 (1987) 333–41 for such a comparison of the Pylos themes (battles, sacrifice, hunt, feasting) to Homeric ones.

[114]Coleman (supra n. 54) and "Frescoes from Ayia Irini, Keos. Part I," *Hesperia* 42 (1973) 284–300; K. Abramowitz, "Frescoes from Ayia Irini, Keos. Parts II–IV," *Hesperia* 49 (1980) 57–85; M. Cameron, "Theoretical Interrelations among Theran, Cretan and Mainland Frescoes," *TAW* 589; Warren, "Miniature Fresco" 127 suggests the "same cycle" as the Theran miniature frescoes (perhaps on the theme of the hunt, rather than battle: cf. *Aspis* 270–305).

[115]E.g., Barber (supra n. 3) 181; Morgan, *Miniature Wall Paintings* 68. A new study of the Kea frescoes by Ellen Davis and Lyvia Morgan is in progress: E. Schofield, *AJA* 91 (1987) 242.

[116]West (supra n. 92) 172.

PART II

ILLUMINATED MANUSCRIPTS

THE LINDISFARNE GOSPELS
Françoise Henry

> *In this review article, Dr Françoise Henry, Director of*
> *Studies in Archaeology and History of Art at University*
> *College, Dublin, discusses fully the new and magistral*
> *edition of and commentary on the Lindisfarne Gospels*
> *produced in Switzerland in 1960.* *

I seem to remember Mr Bruce-Mitford telling me that when he
was in the Laurentian Library in Florence, he asked to have that
monster of all manuscripts, the Codex Amiatinus, weighed for
him. I do not know what the result of the operation was. But
perhaps he will forgive me if I say that, when faced with the
impressive text codex which comes as a companion to the
facsimile of the Lindisfarne Gospels, I was seized with the same
awed curiosity, so that my first impulse was to put it on the scales.
The net result is eleven and a half pounds. No need to say that such
a formidable array of letterpress is difficult to grasp in its entirety,
and that only some aspects of it can be dealt with in a short
article—perhaps of necessity those closest to the personal preoccupations of the present writer.

The volume includes work by various authors, and the publishers are to be warmly congratulated for asking several well-known
specialists to deal with the manuscript from different angles. The
detailed treatment of the interlinear Anglo-Saxon gloss by Alan
S. C. Ross and E. G. Stanley will be no doubt an invaluable
document to linguists and that of the chemical composition of the
colors of the illuminations of the Book of Lindisfarne and a few

---

Reprinted by permission of the publisher from *Antiquity* No. XXXVII, 1963, pp. 100–110.
Evangeliorum Quattuor Codex Lindisfarnensis, by T. D. Kendrick, T. J. Brown, R. L. S.
Bruce-Mitford, H. Roosen-Runge, A. S. C. Ross, E. G. Stanley, and A. E. A. Werner. *Urs
Graf Verlag,* Olten Lausanne, 1960. 125 *guineas.*

related manuscripts by Dr Werner, head of the Laboratory of the British Museum and Dr H. Roosen-Runge—as thorough an examination of the problem as can be made without direct analysis of the pigments—will put the approach to this side of ''Insular'' manuscript decoration on a new footing.

But it is with the main bulk of the volume that I want to deal, with the contributions of two eminent scholars, Rupert Bruce-Mitford, Keeper of British Antiquities in the British Museum, and Julian Brown, who has now left the staff of the Department of Manuscripts in the British Museum for a chair in London University. They give us a joint historical study of the manuscript and then separate to deal one with the text and the other with the decoration.

Now the first point to be examined when dealing with the Book of Lindisfarne is the value and real meaning of the texts concerned with its authorship and origin, the colophon and a passage of the *Historia Dunelmensis Ecclesiae* of Symeon of Durham. As is well-known, the colophon dates from the 10th century. Aldred, prior of the community of Lindisfarne which had taken refuge at Chester-le-Street because of the Viking raids on the island,[1] glossed the Book at that time and tells us that ''Eadfrith, Bishop of the Lindisfarne Church, originally wrote this book for God and for St Cuthbert and—jointly—for all the saints whose relics are on the island. And Ethiluald, Bishop of the Lindisfarne islanders, impressed it on the outside and covered it—as he well knew how to do. And Billfrith, the anchorite, forged the ornaments which are on it on the outside and adorned it with gold and with gems and also with gilded-over silver—pure metal. And Aldred, unworthy and most miserable priest, glossed it in English between the lines with the help of God and St Cuthbert.''

Eadfrith (or Eadfrid) was bishop-abbot of Lindisfarne from 698 to 721. Aldred probably wrote his translation around 970. Usually a colophon later by nearly three centuries than the manuscript itself would be held under grave suspicion. The same applies even more strongly to the confirmation of Aldred's statements given by Symeon of Durham, who repeats what he has no doubt read in the Book and adds to it a few imaginative touches in his usual manner, so that what he tells us has really very little additional value and should not be taken too seriously. When he says for example that Eadfrith wrote the Book ''with his own hand,'' are we to see in this, as our authors do, a "primary Durham source," or simply a figure of speech?[2]

The authors not only consider the authority of the colophon as beyond discussion, but are at great pains to dispose of various hypotheses, such as that of F. C. Burkitt and Abbot Chapman[3] who made Aethelwald (or Ethiluald) the illuminator, or my suggestion that the illuminations are not by the hand of Eadfrith.[4] They have probably made a convincing case (pp. 5–11, 123–125), from a careful study of some alterations to the decoration, for admitting that Eadfrith was the painter as well as the scribe. Having recently come to the same conclusion, partly for historical reasons which will appear later, I am particularly ready to adopt their findings on this point. But perhaps the statements of the colophon are a little too readily considered as binding on their own face value. If we have all more or less accepted their data, it is mostly because they fit well with the features of the manuscript, and also because we have followed that very cogent argument of Baldwin Brown[5] that anyone not relating a well-known tradition would have attributed the Book to St Cuthbert and not to such an obscure person as Eadfrith. So that a slightly less dogmatic and categorical attitude would have been welcome here. All that can be said is that the Book practically certainly comes from Lindisfarne and that the attribution to Eadfrith is likely without being absolutely certain.

At this point, one might have expected to find some kind of history of the monastery of Lindisfarne, from its foundation around 635 to the death of Eadfrith in 721.[6] A sketch of what is known (chiefly from Bede's writings) of its link with Iona from which it was founded by Aidan and of its connexion with the royal house of Northumbria at whose behest it was founded near the royal seat of Bamborough, would certainly have made further statements more intelligible; and a study of how far Lindisfarne may or may not have been in touch with Ireland and Iona at the time when Eadfrith was at work on the manuscript might have helped the authors themselves to make up their minds on some points which are essential in this story.

Instead, we are simply given biographies of the three people directly connected with the manuscript, Eadfrith, Aethelwald and Billfrith. The biography of Eadfrith (pp. 17–18) is a summary of his work as abbot of Lindisfarne. In fact it starts by the statement that "of Eadfrith's life before he became abbot of Lindisfarne nothing at all seems to be known" and ends by the remark that "it has been suggested that Bishop Eadfrith is the Ehfrid [*sic*] to whom a letter was addressed by Aldhelm." To this a footnote is added: "T. F. Tout in *Dictionary of National Biography*, XVI (1888), 306–307. But see R. Ehwald, *Aldhelmi Opera*, M. G. H., Auctorum Antiquissimorum XV (1919), 486–487." Perhaps it is worthwhile to pause a little on these references. The article in the *D.N.B.*, in spite of its ancient date, is of some interest. After the indication (which would need discussion or qualification) that Eadfrith was a disciple of St Cuthbert, one finds this: "He was one of the monastic bishops of the Celtic type rather than the more active Roman organizers. Though . . . he was orthodox in the question which separated the two churches, he lived in the spirit of the Columbas and Aidans," a very true statement, if one examines carefully the little that is known of Eadfrith's life and of his activities devoted nearly entirely to his monastery and the furtherance of the fame of St Cuthbert. And then: "He is probably the Eahfrid to whom, on his return from Ireland, Aldhelm addressed a long and hardly intelligible letter." This letter is certainly one of Aldhelm's most abstruse productions. It has been suggested[7] that it is a parody on a certain contorted Latin style favored in Ireland and represented by the *Hisperica Famina*. Perhaps—though it still remains to be proven that the *Hisperica Famina* are of Irish origin. However, obscure as it may be, enough can be disentangled of that incredible Latin to make a few facts quite clear. Though it is in some cases hardly more than a paraphrase, Bishop Browne's translation,[8] which gives the essential of the meaning, may serve us as a guide.

To his friend, Aldhelm writes: "We have heard from newsmongers that you have arrived safe at the ambrosial shores of British territory, having left the wintry climes and storms of the island of Hibernia; where for a triple two year period ("ter bino circiter annorum circulo")[9] you have drawn nourishment from the udder of wisdom." Then he mentions that the "coming and going of those who pass by the ships-track, the whirlpools of the sea, thence and hence, thither and hither, is so frequent, that it resembles some brotherhood of bees, busily storing the nectar in the comb." He enumerates what they learn: the arts of grammar and geometry, the other six arts of physics[10] and the interpretation of texts through allegory. This worries him: "I, miserable little man, revolved these things as I wrote them down; and I was tortured by an anxious question. Why, say I, should Ireland whither students, ship-borne, flock together . . ., why should Ireland be exalted by some ineffable privilege? As though here, on the fertile turf of Britain, teachers Greek and Roman could not be found. . . . The fields of Ireland are rich in learners, and green with the pastural numerosity of students . . . And yet . . .'' has not Britain got Theodore of Tarsus and Hadrian ''his companion in the brotherhood of learning, ineffably endowed with pure urbanity?'' And he ends by a lurid description of Theodore ''surrounded by a crowd of Irish disciples who grievously badgered him as the truculent boar is hemmed in by a snarling pack of Molossian hounds,'' and tearing them ''with the tusk of grammar,'' and piercing them ''with the sharp and deep syllogisms of chronography, till they cast away their weapons and hurriedly fled to the recesses of their dens.''[11]

This letter is fascinating because of the picture it gives of the state of studies in England in the late 7th century with its two rival poles: Ireland and Canterbury.[12] But in addition it is essential in regard to Eadfrith: if it was really addressed to him, we have to reckon with the fact that he went to study in Ireland and spent six years there before 690 (date of the death of Theodore who is mentioned as alive in the letter)[13] and consequently before he became abbot-bishop of Lindisfarne in 698.

No need to say that there is no complete agreement about the identification of Eahfrid with Eadfrith (or Eadfrid). Ussher, who first published the letter in the seventeenth century,[14] suggests it. Ehwald, in the edition of Aldhelm's works quoted by our authors, infers that the letter is addressed to King Aldfrid of Northumbria, who reigned from 684 to 704. This hardly bears investigation. The letter of Aldhelm is addressed: ''Domino, venerabili praeconio efferendo et sanctorum meritis magnopere honorando, Eahfrido.'' There are letters of Aldhelm (who may have been his godfather) to Aldfrid, and a long poem of Aldhelm is dedicated to him. Everywhere he calls him ''Acircius'' (from the north-west wind), a reference probably to Aldfrid's Irish ancestry.[15] Besides Aldfrid did not go to Ireland as an ordinary student; he went to stay with his mother's people, and uncouth as Aldhelm may be at times he would hardly have had the bad taste of addressing to him his fiery diatribe on Irish scholarship.

The suggestion by Stubbs (*Dictionary of Christian Biography*) that the addressee is an abbot of Glastonbury has nothing to back it.[16] So we are thrown back on Eadfrith as the most likely addressee, both from a historical point of view and by the great similarity of the names, and in this case his biography should include the possibility that he was Irish in education as well as in his way of life. This is of essential importance in regard to the decoration of the Gospels. In fact it is a key-point to the whole problem of "Insular" manuscripts, as it may give an indication of how the Irish style did spread. The only honest statement to make on this is that one cannot be sure one way or the other, but that there is a strong probability that Eadfrith is Eahfrid and that consequently his training was Irish.

A point may be considered here: the question of the date of the manuscript. If it was written by Eadfrith, it has to be dated before his death in 721. But the authors insist that the Book must have been written and decorated before 698, when Eadfrith became bishop of Lindisfarne, because after that date he would not have had the time to attend to such an absorbing task.[17] I must say I find this assertion quite amazing. Surely an abbot is not like a Director of the British Museum who loses automatically all right to work in his Department when he leaves it for the Director's office? In actual fact it would be enough to reflect on what was happening at about the same time in Iona, to think differently. It is shortly after Adamnan had become abbot of the metropolis of the Columban order (a much heavier assignment than the abbacy of Lindisfarne around 700) that his monks asked him to write the life of their founder,[18] and the *Vita Columbae* was written by him in a few years in the midst of embassies to the court of Northumbria and of all the worries of the last stages of the Easter controversy.[19]

If this be taken into consideration, we are left with a much longer period for the writing and decorating of the Book, perhaps 690 to 721. When it was started, we can hardly hope to know. But it is unfinished, as Bruce-Mitford has convincingly shown (pp. 122–123). Why then not assume that it was written in the last years of Eadfrith's abbacy,[20] and not quite finished at his death?

If this late date be adopted, this would make the Book practically contemporary with the heyday of the scriptorium of Jarrow-Wearmouth. Julian Brown has shown (p. 94) that some peculiarities of layout and presentation have been influenced by the habits of the Jarrow-Wearmouth scribes, and, of course, the very pure Vulgate text proceeds from an Italo-Northumbrian exemplar such as were available in the Jarrow-Wearmouth library. If one accepts what is to my mind likely, namely that Ceolfrid took the Codex Amiatinus to Italy as soon as it was finished, this puts its writing, and probably that of the other "pandects," in the beginning of the first quarter of the eighth century, and before A.D. 716, the date of Ceolfrid's departure. This is the very time when one would expect the non-Insular features of the Lindisfarne Gospels to appear under the influence of a fully active Jarrow-Wearmouth scriptorium.

Except for these few points, I do not intend to discuss Julian Brown's elaborate analysis of the problems connected directly with the text of the manuscript and the origin of its archetype, as this is too specialized a realm to venture into, and I shall pass now to the comparisons made by both authors with other manuscripts of the same period. The Book of Lindisfarne is really one of a series of luxury altar-books of more or less similar size which have in common with it the use of large, legible script of imposing appearance, with very few contractions, as well as an elaborate decoration. Of these, two have been singled out in this volume for an elaborate treatment: the Echternach Gospels (Paris, Bibl. nat. Lat. 9389) and the remains of a Gospel-book probably from the Library of Lindisfarne (Durham, Ms. A.II.17); Julian Brown has gone to great pains to study them and compare their script. The Echternach Gospels are written mostly in a large minuscule, but the juxtaposition of the first page, which is written in majuscule, with the script of the Durham manuscript (pls. 2 and 3) shows a remarkable similarity. In his view, they represent, together with the Book of Lindisfarne, the "Lindisfarne scriptorium" (pp. 89 seq.). He considers that they are both by the same hand and that in both cases the scribe is also the author of the illuminations (p. 104, col. 2 [The Lindisfarne scriptorium]). Here intervenes one of these disastrous comparisons which can ruin an argument: we are shown on two opposite pages the Crucifixion of the Durham manuscript and the symbol of St Matthew of the Echternach Gospels (pls. 8 and 9) and we are asked to believe that they are by the same hand. Though minute comparisons of small details have been made here (p. 102), it is enough to stand back and view the photographs of the two illuminations in their general appearance to be convinced that they cannot possibly be due to the same man. So, either the same scribe wrote the two books and different painters were responsible for their decoration, or, much more probably, they are various products of a school of manuscript decoration where the script had become rather standardized (quite a normal thing with such a formal type of writing).

In fact, to reduce the detailed comparisons to these two manuscripts only is the initial mistake of the chapters dealing with these comparisons (pp. 89 seq. and 246 seq.). Several other books have at least as much of a title to be considered here as these two, and they either get hardly more than a passing mention or are not quoted at all: the Lichfield Gospels, first, whose decoration is in places very close to that of the Lindisfarne manuscript and which is referred to only occasionally; and a ruined Gospel-book in the Bodleian (Rawlinson, Ms. G. 167) in which only one decorated page remains, the beginning of the Gospel of St Luke. This is even nearer to the corresponding page of the Lindisfarne Gospel than any page of the Book of Lichfield. Then the Echternach Gospels have a near twin, as far as the drawing of the Evangelists' symbols is concerned: the dismembered Gospelbook of which one fragment (in very bad condition) is in the British Museum (Cotton Ms. Otho. C.V.) and the other (remarkably well preserved) is in the Library of Corpus Christi College, Cambridge (Ms. 197).[21] The relation between the two books would be very interesting to investigate, especially as the Cambridge manuscript shows a peculiarity of which there are one or two examples in the Echternach book, the use of the uncial G instead of the usual Insular type. Before one could start talking about a "Lindisfarne scriptorium," all these manuscripts would have to be examined in detail, and compared one with the other. It would then probably appear that the Book of Lindisfarne has taken undue advantage of its perfect state of preservation. It is the only absolutely intact manuscript we have for that period, except possibly the Echternach Gospels and the Cambridge fragment, whilst it is only by a tremendous effort of imagination that one can visualize what the others were in their original state. In fact its relation to the Lichfield Gospels, which should have been one of the central points of this study, has been left practically out of the comparisons and discussions. Having had, a few months ago, thanks to the kind permission of the Dean of Lichfield, the opportunity to study the Lichfield Gospels with the invaluable help of Roger Powell who was at the time engaged in re-binding it, I have seen the strong suspicion of an early date for Lichfield which had come into my mind at my previous contact with the manuscript, a few years ago, turn into a quasi-certitude. Of the painters of the manuscripts of Lichfield and Lindisfarne, it is that of the Lichfield book who invents, creates, and who is a thoroughly original artist, whilst Lindisfarne has a slightly stilted, a trifle desiccated manner which savors of imitation.

It would be well at this stage to discard the old tripartite pattern which we have all used at one time for the development of Irish illumination: Book of Durrow—Book of Lindisfarne—Book of Kells. This was all right as an easy working hypothesis. But a thorough study of the manuscripts such as the one under consideration ought to bring us to a more flexible view of the problem. The Book of Durrow may well be not so much a forerunner as the representative of a style which may in a way lead to a dead end. On the other hand, in the early part of the 8th century (or perhaps in some cases in the late 7th), we are faced with a collection of large manuscripts. It is essential to remember that they are only the remains of what must have been an abundant production. The fact that we do not have a single psalter, when psalters must have existed by the hundred, and many of them must have been decorated, is the measure of our losses. Of these manuscripts, several (Durham, A.II.17; Rawlinson G.167; Otho.C.V.; Lichfield) are reputed to have a ''mixed'' Irish text. Echternach has it for some parts at least. Lindisfarne is the only one which shows a pure Vulgate text of Italo-Northumbrian type. In view of these facts and until a detailed study of all the texts has been undertaken, it would be extremely unwise to embark on too categorical affirmations as to their origin. There is nothing impossible in the view that they represent a style which developed in some great Irish centre and of which the Lindisfarne Gospels would be a very faithful, but slightly dead imitation. This would fit very well with what may be the early history of Eadfrith and his connexion with Ireland.[22] It would fit also with the atmosphere which may well have existed in Northumbria at the time when it was governed by a half-Irish king like Aldfrid. The hypothesis is in any case well worth considering.

In this case the whole study of the origin of the Lindisfarne ornament would have to be brought back one step further, right into Ireland where Bruce-Mitford seems to be always loth to follow it, instead of being started unconvincingly by comparisons with Sutton Hoo which avoid all the difficulties of the subject.

This hypothesis would even be reinforced by the remarkable study which he has made of evidence already pointed out by Baldwin-Brown but which had never been properly examined. In several decorated pages, especially on the back of the five ''carpet-pages,'' pricks and rulings can be seen and have been photographed, which show how the designs were made, either by the help of a fine grid, or of elaborate compass work (Figs. 1 and 2). For the first time we can watch the draughtsman at work, not through a series of guesses such as those made by Romilly Allen[23] and even by Gabrielsson,[24] but with the certitude of knowing how they proceeded. In fact the secret of the extreme regularity of the decoration lies in the use of these mechanical aids.

This in itself is a splendid discovery of which Mr Bruce-Mitford can be justly proud. Perhaps the conclusion he draws from it is a little too sweeping, but all the same it may help us to understand the special aspect of the manuscript: ''Once these [principles] have been absorbed, anybody, whether Celt, Saxon or Australian aborigine, provided he can hold a pen and take pains, can achieve the most complex-looking Hiberno-Saxon designs of every type.'' From this I would conclude that Eadfrith, being in fact a lot more developed than the Australian aborigine, absorbed the principles inculcated to him by some Irish master, and possessing the method in all its intricacy, contrived to design a perfect ''à la manière de'' of the real Irish stuff. But all the creative spirit which is necessary to make a work of art by means of any such recipe was gone. This is where it would be essential to distinguish between a well perfected *tool* (the geometrical layout), and the mind which uses it.

Another aspect of this is that the origin of the method, as far anyway as the compass-drawn circles and segments of circles are concerned,[23] is to be found in Ireland. The Lough Crew bone-slips where the centres of the circles have remained marked on the bone are a good example of it, and Mr Jope has given another one in his excellent analysis of the various compass-centres from which the ornament of the bronze disc found in the Bann (Belfast Museum) was drawn.[26] This only goes to reinforce the remarks made above.

In fact, if one tries to see where lies the inner defect of an otherwise remarkable study, I would be tempted to say that it is in a refusal to face the problem of the Northumbrian scriptoria. If their

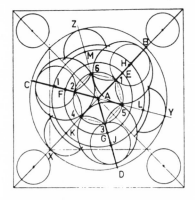

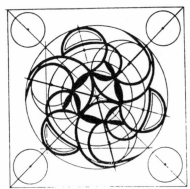

Fig. 1. Pricks and rulings showing elaborate compass work discovered by Mr Bruce-Mitford from the back of some of the decorated pages of the Lindisfarne Gospels; these diagrams illustrate stages in the construction of an ornament of folio 138^V. This discovery is the first certain proof that the extreme regularity of the decoration lay in the use of mechanical aids.

dual orientation had been indicated in the beginning, all would have been clearer: Lindisfarne, where the tradition of seeking inspiration and even tuition in Ireland survived a long time, perhaps in fact late into the eighth century, and Jarrow-Wearmouth which showed a short but intensive spell of imitation of Southern manuscripts under Benedict Biscop and Ceolfrid. This cannot have started before 674, date of the foundation of Wearmouth, and it was in full swing in 716, date of the departure of Ceolfrid with the completed Codex Amiatinus. But here one has to beware of going too quickly: for several years, the monasteries were a-building; Jarrow in fact was not founded until 681 or 682. Then came the plague which lasted, it seems, practically without interruption from 685 to 687 and was so

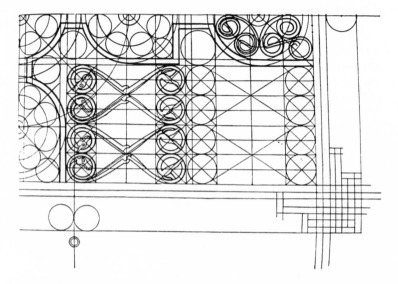

Fig. 2 Geometrical basis of a section of the "carpet-page," folio 26^V, of the Lindisfarne Gospels.

violent that at one time there was nobody left in Wearmouth but the prior and a little boy (probably Bede). These are hardly good conditions for the development of a scriptorium. In fact it hardly seems likely that it got into its stride before the last years of the 7th century.[27] There is no proof whatsoever that the Stonyhurst St John Gospel, obviously a work of the scriptorium, was buried in the coffin-reliquary of St Cuthbert at the time of the translation of the relics in 698,[28] as is often said and as is assumed by our authors. All we know really is that the Amiatinus was finished in 716, when Ceolfrid took it to Italy. So, for fifteen or twenty years there was between Tyne and Wear a centre where Italian script and Italian miniatures were imitated with incredible perfection and very little creative and inventive power.

Meanwhile, everything pertaining to book-art, script and decoration, was learnt at Lindisfarne probably from the time of the foundation (A.D. 635) from Irish masters. The art of the book was by that time very old in Ireland and had seen probably more than two centuries of experiments and improvements. Of this we have an early witness in the Cathach and several landmarks in the seventh century, ending by the Antiphonary written at Bangor[29] in the middle of the century and the copy of the *Vita Columbae* made in Iona probably around 690 by Dorbbene.[30] These are not altar-books, but ordinary reading-books. They show, however, in the second half of the seventh century a well developed tradition of book-writing which is quite compatible with the existence of luxury manuscripts done in the same scriptoria or similar ones.[31] The presence of Adamnan and anyway the importance which the monastery had taken in the course of the centuries would prepare us to accept Iona as one of these centres. The literary personality of Columbanus and his Latin, far better than that currently written on the Continent, casts an extraordinary light on the development of a monastery like Bangor[32] from which he started for the Continent in 590, seven years before the arrival of St Augustine in England. The fact that it produced the Antiphonary some fifty or sixty years later[33] shows that it had quite an efficient scriptorium at that time. Lismore is also beginning to emerge as such a centre of exegetic and hagiographical activities in the 7th and 8th centuries[34] that it must have had a considerable library, and inevitably some scribes. Clonmacnois most probably indulged in similar studies in that period. All these monasteries inevitably produced books which could influence the scriptorium of Lindisfarne.

In the Book of Lindisfarne the two traditions can be felt: the script is of Irish origin, the Vulgate text is of Italo-Northumbrian type. The ornaments are partly Irish in origin and partly (the portraits chiefly) borrowed from Mediterranean models. Whatever Germanic animal-interlacing there is may well have come after being adapted and elaborated in Ireland where it will remain for centuries one of the staple ornaments.

If the clinging to the Irish majuscule script shows the strength of the Irish element in Lindisfarne, it is even more striking to see the use of an Irish script in Jarrow-Wearmouth two or three decades after the death of Ceolfrid, in the Leningrad Bede.[35] There, some of the classical scripts are still used for titles, while a minuscule of Irish type served for the text itself. So even in that stronghold of classical script, the Irish methods reappear once the initial impulsion slows down.

Considering all this, one may well wonder if the type of ornament found in the Book of Lindisfarne is not simply a reflection, and a rather desiccated one at that, of the live and creative schools of book-decoration which probably existed in Ireland at the time when, in my opinion, it is likely to have been decorated, that is to say around 710–720.[36]

NOTES

(1) The community was to settle eventually at Durham.

(2) In the same way the story of the Book being lost at sea and retrieved undamaged—a standard type of legend, told of many manuscripts—ought not to have been taken seriously.

(3) J. Chapman, O.S.B., *Notes on the Early History of the Vulgate Gospels* (London, 1908), p. 9; F. C. Burkitt, "Kells, Durrow and Lindisfarne," ANTIQUITY, 1935, 34.

(4) *Irish Art* (London, 1940), 77.

(5) *The Arts in Early England,* v (London, 1921), 337–41.

(6) The fact that it is to be found in E. G. Millar, *The Lindisfarne Gospels* (London, 1923), 1–3, did not absolve the present book from giving us something similar.

(7) See: J. F. Kenney, *The Sources for the Early History of Ireland* (New York, 1929), 257.

(8) G. F. Browne, *St Aldhelm, his Life and Times* (London, 1903), 262 sqq.

(9) This contorted way of saying *six* is found again in the letter to indicate the *six* arts of physics.

(10) Ehwald suggests for these—from analogy with another text of Aldhelm—the quite likely list: arithmetic, music, astronomy, astrology, mechanics, medicine.

(11) Aldhelm himself had been taught first, as far as we know, by an Irishman, Maeldubh or Maelduin, then by Theodore of Canterbury.

(12) For the journeys of Irish students to Ireland it completes in a very useful way the famous text of Bede (*Hist. Eccles.,* III, 27) which relates to the state of affairs at the time of the plague of 664.

(13) Theodore and Hadrian arrived in England in 669. The letter obviously dates from a time when they had been teaching for a good while, probably 680–85.

(14) J. Ussher, *The Whole Works* (Dublin, 1631), IV (Sylloge), 448–453; see p. 453.

(15) Aldhelm uses the same expression, in the letter quoted above, in connexion with Ireland. Oswy, Aldfrid's father, like his brother Oswald, lived a long time in exile in Ireland, where he became a Christian ('Osuiu a Scottis edoctus ac baptizatus', *Hist. Eccles.,* III, 25). There, as Bishop

Browne tactfully puts it (*op. cit.,* 271) he "married or did not marry" Fina, a princess of the Northern Uí Néill, a grand-niece of St Columba. Aldfrid, in consequence it seems of his alleged illegitimate birth, was first passed over in the royal succession, his younger brother Egfrid succeeding Oswy. Upon the death of Egfrid, however, St Cuthbert advised calling back Aldfrid from "the Islands of the Scots" and he became king (Bede, *Vita S. Cuthberti* (prose)). He is called Flann Fina in Irish documents. The *Annals of Tigernach* mention his death thus (A.D. 704): 'Alfrith mac Ossu—Fland Fina the Irish call him—Rex Saxon fuit'; at the wrong date of 694, the *Annals of Inisfallen* have a similar entry; in the *Fragments of Irish Annals* published by O'Donovan, there is, at the year 704: "The death of Flann Fiona, son of Ossa, king of Saxonland, the famous wise man, the pupil of Adamnan." Adamnan himself calls him: "my friend king Aldfrid" (*Vit. Col.,* II, 46). He enjoys the reputation of a famous poet in Irish, though none of the poems attributed to him goes back to his time. Most of what is known about him is summed up in two notes: one in Reeves's *Life of St Columba* (185–6), the other in C. Plummer's edition of the *Historical Works of Bede* (vol. II, 263–4).

(16) For other identifications, see: Kenney, *Sources,* 227.

(17) Also they assume that it was made to order for the translation of the relics in 698, a not very likely procedure.

(18) *Vita Col.,* preface.

(19) *Vita Col.,* end of Book II. See: Kenney, 431–32 for the date of the redaction of the *Vita Columbae* (mostly before 685, but finished in the following years). A. O. and M. O. Anderson, *Adamnan's Life of Columba* (London, etc., 1961), pp. 5–6, favour a slightly later date. Adamnan's journeys to the court of Aldfrid took place in 686–7 and 688–9.

(20) This is also the time when he got Bede to write his prose *Life of St Cuthbert,* which is dedicated to Eadfrith and was finished just before his death in 721.

(21) Another fragment (canon-tables) in the British Museum (Royal MS 7.C.XII) may also have belonged to the same manuscript. See: E. A. Lowe, *Codices Latini Ant.,* II, no. 125.

(22) That style was probably not fully developed at the time (A.D. 680–85?) when he may have gone to Ireland. But he would be likely to keep in touch.

(23) *Celtic Art* (London, 1904), 272–76.

(24) R. Gabrielsson, *Kompositionsformer i senkeltisk orneringstil* (Stockholm, 1945).

(25) Also probably as far as the grids are concerned, as I hope to show in a coming publication.

(26) E. M. Jope and B. C. S. Wilson, "The Decorated Cast-Bronze Disc from the River Bann near Coleraine," *Ulster Journ. Archaeol.,* 1957, 95 sqq.

(27) This, of course, has a bearing on the Book of Durrow. It is assumed all through the volume under review that it is "a Northumbrian manuscript," by which is probably meant that it is ascribed to the Lindisfarne scriptorium, though the question is not discussed in detail (the clearest statement on its being Northumbrian is probably the footnote 3, page 90). Nobody, so far, has ever demonstrated conclusively that it is (see on the subject, *inter alia:* the articles of A. Clapham and F. C. Burkitt in ANTIQUITY, 1934 and 1935, and F. Masai, *Essai sur les Origines de la miniature dite irlandaise* (Bruxelles-Anvers, 1947) (Lowe's opinions on it seem to have varied greatly (*Cod. Lat. Ant.,* II, no. 273 and Preface)). The main reasons which have been advanced are of various types: *A,* the presence of a page with animal-interlacing of Anglo-Saxon type; *B,* the comparatively pure Vulgate text, thought to be of Italo-Northumbrian type; *C,* the orderly appearance of the script. Of these, *A* is part of the strong Anglo-Saxon influence which is manifest in all Irish metalwork at the end of the seventh century and the beginning of the eighth and may be a consequence of the Irish missions in England and the presence of numerous English students in Ireland, *B* is open to discussion, as the Gospel text is not so very pure Vulgate (see: H. J. Lawlor, "The Cathach of St Columba," *Proc. R.I.A.,* 1916), may not be of Italo-Northumbrian type (see: *Evangeliorum Quattuor Codex Durmachensis* (Olten-Lausanne-Fribourg, 1960), Introduction by A. A. Luce, pp. 3 sqq.) and is accompanied by pre-Vulgate preliminaries; as for *C,* why assume that when a luxury book has an orderly appearance it is necessarily Northumbrian? In fact there, the implied reason is that it would show an influence from these very orderly scriptoria of Jarrow and Wearmouth; but in that case the Book of Durrow would have to be dated very late: one cannot at the same time date it of around 675 and see in it an influence of Wearmouth, founded the previous year, or of Jarrow which did not exist then. Apart from that it looks a bit odd to assume without discussion that it is Northumbrian when there is now a volume in the same collection where Dr Luce is at great pains to show that it is really Irish. Slight lack of co-ordination. . . .

(28) The coffin of St Cuthbert having been opened at the time of the exodus of the monks from Lindisfarne and several relics, including perhaps books, having been stuffed into it at that time, the presence of the volume now in Stonyhurst College on a ledge above the head of St Cuthbert when the coffin was opened in 1104 does not prove anything (see: *The Relics of Saint Cuthbert* (Oxford, 1956), 27 and 356; see also:

E. A. Lowe, *English Uncial* (Oxford, 1960), and D. Wright, "Some notes on English Uncial," *Traditio,* 1961, 441).

(29) Milan, Ambrosian Library, Ms.C.5.inf.

(30) Schaffhausen, Town Library, Generalia, Ms.I.

(31) A comparison of the minuscule script of the *Vita Columbae* with that of the Echternach Gospels would show a great analogy in the script, and even, taking into consideration the very different purpose of the books, in the small initials surrounded with dots.

(32) See: G. S. M. Walker, *Sancti Columbani Opera* (Dublin, 1957).

(33) The Antiphonary is dated to the middle of the seventh century by the poem on the abbots of Bangor which it contains. See: F. Warren, *The Antiphonary of Bangor* (London, 1893–95).

(34) P. Grosjean, S. J., "Sur quelques exégètes irlandais," *Sacris Erudiri,* 1955, 67 sqq; see also K. Hughes, "An Irish Litany of Irish Saints compiled *c.* 800," *Analecta Bollandiana,* 1959.

(35) E. A. Lowe, "A key to Bede's Scriptorium," *Scriptorium,* 1958, 182 sqq.

(36) No need to say that if this view be adopted, there is no more room for the nice little piece of science-fiction by which the Ardagh chalice and the Tara brooch are annexed to Lindisfarne (pp. 250 sqq.).

THE BOOK OF SIGNS: WRITING AND VISUAL DIFFERENCE IN GOTHIC MANUSCRIPT ILLUMINATION
Michael Camille

I. THE BOOK OPENED

The dynamic experience of the medieval book as its layers of skin unfold "flesh side" to "hair side," recto to verso—each opening a verbal and visual revelation ordered for the viewer's gaze—is nowhere more evident than in manuscripts of the Book of Revelation itself, written "to show unto his servants things which must shortly come to pass" (Rev. 1.1). As we move through the great mid thirteenth-century English Apocalypse in Trinity College Library, Cambridge,[1] our eyes are attuned to the integration of text and picture to such an extent that when we come to the beginning of Chapter 10 on fol. 10v, where the picture appears at the bottom of the page, there is no need to look up at the text and gloss opposite. The two-tiered narrative presents a subtle visual equivalent of the written narrative in all its thrust (figure 1). Thus we read it in the same left to right direction as the words around it, starting with St. John, whose self-referentiality opens the chapter "And I saw another mighty angel come down from heaven clothed with a cloud." The next verse of the written narrative is contained in the visual unit formed by two figures to the right of the top band of the visual narrative: "And he had in his hand a little book open: and he set his right foot upon the sea and his left foot upon the earth." Even the adjective's separateness seems visually conveyed in the isolated "book-open," held out to St.

Reprinted by permission of the author and publisher from *Word and Image: A Journal of Verbal/Visual Enquiry,* April/June 1985, v. 1, no. 2, pp. 133–148.

Figure 1. The Angel and the Book. Chapter 10 of the Book of Revelation, *Apocalypse,* Trinity College MS R. 16.2 fol. 10ᵛ (detail). (Reproduced by permission of the Master and Fellows of Trinity College, Cambridge.)

John on the right. Likewise responding to the flow of the following text is the visualization of the next phrase, "and when the seven thunders uttered their voices," by seven human heads spitting fire. St. John is shown again below them, his head tilted as if attentive to the next stage in his visionary experience, which is at once visual, aural and ultimately, scriptural. It has to become writing: "And when the seven thunders had uttered their voices, I was about to write: and I heard a voice from heaven saying unto me, 'Seal up those things which the seven thunders uttered and write them not' '' (v. 4). The "voice" is represented like a cartoon-bubble entering the ears of John below. There is a different, medieval emphasis in its Norman-French translation: "Ne escrivez pas les signes ke les set toneires unt parle" [Do not write the *signs* that the seven thunders have spoken]. The multiple levels of communication here—writing, hearing, seeing, speaking—are an important aspect of the Book of Revelation, which is constructed through a complex of aural, verbal and visual sensations: "and I, John, saw these things and heard them" (22.8); "And I saw another sign in heaven, great and marvellous" (15.1).

The status of the sign, its internal relations (*signans* and *signatum*) and the relation between visual things and words (*res* and *verba*) were no more crucial and problematic than during the High Middle Ages, when people accepted the transformation of the host into the flesh of Christ and awaited the signs that heralded the Last Judgement.[2] "The medieval definition of sign—*aliquid stat pro aliquo*—has been resurrected," according to Jakobson and its contemporary uses have been expounded by critical theorists as diverse as Foucault, Derrida and Kristeva.[3] However, little has been written on the historical context of medieval visual semiotics, with the exception of Meyer Schapiro's study which opens with the warning that "the correspondence between word and picture is problematic and may be surprisingly vague."[4] It is exactly this vagueness, this space between what can be written as language and represented to picture it, which will be examined in this essay. It was a fundamental difficulty for the medieval artist whose framework of representation was almost totally confined to what had been written. Providing the images of Christianity, the religion of the *logos,* was he just "the docile interpreter of great ideas," as Emile Mâle, the systematic iconographer of the cathedral, put it?[5] Were the limits of representation thus the limits of language? The manuscript illuminations (many of them previously unpublished) which are examined in the following essay are taken from a wide range of religious, secular and even scientific texts. The aim is neither to provide a chronology nor any analogic arguments about "the Gothic," but to show how this material can be subjected to synchronic as well as diachronic analysis. The danger of de-historicizing or denying specific contexts must be met by the advantages of asking broader, theoretical questions.

These can reveal facets of function, construction and reception which stylistic criticism tends not to consider.

Confined within the closing and opening shutters of the read text, the spaces of the word itself, the manuscript illuminator's task was more than simply embellishment of the sacred page. The illustrator of the Trinity College Apocalypse (figure 1), for example, has brilliantly discovered a number of visual equivalents, not only for the surface action in the second register (where John eats the book, which makes his "belly bitter" with an almost humorous perception of medieval indigestion) but also for the very pace and concentration of the language itself. The pictorial signification of sounds and voices, for example, continues with "what the angel said unto me" and ends the chapter. John looks over in his discomfort to read the placard held by the angel: "Thou must prophesy again before many peoples and nations, and tongues and Kings" [as gens et as langages et as mus reis]. By the thirteenth century and for the aristocratic, perhaps even royal, reader of this luxurious book, the hegemony of Latin as the official language of religious experience had been loosened. Examples like this very manuscript, with its text, commentary and inscriptions in Norman French, proclaim the evangelizing spread of the word to different "gens" in diverse "languages" after the edicts of the Fourth Lateran Council of 1215. This required every Christian to participate in, be taught and, moreover, understand the articles of the faith, the basic prayers, the signs instituted by God and relayed through the church. Images now assumed a new and vital role in the ideology of medieval religion and in the spaces between writing, in the book, which was opened to a wider audience than had previously been possible.

II. THE ARCHITECTURE OF THE WORD: "PICTURA QUASI SCRIPTURA"

The act of writing is the ubiquitous image in medieval art. Gospel Books pictured not the contents of the text but its production, its "origin" in the four founders of the faithful text, the four Evangelists. It was their special position as first writers that gave them a prestige granted to few of their copyists, since the ordinary medieval scribe had an ambivalent position in medieval society. He was a mere machine for writing, copying and re-copying a visual product, constantly introducing human fallibility and "corrupting" the purity of the spiritually communicated text.[6] The intensity of scribal practice, requiring the labour of the whole body and the fixed gaze, stressed by medieval writers, is visible in a full-page picture, again of St. John, in another thirteenth century Apocalypse, Lambeth Palace Library MS 209 (figure 2). John is here seated as a scribe in his "Gothic" chair on the Island of Patmos, the waters surrounding it making a kind of frame out of which the inspiring angel appears top-left. The Evangelist's narrow eyes look down at the ruled lines of his book, his pen and scraper poised to record the revelation. However, the text which unfolds as a scroll down the front of the lectern is not from the Apocalypse but refers to John's prime role as mediator between Divine and human language in another part of the Bible. Written down the scroll, like an external inscription rather than appearing to be penned by this particular scribe are the opening words of St. John's own Gospel. In Principio erat verbum—"in the beginning was the word and the word was with God and the word was God."

In Augustine's semiotic system, which is a highly evolved and structured hierarchy of the sign, words are "signa propria," arbitrary units which are used in human communication.[7] Totally aware of the contractual basis of sign production, medieval commentators stressed the fact that the written signifier was conventional, technical and representative. According to Gilbert Crispin, Abbot of Westminster (1085–1117) when arguing against an anti-image Jew, "Just as letters are the shapes and signs of spoken words, pictures exist as the representations and signs of writing."[8] It is important to remember this triple level of signification for the user of a medieval illuminated manuscript. We tend to privilege the written above the spoken, but this was reversed in the still semi-oral culture of the Gothic period. Also we lack the relay to a transcendental signified when reading a text, a primary level of meaning which Derrida discusses in relation to the phonocentrism of medieval culture: "reading and writing, the production and interpretation of signs, allow themselves to be confined within secondariness. They are preceded by a truth or meaning already constituted by and within the element of the logos."[9] In this sense, the image of St. John with its "historical"

Figure 2. St. John on Patmos, from an *Apocalypse,* Lambeth Palace Library, MS 270, fol. 47ᵛ. (Permission, Archbishop of Canterbury and Trustees of Lambeth Palace Library.)

representation of the *act* of writing and the visible writing of the logos within it involve two different, though tangential systems that are secondary to the "truth" or "meaning." Both image and text participate in the same upward and outward direction—to utter the same source.

It is necessary to grasp this conventionality of both word and image in order to see their interdependent role in the art of the period. It is too easy to give language the prerogative. One of the most highly respected "philosophers" of visual language, E. H. Gombrich, has stated that the image, because of its lack of "such formators as definite and indefinite articles is unable to signify the distinction between the universal and the particular."[10] On the same lines, someone else has stated that, while it is possible to illustrate a text which says "a horse is red" by drawing a horse and painting it red, a sentence "all horses are red" cannot be depicted.[11] Yet it is exactly the latter kind of statement which the illustrators of Gothic Bestiary manuscripts, which described and illustrated the different animal species, had to convey. We see their illustrations as "general" and not "particular," partly because the universal schemata for animal depiction which they used copied formulae of a thousand-year-old tradition, and put forward animals not as perceived individuals but as concepts. But the best form of representation for refuting the arguments for the non-linguistic nature of visuality and for understanding how an image can function on the same complex semantic levels as a text is the medieval diagram. This was readable as *scriptura* and yet totally dependent on presentation through *pictura*.

A little-known example of a medieval writer using an image to explain meaning occurs in the late twelfth-century tract *De statu Ecclesiae* by Gilbert of Limerick, part of a manuscript now in the Cambridge University Library (figure 3).[12] What looks at first glance like an elaborate architectural design for window tracery is in fact a diagrammatic representation of the hierarchical structure of medieval society. Gilbert's text on the page opposite constantly refers to this *depicta imago* and elucidates it, starting at the base of the pyramidal structure with the parishes and monasteries (indicated by the letters P and M). Each parish consists of seven orders of priests and the congregation of males and females V (*virii*), and F (*feminae*) divided according to the three functions or *ordines* of society, those who pray (*oratores*), those who plough (*aratores*)

Figure 3. Diagram from Gilbert of Limerick's *De Statu Ecclesiae,* University Library MS Ff. 1.27, fol. 18ᵛ. (Reproduced by permission of the Syndics of Cambridge University Library.)

and those who fight (*bellatores*). The same system divides the
ranks of the monastery except that the congregation is of the male
sex only. Over each representative pair of monastery and parish
rise hierarchies of bishops, archbishops over each diocese (D).
The whole is headed by the Pope and his "type" "*Noe*" (Noah's
ark signifying the church). This ecclesiastical edifice has on each
level a secular equivalent, from knights (*Miles*) at the bottom, to
the Emperor (*Imperator*) next to the Pope, the apex of the whole
being, of course, *Christus*. Maria Corti did not refer to such an
illustration in her convincing semiotic analysis of Gilbert of
Limerick's text but stressed what she called "the model's iconic
figuration, on the spatial formalization of culture, for the result is
that verbal message and iconic message are complementary."[13]
There are other manuscripts of the text which display a much
simpler diagram, showing geometrical triangles within triangles.
But this English monastic artist has magnificently embodied
Gilbert's ideas within the smooth arcs and curvilinear crescents
reminiscent of contemporary ecclesiastical structures. "The entire
image displays the shape of a pyramid," according to its author,
"since the lowest part is broad, encompassing the carnal and the
movement, the upper part however, is narrow, as it offers a
straight way for the religious and those in orders."[14] The rigid
ordines of medieval society are made tangible by the text, but it is
the anonymous illuminator who has made the iconic analogy
between church structure on a social level and church structure in
terms of the early Gothic window.

The relationship between writing and image is here integral,
consistent and generated on the creative level. By contrast, when
art historians usually draw analogies between pictures and words
it is on the superficial level of "style." For example, Pierre
Bourdieu, in his "Post-face" to the new French translation of
Panofsky's classic study in formalist analogy *Gothic Architecture
and Scholasticism,* refers to something he terms the "habitus," a
mode of working shared by members of a culture irrespective of
the medium in which they express themselves, which he links to a
notion of a Chomskian "general grammar."[15] In this way he can
illustrate (after H. Marichal) analogies between the style of
written scripts and analogous forms of Gothic window tracery
from the same periods (figure 4). This deterministic notion not
only comes close to the *Zeitgeist* which has so stubbornly been

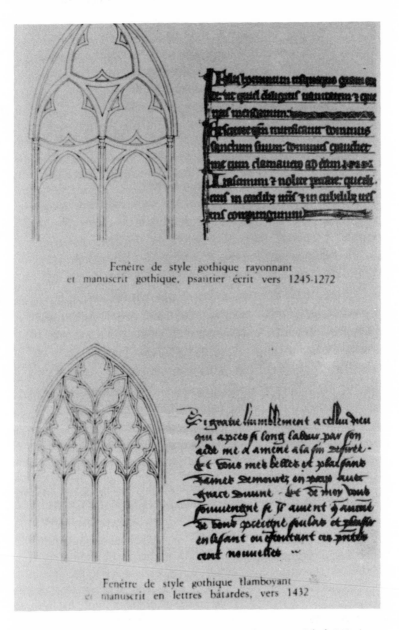

Fenêtre de style gothique rayonnant
et manuscrit gothique, psautier écrit vers 1245-1272

Fenêtre de style gothique flamboyant
et manuscrit en lettres bâtardes, vers 1432

Figure 4. Gothic Windows and Gothic Scripts, after R. Marichal, *L'Ecriture et la Psychologie des Peuples.*

removed from art history over the past decades, it is also generated on a formal level, in isolation from any meaning. Thus it is not noticed, for example, that the two scripts are in Latin and French respectively. Yet one would not want to talk of the second script/architecture comparison as being in a "vernacular" style. We know that Gothic scribes were proud of the variety of different styles of script they could utilize and often advertised the fact.[16] The same artistic "choice" goes for the designer of window tracery. If we were looking for a specific cultural embodiment of the script/architecture relationship we can find it in the carefully designed delineations of meaning in Gilbert of Limerick's diagram, which has become a "window on the world" not in an Albertian sense of a view "through," but in the medieval semiotic sense of *suppositio*—or "standing in place of."

This term is important in appreciating how diagrammatic illustrations like these bypassed the problems outlined at the outset, of distinguishing between universals and particulars. The diagram avoids these difficulties because it is not locked into the particularity of representing "like by like" in the normal iconic means of pictorial representation. In medieval scholasticism it was possible to differentiate between "man at the formal, definitional level" and an example like "Socrates is a man" using the notion of *suppositio*. Michael Evans has shown how in twelfth-century diagrams, the different words on the image do not (like *tituli*) label specific things but signify on a general level, as in the V for *virii* (men) in Gilbert's diagram.[17] Other diagrammatic systems used in teaching, such as *rotae* (wheels) and trees allowed another possible picturing of something usually associated with language—the negative. Kenneth Burke has stated that "Though idea and image have become merged in the development of language, the negative provides the instrument of splitting them apart. For the negative is an idea; there can be no image of it."[18] However, negative statements and relationships are constantly pictured in medieval art as the *distinctiones* in an argument—the *pro* and *con* can be stratified at different sides of a stemmatic tree, virtues can face vices across an opening of a book and an image of evil, like a devil, can be crossed-out or else erased. Other schematic diagrams can embrace, not just abstract categories but temporal ones, presenting the rotation of the year or the stages of life in a wheel, compounding the four elements, humours, seasons, winds, etc.

For these reasons of clarity, immediacy and the avoidance of ontological problems, diagrammatic layout became an aesthetic basis not just for teaching in the cloister or schools but also in the wider spread of images in the Gothic period, especially in stained glass. Churchmen realized the potential of the image in communicating ideology. According to Stephen of Bourbon, "Jesus Christ first taught by things rather than by words and rendered the subtlety of his doctrine in a basic way, as it were in corporeal and visible fashion . . . Corporeal discourse moves more easily from the sense to the imagination and from the imagination to the memory."[19] A less well-known factor in this appreciation of the autonomy of image was the revival of Aristotelian materialism in thirteenth-century intellectual life. This laid stress on sight as the highest of the human cognitive senses and was given doctrinal status in the writings of Thomas Aquinas. An initial to one of Aristotle's scientific tracts by an English artist of c.1270 shows this active perception of the object (figure 5).[20] It heads the book on Memory—"*De memoria et reminiscentia*" which discusses the importance of mental images in thought and how "the soul never understands apart from phantasms." The sage with his book stares at a naked figure and must illustrate Aristotle's contention that "by perception we know neither the future nor the past, but only the present. But Memory is of the past. No-one would say he was remembering what was present, when it was present, e.g., this white thing when he was seeing it."[22]

The function of memory and the distinction between a present perception and its retrieval for later use is a crucial one for the Gothic artist. This very example demonstrates it. The illustrator of Aristotle here did not use his own reading of the text in order to find a subject for the "R" initial. He has to have both the letter "R" itself and its content sketched out by someone else in the bottom margin (figure 5). The integration of text and picture, still possible in the twelfth-century system (figure 3), has broken down. The purely executive function of the new professional illuminator meant that unlike his monastic counterpart he did not produce both text and picture but merely filled in some pre-ordained space.

The artist was also limited not only by the physical confines of the pre-written text but also by the confines of his own contemporary pictorial language. The designer of the Aristotle illustration

Figure 5. Initial to Aristotle's *De Memoria et Reminiscentia* British Library Harley MS 3487, fol. 197ʳ. (Reproduced by permission of the Conway Library, Courtauld Institute of Art.)

(figure 5) follows the conventional patterns of a workshop more used to illustrating religious texts. The particular gesture of the seated figure, for example, economically indicated in the marginal direction to the illustrator is one traditionally used to signify thought or contemplation on the part of dreamers and visionaries like St. John, or is associated with negative ideas of sadness, sloth and melancholy.[22]

The image, rather than being an equivalent for a text as in the Trinity Apocalypse (figure 1), is here extraneous to it and uses its own evolved code of models for reference. A tension develops in thirteenth-century illustrations, outside the continuing diagrammatic genre, as text and picture become distinct acts with separate structures of signification, executed and planned by different skilled practitioners. It is a relationship built on a disruptive difference, a mutual incompatibility of two codes vying for the reader's attention and generating subtle nuances of meaning in the process.

III. THE GOTHIC IMAGE AS SUPPLEMENT

The visual layout or *ordinatio* of the medieval manuscript page clarified the text and provided a frame for the reader. Pictorial elements such as decorative or historiated initials and framed miniatures played their role in this revelatory structure, acting as indexing or heading devices, as well as impressing the text more strikingly on the memory in the language of "corporeal discourse."[23] This choreography of reading was especially important in works with complex marginal glosses, interlinear additions and sub-sections like the Aristotle manuscript (figure 5), where the initials are only one among many accumulated additions, anachronistically clinging like subtly interweaved Gothic pinnacles to a classical temple. But while ostensibly providing an ordered framework for the experience of linguistic meaning, the visual also acts to disrupt any linear unitary response by providing fissures in that smooth progression. Holes of representation, pockets of pictorial narrative, are cracks in the scribal edifice that "lead us away" from the textual hierarchy. Psycholinguists have pointed to this "noise" factor in illustrations and how they in fact run counter to the decoding process in reading.[24] This capacity of the pictorial frame to simultaneously construct and decompose, discussed by Derrida in relation to Baroque title pages, can be seen also in the deconstructive designs of Romanesque and Gothic initial letters, which erupt with independent life within the confines of the *Logos*.[25] An awareness of the conflict between the discursive (the text) and the figural (the image) or at least their tension, meant that more than in any other type of medieval art, the form of manuscript illustrations retained a heavily encoded linguistic component.

A good example of this in another text full of abstract ideas, this time on the psychology of the monastic life, is preserved in a manuscript of Anselm's *De Similitudinibus* in the British Library (*c.* 1220).[26] Here the illustrations are not integral to the text layout but have been placed in the margins as "excess," by an artist who nevertheless struggles to make visible the highly wrought descriptions of this new, original and vivid treatise on the psychology of monastic life (figure 6). On fol. 13ᵛ are two women, *pulchritudine et turpitudine,* personifying beauty and ugliness beneath the first column and on the right two men (one with a heavy load and the other with a light one) signifying ponderousness and agility. These are among the fourteen rewards and punishments of the disobedient will, indicated by the red titles or rubrics in the text above. While we can see how the artist (without any cues in the text) has found a way of expressing the second pair of intellectual traits in a striking visual way, his separation of beauty and ugliness is dependent on a more systematic code of differentiation. This is the semiotic opposition first discussed by Schapiro in relation to medieval art, "profile and frontal—coupled in the same work of art as carriers of opposed qualities."[27] The clearly visible near-frontal or three-quarter face of beauty admonishes the stark profile of ugliness to the left. For the medieval artist there is no need to evoke physical details in the differentiation of two such extremes, only to use the equivalent signs; formal devices that elsewhere can serve to distinguish the frontal hieratic icon-faced Christ from his long-nosed monstrous profile attackers in scenes of the Flagellation, for example. As Schapiro's discussion makes clear, such visual signs convey meaning through arbitrary and conventional units used in combination in the same way as does language.[28] Just as there is no "innocent eye" probing the natural

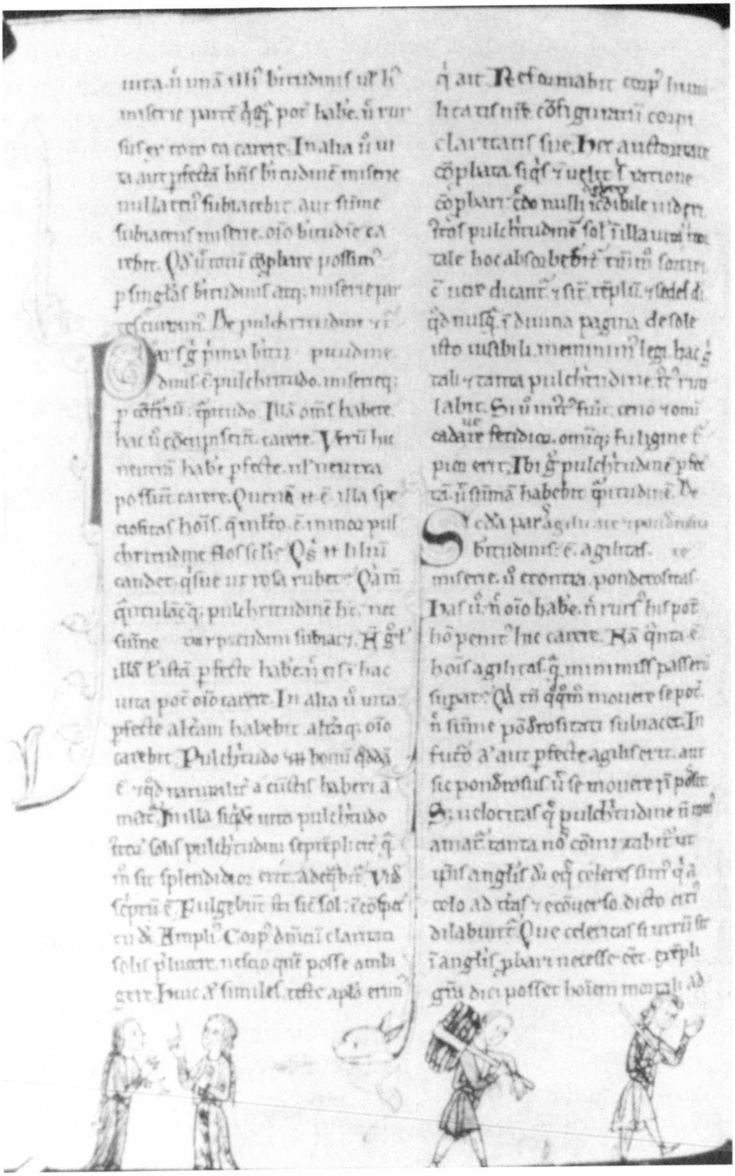

Figure 6. Beauty and Ugliness, Agility and Ponderousness from Anselm's
De similitudinibus British Library, MS Cotton Cleopatra CXI, fol. 13ᵛ.
(Reproduced by permission of the British Library, London.)

world in later painting, there is no innocent illustrator picturing the medieval text as if it were an "open" natural form, simply waiting for translation into the pictorial realm. Rather, the illustrator has to synchronize the units of his own visual vocabulary within the textual pattern, which in this case he must have been able to understand.

In the illustration of one of the most popular of all texts in this period, the Psalter, we can see these artists struggle with the flow of language. The Psalms are non-narrative, almost "imagistic" in the modern sense, read daily and memorized by clergy and laity alike. The devisor of the illustrations in a French Psalter in the University Library, Cambridge,[29] probably utilized his audience's intimate knowledge. Most Psalters in this period contained historiated initials only at the ten major Psalm Divisions but here there is one preceding each poem (figure 7). It is impossible for the artist in each tiny initial to fully convey the multiple shifting metaphors of the whole Psalm text, as did the brilliant artist of the Utrecht Psalter in the ninth century, who literalized each phrase in large half-page pictures above.[30] Yet he is still working in a tradition of "literal" Psalter illustration. At Psalm 118 for example the "C" initial shows a man climbing a tower by ladder (figure 7). This, like all the subjects in the initials, is explained at the front of the book in a table of contents which labels the subject of each initial in French. In this case, the caption reads "Uns home monte par une eschiele sus un tor" [a man climbs by ladder up a tower]. Although it has been suggested that these descriptions originally functioned to tell the illustrator what to depict for each Psalm they also help clarify for the reader the part of the text being visualized. In this example the verse being illustrated is 22, "The stone that the builders refused has become the headstone of the corner." It is a previously unnoticed and important early example of the symbolism of the "corner stone" or *"lapis in caput anguli"* which has been found in later medieval art.[31] With its Christological implications, the metaphor as used by St. Peter (Acts 4.11) and Paul (Romans 9.32) implies that the stone is not at the edge but at the very top of the edifice, like a vault, pediment or pyramid.

This initial "acts out" in the typical way of the thirteenth-century *exemplum* (i.e., by example), the erection of the pre-ordained structure of Gilbert of Limerick's twelfth century *Eccle-*

Figure 7. Initial to Psalm 118, *Psalter* with captions in French University Library, MS Ee. IV. 24, fol. 29ᵛ. (Reproduced by permission of the Syndics of Cambridge University Library.)

sia diagram which also has Christ at its apex (figure 3). The most striking metaphor in the *Psalm* has been chosen. It would have been far more difficult to illustrate verse 2, for example, "Let Israel now say that his mercy endureth for ever." In microcosm we see the principle of selection, important for all medieval textural illustration. As opposed to pictorial images, which are unsystematic, continuous and defined by resemblance, language is articulated by differences, which articulate a chain of simultaneous divisions and discontinuities (what linguistics calls *syntagm*).[32] Visual signs, on the other hand, are not syntagmatic in their normal usage. We have pointed to one case, the frontal/profile opposition, as an example of arbitrary signification through opposition (figure 6), but this is not always possible outside representation of dichotomies such as beauty/ugliness. The problem of finding visual equivalents for more subtle verbal ideas is stressed by Barthes with references to sign systems such as photographs in newspapers. He writes that "the iconic sytagms, which are founded on a more or less anagogical representation of a real scene are infinitely more difficult to divide, and this is probably the reason for which these systems are almost always duplicated by articulated speech (such as the caption of a photograph) which endows them with a discontinuous aspect which they do not have."[33] This is what is going on in the Cambridge Psalter with its illustrated captions pinpointing usually one tiny discontinuous detail in the flow of language that can be appropriated for the visual and made to function as the mnemonic trigger for its complete ingestion.

The discourse of the Christian Faith is, on the other hand, a narrative; the "history" of Christ's ministry and passion, his redemption of mankind and its future Judgement are patterned in a temporal trajectory which image as well as text must follow. But whereas the text is linear, the image is apprehended in unsystematic instantaneousness. This difficulty for the book illuminator is nowhere better displayed than in an English Gospel Picture cycle of the early fourteenth century (figure 8).[34] Writing before each picture refers directly to it with the words "Ici apres est depeint comment," which guides the viewer onto the next picture with this temporal trigger—"Here afterwards is painted." Such momentum in seeing and reading is important in conveying the stages in the visual narrative, for example, in the story of the Raising of Lazarus shown here (figure 8). The first block of text tells us how Lazarus is sick and how "his sisters enter and cry." Their mourning is visualized in the two conventional gestures used for signalling grief, one close to the "thought" pose we saw in the Aristotle (figure 5) while the right-hand sister wrings her hands. In the second description they are both still designated as crying. The same word "seurs" is used (2nd line from the bottom) which we take to refer to the same two people. Yet in the next picture the two figures have changed in dress, colour and even shape. For the medieval artist, visual continuity was not important. The same five letters, "seurs," signify the same thing in two different places and by tracing or other common methods of

Ici apres e deprint cu Lazere le frere carie magdaleine et Marce leur malades et morut. et ses seurs estrit et ploreret p lamor leur frere. et mlt des ieus undrent la pur conforter les deus seurs.

Ici ap e dep comet .i. e. uit et resusciate lazere k auoit est mor qtre iurs. et fer de lier ces mains et ces pies. et frst off le sudarie de sa face e le frst aler hors del monume et plusurs des ieus k uiret cel miracle cruiret en .i. e. e les uns aleret e disoiet as phariseus ce k il auoiet ueu

Et apres est deprint comet Lazere est porte al monument. et puis en seueli. et ces deus seurs toreuoies plurent.

Figure 8. The story of Lazarus, Gospel Picture cycle, St. Johns College MS K. 21 (J), fol. 46[r]. (Reproduced by permission of the Master and Fellows of St. Johns College, Cambridge.)

reproduction the artist could have exactly repeated the two sisters again as if they were a group of letters. But he does not need to. Like the background patterns, which constantly change in this manuscript, the physical characters and their settings are minimal signs for personalities. Their role is assigned by the foregoing text, so they need not remain constantly recognisable throughout. The contiguous aspect of images we later take for granted was not always present in the Gothic period when things were not what they appear to be, but what they are written to be. The third picture is a scene taking place four days later, according to the text, when "many jews" "come to see the miracle." Temporal change is intimated by the stiff upright form of the miraculously raised man in contrast to his horizontal form in the previous two scenes, so that some sense of transition occurs in the differences between essential narrative elements which the reader grasps in scanning the three pictures on the page.

Another way that we can look at the relationship between text and pictures in figure 8 is in terms of what Derrida calls the supplement. Discussing the predominance of speech over writing, he deploys the term to describe how writing has been constructed as an addition to speech. Two important senses of the word are brought out. In the first, "The supplement adds itself, it is a surplus, a plenitude enriching another plenitude, the *fullest measure* of presence" but in the second: "it adds only to replace. It intervenes or insinuates itself *in-the-place-of;* it fills, it is as if one fills a void. If it represents and makes an image it is by the anterior default of a presence."[35]

The idea of the supplement "making an image" is apt, since, just as writing supplements speech, so do images supplement writing. We have already seen Gilbert Crispin's medieval description of this process by which pictures become "representations and signs" of a second order. What this suggests in the case of textual illustration, is that the duplication, or redundancy of the image in relation to the text is an essential aspect of its meaning. This is so in the repeated "cue"—"Here after is painted how . . ."—in the Gospel pictures, whose very redundancy reveals their necessary presence. Another term employed by Derrida— "différance," is also useful to describe how meaning can be activated by "differing" or "deferring." It is certainly at work in our picture cycle in the way that the texts refer forward to the pictures, which in turn defer to the previously written cues, neither admitting responsibility and both pointing to the transcendent signifier of the Biblical moment.[36]

This gives the artist a specific role in relation to language and confines him almost wholly after it and within it. In Gothic manuscript illumination the directives given by the text are not always so clear as they are in the St. John's College Gospel-Picture Book; however, the same power of written orders are often behind the painting of miniatures. Even when illuminators did not follow a pictured directive in the form of a little sketch next to the space they had to fill (figure 5), they often had verbal instructions written in the margins to follow. In most cases these were erased when illustrations were complete but in a few examples they remain. They do in a secular Romance, entitled the *Roman de la Dame à la Licorne* in Paris (figure 9), a different kind of text from those looked at so far but one that was growing in importance in the fourteenth century. Alongside the miniature, a long written instruction to the illustrator ensures that the illustration is correct by providing a "sub-text" between the narrative itself and the task of its visualization. The written instructions are immensely detailed and guide the artist in every possible formal point.[37] He is told to "make a Queen sitting at a table" (note that for the artist's purposes this is not the character in the narrative but the stock-type of "*a* Queen" which has to be utilized) and likewise "*a* woman on the right and two friends." The latter pair are duplicated almost as they are in the textual indication "i" by two exactly replicated female figures gesturing with great flat palms. The details of the two figures in front of the table, "one drinking and the other with his head turned towards the Queen," are likewise precisely adhered to by the artist. The tyranny of the text has not only ordered the visual symmetry of the two halves of the composition but even given the artist his horizontal table top which follows the ruling lines for the script.[38] These sorts of constraints were part of the increasing professionalism of the illuminator's workshop where labor was divided into those who painted frames, initials and even sometimes backgrounds. Illuminators either copied earlier cycles of illustrations or were guided by drawn or written directions as to the appropriate image. They did not have to read the text as such, yet they could read the instructions in the margins. This often results in a highly abstract

Figure 9. Two scenes from the *Roman de la Dame à la Licorne* Biblio-thèque nationale, fr. 12562, fol. 26ᵛ. (Reproduced by permission, Biblio-théque nationale, Paris.)

displaced sort of illustration with figures used almost as mnemonic props rather than characters in action. The artist was not seeking to evoke the visual surface of the text description, like the banquet here, but encode the significant parts of the story in a simplified visual form. The banquet is the subject of the text directly beneath it (this was the more usual practice than having the text followed by its picture as occurs in the previous example). Consequently, the reader first noted the number and layout of characters in the visual frame, then read the rubric title below in red, which outlines the basic subject matter of the next section and finally reads the narrative itself. This system is used in the same workshop's *Roman de la rose* where the stock-motif of the gesticulating interlocuters is repeated again in the text miniature (figure 10).[39] Comparing these two books, we can appreciate the highly conventionalized structure of this narrative style but, because of the survival of the marginal notes in one case, can see that this is a result of the construction of minimal units through the tyranny of writing. Interestingly in the *Roman de la Rose* we witness the artist's liberation from this code in the bottom margin. Here the logic of the supplement reaches its nth degree. Just as writing is marginal in relation to speech and illustration in relation to writing, here we see an image marginalized, literally in relation to other illustrations. Throughout this book a vividly painted subnarrative concerning the sexual exploits of a monk and nun runs in the lower margins, unfolding in the extra-textual realm where both artist and reader sought evocative escape from the wearisome codification of the *logos* and its illustration. In numerous cases in Gothic manuscripts it is the most elevated of languages, Latin, from which these "droleries" or "babewynnes" (literally baboons), as they were sometimes called, provided escape into a realm of *exempla,* satire and social observation. The Word is ridiculed in no uncertain terms in the margins of an Amiens Missal illuminated by Pierre de Raimbaucourt in 1323 (figure 11).[40] The scribe, the writer of the Latin words above with his pen and scraper (see figure 2) is lampooned before his own eyes by a group of monkeys. They are pseudoscribes, like the one furthest right who licks his pen in preparation for writing, a motif used in some Evangelist portraits, or pseudoorators, like the expounding simian *rhetor* furthest left. Of course, although "outside the text" such imagery is not resistant to

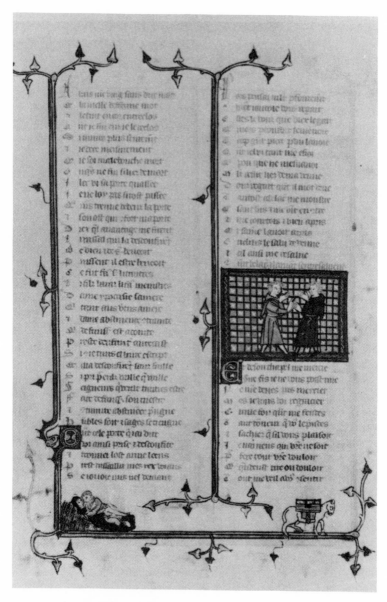

Figure 10. *Roman de la Rose* with *bas de page* scene of copulation: Bibliothèque nationale, fr. 25526, fol. III^v. (Reproduced by permission Bibliothèque nationale, Paris.)

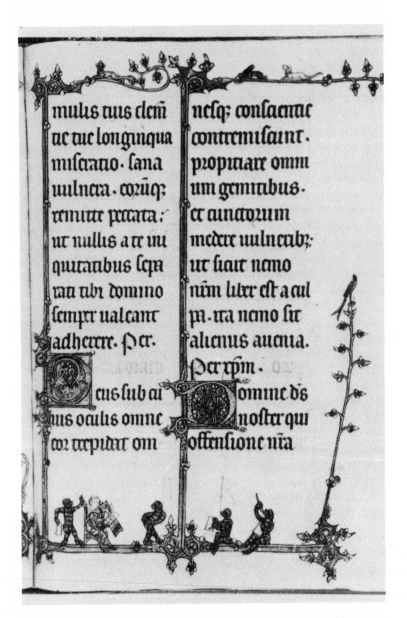

Figure 11. Monkeys mock writing: Page of a Missal illuminated by Pierre de Raimbaucourt, 1323; Koninklijke Bibliotheek, The Hague, MS 78. D. 40, fol. 124ʳ.

semiotic analysis. Just as jokes and nonsense poems can be seen
as meta-cultural or meta-semiotic messages, the strange creatures
and polymorphous perversions of the world of Gothic marginalia
are an unexplored and yet fruitful repository of meanings, attitudes and signs of the medieval unconscious. Significantly, they
are free from the redundancy of that "second-order" status that
we have defined as the supplement.

In this connection we can deploy the second sense of the word
according to Derrida's definition. As well as meaning an "extra"
added to something already complete—it can also mean something whose addition reveals that what was supposed to be
complete, is, in fact, not. The supplement uncovers a lack. Gothic
manuscript illuminations in their normal usage both in secular and
liturgical texts are a confirmation of completeness in the first
sense (figures 7–10) whereas the parodic marginal compositions
(figure 11) challenge the authority of the text and deny its
presentation of the "whole truth."

By subjecting the transcendental signifier to ridicule and
relativism, the riotous blasphemy of this and many other Gothic
marginal scenes is in the transgressive language of "heteroglosia" whose plurality of meanings Bakhtin discusses in his
great study of carnival imagery.[41] Deconstructing and inverting,
turning nose into phallus, face into buttocks, host into excrement,
this was at the same time an imagery of reaffirming humor and
humanity. Just as carnival always took place on the steps of the
church, even sometimes within it, genitalia in marginalia, monkeys and hybrids encroach upon the structure of the *logos*. Their
protest is at the inadequacy of its laws, grammars and semantics
and at their visual equivalents—the schemata, archetypes and
models which were an ideological as well as technical apparatus,
through which the medieval artist expressed the world.

IV. THE SHEPHERD'S SONG:
PICTURE AND "PAROLE"

For art history too, Saussure's distinction between "langue" and
"parole" is an important one. It is a distinction between the
abstract regulating principle of the language system and the
individual motivation of its more material speech acts, the latter

forming the foundations for what Saussure called "a science which studies the life of signs in society."[42] Thus far, the role of the visual sign has been seen mostly within the language system; it is important that we finally also understand the interaction of pictorial representation with speech and ask "who is speaking that image?" Many of the scrolls and inscriptions in medieval pictures are best described as "speech acts." Indeed, the *Trinity College Apocalypse,* with which we began, shows on its first folio, the transformation of a group of pagans into Christians through the power of evangelical speech. The caption above the figures reads "La parole deu al mescreaunz" and the one nearest John holds a scroll, testifying the truth that the prophet has uttered (figure 12). Speech acts like these represented here were crucial in a society where most information was relayed by word of mouth, and where a logocentric religion focussed on the spoken and spiritual *logos* at the expense of the material signifier of the "killing letter" (Corinthians 3.6). "La parole deu" here, of course, is different in emphasis from Saussure's use of the term, yet it still represents the active force of verbal signs in an oral society, where God had spoken directly to man under the Old Law and in the New Testament became the *Word* itself (figure 2).

The angel of the Apocalypse later tells John to carry his message to many people in many different languages (Rev. 10) (figure 1), emphasizing what we have seen as the newer evangelical spirit of the thirteenth century. This multiplicity of languages and their status as institutional and cultural boundaries went back to the building of the Tower of Babel, called so "because the Lord did there confound the language of all the earth" (Genesis 11.9). This important event in human history is illustrated full page in a French thirteenth-century Bible picture-book, with captions in the vernacular to draw out the meaning for the lay reader (figure 13): "Here is the tower to Babel which went against the Will of God: And he transformed the languages so that one did not understand what the other was saying."[43] In attempting to build a tower to reach heaven, an edifice of human will and ambition, man has fallen in terms of language just as he had fallen from Paradise through pride. We have seen the metaphor of architecture before, literally visualized to express the completion and "keystone" in Christ (figure 7) and earlier expressively utilized to convey the idea of order in Christian society (figure 3). These busy builders,

Figure 12. The audience of St. John's *parole: Apocalypse.* Trinity College MSR. 16.2 fol. 1ʳ (detail). (Reproduced with permission of the Master and Fellows of Trinity College, Cambridge.)

Figure 13. The Tower of Babel John Rylands Library MS fr. 5, fol. 16ʳ. (Reproduced by permission, John Rylands Library, Manchester.)

on the other hand, are in a sense deconstructing the very unity conveyed by Gilbert of Limerick's image.

However, the chaos of language that followed Babel was ordered into its own hierarchy by commentators. In the Bestiary we read of "Adam, who first gave names to all the animals, calling each and all of them by something or other by trial and error, according to the sort of nature which each of them had. Moreover, people addressed these animals in the first of languages. For Adam did not award the names according to the Latin tongue, nor the Greek one, nor according to any other barbarous speech, but in the language which was current to everybody before the flood: that is to say Hebrew."[44] In thirteenth-century England the hierarchy of speech was regulated by the Anglo-Norman ruling elite, who used Latin as the most elevated language of power and diplomacy in ecclesiastical and temporal control of the Anglo-Saxon population and also used another "elite" language, Norman-French, for the discourse of leisure and literature at court. English, according to commentators like the Bestiary writer was "barbarous" and used only by the lowest orders of society. This group was not served by the visual arts, which always used Latin as the language of inscriptions on wall paintings of common subjects like the Annunciation. This language had a supernatural as well as political aura, attested by the contemporary tales of clerics frightening away tax collectors with Latin or its miraculous utterance by the otherwise dumb or illiterate.[45] The Norman-French of the ruling elite is sometimes also bestowed as a "gift of tongues" in such miracles. We see it more often in manuscripts in texts of a romance-like nature such as the Apocalypses and Saints' Lives (figure 1). This hierarchy of speech acts existing in medieval England had its influence and relay in the visual realm where separate categories of discourse create their genres of illustration.

This is nowhere more evident than in the famous *Holkham Bible Picture Book* in the British Library (figure 14).[46] Made for a noble Anglo-Norman audience and illustrated in East Anglia in the early fourteenth century, its first page shows the artist painting in the book and being instructed by a Dominican preacher to work well since this, he says, is a book which is going to be shown to rich people. It is a picture book in the tradition we have already

Figure 14. The Shepherds' Song; *Holkham Bible Picture Book*. British Library Add. MS 4762, fol. 13ʳ. (After W. O. Hassall's facsimile).

been looking at (figure 8) but by this time the association between text and image has broken down even further.

The man who wrote the short texts, which play a caption-like, subsidiary role to the half-page narrative illustrations, was a professional "text-artist." He would be called in to fill in the captions on wall paintings or tapestry designs as well as manuscript books. This division of labour and separation of the text from the picture often results in the redundancy and meaninglessness of the words when describing a picture which the text artist does not fully understand.

This is a rare case of the picture preceding and dominating the word and reversing the normal relationship. Indeed, as Pickering has suggested, the text "tells us more about the themes as these were apprehended by the contemporary taxtator, possibly indeed, by all the members of the group of workers involved, including the commissioners of *Holkham.*"[47] A historical "reading" of the image is thus provided in contemporary language, or in the following example, "languages." The two scenes which we shall read, using the text, show the Annunciation to the shepherds on the top and below their adoration of the Christ child (figure 14). In the top scene, despite the angel's standing firmly on the ground beside the startled shepherd, the message it brings is in the conventional, divine language of Latin (the standard *"Gloria in excelsis"* according to the three lines of the text above). The shepherd's reply to this, "Glum glo ceo ne est rien. Allums la, nous le saverums been," is the old *"laicus aut brutus"* or dim-witted "yokel" *topos,* transformed into a joke. The illiterate shepherd, puzzled by the Latin of the Gloria, responds with a gooble-de-gook all his own like the contemporary *Missa Potatorum* performed in the stuttering garble of the inebriated.

This same idea of the twisted speech act of the peasant occurs also in the Conventry Shepherds' Miracle play, which suggests a link between public performance and visual art in the period.[48]

Moreover, in the second picture below, there is a second bifurcation of language, this time from French to the true vernacular of English!

> Et le chant qe le angel ont chaunté
> En le honour de la nativité,
> Songen alle wid one stevene

> Also the angel song that cam from hevene.
> Te Deum et Gloria
> La Contenance veyez cha.

But this in not all. The East-Midland dialect of the third and fourth lines refer in fact to the miraculous singing of the shepherds in proper Latin! Looking at their speech scrolls we can see that they are now fluent in angelic words which previously they had only been able to garble. On the left the hand-held scroll says "Gloria in excelsis deo et in terra," an old pictorial formula of holding the speech (seen in the Trinity Apocalypse figure 12). This separates the revealed word of the Latin *doxa* from the other two languages at play on this page: the Norman-French of the "riche" and courtly reader, and the words in English, still the peasant dialect. "Language is always socialized," according to Barthes, "even at the individual level, for in speaking one always tries to speak more or less the other's language."[49] The user of this book, perhaps as he or she is read the narrative by the Dominican compiler, was able to deal with these three types of discourse and make distinctions between the rude language of the rustics (four if we include the "meaningless" attempt at Latin), his or her own distinguished mode (French) and highest of all, the transcendent Latin. This signals the initial ungodly state of the shepherds by its lack and then by its emission from them their transformation through witnessing God.

For the reader and obviously for the illustrator, the vernacular mode had an ultimately social meaning. Speech or "parole" always indicates a social class, intention or action and its definitions are also integral to the artist's depiction of the bottom scene. This is brought out in the slipping socks of the first bald old shepherd and the wonderfully "observed" detail of how folk-singers drone their song with a finger in one ear. The social distinctions of language are made visually evident in the artist's attempt to translate the shepherd's "Songen alle" into iconic terms. He paints vivid physiognomies, dancing movements and, importantly, the profile opposition between them and the divine characters, signalling their lowness in the moment of their Grace. Compared to the conventional schema of the Nativity, which has hardly changed in the depiction of Joseph, horizontal Virgin, ox and ass, since the twelfth century, the individual shepherds, ironically *"litteratus"* for a moment, are closest to what we might term the medieval vernacular style. The generic and linguistic levels of meaning in this picture prove that Panofsky was quite correct in his general statement that, "a naturalistic mode of presentation was not as yet, a general principle of art. As far as human beings are concerned, it almost amounted to a class distinction."[50]

Throughout this study the fundamental principle of Saussure's theory that language works through "differences"—relationships with other units in relative association—has been carried over to the visual arts and yet it must be admitted that the two kinds of sign, visual and verbal, are not totally co-existent. It would be false to subsume them under the same model derived from linguistics. The units of language are arbitrary and are opposed much more discreetly than the iconic referents of the image-sign, so that while the profile shepherds in the *Holkham Bible Picture Book* example (figure 13) are in conformity to a general semiotic use of binary oppositions in the tradition of distinguishing inferior characters, it is their detailed appearance carrying contextual associations which makes them readable. Unlike the earlier opposition "beauty and ugliness" (figure 6) the opposition of rustic shepherds and Holy Family is one which is built out of specific objects and details rather than arbitrary units. It represents complex characters rather than dual personifications. Only by its interaction with the "parole"—speech acts designated through writing—can this image convey any complex social content.

It is all too easy to see this example as one of Gothic "naturalism" and to equate the lively detail with a perceptual focus on the part of the artist. However, we are still dealing with a visual system dependent on language in the sense that the marvellously systematic diagram of Gilbert of Limerick's was (figure 3). The Shepherd's page carries an inbuilt view of social structure in medieval England which, though "naturalized," is no less strictly demarcated than the twelfth-century pyramidal one. This is where this image seems to lack the experimental rethinking of the text, with its interesting bifurcations in *parole*. Rather than retell the story, find new "words" or phrases for it as a writer might try to do, the Gothic image-maker often falls back on stereotype, schema and convention. This is not just a mechanical or technical factor in the transmission of medieval art (such as copying, tracing or modelbooks), it too is linked to ideological notions of an archetypal language—a system of representation from which all others descend:

> As long as religion, both in literate or pre-literate societies, harks back to a period of revelation and insists on the authority of properly transmitted true texts, either orally or in the written form, its sacred language will contain an archaic component, whether this is represented by a totally different language or older elements in the same language.[51]

Is this archaic component an essential feature of the transmission of Gothic manuscript illumination which seeks to see the "true text" in the "totally different language" of the image? This study has done no more than open up some of the broader theoretical questions which can be addressed by the medieval art historian. As we have tried to show, understanding the analogous parallel system of visual signs as they work alongside verbal ones demands that we see medieval painting as a metalinguistic system. Indeed, the Middle Ages, before the order of things became separated from the words used to describe them, remains a relatively unexplored period and an exciting area for future research into the relation between language and visual representation.

Acknowledgment

Though all the opinions and errors in this study are my own I would like to thank George Henderson and Jonathan Alexander for their continuing insights into the world of the medieval book, Jean-Michel Massing, Nicholas Webb and John Welchman for some suggestions and especially Norman Bryson for his advice and encouragement.

NOTES

[1]Cambridge, Trinity College MS R. 16.2. Facsimiles available in M. R. James, *The Trinity College Apocalypse* (London: Roxburghe Club, 1909), and in *The Trinity College Apocalypse,* introduction by P. Brieger, transcription and translation by M. Dulong, (London: Evgrammia Press, 1967).

[2]See J. P. Charlier, "La notion de signe (σημειον) dans le IVè evangile" *Révue des sciences philosophiques et theologiques*, 43 (1959), pp. 434–48. For Augustinian categories of the sign, see *On Christian Doctrine*, trans. D. W. Robertson, (Indianapolis: Library of Liberal Arts, 1958), p. 34, and the useful theoretical debate with further bibliography by G. B. Ladner, "Medieval and modern understanding of symbolism" *Speculum*, 54 (1979), pp. 223–233. Ladner is one of the few established medievalists to appreciate the value of Saussurian linguistics. See also the recent book by R. Howard Bloch, *Etymologies and Genealogies: A Literary Anthropology of the French Middle Ages* (Chicago: University of Chicago Press, 1983), pp. 30–63.

[3]R. Jakobson, "The phonemic and grammatical aspect of language in their interrelations" *Actes du VIième Congres internationale des linguistes* (Paris: Klinksieck, 1949), p. 6. As well as this analogy made between structural linguistics and Augustinian sign theory, see J. Kristeva, "The semiotic activity" *Screen*, 14 (1973), p. 29, and M. Foucault, *The Order of Things* (London: Tavistock Publications, 1970), pp. 17–30.

[4]M. Schapiro, *Words and Pictures: on the literal and the symbolic in the illustration of a text* (The Hague: Mouton, 1973), p. 1.

[5]E. Mâle, *The Gothic Image: Religious Art in France of the thirteenth century*, trans. D. Nussey (New York: Harper & Row, 1958), p. 396. First published in 1898. Male's conception is here not that far removed from Ruskin's innocent, child-artist. "The medieval artist was neither a rebel, nor a "thinker," nor a precursor of the Revolution.—It is enough to show him as he really was, simple, modest and sincere."

[6]The classic work on the medieval scribe is still W. Wattenbach, *Das Schriftwesen im Mittelalter* (Leipzig, 1896), but see also M. Clanchy, *From Memory to Written Record* (London: Edward Arnold, 1979), pp. 88–116 ("The Technology of Writing").

[7]See Ladner, "Symbolism," p. 226.

[8]Gilbert Crispin, *Disputatio Iudei et Christiani*, ed. B. Blumenthal, *Stromata Patristica et Medievalia*, 3, (Utrecht/Antwerp, 1956), p. 67.

[9]J. Derrida, *Of Grammatology*, trans. G. C. Spivak (Baltimore and London: Johns Hopkins University Press, 1974), p. 14.

[10]E. H. Gombrich, in a review of Charles Morris' *Signs, language and behaviour*, *Art Bulletin*, 31 (1949), p. 72. What art historical journal would carry a review of such a book nowadays?

[11]G. Hermeren, *Representation and Meaning in the Visual Arts: A study in the methodology of iconography and iconology* (Copenhagen: Scandinavian University Books. Lund Studies in Philosophy (1), 1969), p. 78.

[12]Cambridge, University Library MS Ff. 1.27, fol. 18^v (237^v), part of Cambridge, Corpus Christi College MS 66. For this compilation, probably produced at Durham c. 1180, see C. M. Kauffmann, *Romanesque Manuscripts, 1066–1190* London: Harvey Miller, 1975), p. 123, no. 102, for a description, which for some reason does not include Gilbert's splendid diagram.

[13]M. Corti, "Models and antimodels in Medieval Culture" *New Literary History,* 10 (1979), p. 343.

[14]Corti "Models and antimodels," p. 342. For the full Latin text, see *Patrologia Latina,* pp. 159, 997, and for a simpler, much more basic pyramidal version of the *imago,* see R. A. B. Mynors, *Durham Cathedral Manuscripts* (Oxford: Oxford University Press, 1939), no. 47, pl. 42.

[15]E. Panofsky, *Architecture gothique et pensée scolastique* (Paris: Editions de Minuit, 1981), "traduction et postface de Pierre Bordieu," p. 152.

[16]For a scribe advertising the multiple styles at his disposal, see the pages of Oxford, Bodleian Library, MS E. Museo, 198. Reproduced in *Scriptorium,* 10 (1956), pls. 8–11.

[17]M. Evans. "The geometry of the mind" *Architectural Association Quarterly,* 12 (1980), pp. 32–55. The notion of *suppositio* is explained in D. P. Henry, *Medieval Logic and Metaphysics: a modern introduction* (London: Hutchinson University Library of Philosophy, 1972), pp. 47–8.

[18]K. Burke, *Language as Symbolic Action* (Berkeley: University of California Press, 1968), pp. 429–30. Against this notion of the impossible negative, see figures 3 and 4 in Evans, "Geometry," which visualize opposites. An excellent longer study of the medieval diagrammatic tradition is A. K. Esmeijer, *Divina Quaternitas: a preliminary to the study of Visual Exegesis* (Assen: Gorcum, 1979). The false compartmentalization of the pictorial and the linguistic sign is discussed in W. J. T. Mitchell, "Spatial form in literature" *The Language of Images* (Chicago: University of Chicago Press, 1980), pp. 295–297.

[19]*Anecdotes historiques, légendes et apologués tirés du recueil inédit d'Efienne de Bourbon,* ed. A. Lecoy de la Marche (Paris: Société de l'Historie de France, 1887), pp. 3–4.

[20]London, British Library MS Harley 3487, an illuminated schools compilation of the *corpus vetustius,* containing the Aristotelian works of natural history. See my forthcoming article, "The illustrations in British Library, Harley MS 3487 and the perception of Aristotle's *libri naturales* in thirteenth-century England" in *Proceedings of the Symposium on Thirteenth-century English studies held at Harlaxton College, Lincs, 1984* (forthcoming 1985).

[21]Translated from R. Sorabji, *Aristotle on Memory* (London: Duckworth, 1972), p. 47. See also his discussion of "The mental image," pp. 2–8.

[22]For a typology of this gesture with numerous examples, see F. Garnier, *Le Langage de l'Image au Moyen Age* (Paris: le Leopard d'Or, 1979), pp. 182–3 and for its various associations with vice, R. Klibansky, E. Panofsky and F. Saxl, *Saturn and Melancholy* (London 1964), pp. 286–9. The Memory initial as a whole would seem to be based on the conventional initial illustrating Psalm 52, *Dixit insipiens,* showing a seated King and naked fool.

[23]The key study of Gothic page layout is M. Parkes. "The influence of the concepts *Ordinatio* and *Compilatio* on the development of the book" *Essays Presented to R. W. Hunt* (Oxford: Oxford University Press, 1969), pp. 115–41.

[24]"Pictures can be cues which may de decoded as a substitute or supplement to language—These external cues get between reader and written language. In a sense they interfere with the vital recoding process." K. S. Goodman (ed.), *The Psycholinguistic nature of the Reading Process* (Detroit, 1968), p. 24.

[25]See the discussion of the "Parergon" (cadre, vêtement, colonne). in J. Derrida, *La Vérité en Peinture* (Paris: Flammarion, 1978), pp. 66–78.

[26]London, British Library MS Cotton Cleopatra CXI, a copy of Anselm's *Treatises.* For the text, see R. W. Southern, *Memorials of St Anselm* (London: Auctores Britannici MediiAevi 1, 1969), p. 50. A list of illustration is provided by N. J. Morgan, *Early Gothic Manuscripts (1),* 1190–1250 (London: Harvey Miller, 1982), p. 106, no. 60.

[27]Schapiro, Words and Pictures, p. 43: "One of the pair is the vehicle of the higher value and the other, by contrast, marks the lesser— The duality of the frontal and profile can signify then the distinction between good and evil, the sacred and the less sacred or profane, the heavenly and the earthly, the ruler and the ruled, the noble and the plebian," etc.

[28]The linguistic background to Schapiro's notion of the frontal/profile opposition is outlined by M. Iversen, "Meyer Schapiro and the semiotics of visual art," *Block* 1 (Middlesex Polytechnic, 1979), pp. 50–53.

[29]Cambridge, University Library MS Ee. 4.24, described fully in M. R. James, "On a MS Psalter in the University Library," *Proceedings of the Cambridge Antiquarian Society,* 8 (1892–93), pp. 146–167. This and other Psalters with captions (notably Manchester, John Rylands Library MS 22) are discussed by S. Berger, "Les Manuels pour l'illustration du psautier au XIII siecle" *Memories de la societe nationale des antiquaires de France,* 57 (Paris, 1898), pp. 95–134 and G. Henderson,

"Narrative illustration and theological exposition in medieval art" *Studies in Church History,* 17 (1971), pp. 20–24.

[30]See E. T. De Wald, *The Illustrations of the Utrecht Psalter* (Princeton: Princeton University Department of Art and Archaeology, 1932) and for Psalter decoration in general for our period, G. Haseloff, *Die Psalterillustration im XIII* (kiel, 1938).

[31]G. B. Ladner, "The symbolism of the Biblical corner-stone in the medieval west" *Medieval Studies of the Institute of Toronto,* 4 (1942), pp. 43–60, discusses the patristic and textual background but cannot find this image used in the visual arts until the fourteenth century. This is in MSS of the *Speculum Humanae Salvationis,* for which, see J. Lutz and P. Pedrizet, *Speculum Humanae Salbationis* (Mulhausen, 1909), II, pls. 63 and 64. Our example predates this by at least a century. The phrase *"lapis in caput anguli"* refers to the top of the building rather than its corner as shown by A. K. Coomaraswamy, "Eckstein" *Speculum,* 14 (1939) pp. 66, and the representation in the Cambridge Psalter.

[32]The clearest analysis of syntagmatic structure is R. Barthes, *Elements of Semiology* trans. A. Lavers and C. Smith (New York: Hill and Wang, 1981), pp. 58–88. He writes (p. 10) "every semiological system has its linguistic admixture. Where there is a visual substance, for example, the meaning is confirmed by being duplicated in the linguistic message (which happens in the case of the cinema, advertising, comic strips, press photography, etc.) so that at least a part of the iconic message is, in terms of structural relationships, either redundant or taken up by the linguistic system." The same can be said of the medieval manuscript, which bears some affinity with Barthes' "comic strip."

[33]Barthes, *Elements of Semiology,* p. 64.

[34]Cambridge, St. John's College, MS K. 21 (J), once probably part of a Psalter as it has a calender of St. Augustine's Abbey, Canterbury. M. R. James, *Catalogue of Manuscripts in St. John's College Library* (Cambridge: Cambridge University Press, 1913), p. 302, suggests that the order and position of the elaborate picture cycle indicates a monastic owner might have "looked at the pictures" during the long liturgical services before Easter. This would represent the beginning of a trend visible in Books of Hours in the next century, which were often a means of privately following the public liturgy using texts and images in one's own book, but in this case, for the laity.

[35]Derrida, *Of Grammatology,* pp. 144–45. See also pp. 292–293 for discussion of painting: "the image is the supplement; which adds itself without adding anything to fill an emptiness which, within fullness, begs to be replaced."

[36]In *Positions* (Paris: Minuit, 1972), Derrida describes how "The play of differences involves syntheses and referrals which prevent there from

being at any moment or in any way a simple element which is present in and of itself and refers only to itself." Quoted from J. Culler's translation in *Structuralism and Since,* ed. J. Sturrock (Oxford: Oxford University Press, 1979), p. 164 which appears in a useful charting of Derrida's use of the term "différance," pp. 154–79.

[37]Paris, Bibliothèque nationale, MS fr. 12562 (mid-fourteenth-century). The instructions in the left margin in this case read: "Faites bune roynne seant a table/et li dames avech et y compeng/nons mengons sur i bachin devant/la table et tient li et en boirre a/quoi il boit li autre tourne/le teste en regardant la royne." Jonathan Alexander kindly brought this example to my attention.

[38]On the way text ruling can control illustration, see D. Byrne, "Manuscrupt ruling and pictorial design in the work of the Limbourgs, the Bedford Master, and the Boucicault Master" *Art Bulletin,* 66 (1984) pp. 118–135.

[39]Paris, Bibliothèque nationale, MS fr. 25526, fol. III^v.

[40]The Hague, Koninklijke Bibliotheek, MS 78 D. 40.

[41]M. Bakhtin, *Rabelais and his World* (Cambridge and London: MIT Press, 1968) is a fascinating study of the reversal of hieratic levels in language and popular culture of the Middle Ages and can fruitfully be brought to bear on the many pictorial examples in L. M. C. Randall, *Images in the Margins of Gothic Manuscripts* (Berkeley: University of California Press, 1966). Compare especially the *obscenae* (Randall, figs. 528–546) with Chapter six: "Images of the Material Bodily Lower Stratum." Bakhtin's notion of "heteroglosia" as a transgressive language is discussed in K. Arthur, "Bakhtin, Kristeva and Carnival" *Art and Text,* 11 (Melbourne 1983), p. 50.

[42]F. de Saussure, *Course in General Linguistics,* ed. C. Bally and A. Sechehaye, trans. W. Baskin, revised edition (London: Peter Owen, 1974), p. 16. For discussion of the untranslatable terms "langue" and "parole," see the Introduction by J. Culler, pp. xxi–xxiii, and Barthes, *Elements of Semiology,* pp. 13–14.

[43]Manchester, John Rylands Library Fr. MS 5, fol. 16^r. Each of these large imposing compositions is blank on the verso, creating a ditych-like effect of the openings. The lively Genesis series includes a number of unusual illustrations, such as the Birth of Cain (fol. 7^v) and the destruction of Sodom (fol. 19^v). This MS is discussed by R. Fawtier, *Bible en images, Bulletin de la Société Française de Reproduction de Manuscrits à Peintures* (Paris, 1923), pp. 34–87.

[44]T. H. White, *The Bestiary* (New York: Perogree Books, 1980), pp. 70–71 (a translation of the twelfth-century MS, Cambridge, University Library, MS II, 4.26). For the illustrations of this naming scene, see X. Muratova, "Adam donne leurs noms aux animaux" *Studi Medievali,* 18

(1977), p. 376. For "naming" as theological beginning, see Bloch, *Etymologies and Genealogies,* pp. 40–44.

[45]For stories attesting to the "aura" of Latin and Norman-French in England, see J. W. Wilson, "English and French in England 1100–1300" *History* 28 (1943), pp. 50–55 and Clanchy, *From Memory to Written Record,* pp. 175–201. For the effects of levels of literacy on English art of the period, see my article, "Seeing and reading: Some visual implications of medieval literacy and illiteracy" *Art History* 8, 1 (1985), pp. 26–49.

[46]London, British Library, Add. MS 4762. See the facsimile by W. O. Hassall, *The Holkham Bible Picture Book* (London: Dropmore Press, 1954) and M. R. James, "An English Bible-Picture Book of the fourteenth century" *The Walpole Society* 11 (1922–3), pp. 1–5, for the Dominican programme. The text has been printed with notes by F. P. Pickering; *The Anglo-Norman Text of the Holkham Bible Picture Book,* The Anglo-Norman Text Society, 23 (1965).

[47]Pickering, *Anglo-Norman Text,* p. ix.

[48]See R. Woolf, *The English Mystery Plays* (London 1972), p. 183 and J. R. Moore, "The tradition of angelic singing" *Journal of English and Germanic Philology,* 12 (1923), p. 92, for performed parodic language. The *Missa potatorum* is discussed on Corti, "Models and antimodels," p. 354 and published by F. Novati, "La parodia sacra nelle letterature moderne" *Studi critici e letterari* (Turin 1899), pp. 289–300.

[49]Barthes, *Elements of Semiology,* p. 21.

[50]E. Panofsky, *Early Netherlandish Painting* (Cambridge, MA: Harvard University Press, 1953), p. 71.

[51]S. J. Tambiah, "The magical power of words" *MAN,* 3 (1968), p. 182.

THE ILLUSTRATED MEDIEVAL AVIARY AND THE LAY-BROTHERHOOD*
Willene B. Clark

The Latin Aviary, in which real or imagined attributes of birds are the subjects of Christian moralizations, was written in the late years of the twelfth century, and remained popular to the end of the thirteenth. Although the *Patrologia latina* prints it as Book I of the Latin Bestiary, the Aviary is an independent work with characteristics of its own.[1] It is one of several moral treatises by Hugh of Fouilloy, an Augustinian canon whose works are all directed to a monastic audience.[2] His ideas reflect the twelfth-century continuation of the Gregorian Reform, which sought a return to the monastic purity of the Early Christian *vita apostolica.* Hugh was well enough known in his day to be mentioned by the thirteenth-century St. Denis chronicler, William of Nangis, and by two other important thirteenth-century writers, Aubry of Trois-Fontaines and Vincent of Beauvais.[3]

Hugh of Fouilloy was born about 1110 near Amiens, and may have been educated at the Benedictine abbey of Corbie. He entered religion as a Benedictine at the priory of St. Laurent-au-Bois at Heilly (also near Amiens), which came under Augustinian rule in 1148, some years after Hugh's profession. In the prologue to a cartulary which he caused to be written, Hugh states that he was young when he entered religion—perhaps around the years 1128–30—and chose St. Laurent because it was very small and poor.[4] The priory grew in size and substance, however, and even founded a daughter house, St. Nicolas-de-Regny, in 1132.[5] Hugh became prior of St. Laurent in 1152; after an active priorate of more than twenty years, he died sometime before 1174.[6]

As St. Laurent prospered and grew, the canons began to indulge

---

*Reprinted by permission of the author and publisher, from *Gesta,* Vol. 21, No. 1, 1982, pp. 63–74.

in personal luxuries, and trouble arose between them and the lay-brothers of the priory.[7] It will be shown that the Aviary was written for use in teaching lay-brothers; yet in all its allegorical moralizations, there is no suggestion of the trouble which occurred in the middle or late years of Hugh's priorate. Thus, it is likely that the Aviary was one of his first compositions, and was written in the 1150s or early 1160s. The work appears in manuscripts under several titles: *De avibus, De columba argentata, De tribus columbis,* and *Ad Ranierum,* the last in reference to a Brother Rainier at whose request the Aviary was written. It is often associated in the manuscripts with other works by Hugh, with other moral treatises, and in some instances with the Latin Bestiary.

In the first of two prologues, Hugh notes that Rainier had been a knight (*miles*) before his conversion to the religious life.[8] In an illustration for the prologues in several manuscripts, Rainier is depicted as a knight or nobleman (Fig. 1). As one who was not a *clericus,* an educated clerk, he would have become a lay-brother, a *conversus.* The lay-brotherhood was a characteristic institution of the monastic reform.[9] Generally the brothers were men who had come to religion as adults, had little or no education, and did the more menial tasks in the monastery. They were permitted to go out into the secular world, and thus often served as intermediaries between monastery and town. In the prologues, Hugh states that he writes for the unlettered, "to enlighten the minds of the uneducated."[10] He will paint with words his interpretation of a confusing passage in Psalm LXVII, 14, which is the basis for the first six Aviary chapters, and which reads, "If you sleep among the midst of lots you will be as the wings of a dove covered with silver, and the hinder parts of her back with the paleness of Gold."[11] Addressing Rainier in the informal style characteristic of his writing, Hugh states the aim of his book: "Desiring to fulfill your wishes, dearest brother, I decided to paint the dove with silver wings and back of pale gold, and by a picture enlighten the minds of the uneducated . . . and what the ear could hardly perceive, the eye might take in. I wish not only to paint the dove by modelling it, but also to outline it by words, so that through writing I may set forth a picture . . ."[12] Rainier may have had sufficient education to be a teacher for the lay-brothers; among Cistercians, and probably other orders, there is evidence that the teachers could be literate members of the brotherhood.[13] In five of

Figure 1. Prologue miniature. Heiligenkreuz Abbey MS 226, fol. 129v, north France, late 12th century (photo: F. Walliser, Cistercienser Buchkunst, *Heiligenkreuz*, 1969, fig. 93).

the Aviary chapters, Hugh dwells upon the qualities and responsibilities of teachers.[14] As a teacher, Rainier would have translated and explained the moralizations to his simpler brethren; the pictures would be used to keep their attention, as Hugh suggests in the prologues.[15] Hugh's popularizing aim in the Aviary seems to have met with success, for the work survives in a substantial number of copies. Furthermore, the lower corners of pages in the Aviary section are usually the most thumb-marked in manuscripts where it appears with other works.[16]

If the unillustrated manuscripts are included, there are altogether seventy-seven extant copies of all or part of the Aviary (See Appendix list of illustrated copies). Twenty-seven of these are fully illustrated with the characteristic Aviary iconography; two more provide only the three allegorical diagrams (Figs. 2 and 3).

Figure 2. Dove diagram. Paris, Bibl. Nat. MS lat. 2495, fol. 2r, north France, late 12th century (photo: Bibl. Nat., Paris).

Figure 3. Falcon diagram. Douai, Bibl. Mun. MS 370, fol. 105Ar, north France, late 12th century (photo: author).

There are five illustrated fragments which appear to have had the full program, six manuscripts with spaces for the full program, or holes where pictures were cut out, and three with illustrations not based on the Aviary's customary program. The original manuscript is lost; but it was undoubtedly illustrated, for not only does Hugh, in the prologues, emphasize the visual imagery of his work, but he seems also to have established a standard program, apparently even some standard designs, which can be traced through many manuscripts. Furthermore, internal evidence in the cedar illustration, to be discussed, tends to confirm pictures in the original manuscript. The average folio size in extant manuscripts is about 300×200 mm. The painting style tends to be routine, sometimes even coarse, but there are significant exceptions. The majority of copies are of north French production; provenance, when known, tends to be monastic, frequently Cistercian. There are also ten English copies, two Italian, and one south German among the illustrated manuscripts.

Some English copies are extremely interesting, for in these the Aviary text is incorporated directly into the text of well-known Latin Bestiaries. The Aviary appears either in its entirety, or excerpted and combined with bird chapters of the Latin Bestiary or other encyclopedic material on birds.[17] This English exploitation of the Aviary as a new source for Bestiary material began early, for the Aberdeen and Ashmole Bestiaries and MSS Bodl. 602 and 764 (Appendix nos. 26–28) can all be assigned to the early thirteenth century.

Migne's *Patrologia latina* gives only fifty-six chapters for the Aviary, but the usual division in the manuscripts is into sixty chapters. The sixty chapters can be divided into two parts.[18] The first part, consisting of thirty-six chapters, is the more original, and contains the most unusual pictures. The second part, with a picture and chapter for each bird, more closely resembles the typical Bestiary. Hugh's text follows Bestiary tradition by drawing on the *Physiologus.* St. Isidore's *Etymologies,* and Hrabanus Maurus, *De universo.* He also quotes St. Gregory's *Moralia in Job* at length as well as the Bible.[19] The lessons provided in the Aviary are longer than those of the Bestiary, in many cases much longer, reflecting Hugh's rich imagination. The Biblical passages quoted are often those which mention birds, although others are also used, and passages relating to two trees, the palm and the cedar.[20]

Hugh weaves his borrowings and his own ideas into a colorful fabric of allegory and commentary.

THE TEXT

Until now, no one has recognized the Aviary as a textbook for lay-brothers. In the first part, the teachings revolve around three principles laid down in Chapter 1: like Noah cease from sinning, be steadfast like David, seek salvation through Christ. The three personages are illustrated by three doves: a "black but beautiful" (Song of Songs I,4) dove for Noah, symbolizing the sinner saved; the silvered dove (in this chapter called "variegated") for David, and labelled "Sancta Ecclesia," referring to the Church's stead-fastness; and a white dove, labelled "Sanctus Spiritus," for Christ, at whose baptism a white dove appeared. Throughout the Aviary, Hugh's lessons teach repentance, retirement from the world, purity, love of God and neighbor in the monastic commu-nity and the world, and watchfulness for sin in oneself and in the other brothers. In the second part, Hugh reinforces these lessons through a multiplication of allegories using real or supposed traits of the individual birds. In all, we see a concise body of straightfor-ward teaching designed to guide the daily lives of the brothers. Only the most basic doctrine appears in the allegories, and nothing which would require any sort of abstract thinking. The principal doctrinal lesson is: Christ died for us, and thereby furnished us salvation. Such complex problems as God's exis-tence or the nature of sin are carefully avoided. The teachings are, in sum, traditional monastic admonitions, and are presented in a manner which is sometimes elegant, sometimes strained, some-times amusing. In his word painting, Hugh succeeds in creating images which remain today both interesting and entertaining. And the Aviary is a text for which the illustrations are a logical complement.[21]

The Aviary begins with two prologues. In the first, Hugh likens himself to a dove, and Rainier, the former knight, to a falcon, both sharing the same perch, that is, the monastic Rule (Fig. 1). Texts which often appear within the prologue illustration state that the falcon and dove also represent the active life and contemplative life, that is, the lay-brother who does the manual labor of the abbey, and the canon regular or choir monk occupied by prayers of the monastic Office.

Chapters 1 through 11 treat the dove of Psalm LXVII,14 and other Biblical passages. A diagram of the dove summarizes the lessons of these chapters, and is the illustration which is most uniform throughout the manuscripts (Fig. 2). The silvered dove of the psalm is the Church abiding within the "lots" of the two Testaments. Its wings are the active life and contemplative life, which lift the bird to Heaven. The wings are also the love of God and one's neighbor. The gold of the dove's back is eternal blessedness, more precious even than silver, than the Church itself. The dove's eyes are the memory and the intellect, enabling one to see the future judgment and to remember his sins; they appear as gold dots at the top of the picture in Figure 2. The bird's red feet are the blood of the martyrs who wandered the earth. Hugh expands and multiplies the metaphors in terms of the daily experience of the religious. The applications are sometimes strained, but at their best are graceful and appealing: "Silver is divine eloquence; the tinkling of silver like the sweetness of the Word."[22]

Four chapters on the north and south winds preface seven falcon chapters, mirroring the eleven chapters devoted to the dove. The winds chapters show the directions open to the lay-brother, and are based on a text from Song of Songs IV,16: "Arise, O north wind, and come, O south wind." The north wind is temptation and pride; the cold, the torpor of neglect. The south wind comes from the warm, calm region, the serenity of God. It is the spirit of grace, its breeze the blessedness of the Holy Spirit.

The falcon discussion begins with a text from Job XXXIX,26: "Doth the hawk [i.e., falcon] wax feathered by thy wisdom, spreading her wings to the south?" Hugh then cites St. Gregory's story of the falcon spreading its wings to the south wind as it preens.[23] "What is the preening of the falcon," says Hugh, "but one of the saints grown warm when touched by the breath of the Holy Spirit, rejecting the way of the old society as he puts on the form of a new man?"[24] There is a falcon diagram summarizing statements on its preening in the south wind, and other key passages from the winds chapters (Fig. 3).

Hugh describes two types of falcons, the tame and the wild. The tame ones take wild birds, while the wild falcons eat domestic

fowl. Hugh's allegories are nowhere more colorful than in this
essay. The tame falcon, he says, captures wild birds as the
preacher draws laymen into religion (*seculares ad conversionem*).
The bird's master disembowels the captured birds, giving the
hearts to his falcon. So God extracts the heart of a layman through
confession, and "the captive birds come to the table of the Lord
when sinners, chewed by the teeth of the teachers, are converted
into the body of the Church."[25]

The preacher is an important figure in this conversion process,
as noted in the passage just quoted. As Dom Jean Leclercq has
observed, one of the principal differences between Augustinian
canons and the more traditional orders was their preaching
function. The canons had a responsibility "to correct, console,
nourish, recapture" the souls of all people.[26] In Hugh's day,
preaching was being cultivated as a literary form, and would be
codified as such in the following century.[27] The chapters on the
raven and the cock deal at some length with preaching, and show
that many of Hugh's ideas on this subject are drawn from St.
Gregory, *Pastoral Care*.

In the falcon chapters, several references to the lay-brotherhood
give evidence of the brother's training and responsibilities. To tame
a falcon, says Hugh, one must provide it with a safe, warm roost
where it may live except when it is brought out to hunt. Similarly,
the lay-brother lives in the monastery, but is sometimes sent out on
errands, at which time he must always act as prescribed by the Rule,
keeping his thoughts on Heaven. The falcon's perch designates the
Rule; it is suspended above the ground as the monastic life is
separated from worldly desires. The falcon is tied to its perch as one
who is bound by the Rule (Fig. 3). When a falcon has been tamed,
and has molted and gained a new set of feathers, like a monk
stripped of faults and adorned with virtue, the bird is brought out to
hunt. "Similarly, if any lay-brother goes out from the monastery, it
is necessary that he 'come to the hand' of good works; and thus sent
out, that he 'fly' so as to lift himself up with a total effort of mind to
attain the heavenly things he desires."[28]

Three chapters on the turtledove are accompanied by a diagram
similar in form to that for the falcon. The solitary bird symbolizes
chastity; its mournful plaint is the sorrow of a penitent. In our land
the voice of the turtledove is heard (Song of Songs II,12), and we
are in that land "when we occupy our minds in thoughts of the

master and the brothers, so that the soul devoted to God serves the brothers in charity, the neighbor with compassion, itself with modesty, and thus it is made communal."[29] The turtledove loves solitude. Solitude is the cloister; the nest is salvation; the eggs, hope; the turtledove's chicks, the love of God and neighbor. The bird gathers seeds, which are the commentaries of the teachers.

The turtledove nests in the palm tree, for which Hugh's imagery is rich (Fig. 4). The palm is the Church, Christ, and the Cross. Its fronds are the elect, its rough trunk the Church surrounded by

Figure 4. Palm. Paris, Bibl. Nat. MS lat. 2495, fol. 8r, north France, late 12th century (photo: Bibl. Nat., Paris).

tribulation. To climb the trunk is to ascend the Cross to Christ, the sweet fruit of salvation.

Two of the most interesting chapters are those for the cedar (Figs. 5–8). Hugh's text is Song of Songs V,15: "His form as of Lebanon, excellent as the cedars." The cedar is Christ, who in some cases appears within the tree. The tall cedar is the faithful soul excelling others in the height of its desire for Heaven, in the form of its purity, and in the strength of its perseverance. In most cedar illustrations, sparrows nest in the tree (Psalm CIII,17), and symbolize the preachers of the Word. The nests are the place of the tranquil mind, the chicks those persons born again through the sermon. "Therefore, in this cedar nest those who, by living peacefully, hope for eternal blessing."[30] A frequent theme of the Aviary, as of many other twelfth-century monastic works, is the

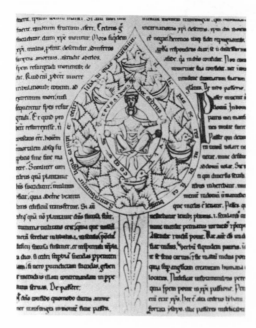

Figure 5. Cedar. Heiligenkreuz Abbey MS 226, fol. 135r, north France, late 12th century (photo: Walisser, Cistercienser Buchkunst, fig. 94).

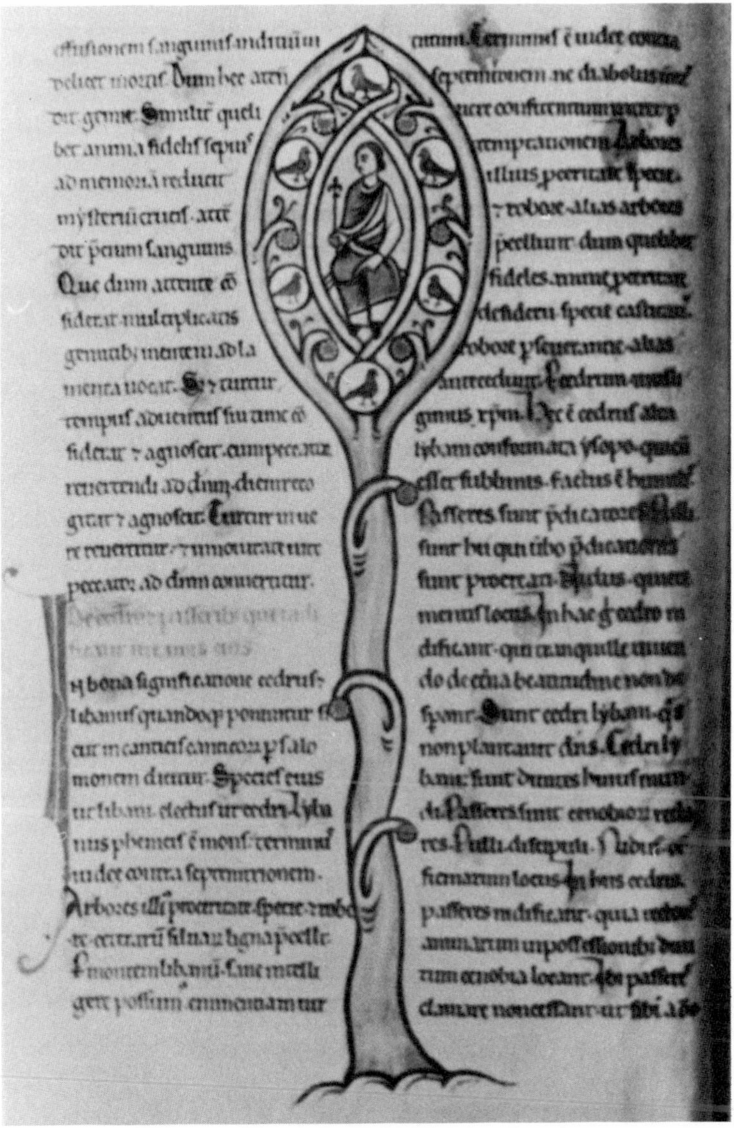

Figure 6. Cedar. Bruges, Great Seminary MS 89/54, page 45, Les Dunes or Bruges, late 12th century (photo: author).

Figure 7. Cedar. Valenciennes, Bibl. Mun. MS101, fol. 176r, ca. 1240 (photo: author).

cloister as a place of spiritual repose, where the soul may be restored to a purity which will bring salvation.[31]

The sparrows nesting in the cedar are also interpreted as "leaders of souls who found monasteries on the lands of the rich."[32] This seems to refer to the placement of monasteries in proximity to benefactors, or as a result of the gift of land on a benefactor's estate. In the second cedar chapter, Hugh goes on to warn that the cedars are also "proud men of wealth." In such cedars one finds nests of herons and falcons, representing greedy people. Herons and falcons hide in the cedars in order to seize prey, just as the accomplices of evil lords threaten other people,

Figure 8. Cedar. Oxford, Bodleian Lib. MS Ashmole 1511, fol. 45v, England, early 13th century (photo: by courtesy of the Courtauld Institute of Art).

both secular and monastic. Hugh's meaning and intent in these passages is not entirely clear, but in such statements he displays a traditional Christian suspicion of wealth and power.

There follow six chapters on the sparrow, which "is an inconstant and restless bird."[33] It represents instability of the mind. The sparrow on the rooftop (Psalm CI,8) is also the faithful teacher making known the heights of virtue. The fowler, that is, the Devil, set three snares for the sparrow: the deceitful rhetoric of demons, deception by heretics, and the charms of the flesh.

Needless to say, this is only a sampling of the wealth of metaphor contained in the first part of the Aviary. The second part is almost as colorful and rich. It consists of single chapters for twenty-three different birds, which, like the birds and trees of the first part, are those mentioned in Scripture, principally Psalms and Job. Hugh's other sources are the *Physiologus,* Gregory, Isidore and Hrabanus Maurus, sometimes quoted at length. Much of the chapters on the raven and cock, and all of the ostrich chapter, are quoted from Gregory's *Moralia in Job.* In most chapters, however, Hugh adds considerable commentary to the material from his authorities. For example, he quotes Isidore's account of the crane setting a watch for the night. "In the watch," says Hugh, "we can understand mature brothers in the community who take precautions for their brethren against temporal things, and spiritually care for them as individuals . . ."[34] The crane at watch holds a stone in its foot, so that if it sleeps, the stone will drop and awaken it. Hugh comments, "The stone is Christ, the foot the passion of the mind . . . Thus if anyone watches out for the safety of himself or his brethren, he bears a stone in his foot, that is, Christ in his mind."[35] The passage continues by saying that if a brother sleeps in sin, the stone will fall, that is, Christ will fall from his mind. "If He should fall, let [the brother] cry out through confession, so that he might arouse the sleepers, that is, the brothers, so that he might invite them to the vigilance of caution . . ."[36]

Confession as a sacrament was new in the twelfth century, and was made a fixed annual requirement only in 1215, at the Fourth Lateran Council.[37] It is interesting that in a number of Aviary passages Hugh notes its importance for salvation. In the passage cited above, public confession is implied; but elsewhere in the Aviary, the then more common private confession to a priest seems indicated.

The importance among Augustinians of public preaching has already been mentioned, and it is not surprising to find an emphasis on preaching in the Augustinian author's text. One of the interpretations of the raven is as a learned preacher. A long quotation from St. Gregory praises the preachers who can judge when their listeners are prepared to hear the inner mysteries of faith.[38] To this and other passages from Gregory relating the preacher to the cock, Hugh adds an amusing image: the cock flapping its wings before crowing is like the preacher who, in preparation for his sermon, beats himself with the wings of contemplation and prayer. Hugh considers the sermon efficacious in the conversion and care of lay-brothers. If Rainier was a teacher, then perhaps he also preached. At times, Hugh even seems to use the terms *magister* and *praedicator* interchangeably.

Another common theme in the Aviary is the importance of the conversion of laymen, presumably to the lay-brotherhood. The jackdaw is known as a garrulous bird, and can be taught to speak. The talking jackdaw represents the converted laymen who have learned "the language of religion." Hugh warns that a garrulous man makes a poor monastic, because he tends to persist in his loquaciousness; and if he then abandons the monastery, he will slander the ways of religion. In other words, the piety and commitment of the garrulous man are questionable. It is at this point that Hugh provides the famous examples of men who are unsuited to the religious life: the mural painters, the physicians, and the entertainers.[39] The principal charge against them is that they are itinerants, and therefore basically unstable.

Occasionally Hugh's metaphors are so earthy as to be comical. Perhaps he meant them to be thus for the benefit of untutored lay-brothers whose spirituality may have been less developed than was their appreciation of a lively image. We have already noted the falcon, or preacher, capturing the wild birds, or laymen, who are then "chewed by the teeth of the teachers." Likewise, the vulture feeds on corpses as a sinner delights in carnal desires. But Hugh's best line, one which must have provoked laughter, comes at the conclusion of the peacock chapter when he equates the bird in display with the prelate who seeks praise for his actions: "when the peacock's tail is raised, its rear end is exposed, and although the action is praiseworthy, the elation is ridiculous."[40]

THE PROGRAM OF ILLUSTRATIONS

A separate study is required for the many interesting questions of style, iconography, and pictorial sources for the Aviary illustrations; but a summary of the visual program will serve to reinforce the Aviary's role as a textbook.

The illustrations of the first part of the Aviary are those most peculiar to the program. The opening miniature accompanies Prologue I, and shows the dove and falcon in an arcade; occasionally Hugh and Rainier are also pictured (Fig. 1). Sometimes the prologue text replaces the figures below the birds.

Next is the dove diagram (Fig. 2), followed by the three doves of Noah, David and Christ; then the falcon diagram (Fig. 3), the palm (Fig. 4), the turtledove diagram, which closely resembles the falcon diagram; and the cedar (Figs. 5–8). The three diagrams tend toward uniformity throughout the illustrated manuscripts. In a few cases, they are the only illustrations.[41] While the dove diagram is a complex summary of the dove chapters, the other two diagrams, with a few essential ideas from the text in the cross-pieces, would be useful as mnemonic devices for students. In many instances, the bird in the dove diagram displays one or more of the metallic colors, or simulations thereof, mentioned in the dove texts.[42]

The palm and the cedar appear in several different forms in the extant manuscripts. The palm is most often seen as a single trunk with a number of fronds (Fig. 4). The most interesting and unique of all the Aviary's miniatures is that for the cedar. The typical cedar design shows a fairly stylized tree with borders, and with sparrows perching or nesting in its leafy top. The cedar from the Heiligenkreuz manuscript (Appendix no. 18) is a good example (Fig. 5). The man seen in this cedar is, in other copies, a king, Christ (Fig. 7), or without any identity (Fig. 6). In the Heiligenkreuz cedar and in three others,[43] the inscription around the man identifies him as "Comes Theobaldus." This refers undoubtedly to Thibaud, Count of Heilly, co-founder in about 1115 and benefactor of Hugh's priory of St. Laurent, and founder also of a family thereafter prominent in the ecclesiastical life of Amiens.[44] With this identification there is little doubt that the cedar appeared in the original manuscript, made for St. Laurent, and contained the portrait of Thibaud. The cedar design must have been close to that of the Heiligenkreuz manuscript, for a substantial number of Aviary cedars are like the Heiligenkreuz one, suggesting a common model in the original. Most other cedars, however, lack the Thibaud identification, which would lose its meaning in manuscripts for most other abbeys. With its excellent text, and cedar with Thibaud, the Heiligenkreuz Aviary probably reflects the original manuscript quite closely.[45] The Aberdeen and Ashmole copies (Appendix nos. 1 and 26) preserve the bordered cedar in an abstracted form, without reference to a tree, and substitute at the center a woman holding a bird medallion (Fig. 8). The woman is probably the Church, and the bird a sparrow, symbolizing the preacher, as in the text.

In a smaller number of Aviaries, the cedar is a simpler and usually more naturalistic tree with a male figure and/or sparrows, as in the copy now in Valenciennes (Appendix no. 43; Fig. 7). The two design types for this important miniature suggest that there may have been two early models for the illustrations. Nevertheless, it seems safe to say that the first part of the original Aviary manuscript must have consisted of the following: a prologue illustration with two birds in an arcade; and the figures of Hugh and Rainier with texts to summarize ideas in Prologue I; the three-doves illustration; the three diagrams; the palm; and a cedar with borders, sparrows, and Thibaud.

The second part of the Aviary consists of chapters on individual birds, each with an illustration. In general these birds resemble those in the birds section of a Bestiary: the bird in profile on a colored or diapered ground, and surrounded by a simple round or rectangular frame. Good examples are the pelican and night heron in a mid-thirteenth-century Aviary from Cambrai Cathedral (Fig. 9). The Aviary's ostrich is often pictured with the cloven feet mentioned by *Physiologus* and the Latin Bestiary, but not by the Aviary (Fig. 10).[46]

In about half the extant illustrated manuscripts, the miniatures are in full color; in the rest they are line drawings, sometimes in colors, or heightened with color. The majority of manuscripts include the above program. In the illustrated English Bestiaries which incorporate the entire Aviary text, some of the Aviary first-part miniatures are used, but more elaborate illustrations appear in the second part, such as for the pelican, the crane, and

Figure 9. Pelican and Night Heron. Cambrai, Bibl. Mun. MS 259, fol. 196r, north France, mid-13th century (photo: author).

the eagle.[47] Where only excerpts of the Aviary occur in English Bestiaries, none of the Aviary pictures appear.

Finally, I would like to suggest still another connection between the Aviary and the Latin Bestiary in the use to which they were put. Where early provenance is known for a manuscript of either text, it is usually monastic—in a surprising number of instances, the austere Cistercians. An explanation of Cistercian use of the Bestiary has been as a source of metaphor and allegory for sermons and moral writings.[48] Both Aviary and Bestiary had a relatively short currency, the Bestiary beginning its rise in the early twelfth century, and the Aviary sometime after mid-century. Production of both declined dramatically at the end of the thirteenth century. Can this parallel currency be only coincidental? Is it not possible that the two books, with their similar literary

Figure 10. Ostrich, St. Omer, Bibl. Mun MS 94, fol. 25r, Clairmarais or St. Omer, early 13th century (photo: author).

structure and popular appeal, were both used to teach lay-brothers? Many orders, and especially the Cistercians, had introduced lay-brothers into their communities in the twelfth century; but by the mid-thirteenth century these second-class monastic citizens were restive, even rebellious, and the whole institution was in decay.[49] The rise and fall of the brotherhood, therefore, closely parallels the period of popularity for the Aviary and Latin Bestiary. To reinforce the relationship between the two texts, one may recall that not only do the two sometimes appear in one manuscript,[50] but also some Bestiaries made in England directly incorporate the Aviary into their texts. Both books, with their moralized accounts of animals, could have been used to teach illiterate lay-brothers who knew no Latin, and whose attention might be held by the pictures, while their teachers translated and explained, in whatever the local dialect, the simplified lessons contained in the texts. This is not to say that such was the only use of the Aviary and Latin Bestiary, but that it was a principal one. Nor were all the manuscripts made for monasteries; but existing evidence of provenance suggests that the majority were.

Although the vogue for the Aviary and Latin Bestiary was over by about 1300, interest in animal allegory continued throughout the Middle Ages, especially in vernacular literature for the courts. It would be a mistake, however, to see courtly literature as a cause of the decline of the Aviary and Latin Bestiary. A French version of the Bestiary had appeared by ca. 1125, and other vernacular versions followed in the thirteenth century.[51] The French rhymed Aviary (Appendix no. 39) was not a success. The vernacular developments almost parallel the rise to prominence of the two Latin texts, and thus would have been at best a long time in forcing them out of favor. Furthermore, the Aviary and Latin Bestiary were texts used in a world that continued to speak and read Latin, regardless of fashions in society outside the monasteries. Had the lay-brotherhood maintained its earlier fervor and discipline, the Aviary, and perhaps also the Latin Bestiary, would almost certainly have remained in production alongside the vernacular Bestiaries.

Hugh of Fouilloy's views on monasticism in the Aviary, and the information therein on the education of lay-brothers, make the text one of interest to historians of monasticism. For the art historian, the illustrations are interesting as a large group based on a single program, providing clearly defined material for study not only of stylistic and iconographic problems, but also of matters concerning the relationship of text and picture. The possibility that the purpose of the Aviary can help explain the patronage and time span of the Bestiary adds further to the value of the Aviary. Thus, there are considerable riches to be found in what may at first seem to be merely an amusing medieval picture book.

NOTES

*I am grateful to Professor Peter K. Marshall for generous help in matters relating to the Aviary text, and for his careful review of my translation; to Professor Florence McCulloch for advice in Bestiary matters, as well as for her kindness in lending me photographic materials; and to Father Louis J. Lekai who read the typescript of this paper and offered suggestions for its improvement. I also wish to thank Dr. Peter Ludwig for permitting me to consult manuscripts in his collection; and the many librarians for their help and courtesy.

(1) Migne, *PL*, CLXXVII, 13–56. F. J. Carmody, 'De Bestiis et Aliis Rebus and the Latin *Physiologus*,'' *Speculum*, XIII (1938), 153–59, correctly separated Book I of the Bestiary from the rest, but failed to follow up the statement in Migne, *PL*, CLXXV, 118, that ''Hughes de Foulois'' might be the author. *Histoire littéraire de la France*, XIII (Paris, 1856), 498, had already named Hugh as author.

I am preparing an edition of the Aviary (based on three of the twelfth-century manuscripts), an English translation, and a study of the illustrations.

(2) H. Peltier, ''Hughes de Fouilloy, Chanoine regulier, prieur de Saint-Laurent-au-Bois,'' *Revue du Moyen Age Latin*, II (1946), 25–44; see also Dom Brial, *Histoire littéraire de la France*, XIII, 492–507; V. Mortet, ''Hughes de Fouilloi, Pierre le Chantre, Alexandre Neckham et les critiques dirigées au douzième siècle contre le luxe des constructions,'' *Mélanges d'histoire offerts à M. Charles Bémont* (Paris, 1931), 105–37; C. de Clercq, ''Hughes de Fouilloy, imagier de ses propres oeuvres?'', *Revue du Nord* XLV (1963), 31–42. Hugh's other works are: the well known *De claustro animae* (Migne, *PL*, CLXXVI, 1017–1182; ed., translated by I. Gobry, Paris, 1965); *Liber de rota verae religionis*, ed. C. de Clercq, *Bulletin DuCange* (Archivuum latinitatis medii aevi), XXIX (1959), 219–28, XXX (1960), 15–37; *De medicina animae* (Migne, *PL*, CLXXVI, 1183–1202); *De nuptiis* (Migne, *PL*, CLXXVI, 1202–18); *De pastoribus et ovibus*, ed. C. de Clercq, *Bulletin DuCange*, XXXI (1961), 77–107. Also important is F. Ohly, ''Probleme der mittelalterlichen Bedeutungsforschung und das Taubenbild des Hugo de Folieto,'' *Frühmittelalterliche Studien*, II, 162–201; and N. Häring, ''Notes on the 'Liber Avium' of Hugues de Fouilloy,'' *Recherches de Théologie ancienne et médiévale*, XLVI (1979), 53–83, which must be read with caution, but which lists most of the manuscripts, with bibliography. The illustrated manuscripts on Häring's list are summarized and expanded in the Appendix to this paper.

(3) H. Gérard, *Chronique latine de Guillaume de Nangis* (Paris, 1843), I, 31: *Claruit praeterea his temporibus Hugo de Folieto sancti Petri Corbienis [sic] monachus, qui librum de claustro animae et corporis composuit. Alii dicunt istum Hugonem in pago Ambiancensi fuisse canonicum regularem.* Peltier, "Hughes de Fouilloy," 25–26, who also puts to rest any notions that Hugh was a monk at Corbie, 27–28. The Renaissance was still aware of at least the *De claustro animae,* for an anonymous sixteenth-century Flemish manuscript of the lives of saints and famous writers (Brussels, Bibl. Roy., MS IV, 204, fol. 105r) mentions it and calls Hugh the "other Hugh" (*Hugo alter de Folieto*) and a man of eloquence (*eloquentiae vir*). The first Hugh is Hugh of St. Victor; other writers included are Boccaccio and Poggio Bracciolino.

(4) Société des Antiquaires de Picardie, MS 62. Peltier, "Hugues de Fouilloy," 29. See also Abbé E. Jumel, *Monographies de Picardie. Heilly* (Amiens, 1870), 96–97, for a translation of much of Hugh's prologue.

(5) Peltier, "Hugues de Fouilloy," 30; Jumel, *Monographies,* 88.

(6) Peltier, "Hugues de Fouilloy," 34. The Necrology of St. Laurent d'Heilly (Paris, Bibl. Nat. MS lat. 12583, fols. 97r–115v) lists "Hugo prior noster" for September 6.

(7) Reported in the Cartulary prologue, fol. 3r; Peltier, "Hugues de Fouilloy," 32.

(8) In a number of manuscripts he is called *Ranierus cognomine Corde Benignus,* "Rainier the Kindhearted." The falcon representing Rainier in Figure 1 seems to have a large heart for a body.

(9) Recent research on the Cistercian lay-brotherhood is summarized, with good bibliography, in L. J. Lekai, *The Cistercians* (Kent, Ohio, 1977), chapter XXI and 435–36. For the present study, the following were also helpful: C. D. Fonseca, "I conversi nelli communità canonicali," *I laici nella "Societas Christiana" del secoli Xle XII* (Atti della Settimana di Studio: Mendola, 1965) (Milan, 1968), 262–95; *idem,* "Hughes de Fouilloy entre l'*Ordo antiquus* et l'*Ordo novus,*" *CCM,* XVI (1973), 303–12; C. Dereine, "Chanoines," in *Dictionnaire d'histoire de géographie ecclésiastique,* XII (Paris, 1953), 315–405.

(10) . . . *simplicium mentes aedificare* (Prologue I; Migne, *PL,* CLXXVII, 14).

(11) *Si dormiatis inter medios cleros pennae columbae deargentatae et posteriora dorsi eius in pallore auri.*

(12) *Desiderii tui, carissime, petitionibus satisfacere cupiens, columbam cuius pennae sunt deargentatae et posteriora dorsi eius in pallore auri pingere, et per picturam simplicium mentes aedificare decrevi . . . et quod vix poterat auditus percipiat visus. Haec tantum columbam volui formando pingere, sed etiam dictando describere, ut per scripturam demonstrem picturam . . .* (Prologue I; Migne, *PL,* CLXXVII, 14).

Similar references to painting occur in the prologues of *De Rota (rotam praelationis . . . pingam); and De pastoribus (duos gregos inter se diversos pingere volui). De rota* usually has two wheel-diagrams with human figures, and *De pastoribus* occasionally has a single full-page illustration of men and animals. C. de Clercq, "Hughes de Fouilloy, imagier de ses propres oeuvres?", on the basis of these passages, supposed that Hugh himself illustrated the original volumes of these texts. There is, however, no conclusive evidence either way.

(13) J. Dubois, "L'institution des convers au XIIe siècle, forme de vie monastique propre aux laïcs," *I laici nella "Societas Christiana,"* 245–46, mentions a master who is an educated lay-brother.

(14) Chapters 28, 33, 39, 40, and 58. See below, note 18, for the subjects of these chapters.

(15) E. Mikkers, "L'idéal religieux des frères convers dans l'ordre de Citeaux aux 12e et 13e siècles," *Collectanea Cisterciensia,* XXIV (1962), 119, describes how Gerard of Heisterbach interrupted a lecture to arouse sleeping lay-brothers with an Arthurian tale. Mikkers' principal topic is Caesar, prior of Heisterbach, who was a teacher of lay-brothers, and whose *Dialogus miraculorum* was evidently used as a text for the brothers, providing lives of saintly religious and lay-brothers as examples of virtues similar to those encouraged in the Aviary: conversion from secular life, simplicity, obedience, humility, and confession, and including also the efficacy of communion and Marian devotion.

(16) This is not to exclude, however, perusals by more modern readers.

(17) M. R. James, *The Bestiary* (Oxford, 1928), 10, 22, and 59, noticed the Aviary text in the English Bestiaries, and F. McCulloch, *Medieval Latin and French Bestiaries* (Chapel Hill, 1962), 36, note 44, and T. S. R. Boase, *English Art* (Oxford, 1953), 294, also comment on the fact. No one since, however, has mentioned these manuscripts in discussing the Aviary. The manuscripts in question are Appendix nos. 1, 10, 19, 26–29, and 32. Further investigations of the Latin Bestiary manuscripts will perhaps uncover a few more examples.

(18) Prologues I and II; (Part I:) Chs. 1–11, Silvered Dove; Chs. 12–15, North and South Winds; Chs. 16–22, Falcon; Ch. 23, Preface to Sparrow and Turtledove; Chs. 24–27, Palm; Chs. 28–29, Turtledove; Chs. 30–31, Cedar; Chs. 32–37, Sparrow. (Part II:) Ch. 38, Pelican; Ch. 39, Night Heron; Ch. 40, Raven; Ch. 41, Cock; Ch. 42, Ostrich; Ch. 43, Vulture; Ch. 44, Crane; Ch. 45, Kite; Ch. 46, Swallow; Ch. 47, Stork; Ch. 48, Blackbird; Ch. 49, Owl; Ch. 50, Jackdaw; Ch. 51, Goose; Ch. 52, Heron; Ch. 53, Caladrius; Ch. 54, Phoenix; Ch. 55, Partridge; Ch. 56, Quail; Ch. 57, Hoopoe; Ch. 58, Swan; Ch. 59, Peacock; Ch. 60, Eagle (the addition of the ibex and coot in a few manuscripts, and in Migne, *PL,* is not authentic).

(19) Gregory was of special importance to Augustinians, for he was one of the sources for the Rule of Aix, the older Augustinian code; see C. Dereine, "Enquête sur la règle de Saint Augustin," *Scriptorium,* II (1948), 34. He was a source for Hugh of Fouilloy in several of Hugh's works.

(20) For a summary of Biblical fauna, see Rev. J. Fisher, *Scripture Animals* (Portland, Me., 1834; new ed. Princeton, 1972).

(21) Despite the illustrations, the Aviary remains moral theology, and was not used as a source by later encyclopedists writing of birds, such as Thomas of Cantimpré or Bartholomew of England.

(22) *Est autem argentum divinum eloquium; tinnitus argenti dulcedo verbi* (Ch. 6; Migne, *PL,* CLXXVII, 18).

(23) Gregory, *Moralia,* Bk. 31, Ch. 46; Migne, *PL,* LXXVI, 623.

(24) *Quid est ergo accipitrem in austro plumescere nisi quod unusquisque sanctorum tactus flatu Sancti Spiritus concalescit et usum vetustae conversationis abiciens novi hominis formam sumit?* (Ch. 16; Migne, *PL,* CLXXVII, 21).

(25) . . . *ad mensa itaque Domini captae volucres veniunt dum in corpus ecclesiae peccatores doctorum dentibus masticati sese convertuni* (Ch. 17; Migne, *PL,* CLXXVII, 22).

(26) J. Leclercq, "La spiritualité des chanoines reguliers," *La vita comuna del clero nei secolo XI e XII,* Atti della Settimana di Studio Mendola, 1959 (Milan, 1962), 121.

(27) J. J. Murphy, *Rhetoric in the Middle Ages* (Berkeley, 1974), 275 and 311.

(28) *Similiter si aliquis conversus de claustro exeat, necesse est ut ad manum bonae operationis accedat; et inde emissus, volet ut ad desideranda celestia toto adnisu mentis seipsum levit* (Ch. 18; Migne, *PL,* CLXXVII, 22).

(29) . . . *dum mentrem nostram cum magistro et fratribus possidemus, ut animus Deo devotus serviat per dilectionem fratribus, per compassionem proximo, per modestiam sibi, et sic communis fiat* (Ch. 28; Migne, *PL,* CLXXVII, 25).

(30) *In hac ergo cedro nidificant qui tranquille vivendo de aeterna beatitudine non desperant* (Ch. 30; Migne, *PL,* CLXXVII, 26).

(31) Peter Damian, *Opuscula* XLII:2 (Migne, *PL,* CXLV, 766), likens the cloister to a zoo, a stall, and an aviary.

(32) . . . *rectores animarum in possessionibus divitum coenobia locant* (Ch. 30; Migne, *PL,* CLXXVII, 26). Cassiodorus presents a similar metaphor, but in different language, in the *Commentary on the Psalms,* CIII, 390–95; see J. J. O'Donnell, *Cassiodorus* (Berkeley, 1979), 191, note 20.

(33) . . . *avis inconstans et instabilis* (Ch. 32; Migne, *PL,* CLXXVII, 27).

(34) *Possumus autem per vigiles intelligere quoslibet discretos fratres quo communiter fratribus temporalia provident, et de singulis spiritaliter curam habent* . . . (Ch. 44; Migne, *PL,* CLXXVII, 41).

(35) *Lapis est Christus, pes mentis affectus* . . . *Si quis igitur ad custodiam sui vel fratrum vigilet, lapillum in pede, id est, Christum in mente portet* (Ch. 44; Migne, *PL,* CLXXVII, 41).

(36) *Si autem ceciderit, per confessionem clamet, ut dormientes excitet, id est, fratres* . . . *ad vigilantiam circumspectionis invitet* (Ch. 44; Migne, *PL,* CLXXVII, 41).

(37) P. Anciaux, *The Sacrament of Penance* (New York, 1962), 46 and 117.

(38) Moralia, III, 9. Similar ideas are expressed in Gregory's *Pastoral Care,* preface to Book III.

(39) *Pictores, medici, ioculatores.* It is subsequently explained that the *pictores* paint pictures on walls (Ch. 50; Migne, *PL,* CLXXVII, 46).

(40) *Cum autem cauda erigitur, posteriora nudantur, et sic quod laudatur in opere derideturin elatione* (Ch. 59; Migne, *PL,* CLXXVII, 54).

(41) Appendix, nos. 12, 15, and 16.

(42) The dove diagram of Paris, Bibl. Nat., MS lat. 2495 is reproduced in color in Ohly, ''Probleme,'' frontispiece to the article.

(43) Appendix, nos. 22, 35, and 44.

(44) W. M. Newman, *Le personnel de la Cathédrale d'Amiens (1066–1306) avec une note sur la famille des Seigneurs de Heilly* (Paris, 1972), 44, correcting errors in earlier accounts of the family's relationship with St. Laurent. Jumel, *Monographies,* 88 and *passim,* while superceded by Newman, is good for documents. Theobald's obituary occurs for May 18 in the St. Laurent Necrology, Paris Bibl. Nat. MS lat. 12583.

(45) It is not clear whether the Heiligenkreuz copy, a French manuscript, was made for the Austrian abbey. To complicate matters, a nearly contemporary copy of it for a daughter house at Zwettl was made by south German hands. The manuscript used by Migne for *PL,* so far not identified, has many variants which do not occur in the majority of manuscripts.

(46) Physiologus says, ''She has feet like those of a camel'' (*Physiologus,* trans. M. Curley, Austin, Texas, 1979, 55).

(47) Appendix, nos. 1, 26, 27 and 29; see B. Rowland, *Birds with Human Souls* (Knoxville, 1978), 131, 33 and 53 for reproductions.

(48) Fr. J. Morson, ''The English Cistercians and the Bestiary,'' *Bulletin of the John Rylands Library* XXXIX (1956), 146–70.

(49) J. S. Donnelly, *The Decline of the Cistercian Lay-Brotherhood* (New York, 1949). In about 1223, the lay-brothers of Ter Doest, the daughter of Les Dunes (Ter Duinen), formed a conspiracy; and the abbot of Les Dunes was asked to quell similar disturbances elsewhere in the region; Donnelly, 35. An important Aviary manuscript, Bruges, Great Seminary MS 89/54 (Appendix no. 3) was probably made for and at Les Dunes.

(50) Appendix, nos. 4, 8, 9, 22, 23, 34, 35, 36, 37, and 43. In no. 37 the rhymed French Aviary appears with the French Bestiary of Guillaume le Clerc, and was almost certainly made for a secular patron.

(51) McCulloch, *Medieval Latin and French Bestiaries,* chapter III.

APPENDIX

The following are the known illustrated copies of Hugh of Fouilloy's Aviary. After the call number is an assigned date, and provenance when known. In parentheses I have suggested the place of production, and provided particulars when necessary. Asterisks indicate those manuscripts which I have added to Häring's list, "Notes on the 'Liber Avium'," 68–83.[1]

1. The following manuscripts in Häring's list do not contain the Aviary, and should be deleted: Cambridge, Engl., University Library MSS Ii.iv.26, Kk.iv.25 and Gg.vi.5. Contrary to Häring, Bodleian Library MS Laud. Misc. 205 has no Aviary illustrations.
2. Bordeaux, Bibl. Mun. MS 995, late 13th cent. (France)
3. Bruges, Great Seminary MS 89/54, ca. 1200, Les Dunes Abbey (Les Dunes or Bruges)
4. Brussels, Bibl. Roy. MS 8536–43, mid-13th cent. (France or Flanders; one picture only, places for the rest)
5. Brussels, Bibl. Roy. MS 18421–29, ca. 1200 (north France or Flanders)
6. Brussels, Bibl. Roy. MS II, 1076, ca. 1200, Aulne Abbey (Aulne)
7. Cambrai, Bibl. Mun. MS 259, mid-13th cent., Cambrai Cathedral (north France)
8. Cambridge, MA, Houghton Library (Hofer Coll.) MS Typ 101, ca. 1270 (north France)[2]
9. Cambridge, Eng., Sidney Sussex College MS 100, ca. 1270 (north France)
*10. Cambridge, Eng., Gonville and Caius College MS 372/621, ca.

---

*[1]Aberdeen, University Library, MS 24, late 12th cent. (England; Bestiary with Aviary text and Part I illustrations)

1300 (England; Bestiary with portions of Aviary text and one Aviary picture)

11. Chalons-sur-Saône, Bibl. Mun, MS 14, early 13th cent. (France; fragment)
12. Charleville, Bibl. Mun. MS 166B, late 13th cent. (north France; one diagram)
13. Chicago, Newberry Library MS 31.1, 14th cent. (Bohemia; places for illustrations)
14. Cremona, Bibl. Statale MS Gov. 199, ca. 1300, St. Augustine Abbey, Cremona (Cremona?)
15. Douai, Bibl. Mun. MS 370, ca. 1200, Anchin? (north France; fragment)
16. Frankfurt, Stadtbibl. MS Barth. 167, ca. 1300, made for a Cistercian abbey (France; diagrams only)
17. Heiligenkreuz Abbey MS 226, late 12th cent., Heiligenkreuz (north France)
*18. Lisbon, Arquivio Nac. Torre do Tombo MS 90, dated 1184, Lorvão Abbey (written at Lorvão)
19. London, British Library MS Harley 4751, ca. 1200 (England; Bestiary with portions of Aviary text, but no Aviary pictures)
20. London, British Library MS Roy. 10 A vii, late 13th cent. (England; fragment)
21. London, British Library MS Sloane 278, ca. 1270 (north France or Flanders)
22. Dr. Peter Ludwig Coll. (formerly Dyson Perrins MS 26), ca. 1270 (north France or Flanders)
23. Dr. Peter Ludwig Coll. (formerly Duke Humfrey of Gloucester Coll, then London, Sion College MS Arc. L402/L28), dated 1277 (north France or Flanders)
24. Namur, Mus. Archiep. MS 48, 15th cent., Aulne Abbey (Aulne)
25. New Haven, Connecticut, Yale Univ, Beinecke Library MS 189, ca. 1200 (England or France; fragment)
*26. Oxford, Bodleian Library MS Ashmole 1511, early 13th cent. (England; Bestiary with Aviary text and Pt. I illustrations)
27. Oxford, Bodleian Library MS Bodl. 602, early 13th cent. (England; fragment; Bestiary with Aviary text and Pt. I illustrations)

---

2. In this manuscript the illustrations are grouped together, separate from the text, and constitute a model-book for the Aviary and the Bestiary; some are pricked for transfer copying. See S. A. Ives and H. Lehmann-Haupt, *An English 13th Century Bestiary* (New York, 1942), Figures 1–8. The text has spaces for the illustrations. Although some of the illustrations in the picture section correspond in design to those in English Bestiaries, the style is Parisian.

*28. Oxford, Bodleian Library MS Bodl. 764, early 13th cent.
     (England; Bestiary with portions of Aviary text, but no Aviary
     illustrations)
*29. Oxford, Bodleian Library MS Douce 151, 14th cent. (England;
     Bestiary with Aviary text and Pt. I illustrations)
 30. Oxford, Bodleian Library MS Lyell 71, ca. 1300 (north Italy)
 31. Oxford, Bodleian Library MS Rawl. G 69 (England?; fragment)
*32. Oxford, University Library MS 120, early 13th cent. (England;
     Bestiary with Aviary text and probable Aviary illustrations; not
     yet consulted)
 33. Paris, Bibl. Nat. MS lat. 2495, ca. 1200 (north France)
 34. Paris, Bibl. Nat. MS lat. 2495A, early 13th cent., Foucarmont
     Abbey (north France; miniatures excised)
 35. Paris, Bibl. Nat. MS lat. 2495B, early 13th cent. (north France)
 36. Paris, Bibl. Nat. MS lat. 14429, ca. 1250, St. Victor (Paris)
*37. Paris, Bibl. Nat. MS fr. 24428, ca. 1270 (north France or Paris)
*38. Rome, Bibl. Casanatense MS 444, late 13th cent., Reims, St.
     Denis Abbey? (north France)
 39. Rome, Vatican Library MS Reg. lat. 221, 13th cent. (France;
     places for illustrations)
 40. Rome, Vatican Library MS Reg. lat. 290, 14th cent. (France;
     places for illustrations)
 41. St. Omer, Bibl. Mun. MS 94, early 13th cent., Clairmarais Abbey
     (Clairmarais or St. Omer)
 42. Troyes, Bibl. Mun. MS 177, early 13th cent., Clairvaux (north
     France)
 43. Valenciennes, Bibl. Mun. MS 101, ca. 1240, St. Amand (Paris)
     (The Vitry-le François manuscript, noted in the earlier literature
     on the Aviary, was destroyed in World War II.)
 44. Zwettl Abbey, MS 253, ca. 1200, Zwettl (Zwettl or
     Heiligengreuz)

OCCUPATIONS OF THE MONTHS IN MEDIAEVAL CALENDARS
James F. Willard

Psalters and Books of Hours hold a high place in the esteem of collectors of mediaeval manuscripts, not so much for their texts, which are largely stereotyped, but for their illuminations.[1] Both were books used for private devotion, the first, in its non-liturgical form, by the clergy and laity, the second, primarily by the laity. When either was made for a wealthy man or a lover of the arts its pages were frequently decorated with the work of the mediaeval miniaturist. The pictures are found in the calendar and in the body of the text; it is with the former that this brief paper is concerned.

The Bodleian Library, like most libraries which possess mediaeval manuscripts, contains a large number of both classes of devotional books. Both were very popular during the later Middle Ages. The Psalter, as is well known, contains the 150 psalms; these make up the bulk of the text and give the book its name. A calendar of saints' days and the chief festivals of the Church usually precedes the psalms. In addition the book usually contains canticles, a litany, the Creed, and various prayers. Psalters are found as early as the Carolingian epoch, but ''from the eleventh to the beginning of the fourteenth century they form by far the most numerous class of illuminated manuscripts.''[2] Psalters of the eleventh century at times contain the Hours of the Virgin. In the thirteenth century these Hours, together with other devotional material, appeared as separate books known as *Horae Beatae Mariae Virginis*. While far from numerous at that time, the *Horae* became more popular in the following century, and during the fifteenth century outnumbered any other kind of manuscripts with illuminations. A Book of Hours normally contains a calendar, the

Reprinted by permission from the *Bodleian Quarterly Record,* Vol. VII, No. 74, pp. 33–39.

Hours of the Virgin, other Hours, the Seven Penitential Psalms and Litany, the Office of the Dead, memorials of the saints and other devotional exercises of less moment. The content of the *Horae* is less formalized than that of the Psalter.

While many of the calendars that appear at the beginning of Psalters and Books of Hours found in the Bodleian bear no miniatures, others have crude or beautifully executed pictures of the occupations of the several months and of the signs of the Zodiac. The latter, though interesting on their own account, lie outside the province of this paper. There are, so far as has been discovered, twenty-three manuscripts in the Library in which the occupations are pictured in their calendars. Seven of these are Psalters, fourteen are Books of Hours, and two are books of private prayers. The latter have been included because of their kinship to the two important classes of devotional books and because of their interesting calendars.[3] The twenty-three manuscripts are:

Thirteenth Century.

Douce 24. Psalter. Northern France. End of the century.

Douce 38. Psalter. Netherlands.

New College 322. Psalter. England. Second quarter of the century.

Fourteenth Century.

Douce 5. Psalter. Flanders. First half of the century.

Douce 48. Psalter. France. Early part of the century.

Canon. Liturg. 126. Psalter. Netherlands. First half of the century.

Fifteenth Century.

Douce 8. Offices and Prayers for Private Use. Flanders. Second half of the century.

Douce 62. Book of Hours. France. About 1400–10.

Douce 72. Book of Hours. France. Second half of the century.

Douce 144. Book of Hours. France. 1407.

Douce 152. Book of Hours. France.

Douce 276. Book of Hours. France. Second half of the century.

Gough Liturg. 7. Private Prayers. England. About 1500.

Canon. Liturg. 99. Book of Hours. France. Second half of the century.

Canon. Liturg. 283. Book of Hours. France.

Misc. Liturg. 41. Book of Hours. Northern France. Fourth quarter of the century.

Misc. Liturg. 60. Psalter. France.

Rawl. Liturg. e. 14. Book of Hours. France.

Rawl. Liturg. e. 20. Book of Hours. France. Second half of the century.

Rawl. Liturg. f. 14. Book of Hours. France.

Rawl. Liturg. f. 31. Book of Hours. France.

Sixteenth Century.

Douce 135. Book of Hours. France. First half of the century.

Rawl. Liturg. e. 36. Book of Hours. France. First quarter of the century.

Scholars who are interested in the Middle Ages frequently dismiss the representations of the occupations of the months as conventional. This is true to a large extent. The men who illuminated the calendars carried on traditions of long standing concerning the proper activities of mankind during the several seasons of the year. These traditions are embodied in writing and sculpture, as well as in mediaeval manuscripts.[4] In the latter it was customary from the thirteenth century, at least, to picture these activities as follows: January, feasting; February, a man warming himself before a fire; March, pruning vines or trees; April, riding or playing in the open air; May, hawking or playing in the fields; June, mowing grass; July, reaping grain or mowing grass; August, threshing or reaping grain; September, treading grapes in a vat or sowing grain; October, sowing grain or treading grapes; November, beating trees for nuts for pigs or killing a pig; December, killing a pig or baking loaves of bread. Most of the Bodleian manuscripts conform to a large extent to this stereotyped programme.

The departures from the purely conventional treatment of the occupations of the month take one of two forms in the Bodleian and other manuscripts. In some manuscripts the illuminator has pictured an occupation that is different from the normal. In others, and these are more numerous, the artist has accepted the conventional activity of the month and has then proceeded to exercise his imagination in the treatment of the scene. While he has pictured a man as mowing in June or as reaping in July, he has so treated the background as to make his miniature a distinctive and individual-istic piece of work.

One manuscript in the Bodleian, Gough Liturg. 7, shows a rather unusual amount of divergence from convention. It is an English book of private prayers of about A.D. 1500 and its illuminator was a well-trained artist. He begins with the conven-tional feasting in January, though the scene is elaborately staged. The February picture shows three men trimming trees and a woman tying faggots. In March a lady directs the setting up of stands for what appear to be flowers—a most uncommon occupa-tion. April shows a usual scene, love-making in a garden. The May picture is missing. In June, instead of mowing, men are pictured moving hay into a fine barn. July has a rather elaborate reaping scene. The August occupation is bringing in grain rather than threshing. The September picture is normal, for a man with bare legs treads grapes in a vat. October is devoted to ploughing with a curious type of plough; in the background is a field enclosed by wattle-work hurdles and to the right a man is sowing. The November scene is also elaborate, for there is a man pulling an ox and in the background a herd of cattle being driven; it would seem that we have here a representation of a cattle market. December presents a most uncommon activity, for people are engaged in selling what appear to be food-stuffs; there is a realistic butcher's shop. So much for what is the finest set of pictures of the occupations of the months in the Bodleian. It may be added here that the earliest and one of the most unique of the Psalters in the Library which has occupational pictures, New College 322, is, like the manuscript already described, English in origin.

Other calendars show occasional departures from the conven-tional. Douce 38, a thirteenth-century Psalter, is a small book with small pictures in its calendar and most of these pictures embody the traditions. In February, however, a woman holding a candle stands before an altar. The picture for June shows a man with a bundle of wood on his back. The November scene is quite unusual in one respect, for though killing a beast is pictured, the latter is not the conventional pig but a calf, or member of the same family, with small horns. Douce 5, another small Psalter, though of the first part of the fourteenth century, is attractive because of the many curious grotesques that are found in its margins. Its calendar, which contains two pictures for each month, shows a few variations from the normal. In January, though a man warms himself before a fire in the usual fashion in one picture, the other depicts a man roasting some sort of animal over an open fire while a vessel catches the drippings. In February there is a man in a small boat who appears to be merely loafing, though he may be a fisherman, while in a second picture we have a service in a church. August shows us a man shooting a deer. Much later than either of these manuscripts, Douce 8, a fifteenth-century Flemish book of prayers, shows the effect of the development of skill in painting. It, like Douce 5, has two pictures of occupations for each month. In most cases these simply portray different phases of the same activity, but in a few instances something new is introduced. In January, for example, while one picture shows the normal warming scene, the other shows a man walking about in the open. The first February picture presents a man digging and his companion drinking from a jug, while in the second another man digs while his fellow mends a hurdle-fence. In March, alongside of the usual pruning scene, a man is pictured tying bundles of faggots. There are other minor variations of the same kind as the latter. Douce 62 is a French Book of Hours of the early fifteenth century with small pictures of the occupations of the month at the bottom of the pages of its calendar. Only two of these are at all unusual. The February scene is of a man fishing, a fish interested in the bait, and a basket for the catch.[5] In March a man is shown in the open blowing two horns at the same time, with an inattentive sheep near at hand. Douce 276, a French Book of Hours of the second half of the fifteenth century, has a profusely decorated calendar. Its occupational pictures are small. Its April occupation is quite unusual, for a man with a long bow is shown shooting at a brown bird on a tree-stump. The June scene, a man with a lamb across his shoulders, is not so uncommon. The latter occupation is also pictured for June in Canon. Liturg. 283, an otherwise conventionalized manuscript in its portrayal of the season's occupations; it has, however, a number of interesting grotesque small boys scattered through its pages. The very simple and rather crudely colored small miniatures in the calendar of Douce 152, a Book of

Hours of the fifteenth century, reduce the portrayal of the occupations of the month to the barest terms. A single figure mows, reaps, or carries a cask of wine. In February, on the other hand, a woman holds a shield. Douce 135, a sophisticated and highly decorated Book of Hours of the first half of the sixteenth century with many interesting illuminations, yields a rather vigorous snow-ball fight in December.

Thus far we have been dealing with variations from the conventional treatment of the occupations of the month. Some of these have been found to be striking, others of no great interest, but the fact that mediaeval artists could depart from the traditional path is obvious. Other illuminators, of equal ability as artists, expressed their individuality in a different way. They accepted the traditions and then sought self-expression in the setting and other details of their pictures. While it is not possible in a brief paper to go into this subject at any length, a few of the more striking treatments may be mentioned. In this connection the simple handling found in a very interesting manuscript now housed in the Bodleian will be given the first place.

The small medallions that are found in the calendar of the thirteenth-century English Psalter, New College 322, are excellent examples of an extremely simple treatment of the occupations of the months. The only background is gold-leaf, the months' work is performed by one man, and the themes are largely conventional. In January a bearded three-faced man feasts. In February a bearded man warms himself. March shows a bearded man digging in a vineyard. In April a king sits on a cushioned bench with branches of foliage in each hand and in May a king on a white horse goes hawking. The unconventional elements are the bearded three faces of January, the beards of February and March, and the kings of the next two months. Precedents may in all probability be found for each of these details—I have found some—but I have not as yet seen all combined in any other manuscript. Douce 24 and Douce 48 have Janus-faced—two-faced—men in January, but they are not bearded.

The gifted illuminator who painted the pictures in the calendar of Canon. Liturg. 99, a fifteenth-century French Book of Hours, accepted the traditional occupations and devoted his attention to the details of his stories. There are some carefully and minutely painted landscape backgrounds and several fine domestic interiors in his pictures, as well as other interesting details. The tables on trestles in January and February are typically mediaeval. There is a castle in the May background. The threshing scene in August is unusually detailed, and the baking scene in December is elaborately developed. In the latter there is a table with loaves upon it, a baker and his helper placing a loaf in an oven, and a well-drawn oven.

The illuminators who illustrated the calendars of Gough 7 and Douce 8, both already described in part, accepted some conventions and introduced some novelties; the latter have received sufficient attention. Their settings of even conventional scenes are full of interest. The first manuscript contains unusually large and fine pictures. January gives us an elaborate domestic interior, March a good castle in the distance, June an interesting barn and the method used to lift bundles of hay into the upper part of the barn, October a realistic ploughing scene, and December a market. The second manuscript, as already noted, has two pictures for each month. These illustrate many phases of mediaeval life. In February a man mends a fence. In June one picture shows hay being raked and taken away in bundles on a barrow. There is a moated castle in the April background and a good boat in a second picture.

It is possible to gain from the various Bodleian manuscripts, even the most conventional, a concrete idea of the shapes of hoes, spades, pruning-hooks, scythes, sickles, ploughs, harrows, carts and waggons. Any one interested will, for example, find a number of variations in the kinds of pruning-hooks that were used. Other pictures give other details. The January miniatures show how a table might be set, as well as the varieties of tables. In the February illuminations are many hooded fire-places, some elaborately decorated, and some constructed simply. Vats in which grapes were pressed under foot, wine casks, and wine cellars are found in September or October. Wooden fences of several varieties and stone walls are pictured in different months. The clothing of the rich is shown everywhere, as well as the artist's idea of the proper dress, in a fine picture, for a peasant. Trees, flowers, domestic animals, and an occasional bird find their place in foreground or background. From the many illuminations in the Psalters and Books of Hours it is also possible to learn something about the methods of mowing, reaping, threshing, sowing, and making wine.

The Bodleian manuscripts containing pictures of seasonal activities in their calendars are not numerous, but they are representative of the different ways of treating more or less trite subjects. They, and others of their kind in other libraries, deserve far more attention than has been devoted to them by scholars interested in mediaeval social and economic life. As long, however, as those who catalogue mediaeval manuscripts dismiss calendar pictures with the barest of descriptive notes it will be difficult to discover which are the most worthy of such attention.

NOTES

(1) Brief descriptions of both classes of manuscripts may be found in J. A. Herbert, *Illuminated Manuscripts,* pp. 324 ff., and in Wordsworth and Littlehalls, *The Old Service Books of the English Church,* see index. For Books of Hours, see V. Leroquais, *Les Livres d'Heures;* M. R. James, *A Descriptive Catalogue of the Manuscripts in the Fitzwilliam Museum,* pp. xxiii ff.; E. Hoskins, *Horae Beatae Mariae Virginis;* S. S. Cockerell, in Sir George Warner, *Descriptive Catalogue of Illuminated Manuscripts in the Library of C. W. Dyson Perrins,* pp. 11 ff.

(2) Herbert, *Illuminated Manuscripts,* p. 327.

(3) Douce 71 is a crudely executed calendar of the fifteenth century.

(4) C. Headlam, *The Story of Chartres,* p. 131, prints the following quatrain which, as he states, is "attributed to the Venerable Bede," though it is probably of much later date:

> Poto—ligna cremo—de vite superflua demo;
> Do gramen gratum—mihi flos servit—mihi pratum;
> Fenum declino—messes meto—vina propino;
> Semen humi jacto—pasco sues—immolo porcos.

(5) The scene probably has its origin in the sign of the Zodiac, Pisces, for the month of February and not in any attempt to picture the current occupation of the month. Men fishing in February are found in the sculptured descriptions of the occupations of the month on the façade of the cathedral at Lucca and about the door of the baptistry at Pisa. Compare B. M. Harl. 2936, a French Book of Hours of the fifteenth century.

EYES OF IMAGINATION AND FAITH: EXPERIENCE, METAPHOR, AND THE IMAGE OF MATTHEW'S "EVERLASTING FIRE"
Glenn Harcourt

In Memoriam, L. D. Ettlinger

> The sum of what is said is, that believers, in order to encourage themselves to a holy and upright conduct, ought to contemplate with the eyes of faith the heavenly life, which, though it is now concealed, will at length be manifested in the last coming of Christ.—John Calvin, Commentary on Matthew 25:31[1]

Within Catholic visual culture as it developed through the Middle Ages and into the Renaissance, the most resilient image of Christian learning (and of its indissoluble link to individual devotional practice) was certainly that of St. Jerome: Doctor of the Church, scholar, and exegete, translator of the Vulgate Bible, and enthusiastic champion of the monastic life.[2]

By the early sixteenth-century, a complex, culturally resonant picture of Hieronymite learning and devotion had been articulated and refined by Catholic artists, both in Italy and in Northern Europe.[3] Pictured within the alien and forbidding world of patristic eremitism, as well as the much more familiar ambit of the contemporary monastic cell, Jerome carried on his work as a translator and commentator, his meditation on death and judgment, as well as the practice of his penitential rigor.[4]

Nor did the saint's importance as an intellectual icon diminish

Reprinted by permission of the author and publisher from *Coranto;* Journal of the Friends of the USC Libraries, University of Southern California, Los Angeles. No. 25, 1990, pp. 34–42.

immediately with the onset of the Reformation. Indeed, Protestants and Catholics alike appropriated Jerome's person and image, at once as a pious exemplar and as a means of asserting the existence of an historical and doctrinal continuity between the world of the sixteenth century and that of the early Church.[5]

Nevertheless, the continuing progress of reform did eventually have a corrosive and finally deconstructive effect, at least on the finely nuanced iconography of the image. In the guardedly Calvinist art of seventeenth-century Holland, for example, the represented synthesis of Jerome's scholarly achievements and his immediate, experiential knowledge of the facts of death, judgment, and salvation (all seen as coordinate aspects of a unified life of the spirit grounded in monastic experience) collapsed under its own ideological weight.[6]

Instrumental in that collapse was an important change in ideas about how a believer's knowledge of eschatological events (the so-called Four Last Things: death, judgment, salvation, and damnation made immediate and concrete as a vision of heaven and hell) could in fact be constituted. This is at once a change that can be defined theologically, for example in the writing of Calvin himself, and one whose effects we can observe concretely, for example in a trenchant and coruscating study of a *Meditating Hermit* (Fig. 1) by Rembrandt's brilliant pupil Gerard Dou, a work which, I will argue, defines quite clearly the limits of the *eschaton* that can in fact be seen "with the eyes of [Calvinist] faith."[7]

As characteristic of the artistic tradition and theological *status quo ante* against which the deconstructive critique implicit in Dou's *Hermit* must be defined, we turn to an early sixteenth-century work: a haunting image of *St. Jerome in his Study* (Fig. 2), dated by the rather eccentric Netherlander Marinus van Reymerswaele in 1521.[8] In Marinus's work, we see the gaunt, cadaverous figure of the saint in half-length, seated before a narrow desk set beneath a shelf in a cramped and cluttered cell or study. The objects displayed suggest both scholarly and devotional exertion, although Jerome in fact turns away from all of them to engage the viewer directly, both with a tired, almost furtive glance and with a languid and ostentatiously rhetorical gesture.

That very gesture invites our attention to the first of a series of objects (the skull that lies on the table before him) which are intended to structure our own devotional experience, as well as

[Figure 1] Gerard Dou, *The Hermit*, National Gallery of Art, Washington, D.C., Timken Collection, 1670

[Figure 2] Marinus van Reymerswaele, *St. Jerome in his Study*, Museo del Prado, Madrid, 1521

our experience of the picture, in a controlled and very carefully circumscribed way. In briefest outline, the path of our visual attention across the surface of the image (a movement up and to the left from the linchpin of the skull framed by the bony hands of the saint himself) maps out for us the stages of a devotional ascent, each stage fixed by means of a discrete image.

The skull, of course, testifies both to the simple *fact* of human mortality and (at least implicitly) to the root of that fact in Man's original sin and Fall from Grace: it is at once "our" skull and the skull of Adam. The historical drama of redemption necessitated by that Fall is objectified in the image of Christ on the cross; and the ultimate outcome of that drama is given in the illumination that identifies the illegible text opposite as that of Matt. 25, even as it figures Christ enthroned at the Last Judgment enacting the final and irrevocable separation of all mankind. In fact, however, the actual path of our visual attention passes first from Fall to Judgment, and then to the promise of salvation embodied in the sacrifice of Christ; and it is just this sequence (Fall–Judgment–Salvation) that structures a typical late medieval or Counter-Reformation devotion or meditation on that subject, for example that given in the *Spiritual Exercises* of St. Ignatius Loyola.

In Dou's *Hermit,* by way of contrast, there is no such overt attempt to structure the course of our visual or devotional experience; nor any address by the represented figure, who appears rather absorbed in the course of his own devotion.

Here, as if in a kind of "history," we are shown an elderly anchorite kneeling full-length before a rough stone table or altar covered by a ragged Turkish carpet.[9] He is dressed in a roughly woven brown habit cinched by a cord that carries a set of eleven rosary beads terminated by a miniature skull and cross. His feet are bare in imitation of the Apostles, and his clasped hands rest on an open book. His eyes stare up at the figure of Christ on the cross, while his mouth is just open, as if in the recitation of a prayer.

The identity of the book from whose text the hermit has turned his attention is not absolutely certain. Its size, the configuration of the text, and the presence of an illustration perhaps suggest a Bible; unfortunately, both text and image are illegible, while the monogram GDou has replaced the heading at the top of the right-hand page.

In addition to the book, the table supports a carved wooden crucifix propped up against a tall wicker pilgrim's basket, and a human skull that wedges the crucifix against it. Just to the right of the skull is an hourglass. The basket itself is pushed hard against the trunk of what appears to be a pollard willow, from which hangs an open and unlit lantern. The skull, which again stands as a physical index of the fundamental fact of death, is once more accorded a place of prominence. Likewise the saving act of sacrifice, which again finds form as the carved image of Christ on the cross.

Conspicuous by its absence, however, is the central visual term of Marinus's devotional sequence: the image of judgment and separation, of ascent into heaven and descent into hell that makes visible for us the text of Matt. 25. Instead, in its place there is only the great open tome with its juxtaposition of illegible text and unreadable image.

Indeed, I would argue that this lack of a readable image at the devotional heart of Dou's work corresponds to an important change in the epistemological structure of individual religious experience. It is a change that grows out of the Reformation. And, as we have suggested above, it is marked by an essential reevaluation of the relationship between image, experience, and a knowledge of God, as we can demonstrate with reference to two key texts.

The first is taken from perhaps the premier work of Counter-Reformation devotion, the *Spiritual Exercises* of St. Ignatius Loyola. It can stand as a kind of verbal pendant to Marinus van Reymerswaele's late medieval *St. Jerome*. And it can materially enrich our feeling for the vividly "experiential" quality of the devotional meditation that can be grounded in images like those presented by Marinus, here specifically an image of the Last Judgment and one aspect of its final outcome:

> The Fifth Exercise is a meditation on hell: it contains, after the preparatory prayer and two preludes, five points [not surprisingly, one for each of the five senses] and one colloquy.
> Let the preparatory prayer be the usual one.
> The first prelude is a composition of place, which is here to see with the eyes of the imagination the length, breadth and depth of hell.
> The second, to ask for that which I desire. It will be here to ask for an interior sense of the pain which the lost suffer
> . . . .
> The first point will be to see with the eyes of the imagination those great fires, and the souls as it were in bodies of fire.
> The second, to hear with the ears the wailings, the groans, the cries, the blasphemies against Christ our Lord, and against all his saints.
> The third, to smell with the sense of smell the smoke, the brimstone, the filth, and the corruption.
> The fourth, to taste with the sense of taste bitter things, such as tears, sadness, and the worm of conscience.
> The fifth, to feel with the sense of touch how those fires touch and burn the souls.[10]

Against this incredibly immediate evocation of the quite physical and sensual torments that await those damned souls enclosed "as it were in bodies of fire," can be juxtaposed another passage from Calvin's commentary on Matt. 25. Although not itself a devotional work, this text makes quite plain the parameters within which a Calvinist meditation on Matthew's image can be developed, and indeed sketches out the structure that such a meditation can easily assume within a Calvinist *milieu.* Calvin here comments on v. 41, Christ's final dismissal of the gathered company of the unrighteous:

> Then he will say also to those who shall be on the left hand, Depart from me you cursed, into everlasting fire, which is prepared for the devil and all his angels.
>
> We are therefore taught how desirable it is to be united to the Son of God; because everlasting destruction and the torment of the flesh await all those he will drive from his presence at the Last Day. He will then order the wicked to *depart* from him . . . [*into everlasting fire*].
>
> We have stated formerly, that the term *fire* represents metaphorically that dreadful punishment which our senses are unable to comprehend. It is therefore unnecessary to enter into subtle inquiries as the sophists do, into the materials or form of this *fire;* for there would be equally good reason to inquire about the *worm,* which Isaiah connects with the *fire; For their worm shall not die, neither shall their fire be quenched.* (Is. lxvi, 34) Besides, the same prophet shows plainly enough in another passage that the expression is metaphorical; for he compares *the Spirit of God* to a blast by which the *fire* is kindled and adds a mixture of *brimstone.* (Is. xxx, 33) Under these words, therefore, we ought to represent to our minds the future vengeance of God against the wicked, *which,* being more grievous than all earthly torments, *ought rather to excite horror than a desire to know it.*[11] [Final emphasis mine.]

For Calvin, then, the torment of hell is not something that can be immediately experienced as an image or vision made manifest and palpable to the other senses through an act of imagination. It is rather a "dreadful punishment which our senses are unable to comprehend," accommodated by God to our understanding, for example, through the metaphor of fire.

Our comprehension of that metaphor (itself an essentially literary configuration, something represented "under these words") does not proceed experientially, but rather discursively, as here through a careful recombination of texts. We understand what hell is like, in so far as we *can* understand it, not through an attempt to visualize and experience it immediately, but rather by means of a series of literary mediations, that take the form of a juxtaposition of texts from Matthew and Isaiah. And I would argue that this is precisely the way Dou's hermit understands it. He indeed sees "with the eyes of faith" both the fact of death and the fact of Christ's sacrifice that seals his own salvation. But as to the events that lead up to his reception into that "heavenly life" that awaits him, he can see no real thing. Rather, there is for him only a text which describes in figure and metaphor the final act of judgment on which the entire drama hinges.

In sum, Dou's *Hermit* presents a quasi-historical image of eremitic devotional practice grounded, despite its ostensibly "Catholic" subject, in an essentially Protestant religious ideology. Fundamentally literary and discursive, that ideology denies the efficacy of sight as an aid in the imaginative constitution of immediate, sensual religious experience, and recasts that experience (at least here with respect to the outcome of Judgment) in figurative and metaphorical terms.

In effect, this denial dissolves the prescriptive, rhetorical connection between Marinus's *Jerome* and its intended audience, and at the same time deconstructs the whole complex system of individual devotional exercise articulated alike by Marinus and Jerome, at the heart of which is embedded a still-powerful image of the Last Judgment. Not yet perceived in terms of figure or metaphor, such an image provided the occasion both for seeing and for visualization, the operation of that Ignatian "interior sense" through which "the length, breadth and depth of hell" could be apprehended, if only with "the eyes of the imagination," and its quite physical torment grasped by the Catholic believer as an immediate, palpable experience.

NOTES

(1) John Calvin (trans. Rev. William Pringle), *Commentary on a Harmony of the Evangelists,* vol. 3, in *Works* 33 (Edinburgh, 1846), p. 174.

(2) For an overall survey, see Eugene F. Rice, Jr., *Saint Jerome in the Renaissance* (Baltimore, 1985).

(3) For an Italian supplement to the material presented by Rice, see Bernhard Ridderbos, *Saint and Symbol Images of Saint Jerome in Early Italian Art* (Groningen, 1984), especially chapters two and three.

(4) Compare, for example, Albrecht Dürer's celebrated engraving of 1514 (reproduced in Rice, p. 110) and the militantly penitent *St. Jerome in the Wilderness* signed and dated by the Antwerper Jan van Hemessen in 1541. For Hemessen's *Jerome* (now in the Museu Nacional de Arte Antiga, Lisbon), see Max J. Friedländer, *Early Netherlandish Painting,* (Leyden/Brussels, 1975), vol. 12, pl. 115, no. 215A (there reproduced in reverse). On the relationship between Jerome's scholarship and his penitential exercise, see also Millard Meiss, "Scholarship and Penitence in the Early Renaissance: The Image of St. Jerome," *Pantheon,* vol. 32 (1974), pp. 134–40, reprinted in *idem. The Painter's Choice: Problems in the Interpretation of Renaissance Art* (New York, 1976), pp. 189–202.

(5) To take but one example, both Martin Luther and his eventual clerical opponent Albrecht of Brandenburg, the Cardinal Archbishop and Elector of Mainz, were portrayed as scholarly Jeromes, Luther in a patent plagiarism of Dürer's famous *Jerome in his Study,* Albrecht (in several versions) by Lucas Cranach the Elder. See Martin Warnke, *Cranachs Luther Entwürfe für ein Image* (Frankfurt am Main, 1984), p. 58, pl. 37; p. 59, pl. 38.

(6) For a more comprehensive discussion, see Glenn Harcourt, *The Representation of Religious Knowledge in the Work of Rembrandt and His Pupil Gerard Dou* (Ph.D. dissertation, University of California, Berkeley, 1990.) The general argument presented here has been developed previously in lectures delivered at Southern Methodist University (November 1987), the University of Toronto (February 1988), and at the 1988 annual meeting of the Midwest Art History Society.

(7) The National Gallery panel (signed and dated 1670) is one of a series of similar works executed by Dou at intervals throughout his career, beginning c. 1635. At least in general, Dou's treatment derives from a type of the meditating Jerome developed initially within the ambit of Rembrandt's Leiden *atelier* (probably c. 1629–30). Compare the etchings B 106 (c. 1629–Rembrandt's earliest and most immediately powerful treatment of the theme), and especially B 101 (dated 1632) for an idea of the conception appropriated and adapted by Rembrandt's talented pupil.

(8) Now in Madrid, Museo del Prado. See Friedländer, *Early Netherlandish Painting,* vol. 12, pl. 92, nr. 162.

(9) On the one hand, Dou quite scrupulously excludes the apocryphal and legendary attributes (notably the lion and the cardinal's hat) almost universally associated with the figure of Jerome himself. On the other, his painstaking and minutely detailed description of primitive monastic

practice corresponds quite closely to the accounts given by a nascent Protestant historiography, for example that found in the so-called "Magdeburg Centuries," the monumental *Ecclesiastica historia* (1559–74) of Matthias Flacius Illyricus *et al.*

(10) W. H. Longridge (ed.), *The Spiritual Exercises of Saint Ignatius of Loyola* (London, 5th ed. 1955), pp. 66–67.

(11) Calvin, *op. cit.,* p. 182.

THE ILLUSTRATED BOOK: AN ADDENDUM
TO THE STATE OF RESEARCH IN NORTHERN
EUROPEAN ART
Sandra Hindman

Although Panofsky is concerned chiefly with panel painting in
Early Netherlandish Painting, which became a kind of catechism
for several generations of students, its influence on the study of
book illustration in Northern Europe during the Renaissance era
has been considerable. My purpose here is twofold: to reexamine
some of Panofsky's biases in order to understand the effect of
historiography upon methodology in the study of book illustration
since Panofsky's groundbreaking work; and to examine a series of
current scholarly issues, in part based on recent research, that are
relevant to the outlining of some desiderata for future research.

At the same time that Panofsky established Flemish art as a
legitimate field of study with the publication of his ambitious
book, he carved out a specific place for the scholarly investigation
of book illustration. When he incorporates manuscripts at three
different moments in his historical chronology, he uses them to
make three points. He opens his book with a chapter on "Book
Illumination," in order to seek the antecedents to the great
Flemings, who, lacking local prototypes in panel painting, must
have turned to the "sister art" of manuscript illumination (p. 27).
Because the manuscript illuminators he considers are most notable for their assimilation of Italian art of the trecento, Panofsky
traces the roots of Netherlandish painting through them to Central
Italy. Later, he devotes a chapter to the Turin-Milan Hours in
order to point out that the miniatures in this celebrated manuscript
must reflect Jan van Eyck's early works, because, he claims,

Reprinted from the *Art Bulletin,* vol. 68, no. 4 (December 1986), pp. 536–542, by
permission of the College Art Association, Inc.

manuscript illumination throughout Europe had lost its impetus
by the 1430's, the decade of Jan's signed and dated works (p.
242). Whenever Panofsky refers, however fleetingly, to manuscript illumination after the 1430's, it is to make his well-known
remark that manuscript illumination, practiced in the shadow of
panel painting, which it came to imitate, would have died—even
without Gutenberg—from an overdose of perspective (p. 28). For
Panofsky, the fate of book illustration, which is characterized in
value-laden language, is thus inextricably linked not only to the
development of panel painting but also to the ongoing conquest of
volume and space by painters in both media. Subsequent scholarship has often reinforced, sometimes in subtle ways, Panofsky's
perception of book illustration as a "minor" art form.[1]

The persistence of this attitude toward book illustration since
Panofsky results partly from the particular way in which art
history is subdivided into specialties in the American university
system. As a field of specialization, "Northern Renaissance Art"
usually takes its intellectual cues from "Italian Renaissance Art,"
which has an older historiography, which imparts not only a
greater legitimacy, but a greater prominence. Since the two fields
are often taught by one individual, some mutual interaction is
inevitable, and there has been a tendency to fashion the study and
teaching of Northern Renaissance art after that of Italian Renaissance art, which remains dominated by a study of "major" art
forms. (For the Italian quattrocento, think of the infrequency of
courses on manuscript illumination or on printmakers other than
those who are celebrated painters, such as Mantegna or Pol-
laiuolo.) It is worth underscoring here the peculiar nature of
art-historical subspecialties by recalling that there is no comparable division within the allied discipline of history. Within the
structure of the university, history has established traditional
breaks in the study of Northern Europe between the medieval
period, that is, before ca. 1500, and the "Early Modern" period,
that is, after ca. 1500, and retained the Italian Renaissance as a
separate field of study. Instead of respecting the traditional break
around 1500, some historians, writing under the banner of the
Annales school, have begun to see a continuum of social organization and cultural mentalities from Europe of the thirteenth century
to Europe around the time of the French Revolution. There is no
basis in either of these schema for distinguishing Northern

Renaissance as a field of specialization in its own right. The different periodization in art history is, then, some measure of the impact of *Early Netherlandish Painting* on the American university.

Of further relevance to an understanding of the institutional study of book illustration during the Northern Renaissance period is its focus on particular countries. Just as a preselected canon of works most deserving of study has become fixed, so a canon of countries—or rather of geographic areas—has become established in large part, I would argue, due to the influence of Panofsky, whose contribution followed not only those of the Belgian and German scholars, Georges Hulin de Loo and Friedrich Winkler for the Flemish world of manuscript illumination, but also those of the French scholars, P. Durrieu and L. Delisle, and the Dutch scholars, A. W. Byvanck and G. J. Hoogewerff.[2] Before Panofsky the historiography of the field had not focused so closely on Flanders. Probably because after the 1950's no equivalent to *Early Netherlandish Painting* addressed in such an erudite way the arts of France or of the North Netherlands, or, for that matter, England and Bohemia, these regions have come to be regarded as being on the periphery of the geographic canon. The exception is France around 1400, which Panofsky included in his book and which Meiss later took up with much the same valuation.[3]

This narrow focus on the art of Flanders cannot be historically justified, since the thirteenth through the sixteenth centuries saw the emergence of national states with geographic boundaries and linguistic identities that led to greater national cultural homogeneity. Flanders was still part of France. Even while the French dukes of Flemish Burgundy spent a large part of their time fighting the French with sword and armor on the battlefield, their writers and artists emulated the French with pen and paint pot in the field of *belles lettres*. At the very least, then, Panofsky's decision to ignore the study of book illustration (or the other arts) in France led to a historical injustice to the art of Flanders. Yet France is not the only area slighted by Panofsky. The northern Netherlands is ignored in large measure because of the entirely different, more modest patronage that was common in the North; and other areas, such as Bohemia and England, are likewise slighted, although to a certain extent these omissions have been redressed by subsequent studies.[4]

One of the most forceful critiques of Panofsky regarding book illustration is by L. M. J. Delaissé, who, in a prophetic review of *Early Netherlandish Painting* that anticipates modern criticism and numerous books and articles, proposes an alternative methodology for the study of the illustrated book.[5] Delaissé praises Panofsky for beginning his history of painting with a history of miniatures, a strategy that Delaissé believes (wrongly, I think) elevated manuscript painting from its usual status as a minor art. He also calls attention to one of Panofsky's greatest accomplishments, that he sought to present a synthesis of style and iconography for the work of art (instead of concentrating primarily on questions of attribution, as scholars before him had done). Nevertheless, Delaissé regrets that Panofsky's treatment of manuscript painting did not result from an "archaeological method." To appreciate this viewpoint requires an understanding of what the "archaeology of the book" means to Delaissé.

For him, the archaeological method entails "observing and analysing all the material data concerning objects of the past and in interpreting them afterwards in order to determine the time and place of their execution."[6] Such a method of analysis and interpretation allows the researcher to uncover evidence about the "life" of the medieval book in order to answer a series of questions: What craftsmen worked on the book? When and where? For whom was the book made? What input did the patron have on the making of the book? Who read the book, both at the time it was written and later? How was the book read, and was it perhaps read differently over time?

Viewed in this way, the illustrations of a book are most meaningful only when they are analyzed with the other textual, historical, and material data that emerge from investigating the total book within its context. Although Delaissé is often thought of as initiating the application of a codicological method for art-historical inquiries, he himself makes a sharp distinction between "archeology" and "codicology," which often is not sufficiently understood.[7] Codicology, which entails the observation and recording of those physical features of an individual book such as quality and arrangement of parchment, pricking, ruling, writing, decoration, illustration, and binding, does not evoke for Delaissé the same historical consequences as "the archaeology of the book." He takes codicology to be an auxiliary discipline rather than a method of historical inquiry. With special reference to *Early Netherlandish Painting,* Delaissé calls attention to some striking historical inaccuracies that result from Panofsky's unfamiliarity with the archaeological method; the most notable is Delaissé observation, based in part on an analysis of the structure of the manuscript, that Jean Bondol as painter for the king of France did not execute the best miniatures in the Bible in the Hague but only the dedication miniature, which is an inserted leaf and which he signed.[8] This leads Delaissé to criticize the "aristocratic approach" in scholarship, by which he means that scholars, including Panofsky, usually focus on works of deluxe quality that were individually created by named artists for patrons of the highest social order instead of on works of routine character that were collectively produced by anonymous craftsmen for the average consumer.[9]

In other words, properly employed, Delaissé's archaeological method yields evidence for the art of the illustrated book about the function of art in its society, that is, about the conditions of its production and of its use (those very issues that most concern Baxandall in *Limewood Sculptures*). It should be evident that many topics of study—such as the role of women as writers, illuminators, and readers and the relationship between text and image—are subsumed under the method of the archaeology of the book, when its implications are fully explored. The challenge to Panofsky posed by Delaissé is thus to take seriously the full historical context of the work of art and to seek "historical explanation" with regard to book illustration. If we are concerned with understanding the production and use of the illustrated book, then we should look, taking our cue from historians, at the social organizations and cultural mentalities that provide the conditions in which illustrated books were made and read.

Once we are aware of the artificiality of a "Northern Renaissance," with its arbitrarily imposed time limits determined partly by the impact of the Italian trecento, we are prompted to push inquiry into the illustrated book back in time. Two important social and cultural changes occur by the thirteenth century that directly link the illustrated book of the fourteenth and fifteenth centuries to the precedents of the earlier period. First, monastic centers of production were displaced by secular urban centers of production.[10] Second, there is a shift from an oral culture, in which the illustrated book functions as an artifact tied to performance, to a written culture, in which the illustrated book becomes an object of silent reading.[11] For the fifteenth and sixteenth centuries, the study of book illustration can be pursued apart from the study of panel painting. This outlook encourages investigation of the interaction between the illuminated manuscript and the early illustrated printed book. The social and cultural changes brought about by printing with regard to the making of illustrated books and the audience for them still merit study.[12] Such investigation would have to include other forms of the illustrated book, e.g., block-books and chiroxylographic books (manuscripts with woodcuts), as well as single-leaf woodcuts.

The study of the illustrated book will thus be more productive if it is freed from the temporal restrictions of a ''Northern Renaissance.'' In seeking to come to terms with the art of this period, we must become specialists both in what historians call the ''Late Middle Ages'' and the ''Early Modern'' period. At either end of the chronological spectrum, issues concerning the production and use of illustrated books are intertwined.

Produced in the thirteenth century, illuminated manuscripts of saints' lives offer an excellent methodological example of how production and use began to distinguish the period from its preceding era. Some of these manuscripts can be attributed to the last great monastic artist. Matthew Paris. who worked at the monastery of St. Albans and who may also have served as a translator of these Latin *vitae* into the vernacular.[13] But although Matthew Paris' life and works have been well documented (a consequence of our post-Renaissance preoccupation with artistic personalities), the ''archaeological method'' has not been used to analyze his works. There is some evidence that he ''devised'' the manuscripts, that is, composed a sort of maquette that remained at the monastery where it served as the model for the presentation copies.[14] The deluxe presentation copies appear to have been made for distribution outside the monastic community to noble ladies at the English court. A series of intriguing questions that bear directly on the production and use of these manuscripts remain unanswered: What exactly was the role of Matthew Paris in translating the texts into the vernacular and then in devising sets of illustrations? Why and how was this group of women readers targeted as the appropriate audience for such deluxe manuscripts, and what do the manuscripts themselves tell us about women as readers during this crucial century when the patterns of literacy were changing?[15] And, finally, what did these manuscripts, which contain lives of English male saints, such as Alban, Edward, Edmund, and Thomas à Becket, but which may take their literary forms from medieval romances instead of from earlier saints' lives, convey in word and image to their readers?[16]

A second example dating from the thirteenth century, the romance, ought to be studied with regard to its production and use.[17] Whereas saints' lives were made in the monastery, albeit for a lay audience, romances seem to have been products of secular workshops, made for use in a society in which the towns and the courts had a greater prominence. The romance was one of the most popular illustrated books of the later Middle Ages and retained its popularity into the Early Modern era. Further investigation of where, by whom, and for whom these illustrated manuscripts (and, later, the early printed books) were made might help answer some of the unresolved questions: Why are the earliest romances unillustrated? Is it because they fit into an essentially oral culture where the telling of tales took its visual form in performance instead of illustration? What caused romances to be illustrated? Once romances were illustrated, what sources provided the conventions of illustration, and what does this borrowing imply about the group responsible for production as well as the meaning of the pictures? How do the conventions of illustration in later romances deviate from the earlier set of conventions, and does this reflect changes in the social organization of the culture and the audience for the books? It has been suggested that the later medieval romance serves not so much as a document of a remote society in which courtly love was a reality but as an antidote to a misogynist society in which courtly love had no place.[18] As artifacts produced by and for a society increasingly attuned to a secular world, the illustrated texts of romances provide a means of recovering the secular life of the late Middle Ages, to which the religious panel paintings and sculptures do not provide ready access.

Many other groups of literary texts emerged in the thirteenth century and remind us that common types of illustrated books from the "Northern Renaissance" originated earlier. For example, historical chronicles and political allegories, which began to proliferate in the thirteenth century and continued through the sixteenth century, offer a means of studying national dynastic concerns and even partisan political disputes, both of which stimulated programs of illustration.[19] Such examples serve to underscore the need to rethink the issue of periodization and to reveal how, ideally, an application of the archaeological method could result in a greater understanding of the patterns of production and use in the later Middle Ages.

Of course, secular book illustration did not wholly supplant religious book illustration between the thirteenth and the sixteenth centuries, as the extraordinary popularity of the Book of Hours, sometimes called the "biggest best-seller of its age," indicates.[20] Delaissé recognizes that, because they existed in large numbers, having been turned out en masse in the fifteenth century, and because they often include local saints and personalized prayers, Books of Hours provide a nearly ideal means not only of localizing production but also of studying the interaction between teams of anonymous craftsmen, such as scribes, decorators, and illuminators.[21] He is not especially concerned, however, with how the readers used the Book of Hours. John Plummer has continued to study the Book of Hours for localization, systematically building up an impressive geography of centers of production throughout France, much as Delaissé does with other types of texts for Flanders.[22] Whereas Delaissé relies primarily, although not exclusively, on evidence gleaned from the book's material character, Plummer has profited from a study of its spiritual content, by observing and recording numerous deviations in the calendars and prayers.

Plummer has thus begun to tap one of the richest but least explored resources for the study of late medieval lay piety. Ultimately this sort of research should enable us not only to localize production with greater precision but also to understand how and why calendars and prayers were so different even in towns located so close to each other, e.g., the Norman towns of Bayeux, Coutances, and Avranches. Once we know more about the ever-variable texts of Books of Hours, we should be able to explain better how pictures in Books of Hours served as aids to devotion. Pioneering work here has been begun by Paul Saenger, who has collected and studied the rubrics in the Books of Hours that refer both to the pictures and to the prayers, in order to address the interrelated functions of word and image.[23]

A thoroughgoing study of fifteenth-century German and Netherlandish block-books would also contribute substantially to our knowledge of late medieval piety.[24] Once regarded as the precursor to printing with movable type, the block-book was much studied as a novel departure from the illuminated manuscript, a transitional form of illustration between the manuscript and the incunable (i.e., a book printed before 1500 in the "cradle" of printing). When, in the 1960's, Stevenson proved conclusively on the basis of an analysis of the watermarks that all the extant block-books postdate printing with movable type by at least twenty years, scholarly interest in block-books waned.[25] A smattering of circumstantial evidence suggests that these block-books were made in monasteries for the clergy, perhaps for parish priests, but almost nothing is known for certain about their production or their audience. Apart from Stevenson, however, no one has submitted the block-books to an "archaeological" investigation, which might still yield evidence about their making. Nor has anyone studied the relationship between their texts and images to understand how and by whom they were actually meant to be read. Just because the block-book no longer holds the position of the harbinger of printing, which stands on the threshold of the modern world, we should not consign it to oblivion. And what can be said of the forms of illustration most closely related to woodcuts in these books: the single-leaf, usually anonymous, woodcut? Too poor in quality to be of interest to many art historians, or, paradoxically, too rare to be given much visibility in museums, these prints remain largely unstudied.[26] Many such prints are found within the pages of the manuscript book, but are rarely consulted by specialists in the history of the print.

Similar overspecialization by media has influenced the study of early illustrated printed books of the fifteenth and sixteenth centuries. There exists a longstanding division between those who study book illustration in manuscripts—usually miniatures—and those who study book illustration in early printed books—usually woodcuts. Yet sufficient material evidence and archival documentation exist to call into question the separability of these categories. Among early printers studied by Sheila Edmunds, Johannes Bämler was certainly both a scribe and an illuminator before he became a printer in Augsburg, and Antoine Vérard appears to have been a scribe before he became a printer in Paris.[27] Other case studies indicate that printers came from other milieus, which must have affected their careers as printers. Examples include Lienardt Holle, who is documented as being a maker of woodcut playing cards before he became a printer in Ulm, where he issued two ambitious volumes before going bankrupt.[28] From a methodological point of view, the material evidence (the manuscripts and printed books themselves) and the archival documentation (guild regulations, tax records, business contracts) taken together should round out our understanding of how books were made (differently?) during the first century after printing. We might find that originally the manuscript responded to the printed book, and vice versa, each assimilating certain features that are more characteristic of the other medium. But ultimately the mechanized production of books was bound to change the very way in which books were conceived and read and in which human beings participated in this techno-cultural revolution.

The work of the miniaturist Johannes Bämler exemplifies another pitfall of overspecialization. In addition to illuminating Christian and secular manuscripts (and printed books), Bämler worked on Hebrew manuscripts, including luxury Haggadahs.[29] His case serves to remind us that we usually mean Christian piety when we speak of late medieval piety; however, there were religious minorities in Europe who were art-makers and consumers. Nonetheless, Jewish illuminated manuscripts of the later Middle Ages rarely appear in manuscript surveys because they are not considered part of "mainstream" art history.[30] To be sure, the difficulty of the language makes Jewish texts less readily accessible than Latin and vernacular texts, but the material is nevertheless important for it provides another example of collaboration in book production even across religious communities.

Even before adequate data can be found to produce a more balanced understanding of the production and use of the arts, it is surely worth reminding ourselves that panel painters and illuminators did not work in isolation. For example, when Hans Memling died in Bruges in 1494, manuscript illumination and printing were flourishing in the city. There in 1486, the illuminator Alexander

Bening joined the Guild of St. John, an association of book illuminators that was distinct from the Guild of St. Luke, to which panel painters belonged.[31] Until 1487, the industrious scribe-turned-printer Colard Mansion operated a press for illustrated books in Bruges.[32] In the same decade Alexander Bening's son, Simon, was born (1483): he was to become one of the most notable illuminators in sixteenth-century Bruges.[33] Simon Bening's last dated works are contemporary with Pieter Bruegel's "theatre of the world" paintings, and Bening's daughter, Levina, became well-established at the English court as a painter of miniatures (a medium in which Simon also tried his hand but which is rarely integrated into a study of "major" art).[34] Bruges is an unusually rich center for the study of how a particular urban setting affected the contemporaneous production and use of different art forms,[35] yet other centers offer parallel opportunities: Utrecht and Haarlem in the North Netherlands, for example, or Bourges and Lyons in France, or Mainz and Augsburg in Germany.

Emphasis here has been on the continuity of secular and religious written culture from the thirteenth through the fifteenth centuries, but as historians we are also interested in signaling change. For Panofsky, change came about with the perfection of panel painting, the *ars nova,* by the great Flemings, Robert Campin, Jan van Eyck, and Rogier van der Weyden. Change thus seems to have been connected primarily with a new medium and the mastery of a new style. But if we really are concerned with explaining the function of art in society, then I ask whether significant change cannot be discerned more clearly when patterns of production and use alter radically. For the illustrated book, patterns of production had changed dramatically in Paris by 1504, when a lawsuit brought by an author, André de la Vigne, against a printer-publisher, Michel Le Noir, was decided in favor of the author, to whom was awarded the right to control all aspects of the printing of his works, which were illustrated.[36] Perhaps as a result of this lawsuit, by 1509 the first "privilege" appears in a French painted work.[37] Patterns of used changed dramatically around the same time, for the author-illustrator-publisher of a printed book sought to identify a collective audience.

It is relevant to retain the French distinction between two sorts of patronage. *Mécenat* refers to the relationship between an individual buyer, who usually commissions the work, and the maker, who produces the work to order. By contrast, *clientèle* signifies the relationship between a group of buyers, who do not participate in determining the character of the work, and a maker, who seeks to address the interests of this group and who may, in so doing, even help to define taste.[38] Of course, the latter system is closer to the socio-economic realities of modern times. The distinction between a *mécenat* and a *clientèle* is not one that is restricted to the illustrated book, for it could be equally useful in discussing, say, painting in Bruges around 1500, when, as Jean Wilson has shown, panel paintings were apparently mass-produced to be sold to the clientele that gathered at the Bruges art fair.[39] It is difficult to know whether the situation in the early sixteenth century represents a rupture with the past, since it might be argued that manuscripts of certain types of texts were already turned out en masse in thirteenth-century Paris for students at the university.[40] But by the early sixteenth century, society at large, not merely a single social group within one institution, was affected by changed means of production and patterns of use of illustrated books.

It might be said that the study of the illustrated book, whether or not it includes manuscripts, block-books, chiroxylographic books, and printed books, remains overspecialized in looking at only one sort of artifact. Yet, if the illustrated book is studied as an artifact that sheds light on the artisans who made the book, on the one hand, and on the audience who used the book, on the other, then such research can have considerable relevance not only for those who study other media but also for those who work in other disciplines. The way readers perceived pictures in books is bound to be linked with how they read other forms of visual culture, such as panel paintings (as James Marrow's work on Passion iconography has shown[41]), posters, dress, theater, and other socio-cultural phenomena that historians seek to include in a "new" history of reading.[42] We should remember as well that different readers read the same book differently over time. Moreover, the way in which readers stored books, as itemized in the library catalogue of Francis I, whose books were housed in the Château at Blois,[43] reflects the architectural environment in which individuals organized their lives. Some books may not have been read (or viewed) at all; they might instead have served as talismans or charms.[44] In sum, the illustrated book is a sensitive artifact of the society that made and used it; therefore study of the illustrated book, both in manuscript and printed forms in Northern Europe from the thirteenth through the sixteenth centuries, can be especially revealing of a society that was in considerable flux.

For their critical readings of this essay, I am very grateful to Larry Silver, who invited it as a complement to his article, and to Susan Weininger and Keith Holz.

NOTES

(1) For example, see the catalogue of the otherwise excellent exhibition organized by The J. Paul Getty Museum, T. Kren, *Renaissance Painting in Manuscripts: Treasures from the British Library*. New York, 1983, and my review, "Renaissance Painting at the Morgan: Miniatures in Context?" *Art Journal*, XLIV, 1984, 169–73.

(2) For these classic works, see G. Hulin de Loo, *Heures de Milan*, Brussels and Paris, 1911; F. Winkler, *Die Flämische Buchmalerei des XV, und XVI. Jahrhunderts*, Leipzig, 1925; P. Durrieu, *Heures de Turin*, Paris, 1902; *idem, La miniature flamande aux temps de la cour de Bourgogne*, Brussels, 1921; L. Delisle, *Le cabinet des manuscrits de la Bibliothèque impériale*, 3 vols., Paris, 1868–81; *idem, Recherches sur la librairie de Charles V*, 2 vols., Paris, 1907; A. W. Byvanck, *La miniature dans les Pays-Bas septentrionaux*, Paris, 1937; and A. W. Byvanck and G. J. Hoogewerff, *La miniature hollandaise et les manuscrits illustrés du XIVe au XVIe siècle aux Pays-Bas septentrionaux*, 3 vols., The Hague, 1922–26.

(3) See M. Meiss, *French Painting in the Time of Jean de Berry; The Late Fourteenth Century and the Patronage of the Duke*, 2 vols., London, 1967, X, for his debt to Panofsky; *idem, French Painting in the Time of Jean de Berry: The Boucicaut Master*, London 1968; and *idem, French Painting in the Time of Jean de Berry: The Limbourgs and Their Contemporaries*, 2 vols., New York, 1974.

(4) For the North Netherlands, see L. M. J. Delaissé, *A Century of Dutch Manuscript Illumination (California Studies in the History of Art, VI)*, Berkeley/Los Angeles, 1968, and A. Chatelet, *Early Dutch Painting. Painting in the Northern Netherlands in the Fifteenth Century*, New York, 1981; for Bohemia, see J. Krasa, *Die Handschriften König Wenzels, IV*, Vienna, 1971; and for England, see a survey of fourteenth-century manuscript illumination by L. F. Sandler, *A Survey of Manuscripts Illuminated in the British Isles*, V, London/Oxford (in press), and a survey of fifteenth-century manuscript illumination by K. Scott, *A Survey of Manuscripts Illuminated in the British Isles*, VI, London/Oxford (forthcoming).

(5) For the review, see "Enluminure et peinture dans les Pays-Bas. A propos du livre de E. Panofsky, 'Early Netherlandish Painting,'" *Scriptorium*, XI, 1957, 109–18. For a list of Delaissé's collected publications, see G. Dogaer and E. König. "A Bibliography of L. M. J. Delaissé, and a Note on the Delaissé Papers Deposited in the Bodleian Library, Oxford," *Quaerendo*, VI, 1976, 352–59.

(6) See L. M. J. Delaissé, "Towards a History of the Medieval Book," *Divinitas*, II, 1967, 423–35 (also published in *Miscellanea André Combes*, II, Rome, 1967, 27–39); more accessibly reprinted in *Litterae Textuales. Codicologica 1: Théorie et principes*, ed. J. P. Gumbert, M. J. M. De Haan, and A. Gruijs, Leiden, 1976, 75–83.

(7) On the debate between codicology and archaeology, see A. Gruijs, "Codicology or the Archaeology of the Book? A False Dilemma," *Quaerendo*, II, 1972, 87–108; and A. Derolez, "Codicologie ou archéologie du livre? Quelques observations sur la leçon inaugurale de M. Albert Gruijs à l'Université Catholique de Nimègue," *Scriptorium*, XXVII, 1973, 47–49.

(8) Delaissé (as in n. 5), 110–11.

(9) Delaissé's most resounding critique of "aristocratic" scholarship is found in his review of Meiss, 1967 (as in n. 3), in *Art Bulletin*, LII, 1970, 206–12.

(10) In the absence of a thorough study that documents this shift, see, for monastic production, M.-C. Garland, "Manuscrits monastiques et scriptoria aux XIe et XIIe sièles," *Litterae Textuales. Codicologica 3: Essais typologiques*, ed. J. P. Gumbert, M. J. M. De Haan, and A. Gruijs, Leiden, 1980, 9–33; and for university production, see the fundamental work, J. Destrez, *La Pecia dans les manuscrits universitaires du XIIIe et du XIVe siècle*, Paris, 1935. For the impact of the university on the book trade in Paris, the classic work is still P. Delalain, *Étude sur le librairie parisien du XIIIe au XVe siècle d'après les documents publiés dans le cartulaire de l'Université de Paris*, Paris 1891.

(11) See S. Huot, *From Song to Book: The Poetics of Writing in the Old French Lyrico-Narrative Tradition*, Ithaca, NY (in press); and P. Saenger, "Silent Reading: Its Impact on Late Medieval Script and Society," *Viator*, XIII, 1982, 369–413.

(12) See C. F. Bühler, *The Fifteenth-Century Book: The Scribes, the Printers, the Decorators*, Philadelphia, 1960; S. Hindman and J. D. Farquhar, *Pen to Press: Illustrated Manuscripts and Printed Books in the First Century of Printing*, College Park, 1977; and the essays in *Manuscripts in the Fifty Years After the Invention of Printing: Some Papers Read at a Colloquium at the Warburg Institute on 12–13 March 1982*, ed. J. B. Trapp, London, 1983.

(13) Awaiting Suzanne Lewis' study, *The Art of Matthew Paris in the "Chronica Majora"* *(California Studies in the History of Art),* Berkeley/Los Angeles (in press), see the study on Matthew Paris by R. Vaughan, *Matthew Paris,* Cambridge, 1958, and the summary treatment by N. Morgan, *Early Gothic Manuscripts,* I, *1190–1250 (A Survey of Manuscripts Illuminated in the British Isles,* IV), London and Oxford, 1982, 21–22. Also see the earlier study by M. R. James, "The Drawings of Matthew Paris," *The Walpole Society,* XIV, 1925–26, 1–26.

(14) Suggested by Vaughan (as in n. 13), 171, 173; also see the summary of research on these manuscripts by C. de Hamel on the occasion of the sale of a newly found fragment of the life of Saint Thomas à Becket in London, Sotheby's, *Western Manuscripts and Miniatures,* July 24, 1986, lot 40, (ill.).

(15) On late medieval literacy, see esp. M. Parkes, "The Literacy of the Laity," in *Literature and Western Civilization,* ed. D. Daiches and A. K. Thorlby *(The Medieval World,* II), London, 1973, 555–77; on the period just before the thirteenth century, see B. Stock. *The Implications of Literacy: Written Language and Models of Interpretation in the Eleventh and Twelfth Centuries,* Princeton, 1981; and for some of the art-historical implications, see M. Camille, "Seeing and Reading; Some Visual Implications of Medieval Literacy and Illiteracy," *Art History,* VIII, 1985, 26–49. On women as readers during this period, see the article by S. G. Bell, "Medieval Women Book Owners: Arbiters of Lay Piety and Ambassadors of Culture," *Signs: The Journal of Women in Culture and Society,* VII, 1982, 741–68.

(16) On earlier saints' lives, see C. Hahn, "Liturgy and Narrative in the Earliest Illustrated Lives of the Saints: Hanover, Niedersächsische Landesbibliothek, MS 180," Ph.D. diss., The Johns Hopkins University, 1982; and B. Abou-El-Haj, "Bury St. Edmunds Abbey Between 1070 and 1124: A History of Property, Privilege and Monastic Art Production," *Art History,* VI, 1983, 1–29.

(17) On illustrated romances, see M. A. Stones, "Secular Manuscript Illumination in France," *Medieval Manuscripts and Textual Criticism (North Carolina Studies in the Romance Languages and Literature: Texts, Textual Studies, and Translations,* IV), Chapel Hill, 1976, 83–102; and on illustrated manuscripts of the troubadour poems, see A. Rieger, "'Ins e.l cor port, dona, vostra faisso,' Image et imaginaire de la femme à travers l'enluminure dans les chansonniers de troubadours," *Cahiers de civilisation médiévale,* XXVIII, 1985, 385–415.

(18) On women as readers of romance, see E. J. Burns and R. Krueger, "Introduction," *Romance Notes,* XXV, 1985, 205–19 (special volume on "Courtly Ideology and Woman's Place in Medieval French

Literature'' with extensive bibliography), and R. Krueger, "Love, Honor, and the Exchange of Women in *Yvain:* Some Remarks on the Female Reader," *Romance Notes,* XXV, 1985, 302–17.

(19) On historical chronicles, see A. D. Hedeman, "Valois Legitimacy: Editorial Changes in Charles V's *Grandes Chroniques de France,*" *Art Bulletin,* LXVI, 1984, 97–117, and *idem,* "Restructuring the Narrative: The Function of Ceremonial in Charles V's *Grandes Chroniques de France,*" *Studies in the History of Art,* XVI, 1985, 171–81. On political allegories, see S. Hindman, *Christine de Pizan's "Epistre Othéa": Painting and Politics at the Court of Charles VI,* Toronto, 1986. On the use of religious imagery for a political agenda, see H. Stahl, "Old Testament Illustration During the Reign of St. Louis: The Morgan Picture Book and the New Biblical Cycles," *Il Medio Oriente e l'Occidente nell'arte del XIII secolo,* Bologna, 1983, II, 79–93.

(20) See Janet Backhouse, *Books of Hours,* London, 1985, 1. In a general fashion, Books of Hours are also treated by R. G. Calkins, *Illuminated Books of the Middle Ages,* Ithaca, NY, 1982, 243–82, and J. Harthan, *Books of Hours,* London, 1977.

(21) L. M. J. Delaissé, "The Importance of Books of Hours for the History of the Medieval Book," *Gatherings in Honor of Dorothy E. Miner,* ed. U. McCracken, L. M. C. Randall, and R. Randall, Baltimore, 1974, 203–25.

(22) J. Plummer with G. Clark, *The Last Flowering. French Painting in Manuscripts 1420–1530,* Pierpont Morgan Library, New York, 1982. See pp. xii-xiii for a discussion of the tests for localization, as well as an announcement of a forthcoming volume entitled "Beyond Use," which is to contain this data. For Delaissé's efforts at localization, see Brussels, Bibliothèque Royale, *Le siècle d'or de la miniature flamande. Le mécenat de Philippe le Bon, 1445–1475,* Brussels, 1959. The importance of attribution for both scholars is considerable.

(23) P. Saenger, "Books of Hours and the Reading Habits of the Later Middle Ages," *Scittura e civitta,* IX, 1985 (in press).

(24) The standard works include: W. Schreiber, *Manuel de l'amateur de la gravure sur bois et sur metal au XVe siècle,* 11 vols., repr., 1969–76, esp. Vols. IX and X, which treat xylographic books; and for Paris, P.-A. Lemoisne, *Les xylographes du XIVe et du XVe siècle au Cabinet des Estampes de la Bibliothèque Nationale,* 2 vols., Paris, 1927–30; and H. Bouchot, *Les deux cents incunables xylographiques du Département des Estampes,* Paris, 1903.

(25) A. Stevenson, "The Quincentennial of Netherlandish Block Books," *British Museum Quarterly,* XXXI, 1965, 85–89.

(26) For 16th-century Germany, see M. Geisberg, *The German Single-Leaf Woodcut, 1500–1550,* ed. W. Strauss, New York, 1974; for

fifteenth-century Netherlands (mostly prints in books), M. J. Schretlen, *Dutch and Flemish Woodcuts of the Fifteenth Century,* London, 1925 (repr., New York, 1969); and for the fifteenth century, R. Field, *Fifteenth Century Woodcuts and Metalcuts from the National Gallery of Art,* National Gallery of Art, Washington, D.C. [1968].

(27) On Bämler, see S. Edmunds, "The Place of the London Haggadah in the Work of Joel ben Simeon," *Journal of Jewish Art,* VII, 1980, 25–34; and on Verard, see M. B. Winn and S. Edmunds, "Verard, Meckenem, and B. N. MS fr. 1686" (in press).

(28) On Holle's place in the history of printing in Ulm, see A. Hind, *An Introduction to the History of Woodcut,* 2 vols., New York, 1935, I, 313–15; and R. Muther, *German Book Illustration of the Gothic Period and the Early Renaissance (1460–1530),* trans. R. Shaw, Metuchen, 1972, 46.

(29) See Edmunds (as in n. 27) and D. Goldstein, *The Ashkenazi Haggadah,* London, 1985.

(30) See, however, J. Gutmann, *Hebrew Manuscript Painting,* New York, 1978; B. Narkiss, *Hebrew Illuminated Manuscripts,* New York, 1969; and on the making of Hebrew books, M. Beit-Arié, *Hebrew Codicology,* Paris, 1976.

(31) See, with earlier bibliography, A. H. van Buren, "The Master of Mary of Burgundy and His Colleagues: The State of Research and Questions of Method," *Zeitschrift für Kunstgeschichte,* XXXVIII, 1975, 286–309.

(32) On Mansion, see the classic work, J. van Praet, *Colard Mansion,* Paris, 1829; and P. Saenger, "Colard Mansion and the Evolution of the Printed Book," *The Library Quarterly,* XLV, 1975, 405–18.

(33) For Simon Bening, see the catalogue of the exhibition cited in n. 1, 69–85.

(34) On Levina and the Flemish background of English miniature painting, see R. Strong, *The English Renaissance Miniature,* London, 1983, and *idem, Artists of the Tudor Court. The Portrait Miniature Rediscovered 1520–1620,* Victoria and Albert Museum, London, 1983, esp. 52–57.

(35) E. J. Mundy, *Painting in Bruges 1470–1550. An Annotated Bibliography.* Boston, 1985, unfortunately includes only panel painting. Also, on manuscript production, see J. D. Farquhar, "Identity in an Anonymous Age: Bruges Manuscript Illuminators and Their Signs," *Viator,* XI, 1980, 371–83; and on painting, J. C. Wilson, "Adriaen Isenbrandt Reconsidered: The Making and Marketing of Art in Sixteenth-Century Bruges," Ph.D. diss., The Johns Hopkins University, 1983.

(36) For the text of the lawsuit, see L. de la Borde, *Le Parlement de Paris,* Paris, 1863, xliii; and for a discussion of the lawsuit, particularly

as it reveals a changed self-consciousness of the author, see C. J. Brown, "Du manuscrit à l'imprimé en France: Le cas des Grands Rhétoriqueurs," *Actes du Ve Colloque International sur le Moyen Français. Milan, 6–8 mai 1985,* Milan, 1985, I, 103–23.

(37) *Ibid.,* 122.

(38) This is a distinction made by A. Viala, *La naissance de l'écrivain,* Paris, 1986.

(39) J. C. Wilson, "The Participation of Painters in the Bruges 'Pandt' Market, 1512–1550," *Burlington Magazine,* CXXV, 1983, 476–79; and *idem,* "Marketing Painting in Late Medieval Belgium," *Artistes, artisans et production artistique au Moyen-Age. Actes du Colloque* [Rennes, 1982], Paris (in press).

(40) See R. Branner, *Manuscript Painting in Paris Under the Reign of St. Louis,* Berkeley/Los Angeles, 1977.

(41) See J. H. Marrow, *Passion Iconography in Northern European Art of the Late Middle Ages and Early Renaissance: A Study of the Transformation of Sacred Metaphor into Descriptive Narrative,* Kortrijk, Belgium, 1979.

(42) See the essays by A. Chartier, R. Darnton, and D. Roche gathered in R. Chartier and A. Paire, eds., *Pratiques de la lecture,* Paris, 1985, and the forthcoming papers of a Franco-German colloquium on the history of reading, esp. the paper by R. Darnton, "First Steps Toward a History of Reading," in *Colloque histoire de la lecture,* Paris, Jan. 13–15, 1986. Many of the points raised by these historians have implications for art historians who study the illustrated book: that the book should not serve as the primary artifact for constructing a history of reading, that there are significant differences between "intensive" and "extensive" reading (that is, reading one book many times versus reading many books, usually once), that there are clear-cut distinctions between public and private reading. Historians, in turn, could profit from a consideration of illustrated books in order to construct a history of reading and from more attention to actual books, what Darnton calls "textual archaeology."

(43) Partially edited in H. Omont, *Paris. Bibliothèque Nationale. Anciens inventaires et catalogues de la Bibliothèque Nationale,* 5 vols., Paris, 1863, I, 1–154.

(44) C. de Hamel suggests that a tiny Psalter, sold at Sotheby's and now in New York (H. P. Kraus), was sewn into clothing for this purpose; see London, Sotheby's, *Western Manuscripts and Miniatures,* November 26, 1985, lot 98.

PART III

ILLUSTRATION FROM PRINTING TO THE 19TH CENTURY

THE EARLY ILLUSTRATED BOOK: HIGHLIGHTS FROM A LECTURE
Philip Hofer

Although one or two illustrated type-printed Western books suddenly appeared just after the middle of the fifteenth century in Germany—one of the "revolutions within a revolution" referred to by Nicholas Barker—illustrated books did not begin to proliferate in Europe until 1472, and then only in Germany and Italy, the heart of the Continent. The first issue of the German *Apocalypse* block book can be fairly closely dated, from its paper, as about 1451. Block books printed from one relief-cut woodblock to a page, with text and woodcut together, soon lost out, however, to the superior technical advantages of books printed from movable type which could be corrected, if necessary, far more easily. Illustrated books printed from movable type—the real technical revolution—began with Ulrich Boner's *Der Edelstein,* issued at Bamberg in 1461. Superior techniques for making engravings, etchings, and woodcuts for illustration were soon being invented in Germany and the Netherlands. Illuminated manuscripts, produced slowly one at a time, had long since become too expensive for scholars and less wealthy individuals to buy. Private libraries were small and public libraries did not really exist.

To be sure, there were single European prints sold as early as 1423 (one so dated is in the John Rylands Library at Manchester, England) and probably before. Paper had arrived in Europe by the twelfth century from the Far East, where printing, paper, and illustration had existed as early as the Buddhist Diamond Sutra, dated A.D. 868, in the British Museum. The invention of the various printing techniques in Europe was a separate development over five hundred years later, but once the idea of illustrated

Reprinted by permission from the *Quarterly Journal of the Library of Congress,* 1978, v. 35, no. 2, pp. 77–91.

Das Goldene Spiel, dated 1472, was the fourth illustrated book printed by Günther Zainer of Augsburg and the first book based on a popular amusement, in this case chess. Meister Ingolt's work was successful but a novelty, for Frederick Goff suggests that it is now very rare. The woodcuts in the copy illustrated here are not hand colored as early German woodcut books usually were.

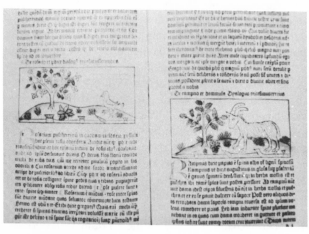

Among the early illustrations done by artists who are unknown to us today is a famous early Dutch woodcut book first printed in Gouda in 1480, the *Dialogus creaturarum.* Both the author and the artist are truly anonymous, but the simple, amusing woodcuts are a delight in their appropriate coloring. Eight different editions of it were made.

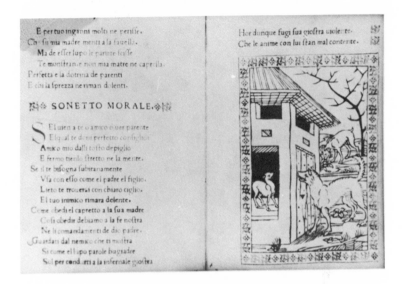

The artistically satisfying woodcuts of the Verona Aesop of 1479 are also by an unknown artist. The pages illustrated are from the only recorded copy of the book that is printed on vellum, a copy which is slightly incomplete, however. There are good reasons to use vellum in printing, costly as it is. Firstly, there is its strength and permanency; secondly, the contrast between the black shiny ink and the white vellum page is brilliant. This is the first book to contain borders made up of type ornament. Aesop's *Fables* has been over the centuries one of the most popular of all books, for it is packed with wisdom told in an amusing and often unforgettable way.

printed books took hold in the West, about 1472, the spread was very rapid. The price and time advantages were enormous and a demand was present.

Early examples of type-printed books were hand-illuminated simulated manuscripts on vellum, but it was scarcely twenty years before inexpensively printed books on paper all but completely superseded such anachronisms. Early type printers usually made little effort to secure the opulent effects of simulated manuscripts,

Present in Italy in the fifteenth century, book jackets and pictorial covers are not a modern invention. This Ferrarese book cover on paper boards, of about 1495, has a different pattern on each cover but no lettering. The purpose of the book jacket must have been, however, the same as it is today: to attract attention. The book is exceedingly rare. The text by Riccias is of little consequence.

which must have cost nearly as much as their prototypes, but rather adapted ideas from manuscripts and invented new ones of their own.

Some artists who did early book illustrations are far from unknown. Great artists have been closely involved with book illustration at all periods—not just in recent times when the School of Paris invented the "livres des peintres." The reputation of book illustration as a minor art is a very underserved one which is rapidly being dissipated. There are more original prints by artists, greater and lesser, as illustrations in books than exist separately.

One of the greatest illustrated books of the fifteenth century, because of the mastery with which the woodcuts were designed and executed by the artist himself, is Albrecht Dürer's *Apocalypse* of 1498. Printed and published by Dürer, the many copies that probably once existed may very well have been broken up so that the woodcuts could be framed separately. The title is very decorative woodcut calligraphy in the Latin edition; a German edition is even rarer. Both are of the same year. (See following page.)

French books were not customarily illustrated with pictures as early as those of Germany, the Low Countries, or Italy. Indeed, the leaf from Valerius Maximus's *Facta et dicta* (1476) reproduced on the cover of this journal is treated like an illuminated manuscript except for the fact that the text is printed from movable type. The rest of the page is all by hand—probably two or three hands, as there was early in the history of printing a division of labor in the making of books. The watercolorist made the pictures, another artist the large initial with its decorations, and the other colored letters were done by a rubricator. From 1481 on, scores of fine French illustrated books were printed in Paris and Lyons, including the many famous small Books of Hours, private devotions illustrated with metal relief plates.

In Italy early books are more rarely found colored than in Germany, but superior Italian coloring and bookmaking are very fine. The Venetians became masters of trade and professional books, such as Johannes de Ketham's *Fasciculo di medicina,* printed in Venice in 1493, a medical treatise and one of the first woodcut books to be colored by stencils. Venetians were great printers of religious texts as well, and, indeed, Venice was the most productive city in Europe at the end of the fifteenth century. The Florentines, on the other hand, were less prolific but more artistic in their presentation.

A small booklet, measuring $7^1/2$ by $5^1/2$ inches, the *Canzone per andare in maschera* was possibly written by Lorenzo de'Medici around 1500. It has a title page bearing a lovely woodcut, illustrated here, showing how Florentine gentlemen persuaded their ladies to go with them to a masked ball. The men hold up what appear to be doughnuts as a temptation. This book has

sometimes been assigned to the school of Ghirlandajo. (See above.)

Florence also produced the first book on commercial arithmetic, in 1491, with dozens of simple but elegant tiny woodcuts. Altogether, the Florentine illustrated books of the 1490s are probably the loveliest of all that decade, with a strong accent of black on white which serves to give a sense of color without its actual use. Slowly we may be able to find the names of the designers, if not the cutters, of these illustrations.

Spanish and Portuguese incunabula are generally larger, more classic, and more severe than German, French, or Italian; but they are nevertheless very ornamental, because of their gorgeous title pages, like the portals of their great cathedrals. The first Iberian illustrated book was *Los Trabajos de Hercules* by Enrique de Aragón, marqués de Villena, printed at Zamora in 1483, which has fascinating but inferior cuts.

An example of the eastern and northern European illustrated books of the fifteenth century, few of which have artistic merit, is the quarto Psalter printed at Cetinje, the capital of the erstwhile small state of Montenegro, now part of Yugoslavia, of which only two copies are recorded. Probably the few relief cuts and many ornamental capitals are from metal rather than wood. Their style is more Slavic then Venetian, although the Dalmatian Coast, where Cetinje is located, was dominated by Venice in 1495. The book was printed by two enterprising Slavs, who give their names as

A fine English book of the early sixteenth century is a large Missal for use at Salisbury, printed by Richard Pynson in London in 1520. The book is printed on vellum and has a limited number of fine illustrations like the one shown here, which is strongly French in style. It is likely that the artist was French, for the Missal is finer than any other English church book done before 1535.

Hieronymus Makarye of Crne Gori and Gjurgja of Crnojevica. (See illustration.)

In England there were no really worthy illustrated books printed in the fifteenth century—not even the well-known Caxton Chaucer, which is, nonetheless, one of the most valuable books of the century because of its text.

The spread of the illustrated book after its beginnings in western Europe was very rapid and its influence exceedingly important, once started. The growth of universities and increasing literacy caused an unexpectedly heavy demand for books. Illustration greatly widened the comprehension of the text for those who read slowly; in fact, pictures plus text gave the book two dimensions, each supplementing the other. Illustrations even attracted attention from the nobles and royalty, who were not always the more literate segment of the population. The invention of printing and the making of prints and illustrations were the most important developments of the years 1450 to 1500, the so-called incunabula period.

Books reached eastern Europe before 1500. A few years later they had reached Turkey, where a few charmingly decorated books appeared, printed in Hebrew by Jews who had been expelled from Spain and Portugal in 1492. The decorations derived mainly from Naples, then a Spanish possession, as did the gifted individualistic designers who produced the glorious, but anonymous, woodcut borders in Moses ben Nahman's *Perush Ha-Tora,* dated 1490.

There was no Western printing or illustration in Russia before 1563. The first printed work did not appear in the Western Hemisphere until 1539 in Mexico; and printing later spread from there into South America. In North America there was no printing until the seventeenth century. The Portuguese voyages around the Cape of Good Hope, however, brought Western printing to Goa, India, in 1557, Macao, China, in 1588, and Nagasaki, Japan, in 1590.

Until the 1520s, northern European illustration was Gothic in style; southern European, notably Italian, was Renaissance; and Spain and Portugal wavered between the two.

As the decades of the sixteenth century passed, more and more secular books were demanded to explain the rapidly increasing exploration and innovations in life-style everywhere. Books became on the average much smaller in size than the folio—some were even small enough to put in a pocket. New subjects were sought, even seemingly frivolous subjects such as emblems. Books of emblems were not considered frivolous at the time they were published, however, since they contained hidden political, social, and religious meanings in their texts and pictures.

Although superficially religious, Robert Gobin's work *Les Loups ravissans,* published in Paris about 1503, is anticlerical. It was printed for Antoine Vérard, the largest French publisher at the turn of the century. The small volume has a most amazingly vigorous set of anonymous woodcuts, like no other of its period. It is essentially a dance of death, rather abstract in cutting, almost modern, powerful, and excessively rare. The artist may have actually cut directly on the woodblocks. He was not a great technician, but his draftsmanship is dynamic.

In Germany another artist besides Albrecht Dürer—who continued to design book illustrations until his death in 1528—drew for books and was nearly as great. He was Hans Baldung, who designed an imaginative woodcut of Christ after the Crucifixion for Ulrich Pinder's *Speculum passionis,* printed at Nuremberg in 1507. The German artist Hans Weiditz, recently become famous, ornamented pages with lovely emblematic woodcut borders of plants and birds. From about 1518 on, and beginning in Basel, Switzerland, ornamental title borders became a high fashion thanks to the great German artist Hans Holbein the Younger.

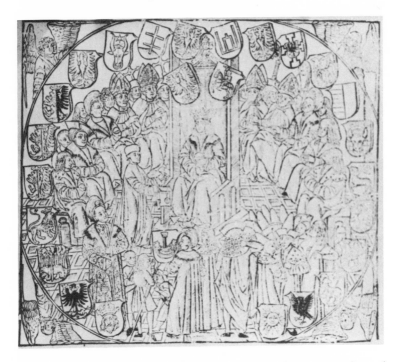

This large folding woodcut is the frontispiece to the earliest compendium of Polish law, printed in Cracow in 1506, and shows King Sigismund I, who had just ascended the throne, surrounded by some of his principal nobles and clergy. In the law folio, printed in the Polish language and for the first time, is the poem "Boga Rodzica," which was the country's national anthem in the sixteenth century.

Hans Weiditz has been identified as the artist who did the drawings for a series of woodcuts in Otto Brunfel's *Herbal*, printed at Strassburg in 1530, which contains the first accurately scientific botanical illustrations. Illustrations from Petrarch done by Weiditz and from other picture books of the 1530s show the beginning of the romanticism that has been characteristic of German art ever since that time.

By the 1540s England was beginning to produce some good illustrated books. The presence in London of Hans Holbein, as king's painter to Henry VIII from 1538 until 1543, when he died, had a real influence in this movement.

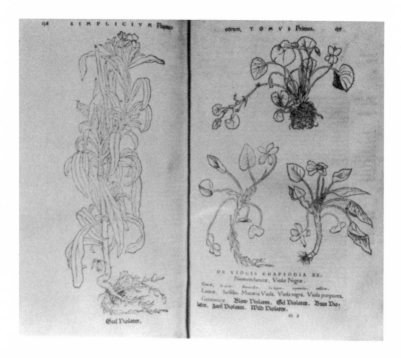

Otto Brunfel's *Herbal*

Italy and France were where most of the more important illustrated books of the sixteenth century were made. Luca Paccioli did the first series of large roman letters to suggest their proper mathematical proportions in Venice in 1509, with some assistance from his friend Leonardo da Vinci, who was also very influential in a folio Vitruvius printed at Como in 1521. Ideas and knowledge had become by then rapidly interchangeable, not only from city to city but among countries remote from one another.

While Paccioli was working on the first alphabet in perspective, a canon of the Cathedral of Toul, near the Franco-Italian border, preceded it by his own general study of perspective, doing amazingly simplified renderings of everyday scenes in a small French city. This excessively rare book, *De artificiali perspectiva* by Jean Pèlerin, printed in 1505 at Toul, may appear Renaissance in style because of the simple classical elements, but it is actually

CARRETA·PELEGRINA·

E V.

De artificiali perspectiva

still Gothic, as books were then in Germany, the Low Countries, and Switzerland.

In Italy the High Renaissance began early and Italian books of the 1520s were more elaborate than elsewhere. A sixteenth-century Italian illustrated book by one of the greatest artists of the century is the Aretino published in Venice in 1537 and illustrated by Titian. It is printed in chiaroscuro, a color-shaded block being superimposed on the basic black-and-white outlines of the first woodblock. Chiaroscuro became high fashion and sometimes gave the effect of the drawings to the prints. The joint publication of two celebrated friends—Titian, the leading Venetian painter, and Francesco Marcolini, one of the best Venetian printers—*Stanze* honors their rather notorious friend Pietro Aretino, whose influence obtained valuable commissions. In a way, the illustration is a bit of a joke: Aretino is seated on the shore, gazing adoringly at a Siren in the sky. As one Angela Serena was Aretino's current mistress, the visions suggests a play upon words, without mentioning her name. The verses are by Aretino. Few books of any period carry as much punch as this small booklet of sixteen leaves.

There are not as many French as Italian books from the second half of the sixteenth century illustrated by known artists since early French artists are, really, lesser known. From 1550 on, engravings were more and more used as book illustrations, particularly in French books. More elaborate effects were possible, and the public had grown to accept the extra cost, both of the copper plates and the necessary double printing. There were even books entirely engraved, text as well as illustration. Then only one printing was necessary.

The French book with the finest early French portrait—that of Henry II, by the French artist Etienne Delaune—was published in Paris in 1560, just after Henry II died, the victim of an accident in a tournament. Another copy of this book, in the collections of Harvard University, contains in place of the Delaune an almost equally handsome portrait of the king in profile by René Boyvin. There is no way to know if the Boyvin portrait was made for a separate issue of the book, but probably not.

Perhaps the most influential book of the century was Hans Holbein the Younger's *Dance of Death,* composed by the great German painter, jeweler, stained-glass-maker, and designer about

1524 in Basel, Switzerland, but not printed as a small book until 1538, at Lyons, France. Meanwhile the forty-one woodcuts were circulated and sold as prints. The cutter of these drawings, made directly on the block by the artist, was Hans Lützelburger, a consummate craftsman who perfectly rendered them. Copies were made in all countries of Europe, death being an ever prevalent phenomenon. Indeed, there has hardly been a decade since 1540 that a new edition, copied from earlier ones, has not appeared, wars, famines, and plagues tending to keep the subject on everyone's mind. (See left.)

From the Iberian Peninsula, this small, thin folio of twenty leaves, almost unknown, is a religious work on an order of nuns and is dedicated to King Manuel the Fortunate of Portugal. The *Misericordia* was printed at Lisbon in 1516. It is splendidly printed and illustrated, Portugal being very rich at this juncture from its control of the sea passage around Africa connecting Europe and the Far East, which it gained in 1498. The woodcuts on the left are by unknown artists. The elaborate interlaced woodcut capitals in red on the right are from late fifteenth-century German sources. (See facing page.)

Illustrated Spanish books of the sixteenth century are less well known than those of any other major European country. J. P. R.

Homo natus de muliere, breui viuens tempo
re, repletur multis miseriis: qui quasi flos
egreditur, & côteritur, & fugit velut vmbra.

IOB   XIIII.

Omnis homo venies grauida mulieris ab aluo
Nascitur ad varijs tempora plena malis.
Flos citò marcescens veluti decedit, & ille
Sic perit, & tãquã corporis vmbra fugit.

Lyell's bibliography of them is now half a century old and woefully incomplete.[1] The Hispanic Society in New York and the Library of Congress are well fitted to supplement Lyell's work.

Because of constant wars, plagues, and disasters, the seventeenth century was not to prove as great a period of illustration as either of the two centuries highlighted here. But it is also still the least known one hundred years, and the century contains many wonders worthy of description. We are still, too, only at the beginning of the study of sixteenth-century illustrated books, particularly of those from the last half of the century, the High Renaissance in all European countries. I most earnestly hope that just as Frederick Goff devoted years to a census of fifteenth-century books in America,[2] some young scholar will tackle the later period.

To illuminate 150 years in a few pages, a highly personal choice of illustrated books is necessary. The commoner works, like Schedel's *Weltchronik* (Nuremberg, 1493), the most prolifically illustrated book of its day, or the equally famous tongue twister, the *Hypnerotomachia Poliphili,* printed in Venice in 1499, have not been included in this overview, for it is doubtful that either book quite lives up to its reputation in the light of many other lesser-known illustrated books from the period. Instead, selections from books that are scarcely known at all, except by specialists, have been presented here, to give an idea of the number and variety of illustrations available.

NOTES

[1]James P. R. Lyell, *Early Book Illustrations in Spain* (London: Grafton & Co., 1926).

[2]Frederick Goff, *Incunabula in American Libraries: A Third Census of Fifteenth-Century Books Recorded in North American Collections* (New York: Bibliographical Society of America, 1964).

EARLY ASTRONOMICAL BOOKS WITH MOVING PARTS
Owen Gingerich

One of the marvelous surprises for anyone who handles astronomical books of the 16th century is to come upon volumes containing movable disks, the so-called *volvelles*. Not only are moving parts found in a few spectacular monuments of the printing art, but many rather unprepossessing octavo textbooks also include these charming assemblies.

Books with moving parts already existed in the medieval manuscript tradition, but like their more durable counterparts of brass, they were individually crafted devices. Hence paper instruments first became widespread and important with the mass production made possible by the advent of printing.

The first astronomical printer, Regiomontanus, opened his shop in Nuremberg around 1470, and his *Calendarium* (1474) contained two instruments with moving parts. One had a jointed brass pointer, while the other was a simple lunar calculator with two moving circles or *volvelles*.

On such simple instruments, it is rather difficult to know if they were primarily for instruction or for actual calculations. In any event, there is a large category of ingenious paper devices whose use was clearly pedagogical.

Barely had printing emerged from its infancy when a class of books called *Cosmographia* became popular. Their mixture of geography and of spherical astronomy sometimes emphasized the one and sometimes the other.

The small volume by Petrus Apianus displayed an outstanding use of *volvelles* for teaching purposes. First issued in 1524, it continued through many editions, including some edited by

Reprinted by permission from *AB Bookman's Weekly*, October 23, 1989, pp. 1505–1508.

Gemma Frisius. Perhaps as a result of Apianus's *Cosmographia, volvelles* became popular at around this same time in astronomy textbooks, that is, in the first half of the 16th century.

The standard introduction to astronomy went back to John of Holywood, a 13th-century English mathematician and astronomer who spent most of his adult life in Paris. There he was known by his Latinized name, Johannes de Sacrobosco.

Although Sacrobosco's *Sphere* had long been used as a standard text for elementary astronomy, and a number of printed versions already appeared before 1500, I believe that the textbook as we know it today was essentially invented in Wittenberg around 1530. That is, for the first time the introductory astronomy books appeared in an octavo format, presumably cheap enough so that each student could afford his own copy.

The idea was almost instantly copied: I have in my own collection a virtually identical pirated edition printed in Venice in 1532, only a few months after its appearance in Wittenberg.

Just a few years later the Wittenberg publishers introduced a new twist into their astronomy text. The first was Joseph Clug, who in 1538 added three diagrams with *volvelles* to his octavo Sacrobosco, closely copying a device of Apianus's for one of the three. The printers in Wittenberg generally passed around the same woodblocks from shop to shop.

Like modern textbooks, those of 16th-century Germany eventually wore out or became obsolete, so that today any particular edition can be pretty uncommon. Hence it was only gradually that I realized that virtually all of them contain almost identical setups; this applies not just in Germany, but throughout Europe.

I was always both amused and bemused by the Latin motto, *Nulla dies sine linea*—"No day without its line"—meaning that the sun draws a line across the sky each day. One day I happened to be reading a book that cited Jean-Paul Sartre's autobiography. Although the French existentialist thought life was without meaning, he nevertheless felt compelled each day to write—*Nulla dies sine linea.*

I jumped to attention, because I realized at once that an ancient proverb must be involved, and that the Renaissance schoolboys were presumably having a great chuckle at some pun every time they used that *volvelle.*

Naturally I turned to Erasmus' *Adagia* (in its splendid new edition from the University of Toronto Press), and there I found that the saying goes back to Pliny, who recorded an anecdote concerning the ancient Greek painter Apelles.

Apelles went off to Rhodes to check up on a rival, Protogenes. Finding Protogenes not at home, Apelles nevertheless went in, and with a fine brush painted a delicate line on the panel on the easel; as he left, he asked the old housekeeper to mention this to Protogenes when he returned. When Protogenes saw the line, he took a finer brush and painted a line down through the middle of the first.

You can guess how the story turns out: Apelles came back again and in turn placed a still finer line on the previous two. This time Protogenes admitted defeat, exclaiming, "Only Apelles could have done that," and he rushed out to find the master painter before he departed from Rhodes.

"And," Pliny adds, "Apelles made it a point never to let a day pass without drawing something, which gave rise to the famous saying."

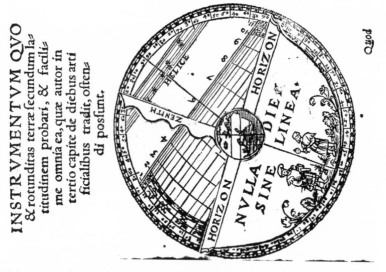

Diagram with *volvelles* from a Wittenberg edition of Sacrobosco's *Libellus de Sphaera*, printed by Petrus Seitz in 1543. The device was used to demonstrate the north-south curvature of the earth by the variation in the height of the pole for observers at different latitudes. The underlying grid was used later in the textbook to deal with more complex problems of solar motion and solar time.

Two other devices are invariably found in the 16th-century Sacrobosco textbooks. The first in the sequence is used to demonstrate from the observed time of lunar eclipses at various locations that the earth is curved in an east-west direction. Taken together, this and the "nulla dies" device establish the sphericity of the earth to the beginning astronomy students.

The third device was used to illustrate the problems of risings and settings, particularly as used by the classical poets. Not only were these three paper instruments found in the numerous editions of Sacrobosco's *Sphere,* but also in the equally numerous commentaries; so it is not uncommon to find two complete sets bound in the same volume, first in the Sacrobosco text and then in the subsequent commentary.

Almost from the beginning, the economics of production made it desirable to furnish uncut sheets and to let the buyer assemble the *volvelles* into his own book. This means that some are fastened with string, and others with glue, which in turn means that many sets were rather insecurely fixed and got lost. In other copies, the assembly was never achieved; sometimes the original uncut sheet can still be found.

I find it rather remarkable that some bibliographers or collectors, who are otherwise fastidious about collations, frequently skip over the moving parts. Hence it is often rather difficult to get good information about just how many pieces are required for a book to be truly complete. However, if a 16th-century Sacrobosco or a commentary on it has at least one diagram with a moving part, then there should almost always be two more. (In a few editions, there is a tiny index pointer on yet a fourth diagram.)

In the latter part of the 16th century other textbooks gradually offered competition to Sacrobosco's time-honored elementary text. Perhaps the most significant was Michael Maestlin's *Epitome astronomiae,* which went through seven editions beginning in 1582. Maestlin abandoned two of the three devices, but retained the more useful one.

My own copy of this work is typical of about half the copies now found. The illustration of the device shown on page 66 lacks the moving part, but the latter is supplied on a sheet that came with the book, complete with instructions on where to place it.

The other great textbook of this period, Peurbach's more advanced *Theoricae novae planetarum* sometimes included

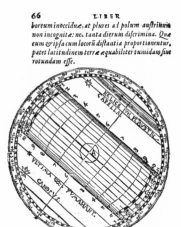

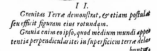

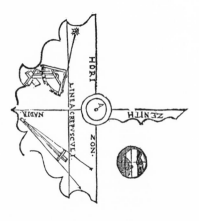

An unassembled copy of Michael Maestlin's *Epitome astronomiae* includes only the underlying diagram on page 66 (left). the movable part (above) was supplied on a separate sheet with instructions for assembly.

volvelles. These illustrated the epicyclic planetary model, where one moving wheel rides on another. It seems that the competitive economics of publishing required having *volvelles* in the elementary Sacrobosco text, whereas in Peurbach's more advanced text they were only optional.

The planetary models of Peurbach's discussion required more complicated devices than in the Sacrobosco, but this may have challenged a few individual workers to make up their own manuscript sets of moving parts for Peurbach's work.

Three splendid examples have appeared in the rare book market in the past decade or so. One was in the Honeyman collection auctioned at Sotheby's in London in 1979. Another, once owned by the New York rare book dealer Hans Kraus, is now at the Getty Museum. A third, slightly smaller, manuscript but clearly from the same general tradition has been acquired by the Adler Planetarium in Chicago.

The paper instruments in these manuscripts, as well as those in the printed editions of Peurbach, are closely related to *equatoria*, a category of devices used to show how the Ptolemaic epicyclic theory works to establish the positions of planets. In this context they are clearly intended to teach the general concepts rather than for actual calculations.

Ptolemaic planetary models that could indeed be used as analog computers have a long history. One of the earliest extant examples, the "equatorie of the planetis" at Peterhouse in Cambridge, was identified some years ago by Derek Price as an original holograph manuscript from the poet Geoffrey Chaucer. While it does not actually have any moving parts, this unique manuscript does explain how to make such a device.

Eventually printed *equatoria* that could be used as actual computational instruments appeared. The rare printed *equatorium* by Oronce Fine (Paris, 1538) is filled with ingenuity so that, with a single graph and sliding rectangles, calculations for each of the planets can be carried out.

Clever as it is, Fine's device does not take advantage of the comparative ease and cheapness of printed sheets; once printing became available, it made much more sense to simplify the *equatorium* by separating each planet into its own instrument.

This was done by Johann Schoner, whose *Aequatorium astronomicum* contained working instruments for the longitude of each planet. His devices are well known through a small-size version in his collected works (Nuremberg, 1551, 1561), but his large original production from 1522 is now quite rare. I know of only a handful of copies in Europe and none in America.

The printed *equatoria* reached their highest state of perfection in Apianus' *Astronomicum Caesareum* of 1540, which was perhaps the greatest tour de force of 16th-century printing. It is a complicated and expensive book for which Tycho Brahe later paid the equivalent of about $1,000. A few years ago a copy auctioned in New York for $80,000.

Although by no means the highest bid offered for an early astronomy book, it was a princely price for a very princely book. Indeed, "Caesar's Astronomy," dedicated to the Holy Roman Emperor Charles V and his brother Ferdinand, was one of the most sumptuous printed works of its century.

Unlike the cheap textbooks, where the buyers were expected to assemble their own sets of moving parts, all of these costly volumes were hand-colored and accurately assembled in Apianus's own printing shop.

Apianus was professor of astronomy in the university town of Ingolstadt (about 70 km north of Munich) where he operated his private press. He made something of a career of being an astronomical popularizer through paper instruments, beginning with the *Cosmographia* mentioned earlier as the work where the idea of moving parts really caught on.

In the 1530s he published a variety of astronomical devices in both Latin and German editions. Many of these included suites of plates printed on one side only so that the instruments could be cut out and assembled. Complete sets of these plates exist in about a quarter of the extant copies, which may mean that a fair share of the original owners actually assembled Apianus's devices.

The planning for a far grander astronomical book apparently took Apianus a number of years, for between 1534 and 1540 he published few other works. Furthermore, some of the elaborate initial capitals, encompassing nearly the entire alphabet and cut with marvelous astronomical vignettes, had already appeared in his 1533 *Introductio geographica.*

The size of the main instruments in the *Astronomicum Caesareum* is almost identical to Schoner's, and Apianus must have got the idea from his contemporary; nevertheless, his scheme is far more sophisticated and self-contained, and it includes a battery of other disks for a variety of unusual purposes.

The *Astronomicum Caesareum* itself grew and changed in the course of production. For example, underneath one of the moving parts is an entirely irrelevant base of an astrolabe, the fossil of a plan that was undoubtedly abandoned when Apianus realized how hard it would be to cut out all the lacework paper structure required for the overlying star chart.

Elsewhere, Apianus decided that the explanation for eclipses was inadequate, and so he discarded a sheet already printed and added two others in its place. Consequently, one of the gatherings has five instead of the usual four pages.

The basic plan of this *magnum opus* was to present sets of disks for the moon and planets according to the detailed circles of the Ptolemaic theory. Not only were these lovely teaching guides to

Ptolemy's geocentric cosmology, but the sets were assembled so carefully that they could actually be used for determining the planetary positions.

This was no mean feat, for the intricacies of the Ptolemaic constructions required different axes for the various disks within a single assembly, and hence demanded considerable ingenuity in order to make all the layers of movable parts functional.

The reason I appreciate the accuracy of the original *Astronomicum Caesareum* so thoroughly is that, about 20 years ago, I took a critical look at the grand facsimile that had just been produced in Leipzig. Like the 16th-century original, the Leipzig reprint is a masterpiece of printing technology, complete with *trompe l'oeil* wrinkles and stains.

But to my consternation, and shortly thereafter to Edition Leipzig's as well, I discovered that many of the moving parts were simply glued to the wrong pages. Furthermore, many of the complex assemblies were mounted in such a careless fashion that the *volvelles* remained correctly concentric only at a single setting.

At first I imagined that fate had played a terrible trick on the press, and that they had by chance selected a defective copy for their reproduction. As a result, I began a systematic examination of copies of this book; now I have looked at more than 100 of them, and I'm filled with ever-increasing admiration for the precision obtained by Apianus and his workshop.

As for Edition Leipzig, apparently they had worked from a copy at Gotha that had come unglued, and someone used his imagination in the reassembly rather than consulting the perfectly correct copy in the Leipzig University Library practically next door to the press. Anyone who has spent the eight to 20 hours required to correct the faulty facsimile can appreciate the sophistication and care required to Apianus' private press.

The *Astronomicum Caesareum* was clearly intended for wealthy buyers, but Apianus did publish a German guide to give his work greater accessibility; this unillustrated handbook is today very rare, and I have located only six examples of it, including a copy acquired several years ago by the Houghton Library at Harvard.

Apianus's paper *equatorium* attracted at least one imitator (just as Apianus had been inspired by the earlier paper *equatorium* of Johann Schoner)—Jacques Bassantin's *Astronomique Discours*

(Lyons, 1557) is a splendid example of printing, though its *volvelles* verge on unabashed piracy.

Other authors simply tried to outdo Apianus in the layers of *volvelles*: G. P. Gallucci's *Theatrum mundi* (Venice, 1588) and his *Speculum uranicum* (Venice, 1593) show the art gone to seed. And the eccentric conceit of Leonhard Thurneysser (Berlin, c. 1574), with six to eight intricately cut *volvelles* on each leaf, brought the entire technique of the *volvelle* to a state of decadent dottiness.

After the elegant Ptolemaic representations of Apianus, no similar creative or educational effort was thrown into the new Copernican cosmology. Nevertheless, there must have been a private tradition for making certain Copernican instruments of paper for instruction purposes. A group of these is today found in the Crawford Collection at the Royal Observatory in Edinburgh, and another equivalent set is bound in the back of a copy of Copernicus' *De revolutionibus* at Aberdeen University.

Since paper instruments are comparatively ephemeral, we can easily imagine that many more originally existed. Such devices must have played their part in teaching both the old and the new astronomy of the 16th century.

Early in the 17th century Michael Maestlin's student, Johannes Kepler, published his own epitome of astronomy. It not only broke new ground by presenting an epitome of *Copernican* astronomy, but it departed from previous practice and did not contain any diagrams with moving parts.

Since the buyers of these books had for many years been expected to assemble the *volvelles* for their own books, a matter of unfavorable economics could hardly have been the reason for the decline of the *volvelles*. Maybe they just became old-fashioned and went out of vogue. In any event, relatively few 17th-century astronomy books of any kind contain these intriguing mobile instruments or teaching aids.

The golden period of astronomical books with moving parts had come and gone in the 16th century, leaving behind an admirable legacy that can even today be copied for educational use.

THE BIBLIOGRAPHY OF ILLUSTRATED BOOKS: NOTES WITH TWO EXAMPLES FROM ENGLISH BOOK ILLUSTRATION OF THE 18TH CENTURY
Edgar Breitenbach

I. The illustration of manuscripts has long been examined thoroughly and with utmost interest. Many famous codices have been reproduced in facsimile, and there exists excellent work on some of the schools and groups of miniatures. And even if much is still to be done, scholarship has in very many instances tried to throw light on the historical development of manuscript illustration.

With early printed books the case is similar. Few stages in the art of the book are so closely studied, even perhaps overrated, as incunabula. The interest taken in them has advantages for the study of their illustrations, as so many sources of knowledge about them exist.

But after this period there is no possibility of getting any general view of the whole subject. As an exception a description of the book illustration of a single country and a single period may be found. It is an even greater exception to find a bibliography as well as a history, and yet this would be of utmost importance for librarians as well as for antiquarians and collectors.

II. Still more difficult is the task of following the illustrations to one specific poetical work through the centuries. So long as one stays in the limits of the Middle Ages one may find a few references. But for the later period almost nothing has been done, with the exception of perhaps an occasional treatise on illustrated Bibles, or on editions of Ovid, Dante and Cervantes, limited to a

Reprinted by permission of The Library Association from *The Library Association Record,* May 1935, pp. 176–185.

297

certain place or period. And yet this method of study is so very enlightening for the manifold problems of book illustration. To give an example: the famous Æsop illustrations by Thomas Bewick, the reviver of the art of the woodcut, are in their composition regular copies of the primitive cuts in an English edition of 1722, which in their turn are nothing else than a coarse imitation of German woodcuts by Virgil Solis of about 150 years earlier. And from thence the way leads backwards over the editions of early printed books to medieval manuscripts. And if we go into details and look at certain rather fabulous foreign animals which Bewick could not have known by actual sight, and trace them backwards, tradition takes its course through medieval bestiaries and the corresponding literary documents right into the mystic circle of the ancient Physiologus. These facts in no way lessen Bewick's merit. On the contrary, it is admirable how he manages to pour new artistic life into his rigid pattern and thus to add a new strong link to the long chain of ancient imagery.

III. Three main groups of book illustrations are to be distinguished: firstly, one in which the main emphasis rests on the pictures and wherein the text only plays the subordinate part of an accompanying explanation, as is the case in sequences by Hogarth and Rowlandson. Here the picture is primary, the text secondary. Secondly, one which consists of pictures for a certain text, these therefore being illustrations in the proper sense of the word *illustrare*. Here the text was first and the pictures serve either to accentuate the climax of the action or to facilitate the understanding of especially difficult parts or for some other purpose of a similar kind. Thirdly, the last group consists of mainly decorative accessories having often very little to do with the text of the book and therefore being sometimes transposed from book to book. All sorts of ornaments belong to this group, but also many vignettes, head- or tail-pieces related to the text without picturing single scenes.

The second group, the one embracing book illustration properly so-called, can be subdivided into two parts: into scientific illustrations and such as belong to works of imagination. To the first appertain, for example, all kinds of medical, botanical, zoological and geographical illustrations, and further most of the ones in topographical publications. Their main aim is accuracy of representation, in favour of which the artistic imagination has to retire. In the second part, the illustrations of works of imagination, there is a difference: the literary matter allows the widest liberty of inspiration to the artist. Although the literary content is constant yet every work of art is subject to the interpretation of its reader. If he is an artist and transposes the impression which the text aroused in him into visual form, that impression will be fixed through the medium of his picture and the spectator will be able to discover the relation between the literary and the visual work of art and to see whether the ideas of both correspond or how far, perhaps, the picture differs from what the poet wanted to express. No literary work is an absolutely fixed thing. Again and again it is exposed to the varying opinions of different individuals, different nations and different times. And each of these three will, according to its character, sometimes add and sometimes omit something.

IV. The bibliography of book illustration in the sense intended here should, then, enumerate all illustrated editions of an imaginative work, arranged according to period and country, subdivided according to authors and works and again according to groups of illustrations. Works often illustrated should be preceded by a short survey by which the student can easily inform himself how many independent sequences of illustrations exist for that same work, which editions contain direct copies of older patterns and which freely elaborate older patterns, as for example, in the above mentioned Æsop pictures by Bewick. The prototype of such groups of illustrations should be treated in greater detail with regard to its pictures, but all dependent editions as briefly as possible. Works only once or rarely illustrated should only be dealt with at length if the quality of the illustrations justifies this. Such editions as are not illustrated by sequences of pictures but only by a frontispiece, vignettes and so forth should be mentioned briefly.

V. Two examples of English eighteenth century book illustration will make all this plain. First let me give you a short survey. For the first half of the century the art of the book in England was much under the influence of France and the Netherlands. We find quite a number of French and Dutch names signing the illustrations of this epoch; often they belong to artists who had to leave their country because of their Calvinistic creed and who found shelter in England: as examples let me name Cheron, Gribelin, van der Bank. With them English artists, for instance Kent, Wootton and especially young Hogarth, were at work. The names only multiply in the second half of the century. Besides a few foreigners (Füseli, Angelica Kauffmann and Cipriani) principally Hamilton, Mortimer, Ryley, Rooker and Thurston ought to be mentioned. Yet the best of English eighteenth century book illustration is only reached at the end of the century and the beginning of the next one. Its most important artists are, besides some of those already mentioned, Stothard, Smirke and Westall as designers for engraving on copper plates, the woodcut-artist, Thomas Bewick, and his school and, totally isolated and hardly recognized in all his greatness by his time, William Blake.

VI. Let the two examples be Thomson's *Seasons,* as the work that soon after its appearance and henceforth through the whole of the century was illustrated, and Young's *Night Thoughts,* to illustrate which the artists only gradually found courage, and which one artist alone really succeeded in transforming into visual form: Blake. We will not give here the proper bibliography, rather presupposing its existence, and we will see what can be found out by examining the sequences of illustrations.

VII. Thomson's *Seasons* holds a very remarkable place in the history of English literature. It was the first time that the description of nature was treated as the main subject of a poem. Up to Thomson's period nature was represented in poems in which idealized rural surroundings served as a frame for long-winded love-stories. Thomson, however, aspired to something new. His aim is to describe a typical day in spring, in summer, etc.; what man meets with in the country on such a day; what labour he has to perform, and how he is subject to the natural phenomena. Philosophical and religious considerations are interwoven with these matters, and several stories. Thomson progresses in his poem by mere enumeration. He puts together piece after piece to get a picture of a typical day, and only in this way combines the single scenes which have no connection with each other. The different parts can be easily separated in the same order

Fig. 1. "Summer," designed by W. Kent, engraved by N. Tardieu. [J. Thomson, *The Seasons,* London (J. Millan & A. Millar), 1730. 4to.] Reduced.

as they are arranged in the summaries placed in front of each season.

In its intellectual attitude as well as its style Thomson's poem stands on the verge of two ages: it is still classical and already romantic. Both are intermingled, but the tendency towards the future is predominant. The poem largely owes its lasting influence in England as well as on the Continent to this double position, and between 1780 and 1820 when once more a classic style changed to romanticism (though now on a different level) the poem flourished again. The very numerous editions of the *Seasons* during these decades give evidence for this.

This introduction could not be spared, as the history of the illustrations for the poem shows an exactly parallel development. Thomson started with *Winter* in 1726; the three other seasons appeared in the following years. J. Millan and A. Millar published the two first complete editions of the *Seasons* in 1730, one in quarto, the other in octavo; both are illustrated, but in a completely different way.

1. *The allegorical group*

The octavo edition of 1730 has one plate to each season, drawn by Picart and engraved by Clark. Picart's illustrations are confined to the spirit of a time which Thomson was just about to overcome. The conception of the seasons is as far from nature as possible: allegorical statues on high pedestals.

These plates only appear once more, namely in the edition of 1735, then they disappear until they experience a short resurrection characteristically in another period of classical thought, in the engravings by Allan, 1778 (used only for Murray's edition, 1792).

2. *The mythological season picture*

In the same year as Picart, Kent produced his engravings for the quarto edition, again one for each of the seasons. The scheme of the picture is each time the same; the sky, vivified by mythological personages; on the earth below an idyllic landscape in which human beings fullfil the tasks and follow the occupations suited to the season.

This way of representation thus answers exactly to the mode of the poem, uniting manifold typical particulars into a whole by mere enumeration.One cannot say that this attempt was successful; the common landscape frame hardly prevents the parts from falling asunder. For not even the proportions in the same picture are the same. The fault is not to be looked for in the otherwise skillful artist, but in the nature of the task.

As far as we can follow the two subjects of pictures *"Seasons"* and *"Months"*—backwards, transcriptive imagery always interchanges with efforts to picture the cosmic flow of the year itself. For instance, the height of the medieval period uses allegory, whilst the later Middle Ages, for the first time in Western art, aim at direct figurative reproduction. Kent's plates belong to the latter kind, although not without certain restrictions. The scheme of composition is astonishingly similar to the ones of the "planet-children" representations in the fifteenth century, which likewise show, under the reign of the astral ruler of providence, a survey of human occupations. But whilst in them there exists mental union between the below and the above, so that the existence of astral divinities is not less real than that of mankind, inevitably subjected to their power, there prevails in Kent's productions an evident dissension: reality below; hollow, worn out metaphorical imagery, whose charm is only formal, above. In the upper half of the picture the plates belong to the past, pseudo-classical period, in the lower one they point out the future. The afterlife of the illustrations is of some interest. First it was made smaller and copied by Foudrinier for the octavo edition of 1744, the plates serving as models for most of the later copies up to their last appearance in 1788 (London, Bowyer). They even made their way to the Continent, where they were copied in 1745 by C. F. Fritzsch, jun., for the Hamburg edition of the translation by Brockes.

In addition to these copies true to the original, there exist three free ones, which show a tendency to reconcile the discrepancy of the mythological and realistic attitude. This is aimed at in two different ways: the plates by Crusius for Palthen's translation (Rostock, 1766), give more space to the mythlogical part and try to remold the landscape more uniformly. The latter is also the evident aim of Dodd's drawings, which show greater nearness of view (engraved by T. Cook) in Rivington's edition of 1788, as well as of Hamilton's, who used the scheme once more in 1797 for the headpiece to the Spring. But the method of mere enumeration is kept up, and all mythological elements renounced, in the commercial engravings by E. Malpas (about 1770). Finally an

Ryley delt.   White sculp

anonymous artist in the Dublin edition of 1773 has tried with rather negative success to show mainly the mythological part.

3. *The sequences of illustrations of single scenes*

Kent's illustrations are the only ones which have found a long succession. In contemplating this third group of illustrative sequences we have, however, to deal nearly always with fresh inventions. The literary model offered so many single aspects, that, as soon as the artist once freed himself from the ideal of a general view, the possibilities for illustration became unlimited. An exception in the series of pictures without tradition is only made in those illustrating the four interwoven tales (see below). The rest of them represent, just as the poetic fiction of the time about the change of the century, all the translations from the classic to romantic feeling for nature. The group possesses a forerunner in the marvellous plates by C. Eisen for the French translation of 1759. Eisen chose for summer and autumn two of the novels, whilst for winter he shows the interior of a peasant's cottage with the inmates amusing themselves on a long winter evening. The giving of an absolute picture of the milieu is not, as yet, achieved, for the things happening all at one time in one room are indeed typical in their single aspects, but unreal in their union. Thus even this plate, little as it seems so on first sight, is nothing more than the combination of single scenes in a fully satisfactory artistic way. Entirely different is the spring illustration. It depicts how boys lift a young bird from the nest to put into a cage. This is the earliest picture for which a single episode of the poem was chosen.

What Eisen commenced in 1759 was continued in England only in the nineties; everything in between belongs to the two former groups. From now onwards the illustrated editions indeed multiply; there follow up to the end of century: in 1793 three different new sets of illustrations, in 1794 two, in 1786, 1797 and 1799 one each.

The series is opened by Ansell, 1792, with pastoral scenes for spring and summer, trifling and wholly estranged from reality. Spiritually related to these are the illustrations by Catton, Metz (1793), Hamilton (1797), and Corbould (1797), which idealize country life and peasantry in a sentimental and falsifying way

(Fig. 2). A new realistic touch appears with Stothard; he is here, as often, instructive in a mild and charming manner, without great pathos, simply depicting the peasants in their rural occupations. In the pictures by J. Cruikshank, 1794, the part of the landscape is more strongly accentuated; the people are hardly more than decorations. Next to him the engravings by F. Genelli, 1796, find their place, and still more advanced, the drawings by J. P. Powell, whose image of autumn is the first purely landscape picture in this display of illustrations. Rural scenes in romantic surroundings are shown by Cranmer (1802), Thurston-Bewick (1805), and an anonymous artist of the Thurston Circle (1806). Here human beings again begin to play a decisive part; the story element imprints its special mark on these illustrations. It dominates in Westall (1816) and above all in the charming scenes composed by Uwins (1811). The line ends with Thomson (1820), who takes up the model of his predecessors.

There the illustration of the *Seasons* stops for a long time. About the middle of the century the poem was again illustrated twice: in 1842 by J. Bell, C. W. Cope and T. Creswick; in 1859 by Birket Foster and others. In our days an artist has attempted to illustrate the poem again (Jacquier, 1927).

4. *The illustration of the stories*

Most illustrations of the third group give special space to depicting the four stories which Thomson interlaced into his poem; these often replace even the season-scenes. The stories have also evoked special literary interest; sometimes they are translated separately, and the one of Lavinia was once even enlarged into a most touching tale. They were so popular that their themes even served high art; Gainsborough's painting of Musidora and his Lavinia give evidence for this.

Especially preferred were the stories of Musidora and of Lavinia, the one because of its erotic charm, the other on account of its sentimental and touching emotion. Kent had already intermixed the Musidora scene with his summer illustration, taking up the first version of the story: the despiser of women, young Damon, is converted by the sight of three bathing girls, Musidora being one of them. It seems to have been a great difficulty to show the looker-on so that in the manifold scenes of the engraving he is still to be recognized, and consequently he appears far too large in proportion (Fig. 1).

Later on Thomson retouched the novel: Damon now is the lover, who by chance witnesses his beloved whilst bathing, and after having thoroughly enjoyed the sight, leaves a few lines for her before running away. Musidora reads his message and scratches an answer on the trunk of a tree. The bathing-scene with the looker-on was a most popular theme for illustration. Usually it was depicted thus: Musidora is standing totally or nearly undressed on the bank of a brook in the woods; between the shrubbery Damon's head appears. The composition was often taken from similar older types of pictures, so from Gainsborough and Crusius (1766) Susanne bathing—(Musidora here sits down)—in aftertime this scheme is influenced by the model of statues of Venus; this is the case, for example, in the drawings by Hamilton, Metz and Stothard. Thurston, 1805, pictures a whole novel, showing not only the bathing scene, but also the running away of the youth. At the beginning of the nineteenth century prudery puts an end to all this, only the scene of the scratching the love letter on the tree remains (Corbould 1799, Powell 1802, Westall 1816).

The other scene chosen equally often is the story of the poor, but noble Lavinia, who must look for work in the fields at harvest time—but whom the proprietor of the estate, Palemon, watching her at work, recognizes as the child of his friend and then marries. Usually this scene of recognition and wooing is represented, in a sentimental way by Ansell, with simplicity by Stothard, Cruikshank and others. The story offered many possibilities for setting, and so occasionally themes of the following kind are treated: the mother tells Lavinia the story of her noble birth (Hamilton, Thurston), or Lavinia decides herself to accept harvest work (Westall), and similar episodes. Another novel relates how Amelia and her lover Geladon are overtaken in the woods by a thunderstorm and how she is killed by lightning. The illustration of this story was undertaken by only a few artists, mostly they show the girl trying to shelter herself in the man's arms, Ansell (1792) again sentimentally; T. Uwins (1811) interestingly. Powell depicts a thunderstorm-scene, Genelli the lament of death.

In ''Winter'' Thomson tells the story of a shepherd who lost his way and was frozen to death in the snow. Two types of illustra-

49

And will not the severe excuse a sigh?
Scorn the proud man that is ashamed to weep;
Our tears indulged indeed deserve our shame:
Ye that e'er lost an angel! pity me.

Soon as the lustre languish'd in her eye,
Dawning a dimmer day on human sight;
And on her cheek, the residence of spring,
Pale omen sat, and scatter'd fears around
On all that saw, and who would cease to gaze
That once had seen? with haste, parental haste
I flew, I snatch'd her from the rigid north,
Her native bed, on which bleak boreas blew,
And bore her nearer to the sun; the sun,
As if the sun could envy, check'd his beam,
Denied his wonted succour, nor with more
Regret beheld her drooping, than the bells
Of lilies! fairest lilies not so fair.

Queen lilies! and ye painted populace!
Who dwell in fields, and lead ambrosial lives;
In morn and evening dew your beauties bathe,
And drink the sun, which gives your cheeks to glow,
And out-blush, mine excepted, every fair;
You gladlier grew, ambitious of her hand
Which often cropp'd your odours, incense meet
To thought so pure: ye lovely fugitives!
Coëval race with man, for man you smile;
Why not smile at him too? you share indeed
His sudden pass, but not his constant pain.

So man is made, nought ministers delight
But what his glowing passions can engage;

Fig. 1. Page from E. Young, *The Complaint and the Consolation (Night Thoughts)*, London, printed by R. Noble for R. Edwards, 1797; illustrating Night III, v. 116–119, designed and engraved by Blake.

tions appear: the shepherd stretched out in the snow (Hamilton, Ansell, Westall), and, less pathetic, the shepherd still walking, trying to find his way (Stothard, Thurston and others).

The editions of the years about the turn of the century show clearly the growing preference for such narrative scenes. Thus occasionally even scenes are illustrated which Thomson only treats as insertions, but which have, when put asunder, no longer any connection whatever with the main theme, the Seasons. Such illustrations are for example the sailor in the thunderstorm by Catton, the wolf's attack by Hamilton, Thurston and Cranmer, Thurston's sturdy drinker, who becomes angry over the weak younger generation, and the resting wood-cutter, whom Hamilton designed in 1797 after Gainsborough's picture.

VIII. The literary position of Young's *Night Thoughts* is similar to that of Thomson's *Seasons* inasmuch as it is placed just as the former on the verge of two epochs and, although it was written during the climax of late baroque and classical mentality, it embodied so many ideas pointing to the future that it exercised a direct and deep influence lasting till long after the end of the century.

How this phenomenon finds its explanation is developed by H. H. Clark in a splendid essay, on *The Romanticism of Edward Young,* 1929. He puts the question: how could the work of a religious poet, supposed to be thoroughly reactionary, meet with such enthusiasm just at the epoch of enlightenment and religious hostility, in England as well as on the Continent, and most strongly in Germany? And he comes to the conclusion that the cause ought to be looked for in the singularity of Young's religious perception.

The *Night Thoughts* are a work of old age; Young wrote them when he was sixty, in a state of deep discontent with the world. After having for a long time led a life that was anything but spiritual, he accepted at the age of forty-five, driven by dejection caused by unmerited neglect, the post of a schoolmaster and country vicar and secluded himself more and more from the outer world. The deaths of his stepdaughter (1736), and her husband (1740), and lastly of his wife in 1741, left him yet more lonely. The poem arose out of this mood.

The Epic shows almost no action, the blows of fate which

struck him in his own experience are scarcely interwoven. The *Night Thoughts* consist of freaks and visions of life and death, love and friendship, full of absolute contempt for everything mortal, and only having roots in the longing for union with God.

Young, like most of the later romantics, found no peace for himself, even though he asserts so in the second part, the Consolation. His Christianity is not that of the active believer who aims in this world at the Imitatio Christi, but that of the mystic, the romantic, who seeks out the solitude of night for the sake of resting undisturbed alone with his world and his God, who always tries to find the eternal light without ever being fully appeased by having part in it. It is the same attitude of soul that later on finds its expression in Novalis and Tieck, Shelley and Keats. Thus it is to be comprehended that Young, much as he belongs in many ways to his own time, yet only reached the climax of his importance long after his death.

The editions of the *Night Thoughts,* beginning in 1741, follow one another quickly. Illustrations are missing, with exception of a frontispiece etched by Vertue for the fifth night, appearing for the first time in 1743, the rather poor drawing of a churchyard by moonlight with the poet before a grave. This engraving is to be found again in a great number of later editions. A further equally primitive frontispiece appears after 1756; Hayman did the design and Grignion the engraving: death at the bedside of a sick person. This plate too turns up frequently. Lastly, the French and English edition (Marseilles, 1770) contains three very insignificant engravings which were adopted for a few Italian translations and a Portuguese. That is all there is of illustrations for the poem, for what the edition by J. French (London, 1777) adds with its six engravings is so insignificant that it cannot be counted. The poem, full of visions as it is resisted all transcription into visual form because its time had no artist capable of the task.

It continued to be thus up to the nineties, the epoch in which book illustration became the great fashion. The first publishers who ordered illustrations were Chapman & Co., 1793, and the artist chosen was Corbould. The choice could not have been more unlucky. The designs Corbould made are nothing but sodden allergories. Another artist took part in these illustrations, Ryley whose name appears on two infinitely superior plates: a Triumph of Death (Fig. 3) and a scene for the third night, in which the poet

transports sick Narcissa into a Southern country. On a barren
highland a sickly young woman, seeking protection, leans towards a man who looks despairingly up to the sky, where the sun
tries to break through a mass of black clouds. The words of the
text say (III, 116–119): "I snatched her from the rigid north, her
native bed on which black Boreas blew, And bore her nearer to the
sun." Later on this passage was chosen once more for illustration
by Blake.

The first five engravings in Chapman's edition are not signed;
two of them, the first and third, might possibly have been done by
Ryley.

Unhappily Corbould received a second order to provide the
poem with pictures. The engravings only appear in 1804 in the
edition of Ottridge & Co., F. and C. Rivington and others. The
spirit of these illustrations is the same as in the former ones: most
insipid allegories of instability, of the seasons, of the crown of
life, and so on. One example for many: Passage I 305–307, "Take
then, O world, thy much indebted tear; How sad a sight is human
happiness, To those whose thought can pierce beyond an hour."
These very beautiful verses look like this in Corbould's imagination and picturing: the poet sits weeping below a willow, armed
with a huge handkerchief, whilst in the background children
dance on a meadow.

Besides the two sequences by Corbould there exist (with the
exception of the one by Blake) only two others till 1830, the one
by Stothard 1798, the other by Westall 1827. The latter does not
differ in spirit very much from Corbould. But Westall takes up
realistic scenes for illustration, such as the funeral or the sickbed,
and thus in his modesty is quite tolerable, although nothing
whatever of the poem's spirit is reflected in these little pictures.
Totally different is Stothard. It is evident that here he submits to
the spiritual influence of Blake. Besides, the poem itself may have
inspired and carried him away: though his creations are not
comparable to those of Blake, yet in his simple, pure and plain
way of depicting he does justice to the poem. Some of the pictures
are very religious: the praying poet perceives in a dream angelic
beings, the Ascension of Christ and so on. It is Stothard's positive
creed that manifests itself in these designs, not the dissent of
Young. Another illustration is as fantastic as a fairy tale: the
Night, a female dressed in black, divides the clouds showing the

sphere of the stars to the poet. Again another one is full of horror, a very uncommon note in Stothard's work: death has taken off the mask that concealed him and sits triumphantly on horseback on the overthrown table holding by the throat one of the people who did not recognize him and crushing him on the floor.

One year before Stothard's sequel appeared, in 1797, the editor Edwards published his folio edition with Blake's engravings which unfortunately was not finished; only the first part, comprising four nights, appeared. As an illustrated book this volume belongs to the most perfect ever done. Rarely is such a high level of artistic union between letterpress and illustration, visual and literary contents reached.

Externally the union is already accentuated by picture and text being joined on one leaf. The letterpress is framed by a line and occupies the middle of the large page, the designs the four spacious borders. Yet these illustrations are in no way margin-drawings. The composition extends itself over the whole leaf, thus trying to give an impression as if the text were only covering part of the picture. Likewise as picture and word are only two different forms of expression for the same contents, by the identity of the paper surface both are already united visually, in such a way that the eye cannot observe the one without perceiving the other at the same time.

Blake designed in all 537 illustrations for the poem, which extend over the nine nights. Only 43 of them were engraved. If the plan had been carried out as conceived by Blake, it would have become the most comprehensive and perhaps the most perfect pictorial work done by him. Here Blake tries for the first time to realize on a large scale his own idea of book illustration. He had already done work like the plates for Gay's *Fables,* where he was only one of the illustrating artists and so had to comply with a fixed scheme; and also, of course, the illustrations for his own poetic writings, for which he invented his well known method of reproduction. It is a fact that at first he only reluctantly began the task, because he felt the necessity of accommodating his designs to a literary pattern not his own as an injury to his artistic force of invention. For him word and picture were only two different forms of expressing his thoughts, they were the medium, not the end, without value in themselves. And as these thoughts always tended to the celestial, their expression had to be dark and incomprehensible to an outer world in which the breach between celestial and terrestrial life, of religion and ethics had already shown itself; that same world destined to introduce nineteenth century realism and materialism, whose climax we are perhaps witnessing just now. Blake's designs have been considered singular and eccentric, they have been disregarded, but also deeply admired for their mysticism. Certainly he uses strange symbols, signs with which he connected a fixed meaning. But this is not the main thing. The force of expression in his pictures does not derive from knowledge of these symbols (for such knowledge is again only a resource, the way, not the end), but from the fact of a personality whose conception of the world is still determined by a centre in God. Here lies the force even of such pictures as have been denied artistic perfection.

Blake enlarged himself during work. He grew together with his literary pattern in such a way as if it were sprung up out of himself. And thus he transposed Young's visions, which finally became his own, into his imagery. He neither interpreted nor explained them, but experienced these visions afresh and represented what he saw by his own artistic means. The reason for the astonishing identity of both works of art lies in the natural relationship of Young and Blake: the latter never would have been able or ready to insinuate himself into ways of thought not corresponding with his own nature.

THE JOURNEY AND THE PICTURE: THE ART OF STERNE AND HOGARTH
William Holtz

"I would give both my Ears," wrote Laurence Sterne to his new acquaintance Richard Berenger in March 1760, ". . . for no more than ten Strokes of *Howgarth's* witty Chissel, to clap at the Front of my next Edition of *Shandy.* . . . The loosest Sketch in Nature, of Trim's reading the Sermon to my Father &c; w^d do the Business."[1] The gist of this letter, which Sterne wrote in his first days of fame as an author, was a plea that Berenger (who knew Hogarth) act as intermediary for Sterne (who did not) in securing the specified illustration for this second edition of *Tristram Shandy* (Books I & II), which Sterne's publisher now undertook on the strength of the immediate success of the initial printing. Berenger accepted the mission and was successful: the result was the first of two illustrations Hogarth did for Sterne's book. The original drawings for both of these are now part of the Berg Collection of The New York Public Library.

The first will occupy our attention here—the famous scene in which Corporal Trim reads the sermon on conscience to the group assembled in the Shandy sitting-room to await Tristram's birth. The passage as it appears in *Tristram Shandy,* even with a paragraph omitted, seems extremely long and detailed; but this, as we shall see, is to a purpose:

> He stood before them with his body swayed, and bent forwards just so far, as to make an angle of 85 degrees and a half upon the plain of the horizon;—which sound orators, to whom I address this, know very well, to be the true persuasive angle of incidence;—in any other angle you may

Reprinted by permission from *New York Public Library Bulletin,* January 1967, pp. 25–38.

talk and preach;—'tis certain,—and it is done every day;—
but with what effect,—I leave the world to judge!

The necessity of this precise angle of 85 degrees and a half
to a mathematical exactness,—does it not shew us, by the
way,—how the arts and sciences mutually befriend each
other? . . .

He stood,—for I repeat it, to take the picture of him in at
one view, with his body sway'd, and somewhat bent forwards,—his right-leg firm under him, sustaining seven-
eighths of his whole weight,—the foot of his left-leg, the
defect of which was no disadvantage to his attitude, advanced a little,—not laterally, nor forwards, but in a line
betwixt them;—his knee bent, but that not violently,—but so
as to fall within the limits of the line of beauty;—and I add,
of the line of science too;—for consider, it had one eighth
part of his body to bear up;—so that in this case the position
of the leg is determined,—because the foot could be no
further advanced, or the knee more bent, than what would
allow him mechanically, to receive an eighth part of his
whole weight under it,—and to carry it too.

This I recommend to painters:—need I add,—to ora-
tors?—I think not; for, unless they practice it,—they must
fall upon their noses.

So much for Corporal *Trim's* body and legs.—He held the
sermon loosely,—not carelessly, in his left-hand, raised
something above his stomach, and detach'd a little from his
breast;—his right-arm falling negligently by his side, as
nature and the laws of gravity ordered it,—but with the palm
of it open and turned towards his audience, ready to aid the
sentiment, in case it stood in need.   (II.17.122–23)

Sterne specified this scene in his request to Berenger because in
his text he had "drawn" the figure of Trim (and, in an earlier
passage, that of Dr Slop) in playful accord with the theories of
form which Hogarth had developed several years earlier in his
Analysis of Beauty (1753);[2] and he saw in this joining of their
talents an opportunity to "transmit us hand in hand together down
to futurity." But this union of the painter and writer was in fact
also sanctioned by the generally received "pictorialist" theory of
literature of the day,[3] which in turn was grounded in a centuries-
old traditional relationship between the "sister arts" that dated at
least from Simonides' observation that "painting is mute poetry,

and poetry a speaking picture," and which was authoritatively reinforced by Horace's recommendation (seldom quoted in context) that "a poem should be like a painting." What I should like to examine here are certain aspects of the work of Sterne and Hogarth that mutually clarify one another when viewed against the background of this close relationship between the arts. The illustration by Hogarth will provide a convenient nexus from which to begin this study.

I

The tradition that brought Sterne and Hogarth together was nourished from two sources: a pictorialist theory of literature and a literary theory of painting; and these in turn rested upon a mimetic theory of art with a strong visual bias. The idea that literature somehow imitated the visible surface of life is expressed by Plato and Aristotle as well as by Simonides and Horace, and the analogy with painting was natural and useful, as was an appeal to the assumed "superiority" of the sense of sight. Neoclassical England knew well the texts in which these ideas occurred; and the veneration accorded classical authority was strengthened by a widespread admiration for Renaissance art and a familiarity with the "literary" theory of painting that Renaissance critics had evolved—a body of doctrine that had grown out of a search for a theory worthy of the manifest glory of Renaissance painting itself. No treatise had survived from antiquity that would serve the painter as the *Poetics* and the *Ars Poetica* served the poet, and it is not surprising that the painter-critics of this period should have appropriated the concepts they found in literary theory. The theory they developed was essentially humanistic, describing painting as an imitation of human action; and it was not uncommon to encounter elaborate prescriptions as to subject, models, historical accuracy, decorum, and moral purpose, all based on literary counterparts.

In neoclassical England, the man of letters was often a connoisseur of painting as well; and the painter was apt to be as concerned with the "history" or "fable" of his work as with the technique of painting. "Painting and Poesy are two sisters," Dryden wrote in

1695, translating Dufresnoy's *De arte graphica;* and Garrick in 1766 simply changed genders in expressing the same idea in the prologue to *The Clandestine Marriage:*

> Poets and Painters, who from Nature draw
> Their best and richest Stores, have made this Law:
> That each should neighborly assist his Brother,
> And steal with Decency from one another.

Reynolds spoke for the painter when he insisted on "that nobleness of conception" which is acquired "by warming his imagination with the best productions of ancient and modern poetry"; and his friend Johnson spoke for the man of letters when he avowed that "of the parallels which have been drawn by wit and curiosity, some are literal and real, as between poetry and painting."[4] Just how far these parallels extended was not clear—both Dryden and Reynolds became involved in some highly dubious analogies between diction in poetry and coloring in painting—but there was a broad common ground assumed. The painter shared with his audience an immersion in classical and Christian literature, and the poet shared a familiarity with a pantheon of Renaissance and Baroque art. Generally speaking, it was accepted that the highest type of painting was the "history," a scene from the literature of antiquity or Christianity which implied the whole of a traditional narrative; and that a central aim of literature was, in the words of Joseph Warton, to raise "*clear, complete,* and *circumstantial* images, and [to turn] *readers* into *spectators.*"[5] In such a context must we view this transaction between William Hogarth and Laurence Sterne.

II

We first must recognize that both Sterne and Hogarth may seem rather out of place in this tradition. For the pictorial tradition was typically heroic, idealized, and eminently serious: Hogarth, in his best work, is none of these, nor is Sterne. This difference aside, however, both can be seen as centrally involved in the literary-pictorial dialogue of their age, each as demonstrating a particularly extreme movement of one art toward the other. We will consider Hogarth first.

Hogarth's work is notable for the attention it has received from literary men. Charles Lamb observed that his "graphic representations are indeed books; they have the teeming, fruitful, suggestive meaning of *words.* Other pictures we look at—his prints we read." William Hazlitt included Hogarth in his *Lectures on the English Comic Writers,* and Thackeray, in *The English Humourists of the Eighteenth Century,* pointed out the value of Hogarth's prints as illustrations to Fielding and Smollett. In this century an entire study has been devoted to Hogarth's role as a literary figure, especially to the influence his pictorial narratives may have had on Fielding's *Joseph Andrews* and *Tom Jones.*[6] These associations reflect the special nature of his art—dramatic, anecdotal, realistic, topical, and comic, often as concerned with narrative content as with visible form. He advertised himself as the "Author" of his works,[7] and his self-portrait of 1745 (the canvas rests upon volumes of "Shakespeare," "Milton," and "Swift") indicates that he saw himself in a line with the great English writers. In his memoirs he asserted:

> I . . . wished to compose pictures on canvas similar to representations on the stage, and further hope that they will be tried by the same test and criticized by the same criterion. . . . I have endeavoured to treat my subjects as a dramatic writer: my picture is my stage, and men and women my players, who, by means of certain actions and gestures, are to exhibit a *dumb shew.*[8]

One measure of his success as a "writer" was that his head appeared as a signboard not only for several print sellers but for a bookseller as well.[9] And Richardson, Fielding, Smollett, and Henry Mackenzie—as well as Sterne—all borrowed from his work.

The works which made Hogarth's fame, and upon which his reputation still largely rests, were his "narrative" series: *A Harlot's Progress, The Rake's Progress, Marriage à la Mode,* and *Industry and Idleness.*[10] Hogarth referred to these as works in a "novel mode"; and although the narrative impulse had been latent in art based on saints' legends and in book illustrations, his claim is valid, for there is no real precedent for his self-conscious and determined effort to embody a unified, highly detailed narrative in picture. His aim, like the dramatic writer he compared himself with, was to present a significant action—a cast of characters involved in a plot with a beginning, middle, and end. Not only do successive plates depict stages in this action, but the individual scenes themselves are so composed as to suggest prior and subsequent events—that is, to be "read" as acts or chapters occupying a segment of time. As Moll Hackabout arrives in London, her future is implicit in the fulsome greeting of the old bawd and the leer of the middle-aged courtier in the background; her background is amply indicated by her plain dress, the country wagon which has brought her to town, and the goose hanging from her basket. As Tom Rakewell carouses in a tavern, the broken lantern and staff at his feet reveal that he has fought with and defeated a watchman, while in the background stands an attendant with a lighted candle and large pewter plate, accessories for an entertainment to be commenced as soon as one of the harlots has finished removing her clothes.[11]

Hogarth achieved a peculiarly temporal dimension by such techniques, and this impression is intensified by his fondness for effects comparable to those of modern high-speed photography. Often his characters are caught in a moment of arrested action—Moll as she kicks over the tea-table, Tom as he lurches from his sedan-chair—or inanimate objects are suspended in mid-fall—a pile of buckets teeters on the point of crashing to the ground, money drops from a secret cache in the ceiling, a sword balances on its tip before clattering to the floor. And the features of the characters also are often frozen in momentary grimaces or transient plays of feeling: as Hazlitt noted, "the expression is always taken *en passant,* in a state of progress or change."[12] Typically the whole picture seems to tremble at the edge of motion; it is as though Hogarth sought to make the barest of concessions to the limits of his medium, to generate for his composition its own continuum of time. Also to this end he fixed his "narratives" firmly in historical time: minor figures are occasionally recognizable as characters on the contemporary scene; the exact date of the harlot's death is labeled on her coffin, which was supposed to indicate also the date Hogarth completed the series;[13] Tom Rakewell's last, disastrous night of gambling at White's can be dated by a fire just breaking out in the background, presumably the start of an actual conflagration that had occurred just two years before the print appeared. And it is but a refinement of this technique to place an event in horological time. As one of his biographers has observed,

> it is noteworthy how many of Hogarth's scenes, both indoors and outdoors, happen to contain a clock, and that the clock he introduces always appears to tell the real hour. Time is perpetually moving, as his personages move.[14]

Without attempting to judge the absolute value of Hogarth's narrative art, we can recognize that many of its unique features derive from his efforts to transcend the limits of his medium. His work in this respect presents a curious and extreme development of the literary theory of painting, a tradition analogous to that of pictorial literature and one which found its more conventional expression in the history of paintings of Reynolds and in Hogarth's own less renowned work in the grand manner. The intermingling of aesthetic premises in this period was congenial to such experiments; and the transition to *Tristram Shandy* can be made by way of analogy and contrast, for this brief examination of Hogarth's work enables us to see Sterne's as a similar kind of experiment. Just as Hogarth, aware of limits imposed by the spatial and static nature of his medium, sought to achieve narrative effects, so Sterne, sensitive to the deficiences of narrative, attempted to render effects that may well be called spatial and static.

III

Sterne was not the first novelist to find inspiration in Hogarth. Fielding and Smollett seem frequently to have had Hogarth's pictures in mind as they visualized the characters of their stories,[15] much as Sterne also invoked Hogarth when he "drew" the figures of Dr Slop and Corporal Trim. My concern here, however, is not with Sterne's debt to Hogarth, but with the way in which Sterne moved toward the painter's domain as he comically explored the outer ranges of his own craft. For if the generally accepted aesthetic of the day viewed painting and writing each as the exemplar of the other, the work of Sterne and Hogarth can be seen as complementary efforts to achieve, in the most extreme sense, this obviously impossible ideal.

We might approach the general problem by considering three passages in which a novelist attempts to "depict" a character in the grip of strong feeling. The first two, by Fielding and Smollett, reveal by allusion to Hogarth the pictorial orientation of the writers: the third from *Tristram Shandy,* is an elaborate extension of the pictorial principle of the other two.

> O, Shakespear! had I thy pen! O, Hogarth! had I thy pencil! then would I draw the picture of the poor serving-man, who, with pale countenance, staring eyes, chattering teeth, faultering tongue, and trembling limbs . . . entered the room.   (*Tom Jones* X.8)

> It would require the pencil of Hogarth to express the astonishment and concern of Strap, on hearing this piece of news. The bason in which he was preparing the lather for my chin, dropped out of his hands, and he remained some time immovable in that ludicrous attitude, with his mouth open, and his eyes thrust forward considerably beyond their station.   (*Roderick Random* III.47)

> The moment my father got up into his chamber, he threw himself prostrate across his bed in the wildest disorder imaginable, but at the same time, in the most lamentable attitude of a man borne down with sorrows, that ever the eye of pity dropp'd a tear for.—The palm of his right hand, as he fell upon the bed, receiving his forehead, and covering the greatest part of both his eyes, gently sunk down with his head (his elbow giving way backwards) till his nose touch'd the quilt;—his left arm hung insensible over the side of the bed, his knuckles reclining upon the handle of the chamber pot, which peep'd out beyond the valance;—his right leg (his left being drawn up towards his body) hung half over the side of the bed, the edge of it pressing upon his shin-bone.— He felt it not. A fix'd inflexible sorrow took possession of every line of his face.—He sigh'd once,—heaved his breast often,—but utter'd not a word.   (III.29.215–16)

The movement through these passages might be described as the expansion of a static center of interest. The "action" in progress, we must assume, is stopped for inspection of its visual detail: the narrative must halt for the picture. This is neither an original nor a profound observation, but it is a means of getting at a central principle in Sterne's strange work. For although Fielding and Smollett arrest the "movement" of their narratives for a significant image, this momentary stasis is in the interest of, and subordinate to, the forward progress of an "action": implicit are narrative conventions as old as the epic—that the action might be judiciously suspended to permit description or analysis, then set in motion again; or that an action so suspended might be assumed to continue unnoticed, then picked up at a later point.[16] But Sterne recognized in these conventions an uneasy compromise with the nature of life itself, which is lived in time and space simultaneously; and in the futile efforts of his hero Tristram to write a "story," he reveals the problems that accrue to the writer from these conventions.

"Oh ye POWERS!" Tristram apostrophizes in a moment of difficulty,

> (for powers ye are, and great ones too)—which enable mortal man to tell a story worth the hearing,—that kindly shew him, where he is to begin it,—and where he is to end it,—what he is to put into it,—and what he is to leave out,—how much of it he is to cast into shade,—and whereabouts he is to throw his light!—Ye, who preside over this vast empire of biographical freebooters, and see how many scrapes and plunges your subjects hourly fall into;—will you do one thing?
>
> I beg and beseech you, (in case you will do nothing better for us) that wherever, in any part of your dominions it so falls out, that three several roads meet in one point, as they have done just here,—that at least you set up a guide-post, in the center of them, in mere charity to direct an uncertain devil, which of the three he is to take. (III.23.207)

Three things are worth noting in this passage. The first is that Tristram sees his dilemma as basically a matter of narrative technique, of selection and arrangement of the parts of his tale. The other two are the metaphors, common in *Tristram Shandy,* that intersect here: the narrative as a journey in one instance, as a painting in another. Together these embody the essence of an aesthetic problem Sterne explored in the pages of *Tristram Shandy:* how to capture in a narrative form the sense of total and simultaneous representation inherent in a painting, how to achieve static effects in the medium of time—in short, how to paint the picture of Tristram's journey through life.

In his more optimistic moments Tristram is confident. "The painting of this journey," he says of a suppressed passage, "appears to be so much above the stile and manner of anything else I have been able to paint in this book, that it could not have remained in it, without depreciating every other scene; and destroying at the same time that necessary equipoise and balance . . . betwixt chapter and chapter" (IV. 25.315). But more typical is his uncertainty which road to take:

> The story, in one sense, is certainly out of its place here; for by right it should come in, either amongst the anecdotes of my uncle *Toby's* amours with widow *Wadman,* in which corporal *Trim* was no mean actor,—or else in the middle of his and my under *Toby's* campaigns on the bowling green,— for it will do very well in either place;—but then if I reserve it for either of those parts of my story,—I ruin the story I'm upon,—and if I tell it here—I anticipate matters, and ruin it there. (III.23.207)

Tristram's uncertainty stems from his refusal to compromise the integrity of his material for the sake of that "equipoise and balance." For although his chosen form offered him conventions for shaping his narrative, to shape meant to sacrifice, to select, and, especially, to leave some things behind as he followed a given line of progress; and Tristram is loathe to omit anything. Very early in his story he warns the reader that "when a man sits down to write a history . . . he knows no more than his heels what lets and confounded hindrances he is to meet with in his way"; and then comes the figure which presages the shape of his work in the volumes to follow:

> Could a historiographer drive on his history, as a muleteer drives on his mule,—straight forward . . . without ever once turning his head aside either to the right hand or to the

left,—he might venture to foretell you to an hour when he should get to his journey's end;—but the thing is, morally speaking, impossible: For, if he is a man of the least spirit, he will have fifty deviations from a straight line to make with this or that party as he goes along, which he can no ways avoid. He will have views and prospects to himself perpetually solliciting his eye, which he can no more help standing still to look at than he can fly. (I.14.36–37)

And late in his book, when the ostensible subject of his narrative coincides with his favorite metaphor, that is, when writing of a journey, he contrasts mere barren progress with the delights of dalliance: nothing, says Tristram, is more fatal to a travel writer than a plain, for it "presents nothing to the eye, but one unvaried picture of plenty," and after a brief description it is of no use to him but to carry him to the next city, then to the next plain, and so on. Tristram, however, determines to manage his plains better; by deliberately pursuing variety, he says, he made his journey across the south of France "the most fruitful and busy period of my life";

> for as I had made no convention . . . as to time—by stopping and talking to every soul I met who was not in a full trot—joining all parties before me—waiting for every soul behind—hailing all those who were coming through cross roads—arresting all kinds of beggars, pilgrims, fiddlers, fryars—not passing by a woman in a mulberry-tree without commending her legs, and tempting her into conversation with a pinch of snuff—In short, by seizing every handle, of what size or shape soever, which chance held out to me in this journey—I turned my *plain* into a *city*—(VII.43.535–36)

One of the stops he makes on this trip is at an inn, where his encounter with the innkeeper's daughter is recorded in a passage which reveals in radical simplicity his desire to salvage from the flux of time something of the actual texture of immediate-experience. Janatone is a charming beauty; she must go into his book; again the pictorial metaphor appears:

> As *Janatone* . . . stands so well for a drawing—may I never draw more . . . if I do not draw her in all her proportions, and

with as determin'd a pencil, as if I had her in the wettest
drapery.—

*   *   *

he who measures thee, *Janatone,* must do it now—thou
carriest the principles of change within thy frame; and
considering the chances of a transitory life, I would not
answer for thee a moment; e'er twice twelve months are
pass'd and gone, thou mayest grow out like a pumkin, and
lose thy shapes—or, thou mayest go off like a flower, and
lose thy beauty—nay, thou mayest go off like a hussy—and
lose thyself.   (VII.9.490)

And later it is Nanette who diverts his progress, a maid whose slit
petticoat halts his narrative for a moment of joyous dance. Here
the journey-metaphor is transformed again, merging into an
allusion to his earlier attempt to graph the convolutions of his
narrative by squiggly lines: the ideal, he had conceded then, was
the straight line, as if drawn by a ruler—or a man planting
cabbages. Now he pulls out a paper of black lines to remind
himself again to go straight forwards: but on the next page he
gives it up:

I defy the best cabbage planter . . . to go on coolly, critically,
and canonically, planting his cabbages one by one, in
straight lines, and stoical distances, especially if slits in
petticoats are unsew'd up—without ever and anon straddling
out, or sidling into some bastardly digression.   (VIII.1.539)

IV

To use Sterne's own metaphors, the tension between the journey
and the picture in *Tristram Shandy* is resolved heavily in the
latter's favor. That is to say, in Tristram's refusal, or inability, to
pursue "a straight line" in his story, Sterne subverts the normal
temporal movement of narrative in favor of other values. Prime
among these is the pictorial: Trim reading the sermon and Walter
collapsed across his bed we have already noticed, but *Tristram
Shandy* is full of such immobilized figures, presented singly and

in tableaux: Walter and Toby conversing upon the stairway, the death-bed of Le Fever, Trim and Toby advancing upon widow Wadman, Trim's oration in the kitchen, Mrs Shandy listening at the doorway. Within the scenes, action is largely subordinated to dialogue or limited to the details of gesture and expression, while the scenes themselves do not merge into a coherent sequence but remain isolated—disconnected fragments of the story Tristram wants to tell. In varying degrees the effect of each scene is pictorial; and Sterne's request for Hogarth's drawing of Trim and his audience is but a further extension of this recurring attempt in *Tristram Shandy* to record in outline and detail the visible surface of life. And Sterne's effort in a narrative-temporal mode to suspend his characters motionless in a moment of time is the exact complement of Hogarth's effort, in a pictorial-spatial mode, to make his characters tremble dramatically on the verge of movement.

But this is only one aspect of a larger problem that Sterne explores in the continuing dialectic of the picture and the journey. For we will recall that, as Tristram puts it, his problem is not only one of halting for "views and prospects" but also of "straddling out, or sidling into some bastardly digression." "Let me stop and give you a picture," he says (VI.25.451); but when he pulls his narrative mule to a halt, it is as often to interpolate comments on the action or to pursue a digression as it is to render a static image. For just to the extent that the narrative of an action must inevitably scant the visible surface of life, so must any analysis from a consistently held perspective leave out much of the complex, simultaneously perceived welter of life-as-experience. As Tristram often tells us, he has many things on his mind at once; and the abrupt shifts and strange veerings of his abortive autobiography reflect his pursuit of this elusive wholeness. Although one result is a series of spatial images and tableaux, the broader aim (impossible of fulfillment) is to mirror the entire inventory of Tristram's mind—which, alas, increases faster than he can write it down.[17]

So that finally it must be said that Sterne's quarrel was not merely with narrative but actually with the very mode of time itself. His subject was the dynamic stasis that is mental life, the sense of immediate wholeness that constitutes conscious being. Language, as a series of symbols operating through time; narrative, as the abstraction from the flux of life of a causally-connected sequence; and logical analysis, as necessarily consecutive inferences and deductions—all of these conventional tools of the writer were inadequate to this design, which the mind weaves by its own laws, obliterating time in its fusion of past, present, and future.

Small wonder, then, that Tristram, in attempting to tell his story, encounters "unforeseen stoppages," "views and prospects" which impede his progress; and if we would accompany him we must share his resolve "not to be in a hurry" (I.14.37). Our representative is the lady who sometimes appears as Tristram's interlocutor. In a curious merging of his journey-metaphor into a dramatic situation, Tristram halts his narrative to discipline her for reading on too fast. "I do insist upon it," he exclaims, "that you immediately turn back, that is, as soon as you get to the next full stop, and read the whole chapter over again." She departs, and Tristram addresses himself to the rest of his audience:

> I have imposed this penance upon the lady, neither out of wantonness or cruelty, but from the best of motives; and therefore shall make her no apology for it when she returns back:—'Tis to rebuke a vicious taste which has crept into thousands besides herself,—of reading straight forwards.

This "vile pruriency for fresh adventures" (as in Fielding and Smollett) must be controlled, and even when the lady has trudged back from retracing her steps, the narrative hangs suspended while Tristram inserts a document on baptism—an expansion of an aspect of Tristram's thought that had been passed over because of the momentum of the narrative. The problem is Tristram's, true, but it is also the reader's if he persists in reading only "in quest of the adventures" (I.20.56–57).

Implicit in the total "thing" that is *Tristram Shandy* is an alternative to the narrative mode, an alternative demanding that the reader abandon his expectation of conventional linear organization (e.g., an ordered plot) and, instead, respond to *Tristram Shandy* "spatially"—suspending any effort to relate parts temporally, while attempting to apprehend the whole in a moment of time.[18] For we must, finally, to make sense of *Tristram Shandy,* ignore the temporal sequence of the passages and assume that the fragments so erratically juxtaposed are the mental furnishings of a being like ourselves, whose identity comprehends simultaneously all that he recalls, perceives, and foresees. Sterne, an amateur painter himself, found in the sister art first an ideal toward which to shape his tableaux, and second a metaphor for the static, non-temporal quality of subjective life that he strove to imitate. "'Tis . . . a picture of myself," he wrote to Garrick, describing his strange book.[19] His turn of phrase is at once conventional and revealing.

V

The informed reader will wonder at having come this far without encountering the name of the German aesthetician, G. E. Lessing. Lessing's *Laocoon* appeared in 1766, when all but the last volume of *Tristram Shandy* had been published; and although Lessing knew Sterne's work, his central concern was with the major developments of the literary-pictorial tradition, descriptive poetry and allegorical painting. Nonetheless, his argument that painting and writing should observe the limits of the categories, respectively, of space and time, that the writer should bend his efforts to the imitation of actions and the painter to imitations of objects, that attempts to represent simultaneity by means of language, and consecutiveness by means of picture, are violations of natural limits—all of this obviously relevant to the works of Sterne and Hogarth. They illustrate the tendency Lessing sought to oppose, while his general principles allow us to see clearly the problems they encountered.

And more clearly, perhaps, than Lessing himself—or, at least, with a greater awareness of their complexity. Bergson has deepened our sense of the "experiential" (as opposed to the purely metrical) aspect of time to an extent that his earlier counterpart, John Locke, did not do for the eighteenth century—except, perhaps, for Sterne, who, as has frequently been noted, found in Locke a rationale for his fractured time-scheme. But from other sources as well comes evidence to suggest that space and time may in fact not be "real" in themselves, but merely ways of talking about things: the physicist admits to a principle of "indeterminacy" in his inability to measure simultaneously the locus and velocity of a body; he invokes a principle of "comple-mentarity" to justify considering light as at once discrete particles and continuous waves; and he informs us that if we could traverse space fast enough, time itself would stop. The world, we sense, is whole and indivisible, but we are forced to limited and distorting perspectives in our discourse about it; and although we attribute "time" and "space" to the "objective" world, it seems likely that these are merely names for alternative modes of organizing our experience, which, at once simultaneous and sequential, occurs in a unified time-space.[20]

The fact of these limitations, coupled with the special principle of "complementarity" of the neoclassical literary-pictorial aes-thetic, led Sterne and Hogarth to the radical departures I have touched on here. Given the objective mode of their art, they in some measure achieved a complementary mode in the subjective realm. For the captive vibrations of time that we find in Hogarth's pictures, the fluid spatiality of Sterne's narrative, both have their locus in ourselves rather than in the works. The next step, for those who wonder at this, is toward psychology, epistemology, and perception theory; but this is a direction that will not be pursued here. It is enough, perhaps, simply to observe that whatever the world may be, it is for the artist (as for all of us) only what his mind makes of it; and the progress from this vision to its symbolic objectification involves an increasingly narrow perspective. Yet to the extent that art becomes meaningful it transcends these barriers, permeating our whole being by means of highly re-stricted sensory stimuli and creating universally valid images from limited personal experience. It is a miracle that cannot be too much admired.

NOTES

[1]Wilbur L. Cross, *The Life and Times of Laurence Sterne* (3rd ed., revised, New Haven 1929) 215, 587–588. References to *Tristram Shandy* will be to the critical edition by James A. Work (New York, Odyssey Press 1940).

[2]I am engaged in a separate study of Sterne's actual borrowings from Hogarth.

[3]This tradition is best described in Jean H. Hagstrum, *The Sister Arts*

(Chicago 1958), and Renssalaer W. Lee, *"Ut Pictura Poesis:* The Humanistic Theory of Painting," *Art Bulletin* XXII (Dec 1940) 197–269, which I draw on here.

[4]Reynolds, *Third Discourse:* Johnson, *Idler* No. 34.

[5]An *Essay on the Genius and Writings of Pope* (5th ed London 1806) II 160. Vol II was first published 1782.

[6]Charles Lamb, "On the Genius and Character of Hogarth," *The Works of Charles Lamb* (London 1889) IV 107. William Hazlitt, "On the Works of Hogarth," *Lectures on the English Comic Writers* (Lecture VII), *The Collected Works of William Hazlitt* (London 1903) VIII 133–149. William Thackeray, "Hogarth, Smollett, and Fielding," *The English Humourists of the Eighteenth Century* (London 1853). Robert E. Moore, *Hogarth's Literary Relationships* (Minneapolis 1948).

[7]In the advertisements of *A Harlot's Progress.* Cited in Moore, p vii.

[8]John Ireland, *Hogarth Illustrated* (2d ed, London 1804) III 25–26. Cited in Moore 26.

[9]Frederick Antal, *Hogarth and His Place in European Art* (London 1962) 230 n 82.

[10]These works can be found conveniently collected in *The Complete Works of William Hogarth,* introd by James Hannay (London, n.d.).

[11]See Peter Quennell, *Hogarth's Progress* (New York 1955) 92–93, 129–131.

[12]"On the Works of Hogarth" 145.

[13]Moore 8.

[14]Quennell 133, 179.

[15]How very frequently is revealed in the chapters on Fielding and Smollett in Moore's study.

[16]Fielding states these conventions clearly in *Tom Jones* II.i.

[17]See IV.13.285–86, where Tristram considers the problem of giving a minute-by-minute account of life. Bertrand Russell, by the way, has proved (for those who can follow him, as I cannot) that Tristram *would* succeed if he persevered. This paradox between "common sense" and mathematical demonstration Russell has used to illustrate a general principle, but he names it in honor of Tristram. No writer, to my knowledge, has been so persuaded by Russell's proof as to try what Russell says *can* be done. See *The Principles of Mathematics* (2d ed London 1937) 358–360.

[18]I am indebted for this insight to Joseph Frank, "Spatial Form in Modern Literature," *Sewanee Review,* Spring, Summer, and Autumn, 1945. Two points need be made. First, Sterne prefigures the form that Frank finds characteristic of modern literature—Proust, Eliot, Joyce. Second, this "spatiality" is attributable to literature only metaphorically, not "objectively," a point which Frank neglects but which is made

clearly by G. Giovannini, "Method in the Study of Literature in its Relation to the Other Fine Arts," *Journal of Aesthetics and Art Criticism* VIII (March 1960) 185–195. I have suggested elsewhere ("Field Theory and Literature," to be published in *The Centennial Review*) that the two kinds of spatiality join at a higher level of abstraction, which might be called a "field" mode of perception. See also Hans Meyerhoff, *Time in Literature* (Berkeley 1955) 37.

[19]Cross 586.

[20]They may be necessary (i.e., universal) modes, or they may be merely a function of our language, if we follow Benjamin Lee Whorf. See his "Science and Linguistics" *Language, Thought, and Reality* (Cambridge, Mass 1956), especially his comments on the non-temporality of the Hopi language; also Kenneth L. Pike, "Language as Particle, Wave, and Field," *Texas Quarterly* II (Summer 1954) 37–54. The problems of modern physics are discussed in a lucid, non-technical style in the essays comprising Niels Bohr's *Atomic Physics and Human Knowledge* (New York 1958).

THE ENGRAVING AND PRINTING OF THE "HOLBEIN HEADS"
Anthony Dyson

Of the years at the turn of the eighteenth and nineteenth centuries, the engraver Abraham Raimbach noted that in Britain "every-thing connected with [the arts] was at its lowest ebb . . . booksellers were, at this time, the only patrons of engraving." The outlook for artists seems to have been so bleak that members and associates of the Royal Academy were exempted from certain taxes. Raimbach spent nine years at the Academy since "the actual state of engraving, still declining from bad to worse, left [him] ample leisure to adopt [this course]."[2] Life was to be very difficult for many artists throughout the Napoleonic Wars. Thomas Uwins was one whose aspirations, like those of so many colleagues, had to be scaled down to suit the smaller compass of book production. In a letter of 14 May 1816, he complained of hard times and artists' unsold pictures; and in 1821 he was still deploring the difficulty of securing patronage as he wrote from Scotland that "Artists here, as well as in every other part of His Majesty's dominions, are something thicker than three in a bed."[3] Such enterprises as Cadell & Davies's 1817 publication of *Don Quixote*, with illustrations printed by McQueen's from plates engraved after the paintings of Robert Smirke (1752–1845), were no doubt typical of the book work doled out to an overcrowded and under-employed profession. Raimbach mentioned working on some of the 74 small plates, newly returned from a post-war journey in the Netherlands. A surviving package of proofs[4] contains the work of no fewer than 14 engravers, including Raimbach. In the production of a book with a large number of illustrations there were considerations of speed; but the shortage

Reprinted by permission of The Bibliographical Society from *The Library*, Sixth Series, v. V, no. 3, September 1983, pp. 223–236.

333

of work must go a long way towards explaining the large number of engravers involved in this, not the most copiously illustrated of projects. The 1812 engravings of the Holbein portraits of members of the court of Henry VIII were the product of a similar collaboration.

It was the Prince Regent who, coming across John Chamberlaine, Keeper of the King's Drawings and Medals, one day in Windsor Great Park, first suggested the idea of a series of small engravings of the celebrated portraits, thinking it would be a "very fine and curious work . . . were [Chamberlaine] to Publish the Portraits in Quarto," and adding that he would allow the publisher "the honor of affixing His Royal Highness's name to the Dedications" (Figures 1A, B).[5]

The 85 portrait drawings of members of the court of Henry VIII were originally executed by Hans Holbein during his two periods of residence in England (1526–28 and 1532–43). Following the artist's sudden death from the plague in 1543 the drawings, contained in a single volume, passed through the hands of various owners until their purchase, evidently by Charles II, brought them again into royal possession, where they have remained ever since.[6] Despite the interest shown by those outside the royal circle privileged to have a sight of them, the drawings were not placed on public exhibition until 1890. There had, however, been several attempts to reproduce them in engraved form: Horace Walpole, who with George Vertue had seen the drawings in Kensington Palace, wrote in 1762 of his chagrin at the absence of engraved versions of these splendid images, and referred to an attempt at their reproduction by Vertue. The latter had apparently spent "part of three years" on the project, tracing thirty-five of the portraits on oiled paper (and, incidentally, leaving the evidence of his efforts in the form of oil-stains on some of the originals) before disconsolately abandoning his task.[7] Shortly afterwards Richard Dalton, the King's Librarian, and an enthusiast for engraving to the extent that he himself actually engaged in the art, endeavored to reproduce a number of the Holbein portraits. Sadly, his efforts have—with justification—been judged "hard and mechanical," beyond which no more is recorded of his labours than that "a quantity of good copper was spoilt" thereby, and that the thirty-six plates eventually issued by 1792 were "very inade-

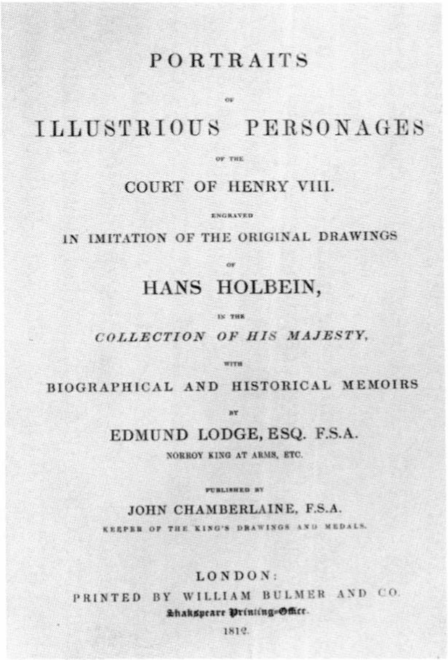

PORTRAITS

OF

ILLUSTRIOUS PERSONAGES

OF THE

COURT OF HENRY VIII.

ENGRAVED

IN IMITATION OF THE ORIGINAL DRAWINGS

OF

HANS HOLBEIN,

IN THE

COLLECTION OF HIS MAJESTY,

WITH

BIOGRAPHICAL AND HISTORICAL MEMOIRS

BY

EDMUND LODGE, ESQ. F.S.A.

NORROY KING AT ARMS, ETC.

PUBLISHED BY

JOHN CHAMBERLAINE, F.S.A.

KEEPER OF THE KING'S DRAWINGS AND MEDALS.

LONDON:

PRINTED BY WILLIAM BULMER AND CO.
Shakspeare Printing Office.

1812.

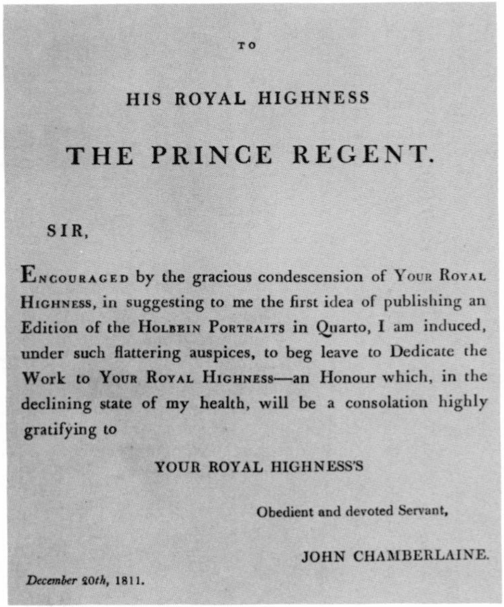

TO

HIS ROYAL HIGHNESS

THE PRINCE REGENT.

SIR,

ENCOURAGED by the gracious condescension of YOUR ROYAL
HIGHNESS, in suggesting to me the first idea of publishing an
Edition of the HOLBEIN PORTRAITS in QUARTO, I am induced,
under such flattering auspices, to beg leave to Dedicate the
Work to YOUR ROYAL HIGHNESS—an Honour which, in the
declining state of my health, will be a consolation highly
gratifying to

YOUR ROYAL HIGHNESS'S

Obedient and devoted Servant,

JOHN CHAMBERLAINE.

December 30th, 1811.

Figure 1A. Title-page, Chamberlaine, 1812. Reduced from
340 by 260 mm.

Figure 1B. Dedication, Chamberlaine, 1812. Reduced from
340 by 260 mm.

quate."[8] It was in this year that the first engraved renderings by Francesco Bartolozzi appeared.

It is necessary, as a prelude to considering the 1812 publication with which we are here principally concerned, to refer to the earlier engravings by Francesco Bartolozzi (1727–1815), for it was on his interpretations of Holbein that the work of the thirteen engravers of the quarto edition was based. To anyone acquainted with the original drawings, the inadequacy of Vertue and, later, Dalton to the task of their reproduction will hardly cause surprise. The freedom of line and the tonal understatement of Holbein's draughtsmanship presented these aspirants with much the kind of problem that J. M. W. Turner's interpreters were later to face in their efforts to render in terms of bitten and graven line the evanescence of the artist's veils of colour (Plate I). Ironically Bartolozzi, an exponent of an approach to engraving described as "the chalk manner"—a style admirably suited to the facsimile reproduction of just such drawings as had teased his hapless predecessors—felt no need to emulate in his engravings the vital shorthand of Holbein, and was quite uninhibited by the challenge. His solution was to produce plates that were frankly equivalents for rather than literally reproductions of the originals; and it was Bartolozzi's *equivalents* that both formed the public's idea of the Holbein portraits until their eventual exhibition in 1890 and, as indicated above, determined the character of the reduced versions of 1812.

Beginning in 1792 and continuing until 1800, when the engraver was 73 years old, John Chamberlaine published "the whole Collection of Portraits after Holbein's Drawings in His Majesty's Cabinet, of the Size of the Originals which [were] Folio." There were 84 prints in all; and, with the exception of one plate by Charles Knight (1743–c. 1825) and three by Conrad Martin Metz (1745/55–1827), Bartolozzi undertook the whole work of engraving. Chamberlaine, in his Advertisement to the series, described the engravings as "the most faithful copies of the originals," maintaining that "it were idle to say more of a work which can require no recommendation—the world need not be told what to expect from Bartolozzi's engravings after Holbein's drawings." There is, too, in the preface to the bound volume, an indication of the continuing interest of Horace Walpole who, with "Mr. Nicol [George Nicol, Bookseller to the King] concerted the plan of the Publication.'' As well as thanking Walpole and Nicol, John Chamberlaine also expressed his gratitude to the illustrious Bartolozzi and to William Bulmer, who had been charged with the letterpress printing. That he went out of his way to acknowledge the latter is a clear indication of the printer's prestige.[9]

Bartolozzi came to England in 1764 and became a full member of the Royal Academy (an honour denied at that time to all other engravers) only four years after his arrival. This inexplicable favoritism—as it must have seemed to the excluded English engravers—coupled with the fact that Bartolozzi was a foreigner who had only just set foot in the country, certainly aroused resentment. He and the technique of engraving with which he had become closely associated attracted virulent criticism—and so, therefore, did those who emulated him in employing the chalk or stipple method. John Landseer (1769–1852) was still grumbling when Bartolozzi, after nearly forty years of dazzling success in this country had already left for Portugal and the prospect of a knighthood there. In his *Lectures on the Art of Engraving* (1807) Landseer attacked the ''infantile indefinity'' of the stipple process, suggesting that Bartolozzi and his followers simply adopted it for speed and were encouraged to do so by unscrupulous dealers more concerned to ''follow, flatter and degrade'' than to ''lead, exalt, and refine'' public taste.[10] It is clear that there was as much emotion as cool appraisal in the criticisms of a method that became, in the minds of its opponents, identified with foreign frivolity and was seen as a rather despicable evasion of the rigors of line-engraving—a technique thought to ''stand before all others'' by its English adherents (who, as late as the mid-nineteenth century when its employment in commercial enterprises was beginning to be considered something of an impracticable luxury, observed ''with regret, though not surprise, its . . . declining state'').[11]

Like any other engraver, Bartolozzi had his failures as well as his successes; but there is no doubt that his Holbein stipple engravings of 1792–1800 are remarkable images of great sensitivity. These strangely remote icons have none of the flesh and blood immediacy of the drawings that inspired them (they reflect ''Bartolozzi's conceits'' rather than ''Holbein's truths,'' insisted Thomas Frognall Dibdin),[12] but this hardly diminishes their charm. They provide us with barometers for the taste of an era

very different from that of their sitters. They offer us a fascinating
view of sixteenth-century court life through the romantic filter of
the late eighteenth century, and they are executed with a Southern
inflection as inescapable for Bartolozzi as the accent with which
he must have spoken his adopted tongue.

An interesting contrast—which would have entirely met with
Dibdin's approval—was shortly to appear in the form of an
engraving by Frederick Christian Lewis (1779–1856) of
Holbein's portrait of Cecily Heron, the youngest daughter of Sir
Thomas More. A comparison of Lewis's rendering with that of
Bartolozzi (a comparison which must necessarily be made in the
Royal Library at Windsor, where the only surviving proof of
Lewis's plate is preserved) instantly and effectively demonstrates
the basis of much contemporary disapproval of Bartolozzi, who
"put into his work three times over what appears in the original
drawings" (Plates II and III). Lewis, with great restraint, confined
himself to a faithful adherence to Holbein's drawing, reproducing
with extreme delicacy all the spontaneity of the original. Bartolozzi, on the other hand, "finished" the sitter's string of beads
and medallion, and the folds and fastenings of the dress merely
suggested by Holbein. An inscription at the foot of Lewis's
engraving indicates that the work was evidence of John Chamberlaine's search for an "engraver of less celebrity [i.e. than Bar-
tolozzi], at a smaller price" in order that he might "give the
public a smaller edition." Chamberlaine was apparently taken
aback by the engraver's rendering of Cicely Heron's portrait, and
"on seeing its truthfulness when compared with Bartolozzi's
print, felt convinced that the reputation of the great work would be
inevitably destroyed if the public ever had a chance of comparing
the faithful rendering of Lewis with the false and mannered prints
of Bartolozzi . . . there is no doubt Chamberlaine had the plate
destroyed." The statement is signed by Sir A. W. Callcott and
dated 22 July 1844 (the year in which Callcott became Surveyor
of the Royal Pictures). The surviving proof seems to have been
one of very few ever taken from Lewis's plate, and was given to
Callcott in about 1819. By this time, Chamberlaine had long since
solved the problem of who should engrave the plates for his quarto
edition: the work had appeared in 1812 and thirteen engravers—
most of them pupils of Bartolozzi—had collaborated in its

production, preserving with great faithfulness Bartolozzi's interpretations of the portraits.

For the 1812 edition, Chamberlaine employed the same letterpress printer as for the folio version of 1792: the William Bulmer
(1757–1830) to whom he had paid tribute in the preface to the
earlier work. Bulmer was born in Newcastle upon Tyne, where he
was a friend of Thomas Bewick the engraver. On arrival in
London, he made the acquaintance of John Boydell (1719–1804),
engraver and publisher, who in 1786 conceived the idea of a
"Shakespeare Gallery," commissioning as the scheme developed
some 170 pictures by British artists on the basis of whose
compositions of Shakespearian subjects engravings were issued.
Between 1791 and 1805 Bulmer was employed in printing the
letterpress for Boydell's Shakespeare publications, and it is
doubtless the Boydell connection that suggested the name of the
printer's workshop at 3 Russell Court, Cleveland Row: the
Shakespeare Printing-Office. Bulmer was evidently a printer of
progressive inclination; he was one of the first to install a
Stanhope press in his office.[13]

The thirteen engravers assembled for the work on the 1812
publication were: *E. Bocquet,* a native of Abbeville, active
between about 1809 and about 1849, who contributed 7 plates;
Marie-Anne Bourlier, also French, who had begun working in
London by 1800 (4 plates) (Plate IV); *Antoine Cardon* (1772–
1813) who came to England from Brussels in 1792 (8 plates);
Thomas Cheesman (*c.* 1760–*c.* 1835), one of Bartolozzi's most
assiduous pupils (9 plates); *R. Cooper,* probably Robert, active
from *c.* 1795 until his death in 1836 (16 plates); *Georg Sigmund
Facius c.* 1750–after 1815), who came from Regensburg (12
plates) (Plate VI); *Samuel Freeman* (1773–1857) (4 plates);
Charles Knight (active from before 1786 until after 1813), one of
Bartolozzi's two collaborators in the 1792 Holbein enterprise (6
plates) (Plate VII); *Henry Meyer* (active before 1799 until after
1833) (5 plates); *James Anthony Minasi* (1776–after 1847) (5
plates); *G. Minasi* and *S. Minasi,* who each contributed a plate;
and *W. Nicholls* (2 plates). Almost all are known to have been
pupils of Bartolozzi or to have been otherwise associated with
him, and all adopted in this work the stipple technique used by the
Florentine and his collaborators in the folio publication. Included

in the total of 84 engraved plates were the portrait of Holbein by
Cooper (after the original at Kensington Palace), that of Holbein's
wife (also at Kensington Palace) by Facius, and the two miniatures (which had already appeared in the 1792 edition) of Henry
and Charles, first and second sons of Charles Brandon, Duke of
Suffolk—both engraved by Bartolozzi.[14]

It is interesting to speculate upon the combination of factors
that brought the thirteen engravers together in the Holbein project.
Bartolozzi seems, of course, to have been the main link, but
publisher-printsellers like Boydell and Ackermann were certainly
prominent in the network of contacts.

Antoine Cardon was one who, like Bartolozzi before him, lost
no time in establishing himself in the artistic milieu of his adopted
country. Upon his arrival in England in 1792 he entered the Royal
Academy Schools, gaining a Silver Medal two years later.[15] He
was subsequently employed by Colnaghi the art dealer, and
produced a great number of plates for Rudolph Ackermann, that
other enterprising expatriate, whose Repository of Arts at No. 101
the Strand provided work for many members of the profession. In
1807 he was awarded the Gold Medal of the Society of Arts for his
large engraving in a mixture of line and stipple of Philip de
Loutherbourg's "Battle of Alexandria."[16] He was a versatile
engraver, not only in terms of the subjects he tackled (from history
pieces to decorative medallions) but also in terms of the techniques he employed, etching, aquatint and stipple all being
included in his repertoire.[17] His reputation grew to the extent that
Ackermann, in an advertisement of 1810, expressed his confidence that "the Public, especially when they are informed that it
is in the hands of Mr. CARDON, whose talents are too well
known to need any eulogium" could not fail to find the shortly-to-
be-published portrait of Princess Maria Louisa of Austria (who
became Napoleon's bride) of great interest.[18] He was indeed so
well established by this time that he felt able to complain to Sir
Thomas Lawrence of the trouble the engraving of the artist's
portrait of Sir Joseph Banks had given him. He was, records
Farington, "incensed and wrote an angry letter to Lawrence upon
the subject [declaring] He wd. never again engrave from a picture
by [him]"; the action, one may suppose, of a confident and fully
employed man.[19] Cardon frequently published prints himself from
31 Clipstone Street, Fitzroy Square, the neighbourhood in which

he died (shortly after finishing the plates for Chamberlaine) at the relatively early age of 40—his end hastened, apparently, by overwork.[20]

It is evident from Rudolph Ackermann's 1830 catalogue that the R. Cooper whose name appears on 16 of the Holbein plates was also frequently given work from No. 101 the Strand. The catalogue lists Cooper's portrait plates of George Canning and of various South American notables, including Señor Egaña, senator of the Chilean Republic (with which country the indefatigable Ackermann had established commercial links).[21]

When Rudolph Ackermann came to England (probably in 1783, when he was 19) it seems he lodged with his countrymen the Facius brothers, Georg Sigmund and Johann Gottlieb, who had already been in this country for several years. From them, he may well have acquired the skills that were eventually to pave the way to the publication of engravings by his own hand. The brothers, frequently in collaboration, produced many plates for the firm of John and Josiah Boydell (at whose behest they seem to have come to London). As well as subjects for the *Shakespeare Gallery,* they engraved a portrait of the Swedish naturalist Carl Linnaeus from an original picture owned by Sir Joseph Banks. The plate, published in 1788, is engraved in stipple, which in the hands of the Facius brothers achieves an effect so rich and so fully tonal as closely to resemble mezzotint. The brothers' connection with Boydell's must certainly have contributed to Ackermann's resolution to set up his own printselling and publishing business; in assisting his hosts, he may even actually have worked on some of the plates they engraved for the Boydells. It is evident that Ackermann in later years repaid his debt with his patronage; at least, his 1830 catalogue lists an engraving by Georg Sigmund after a bust of Lord Castlereagh by Joseph Nollekens.[22]

Charles Knight had already collaborated with Bartolozzi before contributing a plate to Chamberlaine's 1792 Holbein publication. He had done extensive work on the full-length portrait plate of Elizabeth Farren after the painting by Thomas Lawrence, probably under the close supervision of Bartolozzi, who applied the finishing touches with his own graver before the print's publication in 1791.[23] Between 1793 and 1816, Knight exhibited a few miniatures at the Royal Academy; and he had in 1803 become one of the 24 governors of the short-lived Society of Engravers, in

PLATE I

Holbein, portrait of Cecily Heron, black and coloured chalks, 378 by 281 mm (Royal Library 12269; Parker 5). Reproduced by gracious permission of Her Majesty the Queen.

PLATE II

Bartolozzi, engraving of Cecily Heron after Holbein. From Chamberlaine, *Portraits of Illustrious Persons of the Court of Henry VIII,* 1792 (Royal Library 6289). Reproduced by gracious permission of Her Majesty the Queen. Size of original 386 by 276 mm.

PLATE III

F. C. Lewis, engraving of Cecily Heron after Holbein (Royal Library 6290). Reproduced by gracious permission of Her Majesty the Queen. Size of original 371 by 270 mm.

PLATE IV

Marie-Anne Bourlier, engraving of Mary, Lady Heveningham, after Holbein. Chamberlaine, 1812. Size of original 155 by 108 mm.

PLATE V

Detail of No. IV.

PLATE VI

Georg Sigmund Facius, engraving of William Warham, Archbishop of Canterbury, after Holbein. Chamberlaine, 1812. Size of original 169 by 122 mm.

PLATE VII

Charles Knight, engraving of an unknown man after Holbein. Chamberlaine, 1812. Size of original 190 by 142 mm.

PLATE VIII

Detail of No. VII.

which he was joined by such members of the profession as Charles Warren (who was to play an important part in the development of steel as a metal suitable for engraving).[24] Knight published numerous prints on his own account, and he also contributed some aquatints to Edward Orme's idiosyncratic *Essay on Transparent Prints* (London, 1807) in which the author demonstrated a method of applying oil to colored prints so as to make them translucent.

Henry Meyer, a nephew of John Hoppner, R.A., worked both in mezzotint and in stipple, which latter method he studied under Bartolozzi. He is recorded by Farington in 1799 as a student of the Royal Academy Schools; and we learn that his professional work was in full spate ten years later when, in 1809, Reeve and Jones of 7 Vere Street, Bond Street, published his ''Mrs. Jerningham'' after the portrait by his uncle, Hoppner. The same year, his engraving of ''Richard Watson, Bishop of Landaff'' (from a drawing by W. Evans after the portrait by George Romney) was published by Cadell and Davies of the Strand;[25] and his prowess as a mezzotinter found full and spectacular scope of the portrait of another eminent cleric, Samuel Goodenough, Bishop of Carlisle, after the painting by James Northcote. The richness of Meyer's tonal range and the animated rendering of drapery testify to his mastery of rocker and scraper.[26] Inevitably, John Boydell makes an appearance: on 21 June 1814, his portrait engraving by Meyer was published by Cadell and Davies.[27] By at least as early as 1816, Meyer had established contact with Rudolph Ackermann, who on 1 October that year published the engraver's interpretation of Princess Charlotte of Wales, painted by A. E. Chalon.[28] The *Post Office London Directory* for 1820 gives Meyer's address as 3 Red Lion Square, from where he published in his own right such engravings as ''Lady Leicester as Hope'' (1823) after Thomas Lawrence. He was shortly to become (in 1824) a founder member of the Society of British Artists, under whose auspices he exhibited more than a hundred works over the next few years. In addition, from 1821 to 1833, he exhibited at the Royal Academy and the British Institution.[29] A large number of his plates were advertised in Ackermann's 1830 catalogue.

James Anthony Minasi was born in Scilla, Calabria, on 25 July 1776, and came to London in 1793, lodging at 207 Piccadilly with his cousin, Mariano Bovi, who was a pupil of Bartolozzi. He entered the Royal Academy Schools in December 1794. Whilst with Bovi, it seems that the young man received some instruction from Bartolozzi, whom he may also have encountered at the Royal Academy, and to whom in 1797 he eventually became apprenticed. Minasi's precocity was apparently such that the apprenticeship was terminated by mutual consent before it had run its agreed full course. We are told that "at the period when Wellington was at the zenith of his fame" Minasi had the opportunism to produce an engraved portrait of the hero, assisted by Robert Home's painting and the bust by Joseph Nollekens. The bill for "1 Portrait of His Grace the Duke of Wellington highly finished in colours on silk . . . with a rich frame and plate glass [at] £15.15.0," addressed to the Prince Regent on 26 September 1814, was no doubt related to this enterprise.[30]

The work of William Bulmer the letterpress printer was fully acknowledged in Chamberlaine's preface to the 1792 edition of the Holbein portraits. There was, however, no mention of the plate-printer, and it is now time to rectify this matter. It may be assumed that Chamberlaine's careful selection of a letterpress printer would be matched by equal fastidiousness in the matter of finding someone to undertake the extremely tricky business of the printing of the plates, and we have evidence to suggest that Bartolozzi may have had some influence in the eventual choice. Due to the comparative slowness of the intaglio printing process, it was not uncommon for more than one plate-printer to be employed in the production of a book such as Chamberlaine's; and though he may not therefore have been exclusively responsible it seems likely, for reasons which will shortly be given, that prominent among the chosen printers was William Benjamin McQueen.[31] According to family tradition, the McQueens had been copperplate printers since about 1800, though the firm's earliest preserved records are of 1816. William McQueen is known to have occupied a workshop at No. 72 Newman Street, Rathbone Place, from 1817 until 1833 when he moved to new purpose-built premises at 184 Tottenham Court Road. There the family remained for almost a hundred years, to develop during the course of the nineteenth century one of the most celebrated printing-houses in London. Andrew Tuer, writing in 1885, tells us that "Mrs. McQueen, the mother of the present members of the firm of J. H. and F. C. McQueen, fine art copperplate printers, remembers her father having frequently to go to Mr. Bartolozzi's house at Fulham [where he had a copper-plate press], at six o'clock in the morning, to prove his plates under the artist's personal superintendence.''[32] The printer's visits must have taken place before 1802, in which year Bartolozzi left England for Portugal, and it is tempting to suppose that the collaboration began considerably earlier—sufficiently early for some of the proofing at Fulham to have been of the 1792 Holbein plates. Without specifying the edition, Tuer includes the ''Holbein Heads'' in a list of plates printed by McQueen's;[33] and Mr P. N. McQueen, the firm's descendant, has in his collection of family mementoes proofs of plates from both the folio and the quarto editions. These proofs are so brilliant and crisp that they must have been taken from the copper whilst the plates were still in pristine condition. This, and the fact that Mr McQueen owns duplicates of some proofs, the fact that his two proofs of Bartolozzi's miniature of Henry, first son of Charles Brandon, Duke of Suffolk, are colored differently (suggesting early experiment to determine the most satisfactory chromatic scheme), and the fact that at least one of the proofs is spoiled, tempt one to the conclusion that the whole batch comprises printers' proofs which have been in the possession of the family since they were first taken from the press. The presence among these proofs of one of the folio prints (''Lady Rich'') is an indication that McQueen's may have printed the plates of *both* the 1792 and the 1812 editions, and if this is the case, the firm seems to have been in existence for somewhat longer than has been hitherto believed.[34]

Many of the plates of the 1812 edition have survived and are now owned by Thomas Ross & Son, plate-printers, of Putney.[35] The engraving was originally executed on bare copper, though most of the plates are today faced with steel. The steel-facing must have been done many years after the plates were first engraved: the process was developed in France in the 1850s and was only widely employed in England late in the nineteenth century.[36] Those plates bearing a maker's stamp are inscribed ''G. Harris, 31 Shoe Lane, London.'' Shoe Lane, between Holborn Circus and Fleet Street, was in a quarter where plate-makers congregated. Pigot's *London & Provincial New Commercial Directory* for 1822–23 lists, for example, three Pontifexs based in Shoe Lane, describing them all as coppersmiths; and close by, at 14 Lombard Street, was the workshop of Richard Hughes who (with the engraver Charles Warren, already referred to above) was to develop soon after 1820 the steel plates which would revolutionize the engraving trade.[37]

Copper plates for engraving needed to be chosen with great care. Well hammered, densely textured metal was necessary, particularly where work as delicate as that in the Holbein engravings was envisaged. The common procedure was for the engraver or an assistant to make careful working drawings of the images to be reproduced. In this case, it is obvious that Bartolozzi's folio prints were the exemplars. Proofs of his plates would have been scaled down and the main outlines drawn on smooth paper. These drawings would then have been taken to a convenient plate-printer's to be "run through the press." Each sheet would be damped, placed drawing side down on a copper plate (previously warmed and coated with a thin layer of wax which hardened on the metal's cooling) and taken through the rolling-press. The subject was thus transferred to the waxed plate in fine, silvery lines, ready for the first stage of engraving.

Stipple engravers pierced the wax ground with a series of pecks (often in imitation of the granular effect of a crayon line), using an etching point. Each peck revealed a dot of copper which would subsequently be attacked by acid to create a small pit in the metal. The stippling of the Holbein plates has been done with single points, with devices consisting of clusters of points, and sometimes with toothed roulettes. Once the image had been established in this way, a wall of wax would be built round each plate's borders to form a tray into which the acid could be poured. With a protective varnish applied at appropriate stages, the biting could be controlled so as to produce rich variation in tone—the areas most deeply bitten printing more heavily than those left shallow. The metal could, of course, also be engraved. The most delicate passages were usually achieved with the burin rather than by the action of acid. A close examination of the 1812 prints reveals that both etching and engraving were employed: crevices resulting from the former having slightly ragged boundaries, those from the latter being sharper-edged. Etched and engraved areas are sometimes in these plates stippled separately, sometimes intermingled; and in some cases—particularly where hair or drapery is represented—the engravers have enmeshed passages of stipple in a linear network (Plates V and VIII).

The skill of the plate-printer consisted in first filling the crevices of a plate with a dense ink ground in linseed oil, and then wiping (first with a pad of muslin, and finally with the bare palm) the surplus pigment from the surface. The wiping accomplished, the plate would be placed on the plank of the press. Paper, damped so as to accept the ink more readily, would be laid on it; then several layers of resilient woollen felt, and the whole sandwich would be passed between the rollers to produce the impression.[38]

Although it is difficult to judge the span of time over which the engraving and printing took place there is no doubt that the 1812 publication was, like the folio version that preceded it, issued in parts (as well as in complete bound sets of plates) over a number of years. Also, the prints were presented in a variety of ways: for example, in monochrome on buff plate-paper; in monochrome on india paper (mounted on the more substantial plate-paper); and colored *à la poupée* on pink, buff or greyish paper.[39] The plates of the British Museum Print Room copy are printed on paper ranging from buff to off-white and, from print to print, the ink varies from cool black to a warmish hue verging on brown. This underlines the likelihood that more than one printer was engaged; and the variety of sizes and styles of lettering used by the "writing engravers" (as distinct from those undertaking the pictorial work) in the titles and publication lines of the different plates, is further indication of the typically elaborate division of labor.[40]

Holbein made some of the original drawings on unprimed whitish paper and others on paper primed pink. The paper for the 1812 prints *à la poupée* seems to have been colored in conformity with that used by Holbein. Color printing *à la poupée* was a delicate business. The plate was first inked with a neutral "ground" color (rarely simply black; more usually dark gray or sepia) and wiped clean in the usual way. Colors were then applied to the plate's surface and worked into the appropriate areas of the design with stubs of cotton fabric ("dollies") or by the printer's finger covered with a muslin rag. Once all the colors were applied, the plate was very fastidiously wiped with a pad of muslin so as to slightly soften the chromatic frontiers whilst avoiding undue blurring. The fully colored print was thus obtained by a single impression.[41] The colors used in the 1812 plates are, like the paper, chosen to resemble the economical, muted tinting of the Holbein drawings themselves.

Proofs of the 1812 plates began to come from the presses probably late in 1811. On 4 January 1812, John Chamberlaine—then on his death-bed—sent two examples to the Prince Regent in acknowledgment of the latter's encouragement of the project. Though so "extremely low and weak as not to be able to leave [his] Room," he expressed in a covering letter the hope that he would eventually be able to resume work on the publication. By the twelfth of the month, however, he was dead; and the task of seeing the remainder of the plates through the press may well have been undertaken by George Nicol, one of the original enthusiasts for the enterprise.[42] The publication provides us with a typical example of the kind of bookwork which was the major employment for many engravers during what were lean years for all but the most renowned members of the profession. And it helps to amplify our notion of that impulse in the arts that we now call Romanticism.

NOTES

[1]The handy colloquialism of the title is borrowed from Andrew Tuer, *Bartolozzi and His Works* (London & New York, 1885). In the preparation of this paper I have received valuable help from: Iain Bain of the Tate Gallery Publications Department; Gavin Bridson, Librarian of the Linnean Society, London; John Ford, the historian of Ackermann's; Dr Basil Hunnisett of Brighton Polytechnic; Professor Peter C. G. Isaac; Jane Langton, Assistant Registrar, Royal Archives, Windsor Castle; Beryl Pomeroy and her colleagues at Thomas Ross & Son, plate-printers, London; the Hon. Mrs Jane Roberts, Curator of the Print Room, Windsor Castle; and Professor Michael Twyman of the University of Reading.

[2]M. T. S. Raimbach (ed.), *Memoirs and Recollections of Abraham Raimbach* (London, 1843), pp. 22, 23.

[3]Mrs Sarah Uwins, *A Memoir of Thomas Uwins, R. A.,* 2 vols (London, 1858), 1, 167.

[4]Owned by Mr P. N. McQueen.

[5]Letter of John Chamberlaine, dated 4 January 1812, reproduced in *The Correspondence of George, Prince of Wales, 1770–1812,* edited by A. Aspinall (London, 1963–), VIII (1971), 323–24.

[6]See *Holbein and the Court of Henry VIII,* exhibition catalogue, Queen's Gallery, Buckingham Palace, 1978–79 (London, 1978), pp. 8–15.

[7]K. T. Parker, *The Drawings of Holbein at Windsor Castle* (Oxford and London, 1945), p. 20.

[8]Tuer, p. 9; Parker, p. 20.

[9]J. Chamberlaine, *Imitations of Original Drawings by Hans Holbein, in the Collection of His Majesty, for the Portraits of Illustrious Persons of the Court of Henry VIII* (London, 1792–[1800]). For a full discussion of Bulmer and his work see P. C. G. Isaac, "William Bulmer, 1757–1830," *The Library*, V, 13 (1956), 37–50.

[10]Quoted in C. Fox, "The Engravers' Battle for Recognition in Early Nineteenth Century London," *The London Journal*, 2 (1976), 3–31 (p. 7).

[11]T. H. Fielding, *The Art of Engraving* (London, 1841), p. 31.

[12]Quoted in Tuer, pp. 79–80.

[13]In 1800, according to Ian Maxted, *The London Book Trades, 1775–1800* (Folkestone, 1977), p. 34.

[14]The quarto edition was published at £15; and "Cooper was paid thirty guineas for his portrait of Holbein, and ten guineas each for the others bearing his name. Facius was paid sixteen guineas for Holbein's Wife. The remainder of the plates were engraved at prices varying from six guineas upwards, according to the amount of work in them" (Tuer, p. 85).

[15]E. Bénézit, *Dictionnaire des Peintres, Sculpteurs, Dessinateurs et Graveurs,* new edition, 8 vols (Paris, 1948–55) II, 520. Samuel Redgrave, however, in his *Dictionary of Artists of the English School,* 2nd edition (London, 1878), gives the date of Cardon's arrival in England as 1790 (p. 70).

[16]Redgrave, p. 70. There is a fine proof of the engraving in Blackburn Art Gallery.

[17]R. Ackermann, *Catalogue of Prints* (London, 1802). Entries on pp. 6, 7, 8, 10, 11, 13, 15, 16, 17, 19, 24 and 29 give an idea of the engraver's range.

[18]Ackermann's *Repository of Arts,* June, July, August, 1810 (advertisement following p. 403).

[19]*The Diary of Joseph Farington,* edited by K. Garlick, A. D. Macintyre and K. Cave (New Haven & London, 1978–), x (1982), 3693.

[20]Anderson Galleries, Auction Sale Catalogue, Part IV of the *Frederick R. Halsey Collection of Prints* (New York, 1917), lists 22 prints by Cardon (lots 200–21, pp. 39–42; hereafter cited as *Halsey Collection*). Of the 15 with imprints, 5 were published by Cardon himself. For biographical details, see Redgrave, p. 70.

[21]Ackermann, *Catalogue of Prints* (London, 1830), p. 32.

[22]Print in the library of the Linnean Society, London. For details

relating to Ackermann in this paragraph, I am indebted to John Ford, who kindly allowed me to consult the typescript of his forthcoming work on the Ackermann family businesses.

[23]A. M. Hind, *A History of Engraving and Etching,* 3rd edition (1923; Dover reprint, 1963), p. 293.

[24]See B. Hunnisett, "Charles Warren, Engraver," *Journal of the Royal Society of Arts,* 125 (1977) 488–91, 590–93.

[25]*Halsey Collection,* lot 521, p. 90 and lot 527, p. 91.

[26]Print in the library of the Linnean Society, London.

[27]*Halsey Collection,* lot 517, p. 90.

[28]*Halsey Collection,* lot 528, p. 91.

[29]Redgrave, pp. 292–93. For statistical details, see A. Graves, *A Dictionary of Artists, 1760–1893* (London, 1895), p. 190.

[30]For biographical details, see Tuer, pp. 54–61. The bill for Wellington's portrait is in the Royal Archives, Windsor Castle (RA 26973) and is here referred to by gracious permission of Her Majesty the Queen.

[31]For a history of the firm of McQueen, see I. Bain, "Thomas Ross & Son," *Journal of the Printing Historical Society,* 2 (1966), 3–22 (pp. 11–15).

[32]Tuer, p. 29. It is true that only if the printer referred to was Mrs McQueen's father-*in-law* would he himself have been a McQueen; but even if the man was the lady's own father, the story is still an indication of a likely personal link between Bartolozzi and the McQueen family.

[33]Tuer, p. 100.

[34]Mr McQueen has duplicates of Plate IV and X of the quarto edition. The Bartolozzi miniatures are hand-tinted with watercolor. The proof of the "Lord Cobham" portrait is marred by the trace of a hair which has interrupted the transfer of ink to paper.

[35]For a full account of the firm of Thomas Ross & Son (originally Dixon & Ross, founded in 1833) see Bain, and Anthony Dyson, *Thomas Ross & Son: the Nineteenth Century Heritage* (London, 1983).

[36]Anthony Dyson, "Copper- and Steel-Plate Printing in London, *c.* 1830–*c.* 1880" (unpublished Ph.D. dissertation, University of London, 1979), pp. 216–17.

[37]Dyson, dissertation, pp. 208–11.

[38]See Dyson, dissertation (*passim*), for a full account of the engraving and printing processes outlined here.

[39]I am indebted to Charles Newington, who allowed me to study his color-printed copy of the quarto edition.

[40]The manuscript journals of the engraver Samuel Rawle (1771–1860) in the St Bride Printing Library, London, give an insight into the collaborative system and its ramifications (2 volumes covering April 1820–July 1824: Accession No. 34418).

[41]For an account of colour printing *à la poupée,* see J. Frankau, *Eighteenth Century Colour Prints* (London, 1906), chapter 7, pp. 146–51.

[42]For the text of Chamberlaine's letter, see Aspinall's edition of the correspondence of George Prince of Wales, cited at n. 5 above. The letter from Chamberlaine's widow to the Prince Regent, dated 13/1/1812, is inserted in vol. 1 of Chamberlaine's 1792 edition of the Holbein portraits, in the Royal Library, Windsor Castle. It is here referred to by gracious permission of Her Majesty the Queen.

Nicol's role is suggested by Tuer, who refers to the quarto edition as having been "Last published by Nichols [*sic*] in 1812."

WILLIAM KENT'S CAREER AS LITERARY ILLUSTRATOR
Jeffrey P. Widman

William Kent (1684?–1748), famous in the Augustan age as architect, decorator, landscape gardener, painter, and literary illustrator, is remarkable for the wide range of his endeavors alone. His reputation today, though considerably diminished, is justified by his important contributions as architect to the neo-Palladian movement in England and as gardener to the evolution of the picturesque garden. As graphic artist, however, Kent is not considered an original talent.

Yet his career as literary illustrator, which has thus far received little attention, does merit study for several reasons.[1] First of all, his works of illustration span his entire creative period in England, from 1719 to his death in 1748; they reflect not only the variety of Kent's undertakings but also the aesthetic taste of the period, on which the artist had a great influence. Secondly, Kent associated and worked with major poets of the Augustan age—John Gay, Alexander Pope, and James Thomson. His illustrations for their poems are often suggestive from the point of view of literary history and criticism. Although not highly literate himself, Kent apparently possessed the compensating virtue of congeniality, the ability to satisfy the tastes and demands of those educated persons for whom he worked.

In tracing Kent's career as literary illustrator, I shall discuss two chief aspects of his work, the neo-classic and the grotesque. These general terms will be applied mainly to the graphic style of his engravings, but in some measure also to Kent's basic approach to the problem of selecting and ordering poetic materials for the purpose of illustration. The essential characteristics of Kent's

Reprinted by permission from the *New York Public Library Bulletin,* Dec. 1966, pp. 620–646.

neo-classic mode are the following: the use of rational proportions in drawing the human figure; the presence of allegorical figures done in the manner of Italian baroque painting; normal perspective in the composition of scenes, especially landscapes; the unifying of diverse subjects upon a coherent pattern in a single illustration. The characteristics of Kent's grotesque mode are these: disproportion in the drawing of the human figure; the presence of fantastic scenes and creatures; elaborate and fanciful decoration of artifacts; the use of deceptive perspectives in the composition of landscapes with finely detailed features.

As the reader may gather, Kent's grotesque mode is, to some extent, the obverse of his neo-classic; for it largely consists in the artist's abandoning certain techniques that one expects to find in a neo-classic work. Insofar as this is true, the grotesque remains a minor mode, dependent for its effect upon the neo-classicism from which it departs. By the middle of the eighteenth century, it acquires its special province and subject matter—the gothic. In Kent's work for Spenser's *Faerie Queene,* we shall see how his representation of Nature and of gothic chivalry reveals the merging of the grotesque mode with other developments in eighteenth-century culture—the taste for picturesque gardening and the antiquarian interest in the medieval period.

In the following sections of this essay, I shall consider, in turn, Kent's works in the neo-classic and then the grotesque and gothic modes. In this fashion, it will be possible to indicate, finally, certain connections between the culture of the Augustan period, in which Kent played a prominent and versatile role, and the growth of romanticism in the latter part of the century, a development to which Kent indirectly contributed.

THE NEO-CLASSIC MODE: SOME IMAGES OF PASTORAL

Kent's earliest production as illustrator is the designs for the two quarto volumes of John Gay's *Poems on Several Occasions* (1720). Although the drawing in these is decidedly poor and the style often insipid, the illustrations are of interest as examples of the Augustan neo-classicism with which Kent's artistic career begins. However, before considering the relation between picture and poem in Gay's volumes, let us trace the social relations which constitute a significant background to Kent's work and which enabled the artist to become illustrator to the foremost poets of the age.

For the collaboration of Gay and Kent, the influential Third Earl of Burlington, their common patron, was responsible. In 1714, while studying in Rome with the Italian master Benedetto Luti, Kent received this message from his early benefactor, Burrell Massingberd:

> When Ld. Burlington comes you will I hope have his encouragement because he loves pictures mightily and if I had not been so unfortunate as to be out of town all ye time from his first resolution to travel to ye time of his setting out, I had been introduced to him and would have recommended you, and also his assistance to bring over a box of pictures, but I hope your own worth will accomplish ye first and then I shall depend upon you for ye latter . . . I have nothing to add but to beg you'll study and not think of coming over *donec Raphael Secundus eris.*[2]

Kent did, in fact, manage to establish himself in Lord Burlington's favor; and their intimacy grew and endured until the last years of the artist's life, when some breach strangely developed.[3] The publication of *The Designs of Inigo Jones* in 1727 was their joint effort, intended to promote neo-Palladianism in English architecture. It was through Burlington's circle that Kent became acquainted with the poets John Gay and Alexander Pope in 1719, and then with James Thomson some years later.[4]

In the "Epistle to Paul Methuen," first published in the 1720 *Poems on Several Occasions,* John Gay paid his tribute to the illustrator of his volumes:

> Why didst thou, Kent, forgo thy native land,
> To emulate in picture *Raphael's* hand?
> Think'st thou for this to raise thy name at home?
> Go back, adorn the palaces of *Rome;*
> There on the walls let thy just labours shine,
> And Raphael live again in thy design.
> Yet stay awhile; call all thy genius forth,

For Burlington unbyass'd knows thy worth;
His judgement in thy master-strokes can trace
Titian's strong fire and Guido's softer grace;
But, oh consider, e'er thy works appear,
Canst thou unhurt the tongue of envy hear?
Censure will blame, her breath was ever spent
To blast the laurels of the Eminent.   (lines 51–64)

Apparently Massingberd's prophecy—*"donec Raphael Secundus eris"*—was not forgotten by Kent's associates, who very much anticipated his initiating a renaissance in English painting.[5] But the artist, though he always considered himself a connoisseur of "ye Italian gusto" (his own phrase), was not the native son who could equal the Italian masters.

William Hogarth's engraving *Masquerades and Operas* (February 1723/4) satirized Kent's great expectations, or rather pretensions: The artist is seen, in the background, standing atop Burlington Gate, just above the reclining figures of Michelangelo and Raphael.[6] In this fashion, Hogarth implied that Kent owed his eminence less to his own talent than to Burlington's promotion of him at court and elsewhere (which, in the engraving, is a London market-place). In respect to Kent's achievement in the graphic this was more or less the case.

Lord Burlington subscribed for fifty copies of the *Poems on Several Occasions,* perhaps with the intention of distributing some to other courtiers. For his part, Kent attempted to display his best Italianate manner, particularly in the frontispiece opposite the title-page in volume one. On the left in the illustration, five babes are seen busily mounting a wreathed plaque, with the inscription "Mr. Gay's Poems, 1720." Behind this group, a knotty, twisted tree stands upon a slight mound, so that the tree partially hides the classical temple appearing in the background. Unhappily, the temple seems somewhat oval in shape; for the circular roof is unnaturally flattened and lengthened as it is stretched to reach the left edge of the design. One is forced to recognize Kent's miscalculation in the placement of it. In the right foreground, a shepherdess sits with her swain, the latter pointing with one hand to the plaque at the left and with the other touching the breast of his mistress. Here the artist takes care to direct his figures' gaze in significant directions—the shepherdess at the plaque, and the swain at the shepherdess—so as to stress two points of interest: love and poetry.

The execution of this print is poor, in part because Kent engraved his own design—for the first and last time in his career.[7] The movement of his hand is unsteady, and the illustration abounds in curlicues, little indentations breaking the outline of a limb or even of a classical column. Kent was probably unfamiliar with the art of engraving. Some parts of the landscape are done in a rough, impressionistic manner, as though this were a first draft intended for later painting.

This frontispiece relates to the first work in Gay's *Poems,* his serious imitation of Virgil entitled *Rural Sports: A Georgic Inscribed to Mr. Pope.* The lighter and more captivating poems in the first volume—including *The Fan* and *Trivia*—are passed over. Although the poet may have preferred to emphasize his serious pastoral, the strange fact remains that his most interesting works contain a spirit of humor, wit, and mockery which derives from a playful subversion of the neo-classic rules of imitation. Similarly, Kent's comic design for *The Shepherd's Week,* discussed below, far exceeds his frontispiece in liveliness and inventiveness. Both men were at their best, it seems, when having fun with their work.

The symbolism of the frontispiece is easily understood from these verses of *Rural Sports:*

> Here I peruse the Mantuan's Georgic strains
> And learn the labours of *Italian* swains;
> In ev'ry page I see new landschapes (*sic*) rise,
> And all Hesperia opens to my eyes.   (67–70)

In the illustration, the classical temple is seen from below, on the level of the pastoral figures in the foreground. In this perspective, the temple and the entire background as well appear to be emerging from the earth (corresponding to the poet's rising landscapes and opening Hesperia).

Thus Kent bodies forth Gay's imagination of an idealized pastoral world in which idyllic lovers enjoy a new Hesperia without intrusion. Neither the poet's descriptions of hunting and fishing, nor his passing references to turmoil in London are reflected in the design. Rather, it is the nostalgic mood of Gay's closing passage, which reasserts the contrast between city and ideal rural retreat, that the illustrator captures:

> Ye happy fields, unknown to noise and strife,
> The kind rewarders of industrious life;
> Ye shady woods, where once I us'd to rove;
> Alike indulgent to the muse and love. . . . (435–438)

Of this Kent's foreground, with the reposeful lovers observing the mounting of the poet's plaque and wrath, is a symbolic representation. One sees the pastoral ideal that the poet claims to have known; one sees the commemoration of poetic labors. Hence no distinction is made between past inspiration and present achievement, nor between classical model and modern imitation. The essence of the illustration is timelessness and typicality of detail. A fine example of Augustan neo-classicism, this frontispiece, in a sense, is Gay's public image of his role as poet. In the representation of a pastoral world are reflected the moral and aesthetic ideals of a civilization whose order the poet, as teacher, reveals and affirms.

Similar in style and organization is the illustration preceding *Dione: A Pastoral Tragedy* in the second volume. In the foreground, Kent places all the unmistakable emblems: the ornamented pyre, some classical fragments, the pastoral pipes hanging from a tree-limb, five babes in various poses expressing pathos, grief, admonition, and thoughtful concern—attitudes apparently appropriate to the drama. Indeed, one may possibly find amusing the curious intensity and absorption revealed on these cherubic countenances; but this effect, of course, may well be unintentional. The illustration suffers from the exclusion of mature human figures, and is the least interesting of Kent's neo-classic works.

In passing, I might remark that Kent was to employ classical fragments and emblems in this fashion only once again: in his designs for the quarto edition of Pope's translation of the *Odyssey* (1725–6).[8] As the publication date approached, Pope found himself in competition with his publisher, Bernard Lintot, for subscribers to their respective editions.[9] As an inducement to the public on his behalf, Pope advertised, on April 15 1725, that only his copies of the *Odyssey* would have, amongst other features, fifty ornaments by William Kent.[10] By this, the poet meant the elaborate head- and tail-pieces, composed of medallions, emblems of war, and various fretwork which Kent designed and Pierre Fourdrinier engraved. Of special interest is the very last tail-piece following Book XXIV of the *Odyssey.* It is a bust of Pope himself chiseled on a plaque; two cupids are seen embracing above, as a note of special grace.[11] Finally, Kent's frontispiece on the title page is truly noteworthy: The blind bard (Homer) is seen at the moment of his inspiration by a goddess, who beams bright rays into his eyes, while she is seated on a decayed monument against a background of crumbling, moss-covered ruins. The historical time suggested by the setting is peculiarly indefinite, neither wholly antique nor modern. As with the frontispiece to Gay's *Poems,* the theme chosen for illustration is the source of the poet's power to teach and enlighten humanity, and thus to survive the ruins of time as a "classic" bard.

No suggestion of an indefinite time and place exists in the third illustration provided for Gay's *Poems:* that preceding *The Shepherd's Week.* The scene is clearly set in an English country village of the early eighteenth century. The figures wear contemporary costumes. And, in the background, one sees a church-steeple, reminding the viewer that Gay's shepherds are christian. This fact is announced in the Proem: ". . . as he (Spenser) called his Eclogues, the shepherd's calendar, and divided the same into the twelve months, I have chosen (paradventure not overrashly) to name mine by the days of the week, omitting Sunday or the Sabbath, ours being supposed to be christian shepherds, and to be then at church worship."

Kent did not mistake Gay's ironic intention "to describe aright the manners of our own honest and laborious plough-men, in no wise sure more unworthy a British Poet's imitation, than those of Sicily or Arcadie." If the frontispiece to the *Poems* captures the mood of the Golden Age, the illustration for *The Shepherd's Week* provides a sufficiently striking contrast, a sharp descent in style. One may compare the inscription from Virgil placed on the opposite page: "Libeat mihi sordida rura,/Atque humiles habitare casas."

As students of Augustan literature may realize, Gay's purposes in these pastorals were fairly complex. However, one can say in general that Gay's implied position was that the pastoral poet should treat the ideals and simplicity of the Golden Age (as did Pope), but should not imitate the diction of Spenser nor describe the antic manners of real country folk (as Ambrose Philips wrongly did). To some extent, Gay set out to parody the pastorals of Philips, in both diction and moral attitude.

In Kent's illustration, one notices immediately the profuse detail, the cluttered scene, the awkwardness of the figures. Gone are simplicity and typicality of detail. The general theme fails to emerge from the general confusion. It is as though Kent attempted to present in visual terms what Gay believed to be the poetic effect of excessive realism in pastoral. A few lines from "Friday; or The Dirge," in which Bumkinet mourns Blouzelinda, are relevant to the analogy between poem and picture:

> Whilome I've seen her skim the clouted cream,
> And press from spongy curds the milky stream.
> But now alas! these ears shall hear no more
> The whining swine surround the dairy door,
> No more her care shall fill the hollow tray,
> To fat the guzzling hogs with floods of whey.
> Lament, ye swine, in gruntings spend your grief,
> For you, like me, have lost your sole relief.   (61–68)

Clearly our sense of the dignity of the lover's grief is somewhat confused by our associating him with "guzzling hogs" who have likewise lost their "sole relief." A similar effect is achieved in the illustration: A country swain kneels and kisses the hem of a milkmaid's skirt; but the juxtaposition of his posterior with the haunches of a cow reminds us, disturbingly, of a certain likeness between man and beast. This group in Kent's design has no specific source in the poem, though it reflects the tenor of several passages.

The two other main groups in the illustration are drawn from "Monday; or the Squabble":

Lobbin Clout

> On two near elms, the slacken'd cord I hung,
> Now high, now low my Blouzelinda swung.
> With the rude wind her rumpled garment rose,
> And show'd her taper leg, and scarlet hose.

Cuddy

> Across the fallen oak the plank I laid,
> And my self pois'd against the tott'ring maid,
> High leapt the plank; adown Buxoma fell;
> I spy'd—but faithful sweethearts never tell. (103–110)

Is Cuddy's secrecy an act of courtesy or an awkward intimation of Buxoma's secret beauties? If Gay, rather sharply, leaves his reader in doubt ("faithful sweethearts never tell"), it is, perhaps, in order to mock the unquestionable prurience of Philips' shepherds, who artfully manage to intimate but not quite to tell of her amorous acts.[12]

For his part, Kent is faithful to Gay's verse in a more than literal fashion. He illustrates the pranks by which Lobbin Clout and Cuddy contrive to catch a glimpse of their mistresses' charms; but Kent, unlike Gay, refuses even to suggest Buxoma's fall and exposure. Where Cuddy claims "High leapt the plank; adown Buxoma fell," Kent shows the girl triumphantly atop the see-saw, and Cuddy flying toward the ground. The illustrator's slight revision of the poetic action is an added touch of humor, which both Gay and his readers may have fully appreciated as true at least to the spirit of the occasion.

There was also a practical reason for Kent's decision to illustrate this passage from "Monday." The lines first appeared in the 1720 text of *The Shepherd's Week;* they were not in the first version of 1714. In simple terms, the design also served as an advertisement for a new feature, unknown to readers of the original edition.[13]

All in all, the illustration for *The Shepherd's Week* indicates close collaboration and, indeed, understanding between poet and illustrator. Kent, it seems to me, captures those major aspects of Gay's humor and irony which the poet himself might have chosen to point out to a prospective reader. Whether or not this inference is justified, it is true that in this design Kent achieves his most alert visual interpretation of a poetic text.

By comparison, the illustrator of the 1714 *Shepherd's Week,* Lud du Guernier, does not nearly approach Kent in literary sensitivity. For du Guernier's seven designs, fine as they are in execution and realistic presentation of country scenes, lack that essential touch of wit which raises Kent's one illustration above mere literalness in the visual rendering of Gay's poem. In brief, Kent attempts to body forth something of the general idea behind the poem—the essence of the poet's conception considered as a universal quality in the poem, apart from its embodiment in particular details. This neo-classic approach to the problem of literary illustration is even more strongly and independently utilized in the next work that we shall consider.

Kent's illustrations for the quarto edition of James Thomson's complete *Seasons* (1730) constitute, I believe, his most imaginative and successful effort. As visual analogue to the poet's diverse philosophic concern with the natural environment and its bearing upon human life, Kent portrays the great variety as well as the essential unity of natural phenomena. In the heavens, allegorical personae are seen controlling the elements and the seasonal changes; on earth, the landscape and various human activities reflect the potent influence of the heavens. There are both unity of action and unity of composition evident in each design.

The illustration for *Spring* is probably the best known of Kent's works; it has received extensive treatment in Ralph Cohen's study of Thomson's *Seasons* and its critics. Quite rightly, Cohen has suggested an analogy between the structure of Kent's designs and the sense of natural process, of interrelatedness amongst the diverse events in a single season, to be found in Thomson's poem: "In his designs Kent attempted to create a representative picture of the unity of each season, governed by the great chain of being leading in a series of inclined planes from natural to allegorical figures, and including earth, water, clouds, animals, man, and heavenly figures. The analogical unity which the engravings suggested was not that of the subject matter of each season, but of the relation between the distant past and the immediate present."[14]

This interpretation seems valid for Kent's "Spring," although even here I have difficulty in discerning any exact "relation between the distant past and the immediate present" in terms of, for instance, the relation of background to foreground. Nevertheless, it is clear that Kent attempted to depict some successive changes in the weather of springtime, and, perhaps, some causal relation between these and the flowering of the earth. Thus in the sky to the right, one sees a winged figure pushing away dark, heavy storm-clouds; near the center, the sun breaking through some lighter clouds; while the figure of Spring drops new buds upon the earth, and a train of attendant cherubs circles above, holding each other's hands. In addition, a rainbow arches from the upper right down to the earth near the center of the design, behind a lake in which it is reflected. This last touch beautifully symbolizes the beneficence of the heavens in their influence upon the earth.

Still other details of this illustration merit attention: especially the various features of Kent's landscape (including groves, meadows, hills, a pond, tilled fields), and the elegant Palladian mansion at the right. Notably, this edifice not only exemplifies the architectural style favored by Kent and Lord Burlington but also stands directly in a meadow, not at all separated from the surrounding landscape. Nature in Kent's "Spring" is not wild, but civilized Nature; it is not in conflict with human arts, but rather constitutes the medium through which those arts find their perfection.

The essential theme of this illustration is, I believe, the ideal existence of civilized man in the natural environment. It is not strictly the Golden Age, although the peaceful shepherd in the background, the lovers and gamboling sheep in the foreground, all suggest this archetype. Rather, it is the Golden Age as realized in Augustan England. For with the presence of a Palladian mansion and, in the background, a typically English farm, the scene seems less characteristic of Arcadia than of the countryside in England seen under ideal conditions. Needless to say, "Spring" is the appropriate design in which to present the resurrection of the ancient ideal on native grounds. The return of the Golden Age to England is a theme touched upon by Thomson also, in a passage of *Spring* that contains several of the details employed by Kent.[15]

The design for "Summer" is the mate to "Spring." Kent takes care to remind us visually of the affinity between the two seasons. For example, the sun, again at the center of the sky, now shines in full splendor, no longer obscured by clouds. The young cherubs of "Spring" are replaced by a more numerous group of full-bodied youths, who perhaps represent allegorically the circling hours of a typical summer's day. Thomson's argument for Summer suggests this interpretation: "As the Face of Nature in this Season is almost uniform, the Progress of the Poem is a Description of a Summer's Day.'' That is, the poem progresses from dawn to evening.

The heavenly figures in Kent's illustration remind us also of other, somewhat paradoxical aspects of time in this season. To begin with, the figure of Spring, seen shading herself with her cape while fleeing from the advancing chariot of Summer (and the sun), suggests both an affinity and an aversion between the two seasons.[16] The pattern of growth which begins in spring culminates in summer; yet at the same time the mildness and delicacy of the earlier season cannot endure the brutal heat of the later. Kent depicts another aspect of time as well. A sleeping youth and the figure of Father Time, seated upon a cloud at the upper left in the design, both suggest the *seeming* immobility of time in this season. It is the illusory moment of ripeness in Nature. The maturity achieved through time apparently stands untouched by the decay that time must also work.

The lower half of ''Summer'' is of great interest as an example of Kent's use of the analogy between poetry and painting. For his landscape, the artist seems to have chosen to illustrate these verses:

> All in th'adjoining Brook, that shrills along
> The vocal Grove, now fretting o'er a Rock,
> Now scarcely moving thro' a reedy Pool,
> Now starting to a sudden Stream, and now
> Gently diffus'd into a limpid Plain;
> A various Groupe the Herds and Flocks compose;
> Rural Confusion! On the grassy Bank
> Some ruminating lie; while others stand
> Half in the Flood, and often bending sip
> The circling Surface.[17]

The passage itself is an example of Thomson's use of the picturesque analogy; the poem is to create the effect of a landscape painting, as the poet suggests: ''A various Groupe the Herds and Flocks *compose*'' (my italics). Whether or not this effect is or ever can be achieved by poetry is another matter. For the poet employs words set in sequential order; and the impressions produced by sound, rhythm, and verbal meaning are not intrinsically visual. Indeed, Thomson describes his book in a fashion (''shrills along,'' ''fretting,'' ''starting'') that no graphic artist could reproduce in this medium. Nor can the poet truly ''compose'' his scene as the artist does: with all objects fixed in their definite spatial relations and seen, instantly, from a given perspective.

Yet if one takes general features of the landscape as they are mentioned by Thomson (brook, grove, pool, stream, plain, herds and flocks, grassy bank), and then traces the features of Kent's design foreground to background, one will find virtually the same things in the same order. No doubt aware of the poet's attempt to employ the picturesque analogy here, Kent reflected at least the sequence of objects named and tried to lead his viewer's eye along a line from front to rear, past images of these objects. That much could be achieved with techniques of pictorial composition.

Another analogy between the arts appears in the illustration for *Summer:* in this instance, they are sculpture and drawing. In the right foreground of the design, Kent illustrates Thomson's tale of Damon and Musidora.[18] We see Damon at the moment in which he discovers, to his own bedazzlement, three bathing maidens—Sacharissa, Amoret, and Musidora. In the course of an alluring description of these beauties, during which Thomson alludes repeatedly to the three goddesses whom Paris viewed and judged, the poet reaches the height of indirection with this simile:

> So stands the Statue that enchants the World,
> Her full Proportions such, and bashfull so
> Bends ineffectual from the roving Eye.

A footnote informs the reader that this is the "Venus of Medicis." And Kent takes advantage of this opportunity to sport the connoisseur's familiarity with such masterpieces of Italy. In the illustration, the central figure in the group of bathing maidens is, indeed, an image of the famous statue.

Here the analogy between the arts presents no difficulty; neo-classic art regularly employs sculptural models for graphic productions. The difficulty that did present itself was hardly abstruse: it lay in the fact that the statue is mentioned only in Thomson's simile, not as one of the nymphs in the tale of Damon and Musidora. The illustration hence shows four, where the poem has but three, charming bathers. This minor discrepancy was eliminated in the 1744 edition of the *Seasons,* in which three of the figures, including the Medici Venus, were removed from the engraving (leaving but a few traces behind), so as to conform with Thomson's revision of the tale.

Unlike "Spring" and "Summer," Kent's "Autumn" and "Winter" do not suggest growth and ideal beauty in Nature, but rather actual limitations and asperities. Visually, the sun dominates the heavens in "Spring" and "Summer"; but in "Autumn" and "Winter," that symbol of Nature's vitality and potency is absent. Fewer allegorical figures inhabit the heavens. The landscape below is less varied, more rugged and hilly, reminiscent of rough coastal terrain. Notably, human endeavors now receive greater emphasis than heavenly influences.

In "Autumn," two human activities are illustrated: harvesting and hunting. In the heavens, allegorical figures bear the emblems of the harvest season; scythe, sheaf, and cornucopia. On earth, the harvesters in the middle distance and the toying lovers in the foreground also carry scythes. As to hunting, at the very center of the design, one sees a stag pursued by hounds; while the hunters, on prancing steeds, are gathered at the right. Although Thomson describes various kinds of hunting, Kent selects as his main subject the stag at bay—a noble, graceful creature leaping toward the sky. There is, however, little suggestion of Thomson's gruesome and, in tone, slightly mawkish description of the slaughtering of the stag by the "inhuman Rout" (the dogs, after all).[19]

Most of the details of the illustration have some parallel in the poem. But, on the whole, Kent works independently, choosing those themes which are prominent in the poem, susceptible to visual representation, and, at any rate, typical of the season. For this reason, the impression of artistic unity gained from the design may be greater than that obtained from Thomson's poem with its wide-ranging themes and, at times, digressive tendencies. However, this apparent advantage, peculiar to the artist's medium, is accompanied by the disadvantage of being limited to a single, limited scene; and the various groups in Kent's design do appear to be crowded together, rather too large and close in relation to the surrounding landscape.

Kent's emphasis upon man's work (harvesting) and sport (hunting), and upon fruitfulness and death in Nature, provides a forceful transition from the idyllic landscapes of "Spring" and "Summer." And the design for *Winter* offers an even more pronounced contrast. In the earlier illustrations, the influence of the heavens upon the earth is represented as largely beneficent, conducive to growth in Nature and indicative of a cosmic harmony in which man participates. In "Winter," three powerful figures in the heavens are seen stirring up a tempest of wind and rain; a fourth, astride a cloud in a posture reminiscent (I find) of Christ's in Michelangelo's "Last Judgment," reminds the reader of Thomson's persona:

> Then comes the Father of the Tempest forth,
> Striding the gloomy Blast. First Rains obscure
> Drive thro' the mingling Skies and Vapour vile;
> Dash on the Mountain's Brow, and shake the Woods,
> That grumbling wave below.[20]

The poet proceeds to describe the retreat of man and beast to shelter. This section of the poem seems to have been the source for most of the details in Kent's design: the wind-beaten trees, men and cattle fleeing from the storm, the heavy, lowering skies. All these constitute an impressive image of winter's hardships and of the prevalent disharmony between man and his environment.

A unique feature of this illustration is that no one figure upon the earth regards another. And, it follows, the motif of human love completely disappears. One sees essentially isolated men and women seeking safety in a menacing environment.

Still other details in "Winter" enforce our sense of imminent peril and destruction in Nature. In the background to the left, a small ship is seen laboring in heavy seas. To the right, a weird white promontory juts out into the sea and sky. A possible analogue for these details is Thomson's description of the northern Arctic or "frozen zone":

> Where more than half the joyless Year is Night;
> And, failing gradual, Life at last goes out.
> There undissolving, from the first of time,
> Snows swell on snows amazing to the sky;
> And icy mountains there, on mountains pil'd,
> Seem to the shivering sailor from afar,
> Shapeless, and white, an atmosphere of clouds.[21]

This last line especially seems to have caught Kent's imagination.

For the white hill of "Winter" has a most ambiguous appearance: like ice in its whiteness, like a mountain in shape and in respect to the few trees on its brow, yet like a cloud in its amorphousness and proximity to the sky. According to the poet, this is but an optical illusion had by "the shivering sailor from afar." But such an illusion can be readily created in the visual arts for any viewer; and here Kent succeeds admirably.

If Kent's image of the white promontory in "Winter" strikes one as a bold imaginative effect, it is because an unfamiliar mode of perceiving and representing Nature is, after all, a basic function of the graphic arts. In historical terms, the allegorical figures of the illustrations are part of Kent's heritage from the Italian baroque, especially the large frescos of that tradition which the artist imitated while at Rome.[22] The tradition had lost much of its vitality by 1730: Kent's own work attested, in a minor way, to this fact, as many of his contemporaries realized.[23] But new possibilities were appearing and "Winter" suggests those which Kent was to explore. First of all, there was a new subject, Nature in her wilder aspects. Secondly, there was a new view of man as an inhabitant of isolated regions, in retreat from highly civilized society, but in touch with primitive, rude Nature. These two themes, closely related to each other, are present in "Winter." But when considered amongst all the other aspects of Nature— understood in the broad eighteenth-century sense to include all that is natural to man as social being—discernible in Kent's illustrations for the *Seasons,* these themes constitute only a small portion of that truly cosmic view of natural process.

Thus a special emphasis upon wild Nature and man's retreat from civilized society would represent a movement toward particularity, and away from neo-classic generality, in Kent's art. It is such a development that must now be traced: first, through the emergence of his grotesque style and, second, through his work in the gothic.

THE GROTESQUE MODE: SOME IMAGES OF
FANTASTIC REALMS

In the designs for John Gay's *Fables* (1727), we still find Kent's neo-classic style to be present, though circumscribed in application. But the grotesque emerges here quite distinctly in the form of highly fanciful decoration of artifacts and intentional disproportion in the drawing of the human figure.

Kent was not the sole illustrator of this volume; he collaborated with John Wootton, an artist best known for his paintings of animals and sporting subjects. Some division of labor was probably necessary, since each of Gay's fifty Fables, as well as his Introduction, required an illustration. Kent designed twenty; Wootton thirty; and A. Motte—one of several engravers including Pierre Fourdrinier, G. van der Gucht, and B. Baron—apparently contributed one design.[24] The fact that most of the Fables were naturally concerned with the sayings and doings of animals may explain Wootton's doing the major share of the work. Such subjects were his specialty. On the other hand, Kent was assigned the two most important pieces from John Gay's point of view: the Introduction and the first Fable, which was dedicated "To his Highness William, Duke of Cumberland," and intended to gain royal favor.[25] Each of the illustrations simply presents the main characters or incidents of the Fable in a single scene, with no secondary subjects and little of interest placed in the background. This characteristic alone distinguishes them from those of Kent's works previously discussed. In general, the animals and barnyard scenes are quite natural in appearance, the detail being full and realistic. This is particularly true of Wootton's designs, although Kent, in his engraving for "The Two Owls and the Sparrow" (Fable XXXII), equals his partner in this respect. In only two illustrations—"The Monkey who had seen the World" (XIV) and "The Goat without a Beard" (XXII)—is the satiric analogy between human manners and the animal world explored very pointedly. Both designs are by Wootton.

Kent illustrates most of the Fables which include figures from classical mythology. But elements of the grotesque obtrude in his neo-classic subjects. Thus in the design for Fable VI, in which Plutus visits a miser, the god of the underworld seems curiously disproportioned in limb. Similarly, in the design for Fable XXVII, the graceful figure of the good angel contrasts with the haggard, hollow face of the sick man. And in Kent's realization of "The Court of Death" (XLVII), a human skeleton sits in judgment before a drooping woman, who is upheld by another skeleton equipped as soldier (reproduced on p. 385).

Thus the artist creates forceful images of man's vice, depravity, and mortality through a deliberate disfiguration of the human form, a divergence from the perfect proportions characteristic of the neo-classic style. It is, perhaps, in this fashion that Gay's moral concern with man's deviation from virtue is reflected in the designs. Certainly the most deformed of all Kent's figures is that of Care, termed by Gay "The Universal Apparition" (XXXI). Interestingly enough, the poet presents Care (i.e. the moral conscience) as both a pursuing avenger of dissolute living and a monitor who must "go before" any human act. (See reproduction below.)

Purely fanciful, exotic, and esoteric subjects appear prominently among Kent's illustrations. A few may be mentioned: an elephant in a bookseller's shop (X), a Persian praying to his sun-god (XXVIII), the interior of Gresham Hall with its scientific curiosities (XVI), the fairy or "pigmy sprite" appearing to a mother and nurse (III). No less in evidence is Kent's talent for interior decoration, and especially for the creation of fanciful garden ornaments. For example, in the illustration of "The

Butterfly and the Snail'' (XXIV), an elaborate vine-trellis, with classical busts incorporated into its side-supports, easily overshadows the two principal creatures of the Fable. Obviously Kent did not hesitate to illustrate his own ideas in gardening, architecture, and decoration while at work for the poets.

The designs for Gay's *Fables* must be considered one of Kent's lesser works. When the second volume of the *Fables* appeared in 1738, a different illustrator, the talented Gravelot, was employed. His engravings, though fewer in number than those in the first volume, occupied not a half but a full page each. Most important, Gravelot's men and women, dressed in contemporary costume and seen at elegant country estates, possessed a naturalness and grace which Kent's figures never wholly attained. To place the 1727 and 1738 *Fables* side by side is to realize, first of all, that Gravelot's work is a superior and characteristic example of eighteenth-century portraiture and, secondly, that the presence of the fanciful and grotesque in Kent's work represents a rather special development in his own career and, indeed, in the art of the period generally. To grasp in full the ramifications of that development, we must now consider Augustan gothicism and Kent's contributions in that minor mode.

In the Augustan age, the term ''gothic'' had a variety of implications, not all of which could be gathered under the term ''medieval,'' as might be possible today. ''Gothic'' implied some of the following: in civilization, a lack of refinement or a simple barbarism; in art, a lack of rational (i.e. classical) form and a tendency to fancifulness and wildness; in English history, almost any epoch prior to the Restoration, usually the Elizabethan period or earlier (with no certain distinction between Middle Ages and Renaissance).

William Kent, though primarily an advocate of neo-Palladian architecture, designed a few gothic structures during his tenure as Master Carpenter in the royal Office of Works.[26] One such is the gatehouse at Hampton Court Palace, completed in 1732.[27] In style, it is what we might now call early Tudor; and it may be compared with the Holbein Gate at Whitehall, London (1532), to which it bears a certain resemblance.[28] Two other structures—the Hermitage and Merlin's Cave built for Queen Caroline at Richmond Park—were intended as ''retreats''; that is, small houses hidden in the recesses of the Park to which the Queen could retire, ostensibly, for the purpose of solitary contemplation. These buildings were clearly original in conception. For example, in a contemporary engraving, Merlin's Cave is depicted as a squat structure, with a thatched roof formed in three high, conical spires; the doorways have pointed arches surrounded with arabesque decoration.[29] Rustic (i.e. primitive) features, such as the thatched roof, combine with other forms of exotic ornamentation—all this intended to conceal any appearance of regular design.

Merlin's Cave was surely fantastic in conception. Or so at least some of Kent's contemporaries judged it. According to Lord Hervey, upon completion of the building in 1735, and after the attack upon the Queen's extravagance by the opposition in *The Craftsman,* King George II is reported to have told his wife: ". . . you deserve to be abused for such childish, silly stuff, and it is the first time I ever knew the scoundrel to be in the right."[30] A more sympathetic reaction was that of an unknown poetess who, after having visited the Queen at her retreat, was herself visited with the inspiration for a complimentary poem:

But Merlin's Cave had such Impressions made,
And Royal Honours, to his Memory pay'd;
Pleas'd with Reflection, and involv'd in Thought,
Creative *Fancy,* soon this *Vision* wrought.[31]

Indeed, the muse of poetry was a familiar spirit at the Cave. For there Stephen Duck, the thresher-poet whose genius was reputedly untutored, held the office of Royal Thatcher.

It is not difficult to locate a factitious element in the Augustan cult of the gothic: only a thin veneer of primitivism and fancifulness covers an essential sophistication and allegiance to the established orders in society and the arts. But later in the century, the gothic cult was to develop into something far more serious and important, the beginnings of the romantic movement. For this reason alone, Kent's practice of the gothic merits our attention, that this role in the evolution of English culture may be fully appreciated.

Two other phases of that practice must be briefly mentioned here: Kent's painting of medieval subjects and his landscape gardening. The former consists of two small paintings (1729), whose subjects are taken from the life of King Henry V. These are important, first of all, because they are perhaps the first medieval subjects painted in the eighteenth century before 1760 and, secondly, because the artist strives for some degree of historical accuracy in his representation of costume and setting. In this, Kent anticipates later antiquarian interest in medieval culture. As to his landscape gardening, a rich topic fully developed elsewhere, let it suffice to say here that Kent's effort to compose a landscape as though it were a picture resulted in freer flowing outlines for lawns and woods, abandonment of the prevalent geometric designs for the terrain, and hence a relatively less formal and more "natural" appearance, upon which later gardeners were to improve—improve, indeed, to such an extent that they felt obliged to criticize Kent's landscapes as insufficiently grand, wild, picturesque, and true to their conception of Nature.[32]

These various aspects of Kent's career—his grotesque style in drawing, his gothic architecture, medieval painting, landscape gardening, his delight in the fanciful generally—all are relevant to his last and most ambitious undertaking as literary illustrator, the designs for Thomas Birch's edition of Spenser's *Faerie Queene* (1751). It is possible to argue that in his age Kent was a logical choice for illustrator of Spenser. To begin with, his interest in medieval subjects probably corresponded to the editor's concern with a historical criticism of Spenser, not one based upon neo-classic premises irrelevant to the inspiration of this particular poet. Thus Birch, in his prefatory "Life" of Spenser, described his own effort to secure "a just Representation of the genuine Text, not hitherto given in any single Edition, but form'd from an exact Collation of the two original ones of the Author."[33] He also defended Spenser's imitation of Ariosto on the grounds that in the poet's age the Italian poets, not the ancient, had been "in the highest Vogue" and only they had maintained the heroic ethos still alive in that age, the "Remains of the old Gothic Chivalry."[34] And Birch supplied a second reason for Spenser's imitating Ariosto: the poet's desire for a model "which might give the greatest Scope to that Range of Fancy, which was so remarkably his Talent." Here the editor touched upon a familiar point in eighteenth-century criticism of Spenser, one which a predecessor, John Hughes in his edition of the complete *Works* (1715), had already granted a favor of the poet in virtually the same words.[35]

Kent's own "Range of Fancy" probably constituted another of

his qualifications as illustrator of Spenser. In this connection, William Mason later attributed to the artist an interesting, if apocryphal, remark: "It is said that Mr. Kent frequently declared he caught his taste in gardening from reading the picturesque descriptions of Spenser. However this may be, the designs which he made for the works of that poet are an incontestable proof that they had no effect upon his executive powers as a painter."[36] In his poor opinion of Kent's draftsmanship, Mason was not alone in his age. In the admiration of the picturesque quality of Spenser's poetry, mason was no doubt joined by Kent; but it is hardly likely that Kent's innovations in gardening owned more to his familiarity with *The Faerie Queene* than to the works of earlier gardeners or to enthusiasts such as Burlington and Pope.[37]

In considering the illustrations for *The Faerie Queene,* I shall attempt to apply more closely the criteria just discussed: first of all, the criterion of accuracy to historical and textual detail; and, secondly, that of strength of Fancy—Kent's painterly equivalent to Spenser's descriptive power and striking, even surprising imagery.

The first, accuracy of detail, is present to a very great degree.[38] Like the designs for Gay's Fables, each of these thirty-two prints reveals a single narrative event—a practice which is the more notable here because, unlike the *Fables,* Spenser's poem is a long, continuous narrative whose actions could, theoretically, be combined as the subject for a single illustration.[39] No details other than those present in the immediate context in the poem are included. Moreover, each of the plates is marked with the number of the page on which the illustrated action occurs.[40] Thus the reader possesses an open invitation to compare illustration with poetic description.

Compared with the six illustrations for *The Faerie Queene* done by du Guernier in the 1715 *Works,* Kent's designs are more faithful to the medieval costumes appropriate to Spenser's knights and ladies. In addition, whereas du Guernier concentrates upon scenes at court, upon large groups of courtiers and warriors (often in Roman martial dress), Kent presents most often a few isolated figures in a setting virtually devoid of all traces of civilization. Indeed, scenes of urban society appear infrequently. One looks almost in vain for drawings of medieval towns and cathedrals;[41] and only three castles can be found in the designs. These justify

Horace Walpole's opinion that Kent did not succeed in gothic architecture.[42] Certainly there is nothing here to compare with the elaborate fretwork and delicate spires of Walpole's own Strawberry Hill. For instance, the most fully drawn of Kent's castles—that of Pollente in Book V of *The Faerie Queene*—is thick-walled, squat, and mounted with machicolated turrets. It may be compared with a late medieval fort such as the one at Bodiam in Sussex (ca 1386), which was designed for defense against cannon.

It must be admitted that in the matter of architecture Kent does permit himself one anachronism. Spenser's description of Phedria's island in Idle Lake gives the artist some license:

> It was a chosen plot of fertile land,
> Emongst wide, waues set, like a cunning litle nest,
> As if it had, by Nature's cunning hand,
> Bene choisely picked out from all the rest,
> And laid forth the ensample of the best:
> No daintie flowre or herbe, that grows on ground,
> No arboret with painted blossomes drest,
> And smelling sweet, but there it might be found,
> To bud out faire, and throwe her sweet smels all around.
>
> (Bk II, C 6, s 12)

For Kent, an "ensample of the best" means an illustration of his own work as architect and gardener. In the engraving, Phedria's island seems to float between lake and sky like a flat piece of cut cardboard, upon which appears the schema of a country estate. The mansion has a classical portico, while a serpentine stream, waterfall, and several groups of trees suggest the general ground-plan of the park. Another structure, overlooking the water, is similar to the Seven-Arched Portico actually built by Kent at Rousham.[43] In fact, Horace Walpole's description of Rousham serves well for this picture of Phedria's island: ". . . the garden is Daphne in little; the sweetest little groves, streams, glades, porticoes, cascades, and river imaginable; all the scenes are perfectly classic."[44] Kent allows such classicism here only in an instance of the explicitly artful in Spenser's text—the "cunning little nest" of Mirth where Nature, according to the poet, imitates human art with a "cunning hand," or at least seems to do so. The wilder, uncultivated tracts of Faery Land—the realm of Fancy in which the rules of classic art do not prevail—receive, as we shall see, a different treatment from Kent's hand.

In addition to the obvious kinds of accuracy, the use of medieval armor and fidelity to poetic detail, Kent's inclusion of some visual analogues to Spenserian Fancy must also be considered a sincere, if problematic, effort to give the reader a true idea of the poet's peculiar genius. For example, if at times both knight and horse seem strangely diminutive, indeed, toy-like in stature, this may possibly be justified as a pleasing rendition of the elfin nature of Spenser's heroes. Or possibly not. On this point, Horace Walpole, whose standards of judgment were here strangely neo-classic, offered a most unsympathetic criticism:

> Such of the drawings as he designed for Gay's Fables have some truth and nature; but who would search for his faults, will find an ample crop in a very favourite work of his, the prints for Spenser's Fairy Queen. As the drawings were exceedingly cried up by his admirers, and disappointed the public in proportion, the blame was thrown on the engraver, but so far unjustly, that though ill executed, the wretchedness of drawing, the total ignorance of perspective, the want of variety, the disproportion of the buildings, and the awkwardness of the attitudes, could have been the faults of the inventor only. There are figures issuing from cottages not so high as their shoulders, castles in which the towers could not contain an infant, and knights who hold their spears as men who are lifting a load sideways. The land-scapes are the only tolerable parts, and yet the trees are seldom other than young beeches, to which Kent as a planter was accustomed.[45]

Indeed, disproportion is common in these designs. For example, in the illustration of Prince Arthur's defeat of Orgoglio, the disproportion between the slender, armed knight and the bare, fully muscled torso of the giant is so great as to give the impression that Orgoglio stands farther forward than Arthur, when they are actually fighting toe-to-toe (Bk I, C 8). Of course, Spenser also abounds in fantastic disproportions. Unhappily, in this case, Kent fails to approximate the one given by the poet: that Orgoglio in "stature did exceed/The hight of three the tallest sonnes of mortall seed" (Bk I, C 7, s 8). Consequently, one cannot be certain whether Kent's disproportion is an intended but unsuccessful imitation of Spenser, or simply a result of artistic ineptitude.

Thus Walpole's criticism cannot be easily dismissed. For the weakness of Kent's draftsmanship is in evidence here and elsewhere. It would be dangerous to claim that evident faults in the prints are all intentional and significant artistic effects. On the other hand, Walpole's neo-classic standards are not particularly relevant to a work devoted to the realm of Fancy such as Kent attempted to produce, without the aid of an aesthetic theory that might have accounted for the creative independence of the artist's imagination. For this reason, it is difficult to find a critical alternative to Walpole's methods of judgment.

The fact remains that a certain strength of Fancy appears throughout Kent's career as well as in his work for *The Faerie Queene*. I believe that some of the odd effects in these designs are surely the result of the artist's conscious abandonment of certain rules of perspective and proportion—Kent's only method, perhaps, of producing an impression of the fanciful in visual terms. Let us consider a characteristic mentioned by Walpole: the drawing of houses apparently too small for the figures supposed to inhabit them. Even in the earliest of Kent's works, the design for Gay's *The Shepherd's Week,* one discovers in the background a farmhouse whose size is incredibly small in relation to its inhabitant (a girl seen leaning out of a window). This was probably a matter of convenience for the artist, a question of rendering a distant detail distinct in an already crowded design. This practice recurs in the engraving for *The Faerie Queene,* but here another factor must be taken into account. The lower portion of each building seems buried in the ground, as though set in some unseen declivity. One gains this impression particularly from the drawing of Archimago's cell, a small house reminiscent of the Hermitage at Richmond Park and half-obscured by the earth and surrounding trees (Bk I, C 1). In this design, the figures of Redcrosse, Una, and Archimago, all drawn with great naturalness, clearly stand upon higher ground in front of the hermitage. As Spenser describes it: "A little lowly Hermitage it was,/Downe in a dale, hard by a forests side" (Bk I, C 1, s 34). Is it not possible, then, that at least in this case Kent was attempting to portray a partially hidden "dale," in which the hermitage appears, literally, "lowly"?

This is not a remote possibility. Indeed, as a gardner, Kent created similar effects: his landscapes were contrived to reveal

new perspectives, hidden glades and gothic temples, sudden
views across a contoured terrain, as the observer advances. A
characteristic device was the use of the sunken fence or "ha-ha,"
which was named after the cry of surprise usually given by the
walker who suddenly found his path across an open lawn ob-
structed by an unseen ditch.

One cannot say, of course, that the techniques actually employed in the engravings are very effective in surprising the
viewer with the appearance of hidden features in Spenser's
romantic landscape. For the illustrator does not have available to
him the resource of movement; his figures are static and his
viewer cannot enter the two-dimensional picture. This limitation
baffled Kent. For example, in the background of the design of
Redcrosse, Duessa, and Fradubio (Bk I, C 2), the torso of a squire
appears above the line of the hillside, as though his legs were
buried in the ground. It is not immediately apparent that the fellow
is climbing up a hill. For Kent apparently makes no effort to draw
the slope of the ground, so that the viewer, after some puzzling,
becomes aware of the presence of a hidden declivity. Under the
conditions of graphic art, in which both the subject and the viewer
are static, the effect of this technique is liable to be ludicrous.

None of the designs presents a scene with a deep, gloomy forest
such as a post-romantic sensibility might associate with the idea
of gothic; all have open, varied landscapes with relatively small
and sparse trees and with rough, bare, rocky terrain. Thus no
strong contrast between thick woods and a sudden clearing, for
example, is achieved. Only in one illustration, showing the death
of Errour (Bk I, C 1), in which Kent places trees along the
perimeters of the scene and contrasts the rocky hillside with the
opening sky area and emerging sun, does one sense the surrounding presence of those "thickest woods" described by Spenser as
the abode of Errour. But on the whole, the essential characteristic
of Kent's landscapes is the clarity with which the terrain is
revealed, a clarity which exists despite the attempt to conceal
certain features and to present Nature in her uncultivated state.
The artistic spirit of these designs is still that of the Augustan age,
and their image of Nature still one of great clarity and order.

Yet Kent's landscapes also suggest the important step in the
direction of romanticism which was taken before 1750. Even to
conceive of a landscape capable of surprising an observer with the

unseen or to use natural objects in order to express man's sense of the wild and fanciful, this surely was to advance toward an ultimate conjoining of the power of imagination with the independent life of Nature. It is in this light that the illustrations of *The Faerie Queene* become significant in English literary and cultural history. To be sure, other manifestations of the fanciful here are also noteworthy: the surrealistic setting and weird creatures that surround the cave of Merlin (Bk III, C 3), and the drawing of the spotted beast that chases Florimell (Bk II, C 7). But Kent's realization of such fantastic creatures is probably of less far-reaching significance than the landscape that he created as a fit environment for all the figures born of Spenser's Fancy.

By teaching his contemporaries that a relatively wild and "natural" landscape could be experienced as art, a painterly composition, Kent prepared for the age in which men would attempt to experience the wildness and inner vitality of Nature

without the mediation of art, directly and feelingly without the restriction of the picturesque analogy. The romantic approach to Nature, in this aspect, would seem to be an extreme extension of the Augustan program of humanizing the natural environment, adapting it through reason to the needs of human life and civilization. Although romantic writers rejected the rational rules of art as employed by the Augustans, they were, perhaps, better prepared than their predecessors to discover an essential continuity between the human imagination and the life of Nature.[46] In fact, such a continuity was already contained, implicitly, in Kent's visual realization of Spenserian Fancy in the seemingly uncultivated landscapes of his designs. It remained for others to develop the implications of William Kent's exploratory work in the gothic mode—to abjure the art by which he created the illusion of freedom and vitality in his landscapes, and to demand the reality from Nature herself.

NOTES

[1] Margaret Jourdain devotes only one paragraph to the illustrations in her comprehensive study, *The Work of William Kent* (London 1948) 73. Kent's plates for James Thomson's *Seasons* are treated in Ralph Cohen's *The Art of Discrimination: Thomson's* The Seasons *and the Language of Criticism* (Berkeley 1964) 251–265. Brief discussions are found in the following: Edgar Breitenbach, "The Bibliography of Illustrated Books." *Library Association Record,* Fourth Series, II (May 1935) 176–185; Iolo Williams, "English Book Illustration," *Library,* Fourth Series, XVII (1937), 1–21; Bertrand H. Bronson, *Printing as an Index of Taste in Eighteenth-Century England* (New York, The New York Public Library 1963). [This illustrated booklet is still in print.—Ed.]

[2] Quoted from Jourdain, *William Kent* 28–29.

[3] See *The Notebooks of George Vertue,* Publications of *The Walpole Society,* XXII (Oxford 1947) 140–141.

[4] An affectionate portrait of Kent is found in Pope's letter to Lord Burlington (27 Nov 1736): "The greatest news I have to tell you is that the Signior is in perfect tranquillity, enjoying his own Being, & is become a happy but plumper copy of General Dormer. In sweetness of manners, he is allowed on all hands to be a mere Ludovico Dolce. We dined together upon Pictures, Mademoiselle du Parc, and a Mummy. I go frequently to him, not only thro' the affection I bear him & the Respect I

pay to his Genius, but in good earnest to learn what I can, & as often as I can, of your self & my Lady . . .'' (*The Correspondence of Alexander Pope,* ed George Sherburn, Oxford 1956, Vol IV of 5 vols, p 43–44). For a full account of the artistic relations of Pope and Kent, see William K. Wimsatt, *The Portraits of Alexander Pope* (New Haven 1965) 107–136.

5 George Vertue wrote of Kent's early reputation: "*Courtiers* declared him the best History painter—& the first that was a native of this Kingdom." (*Notebooks, Walpole Society* XXII 139). By "Courtiers" Vertue probably meant Lord Burlington and those of his faction. For he also noted that later "his Lordship declared that if Kent was not the first or best painter in England—he was certainly the best architect" (141).

6 Reproduced in Ronald Paulson's edition, *Hogarth's Graphic Works* (New Haven 1965) Vol II of 2 vols, plate 37. Another engraving, *The Man of Taste* (1731) also satirized Pope, Burlington, and Kent. Although traditionally it has been attributed to Hogarth, Paulson now argues against its authenticity. See Paulson I 299–300, and II pl 277.

7 During the rest of Kent's career, Pierre Fourdrinier engraved his designs.

8 See R. H. Griffith, *Alexander Pope: A Bibliography* (Austin, Texas 1922) Vol I of 2 vols, entry no 151.

9 George Sherburn, *Early Life of Alexander Pope* (Oxford 1934) 254 ff.

10 See Sherburn's note in *The Correspondence of Alexander Pope* II 288.

11 This plate reappeared in several of Pope's later publications, but in changed states. See Wimsatt, *The Portraits of Alexander Pope,* 125–127.

12 In the "Sixth Pastoral," *The Poems of Ambrose Philips,* ed M. G. Segar (Oxford 1937) 32–36. The offending lines are, perhaps, the following:

> Hobbinol.
>
> >   Soft, on a Cowslip Bank, my Love and I
> >   Together lay: A Brook ran murm'ring by.
> >   A thousand tender things to me she said;
> >   And I a thousand tender Things repaid.   (lines 53–56)

Whereas Gay's shepherds must use their wits to snatch a glimpse of the girls' beauties, Philips' are purely sensual lovers relishing the wantonness of their mistresses, who themselves behave somewhat in the manner of the naked bathers encountered by the Knight of Temperance in the Bower of Bliss:

> Hobbinol.
>
> >   As *Marian* bath'd, by chance I passed by;
> >   She blush'd and at me cast a sidelong Eye:
> >   Then swith beneath the crystal Wave she try'd

Her beauteous Form, but all in vain, to hide.
Lanquet.
    As I, to cool me, bath'd one sultry Day,
    Fond Lydia lurking in the Sedges lay.
    The Wanton laugh'd, and seem'd in haste to fly;
    Yet often stopp'd, and often turn'd her Eye.   (69–76)

[13] Assuming the original to be the edition "printed for Ferd. Burleigh" in 1714. Another edition, "printed for R. Burleigh," is also dated 1714; but it contains the two stanzas printed as lines 103–110 in the 1720 *Poems.* It has been conjectured that the R. Burleigh volume was actually published sometime after the appearance of the 1720 *Poems* and marked, fraudulently, with the incorrect, earlier date for commercial purposes. See Charles E. Beckwith, "Gay's Eclogues and Georgics: A Critical Edition," Uupubl diss (Yale 1956) li–lvi.

[14] *The Art of Discrimination* 260.

[15] *Spring,* lines 774–792 (in the texts of 1728–38). Most of the details in Kent's design are mentioned in the Table of Contents prepared for the 1729 edition of this poem by Thomson himself. The table is reprinted by J. Logie Robertson in *The Complete Poetical Works of James Thomson* (Oxford 1908) 46–48.

[16] Cf the opening verses of *Summer.* This is the only case in which the figure of the preceding season appears in an illustration.

[17] *Summer,* lines 403–412 (texts of 1730–8).

[18] *Summer,* 972–1036 (texts of 1730–8).

[19] *Autumn,* 428 ff (texts of 1730–8).

[20] *Winter,* 73–77 (text of the 1730 quarto).—The illustration is reproduced on the cover of this *Bulletin.*—ED.

[21] *Winter,* 655–661 (text of the 1730 quarto).

[22] See Edward Croft-Murray, "William Kent in Rome," *English Miscellany,* ed Mario Praz, I (1950) 221–229.

[23] William Hogarth gave a brilliant analysis of the faults of Kent's art, in his engraving *A Burlesque on Kent's Altarpiece at St. Clements Danes,* reprinted in Paulson II pl 57.

[24] Gay wrote to James Dormer (22 Nov 1726): "I am about to publish a collection of Fables entirely of my own invention to be dedicated to Prince Wm, they consist of fifty, and I am oblig'd to Mr. Kent and Wootton for the Designs of the Plates. The Work is begun to be printed, and is delay'd only upon account of the Gravers, who are neither very good or expeditious." (Sherburn, *The Correspondence of Alexander Pope,* II 415–416). Publication was delayed until the spring of 1727.

[25] Unfortunately, Gay was again disappointed in his hopes for a pension; as he wrote to Pope in early 1729: "O that I had never known

what a Court was! Dear, Pope, what a barren Soil (to me so) have I been striving to produce something out of! Why did I not take your Advice before my writing Fables for the Duke, not to write them? . . . It is my very hard Fate, I must get nothing, write for them or against them.'' (Sherburn, *Correspondence* III 20).

26 Jourdain, *William Kent* 38.

27 See John Summerson, *Architecture in Britain 1530–1830* (Baltimore 1954) 238–245 and plate 1B (The Hampton Court Gatehouse).

28 Reproduced by Summerson, *Architecture,* plate 4A.

29 The frontispiece to *Merlin, or The British Inchanter* (London 1736), a drama by W. Giffard (?).

30 *Memoirs of the Reign of George the Second,* ed John W. Croker (London 1855 Vol II of 2 vols, p. 50.

31 *Merlin: A Poem* (London 1735) 4.

32 For an excellent survey and interpretation, see Christopher Hussey, *The Picturesque* (New York 1927) and the same author's ''Introduction'' to Jourdain's *William Kent.*

33 *The Faerie Queene* (London 1751) Vol I of 3 vols, p XXXVII. Prints by Kent will be identified by their location in this text of Spenser's epic.

34 I XXXIV.

35 On eighteenth-century opinion of Spenser, see Earl Wasserman, *Elizabethan Poetry in Eighteenth-Century England,* Illinois Studies in Language and Literature, Vol XXXII (Urbana, Ill 1947) 192 ff. On the work of Hughes and Birch, see Jewel Wurtsbaugh, *Two Centuries of Spenserian Scholarship (1609–1805)* (Baltimore 1936) 55–70. Birch echoed the critical opinions of Hughes and others at several points.

36 Note X to line 511 of *The English Garden,* Book I, in *Works of William Mason* (London 1811) I 385.

37 Cf Jim Corder, ''Spenser and the Eighteenth-Century Informal Garden,'' *Notes and Queries* CCIV (Jan 1959) 19–21.

38 A notable exception is Kent's representation of the procession of Pride (Bk I, C 4). The illustrator arranges the six Vices that draw Pride's carriage in three ranks of two figures each. (Spenser is not precise on this point; he simply states that one Vice is ''beside'' or ''next to'' another.) However, Kent disturbs the sequence in which the poet presents the Vices. According to Spenser, ''The first, that all the rest did guyde'' is Idlenesse, and ''the last of this ungodly tire'' is Wrath. The illustrator, unfortunately, places Wrath in the foremost rank and Idlenesse in the last. This order makes less sense than Spenser's; for the internal contradictions within the procession—for instance, between the lethargic leader Idlenesse and the furious Wrath or the lashing Satan who drives the carriage behind—are lost in the illustration. It is probable that Kent was not sensitive to the psychological nuances of Spenser's allegory.

[39] Iolo Williams mentions only thirty original designs by Kent now in the Victoria and Albert Museum, London (*Library,* Fourth Series, XVII 8). The last three engravings in the 1751 edition of *The Faerie Queene,* Vol III, are not inscribed with the artist's name. It is possible since the volumes were published after Kent's death, that he may not have completed the work himself.

[40] There are some inaccuracies in the marking and inset of the prints; they are minor and attributable to the publisher. A notable one is the placement of a design intended for Bk I, C 8 (Prince Arthur slaying Orgoglio) out of sequence in C 7. The following illustration (Una meeting Arthur) should actually precede and stand in C 7.

[41] Except for the outline of a distant cathedral town set in the background of the design of Prince Arthur with his instructors Merlin and Timon (Bk I, C 9). The image, not at all distinct, represents Merlin's phophetic vision of Arthur's future at the court of the Faerie Queene.

[42] *Anecdotes of Painting in England* (Strawberry Hill 1762) Vol IV of 4 vols, 114–115.

[43] See Jourdain, *William Kent,* figs 106, 108.

[44] *Correspondence of Horace Walpole,* ed Paget Toynbee (Oxford 1903) IV 41.

[45] *Anecdotes of Painting,* loc. cit.

[46] An interesting document in this connection is Uvedale Price's *An Essay on the Picturesque* (London 1794), especially his criticism of Kent's artfulness in landscaping, p 194 ff. As early as 1762, Richard Hurd associated Kent's gardening with the neo-classic mode in art. See *Letters on Chivalry and Romance* (London 1762) 66–68.

THE WORK OF THE IMAGE: THE PLATES OF THE *ENCYCLOPÉDIE*
Daniel Brewer

One of the most frequently commented entries in the vast French *Encyclopédie* is Diderot's lengthy article "Encyclopédie." This comes as no surprise of course, since the article is one of the major manifestoes of eighteenth-century French Enlightenment, providing a detailed picture of how the encyclopedists understood the philosophical, social, and moral context in which they situated their project, the goals they set for themselves, and the criteria and strategies they adopted in order to achieve them. Setting forth the theory of language and epistemology upon which the encyclopedists' concept of an encyclopedia is based, Diderot's article is the most explicitly self-referential entry in the entire work. As such, its importance lies also in its critical position vis-à-vis the encyclopedic text, the way in which it articulates its specific metadiscursive relation with encyclopedic discourse. For much of the article "Encyclopédie" deals with the right way to write an encyclopedia (how to define words, set down the true meaning and significance of objects and concepts, evaluate the relative importance and hence proper proportions of each article and its interconnection with others). By assuming a metadiscursive position with regard to the *Encyclopédie* as a whole, the article "Encyclopédie" also expresses the metacritical function of encyclopedic discourse in general implied in each and every article; in other words, the supposed or at least desired capacity of encyclopedic discourse to double its object, to translate the natural world into language and provide its true reflection, in short to represent.[1]

At the heart of Diderot's article lies the thorny problem of the

Reprinted by permission from *Stanford French Review,* v. 8, no. 2–3 (1984), pp. 229–244. Published for the Department of French and Italian, Stanford University, by Anma Libri, Saratoga, California.

391

relation between discourse and its object, which is one reason why the issue of language receives the attention it does in this text. Given Diderot's keen interest in the question of language, as well as his concern with his reader and the reception his text will receive, it would be an oversight, if not an act of interpretive bad faith, not to realize the extent to which Diderot's discussion of the metacritical function of encyclopedic discourse also implicates us as readers, bearing upon the metacritical position we too establish in producing a discourse "on" the *Encyclopédie*. Putting this negatively and more provocatively, one could say that it is by excluding—or at least radically restricting—the problem of representation as Diderot poses it that the readers of the *Encyclopédie* can comfortably assume that the article accurately and effortlessly describes and represents its object, that like all other entries it translates into language the "idea" or ideal to which it refers, thereby providing us direct access to the "message" of encyclopedism, located in the realm of timeless ideas. Thus, Diderot's article becomes a kind of eighteenth-century artifact, to be dusted off, framed by quotation marks or repaired but ever so slightly by the web of commentary, and placed in the "imaginary museum" (to borrow André Malraux's term) of literary and historical study. This version of how the article "Encyclopédie" may be (and often is) read, although purposefully argumentative, is not uninstructive. For it is based on a misreading, or better an underreading, of Diderot's article as it bears upon the question of interpretation and the relation between discourse and its object.

The crucial oversight of this misreading can be shown by considering a passage in which Diderot explains and defends what he calls encyclopedic order. In addition to the arbitrary order of the alphabet, all articles of the *Encyclopédie* are linked in a way determined by their position on the encyclopedists' genealogical "tree of knowledge." Human knowledge derives from sensory perception, and it is the sensationalist explanation of how perception is transformed into ideas that provides the model for encyclopedic order, the various branches and subdivisions of knowledge. For Diderot and d'Alembert, taxonomy recapitulates epistemology. But is this order natural or arbitrary? Does the *Encyclopédie* represent its object, the natural world, absolutely or relatively? Diderot answers by analogy, likening the natural world to a machine so large and complex, made up of so many interconnecting pieces, that it can be described and figured in an infinite number of ways. "L'univers soit réel soil intelligible a une infinité de points de vue sous lesquels il peut être représenté, et le nombre des systèmes possibles de la connaissance humaine est aussi grand que celui de ces points de vue." The only system of knowledge, he adds, whose order would not be arbitrary, and thus whose authority would be above question, would be "le système qui [existe] de toute éternité dans la volonté de Dieu" (VI, 211). Diderot recognizes of course that such a system is unattainable and hence that encyclopedic discourse cannot provide anything other than an arbitrary and mediated representation of its object. What is more interesting, he goes so far as to suggest that such an absolute and perfectly timeless system of knowledge even runs counter to the goals of encyclopedism. Instead of increasing our knowledge of the world, the ideal encyclopedia—perfect encyclopedic representation—would be just as difficult to understand as the world itself. "Quant à ce système général d'où l'arbitraire serait exclu, et que nous n'aurons jamais, peut-être ne nous serait-il pas fort avantageux de l'avoir; car quelle différence y auraitil entre la lecture d'un ouvrage où tous les ressorts de l'univers seraient développés, et l'étude même de l'univers? presque aucune" (VI, 211). Consequently, the encyclopedists' concern is not with eliminating the arbitrary from the encyclopedic plan, but rather with establishing an order that, although arbitrary, serves to help achieve their goals. This order they derive from their concept of man, "les facultés principales de l'homme." "Pourquoi n'introduirons-nous pas l'homme dans notre ouvrage, comme il est placé dans l'univers? Pourquoi n'en ferons-nous pas un centre commun . . .? Qu'on suive telle autre voie qu'on aimera mieux, pourvu qu'on ne substitue pas à l'homme un être muet, insensible et froid. L'homme est le terme unique d'où il faut partir, et auquel il faut tout ramener . . ." (VI, 212–13). Man, in other words the subject of encyclopedism, is thus placed by the encyclopedists at the center of the unbounded encyclopedic circle, and insofar as it relates everything to this center, the *Encyclopédie* can claim to provide an index to the universe viewed in its relation to man. The spiritual father of the *Encyclopédie* is not Chambers or Bacon but Condillac.[2]

Stated within Diderot's hymn of Enlightenment humanism is a working definition of encyclopedic discourse and the kind of reading that the encyclopedic text calls for. First, encyclopedic discourse does represent its object, but at one remove: there exists a gap or noncoincidence between language and its referent, which discourse cannot fill, but rather only bridge by imposing an arbitrary order upon the world. The order that encyclopedic discourse would produce is designed to make it seem as if the world were indeed structured the way it is represented. Second, for this ordering process to be successful, the reader of the *Encyclopédie* must become a partner to its strategy. The addressee of the encyclopedic text must yield to a discourse whose description of its object is based not on the reflection of man's central place in the universe, but rather on the creation of the powerfully centering notion of "man." To achieve its philosophical, pedagogical, ideal, and above all imaginary order, the encyclopedic text invites its reader to accept and share in the benefits of a discourse one of whose effects is to make it seem as if the true knowledge of all things could indeed be derived from and referred back to the notion of "man." Third, it is not sufficient simply to characterize the enlighteners' understanding of man in the terms they themselves provide. The philosophes' theory of knowledge does define man as sensing, rational subject, yet eighteenth-century epistemological discourse of which the *Encyclopédie* is a part should not be uprooted from its position within a far more extensive discursive apparatus. The epistemological discourse of sensationalism does not so much reflect the enlighteners' idea of their own humanity as it produces a conceptual apparatus that serves to rationalize and justify certain actions and institutions, beliefs and values. The concept of "man" with all its central, centralizing importance may be an ideal concept, but it is certainly an ideologically determined one, especially given the close relation between the rise of materialism in eighteenth-century France and the need to formulate new values and interpretations of the world as a result of a changing class structure.[3]

Viewed from this perspective, the *Encyclopédie* appears less "audacious," yet far more effective, than its "message" would lead us to believe.[4] Proposing that all knowledge of the world be ordered in terms of its relation to man, the encyclopedists relativize knowledge. Questions concerning the nature of ultimate reality need pose no problem, a move on the encyclopedists' part that not only undercuts the authority of traditional discourses of interpretation and social-political institutions that purport to pass judgment on the true and unchanging nature of things, but also avoids direct confrontation with these very discourses and institutions. Thus, the encyclopedists can claim to desire only "useful" knowledge. (The word "utilité" appears repeatedly in d'Alembert's *Discours préliminaire,* for example.) More important, in the world of the encyclopedic text, knowledge guarantees possession through representation. I think therefore I have, or rather, I order so as to possess. The encyclopedists' utilitarian epistemology institutes a notion of the subject that rationalizes and justifies a new relation between man and his world, between subject and object. Knowledge is not simply useful, it is a means of appropriating and mastering a world that has been made into a set of represented objects.[5] The encyclopedists are perhaps far more Cartesian than they themselves admit, for in their project they seek to realize the desire expressed by Descartes in the *Discours de la méthode,* to fashion a philosophical system and produce a discourse that could be imposed upon the world in order to master and possess it ("nous rendre comme maÆtreset possesseurs de la nature").[6]

An additional point needs to be made. The article "Encyclopédie" calls for a specific kind of reading of the encyclopedic text, the double effect of which is to produce both a critique of certain existing values and beliefs and a rationalization of others. But rather than remain with the distinction between the old and the new, which might only lead us to a progressivist, teleological idea of history that begins to emerge in the eighteenth century (by means of certain key exclusions), we should also consider the extent to which the reading called for by the encyclopedic text is ideologically determined. This is to say that it is designed to produce a specific effect, which we should not hesitate to equate with ideology, that is, "the representation of the imaginary relation that individuals in a given society have of their real conditions of existence."[7] If such is the case, what of the effects produced by the encyclopedic text in other, more contemporary readings of it, in our own discourse "on" the *Encyclopédie*? One must ask then to what extent an examination of eighteenth-century encyclopedism, joined with a critique of contemporary interpretations of the Enlightenment, would point the way toward an understanding of the ways in which ideology invests and motivates apparently neutral or at least scholarly academic discourse? Or to put this more positively, how might we take best advantage of the realization that our readings of eighteenth-century texts do not so much describe and reproduce their object as they create it as an effect of an academic, institutionalized discourse whose ideological effectiveness is by no means negligible?

A number of practical and theoretical questions have been raised here regarding reading the *Encyclopédie*. They are designed to introduce the topic of this paper, the plates of the *Encyclopédie*. If reading the *Encyclopédie* has become a topic of creative concern, as is witnessed by a number of fairly recently publications,[8] then equally (if not more) problematic is the question of reading the encyclopedic plates. In attempting to determine the function and significance of the roughly three thousand engravings that fill eleven folio volumes, we must exercise caution in applying uncritically the version of Enlightenment that the enlighteners themselves produced, a quite possibly distorted image that may well lead only to the perpetuation of what was already a myth some two hundred years ago. We must remember too that it is all the more difficult to rely on the plates for the message of encyclopedism precisely because these images of men and machines, complete scenes and fragmented objects, show more than they say, and signify more than they tell. In moving from the encyclopedic text to the encyclopedic image, we leave the realm of the linguistic for that of the visual. The plates provide us with no original discourse we can quote, comment, rephrase. Rather, to speak of the plates, we must supply a language, supplementing the power of the visual image with a discourse that can never simply double its object. In their own way, the encyclopedic plates pose the problem of the relation between the image in general and language.[9] And thus, in writing on the plates, we transform them into language, a process in which we risk diverting them, perverting them through language, and changing them, as Louis Marin puts it, "from what everyone can see into what one person alone can tell him or herself."[10] Yet the danger of critical narcissism should not prevent us from attempting to come to terms with viewing the encyclopedic image. What is there to see in the plates? What are the effects they produce, effects that are the direct result of the force of these images?

From the eighty-three plates on agriculture to its one hundred thirty-five plates on weaving, including engravings that illustrate the manufacture of corks, candles, and nails, describe the technique of glass blowing and silver plating, or demonstrate the fine points of calligraphy, fencing, and military maneuvres, the *Encyclopédie* in its images provides a compendious and detailed picture of the crafts and trades, the arts and sciences, practiced in France in the second half of the eighteenth century. In itself, such a collection was not uncommon at the time. Diderot himself refers in the article "Encyclopédie" to Ramelli's *Le Diverse et artificiose machine* (1558), Leupold's *Theatrum machinarum* (1724–1727), and the *Description et perfection des arts et métiers* that Colbert had called upon the Académie Royale des Sciences to compile some hundred years earlier.[11] Diderot adds though that these collections contain no more than twenty usable plates. Chamber's *Cyclopedia* (1728) included a handful of plates as well, yet they are devoted to such sundry subjects as heraldry, sun dials, geometry, algebra, and navigation. Comparing these two sets of images, one sees that the plates of the *Encyclopédie* begin where Chambers left off, with a step-by-step description of a process of production. If the weakness of previous encyclopedias and technical treatises was that they were addressed either to a broad public of nonspecialists or to a narrow public of specialists, and thus could teach only what was already known, the encyclopedists on the contrary sought to hold to a middle course. What is shown in the plates is technological knowledge, not so much a vast and virtual *savoir* as areas and networks of an applied *savoir faire,* whose utility and value is to be measured in its productivity. Addressed to both the educated reader and the specialist, the plates depict the relative place of each area of technological knowledge in the whole mechanism of economic and social life, as well as the various positions that should be occupied by members of society in order to keep this mechanism functioning smoothly and productively.

Although the techniques and expertise represented in the *Encyclopédie* had changed little from those of the seventeenth century, the encyclopedic plates derive from an idea of technology, a philosophy, and a system of values that belong to the eighteenth century. Bacon, whom the encyclopedists praised, had called for a stronger link between theory and practice, between

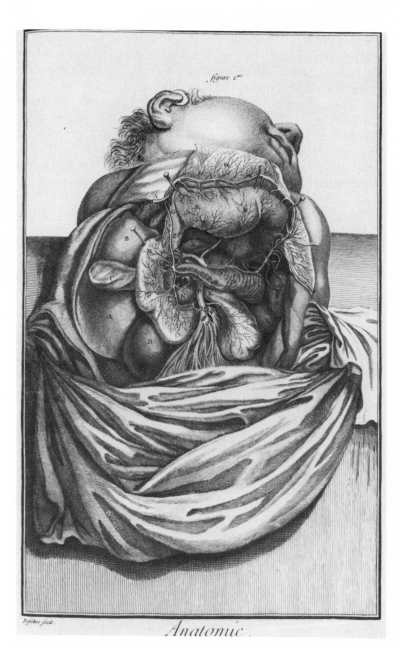

figure 1.er

Desfehes fecit.

Anatomie.

Plate 1

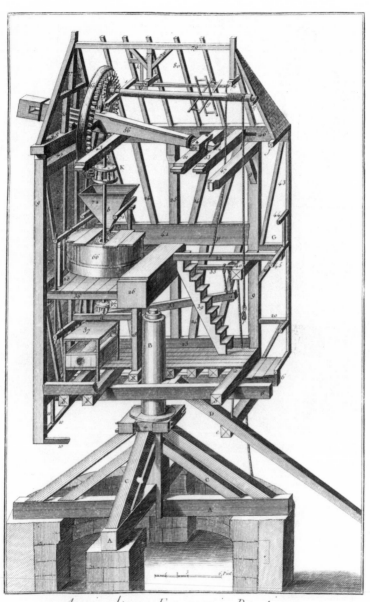

Agriculture, Économie Rustique.
Moulin à l'ail.

Plate 2

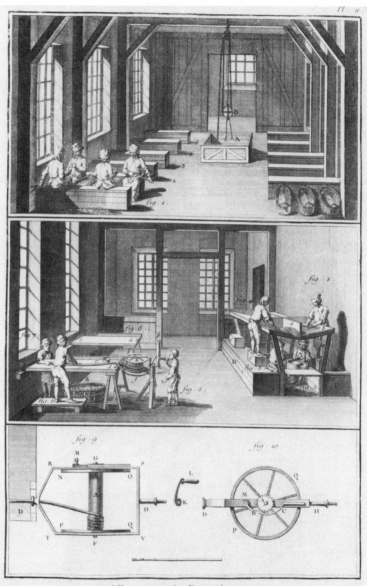

Pl. 11.

fig. 1.

fig. 4.

fig. 3.

fig. 6. *fig. 7.* *fig. 8.* *fig. 5.* *fig. 2.*

fig. 9. *fig. 10.*

Œconomie Rustique,
Fabrique du Tabac.

Plate 3

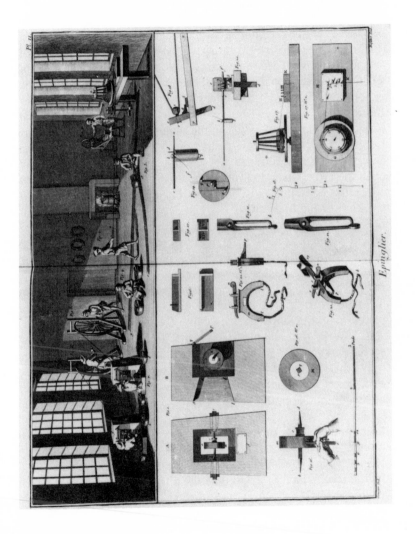

Pl. 11.

Epinglier.

Plate 4

conceptual knowledge and its application in and on the material world. Designed to bridge that gap, the plates reflect an increased valorization of the direct observation of phenomena (witnessed, for instance, in Diderot's visits to studios and workshops while preparing various technical articles, and the use he made of documentation received from specialists working in the different arts and trades). These images constitute a visual counterpart to the utilitarian rationalism, the sensationalist philosophy, and the experimental method that Diderot proposes in his *Pensées sur l'interprétation de la nature* (1753). They also reflect what Roland Barthes in an essay on the plates calls a "philosophie de l'objet" (as well as an "esthétique de la nudité").[12] In the anatomical plates, for example, it is not the surgeon's scalpel, nor even the artist's pen, but rather the look of the reader-viewer that slices through skin and bone, lays back tissue, and exposes the working of the body (plate 1). The encyclopedic gaze disassembles the finished machine or building, dividing it into its parts, and orders them in a series, the logic of which leads from part to whole, from tool to its use, from raw material to finished product. The gaze of the reader-viewer retraces in each set of plates the stages in the object's transformation from matter to object, from thing to property. The spectator's vision follows the logic of the plates, marking what Barthes calls "le cheminement de la raison." With the schematic representation of objects in cross-section and assembly drawings, which became common practice only around the middle of the eighteenth century, the reader of the plates possesses not only an image of the object, but also the rules of its composition, the key to its production and its reproduction (plate 2).[13] And in viewing the object as it is presented in and through the plates, the reader of the *Encyclopédie* comes to know all the natural world, a humanized, fraternal nature, already shaped by the hand of man, its fierceness and roughness mediated by the tool, which is shaping nature alters it so completely that it is recognizable only in its usefulness, known only in its relation to man.

What we have just witnessed is the encyclopedic plate at work, seeming to reflect a preexistent meaning, yet in fact contributing to its creation. We could allow the plates to continue to work, which would produce still further effects. But the point I want to make is that the encyclopedic plates do not so much reflect one stage or moment in a progressivist history of ideas, science, or technology (which could be described, for example, in terms of the industrial revolution that was to come, the rise of rationalism, or the transformation of an old feudal economic order into a more flexible and liberal system).[14] Rather, one of the effects of the plates is to produce such a history. It is the way in which the encyclopedic image represents the natural world, the relation between man, machine, and material, that serves to condition and determine the logic and course of this history, both as it occurred and as we read and write it. To see how this comes about, we must examine more closely how the plates function.

Referring to the plates, Diderot writes in the *Prospectus,* "nous les avons restreintes aux mouvements importants de l'ouvrier, et aux seuls moments de l'opération qu'il est très facile de peindre et très difficile d'expliquer. Nous nous en sommes tenus aux circonstances essentielles, à celles dont la représentation, quand elle est bien faite entra/Æne nécessairement la connaissance de celles qu'on ne voit pas" (v, 103). The plates operate according to a process of inclusion and exclusion, producing a filtering designed not only to explain what is seen but to rationalize what is not, what remains invisible, or at least unrepresented, and thus supposedly insignificant. If we take Diderot at his word, this filtering is simply didactic. And yet, as Jacques Proust rightly notes, the plates' didactic function creates "une sorte d'interférence qui interdit au lecteur de considérer [la planche] comme la transcription naïve de la réalité . . . Entre l'objet de référence et l'oeil de l'observateur [se trouve] l'écran d'une conscience et d'une volonté, celles de l'encyclopédiste, soucieux de témoigner non pas de ce qui était, mais de ce qui pouvait ou devait être."[15] Given this "screen" or veil that the encyclopedic plate places between us and the objects to which it refers, we must step back from these images and find another perspective from which to view them, a point of view that does not necessarily correspond to the one the image assigns to the reader and that may in fact clash with it. One such perspective can be derived from a reconsideration of the representation of men and machines.

The *Encyclopédie* recounts what Barthes in his essay calls the "légende dorée de l'artisanat." This gilding of the crafts takes place, however, at the expense of the actual craftsperson or worker. The encyclopedic engraver is concerned above all with explaining a process of production, and not with depicting the actual condition of people's lives. The plate entitled *Laiterie,* for example, in the section *Agriculture—Economie rustique* shows a vast room with all the equipment for making butter. Yet in this room that should be bustling with activity, all we see is one solitary and rather forlorn-looking milkmaid gazing out at us from behind her butter churn. The second plate in the section *manufacture du tabac* depicts four children seated on benches stripping tobacco. Counting the empty benches shown, we see there is room in the shop for twenty-two children (plate 3). The fourth plate in the same series shows the presses for making tobacco into carrots or plugs. The explanation for the plates notes that "il y a dans la fabrique de Paris jusqu'à soixante rangées le long des quatre faces d'une longue galerie. Vingt ou vingt-cinq ouvriers appliquent leurs forces à l'extrémité du grand levier de fer avec lequel on fait tourner les vis des presses."[16] But instead of the twenty to twenty-five workers on each press, the artist depicts but one press, which only two workers operate easily and expressionlessly. Admittedly, the cost of each plate would have increased drastically if the artist had had to add all these extra figures. But this technically "practical" explanation for what we see and do not see only strengthens the argument that economic determinants govern what is supposed to be seen and what is supposed to be extraneous. Similarly, because of the plate's inability to depict the passage of time, it is possible to avoid trying to show just how working time was actually filled. The explanation accompanying the section *Epinglier* gives us some idea.

> L'ouvrier peut . . . donner soixante-dix coups de ciseaux par minute, c'est par heure quatre mille deux cents; et comme il coupe douze moulées à chaque coup de ciseaux, cet ouvrier peut couper cinquante mille quatre cents têtes de menues épingles en une heure (les grosses étant plus difficiles), ce qui serait néanmoins un travail forcé, parce qu'il n'est point déduit de temps pour les reprises dans ce calcul; mais en y ayant égard, un ouvrier peut communément couper trente milliers par heure . . . Il ne pourrait pas . . . continuer sur ce pied toute la journée, parce que la vue fatigue beaucoup à cette fonction, mais il peut en couper quinze douzaines de milliers, grosses et menues, par jour. (plate 4)

In sum, if the *Encyclopédie* depicts an industrious yet eerily calm and peaceful world, it is because all that must be shown in the encyclopedic plate is the mechanical and technical principle behind a given operation, a requirement that provides the artist free rein to alter or suppress—and the viewer to ignore—any additional aspects of the operation, such as actual working conditions.

The principle of encyclopedic representation operates its filtering not only on workers' numbers, space, and time, but also on their very bodies. The general image of the worker in the *Encyclopédie* is that of a body reduced to its hands. The individual carding cotton, for example, has no existence beyond the wrist and the hand that performs its task. It is not, moreover, the hands of innumerable workers and craftspeople that are shown, but rather two hands, always the same. There is no difference between the hand putting pen to paper to write a letter addressed, as we can see, "A la Reine" (*Art d'écrire*) and the hand weaving fish nets (*Pêche*). Although Diderot does criticize the long-standing prejudice against trades and craftspeople,[17] his defense of the mechanical arts does not prevent the same reductiveness from shaping his discussion of workers and work in other contexts. A *métier* he defines, for example, as "toute profession qui exige l'emploi des bras, et qui se borne à un certain nombre d'opérations mécaniques, qui ont pour but un même ouvrage que l'ouvrier répète sans cesse" (article "Art," v, 496). It is this "manualization" of the worker that allows Diderot to propose the following explanation of why one method of manufacturing is superior to another: "tel ouvrier ne fait et ne fera de sa vie qu'une seule et unique chose; tel autre une autre chose: d'où il arrive que chacune s'exécute bien et promptement, et que l'ouvrage le mieux fait est encore celui qu'on a à meilleur marché" (v, 508). It is the anonymity of workers and their interchangeability ("tel ouvrier") that make it possible to *rationalize* production; that is, not only to subject the production process to the order of reason, but also to capitalize on methods designed to increase efficiency, quality, and finally profitability.

One could argue, as has Arthur Wilson in his biography of Diderot, that although at the time of their publication the plates were received as the most noncontroversial part of the *Ency-*

clopédie, "nothing in fact could disseminate more efficiently than they the subversive doctrine that the daily routine of socially useful labor has inherent dignity and worth."[18] Wilson is certainly right to stress the ideological effectiveness of the encyclopedic plates. Yet is is not certain that we can take them as the simple illustration of the encyclopedists' attempt to rehabilitate the mechanical arts, which would spring from what might be seen as their humane liberalism and their intellectual curiosity. More telling is considering the encyclopedists' views concerning political economic theory and the notion of work and worker that derives from them. Mercantilism had been the prevalent doctrine in mid-eighteenth-century France, a system based on the idea that a nation's wealth is a result of the gold and currency it possesses. Buying foreign products robs a country of its riches, and thus industry must be allowed and encouraged to develop techniques of production and investment policies that will let domestic products compete favorably with foreign goods.[19] According to the logic of mercantilism, it is the wealth of nations and not the "inherent dignity" of those who produce it that must be promoted.

It is not surprising that we find the desire to capitalize on economic theory at work in the plates, visible in the relation depicted between man and machine. In analyzing this relation, we should not forget that the eighteenth-century idea of the machine differs from the way it is understood today. For the encyclopedists, the machine is primarily a more perfect tool, an extension of the hand that increases its speed and accuracy. Correspondingly, their notion of work was that of the artisan whose hand shapes nature according to man's needs and desires. Labor was like man's signature upon the material world. Only later, after the consequences of the industrial revolution had become manifest, would the relation between man and machine have to be rethought. By reducing the worker's role to that of mere agent performing a small task within a far larger process of production, nineteenth-century industrial capitalism transforms the relation between worker and the object produced. Labor becomes less a creative activity, uniting the worker with his fellows and the world; instead, it serves to alienate, the worker's labor becoming an impersonal and generalized object, understood in terms of its exchange value. Although it would be misleading to suggest that

Marx's analysis of nineteenth-century industrial capitalism can be applied just as accurately to the eighteenth-century context, the terms of the analysis remain pertinent for our reading of the encyclopedic plates.[20] By the time the plates appeared, the "gilded legend of craftsmanship" to which Barthes refers may have been no more than that, a myth, and already more than slightly tarnished. In many of the plates, the machine does in fact appear to be a tool, operated by the craftsman's hand or foot. This interpretation of the image of the machine, and the idea of work as craftsmanship to which it leads, is all the more convincing because it corresponds to what Diderot in fact writes about the mechanical arts. Yet, as I have suggested, the function of the encyclopedic plate cannot be thought of as the simple transcription of reality nor as the mere illustration accompanying the encyclopedic text. Viewing the image from another perspective, and not the one given in the encyclopedists' writings, we can see the relation between man and machine somewhat differently. The machine transforms energy, the source of which for the vast majority of machines represented in the *Encyclopédie* is man. All the machines we see are based on the principle of the lever or the pulley. Even the most perfected machine of the time, at least the one that is the object of Diderot's extended and well-known article "Bas," the stocking-weaving machine, is an assemblage of levers and pulleys moved by the worker's hands and feet. It is this reliance on the worker as energy source that explains those plates in which the individual is *not* reduced to two hands; here, instead of being "manualized" as craftsperson, he or she is "instrumentalized" as worker, represented not as supreme master of the machine, but merely as one of its necessary parts. Thus, the encyclopedic plates produce two conflicting notions of worker and labor, one of the creative, independent, and individual craftsperson, the other of the "mechanized," anonymous, and interchangeable worker.[21] Both sets of representations, even in their reciprocal contradiction, were necessary elements of the technological and above all ideological transformations in European theories of production that took place in the late eighteenth and nineteenth centuries.

The plates of the *Encyclopédie* depict a well-ordered world, where man exists in harmony with nature, and where by using his skills and knowledge to their fullest he is able to reap great rewards. Because of the ideal nature of such a world and of the subject who dwells in it, we should not be led to believe that by describing its order we have come to terms with what orders it. The world of the encyclopedic plates is an imaginary one, a fiction, a myth. This is not to say that it is not a real world, outside history, but rather that in the way it is represented the terms of its relation with the real world and with history are not immediately apparent. They must be deciphered, even supplied by interpretation. One such set of terms can be derived by analyzing what orders the world represented in the plates, the instance of desire behind its representation. For it is indeed desire that informs and invests these images, desire to know, yet also, through knowledge, to acquire, possess, and control. As we have seen, this desire operates by means of certain positionings, filterings, and exclusions, from which is derived the ideological force of the plates. The ideological workings of the encyclopedic plates are probably more visible to us today than they were to an eighteenth-century reader. We have learned to read the *Encyclopédie* not only as the encyclopedists wanted it to be read, as a monument to timeless reason, but also as a historically determined and ideologically motivated instrument, and as a text whose language and images escape the intentionality of its authors, thereby exposing the mechanisms of encyclopedic discourse and image, mechanisms at work in the *Encyclopédie* and whose effects extend far beyond the *Encyclopédie*, both textually and temporally. The importance and strength of further rereadings of the *Encyclopédie* will have to be measured by the extent to which they help us understand how our own historical context acts upon our reading of the encyclopedic text, and whether as a result we are better able to come to grips with the contemporary social, historical, and ideological pressures and powers that are at work in our interpretation of the eighteenth century and its texts.

NOTES

[1] Chaque chose étant . . . dans l'*Encyclopédie* ce qu'elle est en soi, elle y aura sa vraie proportion," writes Diderot, article "Encyclopédie," *Oeuvres complètes,* VII (Hermann, 1976), 215. Further references to this edition are given in the text. For an analysis of encyclopedic representa-

tion through a reading of the article "Encyclopédie," see James Creech, "Chasing after Advances: Diderot's Article 'Encyclopédie'," *Yale French Studies*, 63 (1982), 183–97, and my "Language and Grammar: Diderot and the Discourse of Encyclopedism," *Eighteenth-Century Studies*, 13, no. 1 (Fall 1979), 1–20.

2 This intellectual filiation is made by Roger Lewinter in his introduction to *Diderot Encyclopedia: The Complete Illustrations, 1762–1777* (New York: Harry N. Abrams, 1978), p. xxxi.

3 See Bernard Groethuysen, *The Bourgeois: Catholicism vs. Capitalism in Eighteenth-Century France*, tr. Mary Ilford (New York: Holt, Rinehart and Winston, 1968); and Elinor Barber, *The Bourgeois in 18th-Century France* (Princeton: Princeton University Press, 1955). On the relation between Enlightenment philosophy and bourgeois thought, see Lionel Gossman, *French Society and Culture* (Englewood Cliffs, N.J.: Prentice-Hall, 1972).

4 Although outdated, Pierre Grosclaude's *Un audacieux message: L'Encyclopédie* (Nouvelles Editions Latines, 1951), shows how the *Encyclopédie* can be made to seem more revolutionary than it in fact was. A more balanced view is given in Jacques Proust, *Diderot et l'Encyclopédie* (Colin, 1965), and Robert Darnton shows how well the encyclopedic text and project could be adapted to suit the political and intellectual climates of monarchy, revolution, and republic, in *The Business of Enlightenment* (Cambridge: Harvard University Press, 1979).

5 See Bernard Groethuysen, "L'Encyclopédie," in *Tableau de la littérature française*, II (Nouvelle Revue Française, 1939), 343–49.

6 René Descartes, *Oeuvres et lettres* (Gallimard, 1953), p. 168. See the major study on Descartes and Cartesianism in the Enlightenment, Aram Vartanian's *Diderot and Descartes* (Princeton: Princeton University Press, 1953).

7 See Louis Althusser, "Idéologie et appareil d'Etat," *La Pensée* (1970). My translation.

8 In addition to Creech, see Christie Vance McDonald, "The Work of the Text: Diderot's 'Encyclopédie'," *The Eighteenth Century: Theory and Interpretation*, 21, no. 2 (Spring 1980), 128–44; Walter Moser, "D'Alembert: L'Ordre philosophique de ce discours," *MLN*, 91, no. 4 (1976), 723–33; and Patrick Coleman, "The Idea of Character in the *Encyclopédie*," *Eighteenth-Century Studies*, 13, no. 1 (Fall 1979), 21–47.

9 This relation became a more problematic one for Diderot during his preparation of the volumes of plates. He writes in the *Prospectus*, in other words before the plates were printed, that "un coup d'oeil sur l'objet ou sur sa représentation en dit plus qu'une page de discours" (v,

101). Each image was supposed to provide an illustration or condensed version of discourse, yet even so each plate had to be explained and each part of the represented scene or object properly named and labeled. The plates reflect the linguistic ideal and illusion of establishing an exact system of correspondence between work, idea, and thing. If the encyclopedists began by believing in the reciprocal transparency of images, words, and things, they soon realized that the image could not adequately represent words because it could not adequately represent things. Possessing its own logic, the image is always other than what it refers to, a problem to which Diderot returns (and goes beyond) in the *Salons*. See Jacques Proust, "L'Image du peuple au travail dans les planches de l'*Encyclopédie*," in *Images du peuple au dix-huitième siècle* (Colin, 1973), p. 68.

[10] Louis Marin, *Détuire la peinture* (Galilée, 1977). My translation.

[11] On the history of encyclopedias, see Robert Collison, *Encyclopédias: Their History throughout the Ages* (New York: Hafner, 1964). Jacques Payen lists some of the numerous precursors of the encyclopedic plates in his introduction to the Abrams reprint. See also Jean-Pierre Seguin, "Courte Histoire des planches de l'*Encyclopédie*," in *L'Univers de l'Encyclopédie* (Les Libraires Associées, 1964), pp. 25–34; and Georges Huard, "Les Planches de l'*Encyclopédie* et celles de la *Description des arts et métiers* de l'Académie des Sciences," *Revue d'Histoire des Sciences et de leurs Applications,* 4 (1951), 238–49. A good comparison of the *Enclyclopédie* and its antecedents with regard to the treatment of technology as given in Proust, *Diderot,* pp. 177–88.

[12] "Image, raison, déraison," in *L'Univers de l'Enclyclopédie* (Les Libraries Associés, 1964).

[13] See Guy Besse, "Aspects du travail ouvrier au 18e siècle en France," in *Essays on Diderot and the Enlightenment,* ed. John Pappas (Geneva: Droz, 1974).

[14] Industrialization develops much later in France than in England. Charles Ballot's study of the industrial revolution in France, *L'Introduction du machinisme dans l'industrie* (F. Rieder, 1923), for example, begins in 1780. Rejecting the view that the encyclopedists led the battle for the development of mechanization and industrialization, Jacques Proust maintains that by presenting a picture of the current state of technology, the *Encyclopédie* was instrumental in its advancement. Pointing to the large number of treatises on the mechanical arts that followed the *Encyclopédie*, Proust interprets the encyclopedists' desire to make technology more accessible as their wish to have production be the common affair of the most qualified and active persons by circumventing the impediments posed by the *corporations* and the system of *privilèges exclusifs* (*Diderot,* pp. 162–220).

15 Proust, "L'Image," p. 66.

16 This example and the following one are given by Proust, "L'Image."

17 "On a trop écrit sur les sciences: on n'a pas assez bien écrit sur la plupart des arts libéraux: on n'a presque rien écrit sur les arts mécaniques," claims Diderot in the *Prospectus*. Hence, the need to obtain information directly from workers and craftspeople themselves. The time-honored distinction between liberal and mechanical arts, based on whether what is involved is "l'ouvrage de l'esprit [ou] de la main," unfortunately results, he adds, in the "[avilissement] des gens très estimables et très utiles" (v, 99).

18 Arthur Wilson, *Diderot* (New York: Oxford University Press, 1972), p. 360.

19 An example of the application of the mercantilist principle and especially of state protectionism of industry is given in Diderot's history of the manufacture of machine-woven stockings in France in his article "Bas." See also de Jaucourt's article "Industrie."

20 See Marc Le Bot's analysis of the encyclopedic plates as exemplifying the marginalization of art that was performed by emergent industrial capitalism, "Technique et art," in his *Figures de l'art contemporain* (Editions 10/18, 1977), pp. 229–43. See his *Peinture et machinisme* (Klincksieck, 1973).

21 See Georges Friedman, "L'*Encyclopédie* et le travail humain," *Annales de l'Université de Paris,* special issue, 22 (October 1952), who characterizes the mid-eighteenth century as a "remarquable période de transition entre l'atelier corporatif et ce que Marx appellera, dans *Le Capital, la 'machino-facture,'* époque où l'ouvrier qui conduit les machines se double encore, le plus souvent, d'un artisan, au sens actuel du terme," p. 125.

PART IV

ILLUSTRATION FROM THE 19TH
TO THE 20TH CENTURY

Fig. 1. William Blake, *Songs of Innocence*, 1789. *Title page, National Gallery of Art, Rosenwald Collection, Washington, D.C.*

Fig. 2. William Pars, Textile Design, 1756. *Royal Society of Arts, London.*

Fig. 3. William Blake, The Shepherd, from *Songs of Innocence*, 1789. *National Gallery of Art, Rosenwald Collection, Washington, D.C.*

WILLIAM BLAKE'S GRAPHIC IMAGERY AND THE INDUSTRIAL REVOLUTION
Albert Boime

The life and career of William Blake (1757–1827) coincide with the radical transformation of England from an agrarian to an industrial society. Yet when major Blake scholars have related the artist's work to the Industrial Revolution, they have analyzed this relationship mainly in the context of his poetry where it is seen as an essentially negative view of industry. Bronowski systematically explored Blake's development against the background of the industrial epoch, attempting to demonstrate that the artist "turned his pitying and troubled mind against the machine." Schorer perceived Blake as a child of the Industrial Revolution who used "the mechanical in everyday life . . . to express his protest against the mechanical ideas. . . ." Erdman's close analysis of *The Four Zoas* and its industrial implications showed that Blake condemned industry primarily as it was applied to warfare and its impact on the lives of the laborers. At the same time, he sees that Blake's Garden of Eden is attained through a transformation of war-related industry along peaceful lines, and the conversion of weapons into agricultural implements:

> For him the human question was framed not in terms of improved production but as a choice or an issue between the peaceful Looms of Jerusalem . . . and the Mills of Satan casting steel cannon barrels and filling the sky with the smoke of battles and of burning towns.

To Erdman, then, Blake's "dark Satanic Mills" are factories that "produce dark metal, iron and steel, for diabolic purposes."[1]

Most Blake students follow the lead of these scholars in seeing

Reprinted with permission from *Arts Magazine,* June 1985, pp. 107–119.

Fig. 4. Nathaniel Smith, Composition after Nature of Beasts and Birds, 1759. *Royal Society of Arts, London.*

Fig. 5. William Blake, Figures from a Greek Vase, after d'Hancarville: The Apotheosis of Bacchus, c. 1775. *British Museum, London.*

in the poetry a rejection of industry, a threat to be met and mastered. His humanistic opposition to the machine notwith-standing, however, Blake could not avoid its impact on his mind and work. If he protested against the machine's cold, diagram-matic character, its influence was nonetheless apparent in the style and form of that protest. This study will attempt a modest reappraisal of Blake's relationship to the Industrial Revolution, suggesting a more positive connection than has heretofore been established, and providing specific examples of this influence on his graphic imagery.

While Blake's imaginative and visionary mind is often perceived in opposition to the economic transition, and his digs at "dark, satanic Mills" and Newtonian rationalism are endlessly paraded, in fact his art responded to the incipient Machine Age affirmatively, and, on occasion, lovingly. His very style incarnates the marriage of neo-classicism to the Industrial Revolution. His art expressed (directly and indirectly) many of the ideas and sentiments of the progressive wing of the British upper classes, and in particular, those of the Lunar Society.

The Lunar Society—so-called because it met on the Monday closest to the full moon to provide enough light for the return home—embraced a community of provincial manufacturers and professionals who made substantial contributions to the rise of English industry.[2] As such, it was an organization that expressed ultimate confidence in English economic and industrial hegemony.

The founders of the Society were three of England's most distinguished and inventive individuals: (1) Matthew Boulton, an iron and steel manufacturer who collaborated with James Watt in the design and sale of rotary engines; (2) Erasmus Darwin, poet, inventor and physician, as well as grandfather of Charles; and (3) William Small, Thomas Jefferson's professor of natural history at the College of William and Mary in Virginia.

Of the three, Boulton was the prime mover, with his quick and ready mind and ability to see the application of a new idea and its economic possibilities. Darwin, however, was the most creative and versatile. His famous *Botanic Garden* and *Zoonomia* reveal his eagerness to embrace all the latest scientific and technological discoveries of the new age, and to share those discoveries with a wide audience. The *Botanic Garden,* a long poem published in two parts in 1789 and 1791, embraced vast areas of knowledge and their industrial application; in addition to treating botanical and biological concepts, his rich notes contain explanatory comments on meteors, optics, geology, heat, metallurgy, mining technology, meteorology, cotton manufactures, and steam power. Darwin's aim was "to enlist imagination under the banner of Science; and to lead the votaries from the looser analogies, which dress out the imagery of poetry, to the stricter ones, which form the rationation of philosophy."

As an example of his merger of artistic and scientific outlooks, Darwin used his poetic imagination to praise the scientific discoveries of his friend Joseph Priestley, and in particular the diving bell which assured English economic supremacy:

> Led by the Sage, lo! Britain's sons shall guide
> Huge *Sea-Balloons* beneath the tossing tide;
> . . . .
> Buoy'd with pure air shall endless tracks pursue,
> And PRIESTLEY'S hand the vital flood renew.
> Then shall BRITANNIA rule the wealthy realms,
> Which Ocean's wide insatiate wave o'erwhelms; . . . .[3]

Other crucial members of the Lunar Society were Priestley and Josiah Wedgwood. Priestley, a teacher in a religious dissenters' school at Warrington in Cheshire, became interested in Franklin's work on electricity. At Franklin's behest he wrote *The History and Present State of Electricity,* published in 1767. Priestley also wrote on vision, light, and color, but his reputation rests mainly on his work in chemistry, especially that part dealing with the nature and composition of gases and his discoveries of nitrous oxide and hydrochloric acid.

Wedgwood's contributions to the Industrial Revolution were critical and diverse. He created a major ceramic industry, promoted the construction of canals to facilitate the smooth transportation of his fragile wares, and pioneered in factory organization. His industrial complex, which he named Etruria in honor of Etruscan civilization, became a model for the whole of the pottery industry.

Lunar Society members exchanged ideas and shared their collective expertise: in his *History,* Priestley acknowledged Darwin's contributions to the study of electricity; Boulton designed

Fig. 6. The Apotheosis of Bacchus, detail of Greek Vase. (Collection . . . . from the Cabinet of the Honorable Wm. Hamilton, *II, Plate 68.*)

Fig. 7. George Cumberland and William Blake, Psyche Repents, 1794. *Engraving Reproduced as Plate 13 of Cumberland,* Thoughts on Outline, 1796.

Fig. 8. William Blake, Edward and Elenor, 1793. *Engraving, British Museum, London.*

and built a lathe for Wedgwood; mathematician Small worked with Watt and Boulton on the steam engine project while Wedgwood generally had something for everybody. Thus the Lunar Society incarnated the spirit of the entrepreneurs who stimulated the Industrial Revolution: they were not idealists but hard-headed realists who believed that science and industry would mean unlimited opportunities for the English nation and their global empire.[4]

At the same time, their material progress represented breakthroughs in the social sense; they were generally middle-class liberals who espoused *laissez-faire* economics and could support the American and French Revolutions and agitate against slavery in the colonies. In July 1789 Wedgwood wrote to Darwin: "I know you will rejoice with me in the glorious revolution which has taken place in France," and Darwin wrote to Watt in January 1790: "Do you not congratulate your grandchildren on the dawn of universal liberty? I feel myself becoming all French both in chemistry & politics."[5] Even Boulton, perhaps the most conservative politically, tried in 1791 to get a coinage contract from the new Revolutionary government. But the Lunar Society's celebra-

Fig. 9. William Blake, Portland Vase, 1795. *Engraving for Darwin,* The Botanic Garden, *1795, I, p. 352.*

tion of the anniversary of the Revolution sparked the Tory-inspired Birmingham riots in July 1791 in which Priestley's house, library, and laboratory were destroyed. He fled to America and remained ever after divided in his loyalties.

The predominantly dissenting manufacturing middle class favored a number of political, religious, and humanitarian reforms which ran counter to the prevailing climate of conservatism but were consistent with their support of a free and open market, factory

Fig. 10. William Blake, Portland Vase: First Compartment, 1795. *Engraving for Darwin,* The Botanic Garden, *1795, I, p. 355.*

labor, and efficient trade. The most significant case is the agitation for the abolition of slave trading which often involved both Whigs and Tories. The Lunar Society was very much opposed to traffic in slaves: Thomas Day's famous poem, *The Dying Negro* (1773), spurred the nation's conscience while his later *Letter on the Slavery of Negroes* (written in 1776, published 1784) perceived the American as "signing resolutions of independence with the one hand, and with the other brandishing a whip over his affrighted slaves." To illustrate Day's poem, Wedgwood made a cameo in jasper of a slave in chains with the motto: "Am I not a man and a brother?"[6] By 1788 the abolitionist activities of Clarkson and Wilberforce were generating mass support in England and had the participation of the Lunar Society; although there eventually was some limited success, these early drives failed. Clarkson, above all, who continued the struggle, was dependent on the financial support and encouragement of Wedgwood.

Many artists and writers were directly in touch with the Lunar

Fig. 11. Illustration of Vallisneria Spiralis. *(Darwin,* The Botanic Garden, *II, p. 52.)*

Society itself or with the work of its members. Blake collaborated with his friend Fuseli on the illustrations for Darwin's *Botanic Garden;* the book was issued by Joseph Johnson who also published the writings of Fuseli and Priestley, printed Blake's *French Revolution* (which was withheld from publication), and

Fig. 12. William Blake, America, Plate 4, 1793. *Fitzwilliam Museum, Cambridge.*

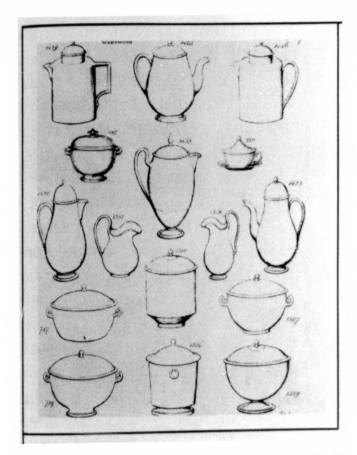

Fig. 13. William Blake, Plate 17 of Wedgwood's Queen's Ware Catalogue, 1817. *Trustees of the Wedgwood Museum, Barlaston, Staffordshire, England.*

hired him for several illustration jobs. The writers include Coleridge, who was for a time a pensioner of Wedgwood, as well as a close friend of Watt's son James and a great admirer of Priestley. Wedgwood also contributed to the support of Wordsworth, Wright of Derby, Flaxman, Stubbs, and Blake.

Blake's father owned a "moderately prosperous" hosiery business (taken over eventually by William's eldest brother,

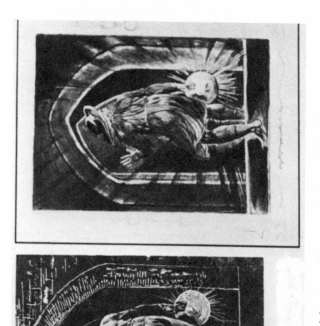

Fig. 14. William Blake, Jerusalem: Frontispiece, 1804–20. *Fitzwilliam Museum, Cambridge.*

Fig. 15. William Blake, Jerusalem: Frontispiece, 1804–20. *Color print. Private Collection.*

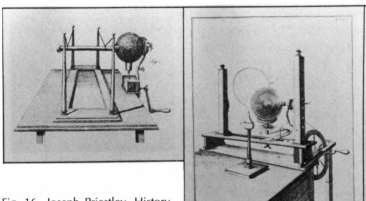

Fig. 16. Joseph Priestley, History and Present State of Electricity, 1767, Plate IV, Figure 1.
Fig. 17. Joseph Priestley, History and Present State of Electricity, 1767, Plate VII.

James); thus Blake and his brothers would have been in touch with the most significant industrial developments of the period. It was the great contemporary hosiers—the Strutts, the Oldknows, the Needs, and the Arkwrights—who organized the first factories and accelerated the arrival of the Industrial Revolution. At the retail level, the hosier generally purchased stockings, nightcaps, socks, gloves, and other goods directly from the factory, but the larger ones—and this would have included Blake's father—employed their own looms and were themselves stocking-weavers. This meant that the senior Blake was involved in all phases of the cotton industry, including printing and dyeing. From his earliest age, therefore, Blake would have experienced directly the major direction of English industrial capitalism.

This is confirmed, moreover, by the fact that his father first sent William to an industrial arts school and then apprenticed him out to an engraver. When he was ten years old Blake was enrolled in Henry Pars' drawing school in the Strand, then the best preparatory school for industrial designers. Several of Blake's fellow students went to work in industry or the crafts. Pars' school had been founded by William Shipley as an adjunct to the Society for the Encouragement of the Arts, Manufactures and Commerce. Shipley's school was founded on the principle that drawing was "absolutely necessary in many employments, trades, and manufactures." The year Blake was born Shipley ran the following ad for the school:

> As it will be Mr. Shipley's endeavour to introduce Boys and Girls of Genius to Masters and Mistresses in such Manufactures as require Fancy and Ornament, and for which the Knowledge of Drawing is absolutely necessary; Masters or Mistresses who want Boys and Girls well qualified for such manufactures may frequently meet with them at this school; and Parents who have Children of good natural Abilities for the Art of Drawing may here meet with Opportunities of having them well instructed and recommended to proper Master or Mistresses. . . .

Shipley further noted in the ad his commitment to the use of drawing in industry as was intended by the Society's prizes "for the most ingenious and best fancied Designs proper for Weavers, Embroiderers and Calico Printers."

Blake's friend and admirer, the miniature painter Ozias Humphry, was sent by his parents to Shipley's drawing school on the understanding that he would learn to draw patterns suitable for the family lace business. The young art student wrote home early in October 1757 that the curriculum consists of "Man's Heads, and Plaster Figures, Birds on Trees, Landscapes, all sorts of Beasts, Flowers, foliages and Ornaments," all of which he hoped would give him "a truer idea in Drawing Lace Patterns" which he began copying toward the end of the month.[7]

Shipley enjoyed a spectacular success with his school through its connection with the Society. When he retired from active management in 1761, he turned it over to Henry and William Pars. Their advertisement in 1762 indicates that they ran the school along the same lines:

> Drawing and Modelling in all branches taught by Henry and William Pars, successors to Mr. Shipley, late Register to the Society for the Encouragement of Arts etc. . . . where Boys of Genius are frequently recommended to masters in such trades and manufactures as require fancy and ornament, for which the knowledge of drawing is absolutely necessary. . . .[8]

They also indicated that Shipley would recommend enterprising graduates for work in the trades, demonstrating that the founder continued to take an active interest in the school after his retirement. One student in this period, Thomas Jones, wrote that after several months of exertion Shipley introduced him "to the Duke of Richmond's Gallery . . . to draw after those fine copies of the most celebrated Antique Statues. . . ."[9]

Jones' statement reminds us of the neo-classic emphasis in Shipley's curriculum. Shipley himself collected antique gems and coins which brought him into contact with Albani's circle. Many of the examples of ancient Roman medals and coins he owned were replicas made by Baron von Stosch from the great continental collections. Shipley in turn made plaster casts of these reproductions covering for the most part the "Roman Commonwealth and Empire," thus following the ideological lead of the wealthy connoisseurs and collectors of the period. The Pars brothers retained Shipley's neo-classic direction: William accompanied the architect Revett to Athens and Ionia to sketch buildings and sculptures, and later Blake made engravings to Pars' sketches for the popular Stuart and Revett portfolios of *The Antiquities of Athens and Ionia.*

The influence of Pars' drawing school is evident in Blake's first major illuminated book, *Songs of Innocence.* The title page integrates word and image in a tightly knit design reminiscent of textile patterns (Fig. 1). The branches of the apple tree on the right are elaborated near the top of the page into plant-like flourishes and form the letters of the word "SONGS." Tiny creatures cavort in and among the letters like playful sprites, consistent with the childhood theme. The "o" of the word "of" lies in the center of the page and is ingeniously encircled by a curving branch bearing apples so that it harmonizes with them like another piece of fruit. The centering of this motif among the intertwined plant flourished and tree branches distinctly recalls textile designs produced at the industrial art school such as the example by William Pars (Fig. 2). It may be concluded that Blake's skill in weaving text and image into successful configurations derives partly from this early training.[10]

Other illustrations for *Songs of Innocence* show the influence of Shipley's basic curriculum. For example, the design for "The Shepherd" (Fig. 3)—with the prominent tree along the right-hand margin serving as a foil for the grazing sheep along the line of the horizon—looks back to designs produced by other Shipley students such as the prize-winning *Composition After Nature of Beasts and Birds* of 1759 (Fig. 4). This pictorial formula recurs several times in Blake's work, recalling Ozias Humphry's remark about the "Beasts, Flowers, foliages and Ornaments" sketched in Shipley's school in preparation for lace patterns.

On the title page of *Songs of Innocence* (and other illuminated books as well) Blake credited himself as "The Author & Printer," thus emphasizing his dual role as artist-entrepreneur. This dual status is literally and symbolically represented by his capacity to combine text and image in a coherent package. Blake's entrepreneurial use of new methods of stereotype printing broke down the distinctions between artist and industrial designer and between type and illustration. It also advanced a pictorial way of materializing imaginative concepts in line with the ideas of the Lunar Society. Blake's imaginative powers consisted of bringing his work into harmony with the new scientific and industrial developments—the aim of Shipley's school on behalf of the Society for the Encouragement of the Arts, Manufactures and Commerce.

At the age of fourteen Blake was apprenticed to James Basire, engraver to the Society of Antiquaries and the Royal Society of the Arts. As in the case of Pars, it is most likely that Blake's father hoped to reap some benefit from this course of action beyond gratifying his son's ambition to become an artist; an industrial designer and engraver could have served a useful function in the hosiery business. Printers in the textile industry hired young art apprentices trained in the workshops of engravers or industrial art schools. At the same time, the success of entrepreneurs like Boydell and the increasing demands of publishers may have also predisposed the elder Blake to apprentice William as he did.

Blake's first friends suggest his early industrial aspirations. Thomas Trotter did calico prints and introduced Blake to Thomas Stothard who had apprenticed to a pattern-designer in Spitalfields, Stepney, a major silk-producing center with the most advanced looms of the period. Stothard became one of the outstanding book illustrators of his day and also executed designs for Wedgwood and the royal silversmiths Rundell & Bridge.[11] Stothard in turn introduced Blake to Flaxman—"one of the best and firmest friends Blake ever had"—who also worked extensively for Wedgwood and Rundell & Bridge. Blake's fellow student at Basire's and his future business partner, James Parker, did interior design for the architect Thomas Leverton at Woodhall Park, Hertfordshire, and also engraved prints for Boydell.

Basire himself engraved the work of West and Reynolds. He was in great demand for his reproductive facility; he illustrated scientific publications, such as histories, geographies, and encyclopedias, while his engravings of ancient monuments gained him the position of official engraver to both the Royal Society and the Society of Antiquaries. As Basire's apprentice for seven years, Blake would have been steeped in antiquities; many of Basire's commissions consisted of engravings of old coins, vases, and gems for such works as the *Archaeologia*. Blake collaborated with the master on a variety of projects (for which he received no credit), including Jacob Bryant's *New System of Mythology* which Blake later drew upon for his own mythological lore. Basire also sent Blake to make drawings of tomb effigies in Westminster Abbey for Richard Gough's *Sepulchral Monuments in Great Britain* which, although Gothic, reinforced in him a taste for linearism and the decorative ensemble.

Blake's identification with artisanal activity is shown by the fact that in June 1780; when he was twenty-three years old, he joined the surging crowd of the Gordon Riots and was swept along "in the very front rank" to witness the burning of the fortress-like Newgate prison. The crowd was composed of thousands of journeymen, apprentices, and servants, demonstrating that the grievances went beyond the religious issue of "No Popery!" Blake and his fellow artisans seized the opportunity to protest the economic burden heaped on the underclasses as a result of the waging of the American War of Independence.[12]

For a short time at the completion of his apprenticeship, Blake attended the Royal Academy where he had the opportunity to draw from life. But he always felt more at home with old prints, plaster casts, and applied art objects. Late in life he claimed: "Natural Objects *always did and do weaken,* deaden and obliterate imagination in me!"[13] He was trained in the mechanical craft of engraving and this predisposed him to conceptualize in schematic outlines. Indeed, his capacity to create dynamic figural movement and fantastic hybrid creatures emerges from his reduction of the world to a kind of visionary blueprint. As he declared in his marginalia to Reynolds' *Discourses:* "Mechanical Excellence is the Only Vehicle of Genius."[14]

Blake assimilated the technical ideal of industry as expressed through neo-classic outline. The linearism of neo-classicism made this style preeminently suited for the new industrial design, exemplified in the work of Robert Adam, Matthew Boulton, and Josiah Wedgwood. Neo-classical silhouetting adapted itself readily to the contours of applied art objects, could be simplified to the point of abstraction (as in textile patterns), and was easy to reproduce. While still an apprentice, Blake obtained a copy of Fuseli's translation of Winckelmann's *Reflections on the Painting and Sculpture of the Greeks* which exalted the human form and emphasized "precision of Contour, that characteristic distinction of the ancients." And like his friends Fuseli and Flaxman he early gravitated to the celebrated d'Hancarville catalogue of Sir William Hamilton's collection of vases.[15] Among his youthful works are two line drawings after d'Hancarville's illustrations, one of which is the Apotheosis of Bacchus reproduced as plate 68 in volume II (Figs. 5 and 6). Blake faithfully reproduced the silhouettes of every figure including the seated Silenus with his lyre at the extreme right and Ariadne holding a cornucopia at the extreme left. It must be emphasized that the illustrations of Sir William's vases were instrumental in the rise of the linear style and its industrial applications.

Blake's notion of a graphic cutting edge was identified in his mind with craft and industry. He set this out affirmatively in his *Descriptive Catalogue* of 1809 under entry XV ("Ruth.—A Drawing"): "The great and golden rule of art, as well as of life, is this: That the more distinct, sharp, and wiry the bounding line, the more perfect the work of art; and the less keen and sharp, the greater is the evidence of weak imitation, plagiarism, and bungling." Then he shows how this relates to the larger social context:

> What is it that builds a house and plants a garden, but the definite and determinane? What is it that distinguishes honesty from knavery, but the hard and wiry line of rectitude and certainty in the actions and intentions? Leave out this line and you leave out life itself; all is chaos again, and the line of the almighty must be drawn out upon it before man or beast can exist.[16]

Blake's obsession with outline informs his life's work; if it is not always consistently applied in his practice, it is of overriding importance to his philosophical ideal. Even his most extravagant visions are subjected to this control. In the *Descriptive Catalogue* he took the opportunity to answer criticism of his method of depicting spirits with solid bodies and firm outlines:

> A Spirit and a Vision are not, as the modern philosophy supposes, a cloudy vapour, or a nothing: they are organized and minutely articulated beyond all that the mortal and perishing nature can produce . . . Spirits are organized men. Moderns wish to draw figures without lines, and with great and heavy shadows; are not shadows more unmeaning than lines, and more heavy? O who can doubt this?[17]

Such a position is analogous to that of Erasmus Darwin in the *Botanic Garden* wherein he would "enlist Imagination under the banner of Science; and to lead her votaries from the looser analogies, which dress out the imagery of poetry, to the stricter ones, which form the ratiocination of philosophy."

Blake shared his outlook with the progressive manufacturing and commercial classes—an outlook perhaps most completely embodied in the writings of his friend George Cumberland (1754–1848).[18] Cumberland had worked for many years as a clerk in the Royal Exchange Assurance Company, a job he hated but which permitted him to accumulate some capital through timely investments. After being turned down for an expected promotion he resigned in 1785, around the time he first met Blake. A few years later he used his savings and a modest inheritance to acquire a small estate and thereafter embarked on an artistic and literary career. Cumberland experimented with new methods of engraving that would substitute for conventional printing and embrace both image and text on the same copper plate. Blake joined him on at least two projects, one of which, *Thoughts on Outline,* was published in 1796.[19] Blake executed some of the plates in the style of classical gems and taught Cumberland how to etch the others, thus enabling the author to—as he put it—"reduce considerably the price of the book." One Blake example, *Psyche Repents* (Fig. 7), was composed by Cumberland and demonstrates to what degree the commercially popular cameo-format dictated the design.

Cumberland identified himself with the commercial classes, and understood the outline method as the only aesthetic approach compatible with British naval, political, and industrial supremacy. In *Thoughts on Outline* and other books he revealed an obsessive competition with the French; he wanted to inspire British industry "so as to rival our neighbors on the Continent." He then addressed his tract to the Whig Leader Charles James Fox. In the wake of the American and French Revolutions, Fox alone is capable of guiding "the mismanaged vessel of the British State, stained, indeed, but not quite ruined, shattered, but not, I hope, out of the reach of repair."

Cumberland's contribution to a regenerated Ship of State is the "chaste outline," the principle of the ancient masterworks. As he stated:

> I have treated principally of *Outline;* for until the importance of it be generally admitted, and its perfection is generally sought; till it be understood, *that there can be no art without it,* and that no man deserves to be called an artist, who is defective in this best rudiment; we may continue to model, carve, and paint; but, without it, we shall never have Artists, Sculptors, nor Painters.

He claims that this principle is central to well-being, "without a knowledge of which, all our justly-boasted manual skill can be of little or no utility, either to this country, or its *commerce,* the source of all our wealth, our pride, our folly, and our crimes. . . ." His hope in writing is to provide a stable base for the fine arts in England, "which alone can insure our future consequence in Europe, and which, I sometimes flatter myself, will be the means of again extending them over the whole world." This encompassed the industrial arts as well; without outline, products bear sloppy and haphazard forms:

> The calico-printer fatigues himself and the public, in inventing patterns without meaning; and religiously believes, that chance alone, and luck, give a print vogue.

The same is true of the potter, founder, engraver, and printer; what alone can insure the success of all is "firm or pure Outline."[20]

Cumberland's position sprang from the neo-classical movement and he appended to his text his own linear designs of "classical subjects invented on the principles recommended in the essay." He perceived his ideal in sculptors like Canova and Flaxman because sculpture by definition "is *all* Outline." And he was certainly inspired by the first catalogue of Sir William Hamilton's vase collection which aimed at setting before English artists and artisans "exquisite models" to inspire a new art direction capable of rivaling antiquity.[21] He further assimilated Sir William's elitist notion of neo-classicism in connection with "pure" outline, for he felt that a "coarse, thick, and irregular Outline, is, like a coarse mode of expression, fit only for the rabble of mankind."

Blake, who often sympathized with the "rabble," was nevertheless dependent on prosperous patrons for his livelihood. While Blake's social and political perspective contained many dissenting attitudes, his thorough association with Cumberland's tract indicates that he too identified with English supremacy. Like the Lunar Society, he could support the American and French Revolutions, attack the slave trade at its roots, but at the same time work in the interests of a powerful Great Britain. Blake's immediate cue came from the commercial middle classes advancing themselves through science and technology; their promise he translated into mystical inspiration, divination, and novelty. In his 1793 prospectus addressed "To the Public," he declared his "powers of invention," and in the advertisement for his *Descriptive Catalogue* he could repeat in the same breath that his "Original Conceptions on Art" were by "an Original Artist." The earlier public prospectus gave him credit for inventing "a method of Printing both Letter-press and Engraving in a style more ornamental, uniform, and grand, than any before discovered, while it produces works at less than one fourth of the expense." Convinced of his public success, he pointed out that his gifts "very early engaged the attention of many persons of eminence and fortune; by whose means he has been regularly enabled to bring before the Public Works (he is not afraid to say) of equal magnitude and consequence with the productions of any age or country."[22]

Among these projected works are singled out a series of subjects drawn from the Bible and a History of England. Blake may have been acting defensively in a year of political repression, but from first to last he appealed to patriotic feelings to sell his work. One of his initial projects as an independent engraver was a series of scenes from English history, one of which was *Edward and Elenor,* engraved and published only in 1793 (and offered for sale in the prospectus), but designed in the late 1770s (Fig. 8). Blake's subject is that of Elenor's courageous act in sucking the poison from her husband's wound by an assassin, a theme exemplifying both domestic and national fidelity to the crown. The composition itself is an amalgam of neo-classic poses and gestures derived from Gavin Hamilton, Benjamin West, and Angelica Kauffmann (who exhibited the same subject at the Royal Academy in 1776).

One of Blake's most "eminent" and devoted patrons was Thomas Butts, who constantly prodded the painter with cash and encouragement.[23] Butts was the same age as Blake, and like Cumberland was a "white-collar" benefactor. He worked as a clerical adjunct of the paymaster in the Commissary General of Musters, an office whose function was to verify that military personnel drawing pay were alive and well, that military hardware was in order, and that enlistments were recorded. By 1788 Butts became the Chief Clerk and received an excellent salary. Through shrewd investments (and probably graft) he accumulated a small fortune; he owned quite a bit of property, including two houses in fashionable Fitzroy Square, and invested the bulk of his estate in such rising industrial and financial enterprises as canals, water-works, mines, banks, and insurance.

Butts met Blake around 1793 and instantly took a liking to the person and his work. Ironically, Butts was both a political and religious conservative, punctilious in his dress and public behavior. Evidently, Blake's so-called "eccentricity" did not prevent him from gaining support from sober, pragmatic, and shrewd business types who knew a good thing when they saw it. As in the case of Fuseli, Blake's high-flown images spoke to the adventurous fantasies and exploits of the new breed of entrepreneurs, complementing their large-scale transactions with grandiose conceptions of the teeming universe. Butts' mansion in Fitzroy Square became a veritable Blake gallery. For almost thirty years he was a steady buyer of the artist's work, at one point purchasing a drawing each week. At other times he bought in large lots or commissioned original works like the series on *Job* which Blake later engraved. At one time or another he must have owned nearly 200 of the artist's pictures, including such outstanding pieces as the tempera designs of *God Judging Adam, Nebuchadnezzar,* and *Newton.* It is no wonder that Blake could boast to Butts that the works he had done for him were equal to those of Carracci and Raphael, and that he was "Proud of being their Author and Grateful to you my Employer & that I look upon you as the Chief of my Friends, whom I would endeavour to please, because you, among all men, have enabled me to produce these things.''[24] Blake's letter expresses the classic artist-patron relationship with one crucial variation: he perceives his backer as an "employer," and himself as an artisan-entrepreneur, working for a stipulated rate of pay.

Blake was actually an entrepreneur in his own right and took on a variety of engraving jobs throughout his career. In 1784 he set himself up next door to the family hosiery business as an engraver, print seller, and publisher in partnership with James Parker, a friend and colleague from the studio of Basire. They hoped to cash in on a market which earned a fortune for the engravers and publishers of such works as *Nightmare* and *Death of General Wolfe*. Blake and Parker hoped to eliminate the middlemen by combining in their enterprise the functions of artist, publisher, distributor, and dealer. Wanting to tap a market beyond the existing institutional network, they began by engraving the mildly erotic scenes of their mutual friend, Stothard. However, after only three years, a rift with Parker ended the relationship and the print-selling. Henceforth, Blake—in alliance with his wife Catherine who worked with him closely on the printing and coloring processes—acted as a self-employed, free-lance designer and engraver.

It was widely felt at this time that any method for simplifying the production of books and newspapers would insure its inventor not only wealth but also unlimited access to the public. Like Cumberland and many others, Blake experimented with fresh approaches to stereotyped printing. Movable type was labor-intensive, putting the author at the mercy of printer and publisher; as both artist and writer Blake sought a cheap means of combining both image and text on the same plate. His solution was to write directly on the plate and replace letterpress altogether. The main problem here was the reversal of the lettering which he resolved by producing a stereotype plate in which the design and the lettering were applied in reverse on the plate. He accomplished this by an intermediate stage in the form of an application to paper with gum arabic or varnish which resisted acid when transferred to the copper surface. Then all the lights were bitten by the acid and the outline of both image and type were left in relief for making impressions.[25]

Blake mocked his own entrepreneurial schemes in a parody of the Lunar Society entitled "An Island in the Moon," written the

438   A History of Book Illustration

year after he opened his shop with Parker. One fragment of the
unpublished manuscript contains an exchange between two of the
characters on a revolutionary printing process which would
guarantee a fortune:

> "Then," said he, "I would have all the writing Engraved
> instead of Printed & at every other leaf a high finished print,
> all in three Volumes folio, & sell them a hundred pounds a
> piece. They would print off two thousand." "Then," says
> she, "whoever will not have them will be ignorant fools &
> will not deserve to live."[26]

The idea of making a killing on the market by creating a cheaply
made "luxury edition" was reiterated by Blake more seriously in
a later exchange with his brother James in 1803:

> The Profits arising from Publications are immense, & I now
> have it in my power to commence publication with many
> very formidable works, which I have finish'd & ready. A
> Book price half a guinea may be got out at the Expense of
> Ten pounds & its almost certain profits are 500 G.[27]

Thus from first to last Blake was determined to make money with
his art—the main justification for his professional life.
   Here again Blake's schemes and ventures place him squarely in
the orbit of the Lunar Society. As stated earlier, he shared their
political and humanitarian interests, exemplified by his illuminated book *America* and his poem on *The French Revolution.*
Solidarity with the Yankees meant the end of the rule of privilege,
civic and parliamentary reform, freedom of the press, and economic justice. A type like Wedgwood was not the least bit
perturbed by the loss of the colonies (knowing that even an
independent America would still have to line up for British wares
and skills). Blake saw in the French Revolution a reappearance of
the civic patriotism that sparked the Americans to action. Again
he shared the attachment to civil and religious liberty of the
Dissenters, large employers, and Lunar Society members, whose
concern for these rights went hand in hand with their attachment
to dogmas of free trade. The warmest welcome to the first stages
of the French Revolution came largely from middle-class and

Dissenting groups among which Blake's artisanal-entrepreneurial category could be counted.

In 1791 Joseph Johnson printed Book I of Blake's *The French Revolution. A Poem, In Seven Books* in conventional typography and without illustrations. The type was set and proofs made, but the work was not published and the remaining books have been lost. Early in 1791 Johnson printed Tom Paine's first volume of *The Rights of Man* (which, among other things, also traced the history of the French Revolution), but the rising tide of Tory reaction decided him against publishing it. In July of the same year, when Lunar Society members were celebrating the second anniversary of the fall of the Bastille, a pre-planned crowd "rioted" in Birmingham and destroyed Joseph Priestley's house, library, and laboratory. Similarly, the project of Blake—who wore the red bonnet of the French Jacobins, and characteristically perceived the French Revolution as ushering in the Millennium— fell victim to the mood of prevailing hysteria.

The same contempt Blake felt for royal tyranny and its subtler tools of oppression is expressed in the lines of Darwin's *Botanic Garden,* published by Johnson in the same year he printed *The French Revolution.* In Canto II of "Economy of Vegetation" Darwin discusses the land of Franklin where "Tyrant-Power had built his eagle nest," and against whom "The patriot-flame with quick contagion ran, / Hill lighted hill, and man electrified man. . . ." Then follows a description of the Bastille, its tortured captives, and its liberation, all of which profoundly influenced Blake's own lines on the subject.[28] Indeed, Blake's involvement with the *Botanic Garden* took place on both a practical and intellectual plane; it may be recalled that Johnson recommended him to Darwin as an engraver, and that he engraved at least five of the ten plates in the 1791 edition, including Fuseli's *Fertilization of Egypt,* and the four illustrations after Wedgwood's replicas of the Portland Vase. Blake's own addition to the *Fertilization* of the winged patriarch flinging lightning and rain from his outstretched arms is an image that recurs in the title page of the *Visions of the Daughters of Albion, The House of Death,* and *The Morning Stars Sang Together* (an illustration for *Job*). The reproduction of the figures in the compartments of the Portland Vase reveals the classical prototypes he used as the point of departure for his more daring imagery (Figs. 9 and 10). The male figure on the left of the first and second compartments with his closely cropped curly hair is the other stock character in his repertoire.[29]

Blake's sympathy for the helpless extended from exploited peoples to "the little winged fly." He loved botanical and entomological forms: floral blossoms of every type—tendril, seedling, and sprout—and insects like the worm, bee, spider, caterpillar, chrysalis, and butterfly; he metaphorically employed these images to exemplify his ideas of renewal and regeneration.[30] Starting with the publication of *Songs of Innocence* and the *Book of Thel* in 1789—the same year which saw the appearance of Darwin's *Loves of the Plants*—Blake was profoundly affected by Darwin's floral and vegetable metaphors. Mingled among his flowers and insects are the forms of fairies and spiritual beings who dart everywhere in the friendly bowers of the *Botanic Garden*. Akin to Darwin's gnomes, nymphs, sylphs, and other creatures that allegorized nature's operations, Blake often anthropomorphized his leafy and floral forms as in the verses and illustration to the poem "The Blossom" in *Songs of Innocence:*

> Merry Merry Sparrow
> Under leaves so green
> A happy Blossom
> Sees you swift as arrow
> Seek your cradle narrow
> Near my Bosom.

Surrounding these verses on Plate II is a burgeoning, flame-like plant on whose leaves cavort naked winged children and an adult winged figure bending over her baby.[31] This may be compared with Darwin's

> So the pleased Linnet in the moss-wove nest,
> Wakes into life beneath its parent's breast,
> Chirps in the gaping shell, bursts forth erelong,
> Shakes its new plumes, and tries its tender song. . . .[32]

Or compare Blake's stanza from "A Cradle Song" (also in *Songs of Innocence*), decorated with flourishing branches and leaves upon which tiny figures lay,

> Sweet sleep with soft down
> Weave thy brows an infant crown.

> Sweet sleep Angel mild,
> Hover o'er my happy child,

with Darwin's

> Closed in an azure fig by fairy spells,
> Bosom'd in down, fair CAPRI-FICA dwells; . . .[33]

Blake's "Infant Joy" shows two enormous blossoms growing from the bottom right corner, one open above the text containing a mother and baby in her lap and a standing sprite with moth wings. But example after example can be called upon to demonstrate Blake's use of imagery derived from the natural sciences, and which he carefully integrated with his text on the basis of his earlier training as an industrial designer.[34]

More concretely, Darwin's plate in *Loves of the Plants* of the *Vallisneria Spiralis* (Fig. 11)—with its root structure, long spiral stalk, wandering tendrils, serpentine leaves, and blossoms—was used by Blake as a model for his decorative foliage in Plate 4 of *America* (Fig. 12), Plates 4 and 12 of *Europe, A Prophecy,* and was probably the source of the large plant at the foot of Plate 2 of *The Marriage of Heaven and Hell.*[35] The striking visual and literary correspondences between Blake and Darwin point up their common philosophical approach to the larger issues of their time. Stimulated by the awesome human potential promised by current scientific and industrial innovation, they tried to grasp the broad implications in a humanized cosmography that would be understandable in both contemporary and prophetic terms.

Here again Blake showed his affiliation with the Lunar Society members. Blake establishes this in his satire on the group entitled "An Island in the Moon," written around 1785:

> In the Moon is a certain Island nearby a mighty continent, which small island seems to have some affinity to England, & what is more extraordinary the people are so much alike & their language so much the same that you would think you were among your friends.

One of the main characters is Inflammable Gass the Wind finder, who is surely a take-off on Priestley. Inflammable Gass conducts all sorts of experiments, makes toys and puppets, and uses an air pump to carry out experiments with the dangerous, plague-bearing "phlogiston." Priestley was well known for his gadgets and toys, and especially for his experiments with the air pump.[36] Another character, the mathematician Obtuse Angle, sings a song about John Locke and Isaac Newton, and must be William Small, who had expounded mathematics and Newtonian physics at the College of William and Mary in Virginia. Steelyard the Lawgiver hosts the group one evening and is not John Flaxman as commonly suggested, but Matthew Boulton, the iron magnate at whose house many of the meetings of the Lunar Society took place. Finally, Etruscan Column the Antiquarian is none other than Josiah Wedgwood whose factory Etruria turned out "Etruscan" objects to order.

Although most of the records of Blake's work for Wedgwood are now lost or destroyed, it is almost certain that Blake engraved illustrations for Wedgwood's *Catalogue of Queen's Ware* assembled in the period 1781–83. According to a surviving Wedgwood account with John Flaxman (who introduced Blake to the potter), the ceiling painting for the drawing-room of Etruria Hall, Wedgwood's residence, was designed by Flaxman and executed by Blake, who was paid 3 pounds, 17 shillings.[37] Blake also made the engravings of Wedgwood's replica of the Portland Vase for the *Botanic Garden*. Perhaps his most notable commission for the firm came from Josiah Wedgwood the younger in 1815; Blake engraved Plates 1–18 for the Queen's Ware Catalogue of 1817 which display cream bowls, butter dishes, soup terrines, salad bowls, and china fruit baskets (Fig. 13). Blake executed these objects with the linear technique associated with neo-classicism; the clear, crisp outlines have now been explicitly deployed in the sale of Wedgwood's products. Blake's systematic turn of mind is exemplified in a note he wrote Wedgwood the younger about the commission: "It will be more convenient for me to make all the drawings first, before I begin engraving them, as it will enable me also to regulate a System of working that will be uniform from the beginning to end."[38]

Perhaps one of the most remarkable graphic examples of his connection with members of the Lunar Society in his frontispiece (Plate I) to *Jerusalem, The Emanation of the Giant Albion*, dated 1804 on the title page but completed only around 1820 (Fig. 14).

It shows a type of nightwatchman or caretaker pushing his way through the door of an arched portal in a stone wall. As he enters the profound darkness of the interior, he carries in his right hand a spherical lantern articulated into concentric circles which give off rays. The lantern is made of a transparent material for the fingers of the caretaker are visible through it, but the globe seems to adhere to his hand rather than be grasped by it. This is especially evident in the color print where the entire scene is illuminated by the curious light (Fig. 15).

This figure clearly represents Los, the protagonist of *Jerusalem* an the persona of Blake himself. Los stands for the Imaginative Mind who perceives spiritual truth but is mired in the materialism of the temporal world. But if he is frustrated in his attempts to make his creations capable of grasping "Eternity in an hour," he continually strives to enlighten human vision. On either side of and above the archway of the frontispiece Blake initially engraved eleven lines which were later delected or obscured in the printing stages. These confirm the identity of the caretaker as "Los/As he enter'd the Door of Death" and who on Plate 31 takes "his globe of fire to search the interiors of Albion's/Bosom. . . ." Albion, the primordial Human Being, the first inhabitant of England, was separated from Jerusalem—his emanation or feminine counterpart—at the Fall. Blake's long poem unfolds the history of Albion's redemption and reunion with Jerusalem after having passed through the experience of Eternal Death. It is Los who enters into the darkest recesses of the material realm in order to bring back to Albion the secrets of a regenerate existence beyond. Los, the perennial seeker after truth, has the responsibility of finding ways of healing divisions and conflicts in the physical and moral structure of the universe—a fictional charge informed by Blake's actual experiences during the ruinous Napoleonic wars.

Los assumes the role of the blacksmith to construct the city of imagination and form the tools of salvation. His attitude is precisely that of Blake himself:

> I must Create a System, or be enslav'd by another Man's.
> I will not Reason & Compare: my business is to Create.

But Los-Blake must carry out his work in the temporal realm; his contradiction lies in the attempt to build a new world from the

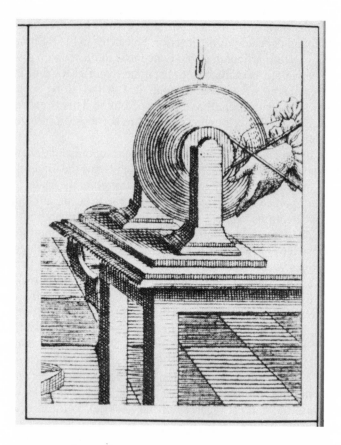

Fig. 19. J. A. Nollet, Recherches . . . électriques, Plate II (detail).

materials and ideas of this one. It is not surprising, therefore, to
find Blake drawing upon the innovations of science and industry
to portray this contradiction, since progressive groups like the
Lunar Society heralded these innovations as the foundation of the
New Jerusalem.

One such innovation which profoundly fascinated Blake and
the Lunar Society was electricity. Among other things, Blake
shared Darwin's faith in electricity as a cure for bodily ailments.[39]
The ball-shaped lantern carried by Los in the frontispiece to

Jerusalem is actually the image of a rotating glass globe used to generate electricity in contemporary electrical experiments. Several examples of the different kinds of electrostatic devices were reproduced in Priestley's *History and Present State of Electricity* (Figs. 16 and 17).[40] Priestley wrote an entire chapter on the construction of "electrical machines," and devotes a major section to his French colleague, the Abbé Jean Antoine Nollet, who pioneered in these contraptions (Figs. 18 and 19).[41] As the glass globe was spun, friction was applied to it by the hand or an emory cloth; the resultant charge was then conveyed by wires to an electrode. These devices were used in primitive electromagnetic experiments, and could also be manipulated to create dazzling light effects in the form of sparking or a more sustained glow when the air around the globe became ionized. Thus Los, Blake's alter-ego or the spirit of prophecy, seeks truth in the dark corners of the material universe with an electric light. Blake was clearly a prophet in more ways than one.

Almost all of Blake's friends accepted the idea of a mechanistic design of the cosmos, a concept indispensable to the Industrial Revolution. The image of the mechanical universe provided the philosophical foundation for harnessing nature through machines. Tom Paine, for example, envisioned God as the archetype of mechanical genius:

> The Almighty is the great mechanic of the creation . . . Had we, at this day, no knowledge of machinery, and were it possible that man could have a view . . . of the structure of the machinery of the universe, he would soon conceive the idea of constructing some at least of the mechanical works we now have.

This is similar to the Lunar Society's benign view of the mechanical world—one that does not contradict contemporary visionary and religious experience so much as reinterpret it. There is no doubt that for many people the actual sight of real machinery in the English environment evoked awestricken and sublime ideas about God's creation. This was certainly the case for Paine, a civil engineer with new and ingenious solutions for building metal bridges.[42]

Blake's mechanistic beings, with their diagrammatic appearance

Fig. 18. J. A. Nollet, Recherches sur les causes particulières des phénomènes électriques, Plate II.

Fig. 20. William Blake, God Judging Adam, 1795. *Color print finished in pen and watercolor. Tate Gallery, London.*

Fig. 21. Rotative Steam Engine made by James Watt and Matthew Boulton, 1784. *Science Museum, London.*

and aerodynamic movements, derive from this point of view. His famous color print (also belonging to Butts) of *God Judging Adam,* although couched in biblical trappings, perfectly supports this conclusion (Fig. 20). The obvious narrative of *God Judging Adam* marks the advent of the Fall, symbolized by the serpent entwined around Adam's leg. It also reveals Blake's condemnation of the Old Testament Jehovah-Urizen during the severe repression and misuse of the legal system in the mid-1790s. The book of laws lies open on God's lap and Adam's body swings forward abruptly in response to the severity of the chastisement. The law declared here is the same as pronounced in the *Marriage of Heaven and Hell:* "One Law for the Lion & Ox is Oppression."

Significantly, the structure of the work depends on an industrial image. The entire composition follows the model of Watt's double-acting rotative steam engine, with the reprimanding arm of Jehovah substituting for the driving arm and piston, and the orbital "fiery chariot" replacing the fly-wheel and furnace (Fig. 21). There is biblical precedent for the latter motif in *II. Kings,* 2:11, where "a chariot of fire, and horses of fire" separated the prophet Elisha from Elijah who was taken "up by a whirlwind into heaven." "Fiery Chariots" were commonly used in Blake's time to characterize steam engines; Darwin referred to the "fiery chariots" of the future which would soar into the heavens powered by steam.[43] The term "horsepower" was not yet used, but people spoke of engines "of three or four horses." Blake's flaming creatures clearly depend on the current metaphors for the new technology.

The largest and best equipped London factory of the period to use steam power was the Albion Mills Company, erected in the years 1783–84.[44] This firm was a flour mill erected on the Surrey side of the Thames near Blackfriars Bridge. But in 1791 it was burnt down (possibly by unemployed workers displaced by the new machinery) and the company never recovered. Watt and Boulton constructed the steam engines, the first of which began in operation in 1786; the second with its set of millstones was installed in 1789. This last was one of the earliest double-acting engines with rotary motion in which the steam pressed alternatively on opposite sides of a piston, enabling the engine to make a power stroke in both directions. Blake could have seen the Watt-Boulton rotary steam engine at work, with its large fly-wheel and connecting rod. While the engine at the Albion Mills had the boiler on the opposite side of the fly-wheel,

Blake's design compresses the complicated mechanism into a compact shape.

Blake's work further resembles the horizontal disposition of Robert Fulton's design for a steamboat mechanism which he submitted to Watt and Boulton for consideration (Fig. 22). While the drawing reproduced here dates from 1809, Fulton had first developed the concept in the 1790s when still a disciple of Benjamin West and an exhibitor at the Royal Academy exhibitions which he looked upon as a means "to create a name that may hereafter produce business." As early as 1793 Fulton drew up a scheme for moving ships and barges by steam, and in November of the following year requested from Watt and Boulton an estimate of the expenses needed for "a Steam Engine with a Rotative movement . . designed to be placed in a Boat."[45] Fulton and Blake had mutual friends who moved in the social circles of Johnson such as Joel Barlow and the poet William Hayley who became an important patron of Blake.[46] Barlow protected Fulton and collaborated with him in many literary, graphic, and technical projects. Barlow dedicated his *Columbiad*—the same book for which Fuseli projected a series of illustrations—to the steamboat pioneer.

But we do not have to demonstrate a direct link between Fulton and Blake; we need only show their participation in the same historical process. A comparison of the Fulton sketch with Blake's print reveals astonishing formal parallels, starting with Blake's fiery orb at the right and Fulton's fly-wheel, moving to the deity whose lower garments are segmented like a gear, his extended arm echoing the connecting rod, and thence to Adam with his legs outstretched, receiving the action akin to Fulton's triangular mechanism.

Adam's body has been impersonalized and transformed into a machine-like object by the concealment of his arms beneath his beard and the geometric configuration of his vertical torso, legs, and the seemingly automatic motion of head and neck which spring forward to meet the staff of Jehovah. It is instructive to juxtapose with Blake's picture the following description of the utopian Age of Steam by Andrew Ure, its foremost apologist in the early years of the 19th century:

> The benignant power of steam summons around him his myriads of willing menials, and assigns to each the regulated

Fig. 22. Robert Fulton, Drawing of Boulton and Watt's Steam Engine adapted for Steam Boat, 1809. *American Society of Mechanical Engineers, New York.*

Fig. 23. William Blake, Whirlwind of Lovers, from Dante's *Divine Comedy*, 1824–27. *Pen and watercolor over pencil. City Museum and Art Gallery, Birmingham, England.*

task, substituting for painful muscular effort on their part, the energies of his own gigantic arm, and demanding in return only attention and dexterity to correct such little aberrations as casually occur in his workmanship.[47]

Could the creation of the first human be considered one of those little aberrations that needed to be adjusted to the demands of the new technology? Here the Machine no longer models itself after the universe but usurps the functions of the Supreme Being.

Blake's design identifies industry with the severe punishment of God and the dehumanization of Creation.[48] When the state is oppressive, technology enslaves people rather than aids them. Blake did not condemn industry in itself, but only its pernicious application in the forging of weapons of war and the enslavement of the people for the sake of their production. During intervals of peace or in the New Jerusalem, technology may produce the implements of peace and then people will enjoy control over production. Under such conditions industry promises unlimited creative possibilities for humankind.

In the mid-1820s Blake worked on a series of watercolors illustrating Dante's *Divine Comedy*. Blake actually rejected Dante's worldview, regarding it as resignation to tyranny and the rule of vengeance. For Blake the *Inferno* exemplified the state of cruelty to which Dante acquiesced, and he could denounce the Italian humanist as an "atheist" and "mere politician." Blake's famous illustration from the series, *Whirlwind of Lovers,* based on the *Inferno,* Canto V, employs a mechanical allusion to go beyond Dante's conception and show a beneficial effect on society (Fig. 23). The picture represents Francesca da Rimini and her lover Paolo in a flame above the prostrate Dante, while a whirlwind draws other couples heavenward. Blake declared that "Dante saw Devils where I see none—I see only good," and used the *Inferno* to both emphasize Dante's fixation on retribution and suggest that those who overcome certain obstacles may attain to a higher union.

The whirlwind carries the couples (who sinned in their earthly existence) beyond the physical to a spiritual union. In the original narrative lustful sinners are driven relentlessly by furious winds, blown hither and thither only to be dashed against the shore. That Blake transformed the wild gusts of wind into a uniform, cylindrically shaped passage indicates a radical departure from Dante's

Fig. 24. William Blake, The Tyger, from *Songs of Experience,* 1789–84. *British Museum, London.*

text. He evidently took as his model for this design hollow tubes or pipes constructed for conveying water, gas, and especially steam which would have been the driving force for most of English industry by the 1820s. Basic to all the steam engines were the suction pipe and air pump.

Blake's sinful lovers rush through the tubes as if into a vacuum created by the difference between the air pressure within and without. Thus his transmutation of the Dantesque punishment into an opportunity for spiritual growth required a mechanical model along the lines of Los and his lantern. Here again it would seem that Blake did not view science and industry as inherently evil, but rather condemned the ways to which they were often applied. Indeed, Blake could perceive the action of steam and vaporizing as a metaphor for the ascendance of sinners into a more spiritual realm—that is, a less solid state of matter.

Thus there is ample evidence of Blake's dependence upon changes wrought by 18th-century science and the Industrial Revolution, keeping in mind that the unprecedented interest in science and its pragmatic applications were inseparable from the economic and industrial developments of the period. Yet critics and historians dwell on Blake's pejorative phrase, "dark Satanic Mills," and conclude that he loathed the new technology. Ironically, this expression appears in the preface to *Milton* (1804), an eschatological work which abounds in scientific and industrial metaphors. Milton's descent is characterized as an "electric flame," and is graphically shown as a rapidly falling star trailing vapor. Los seizes "Hammer & Tongs" to shape on his anvil "a red round Globe hot burning" which separates into the male and female progenitors of creation. The context of "dark Satanic Mills" is itself a prelude to the positive applications of industry:

> And did the Countenance Divine
> Shine forth upon our clouded hills?
> And was Jerusalem builded here,
> Among these dark Satanic Mills?

If Blake calls for weapons to wage a "Mental Flight" against the materialism of his time, the building of the New Jerusalem shall require all the industrial arts at society's disposal:

> Bring me my Bow of burning gold:
> Bring me my Arrows of desire:
> Bring me my spear: O clouds unfold:
> Bring me my Chariot of Fire!
>
> I will not cease from Mental Fight,
> Nor shall my Sword sleep in my hand:
> Till we have built Jerusalem,
> In England's green & pleasant Land.

Darwin's "chariot of fire" was a locomotive steam engine conceived in the early 1760s. It is clear that despite Blake's efforts to combat industrialism, he wound up "fighting fire with fire."

It is true that the birth of Satan in *Milton* conjures up an industrial world:

> O Satan my youngest born, art thou not Prince of the Starry Hosts
> And of the Wheels of Heaven, to turn the Mills Day & Night?
> Art thou not Newton's pantocrator weaving the Woof of Locke?

But this same industrial world coincides with England as a great nation:

> Loud sounds the Hammer of Los, & loud his Bellows is heard
> Before London to Hamstead's breadths & Highgate's heights To
> Stratford & old Bow; & across to the Gardens of Kensington
> On Tyburn's Brook: loud groans Thames beneath the iron Forge
> Of Rintrah & Palamabron, of Theotormon & Bromion, to forge the instruments
> Of Harvest: the Plow & Harrow to pass over the Nations.

And this prolific activity continues to reverberate throughout industrial London:

> Loud sounds the Hammer of Los, loud turn the Wheels of Enitharmon.

Her Looms vibrate with soft affections, weaving the Web of
  Life
Out from the ashes of the Dead; Los lifts his iron Ladles
With molten ore: he heaves the iron cliffs in his rattling
  chains
From Hyde Park to the Alms-Houses of Mile-end & old
  Bow.

Much of this corresponds to the rhythms and ideals of Darwin's
poetry in the *Botanic Garden;* the second book of *Milton* abounds
in references to gnomes, nymphs, and genii and their cosmologi-
cal significance. Plate 31 projects a Garden of Eden with an
inventory that would rouse the envy of Linnaeus and an anthropo-
morphic interpretation that would charm Darwin. The latter's
praise for industry in the context of his love of plants is tied to a
vision of a mechanistic universe. In Canto I of the ''Economy of
Vegetation'' he takes up the origins of the cosmos as a mechanical
operation of Divine Love:

Earth's round each sun with quick explosions of burst,
And second planets issue from the first;
. . . .
Orbs wheel in orbs, round centres centres roll,
And form, self-balanced, one revolving Whole.
—Onward they move amid their bright abode,
Space without bound, THE BOSOM OF THEIR GOD![49]

This may be compared with Blake's verses in *Jerusalem* which
contrast the mechanized nature of tyrannical institutions with the
mechanized operations of his ideal world:

I turn my eyes to the Schools & Universities of Europe
And there behold the Loom of Locke whose Woof rages dire
Wash'd by the Water-wheels of Newton; black the cloth
In heavy wreathes folds over every Nation; cruel Works
Of many Wheels I view, wheel without wheel, with cogs
  tyrannic
Moving by compulsion each other: not as those in Eden:
  which
Wheel within Wheel in freedom revolve in harmony &
peace.[50]

Hence it is not the neutral character of gears and cogwheels that torments Blake, but the cruel ends to which tyrants may apply them.

One of Blake's most persistent metaphors is the tiger which in its various states embodies the full range of human experience. In *Vala* or *The Four Zoas,* the Reign of Harmony (including the conversion of weaponry into implements of peace) is signaled by the metamorphosis of wild animals into pacific symbols:

> The noise of rural work resounded thro the heavens of heavens;
> The horses neigh from the battle, the wild bulls from the sultry waste,
> The tygers from the forests & the lions from the sandy deserts.
> They Sing; they seize the instruments of harmony; they throw away
> The spear, the bow, the gun, the mortar; they level the fortifications.[51]

This brings us to a fitting text to end this discussion of the artist: "The Tyger" from *Songs of Experience* (Fig. 24). Blake's feline has been shaped by a cosmic blacksmith, identified with hammer, anvil, and furnace. If it does not conjure up the Carron Ironworks, it does demonstrate that Blake was not loathe to fuse the creative imagination with an industrial process:

> Tyger Tyger, burning bright,
> In the forests of the night:
> What immortal hand or eye
> Could frame thy fearful symmetry?
> . . . .
> What the hammer? what the chain,
> In what furnace was thy brain?
> What the anvil? What dread grasp
> Dare its deadly terrors clasp!

Here the tiger "burning bright" is the molten material of the New Age waiting to be shaped into the stuff of art and history.

Blake's graphic image of the tiger shows us a docile and lovable beast, like the felines in "The Little Girl Found" (*Songs of Innocence*) who symbolize a non-threatening environment.

Animals and children romp in the biblical paradise heralded by Isaiah, "and the lion and the kid together, and a little child shall lead them." Blake's tiger, too, conjures up a pastoral realm of the innocent, uncorrupted lamb: "Did he who made the Lamb make thee?" The same stanza in which this line is found begins:

> When the stars threw down their spears
> And water'd heaven with their tears:
> Did he smile his work to see?
> Did he who made the Lamb make thee?

The throwing down of spears is analogous to converting swords into ploughshares. It signals an acceptance of peace. Simultaneously, it is the lightning (electricity) and energy required for this transformation. As in the *Vala* or *The Four Zoas,* there is a conversion of war production for the benefit of those who plant and harvest. A major source of inspiration for Blake's poem was Burke, who wrote that the Sublime revealed itself "in the gloomy forest, and in the howling wilderness, in the form of the lion, the tiger, the panther, or rhinoceros."[52] Blake begins and ends his poem in the sublime mode, but its development intimates a dialectical exchange with the category of the Beautiful. The result is a benign tiger who feeds the lamb. Thus the affirmative answer to the final question of the poem may be traced to the impact of the Industrial Revolution on Blake's perception of its potential to promote harmony and freedom in the social realm.

NOTES

This is a condensed version of the Blake section in Chapter IV of my book, *Art in an Age of Revolution,* to be published by University of Chicago Press.

1 J. Bronowski, *William Blake 1757–1827: A Man without a Mask,* New York, 1967, pp. 58ff.; M. Schorer, *William Blake, The Politics of Vision,* New York, 1946, pp. 195ff.; D.V. Erdman, *Blake, Prophet Against Empire,* Princeton, 1977, pp. xxiii-xxiv, 330ff. I wish to take this opportunity to express gratitude to Professor Erdman for his generosity in answering specific queries and in general for his inspired writing on Blake.

Other Blake scholars will recognize my debt to them, but I would like to single out G. E. Bentley, Jr., *William Blake's Writings,* Oxford, 1978; D. Bindman, *Blake as an Artist,* Oxford, 1977; M. Butlin, *The Paintings and Drawings of William Blake,* New Haven and London, 1981; J. Lindsay, *William Blake: His Life and Work,* London, 1978, K. Raine, *William Blake,* New York, 1971. I am grateful to Dan Belanger of the American Society of Mechanical Engineers for the photograph of Fulton's drawing, to Lynn Miller of the Wedgwood Museum, and to Judy Pringle for her many editorial suggestions which greatly improved the text.

[2] For the Lunar Society, see R. E. Schofield, *The Lunar Society of Birmingham,* Oxford, 1963; L. Ritchie-Calder, "The Lunar Society of Birmingham, *Scientific American,* June 1982, pp. 136ff.

[3] E. Darwin, *The Botanic Garden,* London, 1799 (4th ed.). I, Canto IV, verses 207ff.

[4] *Ibid.,* pp. 196–197, note on Priestley; E. Robinson, "Eighteenth-Century Commerce and Fashion: Matthew Boulton's Marketing Techniques," *Economic History Review,* ser. 2, 16, 1963–64, pp. 39ff.; N. McKendrick, "Josiah Wedgwood: An Eighteenth Century Entrepreneur in Salesmanship and Marketing Techniques," *Economic History Review,* ser. 2, 12, 1960, pp. 408ff.

[5] Schofield, *op. cit.,* p. 358.

[6] This cameo was reproduced in Darwin, *op. cit.,* between pp. 100–101, and was used as the title page vignette for much of the abolitionist literature of the 1790s.

[7] D. G. C. Allan, *William Shipley, Founder of the Royal Society of Arts,* London, 1979, pp. 80–81.

[8] *Ibid.,* p. 87.

[9] *Ibid.,* pp. 87–88.

[10] For further analysis of Blake's design in this work and its relationship to the text, see E. Bass, "*Songs of Innocence and of Experience,* the Thrust of Design," in *Blake's Visionary Forms Dramatic,* eds. D. V. Erdman and J. E. Grant, Princeton, 1970, pp. 197–98.

[11] For Stothard, see S. M. Bennett, "Thomas Stothard, R. A.," unpublished dissertation, University of California, Los Angeles, 1977, pp. 7ff., 167ff.

[12] Bronowski, *op. cit.,* pp. 34ff.; Erdman, *Prophet Against Empire, op. cit.,* pp. 7ff.

[13] D. V. Erdman, ed., *The Complete Poetry and Prose of William Blake,* Berkeley and Los Angeles, 1982, p. 665.

[14] *Ibid.,* p. 643.

[15] Bindman, *op. cit.,* p. 17; Butlin, *op. cit.,* I, No. 174.

[16] Erdman, ed., *The Complete Poetry and Prose, op. cit.,* p. 550.

[17] *Ibid.,* pp. 541–42.

[18] G. Keynes, ''Some Uncollected Authors XLIV: George Cumberland 1754–1848,'' *Book Collector,* vol. 19, 1970, pp. 31ff.

[19] G. Cumberland, *Thought on Outline, Sculpture, and the System that Guided the Ancient Artists in Composing their Figures and Groups,* London, 1796.

[20] *Ibid.,* pp. i ff., 8, 12–13, 21.

[21] *Collection of Etruscan, Greek and Roman Antiquities from the Cabinet of the Honorable Wm. Hamilton, His Britannick Majesty's Envoy Extraordinary at the Court of Naples,* Naples, 1766–77, I, pp. vi ff.

[22] *The Complete Poetry and Prose, op. cit.,* pp. 528, 692 (dated 10 October 1793).

[23] G. E. Bentley, Jr., ''Thomas Butts, White Collar Maecenas,'' *PLMA,* vol. 71, part 2, Sept.–Dec. 1956, pp. 1052ff.

[24] *The Complete Poetry and Prose, op. cit.,* p. 719.

[25] Bindman, *op. cit.,* pp. 41ff. Blake's ideas on this were informed by experiments of Cumberland, but he developed his own approach.

[26] *The Complete Poetry and Prose, op. cit.,* p. 465.

[27] *Ibid.,* p. 726.

[28] Darwin, *op. cit.,* Canto II, lines 362ff., 377ff.; D. Worral, ''William Blake and Erasmus Darwin's *Botanic Garden,*'' *Bulletin of the New York Public Library,* vol. 78, Summer 1975, pp. 405–06.

[29] Raine, *op. cit.,* p. 31.

[30] *Ibid.,* p. 113. Darwin, *op. cit.,* Canto I, for worms, spiders, beetles; Canto IV, for seeds, acorns, bulbs and buds, butterflies, caterpillars, and chrysalis.

[31] Bentley, *William Blake's Writings, op. cit.,* p. 32.

[32] Darwin, *op. cit.,* II, Canto IV, lines 435ff.

[33] *Ibid.,* lines 429–30.

[34] Worral, *op. cit.,* pp. 407ff.

[35] Worral compares the Vallisneria illustration to other plates in Blake; *ibid.,* p. 414.

[36] Erdman, *Prophet, op. cit.,* pp. 93–94, notes 13, 13a, recounts the pros and cons about the Priestley identification. Thus far the best alternative suggested has been Gustavus Katterfelto, a lecturer and entertainer in natural philosophy. C. P. Moritz, traveling in England in 1782, wrote that Katterfelto ''understands, besides electricity and a few other tricks of physics, a little of the art of conjuring . . . Every intelligent man regards Katterfelto as a windbag.'' C. P. Moritz, *Journeys of a German in England in 1782,* tr. R. Nettel, London, 1965, p. 70.

However, Katterfelto was only one among a number of itinerant lecturers on science and mechanics who regularly visited the principal towns in the later 18th century, and employed diverting amusements to attract the broad public. Almost all of them took their cue from Priestley, who was perhaps the ablest public lecturer of all. They often publicized his discoveries concerning "different kinds of airs." A. E. Musson and E. Robinson, *Science and Technology in the Industrial Revolution,* Manchester, 1969, pp. 101–102, 106–107. Above all, Priestley invented all kinds of games and toys and put one of them on the market. Priestley, *The History and Present State of Electricity,* London, 1767, pp. xi, 508ff., 556–57; *A Familiar Introduction to the Study of Electricity,* London, 1768, advertisement before title page. These books were published by Joseph Johnson, Blake's friend and occasional client.

Finally, no one enjoyed a livelier reputation than Priestly for his popular experiments on air and gases. As Darwin wrote: "His various discoveries respecting the analysis of the atmosphere, and the production of variety of new airs or gasses can only be understood by reading his Experiments on Airs." Hence Priestley must be considered the prime candidate for "Inflammable Gass the Wind finder"—"O who can doubt this?"

[37] R. Reilly and G. Savage, *The Dictionary of Wedgwood,* Woodbridge, Suffolk, 1980, p. 49.

[38] G. Keynes, *Blake Studies,* London, 1949, pp. 67ff.; Bentley, *Blake Records,* Oxford, 1969, pp. 239ff.

[39] As a medical practitioner, Darwin experimented with electricity in a variety of ways including its use to stimulate paralyzed organs and to dissolve tumors. Blake submitted his wife to electrical treatments in 1804. See his letter to Hayley, 18 December, 1804, in *The Complete Poetry and Prose, op. cit.,* p. 1111.

[40] Priestley, *History and Present State, op. cit.,* Plates IV (p. 525 for explanation), VI, VII.

[41] *Ibid.,* pp. 96, 135ff.; Abbé J. A. Nollet, *Recherches sur les causes particulières des phénomènes électriques,* Paris, 1749.

[42] Paine actually had royal authorization for applying his "method of constructing . . . arches, vaulted roofs, and cielings (sic), either in iron or wood, on principles new and different to anything hitherto practiced, by means of which construction arches, vaulted roofs, and cielings (sic) may be erected to the extent to several hundred feet beyond what can be performed in the present practice of architecture." M. D. Conway, *The Writings of Thomas Paine,* London, 1894, II, pp. 227ff., 230ff.

[43] Schofield, *op. cit.,* p. 29.

[44] H. W. Dickinson and R. Jenkins, *James Watt and the Steam Engine,* Oxford, 1927, pp. 164ff.

[45] H. W. Dickinson, *Robert Fulton, Engineer and Artist: His Life and Works,* London, 1913, p. 30.

[46] Erdman, *Prophet, op. cit.,* pp. 23, 26, 156ff., 159 (note 32), 210 (note 24).

[47] A. Ure, *The Philosophy of Manufactures,* London, 1835, p. 18.

[48] Ironically, Blake's perception reversed that of his contemporaries who saw the steam engine as the means of subduing the earth—the biblical promise of Genesis before Adam's Fall. Here is the definition of the steam engine in an account of Matthew Boulton published in 1803:

> The steam engine, approaching to the nature of a perpetuum mobile, or rather an *animal,* is incapable of lassitude or sensation, produces coals, works metals, moves machines, and is certainly the noblest *drudge* that was ever employed by the hand of art. Thus we "put a hook in the nose of the Leviathan"; thus we play with him as a child, and take him for a servant forever; . . . thus "we subdue nature, and derive aid and comfort from the elements of earthquakes."

See "Biographical Account of Matthew Boulton, Esq.," *Philosophical Magazine,* vol. 15, Feb.–May 1803, p. 60. In this context God's chastisement of Adam may also be understood as a metaphor for the abuse of "the new and stupendous power" of steam engines.

[49] Darwin, *op. cit.,* Canto I, lines 107–114. Also in "Loves of the Plants," Canto II, line 176, "Tooth urges tooth, and wheel drives wheel along," has the Blakean rhythm.

[50] *The Complete Poetry and Prose, op. cit.,* p. 159.

[51] *Ibid.,* p. 393.

[52] E. Burke, *A Philosophical Enquiry into the Origin of our Ideas of the Sublime and Beautiful,* ed. J. T. Boulton, London, 1958, p. 64.

ART AND THE ILLUSTRATIONS OF *VANITY FAIR* AND *THE NEWCOMES*
Stephen Canham

Since William Makepeace Thackeray was the sole major Victorian novelist to illustrate his own work, his novels are unique examples of the relation of text to visual image in the nineteenth century. He illustrated three novels—*Vanity Fair, The Virginians,* and *Pendennis*—as well as a number of other productions, such as *The Paris Sketch Book* and *The Rose and the Ring.* Although he was not opposed to other hands illustrating his work, he maintained a careful, even protective, interest in another artist's rendering of his text. To assess Thackeray's aesthetic ideals and the degree to which the illustrations of his novels satisfy them, I propose to look in some detail at *Vanity Fair,* which Thackeray of course illustrated himself, and at *The Newcomes,* which was illustrated by Richard Doyle. These two examples enable us to survey the rather different problems addressed by an author/ illustrator and by an illustrator distinct from an author, however carefully selected to reflect the author's artistic aims. In their individual ways, the illustrations of both novels are highly successful; to account for that success, we first need to examine some of Thackeray's own ideas about art and to study his skill as an illustrator.

Thackeray's letters offer a good starting point. They give the immediate impression that we are in the presence of a compulsive doodler: many letters, no matter how hastily written, are embellished with some sort of drawing, be it the sketch of a face, an object, or a scene (figs. 1–3). It would be easy enough to attribute these little drawings to the mid-nineteenth century's abhorrence of any void, its desire to fill empty space with dust-collecting

Reprinted with permission from *Modern Language Quarterly,* March 1982, Vol. 43, No. 1, pp. 43–66.

one . O God purify it , and make my heart clean — After dinner and a drive on the sea shore I came home to an evenings reading wh took place as follows It is always so with my good intentions, and I woke about dawn and found it was quite time to go to bed. But the solitude and idleness I think is both cheerful & wholesome. I've a mind to stay on here and begin to hope I shall write a stronger number of Pendennis than some of the last ones have been.

Fig. 1. *A Collection of Letters of Thackeray, 1847-1855* (New York: Charles Scribner's Sons, 1887), p. 63.

And what news w? you have sent? That the baby is well that you have enjoyed yourself pretty well at Sevenoaks? Ah — I would give 6? to hear as much as that Such is a feeble but accurate outline of the view out of my window at this moment and all the time I am drawing it (you will remark how pleasantly the frisk parties in the foreground are with coloured clothes; I cant do anything with ink being black to represent the snow on the mountain behind)

Fig. 2. *A Collection of Letters of Thackeray*, p. 150.

My dear Madam

It was as I feared
on Friday, the
little Printers
devil barred
my door and
I could not
come out

as I should have liked very much to meet Colonel
Cronstade ~ Colonel brown I mean, ~ whom I have
already had the pleasure of meeting at your house
with an exterior w^h the world would call crusty

Fig. 3. *A Collection of Letters of Thackeray,* between pp. 142 and 143.

gewgaws and gimcracks, to fill the borders of pages with ornate floral designs, to fill one's life with social forms and rituals. But Thackeray's sketches are more than this; they are, I think, symptoms of a desire to unite written word and visual image, to achieve accurate expression in both media. To discount them as precursors of telephone-pad scribbling is to discredit his more serious intention, which is to make his audience *see* in a particular way, the way of the artist himself. This goal informs not only the quick letter sketches, but also the more elaborate *Vanity Fair* illustrations.

Thackeray seems often to have thought in visual terms and images. In his youth he studied drawing in Paris, and he initially considered art, not literature, to be his true calling. He once remarked to his mother that "at twenty you know we all thought I was a genius at drawing";[1] though he eventually chose literature, he did not abandon art. In fact, the two disciplines maintain a fine balance in his work, a balance that goes far to explain the power or poignancy of many of his written scenes. Some of Thackeray's best fictional moments combine an eye for pictorial qualities and significant verbal detail with a strong sense of the economy and restraint necessary to achieve a dramatic realization of scene. The pictures accompanying the letters are a good example of this: often humorous, sometimes self-deprecating, they match the witty tone of the writer. In the three novels he illustrated, his intention is similar but his achievement more complex. The drawings here are often sketchlike and lack the detail and fullness of the verbal scenes; this visual economy permits him to focus clearly on his human figures and allows the illustrations to become true, and literal, character sketches.

Vanity Fair (1848) is perhaps Thackeray's best-known attempt to reconcile his two ways of seeing, in words and in visual forms. The results are frequently definitive: having met Amelia or Jos or Becky in the verbal descriptions and in the pictures, we find it difficult indeed to imagine them any other way (figs. 4 and 5). The backgrounds in these drawings are usually vague, merely roughed in or hinted at, for it is not the setting that concerns Thackeray; he has supplied that with the text, and to reproduce it visually would be superfluous. It is enough that the elements of the background— Vauxhall bills, candlesticks, rudiments of architecture, and so on—simply be identifiable: their specific characteristics are left to

Fig. 4. "Mr. Joseph entangled," *Vanity Fair,* I (London: Smith, Elder, 1883), facing pg 42.

the imagination of the reader/viewer. What Thackeray *can* show and elaborate upon are his characters: a "superabundant" Jos, who, "like most fat men. . . . *would* have his clothes made too tight," or an "unprotected" Becky, who confides that "poor

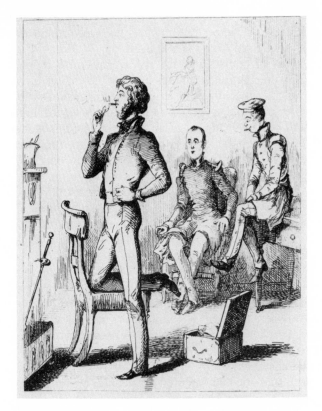

Fig. 5. "Lieutenant Osborne and his ardent love letters," *Vanity Fair,* I, facing p. 124.

Rebecca . . . has only herself and her own wits to trust to."[2] Her sneering smile as she ensnares Jos clearly reveals the efficacy of those wits. Thackeray lavishes careful, even meticulous, attention on his characters, especially their facial expressions, physical attitudes, and costumes. George's uniform is accurately reproduced, as is his vainglorious pride: Becky's sly face peers out of a carefully conventional and proper bonnet. The effect is that of an almost studied offhandedness: a debauched Lord Steyne, a simpering Amelia—they are here in the drawings, seen as we have already been made to imagine them. There is, then, a clear correspondence between verbal characterization and visual rendering. The broad setting, Vanity Fair, is given in the text; the pictures stress the actors, the puppets themselves, and reinforce the images we form from the text itself.

Thackeray of course runs the risk of becoming reductive, of having his often simple drawings become caricatures or cartoons which mock rather than describe his characters. A political cartoon, for example, depends on the reader/viewer's immediate perception of satiric intent, of an intellectual component in the visual image itself which is often complemented by a caption. Such cartoons play off the viewer's prior knowledge or understanding against an exaggerated satiric vision of the subject; the *Vanity Fair* illustrations avoid this kind of discrepancy, along with its ironic potential for another way of seeing than that which Thackeray has already developed with his text. The beauty of these illustrations is that they *are* sketches, seemingly quick views that catch the actors at representative moments; a calculated sneer in a downturned line at the mouth, a vapid ego preening itself, a still-pompous Collector of Boggley Wollah promenading. I am tempted to call them snapshots, almost candid insights into character, where the focus is on the actors and the depth of field is shallow. Thackeray does not deliver a complete visual scene and rarely uses space complexly; almost all of the illustrations simply show the characters from straight on. It is as if Thackeray had lifted an Instamatic and captured his people forever in their most characteristic guises. The resulting images embody the text and give straightforward visual form to the conceptions of the author.[3]

But something rather different occurs in *The Newcomes* (1853–55). Thackeray's novel about art, its ideals and place in society, presents us with a social panorama and a drama of generations as well as individual lives, though it centers on two characters, both of whom are artists. The ostensible hero is Clive Newcome, a young man of modest artistic ability. It is important to note that Thackeray's portrait of Clive, who is depicted as moderately talented, idealistic, and burdened with financial worries and a difficult marriage, contains autobiographical elements.

J. J. Ridley, Clive's lifelong friend and counterpart, is also an artist, but with a difference. J. J. is described in ideal terms, and we should pause for a moment to examine J. J.'s aesthetic, for it echoes the method of *The Newcomes* and will help to clarify the relationship Thackeray established with its then well-known illustrator, Richard Doyle. J. J., nearsighted (as was Thackeray), "always sickly and dirty, and timid and crying" as a child, is the son of a dull-witted butler who is unable to perceive his son's special sensitivity and talent.[4] But Miss Cann, a lodger, is quick to value the boy's worth. She encourages his interest in drawing and shares her meager knowledge with him in the hope that he will one day become famous. The Reverend Charles Honeyman, who also lodges with the Ridleys, evaluates J. J.'s work:

> Honeyman looked at the boy's drawings from time to time and said, "Hm, ha!—very clever—a great deal of fancy, really." But Honeyman knew no more of the subject than a deaf and dumb man knows of music. He could talk the Art-cant very glibly, and had a set of Morghens and Madonnas as became a clergyman and a man of taste; but he saw not with eyes such as those wherewith Heaven had endowed the humble little butler's boy, to whom splendours of Nature were revealed to vulgar sights invisible, and beauties manifest in forms, colours, shadows of common objects, where most of the world saw only what was dull, and gross, and familiar. One reads in the magic story-books of a charm or a flower which the wizard gives, and which enables the bearer to see the fairies. O enchanting boon of Nature, which reveals to the possessor the hidden spirits of beauty round about him! spirits which the strongest and most gifted masters compel into painting or song. To others it is granted but to have fleeting glimpses of that fair Art-world; and tempted by ambition, or barred by faint-heartedness, or driven by necessity, to turn away thence to the vulgar life-track, and the light of common day. (I.xi)

Despite its hyperbole and floridity, this is one of the novel's most explicit statements of the particular qualities ascribed by Thackeray to an artistic temperament. Its ideals are consistent with the views Thackeray espoused in his numerous reviews of gallery exhibitions. The true artist is a visionary, apprehending the sublime in the mundane, the beautiful in the ordinary.[5] The controlling metaphor of the passage is that of vision; the artist is gifted with a special capacity to see more, and to see more intensely, than other people. He is party to a mystery, a beauty which is not only revealed to him but which he also seems to create, so that he discovers what is invisible to others. The

Fig. 6. Decoration, *The Newcomes,* I (London: Smith, Elder, 1869), p. 13.

CHAPTER XXIII.

IN WHICH WE HEAR A SOPRANO AND A CONTRALTO.

HE most hospitable and polite of Colonels would not hear of Mrs. Mackenzie and her daughter quitting his house when he returned to it, after six weeks' pleasant sojourn in Paris; nor, indeed, did his fair guest show the least anxiety or intention to go away. Mrs. Mackenzie had a fine merry

Fig. 7. Initial Letter, *The Newcomes,* I, chap. 23.

Romantic overtones of the passage are clear enough: the notion of
the artist as different from other people not in kind but in degree,
or as a visionary, half-perceiving, half-creating the world, could
easily have come from Wordsworth. J. J. is endowed with what
Thomas Carlyle called "Spiritual Optics," an insight into the
truth of things which goes beyond mere physical sight.[6] It is also
the vision of the poet in Shelley's *Defence of Poetry,* a vision that
"strips the veil of familiarity from the world, and lays bare the
naked and sleeping beauty, which is the spirit of its forms." J. J. is
no Plantonist, but his art does purge "the common Universe" of
"the film of familiarity which obscures from us the wonder of our
being." As Shelley says, such vision "creates anew the universe,
after it has been annihilated in our minds by the recurrence of
impressions blunted by reiteration."[7] In J. J., clearly, Thackeray
has fashioned a modest, functioning example of the more lofty,
more abstract ideals of his Romantic predecessors. J. J. is, in fact,
a down-to-earth example of an artist fashioned in the Romantic
mold, "living" in the midst of Victorian business, imperialism,
and crassness, not a vestigial remnant of an outmoded aesthetic
pose.

In the final sentence of the Honeyman passage, Thackeray
indicates that the world of art is not denied to people other than
artists, but is accessible only momentarily in "glimpses." The
truth of these glimpses is unquestioned, but the force of quotidian
pressures or weakness in the individual causes them to be ignored.
The true artist is the one who manages, by whatever means, to
remain in touch with that "fair Art-world," to exist unsullied and
undeterred by the "vulgar life-track." There is no condemnation
of art as illusion, no undermining of its highest aims; what is
lamented is that it must so often be laid aside in the routine of
existence. The ideal of a "fair Art-world," a limitless realm of
beauty waiting only for the sensitive eye, stands in neat opposition
to a "vulgar life-track," wherein action is repetitive, meaningless,
and, worst of all, unrelieved by beauty. The entire passage must be
considered carefully because of its strategic placement in the
novel: it comes as a conclusion to the descriptions of J. J.'s talents
and as a prelude to the first discussion of Clive's abilities. In this
brief paragraph Thackeray has set forth an ideal for his fledgling
artists, his representatives in the novel; the remainder of *The
Newcomes* examines their (and others') abilities to live up to it.[8]

J. J. in Dreamland.

Fig. 8. *The Newcomes,* I, frontispiece.

Thackeray was no stranger to the formal art world inhabited by J. J. Writing under the pseudonym of Michael Angelo Titmarsh, he contributed a widely read column of gallery criticism to the *Morning Chronicle.* In a representative review, he lauds the "almost *sacred*" pictorical comedy of a painting by Charles Leslie, a scene with a mother and baby, which displays an "exquisite innocent affection."[9] He describes J. J.'s work in a similar manner in *The Newcomes:* "Art is truth: and truth is religion; and its study and practice a daily work of pious duty" (II.xxvii). J. J.'s paintings are "sweet flowers of fancy . . . kind shapes of beauty which he has devised and moulded;" (II.xxvii). For Thackeray, the best art is simple and forthright; it touches elemental human emotions. Its nobility arises from its capacity to reveal the otherwise hidden beauty of ordinary life, not through any didactic scheme, but rather through the innate sensitivity of the artist. Our later tastes might decry these notions as mawkishly sentimental, but to Thackeray immediacy and simplicity evidently came as welcome relief from the trivial prettiness and tedium of his gallery viewing.

The Newcomes seems particularly close to Thackeray's own aesthetic preconceptions. It puts forth ideals about art, tests them, and finds them at least adequate, even successful. It is significant, then, that Thackeray worked closely with his friend Doyle on the novel's illustrations, its graphic component.[10] By this time Doyle was a well-established artist: his reputation had been made at *Punch* (his famous cover design endured for a century), and the interest in fairy mythology which led him to illustrate John Ruskin's *King of the Golden River* in 1851 and William Allingham's *In Fairyland* in 1870 is quite evident (figs. 6 and 7). J. R. Harvey has noted the strong possibility that J. J. may have been modeled on Doyle, almost certain evidence of which is the echo in J. J.'s last name, Ridley, of Doyle's signature mark, "R. D."[11] It has also been suggested that the frontispiece to the first volume, "J. J. in Dreamland" (fig. 8), is a self-portrait by Doyle.[12] But more important, it seems to me, than the simple identification of the two is the fact that in Doyle's art and character Thackeray found expression of his own ideals, proof of his own aesthetic. To base J. J. on Doyle is to acknowledge that one's ideal is practicable, that the aesthetic is workable in the actual world. For Thackeray himself, J. J.'s life must remain a fairy tale, a fiction;

CHAPTER I.

IN WHICH ONE OF THE VIRGINIANS VISITS HOME.

N the library wall of one of the most famous writers of America, there hang two crossed swords, which his relatives wore in the great War of Independence. The one sword was gallantly drawn in the service of the King, the other was the weapon of a brave and honoured Republican soldier. The possessor of the harmless trophy has earned for himself a name alike honoured in his ancestors' country and his own, where genius such as his has always a peaceful welcome.

The ensuing history reminds me of yonder swords

Fig. 9. Initial letter, *The Virginians* (London: Smith, Elder, 1884), chap. 1.

rescued from adolescent poverty by Colonel Newcome, J. J. becomes a successful, contented artist. As an Associate of the Royal Academy, J. J. can, anonymously and charitably, patronize Clive during the latter's waning fortune. But at the very end of the novel, the narrator exclaims, "Ah, happy, harmless Fable-land, where these things are!" (II.xlii). It would be presumptuous, and perhaps beside the point, to suggest that Thackeray may have envied Doyle his professional success. But it seems clear that Thackeray found in the shy Doyle the living prototype for his fictional character, and rewarded J. J. with a fairy-tale life because he realized, as did Doyle, that the real world would not recognize excellence and virtue as consistently as the novel's fiction allowed. By the time of *The Newcomes,* Doyle had resigned from

Fig. 10. "London super Mare," *The Newcomes,* I, facing p. 106.

Punch because of its antipapal position, and in later years he was destined for the social disregard that often confronts those whose fame rises quickly.[13] In Doyle, nevertheless, Thackeray seems to

Fig. 11. *The Newcomes,* I, facing p. 90.

have found living validity for his imaginative creation, and it is no coincidence that *The Newcomes* so closely coordinates text and visual image.

Samples from Thackeray's correspondence reveal how pleased he was (at times) with Doyle's illustrations: "Why, Doyle ought to bless the day that put the etching needle into his hand. . . . He does beautifully and easily what I wanted to do and can't. There are capital bits in almost all the etchings" (*Letters,* III, 362). But Thackeray was demanding as well, and he could be testy when Doyle seemed liable to miss a deadline for serial publication: "If you have not sent in an engraved title can you do one by tomorrow night . . . ? *If not I can and will"* (*Letters,* III, 384). But Doyle seems to have met most of his deadlines, either because of or despite Thackeray's suggestions and nudgings, for the two-volume novel is lavishly illustrated with his work. Doyle completed not only the usual full and half-page drawings, but witty initial letters for almost all eighty chapters as well.[14] Thackeray's taste and influence are evident here, for he too enjoyed the drollery of capital letters and their ability to foreshadow the action, as his own designs for *The Virginians* demonstrate (fig. 9).

The very quantity of illustrations in *The Newcomes* accustoms the reader to their presence. Rather than unexpected pleasures or diversions, they become integral parts of the novel, counter-pointing and expanding its movement. Doyle's drawing is finer, more precise, than Thackeray's, and his backgrounds are usually fuller; even as the drawings recede toward openness, they carry visual meaning. They repay close attention in ways that Thackeray's drawings for *Vanity Fair* do not; Doyle frequently uses space complexly as viewing angles shift from illustration to illustration and faces in crowds reveal distinct personalities (figs. 8 and 10). The general sense is of a carefully composed scene, not a snapshot. His crowd scenes continue the style that won him acclaim in *Manners and Customs of Ye Englyshe* in 1849; like most of his fairy pictures as well, the crowd scenes are filled with bustling, active social comedians, and the point of view is often from above, lending a sense of smallness, even of swarm, to the full illustrations. Many of Doyle's people, with their characteristic wasp-waists and huge eyes, are almost stylized, but the satire that informs a number of the drawings is tempered with more humor and compassion than the work of some of his contemporaries. The wonderfully detailed illustration entitled ''His Highness'' (fig. 11) both accurately renders and subtly mocks the throng of reception-goers. In the foreground, Colonel Newcome receives a salaam from the merchant Rummun Loll with remarkable aplomb, while his nephew Barnes looks on with an air of disdain. These three figures are presented with almost lifelike verisimilitude— we could almost meet them on the street. But behind them the real fun begins. In the crush are lovely admirers of the Colonel, an overweight belle with a pannier of flowers (could this be the hostess, Mrs. Newcome herself?), a short gentleman's head surfacing for air, and a gentleman with electrified hair who seems to have just had a foot trod upon. To the left of center a portly fellow eyes a Turk who, one hand on his scimitar, in turn eyes a typical Doyle beauty, while her friend impassively watches the salaam. Notice the array of hats that Doyle has included: top hats, a turban, a fez, and, far in the back, an odd pointed piece of headgear. And there is still more in the scene, from the Colonel's diamond brooch to the Indian's pointed slippers, all framed admirably by a fountain, a vase, a candelabra, marble columns, and a chandelier. To spend several minutes gazing at "His Highness" is truly to enter the world of *The Newcomes.*

Doyle's vision of *The Newcomes,* like Thackeray's, is one of gentle understanding of human folly and weakness. Pretension and vanity are exposed, but never harshly or cruelly. Again like Thackeray, Doyle usually avoids the lurid and sensational, preferring to dwell on quieter scenes of social involvement or more private emotion. Doyle's art, like the narrative itself, shuns extreme effect; instead of striving for the shock or surprise of the political cartoonist. Doyle is content to present the common and ordinary in a careful, witty manner.

This similarity of point of view suggests a carefully engineered parallelism, one that may have come easily to the two friends and was no doubt intentionally exploited. Thackeray certainly wrote with the illustrations in mind, for there are numerous instances when the "editor" Pendennis addresses the illustrator directly or calls attention to the drawings. These asides frequently come as mock instruction or playful chiding to the collaborator, and are occasionally intended as lightly humorous jabs. The first aside accompanies a description of Clive, and it captures some of the humor of Thackeray's and Doyle's friendship: ". . . and I hope the artist who illustrates this work will take care to do justice to his portrait. Mr. Clive himself, let that painter be assured, will not be too well pleased if his countenance and figure do not receive proper attention" (I.vi). Mr. Clive, it is clear, would not be alone. The operative fiction, of course, is that Clive does indeed exist in the real world; after all, this is the "history" of the Newcomes. Thackeray thinks here in visual terms, translating the imaginary and intangible character into something visible to the reader's imagination, asking it both to conceive and perceive. Only in this way can the metaphor of "sketching a character," used through-

Fig. 12. "A meeting in Rhineland." *The Newcomes,* I, facing p. 317.

out the novel, have any meaning. The figure of speech must have
come instinctively to Thackeray, with his own drawing ability and
his intense involvement with his characters. When he says, ''I

Fig. 13. *The Newcomes,* I, facing p. 121.

Fig. 14. "How 'Boy' said 'Our Father'," *The Newcomes,* II, facing p. 444.

Fig. 15. "The Letter," *The Newcomes,* II, facing p. 234.

know the people utterly—I know the sound of their voices,"[15] we must believe him, for he has clearly seen them already.

In the novel Thackeray often word-paints his way through landscapes, crowds, and drawing rooms with an artist's eye for detail and color. He gives his painter characters this same eye and puts it to good narrative use. When Clive and J. J. unexpectedly meet Ethel on a mountain trail in Germany, for example, Clive assumes that the reader is as interested in her as he is, and grants us a full "portrait":

> Then came . . . Ethel on donkey back . . with a bunch of wild
> flowers in her hand, a great straw hat with a crimson ribbon,
> a white muslin jacket . . . and a dark skirt, with a shawl round
> her feet. . . . As she stopped. . . . the trees there chequered her
> white dress and face with shadow. Her eyes, hair, and
> forehead were in shadow too—but the light was all upon her
> right cheek: upon her shoulder down to her arm, which was
> of a warmer white, and on the bunch of flowers which she
> held, blue, yellow, and red poppies, and so forth.   (I.xxvii)

Although we may heave a sigh of relief at the "and so forth," the
scene is obviously a visual composition, created with a lover's
unfailing attention. The thorough description not only speaks for
Clive's ardor, but also frees Doyle from reproducing this key
scene in a strictly mimetic way (fig. 12). Since we have already
been presented with it visually in the text, Doyle, instead of
repeating Thackeray's exact effect by rendering Ethel in detail, is
able to shift the emphasis to the young men's astonishment and
elation and thus to counterpoint and expand the scene for the
reader/viewer. Thus, Thackeray's own eye for detail frees the
illustrator from slavish reproduction and allows the picture to
assume a complex relation to the text, a relation that goes beyond
simple illustrative definition.

For another example, we might take the illustration titled
"Ethel" (fig. 13). Here the subject, the thematic center of the
drawing, is at the left, her eyes downcast as she concentrates on
her Sunday-school text; she is not at all centered on the page. This
is exactly as Thackeray has "seen" it, but in this case he has not
described the setting in any of the detail provided by the
illustration. Rich and undereducated, Ethel is in the process of
discovering that the "rosy little children" of eight, with "their
fair flaxen heads and pretty faces," are better educated than she, a
girl in her teens (I.x). She is *not* one of them and is separated by
her wealth; note her stylish bonnet and elaborate dress. Doyle has
laid out the scene perfectly: his spatial arrangement develops from
the emotions and psychology of the character. We look first at the
little children, then follow their eyes to Ethel, older, different.
Note also that Doyle has balanced the picture, both graphically
and thematically: at the far right is another older girl, simply
dressed, comfortably reading. Is this a more modest Ethel, the

person she is destined to become in the novel? And yet Doyle has done all this quietly, softly, without blocking out his space rigidly or mechanically. He also manages, in passing, a faithful reproduction of a mid-century Sunday school. Whereas Thackeray merely mentions the setting in a word or two. Doyle allows us to see it, to see the groups of children clustered around their tutors, and even we, at our distance in time, comprehend it instantly. Here, background and detail provide what the text does not; it is a rich illustration, a full and complicated rendering of the textual idea. The complex effects of "A Meeting in Rhineland" and "Ethel" are repeated in other illustrations in the novel and are one of the primary reasons for the enduring appeal of Doyle's drawings.

But not all of Doyle's work for *The Newcomes* possesses such fullness. In some instances he seems to have borrowed Thackeray's technique of focusing strongly on the human actors while leaving backgrounds scantily sketched (fig. 14); in others, there is no effort to reproduce background, as realism gives way to a selective rhetorical emphasis on the illustrated action (fig. 15). Such illustrations remove the action being depicted from a sense of depth and place and allow it to hang suspended in the reader/viewer's undivided visual attention. In *Vanity Fair* Thackeray obliterates background to expose and emphasize character; Doyle similarly obliterates it in *The Newcomes,* but he highlights the action itself. Whereas Thackeray seems to have stopped action permanently by his snapshot technique, thus creating still life, Doyle conveys action, shows us a moment that has just ceased and that will instantaneously continue. He convinces us that his major figures will move, that they have a vitality of their own, that, for all their humor, they are convincing human beings with a credibility beyond Thackeray's meticulous, but still somehow offhanded, depictions. Thackeray shows us the typical, the characteristic pose or expression, and thereby simply corroborates the text, leaving us no choice but to assent that the characters are as we have been made to see them. Doyle's contribution to *The Newcomes* allows us to believe in the imaginative reality of the characters, to perceive the drawings, not as typical tableaux or *exempla,* but as stop-action in an ongoing process, instant pauses in lives that have pasts and futures. From a more practical point of view, it may well have been tempting for Doyle, faced with constant serial publication deadlines, to eliminate all but the essential elements of certain scenes. In any event, no matter what the impulse, the results are usually noteworthy. Because Doyle varies his approach to his subject, he sustains our interest, even amusing and surprising us here and there, as he does with the visual wit of the capital letters.

Doyle's drawings are not completely autonomous, nor do they merely reflect the narrative. They grow out of it, enlarge it, fulfill it. Like Clive and J. J., Thackeray and his illustrator share a common aesthetic, and *The Newcomes'* illustrations are at once adjuncts and extensions of the text, corollaries and integral parts of the work. The practiced and artistic eye of the novelist has released the illustrator from what could have been essentially copy-work.

In *Vanity Fair* Thackeray achieves an imaginative identity, a fusion, between text and illustration. The pictures are designed to re-view and reinforce Thackeray's conception of character as he shares his own private vision with the reader/viewer. But in *The Newcomes,* Doyle's perception of Thackeray's vision creates a more complicated balance. The vision, the way of seeing, is no longer unitary; Thackeray's verbal description releases Doyle, allowing him to complement Thackeray's own way of finding beauty and meaning in simple, ordinary aspects of life. In the one novel there is unity and reinforcement; in the other, expansion and complementarity. But in both a fine harmony results from the careful interplay of idea and image, of conception and vision.

NOTES

[1] *The Letters and Private Papers of William Makepeace Thackeray,* ed. Gordon N. Ray, 4 vols. (Cambridge: Harvard University Press, 1945–46), IV, 270.

[2] William Makepeace Thackeray, *Vanity Fair: A Novel Without a Hero,* ed. Geoffrey and Kathleen Tillotson (Boston: Houghton Mifflin, 1963), pp. 29, 88.

[3] For further discussion of the *Vanity Fair* illustrations, see Robert Colby, *Thackeray's Canvass of Humanity: An Author and His Public* (Columbus: Ohio State University Press, 1979); Jerry W. Williamson, "Thackeray's Mirror," *TSL,* 22 (1977), 133–53; Joan Stevens, "*Vanity Fair* and the London Skyline" and "Thackeray's Pictorial Capitals," *Costerus,* n.s., 2 (1974), 13–41 and 113–40; Patricia R. Sweeney,

"Thackeray's Best Illustrator," *Costerus,* n.s., 2 (1974), 83–111; J. R. Harvey, *Victorian Novelists and Their Illustrators* (New York: New York University Press, 1971); and Joan Stevens, "Thackeray's *Vanity Fair," Review of English Literature,* 6, no. 1 (January 1965), 19–38.

⁴ William Makepeace Thackeray, *The Newcomes: Memoirs of a Most Respectable Family. Edited by Arthur Pendennis, Esq.,* 2 vols. (London: Smith, Elder, 1869), I, 142. Subsequent references to this edition will be made parenthetically by volume and chapter numbers.

⁵ The similarity of these ideas to Robert Browning's "Fra Lippo Lippi" (1855) is important; see especially lines 300–11. The poem is contemporaneous with *The Newcomes* and adds significant weight to Thackeray's aesthetic argument. He was definitely working with ideas central to the Victorian debate over the purposes and utility of art. See David J. DeLaura, "The Context of Browning's Painter Poems: Aesthetics, Polemics, Historics," *PMLA,* 95 (1980), 367–88, for a thorough exposition of the intellectual circumstances surrounding the poems.

⁶ See James Anthony Froude, *Thomas Carlyle: A History of the First Forty Years of His Life, 1795–1835* (New York: Charles Scribner's Sons, 1882), 11, 7–12.

⁷ *The Complete Works of Percy Bysshe Shelley,* ed. Roger Ingpen and Walter E. Peck, VII (New York: Charles Scribner's Sons, 1930), 137.

⁸ A more deprecating view of Thackeray's treatment of this relationship is taken by Winslow Rogers, "Art and Artists in *The Newcomes," BSUF,* 19, no. 1 (Winter 1978), 35–40.

⁹ William Makepeace Thackeray, "The Exhibitions of the Royal Academy," *Contributions to the "Morning Chronicle,"* ed. Gordon N. Ray (Urbana: University of Illinois Press, 1955), p. 145.

¹⁰ Thackeray's reasons for declining to illustrate the novel are outlined by Anthony Burton, "Thackeray's Collaborations with Cruikshank, Doyle, and Walker," *Costeras,* n.s., 2 (1974), 155–56. Burton notes that Thackeray also provided Doyle with rough sketches of some of the illustrations, Burton tends to see the collaboration from a more technical point of view than I do.

¹¹ Harvey, p. 95. Viola Hopkins Winner also makes this suggestion in "Thackeray and Richard Doyle, the 'Wayward Artist' of *The Newcomes," III.B.* 26 (1978), 193–211.

¹² Susan Dean, comp., *Victorian Illustrated Literature: A Catalogue of an Exhibition at the Newberry Library, Winter 1976* (Chicago: Newberry Library, 1976), p. 19.

¹³ Daria Hambourg, *Richard Doyle: His Life and Work* (London: Art and Technics, 1948), p. 28.

¹⁴ Edgar F. Harden, "The Artistry of a Serial Novelist: Parts 10, 14, and 15 of *The Newcomes," SEL,* 16 (1976), 622, contends that Doyle's

capitals were often designed to fill up page space rather than to perform an integral function in the development of the novel. Winner examines the history of the collaboration in detail and corroborates a number of the ideas of the present study. She finds, however, that a disposition in Doyle "to find beauty wherever he looked" both detracts from his ability to portray "circumstantial realism" and minimizes Thackeray's "social indictments" (p. 211). Such a view completely ignores the reforming power of beauty and the artist's vision which is at the heart of Thackeray's rendering of J. J.

15 "De Finibus," *Roundabout Papers* (London: Smith, Elder, 1869), p. 277.

THE ART OF NOT "GOING HALFWAY": ROSSETTI'S ILLUSTRATION FOR "THE MAIDS OF ELFEN-MERE"
Allan R. Life

Considering the prevalence of interdisciplinary approaches to Rossetti, his book illustrations have received surprisingly little attention. In Rossetti's designs for William Allingham's *The Music Master* (1855), Tennyson's *Poems* (1857), and his sister's *Goblin Market* (1862) and *The Prince's Progress* (1866), the literary basis of much of his visual art is manifested in the juxtaposition of pictures and texts. As abundant documentation attests, Rossetti incorporated as much "fundamental brainwork" into these illustrations as into any of his works. Nor is this fact remarkable, considering this artist's aversion to exhibiting. As he labored on his illustration for *The Music Master,* he reflected that "it is a book which everyone will be sure to see." The specter of the Dalziel Brothers, whose firm would engrave the drawing, consequently haunted him, and he spoke of impressing upon Allingham's publishers "that there was a reputation of some sort in some quarters that I had to take care of" (DW 190).

Far from damaging Rossetti's reputation, the Dalziel's rendering of his design for Allingham's "The Maids of Elfen-Mere" extended his fame, and soon after his presence, into the circle headed by William Morris and Edward Burne-Jones. The circumstances leading to these results are well known, and so indeed is the ironic prelude: the abuse poured by Rossetti upon "that—thing of—Dalziel's," which at first he refused to publish and ultimately tore from his copy of *The Music Master* (see DW 206). What remain to be explored are the formal and interpretive qualities of this supposed abomination. Rossetti himself has

Reprinted with permission from *Victorian Poetry,* 20 (Autumn/Winter 1982), pp. 65–87.

provided guidance for this enquiry, for it was during the preparation and immediately following the completion of the "Elfen-Mere" design that he articulated his basic approach to illustration. This paper will clarify that approach and show how it is exemplified in the relationship between Rossetti's design and Allingham's poem. First, however, it should be noted how Rossetti came to undertake this commission, for this documentation in itself suggests the unique place in his aesthetic assigned to book illustration during this period.

Rossetti's conception of book illustration is implicit in his letter to Allingham on July 23, 1854 (DW 177). Here, Rossetti promises "to join [Arthur] Hughes in at any rate one of the illustrations of *Day and Night Songs,*" a collection of Allingham's poems published by Routledge about a year later as *The Music Master, A Love Story. And Two Series of Day and Night Songs.* Significantly, this assurance is preceded by an eruption of literary enthusiasm. The professional painter who had declared two years before that "I have abandoned poetry" (DW 78), and who since then had confessed to only vestigial literary activity, suddenly speaks of publishing "as soon as possible" his translations of early Italian poetry, and leaves little doubt that he intends to civilize the "aboriginal state" of his original poems. As a specimen of his current writing, Rossetti includes the first version of "Lost on Both Sides," a sonnet related to a confession in his next letter to Allingham: "I believe my poetry and painting prevented each other from doing much good for a long while— and now I think I could do better in either, but can't write, for then I sha'n't paint" (DW 180). In fact, his previous letter contains not a single reference to painting. Yet besides offering to contribute to *The Music Master,* it also reports Macmillan's desire to "propose to Millais, Hunt, and me to illustrate a life of Christ" and suggests that this publisher might consider a collection of ballads Allingham had been editing, and which Rossetti and Elizabeth Siddal had begun to illustrate.[1] Even his plans for his translations implicitly relate to illustration: he only relinquished the idea of preparing at least one etching for *The Early Italian Poets* when the book had actually appeared in 1861. Also revealing is the leap in Rossetti's next letter to Allingham from his melancholy reflections on conflicting arts to his jubilation at a "capital" "plan of a joint volume among us of poems and pictures" (DW 180).

It seems that, for Rossetti during this period, book illustration could reconcile the creative processes underlying his painting and his poetry. On the face of it, this proposition is dubious enough, since a painting like *The First Anniversary of the Death of Beatrice* (S. 58), which Rossetti finished early in 1854, is as literary in content as his design for Allingham's poem. But although these works may seem to be similarly illustrative, they do differ in the sense that the Dante picture is divorced physically from its literary source. And this circumstance limits further the communicative potential of a painting that, as Rossetti informed its first owner Francis MacCracken, invests a scene in the *Vita Nuova* with "notions of my own . . . which would only be cared about by one to whom Dante was a chief study" (DW 172). This hardly applied to MacCracken or to most of the other merchant patrons he heralded; as Rossetti declared in 1866, "it is pleasanter sending a poetic work where it will be seen by cultivated folks than to a cotton-spinner or a dealer" (DW 683). By illustrating an author like Allingham, Rossetti could juxtapose his art with the text that inspired it, in a volume that would be seen by "everyone" whose sensibility he valued. In the process, he could enhance literature he admired, while achieving the publication for his visual art that he was contemplating with wavering assurance for his own poetry. To some degree, book illustration conformed to Rossetti's notion of "poetic" art: his desire, expressed in a letter to Patmore, "to do for painting, as far as possible, what you and a very few more poets are doing now for poetry" (DW 225); his sense, Neo-Platonically epitomized in one of his notebooks, that "picture and poem bear the same relation to each other as beauty does in man and woman: the point of meeting where the two are most identical is the supreme perfection" (*Works,* p. 606). Potentially, such a synthesis could be experienced by the "cultivated" reader of a successfully illustrated book.

Admittedly, what was compelling to Rossetti in conception often proved less congenial in execution, and his abuse of the Dalziel Brothers must be weighed against his own failure to master any graphic process except lithography. In addition, there is a more profound reason for the fluctuations in Rossetti's commitment to illustration. Though in periods of literary enthusiasm he might wish to adorn a favorite author, the same literary impulse made him question the effect of illustration on the reader. He entered the *Music Master* project with the hope that Hughes' designs "and mine will both be worthy" of Allingham's poems "—else there is nothing so much spoils a good book as an attempt to embody its ideas, only going halfway" (DW 177). His obsession with this hazard continued past the completion of his drawing, for on January 30, 1855—less than a week after he had delivered the "Elfen-Mere" woodblock to Routledge—he informs Holman Hunt:

> I think illustrated editions of poets . . . quite hateful things, and [I] do not feel easy as an aider or abettor. I have just done one for Allingham's forthcoming volume, and know that were I a possessor of the book I should tear out the illustrations the first thing.

In the case of his own contribution, this is just what he did! Yet the circumstances of this tirade must be kept in mind. A few days before he wrote to Hunt, Rossetti was invited to contribute to Moxon's illustrated Tennyson by the publisher himself, who lent him a copy of the *Poems* in which works were already assigned to various artists. "What do you think?" Rossetti asks Allingham on January 23. "Stanfield is to do *Break, break,* because there is the sea in it, and *Ulysses,* too, because there are ships" (DW 196). Still more exasperating was the discovery that "all the most practicable subjects have been given away already" (DW 194). In his letter to Holman Hunt, he laments that he "can find few direct subjects left . . . , and shall probably do *Vision of Sin, Palace of Art,* and things of that sort . . . ." His denunciation of illustrated editions follows, but suddenly a different note is struck. Confessing that "I have long had an idea for illustrating the last verse of *Lady of Shalott,* which I see marked to you," Rossetti inquires: "Is that a part you mean to do, and if not and you have *only* one design in prospect to the poem, could I do another?"[2] When he returned to England over a year later, Hunt found Rossetti still complaining that "all the best subjects were now taken" for the illustrated Tennyson. When Hunt cited "The Palace of Art" among the poems still available. Rossetti declared that "what he had wanted was the 'Lady of Shalott'." And Hunt maintains that it was only when he surrendered the conclusion of this poem that Rossetti "was . . . persuaded to see Moxon with a view of embarking on his work."[3]

It was during his initial discontent with the Tennyson project that Rossetti sent Allingham his central pronouncement on illustration:

> I . . . fancy I shall try the *Vision of Sin* and *Palace of Art,* etc.—those where one can allegorize on one's own hook on the subject of the poem, without killing, for oneself and everyone, a distinct idea of the poet's. This, I fancy, is *always* the upshot of illustrated editions,—Tennyson, Allingham, or anyone,—unless where the poetry is so absolutely narrative as in the old ballads, for instance. . . . There are one or two or more of Tennyson's in narrative,— but generally the worst, I think,—*Lady Clare, Lord of Burleigh,* to wit. (DW 196)

According to every critic who has quoted from this passage, "allegorize on one's own hook" epitomizes Rossetti's conception of illustration, and is synonymous with unrestricted interpretive license. This reading in fact is wrong on both counts. Rossetti intends to employ this method in illustrating—not *all* literary works, but "the *Vision of Sin* and *Palace of Art,* etc." The second poem, in particular, is about as close as Tennyson comes to traditional allegory, in which interrelated concepts are symbolized within a sequential narrative. To adopt the terms employed by Angus Fletcher in *Allegory* (1964), what Rossetti evidently proposes is to embody the tenor or the "primary" meaning of such poems in a "secondary" vehicle which is distinct from that employed by the poet. Thus, in illustrating "The Palace of Art" in Moxon's edition, Rossetti does not compete with Tennyson's description of the soul's experiences; instead, he portrays two of the pictures described in the fourth section of the poem. And, though the precise relationship between these designs and the primary meaning or "subject" of "The Palace of Art" cannot be explored in this paper, Rossetti's intention to "allegorize on one's own hook" cannot sanction obliviousness to the literary content of these illustrations. "Allegorize" corresponds here with the standard intransitive usage: "to give allegoric explanations, to expound allegorically" (*NED*), in this case "on the subject of the poem." As for "one's own hook," this is Eric Partridge's definition: "on one's own account, at one's own risk and/or responsibility."[4] These definitions are perfectly consistent with embodying the tenor of the "sort of allegory" that Tennyson achieves in "The Palace of Art."

As his reluctance to undertake "The Palace of Art" suggests, however, and as his other contributions to the Moxon *Tennyson* confirm, Rossetti's approach to this poem is not typical of his work as an illustrator. His designs for "Sir Galahad" and "Mariana in the South" depict the protagonists in central scenes from these poems, while his illustration for the last stanza of "The Lady of Shalott" shows Lancelot "musing" upon the Lady amid the fearful citizens of Camelot. That all these designs transcend through formal and iconographic means the events they portray does not discount their relevance to these events. And this fact reflects this illustrator's characteristic procedure: the portrayal of a concrete narrative situation—a "direct subject," to adapt his language to Hunt—through which he epitomizes his reading of an entire literary source. Similar interpretations of central narrative events are effected in such pictures as *The First Anniversary of the Death of Beatrice* and "Hamlet and Ophelia" (S. 108), an elaborate drawing "so treated as I think to embody and symbolize the play without obtrusiveness or interference with the subject *as a subject*" (DW 186). By contrast, "going halfway" in illustration means divorcing literary imagery from its emotional and figurative context. This is the kind of failing Rossetti expected from Clarkson Stanfield, who in the Moxon *Tennyson* treats the sea in "Break, break, break" and the ship at the conclusion of "Ulysses" as picturesque motifs, dependent on the accompanying texts for what little iconographic meaning they possess.

In theory, Rossetti maintains that an illustrator is least likely to go halfway when treating poetry that is "absolutely narrative as in the old ballads, for instance." In practice, however, he was most readily inspired by poems like his first choice from Tennyson, "The Lady of Shalott." If "this tale of magic 'symbolism'," as Hallam Tennyson calls it,[5] is not a consistent allegory, it is as far from being "absolutely narrative" as Rossetti's tailpiece in Moxon's edition, which, like the final stanza, portrays a temporal encounter between the miraculous and the mundane. Perhaps it was a vaguely comparable situation in one of Allingham's ballads that ignited Rossetti's equally strong desire to illustrate that poem. No sooner has Rossetti offered to contribute to his friend's volume than he inquires: "Is *Saint Margaret's Eve* to be in? That would be illustratable" (DW 177). His preference for his ballad is maintained even when he has read "The Maids of Elfen-Mere," and he repudiates illustrating it only after several weeks (see DW 180, 186). "St. Margaret's Eve" (*MM*, p. 161) tells of the visit paid to the narrator's castle by "a fair lady" holding a gold cup "full of wine": "Drink, said the lady, and I will be thine." But no sooner has the narrator proclaimed his love and lamented, "I know not how to woo," than "down dash'd the cup, with a sudden shock, . . ./ The wine like blood ran over the rock," and the lady "vanish'd" with a shriek. To the extent that this plot can be extracted from it, the ballad can be called a "narrative." What is less certain is that it affords the kind of "direct subject" that Rossetti sought for illustration. Depicting the encounter between the narrator and the lady would be almost inescapable, yet in the process the illustration would clash with the elliptical presentation which reinforces the erotic allusiveness of the ballad. Perhaps Allingham himself felt such misgivings, for when he sent Rossetti a copy of "St. Margaret's Eve" he actually proposed a subject from a second ballad, "The Maids of Elfen-Mere." Presumably, the version of the second poem he provided is the same that was to appear with Rossetti's engraving (*MM*, p. 202):

> 'Twas when the spinning-room was here,
> There came Three Damsels clothed in white,
> With their spindles every night;
> Two and one, and Three fair Maidens,
> Spinning to a pulsing cadence,
> Singing songs of Elfen-Mere;
> Till the eleventh hour was toll'd,
> Then departed through the wold.
> *Years ago, and years ago;*
> *And the tall reeds sigh as the wind doth blow.*
>
> Three white Lilies, calm and clear,
> And they were loved by every one;
> Most of all, the Pastor's Son,
> Listening to their gentle singing,
> Felt his heart go from him, clinging
> Round these Maids of Elfen-Mere;
> Sued each night to make them stay.
> Sadden'd when they went away.

In the third stanza, the Pastor's Son delays the departure of the Maidens by setting back the village clock; when "the false 'eleven' " sounds, the visitors depart "like three doves on snowy plume."

> One that night who wander'd near
> Heard lamentings by the shore,
> Saw at dawn three stains of gore
> In the waters fade and dwindle.
> Nevermore with song and spindle
> Saw we Maids of Elfen-Mere.

As for the Pastor's Son, he "did pine and die; / Because," the narrator explains, "true love should never lie."

After receiving this ballad, Rossetti assures Allingham of its "many beauties, . . .—indeed, [it] is all beautiful, except, I think, the last couplet, which seems a trifle *too* homely,—a little in the broadsheet-song style." He then pronounces "first-rate" the subject from the poem proposed by Allingham and adds, "I have already made some scratches for its arrangement" (DW 180). Allingham's letters to Rossetti are unfortunately lost, but he probably asked his friend to portray the night when the Pastor's Son delays the Maids' departure. The brooding aspect of the youth in the engraving (Plate 6) encourages this hypothesis, and so does the clock in the upper-left corner, which reads 10:46 in the mirror image corresponding to Rossetti's design on the woodblock. In this same mirror image the crescent in the upper-right corner resembles the moon's twenty-fourth phase, which rises about two in the morning. Could Rossetti, amid his eleventh-hour exertions to complete this design, have forgotten to draw these motifs in reverse? Few mistakes could be more ironic, for it was his initial failure to portray the Maids spinning left-handed that led to a "second edition" of the block (see DW 187, 196). Yet additional evidence that he did forget is found in a study for the design (S. 67A; Plate 7), where the Maids are left-handed and where the clock, if reversed by engraving and printing, would be nearing midnight.

Perhaps the very concreteness of the youth's situation aroused Rossetti's fears of "going halfway," of visualizing the narrative to the detriment of the symbolic. As late as September 19 he is still

PLATE 6

PLATE 7

doubtfully committed to this subject even as he ventures that his first sketch "would come nice" (DW 186). By the following January, however, Rossetti had created a design which on every level is "worthy" of its source. This success is scarcely surprising, for "The Maids of Elfen-Mere" shares with "The Lady of Shalott" the conjunction of the supernatural and the mortal, portrayed within a narrative that lacks the definitive metaphysical context of an allegory like "The Palace of Art." As he seeks to transcend the mundane perspective of Allingham's narrator, the reader draws on associations of a kind that Rossetti had ready to hand. From the first, Rossetti found the plot tantalizingly familiar: after beginning his design he asks Allingham if the poem is "founded on some Northern legend or other [.] I seem to have read something about it in Keightley or somewhere" (DW 180). In fact, there is no story of precisely this kind in Thomas Keightley's *The Fairy Mythology,* a standard treatment of the *Romance and Superstition of Various Countries* first published in 1828 and issued in expanding editions for the next half century. However, Keightley does refer to German legends about the nixes, or water people, whose females sometimes adopt human dress and even go to market. Similar accounts of these beings are found in other works of the time, and one legend in particular may well have influenced Allingham's ballad. In his 1839 collection of Rhine traditions, Joseph Snowe tells of three strange and beautiful maidens, "garbed in white from head to heel," who dance with three youths one evening at a rural festival. "As the clock [strikes] eleven" the maidens depart, warning their partners "in mournful cadence" not to follow them. The youths disobey, and they promptly sink when they accept the nixes' invitation to trip over the surface of the river. "Three small ensanguined streaks, reaching from the centre of the stream to the shore," testify to "this dreadful catastrophe on the following morning."[6]

Though these femmes fatales are far removed from Allingham's "doves on snowy plume," they must depart at the same hour as the Maids of Elfen-Mere, and the "mournful cadence" in which they warn the youths recalls the "pulsing cadence" to which their counterparts spin. And whereas in Snowe's version the "ensanguined streaks" denote the fate of the men, the situation is reversed in a Netherlandish variant of this legend, published in 1843 as "Die drei Nixen von Jupille." Here, the three white-clad maids (*Jungfrauen*) are crowned with water lilies, and besides dancing at a village festival they further infatuate their partners with their singing. They leave abruptly— at midnight, in this version—but they return the next evening and dance again with the young men, one of whom is entrusted with his partner's gloves. When twelve sounds and she requests their return, he not only refuses but pursues her to the river Meuse, into which she and her companions disappear. The following morning the lovesick youth finds the water at this spot blood-red; the maids never return.[7]

In this version, the maiden's gloves function as passports to her supernatural realm, and the refusal to return them is signalled by the blood-red spot in the water, a profanation that in Allingham takes the more startling form of "three stains of gore." The nearest approximation in the rest of the *Music Master* volume to this imagery comes in "St. Margaret's Eve," where "the wine like blood ran over the rock." Both passages connote sexual violation; indeed, judging from other poems in the collection "violation" might be called as readily "initiation." There is a notable tension in Allingham's volume between yearning for ideal women and extolling virginal innocence, and the aftermath of sexual consummation in these works is generally disastrous. "The Girl's Lamentation" (*MM*, p. 171) is uttered by a betrayed woman who has contemplated suicide "in the stream below"; "Lady Alice" (*MM*, p. 64) presents the bleakest possible sequel to "The Eve of St. Agnes," with the heroine appearing in rags at her father's funeral, where "like a statue built of snow, [she] sinks down upon the ground." This metaphor for blasted innocence, like the sanguinary "wine" and the "stains of gore," reinforces an ambivalence in the volume towards not merely sexual initiation but the onset of puberty, especially in women. But not only in women: in "The Witch-Bride" (*MM*, p. 72) a young man is impeded by the "foul" spouse of the title in his quest for the "snowy light" of an ideal "Shape." Elsewhere the search for the elusive ideal itself is questioned; "Therania" (*MM*, p. 67) concludes with the enquiry so often reiterated by the Pre-Raphaelites: "Art thou Love indeed, or art thou Death, / O Unknown Belov'd One?"

Poems like "Therania" recall "Love's Nocturn," which in *Works* is dated 1854. According to Rossetti himself, "the first conception of this poem was of a man not yet in love who dreams vaguely of a woman who he thinks must exist for him" (DW 869). In Allingham, however, the yearning for the ideal woman is at times so "vague" as to be indistinguishable from the vaporous mysticism that he often associates with music: with the Aeolian harp; with the "harmony of words" through which "may murmur the harmony of things" (*MM*, p. [x]); above all with the "endless tune" of "Day and Night and Day" (*MM,* p. 23) alluded to in the subtitle of the volume. Cumulatively, such references evoke the melodious cosmic force which Rossetti had already epitomized in "The Sea-Limits" (*Works,* p. 191).

Within the "pulsing cadence" to which the Maidens spin, this same "harmony of things" seems to be supernaturally embodied. An equally profound significance is implicit in the act of spinning itself, which though rarely associated with water spirits is an attribute of their equivalents on land. In this, as in their prophetic powers, the fairies of legend recall the three Parcae or Fates; indeed, the Latin plural *fata* probably gave rise in popular Latin to the feminine singular *fata* or "fairy." The mythical and etymological associations between the Parcae and the fays are outlined by Keightley,[8] and even without such guidance Rossetti would have recognized this connection through his fluency in Italian. Read in this context, "when the spinning-room was here" denotes a time when men could still be enlightened by embodiments of occult revelation. And embodiments, furthermore, of a distinctly sacramental kind: the enumeration of the Maidens ("Two and one, and Three") is resonantly Trinitarian, while their metaphorical status as "doves" and "Lilies" reinforces the Christian dimension of their chastity.

These associations clarify the situation of the Pastor's Son, who is trying to prolong his contact with three intermediaries between the temporal sphere and a supernatural one that seems infused with the essence of the natural world. In their presence he experiences an amorous ecstasy that combines the ideal and the erotic sides of Allingham's mysticism. Presumably, he finds in the Maidens and their singing a wisdom that transcends that of his father's religion, but it is his heart that clings "round these Maids of Elfen-Mere." When he tampers with the temporal measure to which the Maids submit, he perpetrates a "lie" with connotations of sacrilege, for the "eleventh hour" recalls not only the parable of the laborers in the vineyard (Matt. 20.1–16) but another parable inevitably associated with it, that of the wise and foolish virgins (Matt. 25.1–13). The question indeed is whether the true equivalent of the foolish virgins is the Maidens, or the Pastor's Son whose violation of "true Love" is blazoned in the light of dawn. It is after all the youths in the legend related by Snowe whose fates are denoted by ensanguined streaks, and in numerous tales collected by such authorities as Keightley and the Grimms equally terrible punishments befall intruders into what the manuscript of "Love's Nocturn" terms "unpermitted Eden" (DW 869, p. 739, n. 2).

For an illustrator like Rossetti intent on not "going halfway," the subject that Allingham evidently proposed from "The Maids of Elfen-Mere" presents a formidable challenge. The artist must suggest the ontological difference between the Pastor's Son and the Maids without diminishing either the corporeality of these "Lilies" or the reality of the temporal moment he is portraying. For guidance in treating such a subject Rossetti could turn to Dürer and the Early Netherlandish painters, and also to several modern illustrators whose works exemplify various solutions to similar interpretive problems. Some of these artists adhered to the "outline school" associated with John Flaxman, which bounded natural and supernatural motifs with identical linear contours, and replaced illusionistic space with extensive white grounds. One follower of this school, David Scott, produced etchings for *The Rime of the Ancient Mariner* (1837) which Rossetti lauded in 1850 for being "in the truest Coleridgean vein" (*AN*, 2, 284). In his portrayal of the scene after the Mariner has shot the Albatross (Plate 8), Scott suggests the symbolic importance of the event by contrasting the frontal attitude of the mariner with the contorted poses of his shipmates—poses which accentuate not only their gestures but also the planar nature of a composition in which figures are disposed for thematic as much as for pictorial effect.

Though he experimented with this "outline" method, Rossetti by the fifties (see "Gallery," Plate 32) had abandoned it for a more painterly rendering of chiaroscuro. But the kind of symbolic compositions employed by David Scott continued to fascinate him. Other styles of book illustration must have encouraged this orientation; particularly interesting, given the subject of Allingham's poem, is one of the engravings in an 1843 edition of *Der Nibelungen Noth* that Rossetti knew well in the mid-forties (Plate 9).[9] Here, Schnorr von Carolsfeld employs the same emphatic contours and shading for the human (Hagen) and the daemonic (the Rhine maidens). The only formal distinction between the mundane and the subterranean realms is achieved through the composition, in which the frontal plane is accentuated by botanical motifs and by the accompanying typography. For a vertical

ieweile hatte Hagen
Den Schaz viel gar genommen,
Eh' der reiche König
Wieder war gekommen;
Er senkte ihn zu Loche
Allen in den Rhein.
Er wähnte sein zu genießen;
Das sollt' ihm nicht beschieden seyn.

Die Fürsten kamen wieder,
Mit ihnen viele Mannen;
Kriemhild mit Frauen und Mägden
Zu klagen da begannen
Ihren großen Schaden;
Ihnen war bitter leid.
Gerne wär' Giselher
Zu allen Treuen ihr bereit.

Da sprachen sie in Gleichem:
„Er hat viel übel gethan."
Er entwich der Fürsten Zorne,
Bis wieder er gewann

PLATE 8

PLATE 9

version of the horizontal bisecting of Schnorr's illustration, Rossetti could turn to a design by a still more naturalistic artist, Tony Johannot. In one of his bizarre inventions in *Voyage ou Il Voùs Plaira* (Plate 10), a volume Rossetti purchased a few months after its appearance in 1843 (see DW 18, p. 23, n. 5;20), Johannot invests not only the figure of a dreamer but also the "interminable procession de graves personnages" of his nightmare with a concreteness that approaches the visionary.

Rossetti employs a composition reminiscent of Johannot's in one of his drawings illustrating "The Raven" (S. 19A; Plate 11).[10] Here, the speaker yearns towards the procession of angelic spirits, or rather towards that one among them whose name reverberates through Poe's lyric. And though the angels are evanescent compared to Johannot's monumental grotesques, Rossetti might well have increased their solidity had he completed his drawing. Certainly, his canvases of *The Girlhood of Mary Virgin* (S. 40) and *Ecce Ancilla Domini!* (S. 44) manifest his willingness to invest angelic figures with full corporeality.

It is hardly surprising, therefore, that in his study for the "Elfen-Mere" illustration (Plate 7) Rossetti portrays the Maids with considerable naturalism. The ragged contours and the painterly hatchings of their gowns make these figures almost as kinetic as those in the "Raven" design. The youth seems by comparison static, and the dark shading on his figure has metaphorical undertones of brooding and guilt. By partially superimposing this figure upon those of two of the Maids, Rossetti adopts a more daring composition for such a subject than that of "The Raven." And whereas the protagonist in the Poe design gazes at his vision, the youth here looks downward and even inward, as though the figures behind him were projections of his own psyche. Reflection, however, cannot sustain such a reading of this design, in part because of the very success with which Rossetti has suggested a momentary interaction between corporeal figures. Though the youth's pose is essentially a seated version of the anguished man's in *Found* (S. 64), it has almost a casual quality, and the shadow sweeping across his torso is a naturalistic rendering of back-lighting. As for the Maids, their gestures are too animated and their expressions are too variable to invest this design with the monumentality demanded not only by this figurative reading but by the narrative level of the literary source.

PLATE 10

PLATE 11

Admittedly, these limitations of the study seem obvious because they have been eliminated in the final version of Rossetti's design. Yet this statement itself requires a further admission: we do not have what Rossetti considered his "final version," which was engraved in the Dalziels' workshop. It arrived there, furthermore, in a state the engravers never forgot: "Rossetti made use of wash, pencil, coloured chalk, and pen and ink, producing a very nice effect, but the engraved reproduction of this many tinted drawing . . . failed to satisfy him."[11] This reminiscence illuminates Rossetti's protest against the engraver's "stupid preconceived notion . . . about intended 'severity' in the design." He further laments that "the human character" of his drawing had yielded to an "oyster and goldfish cast of features" (DW 198, 199). These and related blemishes he attempted to correct through directions to the Dalziels, and though he despaired of making the engraving a literal facsimile of his drawing, the published version of the print (Plate 6) hardly conforms to his description of its first state: "as hard as a nail, and yet flabby and vapid to the last degree' (DW 198). For one thing, the basic forms of the figures testify to the careful drawing "from nature" that Rossetti invested in them (see DW 190). Note for example the hands of the Maids, whose every fingernail is accurately delineated. In their poses and their setting, furthermore, all four figures correspond so precisely to the narrative level of Allingham's ballad that at first sight the engraving can be accepted as a naturalistic representation of the crisis of the poem.

But only at first sight. When the viewer relates the individual motifs to the structuring forms of the work, he encounters intrusions on a literal reading of the picture for which the artist alone could be responsible. Though Rossetti's figures are more naturalistic than those in Johannot's illustration, they are disposed in a composition which recalls David Scott's in its fragmented spatial units and its unnatural symmetry. Symmetry is in fact the most striking characteristic of the design: the vertical center of the composition passes through the form of the middle Maiden, and her fellow spinners stand equidistant from her on the wings of a platform. Diagonally crossing these figures is the youth, his body twisted in a partial *contrapposto* rendering it parallel to the frontal plane, the crown of his head virtually touching the horizontal center of the composition. Instead of recalling that of the lover in

Found, his pose now parallels that of a young mariner in David Scott's etching, gazing horrorstruck at the Albatross whose murder he will soon enough condone. Even more than that of Scott's mariner, the figure of the Pastor's Son constitutes a triangular configuration that reinforces the symmetry of the design, which is further emphasized by the schematic interior of the spinning-room. It is this interior, too, which alerts the viewer to the unnaturalistic rendering of space throughout the picture. As even a casual examination of their angles shows, the borders of the side windows have divergent focal points, and the floorboards also violate linear perspective. Though suggesting three-dimensional space was not Rossetti's forte, his study for the design is more consistently related than the engraving to a single stationary viewpoint. Perhaps his most glaring deviation from this principle is found in the prospect of the town, which would not be visible through windows viewed from the kneeling position suggested by their variable perspective. Like the figures of the Maids and the youth, furthermore, the town and its clock tower are devoid of vertical recession.

Combined with this unnaturalistic treatment of space is a complex disposition of light and dark within the design. In good impressions of the engraving, the print is diffused with subtly modulated illumination—an effect which must have been more apparent in Rossetti's tinted original but which the engraver has translated into the parallel flecks of white that crisscross the otherwise black areas of the work. The highlights on the robes and faces of the Maidens remain, nevertheless, preternaturally brilliant, and this quality is reinforced when one seeks the source of this illumination.There are as many possible light sources as there are focal points in the design: a lamp could, for example, be placed on the floor to the left of the figures or, alternatively, be suspended from the ceiling above them. But no single light source could account for the illumination within the engraving, which, as much as the disposition of motifs, violates naturalistic presentation.

Through this subtle tension between naturalistic form and unnaturalistic composition and chiaroscuro, Rossetti suggests the youth's incomplete and mutually destructive relationship with the Maids. For the figure of the Pastor's Son seems confined within the lower half of a design where his form is partially superimposed upon those of his companions, not integrated with them in terms of natural space. His torso, furthermore, is restricted almost entirely to the left side of the composition. By contrast, the Maidens not only are disposed laterally across the picture, they seem also enshrined within a niche whose openings encapsulate symbols of human time (the clock) and natural time (the moon). Behind the clock tower are shapes suggesting the domes of a basilica; further to the right a Norman tower ascends above the left Maiden. As the verticality of the form of this Maiden emphasizes, the symbols of mortal time and institutions are directly above the Pastor's Son, who therefore occupies what can be considered the mundane side of the composition. To a notable extent, Rossetti has united the horizontal division found in Schnorr's illustration with the vertical cleaving employed in Johannot's design and in his own "Raven" drawing. Both the vertical and the horizontal divisions of this illustration suggest the spiritual gulf between the Pastor's Son and the Maids.

Yet it is equally true that the form of the Pastor's Son does touch those of all three Maids, not just of two of them, as in the study. And this fact signals that the gulf between the youth and his companions may be less wide and less definitive than has so far been suggested. A similar implication can be found in the images flanking the Maids. Through the disposition of the clock and the moon, Rossetti may be indicating that the Maids owe their temporal existence to their own suspension between the forces symbolized by these images, which they therefore succeed in reconciling. But it has already been ventured that Rossetti intended to draw a waning moon in the right window, and this image would signal the imminent end of this reconciliation. A waning crescent would be, furthermore, an ominous image here: the energy of elves and kindred spirits is considered proportional to the fullness of the moon, and since the waters are subject to lunar control, the Maids of Elfen-Mere would be especially susceptible to such influence. Equally significant in this context is the association of the moon with chastity and with the feminine principle in general.

In both his conception and his rendering of the Maids, indeed, Rossetti does more than visualize the whiteness, the calmness and clarity, that Allingham attributes to these figures. With their tresses cascading over their shoulders and their long necks bent forward, with their heavy lids drooping and their lips half apart, they appear absorbed in a trance that is distinctly sensual. And the unnaturalistic illumination in the design supports this impression: foiling the white areas of their robes are linear shadows that are ominously substantial compared with the painterly hatchings in the study. The fact that this shadow is most prevalent on the head and torso of the left-hand Maiden both reinforces the sense of the greater temporalness of this side of the composition and relates the shading on all three Maids to the dark form of the youth beneath her. Given the connotations of whiteness in the poem, this vivid chiaroscuro parallels the transition in the ballad from images of Lilies and doves to stains of gore. Rossetti even seems to have anticipated this conclusion with the shadows in the water beneath the moon.

As in the study, the youth's form is heavily shaded, but here too Rossetti's hatchings have increased in both solidity and metaphorical ambiguity. The flecks of white crossing his form in the engraving confer on the Pastor's Son a distinct luminescence, and this impression is reinforced by the brilliant highlights on his face and hair. With his rapt expression and his metallic locks flowing into fiery curls, he seems both inspired and satanic. To accentuate this duality, Rossetti has apparently indulged in a visual pun; flanking the head of the youth are two spindles, hovering like emblems of divine inspiration or, alternatively, of demonic possession.

The unnaturalistic disposition of the youth's form across those of the Maidens and the ambivalent portrayal of all four figures encourage a figurative reading of the design that the study for the engraving could not sustain. This reading posits that the Maids are embodiments of the youth's psyche, or more specifically of a tension within that psyche between the ideal and the sensual. The darkness of the spindle to the left of his head and the comparative lightness of the one to the right accord with this interpretation. And there is a further dimension to this reading: one that also informs much of the aspiration toward an ideal beloved in Allingham as well as in Rossetti. This concerns the Neo-Platonic doctrine of the soul mate which Rossetti epitomizes in the sonnet, later entitled ''The Birth-Bond,'' which he composed as he began the ''Elfen-Mere'' design (see DW 180). Admittedly, there are three Maidens in his illustration, but these Maidens resemble a single figure reflected in a triptych mirror. As he had already intimated in his poem "The Mirror" (*Works,* p. 194), Rossetti was fascinated with the idea that the image of a man's soul mate could reflect his own spiritual identity, and a triple image of the female paragon affords a resonant extension of this concept. It also serves to extend and clarify the predicament of the Pastor's Son, who in this reading must decide whether chastely to adore the tripartite ideal in her moments of incarnation, or through deception to pull her from her niche into the world which in Allingham is often the scene of profanation, and in Rossetti has been termed by one critic "the hell of love."[12]

One final implication of this reading is suggested by a famous entry in Madox Brown's diary. In March 1855, Brown notes of the model for the Maids in Rossetti's design, Elizabeth Siddal: "Rossetti once told me that, when he first saw her, he felt his destiny was defined" (*RRP,* p. 33). So it would be for any aspiring Neo-Platonist who had found his "life's own sister,"—to quote the first version of "The Birth-Bond." As has already been noted, the three Maids in the poem recall the three Fates, and in the design the rhythmic parallels between their forms reinforce the symbolic implications of the "pulsing cadence" to which they spin. To this extent, the illustration parallels a sketch by Rossetti of c. 1851, showing "a youth wearing a loin-cloth lying whole-length on the ground with the Three Fates seated behind him, holding scissors and a shuttle" (S. 589). In the "Elfen-Mere" design, of course, there are at best three images of Clotho, the spinner. But as Rossetti was well aware, the Fates or Parcae are not invariably represented as individualized figures with separate attributes.[13] In the Allingham illustration, the setting and the rendering of the tripartite ideal woman seem to mirror the destiny of a youth who, crawling like Hamlet between heaven and earth, sinks to the mundane.

It may be objected that such a reading goes far to justify the allegation that Rossetti in his illustrations deviates widely from his literary sources. But, characteristically, Rossetti has grounded his interpretation of "The Maids of Elfen-Mere" on the narrative level of the work. Through imagery strategically disposed and rendered, he not only epitomizes the enigmatic relationship between the Maidens and their suitor, he also intensifies its most compelling dimensions. Rossetti's misgivings about the Dalziels' handiwork should not obscure his achievement here: the creation of a design "worthy" of Allingham's book and of his own refusal to go "halfway" as an illustrator.

NOTES

[1] For earlier references to this abortive project, which Routledge at first was expected to publish, see DW 165, 167, 170, 174, 176. Following George Birbeck Hill's edition of *Letters of Dante Gabriel Rossetti to William Allingham: 1854–1870* (London, 1897), p. 12, DW incorrectly identifies (165, p. 189, n. 1) the first of these references with the *Music Master* volume (1855; hereafter internally documented as *MM*, followed by the first page of the poem cited).

[2] These quotations from Rossetti's letter to Hunt are from the manuscript in Special Collections, Arizona State University. For a published transcription of the entire letter, see W. Holman Hunt, *Pre-Raphaelitism and the Pre-Raphaelite Brotherhood,* 2nd ed. (London, 1913), II, 1–3.

[3] "Introduction," *Some Poems by Alfred Lord Tennyson* (London, 1901), pp. xxi–xxii.

[4] *The Dictionary of Slang and Unconventional English,* 5th ed. (London, 1961).

[5] *Alfred Lord Tennyson: A Memoir* (London, 1897), I, 116.

[6] *The Rhine, Legends, Traditions, History, from Cologne to Mainz* (London, 1839), II, 92–93.

[7] Johann Wilhelm Wolf, *Niederländische Sagen* (Leipzig, 1843), pp. 611–612. Though another version of the legend in Snowe and Wolf may have served as Allingham's source, none has been found in print before 1850, when the first version of "The Maids of Elfen-Mere"— different in form but little in content from that of 1855—appeared as "The Maidens of the Mere" in Allingham's *Poems* (London, 1850). In a concluding "Note" to this volume, Allingham states that the legend is "I believe, originally the property of Germany": a speculation which suggests that he drew on Wolf or a similar collection of *sagen* from outside Germany. An admitted problem with Wolf as a source for the poem arises from Allingham's rudimentary knowledge of German at this period; as late as 1850 Thomas Carlyle advised him about a course of study to learn the language (see *Letters to William Allingham,* ed. H. Allingham and E. Baumer Williams [London, 1911], p. 132).

[8] In the first edition of *The Fairy Mythology* (London, 1828), I, 10–11, Thomas Keightley comments on "the connexion between the Parcae and the Fairies of romance"; the etymology of "fairy" is treated

more thoroughly in the second edition (London, 1850), pp. 5–7. Keightley's writings are especially relevant here because of his friendship with Gabriele Rossetti and his family; see *Memoir*, p. 44. In October 1854—during the period when he executed the "Elfen-Mere" design—Rossetti stayed with Keightley at his home in Chiswick (see DW 187, 188).

9 In *Memoir*, W. M. Rossetti states that his brother was assisted by "Neureuther's illustrated edition" in translating the *Nibelungenlied*. However, it is not Eugen Neureuther's decorative contributions to this edition but Schnorr's narrative ones that would have aided him in following "the course of the narrative" (p. 104).

10 Dated by S. "c. 1847," although the style suggests 1850 or later. Writing to Holman Hunt between April and August, 1850, Rossetti declares that "Hannay will be there, and we can come to conclusions about the Poe project" (unpublished letter in Special Collections, Arizona State University). This presumably refers to one of the proposals for illustrated editions that the Pre-Raphaelites were considering at this time. James Hannay published an illustrated edition of Poe's *Poetical Works* in 1853 with a dedication to Rossetti, and perhaps his friend prepared this study with some stage of Hannay's "Poe project" in mind.

11 [George and Edward Dalziel], *The Brothers Dalziel: A Record of Fifty Years' Work* (London, 1901), p. 86n.

12 Jerome J. McGann, "Christina Rossetti's Poems: A New Edition and A Revalutation," *VS,* 23 (1980), 241.

13 One source of this insight would have been a work regularly consulted by Rossetti's father, Vincenzo Cartari's *Le Imagini de i dei de gli Antichi.* In an engraving on p. 304 of the first illustrated edition (Venice, 1571) the Necessity of Plato's *Republic* turns a giant spindle with the aid of her three daughters the Parcae, portrayed as identical women with curling locks and white gowns. In Gabriele Rossetti's *Il Mistero dell' Amor Platonico* (London, 1840), this edition of Cartari is cited frequently (e.g., see I, 20n). Woodcuts of the engraving of Necessity and her daughters appear in two Latin editions of Cartari published in Lyons in 1581; one of these editions appears in a manuscript catalogue of Dante Gabriel Rossetti's library prepared by his brother William (c, 1867, in AP). New illustrations were introduced in the Padua edition of 1615, with Necessity and her daughters—the latter still identical and still attired in the same manner—portrayed on p. 272; a later edition (Venice, 1647) including this woodcut (p. 160) is also listed in the manuscript catalogue of Rossetti's library.

GOVERNMENT GRAPHICS: THE DEVELOPMENT OF ILLUSTRATION IN U.S. FEDERAL PUBLICATIONS, 1817–1861*

Charles A. Seavey

INTRODUCTION

The U.S. Congressional Serial Set is viewed by researchers and librarians alike as a vast, if somewhat forbidding, source of information about the United States as it developed. However, it is only recently that the physical volumes of the Serial Set have been considered as items of interest in their own right.[1] There has been a growing recognition that some nineteenth century federal publications, if not exactly rare in the conventional sense of the word, are special enough to merit special handling and, in some cases, transfer to a restricted use area.

The Congressional Research Service *U.S. Serial Set Index* provides access to the textual information in the Serial Set. There is information contained in nontextual format which is less accessible, however. A project is underway at Kansas University to produce an up-to-date index to the thousands of maps contained in the Serial Set.[2] This paper is an initial survey of the development of illustration in federal publications prior to the formation of the Government Printing Office in 1861.

Illustrated federal publications of today are common enough to cause no major comment, and some agencies make excellent use

Reprinted with permission from *Government Publications Review,* Vol. 17, pp. 121–142. Copyright 1990, Pergamon Press plc.

*The author would like to thank the late Valmai Fenster who read an early version of this work, and the unknown *GPR* referees whose comments made for a stronger paper. Illustrations are courtesy of Special Collections, University of Arizona Library.

of illustration. The outer space visions of the National Aeronautics and Space Administration come to mind. Other federal publications use no illustration at all. The point is that illustration is unremarkable in that it is simply part of the mainstream of federal publications. Such has not always been the case. Practice in publishing and printing of illustrated federal publications evolved during the nineteenth century. In the course of that evolution the government produced a number of volumes that are remarkable by virtue of their illustrations alone.

The questions investigated in this paper are: What are the origins of illustration in U.S. federal publications? Where, in that great enigma of the Serial Set, are the beginnings of what is now widely accepted practice? Which government agencies took the lead in developing illustrated publications?

METHODOLOGY

The unit of analysis selected for the investigation was the collection of congressional publications known as the Serial Set. While it is true that not every federal publication in the nineteenth century appeared in the Serial Set, the vast majority of them did. In only one instance were non-Serial Set volumes inspected for illustration: the reports of the U.S. Exploring Expedition, in which the author had previously noted the presence of illustration.

It was decided to concentrate on the period 1817–1861, prior to the formation of the U.S. Government Printing Office (GPO). By 1861, use of illustration had become well established in federal publications. There have been accounts of the printing and distribution of federal publications during the pre-GPO period, but none of them consider the development of illustration.[3]

Approximately 1000 volumes of the Serial Set, shelved in the State Historical Society of Wisconsin (SHSW), were inspected for illustrations. The 1000 volumes included every volume on the shelf at SHSW. No Serial Set collection is complete, but the SHSW collection is so large and well maintained that it doubtlessly contains a very substantial portion of potential universe of volumes.

Maps were not included in the investigation, as they are being reported on elsewhere. Also excluded were items that were essentially exercises in mechanical drawing, such as engineers' plans or illustrations of mechanical devices being patented. While this initially appears to call for a great deal of subjective judgment on the part of the author, in the end this restriction did not affect the overall conclusions of the study nor greatly change the descriptive portion.

Each illustration, or series of illustrations, was noted, along with the names of any artist, engraver, or other person visible on the print, as well as the name of the printer/publisher who produced the actual volume. This data, a list of over 150 names, will be further analyzed and reported on at a later date.

Forty-nine items (volumes or collections of volumes) containing illustration were identified. They are bibliographically presented in Appendix 1. In the main text, items will be identified by Serial Set number and date of publication only.

A CHRONOLOGICAL FRAMEWORK

After collection, the raw data were used to establish a chronology of the development of illustration in federal publications. The time span studied (1817–1861) may be divided into four periods as follows:

- 1817–1843. A period of sporadic illustration.
- 1844–1850. Illustration becomes integrated into textual material.
- 1850–1857. A period of heavy publication of illustrated material.
- 1857–1861. A "cooling off" period in which incidence of illustration returns to that of 1844–1850.

1817–1843: Sporadic Illustration

During this 26-year period only six volumes of the Serial Set contain illustrations. The six volumes may be viewed in three groups.

The first group consists of Serial Sets 172 and 317. Serial Set 172 (1828) contains the first illustration encountered in the investigation. The text is a treatise on the rearing of silkworms. Part of the text is keyed to a full-page illustration "Representation of the Different Ages of the Silk Worm." The illustration is slightly oversized and is hand colored. No tree branch will ever display all the depicted stages of the silkworm's life as does this illustration.

Serial Set 317 (1838) is an octavo volume containing a petition for land in Florida upon which to grow tropical plants. Almost incidental to the text are 24 full-page engravings in black and white. The plates are grouped together following the text. They are all simple line drawings of plants.

The second group of illustrations is more technical in orientation. Serial Set 198 (1830) provides evidence of continued congressional curiosity about the manufacture of silk and contains a 6 × 10 cm. woodcut of a silk reel with an accompanying explanation.

Serial Set 322 (1837) contains plans for a new building for the General Land Office, but the item of interest is a foldout elevation of the proposed structure. Measuring 21 × 32 cm., it depicts something as it might be, not as it existed. Serial Set 331 (1838) is the first instance of a work containing more illustration than text. The 28 plates, showing aspects of work on the Potomac Aqueduct, are considerably thicker in bulk than the accompanying text. There are two maps, 21 illustrations that are strictly engineering plans, and five perspectives, or views, showing both completed and planned construction. Most of the views contain human figures added, one suspects, to give a sense of scale to the illustrations.

The final group in this early period consists of a single item contained in Serial Set 360 (1840). Senator Daniel Webster (he who debated with the Devil) had become concerned about postage rates. As part of his report to Congress on the subject, he included a reprint of a poster (or broadside) dealing with postage rates in Britain. The illustration has the usual Rule Britannia theme, with various colonial types of all colors being watched over by Britannia and a sleepy-looking lion. The illustration is not mentioned in the text, nor is it at all clear what its meaning is, but it does serve to inject a note of whimsy into an otherwise dull volume.

1844–1850: Illustration Comes to Age

This brief period encompasses two mighty egos representing the Army and the Navy, who used illustration as an integral part of the reports of their explorations to strange and mysterious lands. In a sense, they created the pattern of illustration that would dominate government reports for the rest of the pre-Civil War era. Charles Wilkes and the Navy will be considered first, then John Charles Fremont and the Army.

The U.S. Exploring Expedition

In the 1830s the United States Navy assumed responsibility for producing nautical charts for the growing American seaborne commerce. Because a substantial portion of that commerce involved going far from the coastal waters of North America, the Navy also had to venture far from home.

The U.S. Exploring Expedition of 1838–1842 was the first major government exploration effort to areas other than what could reasonably be called United States territory. Led by Navy Lieutenant Charles Wilkes, who appears to have been something of a tartar, the expedition mapped parts of the Pacific Northwest and then pushed on into the Pacific, eventually accomplishing the first extensive mapping of Antarctica and circumnavigating the globe.

Wilkes was determined that the publication of his report would be a worthy effort, consciously basing it upon *The Voyage of the Astrolabe,* a publication of the French government. The publication of the Wilkes report eventually raised congressional ire, partly expressed in a suggestion that the whole effort be consigned to the Potomac River.[4]

The narrative portion of the Wilkes report was published in five volumes and is a trove of illustration. These volumes are important in that they mark the first instance of illustration totally integrated into the text of the work. The Wilkes volumes were obviously *designed* as illustrated works; they were not just reports to which some illustration had been added. The report gives full credit to the various artists who drew the original works and prepared the published versions. The "List of Illustrations," pages lvii–lx, lists the title of each work, the original artist, and the individual or firm who prepared the published plate. The "List of Officers and Men" in volume 1, pages xxxiii–lvi, lists the

Figure 1. The Wilkes expedition: illustration integrated into the text (*Narrative of the United States Exploring Expedition during the Years 1838–1842. . .*, volume 1, N 1.8:W 65/1).

Figure 1. The Wilkes expedition: illustration integrated into the text (*Narrative of the United States Exploring Expedition during the Years 1838–1842 . . .*, Volume 1, N 1.8: W 65/1).

personnel for each vessel on the expedition. Among the individuals listed in the category of "Scientific Corps" for the *Vincennes,* for instance, is Joseph Drayton, Artist. Wilkes was giving full credit and setting a pattern that future Naval officers would emulate, at least in part.

Three types of illustration are employed in the Wilkes volumes.

Full-page plates, engraved on either copper or steel (both media are employed), depict major scenes or events from the course of the expedition. There are 66 plates of this type distributed throughout the text. Vignettes, also engraved on copper or steel, and smaller in size than the full-page plates, are integrated into the text. There are 47 such vignettes distributed throughout the five volumes. Two hundred fifty woodcuts are distributed through the volumes. These include small head and tail illustrations beginning and ending each chapter and insets such as Figure 1, "Coffee Carriers" which was drawn by Drayton and cut for publication by F. E. Worcester.

Wilkes insured that the binding of his report would set it apart from the ordinary federal publication. The Serial Set volumes of the day were generally bound in smooth sheepskin. Data were carried only on the spine. The Wilkes volumes were bound in a deep blue cloth, with an embossed gold American eagle (obviously a Navy eagle) on the cover.

Wilkes was a very determined man, and, in his effort to create a worthy report, he set a pattern that would be followed by future Navy authors.

Fremont and the Topographical Engineers

The period before the Civil War has been characterized as The Great Reconnaissance of the western portion of what would become the United States.[5] Beginning with Thomas Jefferson's instructions to, and support of, Lewis and Clark, the federal government was closely involved with the exploration of the vast territory west of the Appalachians. The agency that carried a great deal of the responsibility for government exploration, particularly west of the Mississippi, was a small army unit, the Corps of Topographical Engineers (USTE). The Topographical Engineers' story has been well told elsewhere,[6] and this paper will consider only the illustrated portions of its reports. Critical to an understanding of those illustrations is the knowledge that the USTE, in the middle third of the nineteenth century, had a status vastly different from that of virtually any part of the military organization of today. The USTE was not simply a small exploratory part of the Army, but an integral part of American science. Academic researchers vied for positions of USTE expeditions, and USTE officers were regarded as part of the scientific establishment of the day.[7]

John Charles Fremont, the Pathfinder, is the most well known of the Topographical Engineers, although not the most accomplished. His explorations, with a little help from his father-in-law, Senator Thomas Hart Benton, helped fire the public imagination about the wide open west in the 1840s and set the style of subsequent Topographical Engineer reports.

Fremont's reports were first published in Serial Set 416 (1845) and later in Serial Sets 461 (1845) and 467 (1845). Volume 416 deals with the 1842 exploration that crossed the Great Plains and continued into the Rocky Mountains. In terms of illustration, the report is nowhere near as grand as that of Wilkes. There are six full-page lithographs showing views of various points along the path of exploration. The work is crude and the scenes are rather imaginatively portrayed, probably in an attempt at dramatic effect.

Typically on most USTE expeditions, the original illustrations were done by members of the expedition. Fremont and his topographer, Charles Preuss, did the original drawings for the reports. Fremont was not a West Point graduate, but most of the Topographical Engineers were and had received training in topographical drawing as part of their civil engineering curriculum.[8] Illustrations for later USTE expeditions were accomplished by USTE officers, scientists accompanying the expeditions, or artists brought specifically for the purpose. In most cases, the final published versions were cut or engraved by artisans in the east, working either on a contract basis or for established lithographic firms like A. Hoen of Baltimore or Julius Bien of New York.[9] Unlike the Wilkes report, the USTE volumes mentioned in this study do not usually identify the artists responsible for either original art or preparation for publication in a list of illustrations.[10]

Serial Sets 461 and 467 reprint the original report from the 1842 expedition and add the report for the epic exploration through Oregon and California in 1843 and 1844. The original illustrations are reprinted and integrated into the text rather than in a separate section. There are an additional 16 plates derived from the 1843–1844 expedition. Seven of the plates are general views, and the other nine are of fossils or plants. All are full-page in black and white. The fossil plates are the first indication of interest in a subject that produced much illustration in later reports. Serial 467 differs from 461 only in attributing a different lithographer to the nine fossil/plant plates.

Three additional exploration reports from the USTE fit into the 1844–1850 period. Serial Set 477 (1846) reported on Lt. James W. Abert's exploration in the Southwest in 1845. It contains 11 lithographed views, one of which is a foldout by virtue of being 1 cm. wider than the octavo-sized page. Some artistic originality is shown on two of the plates that employ an oval framing technique instead of the standard rectangular format. The views in this report are rather more realistic than those of Fremont. Abert reported again in Serial Set 506 (1848) on his exploration in New Mexico in 1846–1847. Abert favored individuals rather than general scenic views in this report. Twenty-one of the plates are of people or situations with people in them.

Serial Set 505 (1848) marks the first appearance of William Helmsly Emory, an individual who produced a great deal of illustrated material that will be discussed later. Emory was a major figure in the exploration of the trans-Mississippi West, in terms of both maps and illustration. This volume contains the report of a fast reconnaissance in 1846 from Fort Leavenworth, Kansas to San Diego. It contains 38 lithographs gathered after the text. There are the usual views of the western scenery, plus some departures: three Native Americans, a fish, a cactus, a goat, some hieroglyphics, and some botanical specimens.

The remaining two reports from this period are important in that they are not USTE or Navy publications. Other agencies were starting to use illustration, and one of them, the Patent Office, was to be an annual producer of illustrated reports for the rest of the period under investigation.

Other Agencies: Patent Office and the General Land Office

Starting in 1837 the Commissioner of Patents included a report on agriculture as part of his annual report. This agricultural section would become a separate volume after 1849 and continue until 1862 when the Department of Agriculture was established. Serial Set 451 (1845) contains a full-page woodcut showing 24 types of grain. It is not keyed to any one report in the section but relates to many of them.

The last report considered in this period is Serial Set 509, which is from the General Land Office (GLO). The report is of a geological reconnaissance of Wisconsin undertaken by David

Dale Owen at the request of the GLO. Owen's report contains 23 plates, most of which are views concentrating on the geologic features of the Chippewa land district. In addition, there are 13 hand-colored geologic sections. All the illustrative material is placed at the end of the text.

The 1844–1850 period represents a maturation of illustration in federal publications. Illustration in this period, for the most part, was no longer incidental to the textual material. Indeed, Wilke's reports are a totally integrated illustrated/textual package. In addition, the first of many agricultural illustrations appeared during this period, and the GLO report foreshadowed later illustrated nonmilitary exploration reports. There were no major technical innovations during this period. Hand-coloring was still used where color was desired. Lithography dominated the production of plates, although steel and copper plate engraving were also used. Woodcuts continued to be employed when illustration was integrated with textual material.

1850–1857: The High Point of Illustration

The years 1850–1857 saw a very high incidence of heavily illustrated federal publications. Of the 49 items listed in Appendix A, 26 were published during this period. Of those 26, several are multivolume efforts, bringing the actual number of volumes to 44. The great reconnaissance was in full swing, the Navy was venturing further afield, and the Patent Commissioner continued to use illustration for the agricultural portions of his reports.

Twelve of the reports to be considered in this section deal with explorations of the land west of the Appalachians (mostly west of the Mississippi) and form the richest vein of illustration. Most of the military expeditions were planned explorations by the USTE, although other Army organizations and the General Land Office were involved.

Western Exploration, 1850–1857

Serial Set 558 (1850) is a report of one of the non-USTE explorations, although three USTE officers were with the expedition. As part of the Mexican War effort, a division of the Army marched from San Antonio, Texas, to Saltillo, Mexico. There are eight plates in the report of the march, including four plates showing the ruins of the Alamo drawn by Edward Everett, nephew of the Senate orator of the same name.

Serial Set 562 (1850), contains a major breakthrough: the first example of an illustration printed in color noted this study.[11] The document itself is a collection of seven reports dealing with various USTE activities. The most important is the report of Lt. James H. Simpson detailing an expedition to Navajo country in 1849. It contains 73 plates, 26 of which are printed in color by the P. S. Duval Steam Lithographic Press in Philadelphia. Simpson's report is notable not only for the use of color. It contains three foldouts; the longest of these measures 84 cm. and shows the graffiti on Inscription Rock, New Mexico. Inscription Rock was used by virtually all who passed through that area to record their names for posterity. There are several varieties of Indian inscriptions and messages from various Spaniards. There are seven single-page plates devoted to Inscription Rock. Simpson had a discerning eye for other subjects of interest. Among the views are plates of Chaco Canyon and Canyon de Chelly (both now national parks) and three plates of the Rio Grande basin Pueblo Indian cities of Jemez, Isleta, and Zuni.

Simpson reported again in Serial Set 577 (1850). There are only two plates, one a view of Santa Fe, the other depicting a creature that apparently amazed Simpson: the axolotl, an amphibian, resembling a large tadpole. The illustration of the axolotl shows the kind of attention to detail with which the men of the USTE looked at their surroundings, because they were ordered to record in word, picture and specimens examples of the flora, fauna, and geology of the land they traversed.

Serial Set volumes 578 (1850) and 609 (1851) shift from the exotic Southwest to the more economically important upper Midwest. The two volumes are a report of the geology of the Lake Superior land district done under the aegis of the General Land Office. *Part 1, Copper Lands,* contains 12 plates that are mostly views of the area. There are numerous small inset illustrations in the text, mainly schematic in nature, but occasionally from life. Part II, which deals with the iron region, has a frontispiece and 22 views printed in color. This color is not like the full color found in Serial Set 562, but is rather the result of a tinting process involving two or more lithographic stones and two or more passes through the press. The effect is not brilliant, but subtle and sometimes quite beautiful. There are also 13 black and white plates showing fossils.

Serial Set 587 (1850), like 558, is the product of a non-USTE military march, that of the Regiment of Mounted Riflemen, to Oregon in 1849. There are 35 plates in black and white, including three foldouts.

The next three reports are all USTE productions and show a great increase in the number of illustrations and the variety of subject matter depicted. Serial Set 608 (1852) is Howard Stansbury's report of his expedition to the Great Salt Lake. It contains five general views, some tinted in single or dual colors, as well as eight plates showing reptiles, two plates of insects, nine plates of plants, and four plates depicting fossils.

Randolph Marcy and George B. McClellan, in Serial Set 666 (1853), report on an exploration of the Red River in the Texas-Oklahoma area. There is a total of 66 plates: 12 views, 9 geologic sections, a handcolored foldout view, 6 plates of fossils, 18 plates devoted to zoology and 20 plates of botanical subjects. The plates were apparently intended to be distributed throughout the text, as they are listed at various locations in the "List of Illustrations" in the table of contents. However, the copy in the SHSW has been rebound, and is defective in that several plates are bound upside down and are out of order. Plates in copies inspected at other locations are gathered at the rear of the book, apparently the original condition, despite the intentions expressed in the "List of Illustrations."

Serial Set 668 (1853), is a report describing the expedition of Captain Lorenzo Sitgreaves on the Zuni and Colorado Rivers. Seventy-eight plates on a wide variety of subjects accompany this report: 23 views, 6 mammals, 6 birds, 20 reptiles, 3 fish, and 20 plants. One of the views is a foldout of the Buffalo Dance at Zuni Pueblo, shown in Figure 2. A number of the other views show interiors at Zuni Pueblo or individual Indians. Figure 3 is representative of the zoological drawings of this and other USTE expeditions.

"Buffalo Dance at Zuni . . ." was drawn by Richard H. Kern, one of three brothers who were involved in illustrating western exploratory expeditions. Richard Kern accompanied the expedition and did the original drawings for all 23 views in the Sitgreaves report, as well as some of the zoological drawings.

Figure 2. "Buffalo Dance." Illustrating the American Indian (*Report of an Expedition Down the Zuni and Colorado Rivers. . .*, volume 10, Serial Set 668).

Figure 3, "Hesperomys Texana," is credited to Richard's brother, Edward M. Kern, although we have no evidence that Edward was actually on the expedition. It is possible that he worked from a specimen or from his brother's rough field sketch. The printed versions of both illustrations were done by Ackerman Lithography of 379 Broadway, New York City. Ackerman Lithography was the corporate name for the brothers George W. and James Ackerman, who operated either separately or as a team for over 20 years in New York. In addition to government reports, they illustrated botanical and bird books, worked for the *Union Magazine,* and did general commercial lithography.[12]

All of these USTE expeditions were, in a sense, just a warmup for the massive effort that produced Serial Set volumes 759–768 (1855–1858), the Pacific Railroad Reports.

The Pacific Railroad Reports

Building a transcontinental railway was much on the American mind during the mid-nineteenth century. The assumptions were that

Figure 3. "Hesperomys Texana": typical zoological illustration (*Report of an Expedition Down the Zuni and Colorado Rivers. . .*, volume 10, Serial Set 668).

only one route would be built, and that anybody at either terminus and those along the chosen route would become wealthy and powerful through the riches that the railroad would bring. This had the unfortunate effect of making the selection of the route an incredibly complex political issue that exacerbated normal regional disputes (mainly the tension between the North and the South) and added intraregional competition for the eastern terminus to further complicate the issue. A number of routes seemed possible, and all had equally vociferous champions and challengers in Congress.

By 1852 events had reached a total impasse, and Congress decided to settle the issue scientifically by having the Topographical Engineers survey all possible routes at once and select the best on merit alone. The surveys took most of 1853 and all of 1854. It was not until 1857 that publication of the final version of the report began.

Six separate parties of Topographical Engineers explored the four major routes or segments thereof. A preliminary version of the report was published in 1854, but what is normally referred to as the Pacific Railroad Reports (PRR) did not commence publication until 1857. Due to the peculiarities of federal publication at this time there are several versions of the PRR in existence. There is the Senate version used for this investigation, there is a House version, and what is called the departmental version, printed for the War Department.[13] None of the versions has an index or a comprehensive table of contents. The pagination is not always consistent within individual volumes, let alone through the various versions. Although they cost as much as a million dollars to produce and were, as historian William Goetzmann said.

> . . . one of the most impressive publications of the time, (they) were a little like the country they were intended to describe: trackless, forbidding, and often nearly incomprehensible.[14]

Given the accuracy of that description, it is not necessary to describe the illustrations in detail. The nine quarto volumes have nearly 400 plates depicting the usual general views of the landscape, such as Figure 4 "Sierra Nevada from the Four Creeks," botany, zoology, geology, and fossils. Several volumes have woodcuts interspersed with the text in addition to the separate page plates. Many of the plates are in color. Where color is used in the general views it is of the tinted variety. Many of the plates, measuring about 21 × 29 cm., are exquisite in appearance, particularly some general views, such as Figure 4, and the bird plates. The majority of the plates, however, are black and white lithographs, although there is some hand coloring in evidence in addition to the tinted lithographic plates.

Figure 4 is typical of the appearance and scope of the general views in the PRR volumes. Unfortunately, black and white reproduction does not fully carry the impact that the full-size colored versions do. "Sierra Nevada" was drawn by William P. Blake, who was on the expedition as a naturalist and geologist and went on to a distinguished career in academe, culminating in the directorship of the School of Mines at the University of Arizona.[15]

In addition to Blake, 10 other artists involved in preparing the original illustration accompanied the various survey parties. One of them, Richard H. Kern, mentioned above, was slain when the party of Capt. John W. Gunnison was killed by Indians.[16] Several of the men, Albert H. Campbell and John Young, for instance made virtual careers of illustrating federal publications. Others

Figure 4. "Sierra Nevada from the Four Creeks": typical illustration of the western landscape (*Reports of Explorations and Surveys to Ascertain the Most Practicable and Economic Route for a Railroad from the Mississippi River to the Pacific Ocean. . .*, Serial Set 762).

were multitalented men like F. W. von Egloffstein who prepared both illustrations and striking maps for other expeditions, and Heinrich Mollhausen, a scientific gadfly and author of 45 novels or collections of short stories.

The PRR were a monumental accomplishment. They are very rich in illustration although no new techniques were employed in their production. Clearly, like Wilke's earlier report, they were designed as illustrated pieces and, in spite of being "trackless and forbidding," can be quite lovely at the same time.

After the PRR, Serial Set 822 (1856) is a distinctly minor effect that contains only two large woodcuts as illustration.

The Mexican Boundary Survey

The Mexican Boundary Survey (Serial Set volumes 832–834, published in 1857) was a strange military/civilian hybrid. The United States and Mexico fought a war from 1846 to 1848 over the issue of the legality of the American annexation of Texas. At the conclusion of the war, the peace treaty described the new Mexican-American boundary in general terms based on a map known to be inaccurate at the time and provided for a joint commission to survey and map a precise border as soon as possible.

The survey lasted from 1849 to 1857. The original American commissioners were comprised of military and civilians responsible to the Secretary of the Interior. There were difficulties, various forms of incompetence and malfeasance, and the Gadsden Purchase (a large tract of land in southern Arizona purchased by the U.S. in 1853) to complicate the issue. The mainstay of the operation on the American side was William H. Emory of the USTE, who began as Chief Astronomer and commander of the escort troops in 1849. By 1854 he was the American Commissioner, and it is his name that is on the final report.[17]

Like other USTE efforts this was not simply a report on the boundary. It was intended from the beginning to be "... a scientific description of the entire Southwest as a physical region ... (including) the findings of scientists in all other disciplines, including ethnology."[18] Certainly the illustrations in the report cover a wide variety of disciplines. The three quarto volumes contain approximately 370 full-page plates. The subject matter

Figure 5. "Military Colony Opposite Fort Duncan, Texas": Emory's use of the steel plate engraving technique (*Reports of the United States and Mexican Boundary Surveys . . .*, Serial Set 832).

Figure 6. "Co-Co-Pas": Color tinted lithography (*Reports of the United States and Mexican Boundary Surveys . . .*, Serial Set 832).

shows the same diversity as did the plates in the PRR—animals, plants, fossils, fish, and no fewer than 75 plates of cacti. A number of plates are steel engravings similar to Figure 5, "Military Colony Opposite Fort Duncan, Texas." The steel engraving process is noted here for the first time in an Army publication. In addition, there are some woodcuts interspersed throughout the text, and the balance of the illustrations being the familiar full-page lithographs, either black and white or, like the original of Figure 6, "Co-Co-Pas," tinted in subtle colors. The bird plates are brilliantly colored, whether by hand or chromo-lithography is undetermined.

The original of Figure 5 is black and white, but has a remarkable sense of depth and fineness of detail imparted by the steel engraving process. The original drawing for illustrations 5 and 6 was by Arthur Schott, who accompanied the expedition as geologist and illustrator. Schott was an ardent naturalist who was later associated with the Smithsonian Institution. The actual engraving on steel for Figure 5 was done by either James or James D. Smillie, a father and son team of engravers in New York. James D. Smillie went on to distinguish himself as an artist and founded the American Water Color Society. The printed versions of both illustrations were prepared and lithographed by Sarony, Major & Knapp, a major New York lithographic firm that produced a great deal of illustration for government reports as well as commercial publications.[19]

While the results of more Army exploration in the American west will be noted later in this article, the Pacific Railway Reports and the Mexican Boundary Survey represent the apogee of activity and illustration for this period. In sheer volume and number of illustrations the post-1857 reports do not compare with this brief golden era.

The Navy, 1853–1856

While the Army was producing the previously discussed material, the Navy was also publishing some heavily illustrated works. Reports totaling seven volumes on three separate expeditions were produced during this period. Two of the expeditions are virtually forgotten today, while Matthew Calbraith Perry's expedition to Japan had literally earthshaking consequences.

Lt. Matthew Maury, the great oceanographer, had noted the relationship between the Amazon River and certain currents in the Gulf of Mexico. He persuaded the Navy to mount an expedition to South America to study the phenomenon in more detail. Lt. William L. Herndon and Midshipman Lardner Gibbon undertook the exploration, and their report, *Exploration of the Valley of the Amazon,* Serial Set volumes 663 (1853) and 664 (1854) helped open up the theretofore forbidding river to merchant vessels.[20] The two volumes were designed as illustrated works. Both have frontispieces and plates distributed throughout the text. Gibbon's report, Serial Set 664, contains 38 woodcuts of sketches by the author integrated into the text. There are a total of 52 lithographic plates in the two volumes, with an emphasis on people as subjects, although other denizens of South America do appear.

Serial Set volumes 728–733 (1855) report on a four-year naval expedition to South America dating from 1849 to 1852. The Navy was there primarily to make astronomical observations, but that did not prevent the investigation of other matters and the resultant breakthrough in federal illustration. Serial Set 728 contains evidence of the first use of photography to produce illustrations. There is no direct reproduction of photographic images, but a number of the plates are based on daguerreotypes, or what are termed "camera sketches" in the text. The first item so labeled is a huge (29 × 178 cm.) foldout, "Panoramic View from the Summit of Santa Lucia." This foldout is a lithograph done in black with brown tint added from another plate, and native costumes and flags were colored by hand. There are other plates based on photography, including a portrait of an Araucanian chief painted from a daguerreotype by John Mix Stanley. Stanley was a noted artist of the day who had made his reputation with a series of paintings of American Indians. Serial Set 728 contains 12 more plates, all lithographs of the color-tinted variety. Serial Set 729, the supplementary papers, contains an additional seven plates and 11 woodcuts distributed throughout the text. Seventeen of the plates are chromolithographic prints of birds, including a vibrantly green parrot.

The Perry Expedition to Japan

The final Naval report to be considered here is significant both in terms of illustration and in what it represents. Serial Set volumes 769–771 (1856) are Matthew Calbraith Perry's report on the opening of Japan in 1852 and 1853. Few events of the nineteenth century have had more far reaching consequences.

The first two volumes of the report contain 116 plates, with an additional 76 woodcuts integrated into the text in volume I. Like Wilkes before him, Perry used head and tail pieces for his chapters. Like the Wilkes report, Perry's "List of Illustrations" (volume 1, pages xv–xvii) credits the artist responsible for each original sketch or daguerreotype. Unlike Wilkes, the Perry report does not mention the artists or firms responsible for preparing the published plates, although credits are sometimes carried on the plates themselves. The plates include a number of oval portraits based on daguerreotypes, similar to Figure 7. Like many of the lithographs, they are lightly tinted rather than flat back and white. Two brilliantly colored facsimiles of Japanese drawings are included in volume I. Volume I was Perry's general report. Volume II, Serial Set 770, contains over 40 individual reports on aspects of the trip both in the Far East and on the Atlantic Ocean. There are plates dealing with agriculture, birds, and seashells, as well as a facsimile of the Japanese text of the treaty of Kan-a-ga-wa which opened Japan to American trade and influences.

"China Girl" is an excellent example of both the amount of

Figure 7. "China Girl": Use of the camera as an aid in preparing illustration (*Narrative of the Expedition of an American Squadron to the China Seas and Japan...*, volume 1, N 1.8:P 42).

cooperation necessary to produce illustrations for publication, and the essentially cautious use of photography at the time. The portrait is not a photographic reproduction, but a drawing based on the original photograph. The daguerreotype was taken by E. Brown, who is listed in the roster of the expedition's officers as an artist and in the text as "daguerreotypist." The published version was drawn by Peter Kramer who was working at the time for the lithographic firm of P. S. Duval in Philadelphia. Kramer subsequently established his own business in New York and was active as late as 1898. The P. S. Duval company has a long and complex history stretching from roughly 1835 until 1893 when the last variant of the firm, apparently bankrupt, was sold by the Sheriff. It was a sad end to a firm that had been a pioneer in the development of color printing in the United States.[21]

While the Army explorations of the trans-Mississippi West certainly produced more illustrations during this period, in terms of overall quality the Navy productions are superior as well as more technically innovative. All three Navy reports are clearly designed as illustrated works, with frontispieces, insets, and in some cases, chapter head and tail pieces. Furthermore, Perry, at least, goes to some length to identify the artists and technicians associated with each work, whereas one is left guessing about many of the Army produced items. The Navy clearly can take credit for the first U.S. government use of the camera as an illustrative tool. It must be noted, however, that it was a lot easier to transport the cameras of the day on an ocean-going vessel than on an Army mule!

The Patent Office, 1849–1856

The Patent Office, as mentioned above, reported annually on American agriculture from 1837, and the agriculture report formed a separate volume after 1849. With one exception, the Patent Office volumes to be described are from the agricultural works. The exception is Serial Set volume 574 (1850), chapter 8 of which is titled "On the Propulsion of Steamers." In that chapter Thomas Ewbank (Commissioner of Patents) relates how he was pondering the problem of steam powered vessels one morning while on his way to work. As he passed by a fish market he realized that fish fins were superbly designed to propel objects through water. The results appear in the report as six plates and numerous drawings of the fins of fish, seals, and porpoises, and of a number of bird wings.

The agricultural reports for this time period are included in Serial Set volumes 575 (1850), 625 (1852), 683 (1852), 697 (1854), 755 (1855), and 818 (1856). Each volume usually contains seven to nine plates illustrating scenes such as grazing sheep or dairy cattle. The plates are usually gathered at either the end or the beginning of the report and sometimes appear to bear no relationship to the text. Serial Set 697 (1854) is worth particular note because it contains the first use of color in an agricultural report, a practice continued in Serial Set volumes 755 and 818. The precedent of illustration set in these early agricultural reports carried through to the publications of the Department of Agriculture when it was formed in 1862.

1857–1861, The Flood Diminishes

This period contains little that is remarkable. No new technical ground was broken, and the sheer volume of illustration is far below that of the previous period. On the other hand, it is possible to advance the suggestion that illustration in federal publications had become routine by this time. The pattern of illustrated annual reports was well established by the Patent Office, and the Army and Navy were familiar with illustrated reports as well.

The Patent Office

Serial Set volumes 885/905 (1857), 928 (1858), and 988 (1859) are the agricultural sections of the Patent Office annual reports for 1856–58. In the main they show the same pattern described above. An interesting anomaly occurs in Serial Set volumes 885 and 905. Serial Set volume 885 is the Senate version of the 1856 report, and volume 905 is the House version. Textually they are exactly the same. Their illustrations, however, are rather different. Serial Set 885 contains two color plates, one of which is titled "South Down Sheep." There are an additional 46 black and white plates to complete the illustrated section. Serial Set 905 contains exactly the same number of plates, and there is also a color plate titled "South Down Sheep." However, the Senate sheep is white faced and facing right while the House sheep has a black face and ears and is facing left. Different lithographers printed the two versions, but no artist is noted on either. This certainly raises some interesting, if minor, questions about what is going on. What did the lithographers use as a source? Which is the *real* South Down sheep?

The Army, Part I

The last of the Pacific Railroad Reports appeared in Serial Set 982 (1859) and is much the same as earlier reports. There is a total of 119 plates covering the usual range of subjects. The bird plates are in full color.

Because of the South Down sheep episode, Serial Set volume 1054 (1860), the House version of Serial Set 982 was inspected for this study. The plates, although printed by different lithographers, show great similarity. A close inspection with a large magnifying glass, however, reveals significant enough variation in small detail to suggest that two different plates are involved, perhaps prepared by different printers-engravers from the same original drawing. The Senate version (1054) lithographed by J. Bien has the more realistic color, while the House version (982) appears sharper, or better focused, to the eye.

The Army was interested in areas beyond the continental United States during this period. Russia, Turkey, France, and the United Kingdom were at war in the Crimea and the Army sent observers to see how the Europeans waged war. Serial Set volumes 916 (1857) and 1037 (1860) contain reports on the war, and, in the case of volume 1037, other aspects of the European military establishment. Serial Set volume 916 contains many sketches of military equipment and plates showing cavalry maneuvers in a schematic fashion. There is a large, and colorful map of Sebastapol that is more interesting than the illustrations. Serial Set volume 1037 contains 21 plates, most of which are schematics, and there is a large foldout of the Arsenal at Vienna as well.

It was at this time that the Army began its famous investigation into the possible use of camels as beasts of burden in the Southwest. Serial Set volumes 881 (1857) and 937 (1858) contain reports on the subject. Since the camel might be perceived as a fairly peculiar creature, the reports are well illustrated. Serial Set volume 881, the longer of the two, contains 20 woodcut plates and a few insets. Serial Set volume 937 contains a letter from W. Re Kyan Bey on the subject of the dromedary and some inset woodcut illustrations.

The final report reviewed in this paper is technically outside the parameters of the study in that it was published by the Government Printing Office (GPO). However, it is the last report to be published by the Topographical Engineers prior to their absorption into the Engineer Corps during the Civil War. In addition, it offers evidence that the pattern of illustration established in the pre-GPO period was not affected by the establishment of the GPO as a centralized printing office.

Serial Set volume 1058 (1861) is the report of Joseph Christmas Ives, USTE, on the first American exploration of the Grand Canyon. Ives was also the first person known to map portions of the canyon. In addition to the maps there are 11 black and white engravings, eight color lithographs, eight foldout panoramas, and 41 woodcuts included in the text. Some of the engravings are noted as being taken from photographs by Ives; this provides the first acknowledged Army use of the camera as a tool for illustration.

CONCLUSION

It has been established that illustration of federal publications was almost incidental prior to 1844. After that date, illustration became an integral part of many reports. The main drive behind the development of the illustrated report was exploration, both at home and abroad. The Army, the Navy, and, to a lesser extent, the General Land Office, were the principal agencies that used illustration to convey the sense of locales far from Washington better than their textual reports, no matter how well written, possibly could. William Goetzmann explains it this way:

> Finally there was a noticeable kinship between science and art . . . what lay at the heart of this artistic approach was the desire not only to measure, but to get at the quality of the new-found data . . . Perhaps the best evidence for this instinct is to be found in the lithograph drawings made by the artists who accompanied the expeditions . . .[22]

It has also been established that exploratory agencies were not alone in producing illustrated reports. The Patent Office established the principle of an illustrated annual report that would be much used in the post-Civil War era. By 1861 the fundamental pattern of federal illustration was well established, and the coming of the Government Printing Office would not disturb that pattern.

POSTSCRIPT

Two lines of further inquiry to follow this initial survey suggest themselves. First, the field needs a complete inventory of at least the single-page plates in federal publications in the 19th century. The map indexing project at Kansas University estimates there are 12,000–13,000 maps in the Serial Set; there are nowhere near that many plates to be inventoried, even when considering the non-Serial Set material. The second line of research is rather broader in scope. This paper did not consider in any detail the actual processes used to produce the federal illustrations, particularly the color plates. The nineteenth century saw a period of rapidly changing print technology. The development of government graphics needs to be placed in this larger context. Were the federal printers leading the way in developing color illustration; or were they in the mainstream, or were they even lagging behind? This avenue of research seems to lend itself to a book length treatise on the topic.

NOTES

1. This awareness of the special nature of some federal publications led to the creation of an ad hoc committee of the American Library Association (ALA). Representatives of the Association of College and Research Libraries' Rare Books and Manuscripts Section, the Government Documents Round Table, and the Map and Geography Round Table, have been discussing the issue. These discussions resulted in a well attended program, ''Government Documents as Rare Books'' at the New Orleans meeting of ALA on July 10, 1988. At that meeting various aspects of ''special'' federal publications, among others, were discussed. While there are no specific guidelines for evaluating whether or not a federal publication is worthy of special handling per se, one aspect that was considered is illustration. David Heisser's introductory survey at the ALA session was illustrated with slides from the Serial Set. The slides made an obvious impression on the audience.

2. There is a growing interest in nineteenth century mapping by agencies of the U.S. government. Recent years have shown a sharp increase in the literature devoted to nineteenth century government mapping. Prior to the last 15 years, most carto-historians stopped their investigations at 1800.

3. Orvin Lee Shifflett. "The Government as Publisher: An Historical Review," *Library Research* 4 (Summer 1982).

4. For a complete publishing history of the reports, see "Resolution on Progress Towards Completion of Publications of Exploring Expedition under Captain Charles Wilkes, etc. . ." 35th Congress, 2nd session, Senate Report 391, Serial Set 994; and "Memorial of Rear Admiral Charles Wilkes on Publication of Report of Wilkes Exploring Expedition . . ." 44th Congress, 1st session, Senate Report 60, Serial Set 1667.

5. Edward S. Wallace, *The Great Reconnaissance* (Boston: Little, Brown & Co., 1955).

6. William H. Goetzmann, *Army Exploration in the American West, 1803–1863* (New Haven: Yale University Press, 1959). See also Goetzmann's *Exploration and Empire; The Explorer and the Scientist in the Winning of the American West* (New York: W. W. Norton, 1978).

7. Goetzmann, *Army Exploration,* 14–17, in particular; *Exploration and Empire* in general.

8. Goetzmann, *Army Exploration. . .,* 15–16.

9. A major source of information on the nineteenth century lithographic industry is Harry Twyford Peters, *America on Stone* (New York: Arno Press, 1976, originally published by Doubleday, Doran & Co. in 1931). A subsequent article will deal with the firms and artists involved in preparing illustration for nineteenth century federal publications.

10. Many times, the names of both the original artist and the publication artist are visible on the plates, but this is not universal practice in USTE publications.

11. The first use of color located during the inspection of the volumes in the SHSW was seen on the hand colored borders of a map, "Bay on Pensacola," located in "Letter from the Secretary of the Treasury Transmitting Copies of the Reports of the Commissioners of Land Claims in East and West Florida," 18th Congress, 2nd session, House Document 111, Serial Set 120. (Washington: Gales and Seaton, 1825).

12. The material on the Kerns is drawn from Robert Taft, *Artists and Illustrators of the Old West, 1850–1900* (Princeton, NJ: Princeton University Press, 1982, originally published by Charles Scribner's Sons, 1953) 258–259. The Ackerman material is drawn from Peters, *America on Stone,* 72.

13. While familiar to most documents librarians, the practice of printing two or three separate versions of federal publications during the

nineteenth century may not be obvious to other scholars. Despite the expense, the practice continued for most of the century, even after the formation of the Government Printing Office in 1862.

14. Goetzmann, *Army Exploration,* 313.

15. The material on Blake is drawn from Taft, *Artists and Illustrators,* 256, and Goetzmann, *Army Exploration,* 317.

16. Taft, *Artists and Illustrators* . . . devotes an entire chapter to John Mix Stanley, who was with the Stevens, or northern, expedition. Many other PRR artists are discussed in the book. Taft's notes for chapter 1, pages 252–278 are particularly detailed. While Taft does discuss the principal artists, neither he nor other writers, have investigated the individual engravers or lithographers who prepared the artists' work for publication.

17. This is a simplification of a complex topic. There were actually two commissions, one succeeding the other. See Goetzmann, *Army Exploration,* chapter 5, particularly pages 192–197 for details.

18. Goetzmann, *Army Exploration,* 197.

19. The material on Schott is drawn from Taft, *Artists and Illustrators* . . . 276–277, and Goetzmann, *Army Exploration* . . . 201–205. The Smillie material comes from Taft, page 277, and Mantle Fielding, *Dictionary of American Painters, Sculptors, and Engravers* (Greens Farms, CT: Modern Books and Crafts, originally published 1926), 336. The Sarony, Major and Knapp material is drawn from Peters, *America on Stone,* 350–357.

20. U.S. National Archives and Records Service, *Geographical Exploration and Topographical Mapping by the United States Government, 1777–1852: An Exhibit Catalog* (Washington, DC: U.S. Government Printing Office, 1952, reprinted 1966, 1971), 10.

21. The Kramer material is drawn from Peters, *American on Stone,* 255. The P. S. Duval story is taken from the same source, 163–168.

22. Goetzmann, *Army Exploration,* 19.

APPENDIX A
CHECKLIST OF ILLUSTRATED SERIAL SET VOLUMES NOTED IN THIS PAPER

To simply the citations to the Serial Set volumes noted in this paper, the following pattern is employed:

172: Serial Set Number

20/1: Congress and Session number; i.e.: 20th Congress, 1st Session.

HD 226: Document number; i.e.: House Document 111.
Document types vary over the years. The most common are:
HD: House Document
SD: Senate Document
HR: House Report
SR: Senate Report
HMD: House Miscellaneous Document
SMD: Senate Miscellaneous Document
HED: House Executive Document
SED: Senate Executive Document

Other elements such as title, responsible authority, etc. are not always so evident in congressional publications, nor, in terms of federal bibliography, are they as important. Variation in title is almost guaranteed from bibliographer to bibliographer, but the congressional numbering system never varies and is the main element of the citations below.

The first date given is the date the material was ordered to be printed, the second is the actual imprint date. Either or both are occasionally missing.

The single exception to the congressional numbering scheme is found in item 7, which is simply coded USEE. There were items published by the federal government that were not part of the Serial Set, and the report of the Wilkes expedition is one of them.

Most documents librarians will recognize that with few exceptions the citations below represent only one of at least two, and sometimes three, versions of a particular report or document. As always, the *1909 Checklist* should be consulted in any search for alternative versions.

1. 172 20/1 HD 226
   Letter from James Mease Transmitting a Treatise on the Rearing of Silk-Worms, by Mr. DeHazzi of Munich.
   February 2, 1828. Gales and Seaton, 1828.
2. 198 21/1 HD 126
   Report of the Committee on Agriculture on the Growth and Manufacture of Silk, to which is Annexed, Essays on American Silk. . . May 14, 1830. Duff Green, 1830.
3. 317 25/2 SR 300
   Memorial of Dr. Henry Perrine Praying for a Conditional Grant of Land in Southern Florida to Encourage the

Introduction and Promote the Cultivation of Tropical Plants.
. . March 12, 1838. Blair and Rives, 1838.
4. 322 25/2 HD 23
Affairs of the General Land Office (main title) *Report of James Whitcomb, Commissioner,* December 12, 1837. Thomas Allen, 1837 (?).
5. 331 25/2 HD 459
Report on the Potomac Aqueduct. July 2, 1838. Printer not identified.
6. 360 26/1 S(?) 547
Mr Webster . . . Relative to a Reduction of the Postage on Letters. June 10, 1840. Blair and Rives, 1840.
7. USEE
Narrative of the United States Exploring Expedition during the Years 1838–1842, by Charles Wilkes, USN. 5 volumes. Lea and Blanchard, 1845.

This is a woefully incomplete citation for a very complex set of publications. In addition to the five-volume *Narrative,* 14 more volumes (out of a planned 24) were published. The supplemental volumes, not authored by Wilkes but by various scientists on the expedition, were printed in very limited quantities. Horatio Hale's volume on ethnography was limited to a run of 250 copies, and James D. Dana's volume on zoophytes to only 200, for example. The *1909 Checklist* contains a list which may or may not be complete.

8. 416 27/3 SD 243
Report on an Exploration of the Country Lying Between the Missouri River and the Rocky Mountains along the Line of the Kansas and Great Platte Rivers. By Lt. J. C. Fremont. March 2, 1843. Thomas Allen, 1845.
9. 451 28/2 SR 75
Report of the Commissioner of Patents Showing the Operations of the Patent Office during the Year 1844. Gales and Seaton, 1845.
10. 461 28/2 SR 174
Report of the Exploring Expedition to the Rocky Mountains in the Year 1842 and North California in the Years

1843–44, by Brevet Captain J. C. Fremont. . . Gales and Seaton, 1845.

11. 467 28/2 HD 166

    (same as item 10) Blair and Rives, 1845.

12. 477 29/1 SD 438

    Report of an Expedition Led by Lieutenant Abert on the Upper Arkansas and through the Country of the Camanche (sic) *Indians in the Fall of the Year 1845.* Ritchie and Heiss, 1846.

13. 505 30/1 SED 7

    Notes of a Military Reconnoissance (sic) *from Fort Leavenworth in Missouri to San Diego in California . . . by Lt. Col. W. H. Emory.* December 16, 1847. Wendell and Van Benthhuysen, 1848.

14. 506 30/1 SED 23

    Report of Lieut. J. Abert of His Examination of New Mexico in the Years 1846–47. February 10, 1848. Wendell and Van Benthuysen, 1848.

15. 509 30/1 SED 57

    Report of a Geological Reconnoissance (sic) *of the Chippewa Land District of Wisconsin and the Northern Part of Iowa.* June 22, 1848. Wendell and Van Benthuysen, 1848.

16. 558 31/1 SED 32

    Memoir Descriptive of a March of Division of the United States Army under the Command of Brigadier General John E. Wool from San Antonio de Bexar, in Texas, to Saltillo, in Mexico, By George W. Hughs, Capt. USTE. February 18, 1850. Wm. H. Belt, 1850.

17. 562 31/1 SED 64

    A conglomeration of seven reports dealing with exploration in the trans-Mississippi West. The illustrated one is *Report of Lieutenant J. H. Simpson of an Expedition to the Navajo Country in 1849. . .* August 10, 1850. Wm. H. Belt, 1850.

18. 574 31/1 HED 20

    Report of the Commissioner of Patents for 1849. Part I, Arts and Manufactures . . . Office of Printers to the House of Reps., 1850.

19. 575 31/1 HED 20

Report of the Commissioner of Patents for 1849. Part II, Agriculture. Office of Printers to the House of Reps., 1850.

20. 577 31/1 HED 45
    Report of Exploration and Survey of Route from Fort Smith, Arkansas, to Santa Fe, New Mexico, made in 1849 by First Lieutenant James H. Simpson, USTE. February 21, 1850 (no printer noted).

21. 578 31/1 HED 69
    Report on the Geology and Topography of a Portion of the Lake Superior Land District in the State of Michigan by J. W. Foster and J. D. Whitney, Part I, Copper Lands. May 16, 1850 (no printer noted).

22. 587 31/1/SED 1
    Report of the Secretary of War . . . A Report in the Form of a Journal, to the Quartermaster General, of the March of the Regiment of Mounted Riflemen to Oregon . . . 1849, by Major Osborne Cross. December 2, 1850 (no printer noted).

23. 608 32/special session SED 3
    Exploration and Survey of the Valley of the Great Salt Lake of Utah, Including a Reconnoissance (sic) *of a New Route Through the Rocky Mountains. By Howard Stansbury, USTE.* Lippincott, Grambo & Co., 1852.

24. 609 32/special session SED 4
    Report on the Geology of the Lake Superior Land District by J. W. Foster and J. D. Whitney . . . Part II, The Iron Region . . . March 13, 1851. A. Boyd Hamilton, 1851.

25. 625 32/1 SED 118
    Report of the Commissioner of Patents for 1851 . . . Part II, Agriculture. Robert Armstrong, 1852.

26. 663 32/2 SED 36
    Exploration of the Valley of the Amazon . . . by Wm. Lewis Herndon and Lardner Gibbon, Lieutenants, USN . . . Part I, by Lieut. Herndon. February 10, 1853. Robert Armstrong, 1853.

27. 664 32/2 SED 36
    (same as above) . . . *Part II, by Lt. Lardner Gibbon.* March 3, 1853. A. O. P. Nicholson, 1854.

28. 666 32/2 SED 54
    Exploration of the Red River of Louisiana in the Year 1852

by Randolph B. Marcy . . . assisted by George B. McClellan.
February 4, 1853. Robert Armstrong, 1853.

29. 668 32/2 SED 59
*Report of an Expedition Down the Zuni and Colorado
Rivers by Captain L. Sitgreaves, USTE.* March 3, 1853.
Robert Armstrong, 1853.

30. 683 32/2 HED 65
Report of the Commissioner of Patents for 1852. Robert
Armstrong, 1852.

31. 697 3/1 SED 27
*Report of the Commissioner of Patents for 1853 . . . Part II,
Agriculture.* A. O. P. Nicholson, 1854.

32. 728–733 33/1 HED 121
*The U.S. Naval Astronomical Expedition to the Southern
Hemisphere during the Years 1849–1852.* July 13, 1854.
A. O. P. Nicholson, 1855.

33. 755 33/2 SED 42
*Report of the Commissioner of Patents for 1854 . . . Part II,
Agriculture.* Beverly Tucker, 1855.

34. 759–768 33/2 SED 78
*Reports of Explorations and Surveys to Ascertain the Most
Practicable and Economic Route for a Railroad from the
Mississippi River to the Pacific Ocean . . .* 8 volumes.
February 24, 1855. Beverly Tucker, 1855–.
Like the citation for the USEE (item 7, above) this citation
will only get the reader to one of several versions of the
vastly complex set of documents known as the Pacific
Railroad Surveys.

35. 769–771 33/2 SED 79
*Narrative of the Expedition of an American Squadron to
the China Seas and Japan . . . Under the Command of
Commodore M. C. Perry, USN.* January 22, 1855. Beverly
Tucker, 1856.

36. 818 34/1 SED 20
*Report of the Commissioner of Patents for 1855 . . . Part II,
Agriculture.* A. O. P. Nicholson, 1856.

37. 822 34/1 SED 76
Explorations in the Dacota (sic) *Country in the Year 1855 by
Lt. G. K. Warren.* May 22, 1856. A. O. P. Nicholson, 1856.

38. 832–834 34/1 SED 108

Report on the United States and Mexican Boundary Surveys . . . by William H. Emory, Major, First Cavalry and United States Commissioner. 3 volumes. August 15, 1856. A. O. P. Nicholson, 1857.

39. 881 34/3 SED 62
Reports on the Purchase, Importation and Use of Camels and Dromedaries, to Be Employed for Military Purposes . . . 1855, '56, '57. February 26, 1857. A. O. P. Nicholson, 1857.

40. 885 34/3 SED 53
Report of the Commissioner of Patents for 1856 . . . Part II, Agriculture. A. O. P. Nicholson, 1857.

41. 905 34/3 HED 65
(same as above, House version) Cornelius Wendell, 1857.

42. 916 35/special session SED 1
The Report of Captain George B. McClellan . . . (on) the Seat of War in Europe in 1855 and 1856. March 14, 1857. A. O. P. Nicholson, 1857.

43. 928 35/1 SED 30
Report of the Commissioner of Patents for 1857 . . . Part II, Agriculture. William A. Harris, 1858.

44. 937 35/1 SMD 271
Letter of W. Re Kyan Bey . . . on the Treatment and Use of the Dromedary . June 12, 1858. William A. Harris, 1858.

45. 988 35/2 SED 47
Report of the Commissioner of Patents for 1858 . . . Part II, Agriculture. William A. Harris, 1859.

46. 982 35/2 SED 46
(supplement to the Pacific Railroad Reports, item 34). William A. Harris, 1859.

47. 1037 36/1 SED 60
Military Commission to Europe in 1855 and 1856 . . . (by) Major Alfred Mordecai. June 16, 1860. George W. Bowman, 1860.

48. 1054 36/1 HED 56
(same as item 46 above, variation in illustrations). Thomas H. Ford, 1860.

49. 1058 36/1 HED 90
Report on the Colorado River of the West, Explored in 1857 and 1858 by Lt. Joseph Christmas Ives, USTE. June 5, 1860. U.S. Government Printing Office, 1861.

"EITHER IN BOOKS OR IN ARCHITECTURE": BERTRAM GROSVENOR GOODHUE IN THE NINETIES

James F. O'Gorman

To James S. Ackerman, Teacher

In a letter of 28 June 1894, Bertram Grosvenor Goodhue (1869–1924) reported to the photographer-publisher F. Holland Day that he was experiencing a momentary lull in his labors, "either in books or [in] architecture."[1] Within three years of his arrival in Boston, then, Goodhue was looking for work in two specialized fields, the two on which his fame principally rests, and the lull he then remarked was the last he was to enjoy for many years.

In preparing this brief profile of Goodhue that emphasizes his double-barreled career in the 1890s, I have visited some of his major buildings, held in hand some of his finest volumes, and cast an eye on some of his original decorative drawings at the Grolier Club and elsewhere, but I must confess to having drawn primarily on the work of other, more specialized scholars. Whoever seeks the historical Goodhue must use and acknowledge the contributions of such recent students as the late Richard Oliver, whose monograph on the architecture is currently definitive; Susan Otis Thompson, writing on the influence of William Morris in American book arts; Estelle Jussim, on the career of that "slave to beauty," F. Holland Day; Beverly Brandt, on the local Arts and Crafts Society; and Nancy Finlay in her fine exhibition catalogue on artists of the book in Boston.[2] Collectively, these publications provide an indispensable context for Goodhue's career. In short, I hold no special brief in the study of design in Boston in the 1890s; I draw upon the work of others and here attempt merely to make

Reprinted with permission from *Harvard Library Bulletin,* Spring 1987, pp. 165–183.

again whole that which specialized scholarship has tended to pull asunder.

We generally split art history in a way that separates fields such as architectural design from book decoration, and rarely do we discuss the two at the same time, but Goodhue was not the first to excel in both areas (I am thinking particularly of his Boston progenitor, Hammatt Billings),[3] and in his case, at least, books and buildings must be thought of as variant flowers from a common stem. One cannot approach his bookwork without recognizing his origins, early development, and ultimate stature as an architect as well.

Born in 1869 in Pomfret, Connecticut, Bertram Goodhue was the scion of old New England stock.[4] He was from his early years a student of design in all of its phases, with special attention to the medieval. Oliver reports that at the age of ten Goodhue set up a studio in the attic of his parents' house and painted its windows in imitation of stained glass. Although allowed to grow up unburdened by much formal learning, he was bookish, reading the Arthurian legends and other romantic literature. His precocious talent as a graphic artist led him at fifteen to an apprenticeship in New York with the architectural firm of Renwick, Aspinwall & Russell, whose principal partner, James Renwick, Jr., was, with Richard Upjohn, a leading figure in the early Gothic Revival in this country.[5] Renwick had provided Manhattan with two of its finest midcentury medieval churches: Grace on lower Broadway, begun in the 1840s, and Saint Patrick's Roman Catholic Cathedral on Fifth Avenue, begun in the 1850s and completed a few years prior to Goodhue's arrival in New York. It was this neo-Gothic world into which the budding designer plunged in 1884.

Grace and Saint Patrick's, like Upjohn's Trinity at the head of Wall Street, represent the earliest phase on this side of the Atlantic of a design movement that originated in England, so far as Americans were concerned. Its chief voice was Augustus Welby Pugin, whose vision of an exclusively Gothic world (filled with churches of his own design) appears as frontispiece to his *Apology for the Revival of Christian Architecture* (1843). Through Renwick, Goodhue's professional lineage reached back to Pugin, the theoretical rock upon which rested English medievalism of the later nineteenth century, whether championed by Ruskin or Morris, the high Victorians, or the Arts and Crafts Movement.

FIGURE 1. "Church Furniture Revived at Birmingham," from A. W. N. Pugin, *An Apology for the Revival of Christian Architecture in England,* London, 1843

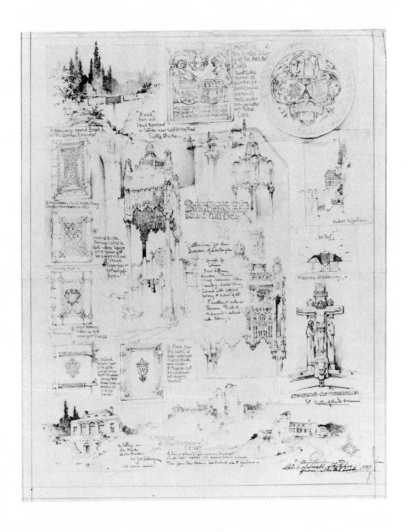

FIGURE 2. B. G. Goodhue, miscellaneous sketches for architecture and decorative arts, various dates

Pugin's influence went far beyond mere building design. In his view reform was all-encompassing, and from his feverish talent stemmed drawings for churches and everything they contained. Another plate in the *Apology* drives home his program (figure 1). In it Pugin displays his wares, his designs for a spectrum of medieval liturgical hardware ranging from miters and incense burners to altar cloths and book covers.

Pugin died seventeen years before Goodhue's birth. One might suppose that his influence had weakened by the 1880s, when Goodhue joined Renwick, but in fact it remained for the younger man focused and potent. We know from Goodhue's early partner, Ralph Adams Cram, that Pugin's books were an important source for Goodhue's designs in architecture.[6] And we have visual confirmation of continuity in the realm of the decorative arts in sheets of sketches such as the one (figure 2) that contains studies for the seal of the Boston Arts and Crafts Society, founded in 1897. Here Goodhue's pen explores a host of design problems ranging from buildings to ecclesiastical furniture to book covers, all of medieval inspiration. On such a page, and on others like it, Goodhue practices the profession of total design prescribed by Pugin and reiterated by the English Arts and Crafters.

Goodhue was, then, an all-round designer, but at least through the 1890s he wore two principal hats. In the one guise, as he is portrayed in a grotesque in his chapel at West Point, he practiced architecture; in the other, he embellished books for the trade and private presses of Boston.

While still a teenaged apprentice to Renwick, Goodhue was publishing pen sketches of Pomfret buildings in professional magazines. At twenty he entered a Richardsonian Romanesque project in the competition for the Anglican cathedral of Saint John the Divine in New York. This early perspective already shows the low angle of vision characteristic of his presentation drawings. Although his scheme for Saint John went unnoticed, two years later, now at age twenty-two, he won a competition for the cathedral of Saint Matthew in Dallas. Recognizing his lack of experience in actual building, Goodhue associated himself in 1891 with the Boston architectural firm headed by Cram. By the next year he was Cram's partner.

The firm's first triumph was All Saints' in the Ashmont section of Boston, a stylistically transitional work combining the seem-

FIGURE 3. B. G. Goodhue, presentation drawing for the U.S. Military Academy, West Point, New York, 1903

ingly irreconcilable characteristics of Richardsonian robustness and Gothic grace.[7] Winning the competition for the major additions to West Point in 1903 established the firm on a national basis. Goodhue's drawing for the project, showing cliffs of architecture rising sublimely above the Hudson's waters, their picturesque silhouettes darkly emphasized against the blank sky, is an enhanced version of the low angle of vision in the perspective of Saint John's (figure 3). This trademark of Goodhue's graphics recurs over and over, for example in the drawing for the Frederick Peterson house at Brewster, New York, of 1915. The low eye level dramatizes the image, urging the building to body upward for its geological base. This viewpoint is also characteristic of architectural perspectives in English romantic book illustration, such as the view of Ludlow Castle, after J. M. W. Turner, in an 1858 Boston edition of Milton's poetry (figure 4). The sublime may be tempered somewhat in Goodhue's presentation, but it remained the underlying aesthetic assumption on which his sensibilities rested. As Cram reported, "the sense of romance possessed him . . . and made him a Mediaevalist in all things."[8]

With the need to supervise the work at West Point, Goodhue moved to New York, where, starting in 1905, the firm created in Saint Thomas's on Fifth Avenue (across and down from Renwick's Saint Patrick's) one of the glories of turn-of-the-century urban Gothic. Goodhue's creative energy lingers in the smallest detail, and in such decorative accents as the ornamental door hardware, the spirit of Pugin lives on into the early twentieth century. When Saint Thomas was completed in 1913, Goodhue split with Cram and began a period of stylistic experimentation in architecture that eventually materialized in buildings such as the Nebraska State Capitol in Lincoln, begun in 1920, in which Gothic drive joins classic calm to emerge as modern synthesis. Goodhue died as its tower began to rise above the prairie.

Goodhue's winning design for the cathedral at Dallas was never built, but it represents a pivotal moment in his career. It brought him to Boston and into a circle called by various recent writers the "local bohemian intelligentsia,"[9] or "those brilliant young men of the nineties,"[10] that took for granted the totality of the design reform stemming from Augustus Pugin and reinvigorated by William Morris. The circle included the architect and polemicist Cram, the aesthete publisher-photographer F. Holland Day, Day's partner, Herbert Copeland, the designer-printer D. B. Updike, the poet Bliss Carman, the architects and designers who collectively formed in 1897 the earliest Arts and Crafts group on this side of the Atlantic, and the intellectuals who gathered into such social clubs as the Pewter Mugs and the Visionists. It was a heady world for a twenty-two-year-old, even one as gifted as Goodhue. In this ripe atmosphere his abilities and inclinations flowered in memorable works of architecture and book design. Nor was he merely one of the crowd. As Cram wrote in the 1925 memorial volume to his former partner: "It was he, more than any one else, who was instrumental in bringing together that extraordinary group of young men who found such joy in life. . . . He would design a font of type or a sumptuous set of initials as quickly as he would clothe an architectural form with the splendid vesture of intricate Gothic ornament."[11]

In his *Decorative Illustration of Books* (1896), Walter Crane

FIGURE 4. Ludlow Castle, after J. M. W. Turner, from John Milton, *The Poetical Works*, Boston, 1858

distinguishes between what he calls a volume's "pictorial statement" and its "decorative treatment"; that is, between illustration and ornamentation.[12] If artists of the book in Boston are
divided into such camps, then Hammatt Billings falls into the
pictorial fold, and Goodhue must be counted a decorator. His
illustrations, while significant, take second place to his borders
and full-page designs, covers, bookplates, printers' marks and
seals, miscellaneous decorations, initials, tailpieces, endpapers,
and printing types.[13]

If Goodhue's architecture was deeply rooted in the English
medieval revival, his work as book designer stemmed from both
old and new layers of the same soil. The cover of the *Knight
Errant,* that evanescent art magazine edited by Goodhue and
Cram, with contributions by Day, Walter Crane, Bliss Carman,
and others of the crowd, visually conveys their editorial stance
(figure 5): sir knight, somewhat hesitantly to be sure (for he
glances back toward a kerchief being waved from the open
window of the castle-keep), rides forth to do battle with the forces
of materialism and ugliness represented by snakes, turtles, toads,
and other crawling things. The failures of previous aesthetes are
graphically depicted by the skull half-submerged in the dank tarn
lying athwart his path. This image reeks of Scott or Tennyson
while it anticipates Howard Pyle; it is the illustrative equivalent of
the romantic associations of Goodhue's architecture. At the same
time, the cover's heavy black-and-white design punched up with
red, and the magazine as a whole, a large quarto on handmade
paper set in old-style type with wide margins and embellished
with initials and tailpieces by Goodhue, shows an early awareness
of the English Arts and Crafts book, especially of William
Morris's new Kelmscott press.

His high-minded, high-art *Knight Errant* having succumbed to
the forces of materialism within a year, Cram retreated to the
opposite extreme, producing in 1893 a call to idleness entitled *The
Decadent: Being the Gospel of Inaction.* We might think of it as
the 1890s mild equivalent to Timothy Leary's 1960s call for a
drop-out drug culture. Copeland and Day published it; it was
dedicated to Goodhue, who provided the cover, three initials, and
a frontispiece. This last reflects Cram's change of mood, for here
the designer is toying with a variant stream of current English art,
the Aesthetic Movement. This linear, flat, sanguine, asymmetri-

FIGURE 5. B. G. Goodhue, cover design for the *Knight Errant,* 1891

cal, Japanese-influenced plate shows Aurelian Blake, the opium-beclouded hero (if a tract on inaction can have a ''hero''), lounging in a hammock full of books and flowers, smoke from his hookah swirling around Shiratsuyu, his Oriental serving girl. The art of Aubrey Beardsley comes to mind, but this is Beardsley denatured and, in truth, banalized. Cram's fin-de-siècle text and Goodhue's derivative illustration do nothing to enhance the reputation of either, and from this moment on, with notable exceptions, Goodhue stuck largely to decoration, leaving illustration to others.

Susan Thompson sees the frontispiece to *The Decadent* as clearly an Aesthetic creation, but she finds the book as a whole, with its heavy black letter scarcely relieved by a few historiated initials, decidedly Arts and Crafts. The Arts and Crafts book was known in Boston as early as 1891, the very year Morris opened his Kelmscott Press; in October, five months after it was published in Hammersmith, the Boston trade publisher Roberts Brothers issued *The Story of the Glittering Plain* in photofacsimile. The heavy type, engraved initials, and swirling vegetable borders were to become standards of Morris's work. The speed of *The Glittering Plain's* publication in Boston attests to the anglophilia of local taste; and the speed with which Morris's example affected the Boston publishing world in general and the work of Goodhue in particular attests to the permeation across the ocean of the Arts and Crafts spirit.

By 1892 this spirit had generated a native design, although not one from a fine-art press, nor one by Goodhue. The first American book to show Morris's influence was a collection of sketches by F. Hopkinson Smith, published by Houghton Mifflin and designed by D. B. Updike.[14] This has a title page border drawn by Harold Van Buren Magonigle, a man better known as a Gothic-revival architect than as a book decorator.[15] Two years passed before Goodhue's more accomplished emulation appeared, in Rossetti's *House of Life,* from the house of Copeland and Day. According to the colophon, this exists in five hundred copies on French handmade paper plus fifty on Michallet paper, with three borders and one hundred fourteen initials by Goodhue. It is dated 1894, although printed in 1893 and—again according to Susan Thompson, upon whose research I draw heavily—was probably designed in 1892. A review in the *Knight Errant,* while recognizing the origin of Goodhue's inspiration in this work, self-consciously sought to distance its editor from his source, and concluded that "while Mr. Goodhue's style would hardly have been possible without Mr. Morris, it cannot be justly said that he has copied

FIGURE 6. B. G. Goodhue, title page to [Bliss Carman], *Saint Kavin: A Ballad,* 1894

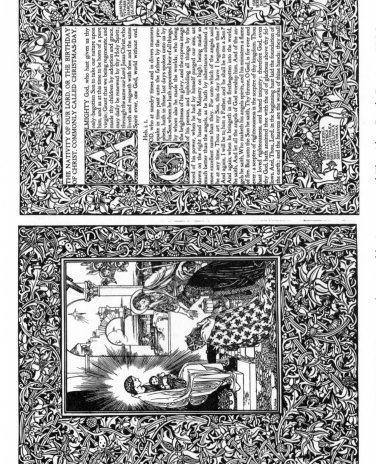

FIGURE 7. Verso and recto of facing pages of *The Altar Book*, Boston, 1896

him."[16] I leave it to others to decide the size of Pugin's American follower's debt to Pugin's English successor.

After the *House of Life,* Goodhue turned out one Arts and Crafts book after another for Copeland and Day, Updike's Merrymount Press, and other Boston publishers. In some work, like the title page to the ballad of Saint Kavin, Goodhue's tiny 1894 masterpiece for the guild of Visionists shown in apostolic assembly at the top (figure 6), the page spread for Louise Imogen Guiney's *Nine Sonnets Written at Oxford* (Copeland and Day, 1895), or the *Description of the Pastoral Staff . . . at Albany* (Merrymount, 1900), Goodhue's use of architectural rather than floral borders seems to penetrate through the Kelmscott influence to its Puginesque roots. Other work, such as the folio *The Altar Book* published in 1896, achieves, despite the noticeable stylistic differences between illustrations and decoration, a kind and quality of design equal to the master of Hammersmith himself (figure 7). *The Altar Book* was a collaborative effort overseen by Updike, with heraldic designs by Charles Sherman of London, illustrations by Robert Anning Bell of Liverpool, and borders, initials, and type (the first of two fonts to his credit) by Bertram Goodhue.

Goodhue's work as book decorator seems largely a function of his Boston days and milieu. His design for the cover of the *Knight Errant* is dated in the lower right corner 1891, the year he joined Cram; his last works are dated 1903–04, the year he moved to New York. Thereafter, lacking the stimulation of the Boston crowd, and increasingly becoming slave to a burgeoning architectural practice, with few exceptions (for example, one drawing for initials at the Grolier Club dated 1914), he abandoned his second design career.

Goodhue's output in both books and architecture was far richer than suggested here, but the medievalist roots and characteristics that have been emphasized are fundamental in any attempt to understand his historical position as a designer. It is possible, in fact, to envision him at work looking something like figure 8, at least during the first decade of his career, perhaps not dressed in a robe but totally immersed in a world of Gothic things. The fact is, this is not Goodhue, but Pugin; at least, this is the frontispiece to Pugin's *The True Principles of Pointed or Christian Architecture* (1841), depicting the medieval designer at work. Perhaps the parallel is forced, perhaps not. Goodhue shows what is presum-

FIGURE 8. Frontispiece to A. W. N. Pugin, *The True Principles of Pointed or Christian Architecture,* London, 1853 (first ed., 1841)

ably himself looking a lot like that medieval designer in his personal bookplate (figure 9); he would certainly have acknowledged his descent from the English polemicist.

But this bookplate suggests another dimension, a decidedly

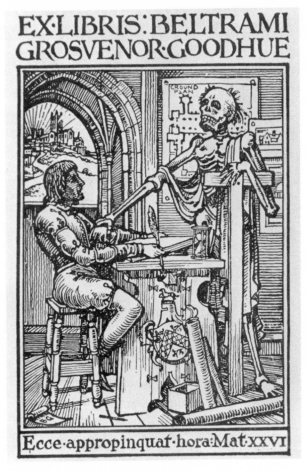

FIGURE 9. B. G. Goodhue, his bookplate (after Whitaker, *Goodhue,* 1925)

macabre one, to Goodhue's self-image. Here Death stays the designer's hand, just as death in fact stayed Goodhue's hand in 1924 when he was only fifty-five. In his biography of Goodhue for the *Macmillan Encyclopedia of Architects,* Richard Oliver characterizes Goodhue's death as coming at an ''awkward moment.'' It can be argued that most deaths are inconveniently scheduled, but what Oliver meant to emphasize was that Goodhue died just as he had begun to emerge in architecture from the Gothic Revival of

FIGURE 10. B. G. Goodhue, cover to *Alice in Wonderland: A Play*, New York, 1898

his origins to a twentieth-century interpretation of historical materials in buildings such as the Lincoln State House. Goodhue's work in the book arts was cut off even earlier and more awkwardly, not by death but by the press of architecture. If we wish that he had had more time to work out his reinterpreted architectural style, what can we say of his potential as a book designer? All is speculation, of course, but one piece of evidence at least suggests that Goodhue would have continued to develop in the realm of the book arts. The work that stands out from the line of Arts and Crafts designs listed earlier in his contribution, including endpapers, illustrations, and covers, to Emily Delafield's *Alice in Wonderland,* printed by Updike at the Merrymount Press and published by Dodd, Mead in 1898 (figure 10). Here, as at the beginning of the decade, Goodhue works as both pictorial and decorative artist, to reiterate Crane's distinctions, and has broken out of the black and white straightjacket of his coeval production. He works in the firm, flat, colorful style that marks and perhaps anticipates the product of contemporaries such as Maxfield Parrish. Here, in the book arts, he seems to prefigure the modernized medievalism that was to mark his last works in architecture. A full study of his achievement in book design will have to recognize the variety suggested by this image.

NOTES

1. Houghton Library MS Am 800.14.

2. R. Oliver, *Bertram Grosvenor Goodhue* (New York, Cambridge, and London, 1983); S. O. Thompson, *American Book Design and William Morris* (New York and London, 1977); E. Jussim, *Slave to Beauty* (Boston, 1981); B. Brandt, "The Essential Link: Boston Architects and The Society of Arts and Crafts," *Tiller Magazine,* 2 (1983), 7–32; N. Finlay, *Artists of the Book in Boston, 1890–1910* (Cambridge, 1985).

3. J. F. O'Gorman, "War, Slavery and Intemperance in the Book Illustrations of Hammatt Billings," *Imprint,* 10 (1985), 8–10.

4. Oliver, *Goodhue* (note 2), pp. 2 ff.

5. William H. Pierson, Jr., *American Buildings and Their Architects, Technology and the Picturesque: The Corporate and the Early Gothic Styles* (Garden City, N. Y., 1978), pp. 206 ff.

6. R. A. Cram, *My Life in Architecture* (Boston, 1936), p. 78.

7. Douglass Shand Tucci, *All Saints' Ashmont* (Boston, 1975).

8. R. A. Cram, "Partnership," in *Bertram Grosvenor Goodhue, Architect and Master of Many Arts,* ed. Charles H. Whitaker (New York, 1925), p. 31.

9. Oliver, *Goodhue* (note 2), p. 26.

10. Thompson, *American Book Design* (note 2), p. xiii.

11. Cram, "Partnership" (note 8), pp. 30–31.

12. W. Crane, *Of the Decorative Illustration of Books Old and New* (London and New York, 1916; 1st ed., 1896), p. v.

13. *Book Decorations by Bertram Grosvenor Goodhue* (New York, 1931).

14. Thompson, *American Book Design* (note 2), pp. 77–78.

15. Finlay, *Artists of the Book* (note 2), p. 4.

16. *Knight Errant* (January 1893), quoted in Thompson, *American Book Design* (note 2), p. 44.

COCKERELS AND AMAZONS: LETTERS OF CHRISTOPHER SANDFORD TO CLIFFORD WEBB, 1946–1947
Roderick Cave

Christopher Sandford, partner in (and later sole owner of) the Golden Cockerel Press from 1933 to 1959, carefully preserved nearly all the letters he received from the authors, artists and others with whom he worked on the production of the long and distinguished series of Golden Cockerel books. It was his intention eventually to produce a book which would include their comments on art, theories of illustration and so forth. In his annotation to the entry for *The Vigil of Venus* in *Pertelote,* the bibliography of Golden Cockerel books October 1936 to April 1943, Sandford referred clearly to his wish to write this book "when peace comes and we can return to literary work," but the volume was never written. Some of the materials for it survive in the collections of Cockerel papers in the William Andrews Clark Memorial Library at the University of California (Los Angeles) and in the Harry Ransom Humanities Research Center, University of Texas. Research in these collections is therefore really incumbent on anyone attempting a serious study of the Golden Cockerel and how its books came into being.

In many instances, however, use of these collections is not enough as the correspondence they contain gives only one side of the exchange of letters. Sandford seldom retained copies of the letters he wrote—and "wrote" is the correct word, as most of his correspondence about Golden Cockerel matters was written longhand. Very occasionally indeed when an exact record was required Sandford would make a longhand draft of a letter which he

Reprinted with permission from *The Private Library,* Spring 1988, V.1, N.1, Fourth Series, pp. 27–42.

would then have typed, and would retain a carbon copy. Rather more often, he would draft a letter in pen or pencil and keep this draft in his files as a record after he had copied it out in his characteristic clear handwriting and sent the copy as his reply. Sometimes when the correspondence was irksome he would draft a cutting rejoinder but (having thus worked off his irritation) would then send a more diplomatically worded response in its stead. Usually, however, his procedure was simply to make a scribbled record in a sentence or two of the gist of his own letter, in the margin of the one he was answering.

Even in the relatively relaxed, comfortable and unbusinesslike world of the private press this could (and did) cause difficulties when queries arose long after the event, and it cannot have been very satisfactory for Sandford himself. There is some indication that even after he had sold the Golden Cockerel to Thomas Yoseloff he made attempts to round out his own record of the making of its books by getting back his own letters. Thus, some time after the wood-engraver Clifford Webb had died in 1972, and Sandford was in touch with his widow Ella, he asked if he could have back any of his own letters that Ella Webb might have come across in sorting through her husband's papers. In a letter dated from Kibworth Beauchamp, Leicestershire, ''Boxing Day,'' Mrs. Webb sent him all she had been able to find; the text of these is printed below.

Clifford Webb illustrated eight books for the Golden Cockerel Press, starting with *Ana the Runner* by Patrick Miller published in 1937 (*Pertelote* no. 122) and ending with Eurof Walters' *The Serpent's Presence* issued in October 1954 (*Cock-a-hoop* no. 197). Eight books—some of them among the most successful and important Cockerels of the time, as well as being outstanding examples of Webb's work in wood-engraving—was a substantial number, and would have generated quite a considerable correspondence between the artist and his publisher. Ella Webb, however, was able to find only a small number of letters: ''there must have been a lot more that he did not keep'' she reported to Sandford. Those that she did find were written in 1946–47, and concerned mainly with the preparation of Ivor Bannet's *The Amazons,* eventually published by Golden Cockerel in 1948 (*Cockalorum* no. 181).

In the transcript of Sandford's letters given below, I have

Wood-engraved title-page device by Clifford Webb from The Amazons, 1948

Wood-engraved title-page device by Clifford Webb from The Amazons, 1948

followed Sandford's orthography and punctuation exactly. The letters were written on paper with Golden Cockerel letterheads, usually with the address for ''Production'' which was Sandford's home address at Eye Manor, Leominster, Herefordshire, but occasionally (when he did not have the right paper to hand, or when he happened to be in London) with the address 1–5 Poland Street, London W.1, the office Golden Cockerel had on the premises of the binders Sangorski & Sutcliffe who bound most of the deluxe copies of Cockerel books at that period. Sandford's home address was always added in longhand at the head of these letters.

Though business letters, there was an air of informality about the physical appearance of these letters written to Webb, just as there was in the easy style Sandford adopted in them. A final paragraph written in the margin rather than starting a fresh page; words crossed through; words interpolated—all testify to the relaxed way in which Sandford conducted the Golden Cockerel Press. It may have been Horace Walpole who hoped that the books from his private press would reveal ''all the beautiful negligence of a gentleman,'' but Sandford's letters show how his own gentlemanly negligence was more in appearance than reality, being combined with an informed mind, a caring heart and an attentive eye, which helped to make Golden Cockerel books some of the handsomest of their generation.

The correspondence starts in the summer of 1946, just after the publication of Somerset de Chair's translation for the Golden Cockerel of *The First Crusade* for which Webb had provided some powerful and effective engravings.

[i]   The Golden Cockerel Press, Eye Manor, Leominster
                                                            29 June 1946
Dear Webb

I'm so glad you like the book. Although your blocks for *Ana* could not have been bettered & I shall always be fond of that little book, I think that, taken all round, the *Crusade* is our finest joint effort so far. Even at this early stage, there is every indication that the book is being greatly admired & liked. The text makes most enjoyable reading, your pictures are extremely powerful (I find that they *grow* on one), & the whole thing was pleasantly lavish & pre-war & un-proletarian.

I am glad you are coming down this way, as I want to show you the one copy of the 'specials' which I have kept. In full vellum, &

with your *admirable* designs on front & back covers, they are, I think, quite delightful.

If you should want any more ordinaries, please write *at once* to W. Green, Golden Cockerel Press, 1–5 Poland Street, [London] W.1, as I feel sure that there is being a scramble for this book, there being only 500 copies. (At the time we put it in hand 500 was the limit we were allowed by the Board of Trade to print in large type & with margins). The cost is 5 gns less 33 $\frac{1}{3}$% to you (105/– minus 35/–= 70/–).

We shall discuss a new book for you when you are down here. I have one which both I and the author particularly want *you* to illustrate. Alas! it is not about animals, unless you could call Amazons such! It is a reconstruction of the wars of the Amazons by Ivor Bannet, an Oxford historian at present in the civil service. It is rather terrific, in a Salambo sort of way—*not sexy*—& nobody would handle it as well as you would. According to legends, they came from, & returned to, Atlantis, & *that* comes in too. I suggested various alterations which are now being made. As soon as I receive a revised typescript, I shall send it to you for persual [sic].

Yrs ever
Christopher Sandford

Sandford wanted Webb to undertake the commission, but was a little less than completely honest in suggesting that he was specially anxious to have Webb's engravings in *The Amazons*. By June 1946 he might have been, but at the beginning of March that year he had been trying to tempt John O'Connor with it:

> . . . your next 'fence' must be to master the figure & its inclusion in all the rest of your picture. . . . You are such a good artist, you can surely master this. And if you can, I can give you book after book. For instance, I have one by me now, called *The Amazons*—a romance founded on all the old myths concerning that strange tribe. Now that Gill is dead, there are only three practising engravers in this country who *could* handle this book adequately . . . .

The engravers Sandford meant were John Buckland Wright,

Dorothea Braby and his own wife Lettice Sandford. His use of *The Amazons* as bait hove out to persuade O'Connor to make his engravings more arousing (like those of Buckland Wright) has been described elsewhere[1] and need not detain us further. It seems clear however that at his first reading of Ivor Bannet's text Sandford *had* seen *The Amazons* as a vehicle for sexy illustrations of the kind appreciated by many purchasers of Cockerels, and had by no means thought of Webb as an appropriate artist for the book. Indeed, as a part of his attempt to mould O'Connor into an artist who would provide Golden Cockerel patrons with pictures of "girls whom discerning men would want to pick up & who have ... shapely arms & legs" (as he had put it) Sandford had sent O'Connor a print from *Ana the Runner* showing some of the faults in Webb's figure-work which O'Connor should try to avoid. When on 16 May 1946 Sandford told O'Connor that he had been compelled to give *The Amazons* to another artist because the author did not like O'Connor's style of engraving, he had not yet made any approach to Webb. Does the fact that six weeks intervened between this letter, and his first suggestion of the book to Webb, indicate that Sandford had unsuccessfully sought to interest another engraver in the meantime? It is hard to tell, but there is no doubt that in the letter he wrote on 29 June to Webb, and in their subsequent meeting, Sandford was successful in persuading him he was the right artist for the book. Before the next letter they had met at Eye Manor, during one of Webb's camping trips which so surprised Sandford.

[ii]   The Golden Cockerel Press, Eye Manor, Leominster
                                                          25 July 1946
My dear Webb

It was very nice seeing you again. I was cross with myself afterwards for not having suggested that, if the weather turned wet, you should move in here till the end of your stay. In fact it did turn wet on Friday. But, on the other hand, you may have been able to work in the farm & no doubt wanted to remain on the scene of your pictures till finished. But this is to say, as I may have said before, that we are *always* keen to put you up here, should it suit your plans for work you may be doing down here in Hfds: [i.e. Herefordshire].

About *The Amazons,* I am so glad that this appeals to you, as you will do it marvellously. When I saw you, you had not read the best of it &, as you had already liked the least good, I am taking for granted that you *will* be doing it, even to the extent of ordering the paper & sending the typescript for typesetting! The paper & typesetting will both take some six months, so I am not being as premature as I might seem. I have learnt by experience that one must jump one's books into the queues or else miss the boat.

Regarding your illustrations, I confirm that we shall pay you £100 on rct: of the engravings (or part in advance at any time, should this be helpful). The book makes some 240 pages, so that, say, about 10 (on an average of every 24 pages) would suffice. If, however, you feel much drawn to this book & would like to do 16—a frontispiece & one for each of the 15 chapters—I must pay you more, & trust to the enhanced attractiveness of the book to sell more copies & recover the additional outlay.[2] But, as I said, what you do (for whatever we pay you) is whatever you yourself choose to do. It is far best to leave it like that, as we did with *The First Crusade.*

Also about *time,* I want to leave you free. I suggest, tentatively, that you should sound a "dressing-gong" at the end of December, & "dish up" between then & Easter, which would be about the latest if the book is to be printed & bound by Sept 1947. But much will depend on how much work you decide to put into this book, & it would be a pity to hurry it. I would rather publish in February 1948 than hurry you.[3]

About size, I think I know just what you like now, & spent this morning going into sizes & shapes relative to types available, & have decided on Imperial 8vo, page 11 in. [high] by 7 1/2 in., 16 pt. Poliphilus type (same as *The First Crusade*), the size of the blocks to be 7 1/4 in. [high] × 5 in. I am quite unusually excited about this book, because it is something new, rather terrific, & with, I guess, a very considerable appeal. In this shape, it should be exceptionally well proportioned in its *three* dimensions. So often our books are grand in height and width but too slim. This should be just right. And it will have enough margins to be rich, without so much as to be gaudy. It should be just what a book *should* be— admirably worth reading, & readable, & pleasantly embellished.

I shall greatly look forward to a line from you, saying that we are progressing in step. If anything is *not* as you would wish, I can still (if I know at once) stop the paper, or the typesetting, pending further discussion. I may have been premature. What I did *not* want was to lay this book on one side, where it would gradually sink to the bottom of a pile (as, I find, things *do*) & not reappear for months or even *years*!

Yrs ever
Christopher Sandford

[*Postscript, written in margin*] My address from Wed. until 14th Aug: c/o Mrs Lee, Gelligemlyn, Dolgelley, Merioneth, Wales (then back here).

[iii]   The Golden Cockerel Press, Eye Manor, Leominster
23/12/46

My dear Webb

I am thinking of you & your Happy Family & hoping that you will all be having a very Merry Christmas & success in all your endeavours during 1947.

I hope that *The Amazons* progresses slowly but surely. My most recent information from the Mill is that I cannot expect delivery of the paper (ordered in July!) until about April next. What times we live in! So, if you complete by Easter, so that the whole thing can be got ready for when the paper is ready, that will suit me well.

All the best
Christopher Sandford

I should naturally be excited to see prints of any blocks you may already have got done.

Paper supplies were only one problem in those difficult post-war years. Sandford was finding delays of a kind he had never

Wood-engraved colophon device by Clifford Webb from The Amazons, *1948*

Wood-engraved colophon device by Clifford Webb from The Amazons, *1948*

encountered before or during the war in composition, press-work, and binding as well. In addition to all these troubles, there was one problem which worried several of the other Cockerel artists as well as Webb and Sandford: getting boxwood blocks. Stanley Lawrence, the proprietor of T. N. Lawrence, was something of a character who ran his business the way *he* thought best, as readers of his grandson's affectionate memoir printed in *Matrix* 7 will know. In the difficult post-war years he suffered periodically from bad stomach ulcers, and in December 1946 had been completely incapacitated by them.[4] There were likely to be considerable delays before orders for boxwood blocks could be filled from the shop in Bleeding Heart Yard.

[iv]   The Golden Cockerel Press, Eye Manor, Leominster
31.12.46
Dear Webb

Your two prints—most especially the one of the ship—are perfectly delightful. What tremendous effect you get with your 'zig-zaggery'. You always manage to remain powerful & personal. It is going to be a great book.

Yes, it is an awful bore about Lawrence. There used to be him, & his pa, & also his old uncle (in opposition round the corner). Now there is only him, & he himself very ill. By every post I hear groans, from all of you engaged on books for the G.C.P. As we specialise in books with engravings, L's illness is going to slow us down seriously presently, I'm afraid.

Considering that you & others depend on him so much, I think it is very wrong of Lawrence to have got himself into this position. It is surely one of the understood things that a good craftsman always provides for the continuation of his craft in the event of any thing happening to him. I've written to him along these lines, so that, perhaps, when he is well again, he will do something so that it does not happen again.

What about *trying* one of the other block-makers you speak of? I did not know there were *any* others. Could you give me the name of one?[5] I would go & see him when in London next week & see whether he considered he could perhaps do as well as Lawrence in some way—as perhaps by charging Lawrence's prices. There's a lot in that. Lawrence's cheaper blocks were always unsatisfactory. [*Remainder of letter written in margin*] Well, I hope all will be right in the end. It is very disappointing for you, but having anyhow to wait for the paper consoles one a little.

All the best
Christopher Sandford

I shall look out for the two others from you with keen anticipation.

[v]   The Golden Cockerel Press, Eye Manor, Leominster
                                                                19.3.47

My dear Webb

Many thanks for yours of the 14th. How delayed posts are! Your
letter took 4 days coming, & my reply may never reach you, as we
are surrounded by deep floods, & no doubt you are too. But I shall
duly put this in the box, & hope that some amphibian postman will
win his way through sooner or later.

You asked for a date to work to & I suggested Easter, but you have
had your delays with [getting] blocks & I with paper, & don't let
us allow the book to suffer on that account. Let its printing await
your completion, whenever it may be. I would hate, by quite
unnecessary haste, to rob it of the 8th picture. Every one of the 8
will be treasured, not only by me but by 750 enthusiastic
book-lovers.[6]

In any case, I should hate to hurry you. I am a *great* believer in the
artist & designer taking their time. Rushed work is never first
class. The very fact that each of your pictures takes you so long, as
a result of careful experimentation & thought, appeals to me
greatly. This makes all the difference in the world to the finished
article.

It will be lovely if you come our way at Easter. You wouldn't
rather have a bed? For the first week of April we shall be rather a
full house, but there'd always be a bed for you. After the 8th a
double bed, in which you could stretch far & wide. Camping
sounds very moist just now. But I do understand anyone liking a
dose of complete solitude now & then. It is a spiritual necessity—
as Christ knew when he went into the wilderness & even old-man
Hitler when he buzzed off to Berchtesgaden.

The curlews arrived on Saturday—or rather the first. He came &
flew round calling, & now there is quite a gaggle or wisp, flying
about & searching (like Noah's birds) for some not-too-dry dry
land.

The plovers came today, and are tumbling about pee-witting, bless
them! It is charming of you to suggest a couple of head or tail

blocks for the book. It will just make all the difference if you feel you *can* do, say, a vignette for the title page (the same sort of size as the two horsemen you did for *The First Crusade*) & a pressmark for the End (again that same sort of size). The latter might be mildly humourous, if you like—an Amazon petting a cockerel or each of them looking very fierce & trying to frighten each other? I think that would be better, for this book, than formal head- pieces. It will be really grand if you do feel drawn to do anything of the kind suggested. Let's aim at going to press some time about the middle of May. Its [sic] going to be a truly delightful book!

Yrs ever
Christopher Sandford

[vi]   The Golden Cockerel Press, Eye Manor, Leominster
23/3/47
My dear Webb
The prints of the blocks have come. They are *lovely*! They seem to me to be far the best you have done so far, for the Cockerel or anyone else. How is it that you are all surpassing your previous work so greatly now? Maybe it is the return to art after the fallow years—the 'winter'—of war. Maybe a healthy competition helps: our socialist friends would deny this, but it is true.
Anyway, believe me, the receipt of these prints has made me very happy. One thing good about them is that each is a picture on its own: though they all combine & are good illustrations, they are not merely such but good as pure pictures too.[7]
The one of the Garden of the Hesperides is a really beautiful conception, as lovely as any print I have ever had from anyone. But I like them all, with their gentle under-current of humour, the va et vient of the crowd, giving life & humanity, & your technical effects. You have cleverly managed to bring a lot of animals into the pictures, &, where there are none in the context, you have brought in those quaint ships & treated them as such. It is all *grand,* & you have done wonders with the text. The author has not yet seen these latest prints, but is wildly enthusiastic about the first two he saw. These will all need very careful printing. I shall probably print the text first & then cut up the sheets on which these are to be blocks, & print the latter on damped paper in small size on a platen machine. If one *ought* to temper appreciation with

criticism, I myself would prefer a little more naturalistic treatment
of the girls' figures—a little more feeling for flesh, bone & sinew.
Your wolves, horses, & sea-gulls are also symbolised but less so
than your girls. I should like more sex-appeal. I feel you *could*
have this, & all the rest *too*—that a greater feeling for 'the flesh'
would add something without lessening your total effect.
But this is only a suggestion—*for the future.*[8]

Yrs ever
Christopher Sandford

Would you like some money yet?
The Studio is letting me do some articles on contemporary
wood-engravers, who are not, I think, getting enough notice. I
want you to let me do one on you before long.[9] Let's discuss this
when we meet—if, as I hope, you come down this way.

[vii]   The Golden Cockerel Press, Eye Manor, Leominster
29.4.47

Dear Webb
Your Cave of Chronos block is really 'super'—your best ever, I
think. I do think it astonishing that you can take, for instance, the
garden of the Hesperides & the Cave of Chronos, & not only
portray the magic of these romantic & 'ideal' literary conceptions,
but actually improve on the pictures evoked by the words.
Technically this latest work of yours for *The Amazons* is, of
course, faultless, but it seems to me also to have a new 'magic' of
poetic conception which lifts it above all your previous work.
As you ask for Ivor Bannet's latest criticism, I enclose it.[10] [*Not
now present with the letters.*] As criticism, I suppose it is very
clever, & there is, of course, powerful structural design in your
work which can, if need be, be interpreted in terms of geometry.
But that sort of criticism is, for me, too glib & too mechanical.
However, for what it is worth, here it is. [*Written in margin beside
this paragraph*] As a matter of fact, do you *consciously* adopt
geometric shapes in your composition? I *doubt* it.
I see he has singled out the Pegasus block for criticism. Of course,
as you explained, it was difficult to translate his nebulous
conception of a man astride a 'huge' ship. I think you did it very
well, & personally I think it is a very fine block—your contrasts of

"The Pegasus," engraving by Clifford Webb from The Amazons, 1948
(reduced from 5 inches wide)

"The Defeat of the Argives," engraving by Clifford Webb *from* The Amazons, *1948 (detail)*

black & white masses being extraordinarily effective in that block.

Before you leave the subject altogether, could you do a simplified drawing for the binding brass? I suggest you might quite simply do a very plain outline drawing with bold lines (& the minimum of them) of enclosed print from your title-page block. Actually the size of the book is $11 \times 7^{1}/_{2}''$, thus:

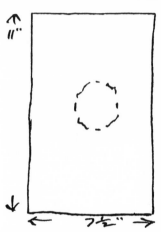

So this design is on the small size, but not really *too* small. The ideal, of course, would be to have *two* brasses to match (as for the 'special' bindings of *The First Crusade,* but I think I could get two out of one, as it were, by making one block the way of your drawing (when it comes) & the other the same thing photographically reversed. But two, balancing each other but *not* the same, would be ideal—and in size say 5 $^{1}/_{2}''$ to 6" $\updownarrow \times 3^{1}/_{2}''$ to 4".

I'll give you a 'special' copy this time. It will be a small return for the extra sweat.

Here's the cheque.

It will be nice seeing you again in July. I was sorry to miss you when you called. Since then we have most of us had chicken pox, including myself, rather badly. My scabs are all gone now, so this letter won't infect you. By the way, the blocks as well as the prints, arrived safely.

                                    Yrs ever Christopher Sandford

    The surviving correspondence closes with this letter, nineteen months before *The Amazons* was actually published—such were the delays in production which afflicted Golden Cockerel at that time. Several months before it was published Ivor Bannet died at the early age of 37. Whether he had become reconciled to Webb's interpretation of some of his imagery we do not know, though we can guess that any coolness between him and Sandford over the illustrations was of no real importance since at the time of Bannet's death his second book, *The Arrows of the Sun,* was being considered by Sandford. Although it was published later, it was not as a Cockerel.[11]

Webb's work—and Bannet's text—was damned with faint praise in the *Times Literary Supplement* of 18 November 1949, in which the anonymous reviewer commented that

> The engravings by Mr Clifford Webb do not seem to express with quite sufficient sense of classicism the scenes they illustrate, just as the writing falls short of the epic quality required.

But in the minds of those in Printing House Square in the late Forties, the Golden Cockerel could do nothing right, or so Sandford believed. Sandford himself thought very highly of Webb and of his engravings for *The Amazons,* "the finest yet produced by this master of black and white" as he put it in *Cockalorum.* Whether it is the finest of the Cockerels illustrated by Webb is a pleasant topic for collectors to debate. . .

NOTES

1. In my article "Fanfares, Amazons and Narrow-Boats: Correspondence Between John O'Connor and Christopher Sandford, 1944–47," in *Matrix* 7, 1987, pp. 128–46.

2. In the end the volume of 252 pages was published with twelve wood-engravings by Webb, plus three maps by Mina Greenhill which were reproduced by line-block.

3. Though dated December 1948 in *Cockalorum,* it was not, in fact, published until several months later.

4. cf. Simon Lawrence, "My grandfather, Stanley Thomas Evans Lawrence," in *Martrix* 7, 1987, pp. 1–3. I am grateful to Simon Lawrence for telling me what was the nature of his grandfather's illness forty years ago.

5. If there were any other London blockmakers working in the late Forties, I have been unable to find out anything about them. T. N. Lawrence & Son in fact had a monopoly in Britain.

6. Sandford seems to have been planning a much larger edition than the 500 copies actually published. Several Cockerels between *Flinders' Narrative* in October 1946 and Swinburne's *Laus Veneris* in July 1948

were issued in editions of 750 copies, but this was really more than the market could readily absorb, as Sandford soon discovered.

7. In conversations with me in the late Sixties, Sandford emphasized the way in which he had tried to allow artists to produce illustrations which could stand alone as pictures away from the text.

8. Sandford was no more successful in persuading Webb to show "a greater feeling for the flesh" than he had been with O'Connor. Evidently there *were* some Golden Cockerel clients for whom sex-appeal was important—or so Sandford believed—but there were as many potential customers who were slightly scandalized by it.

9. It appeared in the August 1949 issue. Another version of the text was printed by Sandford in *Cockalorum,* pp. 65–71.

10. Sandford often protected his illustrators from the sight of criticism he thought likely to wound them, and it seems clear that in this instance he had not wanted Webb to see Bannet's comments. In other cases when authors made adverse comment on the illustrations provided, Sandford was swift to support the artists against attack, and it is likely that he brushed off Bannet's criticisms in this instance.

11. It was published by the Cresset Press.

OPENING PHOTO

AUTHOR AND ILLUSTRATOR: IMAGES IN CONFRONTATION
Sybille Pantazzi

In 1842 the *Illustrated London News* announced that art had become the bride of literature. This union was a *mariage de:cove-nance* promoted for commercial reasons by the publishers and engravers. In fact it will be seen that, although the bride was sometimes restive, she was generally docile but that in many cases the groom would have preferred to remain a bachelor. The inherent rivalry between writer and artist did not prevent some

Reprinted with permission from *Victorian Periodicals Newsletter* (now *Victorian Periodicals Review*), V.9, no. 2, 1976, pp. 39–49.

fruitful collaborations but it was nevertheless a constant factor (see G. Du Maurier's Tail-piece [*Magazine of Art* XIII, 1890, p. 375] above). This paper deals with some aspects of this rivalry and with the uneasy marriage of text and picture which resulted from it.[1]

The illustration of books is generally assumed to be the graphic interpretation of situations in pre-existing texts. However, the matching of text to preexisting pictures was also a wide-spread practice which continued late into the 19th century. This practice, which subordinated the writer to the artist, partly explains the distaste of many authors for illustration. The following examples range from 1810 to the 1880s.

For the *Tours of Dr. Syntax,* William Combe received each month from Rowlandson a comic design for which he was expected to provide the verses, without ever knowing what next month's subject would be. Mrs Sherwood wrote tracts to fit miscellaneous assortments of wood-cuts sent by the publishers. In the 1820s Scott was asked to supply the text for *The Provincial Antiquities of Scotland* for which Turner had been commissioned to supply drawings. Dickens also was originally engaged by Chapman and Hall to write the text to a series of sporting pictures by Robert Seymour. This was the genesis of *Pickwick Papers,* but Dickens from the first expressed his strong conviction that illustrations should arise from the text and ever after exercised a firm control over his illustrators with the admirable results we all know.

The preface to an 1838 annual described the poetry and prose it contained as "being no unfit companions to the beautiful engravings which they are intended to illustrate."[2] Thackeray, among others, made fun of these fashionable annuals. In *Pendennis* the hero is commissioned to write some verses to "illustrate" the *Church Porch,* a pretty picture which depicted a Spanish damsel hastening to church with a large prayer-book, watched by a youth in a cloak who is hiding in a niche. Thackeray ironically explains: "as these plates were prepared long beforehand, requiring much time in the engraving, it was the eminent poets who had to write to the plates, and not the painters who illustrated the poems."[3]

Birket Foster's *Pictures of English Landscape* is a good example of the 1860s. The drawings were commissioned by the Dalziel Brothers and, through the intervention of Millais, Tennyson was invited to write the poetry. Lady Tennyson wrote to Millais: "I am sorry to have to answer the thing is impossible. Poems do not come to him so. . . "[4] However, Tom Taylor, the playwright and contributor to *Punch,* accepted the commission. In the preface to the volume, which appeared in 1863, he defends this method of illustrating a book in the following terms:

> Birket Foster's drawings were made quite independently of the verses I have attempted to set to them . . . The verses which I have associated with his designs are meant to harmonize with and illustrate, without pretending to describe, the inventions of the painter. In this free way, I believe pen and pencil will be found to work best together. The painter as a rule, succeeds as ill in painting after the writer's descriptions, as the writer who tries to produce a picture in words after the painter. But picture may be set to poem, or poem to picture, as music is set to words, with an effect that enhances the enjoyment both of one and the other.[5]

Publishers of illustrated works like Cassell accumulated large stocks of used wood engravings and electrotypes which were drawn on by periodicals like *Once a Week* (under Manville Fenn's editorship) and *Onward,* Mayne Reid's magazine. Many of the blocks were imported from France but Reid removed the names of the French artists and engravers. Clement Scott and others provided appropriate verses for old blocks in the *Quiver.* George Augustus Sala was commissioned to provide the text for the drawings by Gustave Doré, and W. H. G. Kingston wrote adventure stories around old cuts.[6]

Unlike Tom Taylor, the talented authors quite naturally resented being under the disadvantage of having to write to the plates of the artists—a practice scarcely favourable to literary merit. In view of this, the following letter from Henry James, written to the publisher of *Lippincott's Magazine* in 1878, will not seem surprising: "I am afraid I can think of no suggestions for plates for my 'English Vignettes'," he wrote. "The purpose of these few lines is to express my grief at my would-be-delicate and to-be-read-on-its-own-account prose being served up this manner. The thought is painful to me . . . But I earnestly beseech you not to equip anything I may in future send you in the same fashion. I think the text of illustrated articles is always supposed to be poor and perfunctory—written to the plates and not read by those to whom I address myself."[7] The article in question was indeed illustrated with undistinguished topographical engravings. And again fifteen years later, in 1895, he wrote to Howells à propos of the illustrated magazine world: "I hate the hurried little subordinate part that one plays in the catchpenny picture-book and the negation of all literature that the insolence of the picture-book imposes."[8]

When Samuel Rogers complained that nobody read his poems, Turner exclaimed "Then they shall read them, and no lady's boudoir shall be complete without a copy, for I will make them attractive with illustrations."[9] As is well known, the illustrated editions of Rogers's *Italy* (1830) and of his *Poems* (1834) were best-sellers and their success was due to the illustrations by Turner and Stothard. Rogers said afterwards: "I never had any difficulty with Stothard and Turner about the drawings for my works. They always readily assented to whatever alterations I proposed and sometimes I even put a figure by Stothard into some of Turner's landscapes."[10]

In a letter to Rogers acknowledging the receipt of *Italy,* Sir Walter Scott wrote that his "beautiful verses of Italy are embellished by such beautiful specimens of architecture as to form a rare specimen of the manner in which the art of poetry can awaken the Muse of Painting."[11] Nevertheless, when Cadell suggested to Scott that Turner should be commissioned to illustrate his Works, the writer was not enthusiastic. He regarded the illustration of his poems as a concession to popular taste and considered the artists as incapable of historical accuracy in costume or topographical accuracy in landscape as well as incompetent to choose the subjects of illustrations.

"Perhaps nothing is more difficult than for a painter to adapt the author's ideas of an imaginary character," Scott wrote in August 1804, "especially when it is founded on traditions to which the artist is a stranger. I should like at least to be at his elbow when at work." About Westall's illustrations for *The Lay of the Last Minstrel* and *Marmion* he replied to Joanna Baillie, "You are quite right as to my private opinion of Westall's illustrations, they are basely devised like almost everything of the kind I ever saw—but what would it have availed to have said so to the artist or to poor Longman—the deed was done.'' And again, in the same letter, about the forthcoming illustrations for *The Lady of the Lake,* ''both will probably be execrable for if Westall who is really a man of talent fail'd in figures of chivalry where he had so many painters to guide him, what in the devil will he make of Highland figures. I expect to see my chieftain Sir Roderick Dhu in the guise of a recruiting sergeant of the Black Watch and his Bard the very model of Auld Robin Grey upon a japan'd tea-tray.''[12]

About the Turner illustrations he wrote to Cadell, ''I foresee that if Mr. Turner is to have his way in the illustrations, the work is to be void of that propriety which gives interest to an illustrated poem which I conceive to be the propriety of the union between press and pencil which like the parties in a well chosen marriage, should be well considered before hand.''[13]

Westall and Turner may not have satisfied Scott's requirements but none the less they were keenly aware of the difficulties of illustrating a text. Thus Westall in a letter to Scott defines one of the major dilemmas in illustrating a work of imaginative litera- ture: ''The reason why I judge highly of your opinion in paint- ing,'' he wrote, ''is the great, the minute, the picturesque skill with which you have wrought every important scene in your works; and in proportion as you are in this respect a painter, you are more difficult to paint from, for you have embodied your own ideas and presented them to the mind so completely that little is left for the pencil to perform.''[14] Turner also, in his lectures on perspective at the Royal Academy, warned that ''poetic descrip- tion most full, most incidental, and displaying the greatest richness of verse is often the least pictorial.''[15]

In the late 1860s, Luke Fildes, who was commissioned to illustrate *Edwin Drood,* found Dickens difficult to work for because the scenes the author wished to have illustrated were those into which he had put the utmost of his descriptive powers. Fildes contended that those were the scenes which least required graphic illustration and that an illustrator's usefulness could best be put to commenting on and emphasizing the least outstanding passages in the text.[16]

Dickens's views on this matter and on the new school of illustrators which Fildes represented were expressed in *All the Year Round* in 1867. He deplored that the illustrator of the eighteen-sixties ''chooses those situations which are the tamest

Illus. I. Millais: *The Small House at Allington* (*Cornhill,* July 1863).

Illus. II. Du Maurier: *Sybil's Disappointment* by Harriet Parr (*Cornhill,* June 1863).

Illus. III. Bush: *The Moonstone* (*Harper's Weekly,* Jan. 1868)

Illus. IV. Leighton: "Escaped," *Romola* (*Cornhill,* Jan. 1863).

and least dramatic, because they fetter him less and lend themselves more readily to producing a complete and agreeable picture, than those more stirring situations which both the author and the public would have liked to see illustrated.'' In contrast to Cruikshank and Browne's lively style, the drawings of the new school, he complains, ''represent scenes wholly devoid of action or stir: two or three people seated around a table; a couple of young fellows chatting over their wine; a lady showing a picture-book to her little girl; lovers in pairs, without end, single figures, also without end; young ladies reading love-letters, or overwhelmed with some piece of ill news just received.''[17] Illustrations I and II are from *The Cornhill Gallery* (1864) where Dickens could have found many examples of the type of scenes he describes. It was an anthology of engravings which had appeared in *The Cornhill Magazine*.

Tennyson's attitude to the illustration of his poems was a mixture of distaste and incomprehension. He disliked Moxon's project of the Illustrated Edition which was published in 1857. According to his son, he found many of the drawings antipathetic and ''some, such as Rossetti's St. Cecilia, which he admired, seemed to him to have no relation to the text.''[18] His reaction to Holman Hunt's illustrations are amusingly related by Layard:

> ''My dear Hunt,'' said Tennyson, when he first saw [the] illustration [of the Lady of Shalott], ''I never said that the young woman's hair was flying all over the shop.'' ''No,'' said Hunt; ''but you never said it wasn't,'' and after a little the poet came to be wholly reconciled to it. Not so easily did he allow himself to be pacified, however, when he saw the long flight of steps which King Cophetua descends to meet and greet the Beggar maid . . . ''I never said,'' he complained, ''that there were a lot of steps; I only meant one or two.'' ''But,'' said Hunt, ''the old ballad says there was a flight of them.'' ''I dare say it does,'' remonstrated Tennyson, ''but I never said I got it from the old ballad.'' ''Well, but,'' retorted Hunt, ''the flight of steps doesn't contradict your account; you merely say: 'In robe and crown the king stept down'.'' But Tennyson would not be appeased and kept on declaring that he never meant more than two steps at the outside.[19]

Rogers, as we have seen, needed the support of a sister art to sell his poems but neither Scott nor Tennyson felt that necessity and only reluctantly consented to the demands of their publishers. A good number of novelists also yielded to the fashion for illustration but with many reservations.

Charles Reade's "The Good Fight," the first version of *The Cloister and the Hearth,* began appearing in the first issue of *Once a Week* in July 1859. The illustrations were by Charles Keene. Unfortunately the story was unpopular and as the circulation of the magazine began dropping, at the request of the publishers (Bradbury and Evans) it was terminated abruptly in October. Reade was naturally displeased and he commented in a letter: "the story has done great things for them [the publishers] as far as I can judge. I don't think this is their opinion. They fancy their paltry illustrations, which are far below the level of the penny press, do the business." Bradbury and Evans, who had launched *Once a Week* in competition with Dickens's new magazine *All the Year Round,* were in fact counting on the numerous illustrations to win subscribers, but these were not immediately appreciated. Reade also resented the fact that Keene was paid three guineas for each drawing and the blocks cut by Swain came to an average of two pounds and ten shillings each, the cost of the illustrations being more than one third as much as Reade received for the text.[20]

This unfortunate experience was not forgotten when twelve years later he wrote to Manville Fenn, the editor of *Cassell's Family Magazine:*

> In black and white it generally takes three at least to make a picture: on the vertical block there is not room for three figures well placed—even two are often huddled. To the vertical block we owe that system of amusing duet, of which the magazines are full. A ponderously tall gentleman is seen talking to a ponderously tall lady in a room furnished with the section of a tea-table. What are they talking about? Oh, you must read the text to learn that. In other words the writer must illustrate the sketch that is paid for to illustrate the writer.[21]

Reade's serial was followed by George Meredith's *Evan Harrington* which was also illustrated by Keene. Meredith had no

Illus. V. J. E. Millais: "Was it not a lie?" *Framley Parsonage* (*Cornhill Mag.*, June 1860).

objection to the artist whom he said "would do capitally." He wrote to Lucas, the editor of *Once a Week:* "We will leave the artist to his devices. Just tell him from me (with a multitude of thanks) that it will be as well not to insist too much on the costume—especially dealing with the younger people. A young lady in a poke [bonnet] is hardly presentable."[22] Some thirty years later, in answer to a query, he wrote: "I have a recollection of Charles Keene's illustrations to the novel and that I generally thought them apt, as his hand could be."[23] Faint praise for an artist who was one of the outstanding draughtsmen of the period. Scott and Meredith's preoccupation with costume was shared by Wilkie Collins. Regarding the illustration for *The Moonstone,* one of which is reproduced (Illus. III), he wrote to his American publishers, Harper: "The illustrations to the first number are very picturesque, the three Indians and the boy being especially good, as I think. In the second number there is the mistake (as we should call it in England) of presenting Gabriel Bettere in *livery.* A head-servant, he would wear plain black clothes—and would look, with his white cravat and grey hair, like an old clergyman. I only mention this for future illustrations."[24]

So far we have encountered irritation (Scott), resentment (Reade) and indifference (Meredith) in our authors. A graver doubt about the desirability of illustrations was expressed by Charlotte Brontë. To her publisher's suggestion that she provide some illustrations to *Jane Eyre* she replied: "If then Jane Eyre is ever to be illustrated, it must be by some other hand than that of its author. I hope no one will be at the trouble to make portraits of my characters. Bulwer and Byron heroes and heroines are very well, they are all of them handsome; but my personages are mostly unattractive in looks, and therefore ill-adapted to figure in ideal portraits. At the best, I have always thought such representations futile."[25]

George Eliot's misgivings are expressed in her letters to Frederic Leighton about the illustrations for *Romola* which appeared in the *Cornhill Magazine* in 1862. "I feel for you as well as for myself in this inevitable difficulty—nay impossibility of producing perfect correspondence between my intention and the illustrations," and again, "I am convinced that illustrations can only form a sort of overture to the text. The artist who uses the pencil must otherwise be tormented to misery by the deficiencies

Illus. VI. W. M. Thackeray: Sketch of "A Quarrel," *The Adventures of Philip*, 1861.

or requirements of the one who uses the pen, and the writer on the other hand, must die of impossible expectations.'' Her passionate concern with every detail is illustrated in still another letter: ''Romola's attitude is perfect and the composition altogether such . . . her face and hair though deliciously beautiful are not just the thing—how could they be? Do not make your self uneasy if alteration is impossible but I meant the hair to fall forward from behind the ears over her neck, and the dress to be without ornament.'' The following day, however, she generously admits that "the exigencies of your art must forbid perfect correspondence between the text and illustrations; and I came to the conclusion that it was these exigencies which had determined you as to the . . . fall of Romola's hair. You have given her attitude transcendently well, and the attitude is more important than the mere head-dress." In a subsequent letter she remarked on the "exquisite poetry" in the scene where Romola is standing above Florence.[26] (Frontispiece and Illus. IV)

As Allan Life's paper in this issue is devoted to the illustrations of Millais, I shall only mention the incident of Trollope and "the flounced dress." In February 1860, when Trollope forwarded the MS of *Framley Parsonage* to George Smith, the publisher and owner of the *Cornhill Magazine,* he included a note saying, "Should I live to see my story illustrated by Millais nobody would be able to hold me." However, on May 23rd of the same year he was writing to Smith: "I can hardly tell you what my feeling is about the illustration to the June No. of F. parsonage. It would be much better to omit it altogether if it still be possible— tho I fear it is not—as the copies will have been sent out. The picture is simply ludicrous, and will be thought by most people to have been made so intentionally. It is such a burlesque on such a situation as might do for Punch, only that the execution is too bad to have passed muster for that publication. I presume the fact to be that Mr. Millais has not time to devote to these illustrations, and if so, will it not be better to give them up?" And after signing the letter he added: "Even the face does not at all tell the story, for she seems to be sleeping. I wish it could be omitted" (Illus. V).

The illustration which depicts Lucy Robarts after she has refused the proposal of Lord Lufton (at the end of Chapter XVI) shows her wearing a dress with a billowing flounced crinoline which submerges the bed she is lying on, apparently dozing. In July Trollope wrote to thank Smith for the August issue. He commented: "The Crawley family is very good, I will now consent to forget the flounced dress. I saw the *very pattern of that dress* some time after the picture came out."[27]

Like Dickens and Trollope, Thackeray felt that the author should select the subjects and provide the artist with precise hints, among others about the costume. He had intended to illustrate himself *The Adventures of Philip* and had engaged a young artist of twenty-one named Frederick Walker to transfer his designs on

Illus. VII. F. Walker: "A Quarrel," *The Adventures of Philip* (*Cornhill Mag.*, October 1861).

to the wood block. But Walker soon rebelled at this hack work and Thackeray was so satisfied with his first blocks that he consented to let him invent his own designs. In August(?) 1861 he sent Walker a sketch with the following annotations: "Lord Ringwood on his sofa in the gout. Philip puts on his hat and makes him a bow. Lord Ringwood dressed in an old-fashioned tail-coat of 1824 date, high stock and collar."[28] Illustrations VI and VII reproduce Thackeray's sketch and Walker's illustration.

George Du Maurier believed that Thackeray "was more pleased with the outward shape that Fred Walker had given his Philip than with even his own mental conception of the same, which was quite different."[29] In fact Thackeray exemplified Du Maurier's contention that "it would be a great boon if [authors] could, however roughly, illustrate their own work, that the artist might have some idea of the characters and scenes as these present themselves to him who imagined them first." "If, authors would learn a little how to draw themselves," Du Maurier continues, "they would not put such difficulties in the artist's way, and expect the impossible from him, such as that he should draw three sides of a house in one picture, or show the heroine's full face, tearstained, as she gazes on the lover vanishing in the middle of the background."[30]

The Dalziel Brothers have recorded that on each page of the manuscript of Christina Rossetti's *Sing Song* (1872), the author had placed a pen sketch suggesting the subject to illustrate, but, they add, "of these Mr. Hughes made very little use and in only two instances actually followed the sketch."[31] Indeed, as George Eliot wrote, "the writer must die of impossible expectations."

NOTES

[1] For a late Victorian discussion about the rivalry between art and literature see P. G. Hamerton, "Book Illustration," *The Portfolio* XIX (1888), 17–21; reprinted in P. G. Hamerton, *Portfolio Papers* (Boston: Roberts, 1889), pp. 293–311.

[2] *Finden's Tableaux . . . of National Character,* ed. Mary Russell Mitford, 1838.

[3] W. M. Thackeray, *The History of Pendennis* (1848–1850), Chap. XXXI.

4 *The Brothers Dalziel, a Record of Fifty Years' Work* (London: Methuen, 1901), p. 143.

5 *Birket Foster's Pictures of English Landscape with Pictures in Words by Tom Taylor* (London: Routledge, Warne & Routledge, 1863). According to the Dalziel Brothers (pp. 140, 144) Foster was paid at least twice as much for the pictures as Taylor was for the poems.

6 Simon Nowell-Smith, *The House of Cassell 1848–1958* (London: Cassell, 1958), pp. 105–106.

7 Henry James, *Letters,* ed. Leon Edel (Cambridge: Harvard University Press, 1975), II, 181.

8 Leon Edel, *Henry James: The Treacherous Years, 1895–1901* (Philadelphia: Lippincott, 1969), p. 95.

9 Quoted by Mordechai Omer, *Turner and the Poets. . .* [Catalogue of an exhibition held at] Marble Hill House, Twickenham 12 April–1 June. (London: Greater London Council, 1975) (unpaged) [p. 19].

10 Quoted by T. McRobert, *Fine Illustrations in Western European Printed Books: Victoria & Albert Museum* (London: H.M.S.O., 1969), p. 21.

11 Omer, [p. 19].

12 Quoted by Catherine Gordon, "The Illustration of Sir Walter Scott: Nineteenth Century Enthusiasm and Adaptation," *Journal of the Warburg & Courtauld Institutes,* XXXIV (1971), pp. 301–302.

13 Adele M. Holcomb, "Turner and Scott," *JWCI,* XXXIV (1971), 391.

14 Gordon, p. 301.

15 Omer, [p. 40].

16 L. V. Fildes, *Luke Fildes* (London: Michael Joseph, 1968), p. 15.

17 [Charles Dickens], "Book Illustrations," *All the Year Round,* (10 August, 1867), p. 152.

18 Charles Tennyson, *Alfred Tennyson* (London: Macmillan, 1968), p. 303.

19 G. S. Layard, *Tennyson and His Pre-Raphaelite Illustrators* (London: Elliot Stock, 1894), p. 41.

20 R. A. Gettmann, "The Serialization of 'A Good Fight', " *Nineteenth Century Fiction,* VI (1952), 25–26.

21 Quoted by Nowell-Smith, p. 94.

22 George Meredith, *Letters,* ed. G. Cline (London: Oxford University Press, 1970), I, 56.

23 Meredith, *Letters,* III, 1276.

24 Quoted by M. L. Parrish and E. V. Miller, *Wilkie Collins and Charles Reade: First Editions Described with Notes,* (London: Constable, 1940), pp. 74–75.

25 Clement Shorter, *The Brontës: Life and Letters* (London: Hodder

& Stoughton, 1908), I, 402.

[26] George Eliot, *Letters,* ed. G. S. Haight (New Haven: Yale University Press, 1955), IV, 40–41, 55–56, 63.

[27] Anthony Trollope, *Letters,* ed. B. A. Booth (London: Oxford University Press, 1951), 56, 59–60, 64.

[28] J. G. Marks, *Life and Letters of Frederick Walker* (London: Macmillan, 1896), p. 24.

[29] George Du Maurier, "The Illustrating of Books from the Serious Artist's Point of View," *Magazine of Art* XIII (1890), 350.

[30] Du Maurier, p. 371.

[31] *The Brothers Dalziel,* pp. 91–92. Christina Rossetti's manuscript, with her drawings, is in the British Library, Ashley MS 1371.

PART V

CHILDREN'S BOOK ILLUSTRATION

EMBLEMS AND CHILDREN'S BOOKS IN THE 18TH CENTURY
Samuel Pickering, Jr.

In *Some Thoughts Concerning Education* (1693) and *An Essay Concerning Human Understanding* (1690), John Locke convinced the 18th century that childhood shaped the adult. Locke had an incalculable secularizing effect upon education, of which early reading came to be thought an important part.[1]

As commercial prosperity created then enriched the middle classes, parents, nurtured on Locke's ideas, envisioned children's futures in secular as well as religious terms. As a result children's books which seemed to promote both moral and worldly success became popular among the middle classes while "godly books" which minimized worldly success lost much of their appeal and rarely appeared on the lists of the leading publishers for children.[2]

In John Newbery's books, for example, a good early education inevitably brought financial success. Instead of climbing Jacob's Ladder and receiving rewards in heaven, Newbery's heroes and heroines—characters like Giles Gingerbread and Goody Two-Shoes—achieved prosperity and comfort on this earth and rode out of their histories in coaches and sixes.[3]

Paradoxically, however, the narratives through which the Giles Gingerbreads and Goody Two-Shoes traveled were often created out of the matter of traditional Christian allegory. Although authors may not have been consciously aware of the extent to which they relied upon religious material, many early children's books seem organized around emblematic scenes similar to those found in books like John Bunyan's *The Pilgrim's Progress* and Francis Quarles' *Emblems Divine and Moral*. Among the most commonly used emblems were the maze, the shipwreck, the

Reprinted with permission from *AB Bookman's Weekly,* November 9, 1987, pp. 1798–1805.

603

sleeping traveler, the cage or prison, the cure-all, the fight, the garden, and the precious jewel.

In hopes of "seeing" early children's literature in a new way, I examine the use made of two related emblems in eighteenth-century children's books: the looking glass or vanity mirror and the perspective glass or telescope.[4]

The 39th emblem in John Bunyan's *Divine Emblems: or, Temporal Things Spiritualized. Fitted for the Use of Boys and Girls* depicted a woman primping before a mirror. In the poem "Upon a Looking-glass," which accompanied the woodcut, Bunyan wrote, "In this, see thou thy beauty, hast thou any;/Or thy defects, should they be few or many./Thou may'st (too) here thy spots and freckles see,/Hast thou but eyes, and what their numbers be."

The spots to which Bunyan referred were inner, not outer. Looking only at the surface, the woman in the emblem was spiritually blind. "Without eyes" opened by Christianity, she was seduced by luxury and could not foresee her "eternal fate." "Many that seem to look here," Bunyan wrote, "blind men be./This is the reason. They so often read/Their judgment there, and do it nothing dread."

Francis Quarles' vanity mirror resembled Bunyan's looking glass. "Believe her not," Quarles urged, "her glass diffuses/False portraitures." The mirror abused "her mis-inform'd beholder's eye" and instead of a "true reflection" scattered "Deceitful beams." Like the Mirror that made the observer "fairer, goodlier, greater," the prism deceived and focused attention on "present toys" instead of "future joys."

In a discussion between Flesh and Spirit in book three of *Emblems Divine and Moral,* Quarles used the prism and the telescope to elaborate upon vanity and seeing. Noticing the telescope at her "sister's eye," Flesh asked Spirit what she saw. When Spirit replied that she was looking at "Grim death," Flesh asked, "and is this all? Doth thy prospective please/Th'-abused fancy with no shapes but these?"

Spirit then described another sight: Judgment Day. While "the angel-guarded Son" sat on his " high tribunal," the battlements of heaven sweltered in flames. Far below, Spirit said, was a "brimstone sea of boiling fire." There fiends "with knotted whips of flaming wire" tortured "pour souls" that gnawed "their flame-tormented tongues for pain.'' Into these purple waves ''queasy-stomach'd graves'' vomited the dead, who cursed ''all wombs for bearing and all paps for nursing.''

Not attracted by this picture, Flesh invited Spirit to put aside the telescope and look into her prism. There she would see, Flesh said in lyrically seductive language, ''the world in colours; colours that distain/The cheeks of Proteus, or the silken train/Of Flora's nymphs; such various sorts of hue,/As sun-confronting Iris never knew.'' ''Ah, fool,'' Spirit replied, ''how strongly are thy thoughts befool'd, alas!/To doat on goods that perish with thy glass.''[5]

At the beginning of the 18th century, godly books for children not only used Quarles' emblems but also similar language. In *A Looking-Glass for Children. Being a Narrative of God's gracious Dealings with some little Children,* Abraham Chear asked ''what are the Toyes, of Wanton Boyes,/To an Immortal Spirit?'' ''If naughty boys, allure with Toys,'' he wrote, ''to sin, or lies to tell; Then tell them plaine, you tempt in vain,/such wayes go down to Hell.'' In the poem, ''Written to a young Virgin,'' after looking ''in a Glass'' and thinking ''how sweetly God did form me,'' the narrator moaned, '' 'Tis pitty, such a pretty Maid,/as I should go to Hell.''

Chear's book celebrated the holy deaths of young Christians. To escape Hell, Chear implied, the young virgin had not merely to reject vanity but life itself.

By the end of the century, although the emblem of the mirror was the same, the ends and language of children's books had changed. Instead of reminding children of their mortality, mirrors taught morality.

Among the most popular children's books at the end of the century was Arnauld Berquin's *A Looking-Glass for the Mind,* a collection of instructive stories. Instead of directing her to Bunyan's Celestial City, the *Looking-Glass* directed the child to an earthly ''*Temple of Honour and Fame.*'' ''As a useful and instructive *Pocket* LOOKING-GLASS,'' the preface of an edition of 1794 stated, ''we recommend it to the Inspection of every Youth, whether Miss or Master; it is a MIRROR that will not flatter them, nor lead them into Error; it displays the Follies and improper Pursuits of the youthful Breast, points out the dangerous Paths they sometimes tread and clears the Way to the *Temple of Honour and Fame.*''[6]

Among the many early children's books which relied heavily upon traditional emblems and religious allegory was *The Prettiest Book for Children; Being the History of the Enchanted Castle; Situated in one of the fortunate Isles, and governed by Giant Instruction.* Ostensibly written by Don Stephano Bunyano, Instruction's secretary and "a distant relation of the famous John Bunyan," *The Prettiest Book* adapted Bunyan's Interpreter and his house to suit the educational climate of the 18th century.

To lure children to learning, Instruction was a blend of the moral and the exotic. The seductive world of Flesh and the didactic world of Spirit which were adversaries in Quarles came together in Instruction's appearance and life. Instruction was 10 feet tall and had a gold beard and gold hair which hung over his shoulders "in flowing ringlets." On his head he wore a green turban decorated with gold and diamonds while about his waist he wore a purple vest ornamented with pearls.

Despite his Turkish or Arabian appearance, however, Instruction was a Christian, who believed the Bible was the best book in the world and who said his prayers every morning and evening. His wife was Lady Good-Example, and his daughters were Piety, Patience, Charity, Sobriety, and Prudence.[7]

The Enchanted Castle was located on "the *seat of education,*" the smallest of the Fortunate Isles. Tutors lived in the castle, and the children of both the rich and poor traveled "hither to be educated" from other Islands. As sinners avoided Interpreter's House, so Instruction refused to admit children who believed that birth, not education and good behavior, determined success in life. "No man can be so great, or so rich and powerful," Instruction said, "as to have any right to excuse himself from his duty. Some little boys, indeed, because they are gentlemens sons, and are finely dressed, and eat and drink, as we say, of the best of every thing, are silly enough to think that they may do all manner of wickedness and mischief. But these are very stupid and naughty children; and if they were even to set their feet in the *Enchanted Castle,* or even to come near to the door of it, the good giant would spurn them out of his sight, or perhaps do something worse with them."[8]

The author of *The Prettiest Book* changed Christian allegory into educational matter. As Watchful the porter challenged pilgrims before the house built by the "Lord of the the Hill," so the porter of the castle was Mr. Alphabet. Once admitted to castle, children examined instructive curiosities, much as Christian viewed the *"Rarities"* of the Lord of the Hill, and the contents of Interpreter's *"Significant* Rooms.''

First children came to the Picture Gallery where they were met by Mr. Interpreter, who like his namesake showed them pictures, including Mr. Dutiful's depiction of Absalom's death and Mr. Good's painting of the cruel steward.

After the Gallery, children visited the Museum where Mr. Set'em-right pointed out rarities. Among them were a 12-foot long telescope, made by Mr. Faith-and-Hope through which children could glimpse ''a noble city'' in comparison to which the Enchanted Castle was but ''a fool'' and a looking glass invented by Mr. Flatter-none which reflected the inner rather than outer person.[9]

Unlike the person blinded by vanity who looked into the mirrors of Bunyan and Quarles, the child who looked into Mr. Flatter-none's glass learned a lesson. Not simply, to use Quarles' words, a ''falsely steel'd'' crystal, this mirror revealed helpful truth and pointed the way to reformation. The device that for Quarles was an emblem of luxury and pride had now become positively instructive.

As Locke convinced the age that early reading could shape success here as well as hereafter, so the things of this world became less reprehensible. If not abused and turned into a vanity glass, the mirror could reflect truth. Despite the traditional moral lessons suggested by its contents, the Enchanted Castle prepared children for secular success. Although Instruction refused to admit proud, selfish children—the sort of child who would sit before Quarles' mirror and admire himself—humility similar to that of Bunyan's Christian would not itself gain a child entrance. Learning was also necessary, and if a child did not know his letters, Mr. Alphabet sent ''him packing like a dunce and a blockhead.''[10]

Few children's books published by the leading London publishers drew so extensively upon Christian allegory as did *The Prettiest Book.* Several, however, used the device of rarities. Although such books used emblems and allegory, they taught good rather than doctrinaire religious conduct. In *The Lilliputian Auction,* Master Charly Chatter sold the contents of his uncle's estate. "A celebrated Lilliputian Virtuoso," Charly's uncle, Timothy Curious, Esq., had "not only collected what was rare and curious, but what would likewise be beneficial to Mankind," including a Brazen Head which urged children to read and a packet which contained a recipe for making young ladies beautiful. "*If beautiful you would appear,*" it stated, "*Always be good humour'd Dear.*" Among the lots auctioned was "a curious Looking-Glass," which Charly explained, "will be of use to any little perverse Lilliputian, since it shews what a disagreeable figure any person makes, when in a passion, or shewing unnecessary Airs." Master Mulish, Charly recounted, had once owned it.

One day after beating his brother "heartily," Mulish looked into the "faithful Glass." He appeared "so extremely ugly" that he frightened himself; immediately he ran "to his Brother and begged his pardon," after which he returned to the glass and "found he had recovered his original prettiness." On another occasion, "seeing a beggar Woman before Door, he flew to her like lightening, and gave her a shilling, which was all the Money he had. As soon as he looked into his glass, he found himself as beautiful as an Angel." When Charly offered the glass for sale, Master Froward declared that he did not want it, saying "I have no occasion for it, for I have no faults to be told of; and if I had, I should not like to be told of them." "Indeed, Master *Froward,*" Master Affable answered, "you have great occasion for it; so I'll buy it myself, and make you a present of it."[11]

Perhaps the most popular collection of rarities in early children's books was *The Exhibition of Tom Thumb; being an Account of many valuable and surprising Curiosities which he has collected in the Course of his Travels.* Collected "for little masters and misses," Tom said, "who are little and good like myself," the exhibition was moral. It was held "in a large commodious room of *Mr. Lovegood's,* No. 3, in *Wiseman's* buildings, at the end of the upper end of *Education-Road.*"

Among the objects exhibited were the stone with which Master Stephen Hot-spur killed his brother and a diamond found by "Messrs. *Temperance* and *Wisdom,* in one of the walks of *Paradise,* exactly upon the spot where stood the evening bower of *Adam.*"

The most striking curiosity, however, was "the *intellectual perspective-glass,*" made by Mr. Long-Thought. Unlike Spirit's telescope which revealed eternal reality, this telescope only exposed the true nature of dangerous things. Thus, Tom explained, "this truly wonderful optickglass, has the property of making every object which is viewed through it appear in such a form, as is most suitable to its natural qualities or probable effects."

When examined, through the glass "a basket of unripe apples or gooseberries" was changed "into a swarm of worms and other devouring reptiles" while "a bowl of punch, or a bottle of wine" appeared "to be full of snakes and adders." Like Interpreter explaining the significance of a painting to Christian, the perspective glass "explained" a series of pictures to children.

In a painting by Mr. Josiah Thrifty-man, for example, the principal figure was a young prodigal who seemed "highly delighted with the expensive follies and gratifications to which he had eagerly resigned himself." Seated in a public garden, he was surrounded by a "crowd of harlots, pimps, musicians, bullies, and sharpers," all of whom were "eager to court his favour, and ready to assist him in his foolish amusements." When viewed through Mr. Long-Thought's glass, the prodigal changed into a beggar "bedewing his face with a plentiful shower of tears, and stamping on the ground, and wringing his hands like a mad-man." Nearby were "a surly bailiff and his followers" who had just arrested him and were "dragging him to a gloomy prison." In the corners of the picture stood "the late companions and ministers of his folly," all of whom ridiculed him.[12]

As early children's books stressed the proper nurturing of Flesh and Spirit, instead of antagonism between them, so such books blended characters drawn from pagan or secular literature into Christian allegory. Thus in *The Prettiest Book,* a geni became the giant Instruction.

Throughout the century fairy tales had been criticized by most educators concerned with religion. By the end of the century, though, even the matter of fairy tales was being mixed with traditional allegory.

In *The Fairy Spectator,* Miss Sprightly described a dream she had about a fairy to Mrs. Teachwell, her governess. Mrs. Teachwell said she would write stories in which the fairy appeared. Miss Sprightly said she was pleased "because she would teach me to be good; for I should be ashamed to have even a naughty thought." "I love you for your earnest wish to be good,"

Mrs. Teachwell said, "but tell me, is not every action, word, and thought known?" "To whom, Madame," Sprightly asked, "Consider!" Mrs. Teachwell responded.[13]

After this evocation of the divine, Mrs. Teachwell began her account of the fairy. Lady Child, she said, had "fitted up" a closet of instructive books and toys for her daughter, Miss Child. Unfortunately Lady Child died when her daughter was five years old, and Miss Child's education was taken over by a governess, interested only in the "outward person."

One day when Miss Child sat in her closet looking over feathers and artificial flowers "in order to make choice of such as should be most becoming to her complexion," a beautiful fairy appeared, carrying "ENCHANTED GLASSES." Like Timothy Curious's mirror, one glass reflected the child's actual moral state. In contrast the other glass projected what the child could and should be. In presenting the glasses to Miss Child, the fairy described their history, saying that they had cured Miss Pettish of peevishness and Miss Lavish of prodigality.

With the glasses, the fairy also gave Miss Child a book in which she could keep account of her moral progress. "Look in *this*," the fairy said of the glasses, "nay, never start; you must first see your faults, before you can mend them," "Record in this book," she continued, "the report of the glasses; on the one leaf *what you are;* on the opposite, *what you should be.*" The mirror was one of several curiosities which aided in bettering children in *The Fairy Spectator.* The fairy's companion *Amiable* gave a rose to Miss Playful and instructed her to place it in her bosom. "It will adorn and delight you," Amiable said, "but it has a Thorn, which you will feel whenever you do amiss."[14]

Although emblems lost much of their Christian didacticism in the company of fairies and moral Genii, they furnished outlines for stories in other children's books and gained a new dramatic power.

Inherent in the use of emblems like the mirror and telescope was the danger that children would be so attracted by the marvelous paraphernalia of allegory that they would miss the lessons conveyed. Moreover in depending upon the marvelous, emblems appealed to the imagination, always suspect as a moral guide, and led children to, if not the eternal world, a world far different from that in which they spent their lives.

Unlike emblems and allegorical stories, moral tales, which became very popular in the 18th century, usually eschewed the fantastic and described, if not always ordinary events, at least the paraphernalia of middle-class life. Significantly a great number of these moral tales were actually "mirror" tales. Almost as if the reflections in Miss Child's enchanted glasses had been rounded into actual characters, these tales often depended upon the contrast between physically or socially similar but morally different individuals.

As Miss Child's glasses, or Spirit's telescope revealed the ends of good and bad behavior, so the stories followed the fortunes of good and bad characters or reflections in order to persuade young readers to live better lives.

Often such stories described the fortunes of two sisters, one of whom was beautiful but bad while the other was homely but good. In *The Sugar Plumb,* a poor farmer, typically, had two daughters. "A very great beauty," Betsey unfortunately was "very affected, and proud." "She only loved her own dear Self, was hardhearted to the poor, and behaved unmannerly to every one, and would not do any kind of work, for fear of spoiling her fine white hands."

In contrast Laura "had been very handsome before the small-pox; But this disorder had robbed her of her beauty, without giving her much concern, as she put no great value on such a fading flower. She was loved by all her neighbors for she endeavored to oblige every body, and frequently deprived herself of bread to give to the poor."

As Locke convinced the middle classes that a good education brought success in this life, so the rewards offered by the good reflection in mirror tales were usually marriage and money.

One day as the sisters were milking cows, "a rich gentleman" passed by on the road. Betsey's beauty was so great that he fell in love and began to court her. Much like the child, however, who learned from the story that physical beauty was of little value in comparison to moral beauty, the gentleman soon discovered Betsey's nature, and he rejected her and married Laura.[15]

Many variations of the mirror formula appeared in moral tales. In *The Histories of More Children than One,* there were two pairs of children, Polly and James Homespun and Kitty and Thomas Bloomer. "At first sight," Dorothy Kilner wrote about the Bloomers, "every body admired them; for they were the prettiest children that were ever seen, looked so pleasant, and had such rosy cheeks and nice curling hair and fine complexions, held up their heads so well, and moved so very gracefully, that they were much taken notice of." The children did not improve upon acquaintance, however, and once "in their company," admirers discovered them to be "the most tiresome disagreeable children they knew."

In contrast the appearance of the Homespuns was not prepossessing. James had "a frightfully large mouth and flat nose" and Polly "had the misfortune to have but one eye, and to be very much marked with the small-pox." Yet, they "were so extremely good and civil to every body: and spoke so politely if they were asked a question, that every body who was acquainted with them loved them dearly."

Because childhood shaped the adult in Locke's view, the Bloomers seemed destined to fade while the Homespuns were headed for successful happy lives. In another variation upon the formula, mirror tales frequently relied upon reflections of "before and after." In *The Blossoms of Morality* Bella was "an indolent beauty." Because her father was wealthy and she was beautiful, Bella saw no reason why she should study and become educated. When Honestus "a young gentleman of fortune and character" met her, he considered "paying addresses to her." Once he discovered her character though, he changed his mind. Fortunately for her if not her family, Bella was "instructed by misfortune." Her father died after going bankrupt, and Bella and her mother were forced to move into a small cottage in the country. Next Bella caught smallpox which destroyed her looks. After recovering from the illness, Bella devoted her time to study. "Before she was a beauty without sense," Richard Johnson wrote, "now she had lost the charms of her face, but had found those of the mind, which are infinitely the most to be valued." Two years passed, and then Honestus who happened to be nearby on business stopped to pay his respects to Bella's mother. At first Honestus did not recognize Bella, and after he did only began to talk to her "out of politeness." Conversation quickly showed Honestus that the changes in Bella were more than external; he fell in love, and shortly afterwards proposed and was accepted.[16]

One of the effects of Locke's secularizing influence upon early education and children's literature was the possibility that material things would become ends in themselves. Although mirror tales did not direct readers to the other-worldly, they nevertheless criticized luxury. In these stories, luxury seduced children, not from Christianity, but from natural decent lives.

In *The Adventures of a Pincushion* Mary Ann Kilner used the contrast between two cousins to criticize luxury and vanity and to celebrate simplicity and naturalness. Hannah Mindful's father was a small farmer. At 14, Hannah, the oldest of six children was "a healthy looking country girl." "Her complexion," Kilner wrote, "was burnt by the sun, and her hands hardened by laborious toil; she was not ornamented by dress, though her person was at all times made agreeable by neatness: She had never been taught those graces, which so forcibly recommend the possessor to general observation; but a constant cheerfulness, and a desire of obliging, which was never interrupted by petulance, made her beloved by every one who knew her."

In contrast, Sally who was a year older than Hannah, "had been a half boarder at a great school near *London.*" There she had been taught to worship glittering images or fashion and had grown vain and luxurious. When she was suddenly an orphan, her Uncle Mindful welcomed her to his family. Unfortunately she was incapable of appreciating simplicity, and like the contrasting reflections on Miss Child's glasses, her behavior and that of Hannah showed "what we are, and what we ought to be."[17]

Instead of helping Hannah in the morning with chores, Sally "Would disdainfully turn around to sleep." The simple clothes she wore particularly upset Sally, and conversation between Hannah and her resembled that between Quarles' Flesh and Spirit. Seduced by the "world in colours," Sally could not appreciate the natural, not only in dress but within herself and others. "O! Hannah," she said, describing her schoolmates' clothes, "had you seen the caps, and feathers, and muslin, and gauze frocks, which they used to wear on a dancing day, and how smart they looked in their silk shoes, or else red morocco ones, you would not wonder that I do not like these great black leather things. Indeed, Hannah, I could cry, whenever I see you and your sisters clothed in such coarse gowns, with your black worsted stockings, and that check handkerchief on your neck, and your round cloth caps, with that piece of linen for a ribbon." After hearing Flesh praise the prism, Spirit responded, "Ah, fool! that doat'st in vain, on present toys/And disrespect'st those true, those future joys." Although her response was more restrained, Hannah's reply to Sally was similar in tone. "O, fie, *Sally*!" she said, "that is quite ungrateful for the good things which you are blessed with."

Like Bunyan's woman before the looking glass, Sally was "without eyes" and unable to see clearly, she asked, "what good things?" "Do you call this dowlas shift, this coarse apron, this linsey wolsey gown, *good things*? Or do you call the brown bread we eat, or the hard dumplings, you was making just now, *good things*? And, pray this old worm eaten bed without any curtains to it, and this little window which is too small to admit one's head out, and what a little hole there is, quite crammed full of honeysuckles; or this propped up chest of drawers, or that good for nothing chair with a great hole in the bottom, which you know, Bet nearly fell through yesterday, when she got upon it to reach the box which holds her *Sunday* straw hat; do you call these *good things*? because if you do, I am sorry you know no better."[18]

Milton's Satan appealed to Eve's vanity to undermine paradise. Hannah's world with its simple food and furnishings and the honeysuckle filling the window was, if not an Eden, certainly a natural garden. Led astray by vanity, Sally was not home in the garden and did not listen to Hannah when she, like Miss Child's helpful mirror, urged her to appreciate her surroundings. "I think our bread is as good as any body need wish for," Hannah said, "and I am sure the dumplings you so scornfully mention, will be very well tasted and wholesome. As to the furniture, if it is old, I will answer for its being clean, *Sally*; and my father says he can nail a piece of board over that chair, which will last as many years as the back does." "And as to our clothes, I am sure they are whole and right," she continued; "they are coarse to be sure; but they are as good as our neighbours, and many a one would be thankful to have such to put on."[19]

In his *A Christian Dictionary* (1673), Richard Baxter warned against love of dress. "If it be fine Clothes and gaudy Ornaments that you are proud of, it is a sin so foolish and worse than childish, that I shall give it no other confutation, than to tell you, that it contradicteth it self, by making the person a scorn and laughing stock to others, when their design was to be more admired."

Almost as proof of the truth of Baxter's warning, Sally's "sin" made her ridiculous. To celebrate his daughter's 18th birthday, the local squire, Squire Goodall, invited his tenants and their families to an entertainment at Oakly Hall. Hannah and her two sisters appeared "as neat as rustick simplicity could adorn them." Each wore a nosegay of flowers, a light brown stuff gown, a white apron, handkerchief, and a straw hat. Hannah decorated her hat with green ribbons while her sisters decorated theirs with pink. Not satisfied to wear the garnet colored stuff gown she had been given, Sally waited until the rest of the family left for Oakly Hall, then put on a silk coat which she had worn at school.

Hannah's waggish brother Jack helped Sally prepare for the party. Although the coat did not fit, Sally did not know it because Jack hid the mirror. When she put on a hat "which exhibited the most tawdry collection of old gauze, bits of ribbon, and slatternly tassels, that can be imagined," Jack praised it, and when Sally was not looking stuck pieces of straw on it. On a ribbon which he pinned to Sally's shoulder, he tied two sheep's feet and so rigged them that Sally would not notice them until he pulled the ribbon and they tumbled down her back and bounced loudly on the floor. Like the woman sitting in front of Quarles' mirror, Sally thought she was "fairer, goodlier, greater" than she was. "The laugh which her appearance occasioned" at Oakly Hall undeceived her, and she quickly left, "mortified" to be, in Baxter's words, a "scorn and laughing stock."[20]

In "Directions for young Christians," Baxter said that "Books are (if well chosen) domestick, present, constant, judicious, pertinent, yea, and powerful sermons."[21] Not only did many early children's books preach sermons, but they took for their texts the matter of traditional emblems and Christian allegory.

Adapted to an age in which education was being rapidly secularized, the truths taught by children's books resembled and differed from those taught by conventional allegory and reveal much not only about education and children's literature in the 18th century but also about middle class aspirations and Christianity itself.

NOTES

1. For a discussion of Locke's influence see my *John Locke and Children's Books in Eighteenth-Century England* (Knoxville: University of Tennessee Press, 1981).

2. For more on godly books, look at my *John Locke* and "The Grave Leads but to Paths of Glory: Deathbed Scenes in American Children's Books, 1800–1860," *Dalhousie Review,* 1980, pp. 452–464.

3. The full title of Goody Two-Shoes is: *The History of Little Goody Two-Shoes; otherwise called, Mrs. Margery Two-Shoes. With the Means by which she acquired her Learning and Wisdom, and in consequence thereof her Estate; set forth at large for the Benefit of those, Who from a State of Rags and Care,/And having Shoes but half a Pair;/Their Fortune and their Fame would fix,/And gallop in a Coach and Six.*

4. For my approach I am indebted to Barry Qualls. His *The Spiritual Pilgrims of Victorian Fiction* (Cambridge: Cambridge University Press, 1982) is splendid and should be of interest to all concerned about the relationship between Christianity and literature.

5. John Bunyan, *Divine Emblems: or, Temporal Things Spiritualized. Fitted for the Use of Boys and Girls* (New York: James Carey, 1794), p. 68. Francis Quarles. *Emblems Divine and Moral* (London: H. Trapp, 1777), pp. 71, 142–43. Those interested in emblem books for children in the 18th century should consult: John Huddlestone Wynne, *Choice Emblems, Natural, Historical, Fabulous, Moral, and Divine, for the Improvement and Pastime of Youth.* Wynne's book was very popular in the 18th century; it did not, however, contain emblems of the telescope or vanity mirror.

6. Abraham Chear, *A Looking-Glass for Children, Being a Narrative of God's gracious Dealings with some little Children* (London: J. Marshall in Gracechurchstreet, fourth edition, 1708), pp. 27, 30–31, 42. Arnauld Berquin, Richard Johnson, compiler, *The Looking-Glass for the Mind* (Providence: Carter and Wilkinson, 1794), preface.

7. Don Stephano Bunyano, *The Prettiest Book for Children* (London: J. Coote, 1770), pp. 15, 26–27, 68.

8. Bunyano, pp. 19, 24–25.

9. Roger Sharrock, ed., *John Bunyan: Grace Abounding to the Chief of Sinners and The Pilgrim's Progress* (London: Oxford University Press, 1966), pp. 175–76, 182, 302. Bunyano, pp. 33, 43, 52, 55.

10. Quarles, p. 71. Bunyano, p. 33.

11. Charly Chatter, *The Lilliputian Auction. To which all little Masters and Misses are Invited* (Philadelphia: Jacob Johnson, 1802), pp. 5–6, 9–14, 28–29.

12. *The Exhibition of Tom Thumb* (Worcester, Mass.: Isaiah Thomas, 1787), pp. 5–6, 12–14, 21–24, 34–35.

13. See my *John Locke* for criticism of fairy tales. Ellenor Fenn, *The Fairy Spectator; or, the Invisible Monitor* (London: John Marshall, 1790?), p. 17.

14. Fenn, pp. 21, 23, 27, 31, 42–43, 76.

15. *The Sugar Plumb; or, Street Amusement for Leisure Hours: Being an Entertaining and Instructive Collection of Stories* (Worcester: Isaiah Thomas, 1787), pp. 79–80.

16. Dorothy Kilner, *The Histories of More Children than One* (London: John Marshall, 1783), pp. 43–45, 56–57. Richard Johnson, *The Blossoms of Morality* (Philadelphia: William W. Woodward, 1795), pp. 81–82, 86–88.

17. Mary Ann Kilner, *The Adventures of a Pincushion* (Worcester: Isaiah Thomas, 1788), pp. 80, 88. Fenn, p. 21.

18. Mary Ann Kilner, pp. 80–85.

19. Mary Ann Kilner, p. 85.

20. Richard Baxter, *A Christian Dictionary: or, A Summ of Practical Theologie* (London: Robert White for Nevill Simmons, 1673), p. 251. Mary Ann Kilner, pp. 92, 95. Quarles, p. 71.

21. Baxter, p. 60.

VICTORIAN CHILDREN IN THEIR PICTURE BOOKS
John Vaughan

The range and variety of printing processes available in the last quarter of the nineteenth century made possible an abundance of illustrations in publications for children. The quality of production associated with the names of the printer Edmund Evans and of the artists Walter Crane (1845–1915), Kate Greenaway (1846–1901) and Randolph Caldecott (1846–1886) is well known. At the other end of the scale there are some very dull, ill-drawn and worse printed cheap magazines and reward books for the pious if inartistic part of the market.

Covers of a series by G. Manville Fenn *The little skipper* (1897), *Our soldier boy* (1898), *The powder monkey* (1904) and *A young hero* (1903), published in London by Ernest Nister and in New York by E. P. Dutton, illustrated by Archibald Webb and printed in Bavaria, will serve as examples of the "chocolate box" genre at the turn of the century. Percy Muir commented (*English children's books 1600 to 1900,* 1954, p. 236) on Nister's keen eye for the English market and that, although his productions were of a high standard, the art work was "in the insipid style then thought suitable for children's books." Robert Ellice Mack's *All round the clock* illustrated by Harriett M. Bennett and published by Griffith, Farran & Co., 1887, was printed at Nuremberg by Nister together with lithographic illustrations. A series of full-page illustrations depict young cherubic children in a variety of idealized situations: "Good morning pussy" (a blue-ribboned cat on the bed of a golden-haired child); "Bread and milk" (dog and cat sitting expectantly at breakfast with pink-cheeked and petticoated small boy); "Sympathy" (golden-haired girl nursing sick

Reprinted with permission from *The School Librarian*, February 1987, pp. 6–11.

mongrel); "Kept in" (tearful small boy, socks down, laces untied, clutching slate with rude picture of teacher); "The little librarian" (golden- haired child in white nightdress with kitten appearing from shelf of folios); "A donkey race" (sailor-suited boy and other children on beach); and "Pray God bless" (golden-haired boy, with pink toes peeping from under nightdress, kneeling at his mother's lap at side of cot). This single volume contains examples of many of the favorite themes of the "chocolate box" school of well-fed cherubs living in an idealized landscape with sunny skies and flower-bedecked fields and gardens, whose major tragedy is a sick pet or a scholastic peccadillo and whose closing prayer is:

> Pray God bless my dear Mamma,
> And please take care of dear Papa,
> Let no ill dreams my sleep annoy
> And make Freddy a good boy,
>
> Amen.

Popularly assumed to be a prime example of this genre, but in fact having much more complex origins in the Victorian adult novel, is Little Lord Fauntleroy, who first appeared in the American *St. Nicholas: An Illustrated Magazine for Young Folks* (Volume 13, Part I, November 1885) illustrated by Reginald Birch, to whom Mrs Burnett sent a photograph of her second son Vivian. First, "When he was old enough to walk out with his nurse, dragging a small wagon and wearing a short white kilt, and a big white hat set back on his curly yellow hair he was so handsome and strong and rosy that he attracted every one's attention." Then appeared the famous suit of velvet coat, with long sash and lace collar, and velvet kneebreeches, long stockings and buckled shoes already familiar on Mrs Hodgson Burnett's own children by 1882. This may have been derived from the attire of Oscar Wilde on his visit to Washington in 1881. Although mocked in Gilbert and Sullivan's *Iolanthe* (1882), the suit established itself as fitting formal dress for boys at parties and major social events. The book, after adaptation for television, may have recovered from the verdict that it was to adults "repellent" (Marghanita Laski, *Mrs Ewing, Mrs Molesworth and Mrs Hodgson Burnett,* 1950, p. 83); but to contemporaries, "The lovely portraiture of a sweet child-nature in Little Lord Fauntleroy is irresistible'' (Oliver Wendell Holmes to Mrs Hodgson Burnett, 28 October 1888). Birch's illustrations are in a variety of styles: that showing the little lord playing with a large white cat on a tiger skin (''The big cat was purring in drowsy content: she liked the caressing touch of the kind little hand.'') is clearly related to the Nister style although in black and white.

Another illustrator of influence on sartorial matters was Kate Greenaway. The demand for Greenaway designs resulted in the redrawing of her figures for a variety of purposes including the design of children's clothing in the style the French called *Greenawisme*. Criticisms of her work were plentiful and her limitations manifest. It is true that apparent lack of knowledge of anatomy led to a class of child almost instantly recognizable as hers. Together with a limited skill in the technique of drawn perspective this gave, particularly, her groups of children with their delicate colors, an almost hieratic quality of great charm and full of grace and light.

The other side of life was not neglected by the publishers of illustrations for children. Children were reminded that life could be nasty, brutish and short. The pictures of happy families and luxurious Christmas parties in *Happy little people,* by Olive Patch, published by Cassell, Petter, Galpin in 1882 with copious illustrations of musical games, magic lantern shows and outdoor sports, includes a reminder of the less fortunate. Facing a full-page illustration of a little girl acting as ''queen for the evening'' (distributing Christmas gifts helped by a butler in the background) is another picture. ''Huddling under the leafless trees was a little girl about the size of May. She was thinly clad and trembled with the cold, and she held in her hand some matches which she tried to sell to passers by. She looked entirely wretched, uncared for and sad. Further up the street . . . we saw an old man and woman making their way through the snow. They were not so utterly forlorn looking as the little match girl, but they were evidently very poor. 'Do you not see that there are people in the world to whom Christmas is not what it is to you, dear Hughey,' said mother.'' Even someone writing under the pseudonym of ''Chatty Cheerful'' in *The little folk's out and about book* published by Cassell in 1884 could include a chapter called ''Out in the streets'' with illustrations of shoe-blacks and crossing-sweepers. ''Here is a poor, ragged, dirty little street Arab—a boy who was carried into the streets before he could walk into them, he was so little, and he has been in them ever since. He is always hungry, and often dinnerless, tealess, and supperless.''

The picture could be sentimentalized and the match girl Kitty in *Out little dots,* an annual published by the Religious Tract Society in 1898 with a ''chocolate box'' cover and frontispiece, is unrealistically plump, well groomed and well clothed. The religious societies did illustrate the poor in their magazines—for example, the crippled pedlar for the January 1887 number of *Our Own Magazine* issued by the Children's Special Service Mission, or the homeless waif Joe Martin found sleeping on the Thames Embankment in *Chatterbox* annual for 1900, edited by the Revd. J. Erskine Clarke. The causes of such poverty might be explained, as in the poem ''Mike's day-dream'' in *The boys' and girls' companion,* published by the Church of England Sunday School Institute in 1889:

> I wonder what it feels like
> To have a lot of tin,
> Like folks that live in this street,
> And others where I've been.
>
> To have hot meat and cabbage
> For dinner every day,
> Fried fish, or soup and dumplings,
> Or tripe and onions, say,
>
> But there, it's no good thinking
> Of what it must be like,
> For Mother's got no money
> Now Father's out on strike.

The shoeless Mike props up a street bollard. This volume has other illustrations of ragged children contrasting with at least one contribution by Kate Greenaway. There is also the illustrated poem ''Charlie's mistake'' (a child who hates soap and water) but:

> There's One who love us better
> Than Mother does her boy.

His Hand directs our footsteps,
Sends pain as well as joy.

Children were reminded that even the good and the great faced
hardships and had endured privations. The March 1893 issue of
Our Own Magazine has an illustration of a Fauntleroy-like boy
who is the future Lord Shaftesbury. "So the poor little lad grew
on, neglected, and almost forgotten by those who were nearest and
dearest to him, living his lonely life all to himself."

The earlier Evangelical tradition of the pious deathbed scene
remained alive in the accounts of orphans, or "single parent
families." A deathbed is illustrated in *The Children's Prize* for
1866 (edited by the Revd. J. Erskine Clarke) in which the child
Hughie is held aloft while one of the servants writes down his
father's dying words in a Bible. The following year this magazine
showed Charlie Gordon orphaned at six or, "left without an
earthly parent to love him. His father was a hard-working
clergyman, who caught a fever whilst visiting a poor woman, and
his mother died of consumption only a year afterwards." This
volume includes pictures of crippled children, wealthy children in
happy families and an illustration to the text "Suffer little children
to come unto Me" from St. Matthew's gospel. A special genre of
stories of deprived children developed. One still in print is Silas
K. Hocking's *Her Benny,* first published in 1879. By a Methodist
minister, it is based on his three years' experience of the "poorest
neighbourhoods" of Liverpool. The illustrations show the children as street sellers and roasters of hot potatoes at watchmen's
fires, but also the interior of their poverty-stricken (cause: drink)
"home." An important theme in the book is the influence of the
death of little Nelly Bates on her brother and their watchman
friend Joe.

Even in *Her Benny* there are scenes of happy family life, and
pictures of aristocratic and royal family groups appeared regularly. *The Children's Friend* of 1877 (price one penny per issue)
began with a frontispiece "H.R.H. Princess Christian and her
daughter the Princess Victoria," and included "The Duchess of
Teck and three of her children," "The Queen of Greece and her
sons," and "The Princesses Victoria and Elizabeth." These were
engravings based on photographs. An important consequence of
these technical developments was that not only could foreign

royalty be portrayed with reasonable accuracy but also the lives of more ordinary families. For example, *Our Own Gazette and Y.W.C.A. News* of 1896 has a series of articles by Miss M. F. Billington (Special Correspondent of the *Daily Graphic*) and her "with my camera in India" is illustrated by "A Parsee family at home," which is such a contrast to the pictures common earlier in the century in school geography books.

Other examples from this range of illustrations, from the pink-cheeked angels of Nister and the "chocolate box" school to the often crude engravings of the cheap religious annuals showing royalty or street urchins, can be found to illuminate the whole variety of late Victorian child experience as reflected in the pictures in the books of the period. The most obvious form of activity is that of being educated. Pictures of school teams and other formal depictions appeared in the annuals together with less authentic and stereotyped illustrations of school stories. Gordon F. Browne (1858–1932), the younger son of "Phiz," illustrated a truly amazing quantity of boys' stories. There is a sameness in his work which makes it impossible to ascribe immediately any example of it to a particular author, but it was clearly very acceptable to publishers. As an example, his work for the illustrated 1895 edition of Farrar's *St. Winifred's or the world of school* may be taken, for it was reprinted frequently. Similar pictures were published for girls. Everard Hopkins (1860–1928), the brother of Gerard Manley Hopkins, worked extensively for magazines. Examples of his work were used in A. E. Ward's *A girl governess: or Ella Dalton's success,* published by the Sunday School Union in 1894. Much more attractive, but possibly even less authentic, is the version of the traditional picture of chaos in the village dame's schoolroom by Francis Donkin Bedford in his *Four and twenty toilers,* published in 1900 with verses by E. V. Lucas; or the lovely "In the corner" in *At home,* illustrated by John G. Sowerby and decorated by Thomas Crane (Walter's elder brother) and published by Marcus Ward in 1881. This is a book designed in the height of current artistic fashion in a style combining the best features of Walter Crane and Kate Greenaway. It has many delightful indoor schemes recalling the "house beautiful" school of interior designers and such details as fans of peacock feathers and cupboards displaying blue and white china. "In the corner" has many of these features illustrating a poem which concludes:

This is why our little Lettice
In the corner there you see,
Till it pleases her to know her
A.B.C.

Other examples illustrating good and bad behaviour can be found, from the tragedy of a blot of ink on a copy book (in R. Sinclair's *Pictures and stories for little folks*, 1902) to the common denunciation of the evils of bird-nesting (colored cover and frontispiece "The young robbers" of the *Child's Own Magazine*, 1875, published by the Sunday School Union) or the temptation to shop-lifting (*Her Benny*). Good works were encouraged. Hilda's penny goes into a slot "For the sick poor" and Dorothy's to a poor crossing-sweeper (*Our Sunday stories*, Cassell, *c.* 1888). Both these examples emphasize the religious origins of these actions. Contrary behavior such as disobedience and gluttony brought pain and repentance. Bertie resolves, "I'll ask Jesus to forgive me, and help me always to obey mother" (the Religious Tract Society's *Our little dots*, Volume 8, 1894).

Joyful outdoor activities were also illustrated and such events as winter sports provided good material for the artists and printers. The frontispiece to *Chatterbox* for 1890 is "The slide" by Stanley Berkeley (*fl.* 1878–1907) who was noted for his animal paintings. James Weston's *Sunny hours: a picture story book for the young* (published in 1891 by S. W. Partridge in a style rather superior to their usual offerings) has an idyllic cover of a family in a rowing boat, a frontispiece of a triumphant cricket team, children by the sea, "Harold and his prize yacht," and a very superior ice-chair in a skating scene. All these are in full color; but there are black and white pictures including those of "Our Band of Hope meeting" and the sadly familiar ink blot on a new copy book. Mrs Ewing's *A soldier's children and five other tales in verse* (of 1879 but published in book form by SPCK in 1883) has illustrations by R. Andre (she realized his selling power was less than Caldecott's) of groups of children playing soldiers, washing clothes for dolls (a favorite subject), "helping" in the house, by the seaside, and bird-nesting (again leading to tragedy for the nestlings):

The bitterest tears that we could weep
Wouldn't wake them out of their stiff cold sleep.

Kate Greenaway's *Book of games* (engraved and printed by Edmund Evans and published by Routledge in 1889) was one of her happiest illustrated compilations recording and depicting traditional games, from the well-known ''Hide and seek,'' ''Musical chairs,'' and ''Hunt the slipper,'' to the less familiar ''Up Jenkins,'' ''Dumb Crambo,'' ''Russian scandal,'' ''Buz,'' ''Mary's gone a-milking'' and ''Queen Anne and her maids'' amongst many others (not all, sadly, illustrated).

Victorian children opened their picture books sometimes to be lost in a never-never-land of fantasy and fashion, but also to be reminded of the seriousness of life, its moral problems, and the need to be aware of the sufferings of others (human and animal) who were less fortunate than themselves.

BEATRIX POTTER: NATURALIST ARTIST
Catherine Golden

Although in recent years there has been extensive critical interest in the art and accomplishments of Beatrix Potter (1866–1943),[1] she most frequently is recalled with affection as the author and illustrator of *The Tale of Peter Rabbit* (1902), her first book. Potter has often been misconstrued as a Victorian spinster sublimating her childlessness by writing and illustrating endearing books for other people's children. Such a perception, however, denies the self-reliant artist her multifaceted personality and her accomplishments as a conservationist and a naturalist artist.

Although she was born into a family avidly interested in the fine arts, Potter had little formal art training. Her father, Rupert, a prosperous businessman and lawyer, was an amateur artist and photographer who collected paintings, attended gallery exhibitions, and encouraged Beatrix and her younger brother Bertram (1872–1918) in their art. Her mother, Helen Beatrix, was accomplished in the arts and joined the family in frequent drawing excursions during summer vacations in Scotland and northern England's Lake District. From age eight Beatrix studied the animals, insects, plants, fungi, and fossils that she and Bertram collected during these family holidays. They smuggled rabbits, mice, bats, owls, and hedgehogs into the upper-floor nursery of their London home at No. 2 Bolton Gardens, West Brompton. Live models doubled as pets, but the dead specimens proved invaluable as well. She and Bertram secretly skinned and boiled dead birds, rabbits, and even a fox, in order to articulate the skeletons for anatomical drawings.

Bertram was sent to boarding school at a young age, and Beatrix, educated at home, endured a loneliness and seclusion that was broken only when the family moved to its various rented

Reprinted with permission from *Woman's Art Journal,* Spring 1990, pp. 16–20.

country houses during holiday seasons. In the solitude of the nursery, her creative imagination and thirst for knowledge grew. She read avidly, selecting books from the well-stocked household library (which included illustrated natural histories); memorized several of Shakespeare's plays; invented her own private journal code; and made detailed, meticulous drawings of animal and plant specimens as viewed through Bertram's microscope.

A series of governesses instructed Beatrix in the ladylike accomplishments of painting and drawing and, as she grew older, took her to the South Kensington Museum (now the Victoria and Albert) and the Museum of Natural History. At considerable expense, the family also engaged art teachers. In addition to occasional lessons with an unidentified "Mrs. A," Beatrix studied with a Miss Cameron (from 1878 to 1883), who prepared her for the Art Student's Certificate offered by the Science and Art Department of the Committee of the Council on Education. Issued July 1, 1881, just before Beatrix turned 15, this certificate affirmed her skill in freehand and model drawing, practical geometry, and linear perspective.[2] She also received artistic advice from a close family friend, the Pre-Raphaelite painter Sir John Everett Millais, who complimented her: "Plenty of people can draw, but you . . . have observation."[3]

In fact, Potter, a gifted observer of the natural world, questioned the value of art instruction and concluded of her drawing and painting teachers: "I may probably owe a good deal to Mrs. A as my first teacher. I did to Miss Cameron, but I am convinced it [artistic mastery] lies chiefly with oneself."[4] Although she was cognizant of and influenced by contemporary art and illustration, including the imaginative animal illustrations of Randolph Caldecott (whose whimsical frog in *The Frog He Would Go A-Wooing* [1883] foreshadows Potter's Jeremy Fisher) and the landscape details of Millais and John Constable, as an artist she relied heavily on her own powers of "observation." At age 16, Beatrix began attending the biannual exhibitions of the Royal Academy, often in the company of her father. Her journal records critical observations of the art and her search for female role models. At the Summer Exhibition of 1882, she praised the anatomical detail of Rosa Bonheur's *The Lion at Home.*[5] Of the 1883 Winter Academy Exhibition of Old Masters, she noted the inclusion of only one canvas by a woman, Angelica Kauffmann's *Design.* She

Fig. 1. Beatrix Potter, A. (*Lepiota*) *cristatus* (Sept. 9th 1893),
watercolor. © Frederick Warne & Co., 1955, 1972.

remarked that it was "rather cruelly hung near Reynolds's five
figures," but it "raised my idea of art, and I have learnt some
things by it. I was rather disheartened at first, but I have got over
it. That picture by Angelica Kauffmann is something, it shows
what a woman has done."[6]

Potter's biographer, Margaret Lane, explains: "Art, only art
. . . the animal detail of Rosa Bonheur and Landseer, the bucolic
vision of Palmer and Constable, these were what fascinated her;
yet here was the inevitable impediment—how could she presume
to think of entering the grandiose world so genially dominated
both at home and at the Academy by Millais."[7] At age 24 the shy,
aspiring artist started her professional career as a greeting card
designer; she then illustrated tales and fables by Lewis Carroll,
Joel Chandler Harris, and Edward Lear. During the 1890s she

Fig. 2. Beatrix Potter, illustration for *The Tale of Squirrel Nutkin* (1903), watercolor, 3" x 3⅛". © Frederick Warne & Co., 1903, 1987.

wrote and illustrated "picture letters," as she called them, to the children of her former governess, Annie Carter Moore.

Potter's main goal, however, was to become a naturalist artist and have her works accepted by the leading organization of London scientists, the Linnaean Society, or even someday hang in a Royal Academy exhibition. Although aware that neither the Linnaean Society nor the Royal Academy permitted women as full members (though the Royal Academy had in the 18th century admitted Mary Moser and Angelica Kauffmann as founders), she avidly pursued her early passion for studying and drawing plant and animal life throughout the 1890s, with the hope of publishing a natural history book. To ensure scientific accuracy, Potter dissected, classified, and compared the specimens she collected to those of the Natural History Museum, all without help from the

Fig. 3. Beatrix Potter, *Squirrels on a Log*, watercolor, 21" x 18". © Frederick Warne & Co., 1955, 1972.

curatorial staff. In her journal (1896) she records that ''the clerks seem to be all gentlemen and one must not speak to them . . . they take the line of being shocked [and] it is perfectly awful to a shy person.''[8] She was forced to peer painstakingly through the glass cases at the small specimens and labels and suffered from lifelong eye problems as a result.

In 1896 Potter's uncle, Harry Roscoe, arranged for her to show these specialized studies to the botanists and director of the Royal Botanical Gardens of Kew. Her portfolio contained more than 250 drawings and watercolors of fungi and mushrooms. The water-color study of the *A. cristatus* (formerly classified as *Lepiota*) (1893; Fig. 1) clearly demonstrates her talent as a naturalist. The image details the markings on the rounded curving cap of the mushroom, the ridged lines on the underside of the cap, and the nodules along the stem. It also shows the beauty of the mushroom in its natural surroundings; pale green blades of grass accentuate the reddish markings on the cap, much as they would in nature.

Although Potter perceived that the Director of Kew "seemed pleased with my drawings and a little surprised," she reported that during the interview he "did not address me again, which I mention not with resentment, for I was getting dreadfully tired, but I have once or twice an amusing feeling of being regarded as young"[9]—she was 30. Not only did the botanists of Kew dismiss her because of her gender and age, but they also were skeptical that one so young, and female at that, had illustrated theories drawn from independently conducted scientific experiments.[10] For example, her drawings showed lichens to be dual organisms, a species of fungi living in close association with algae. This theory and her ideas about the propagation of mold spores were in advance of those held by the Linnaean Society, of which these men were all members. Following her rejection by Kew, she wrote a paper, "On the Germination of the Species of *Agaricineae*." Since women were not allowed to attend meetings of the Linnaean Society, Potter requested her paper be read for the society's members.[11] Although having the paper read was in itself an achievement, Potter realized that her interest in mycology would lead nowhere, and she laid aside her carefully prepared portfolio.

Potter's rejection by Kew increased her awareness of the limited opportunities for women artists in Victorian England. Many became book illustrators—a field "then as now . . . viewed as a stepchild among the arts."[12] During the 1890s, as the popular publishing field expanded, there were unprecedented opportunities for women to work as illustrators, particularly of texts for children and women with themes of fantasy, romance, mother-hood, and childhood. Like accomplishment in many of the "lesser" arts, illustration was deemed eminently suitable for women because it was thought to require only mediocre talent and

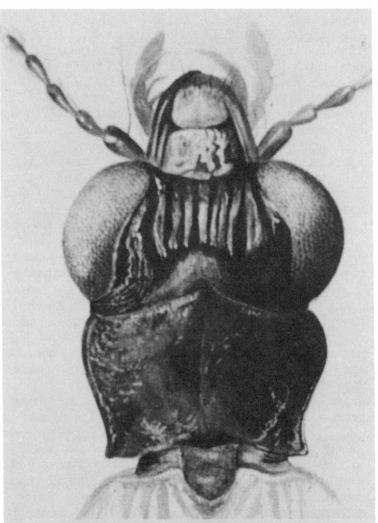

Fig. 4. Beatrix Potter, *Highly Magnified Study of a Beetle* (1887), pen-and-ink and watercolor. © Frederick Warne & Co., 1955, 1972.

to be an extension of the domestic role. Further, the work could be done at home, thereby not compromising a woman's social position.

Potter's ultimate success as an author-illustrator perhaps reflects the fact that she became a children's writer at a time when female authorship was no longer an anomaly. She was part of the "third generation" of feminine novelists—"business-like, unconventional, efficient, and productive"[13]—many of whom became children's writers and sensation novelists as well as editors and publishers. Kate Greenaway (1846–1901) was another. Potter's famous first story about a playfully disobedient rabbit began as a picture letter (September 4, 1893) to Annie Moore's ailing son, Noel. Aware of the growing market for children's books, she revised it for publication. *Peter Rabbit* was rejected by at least six publishers, so in 1901 she published it herself. She eventually contracted with children's book publisher Frederick Warne and Company, who produced *Peter Rabbit* (1902) and her entire series of 23 storybooks. Potter's correspondence with Warne reveals her well-developed business sense and practical plan for promoting her books—they should be reasonably priced, small enough to fit into a child's hand, and amply illustrated.

In her book illustrations, which are all carefully coordinated with her narratives, Potter capitalized on her keen observation and love of the natural world. As inspiration, she returned to her portfolio of natural history studies. This is not surprising given her philosophical musing in her journal (1894): "The funguses will come up again and the fossils will keep."[14] Still lifes of flowers and fungi do indeed "come up again" in *The Tale of Squirrel Nutkin* (1903); studies of waterlilies and beetles reappear in *The Tale of Mr. Jeremy Fisher* (1906); and numerous plant and animal renderings reemerge as illustrative details in the Peter Rabbit series. By translating her naturalist art into illustrations, Potter urges us to consider her a naturalist artist.

Potter's skill in drawing flora, fauna, and landscape is sustained throughout all her illustrations,[15] even in those stories that move animal characters to human settings.[16] *The Tale of Squirrel Nutkin* (1903) derives its plot from animal behavior in wildlife: Squirrel Nutkin and his cousins gather nuts on an island ruled by an old owl. The story is set in Derwent Water, part of the Lake District where Potter eventually settled (the owl's island is really St.

Fig. 5. Beatrix Potter, illustration for *The Tale of Mr. Jeremy Fisher* (1906), watercolor, 3¼" x 3". © Frederick Warne & Co., 1906, 1987.

Herbert's Island of Derwent Water). Although the story evolved from a "picture letter" Potter wrote to Norah Moore (September 25, 1901) while vacationing in the Lake District's Keswick, she purchased some squirrels in 1903, which she drew from directly to ensure accuracy.

As was typical of her design process, Potter's illustrations for *Squirrel Nutkin* began as rough pencil sketches pasted into the corners of a paper-covered exercise book. From these she made detailed pen-and-ink drawings to which she added watercolor wash. In her early color designs, such as those for greeting cards, she used a fairly dry brush technique particularly suited for rendering the fur of small animals, but over the years she developed a more fluid illustrative style and relied more heavily on color wash.[17]

In the illustration of Nutkin gathering pincushions from a rose briar bush (1903; Fig. 2), Potter's anatomical accuracy parallels Bonheur's. The anatomy and behavior of the fictional Nutkin are drawn from numerous pencil and watercolor studies of squirrels on tree branches, particularly the undated watercolor *Squirrels on a Log* (Fig. 3). This study, among others, displays Potter's understanding of the British red squirrel, *sciurus vulgaris*,[18] which she fully intended Nutkin to be. The book illustration accurately shows the animal shifting its weight to its back paws, freeing its forepaws to grip the rose (one paw on either side of the object). Potter positioned Squirrel Nutkin's fluffy tail to fan his back and curl around his head and small tufted ears. In fullness, proportion, and position, Nutkin's tail resembles Potter's British red squirrel study. His reddish-brown back coat, red markings on the arms and legs, and white patch on the underside are also authentic.

The accompanying text focuses on Nutkin's gathering "robin's pincushions off a [rose] briar bush."[19] Potter had been drawing rose hips since childhood, and the tearlike shape of the rose hip's seed receptacle, the angled projections extending from the hip, and the flower's cranberry-red hue are some of the details that inform the text.[20] Mushrooms, fir cones, and oak apples add authenticity to the wood setting and reframe Squirrel Nutkin's whimsical activities of playing "ninepins" with fir cones and "marbles" with oak apples.[21] In the brownish color of the upturned caps and curves of the leggy stems, the mushrooms in the illustration of Nutkin playing "marbles" resemble a watercolor study of the *Cortinarious torvus* that Potter completed in 1893 in the Lake District town of Dunkeld.[22]

In its allegiance to specific geographical sites, Potter's illustrative style differed from that of her contemporaries Kate Greenaway and Randolph Caldecott, both of whom used more idealized country settings. Potter's recognizable landscape, flora, and fauna were more akin to those found in the paintings of specimens from nature used to illustrate natural history books, such as those of P. H. Gosse in *Evenings at the Microscope* (1859), popular among Victorian Britain's upper classes, then experiencing a growing interest in scientific investigation. However, Potter's habits of taking expeditions to collect specimens, observing directly from nature, and tirelessly studying specimens under the microscope liken her to the best naturalists of her day.[23] For her children's tales she blended this kind of scientific study with the expressive quality and fanciful depiction of animals in clothes found in Caldecott's works to create books that have appealed to generations of children.

In developing most of her animal storybook characters, Potter returned to her early natural history studies of animals. The light brown fur, white underside, and almond-shaped eyes of her storybook rabbits, Peter and Benjamin, identify them as Potter's two pet Belgian rabbits.[24] Some of the plates within *The Tale of Benjamin Bunny* (1904) show more skill in the depiction of plant than animal life. For instance, the naturalism of the rabbits in the illustration of Peter and Benjamin gathering onions suffers because Potter focused on the onions, which are central to the story's outcome; in *Benjamin Bunny,* Peter is welcomed in the fir-tree home once again because he retrieves his clothes from Mr. McGregor's garden and adds onions to the family larder. The rendering of the onion that Benjamin pulls from the ground reveals Potter's keen observation of the bulbous shape and red-dish-gold color of the skin of the onion, the wiry shape of the roots, and the long green stems that fold and bend, and lends a natural history emphasis to the whimsical depiction of rabbits harvesting onions.

The illustrations of the hedgehog character in *The Tale of Mrs. Tiggy-Winkle* (1905) and the frog character in *The Tale of Mr. Jeremy Fisher* grew out of studies of her pets, including her pet frog, Punch. Frogs and hedgehogs do not seem likely choices for storybook characters—or pets—but Potter was unusual in her ability to realize the charms of nearly all animal behavior. The plotline of *Jeremy Fisher* has Jeremy fishing on a waterlily leaf when he inadvertently becomes bait for a hungry trout. Like *Squirrel Nutkin,* this tale grew from a "picture letter" to Eric Moore (September 5, 1893), written in Scotland's Eastwood by the river Tay. Jeremy's home is Esthwaite Water, near Sawrey, the southern part of the English Lake District, where, beginning in 1905, Potter made her home at Hill Top Farm. The story offers the full range of Potter's skill in drawing animals and waterlife. In fact, five of the twenty-six plates are naturalist close-ups featuring a beetle, a water rat, a trout, and waterlilies. Potter illustrates how "a GREAT big water beetle came up underneath the lily leaf and tweaked the toe of one of [Jeremy's] galoshes. Mr. Jeremy crossed his legs up shorter, out of reach, and went on eating his sandwich."[25] The passage demonstrates Potter's precise word choice. The capitalization of "GREAT" followed by "big" increases the size of the beetle caught visually in the act of "tweaking" Jeremy's toe. Although Potter includes the tip of one of Jeremy's galoshes as a small detail in the accompanying illustration, the hard-shelled black water beetle dominates the accompanying illustration so we can see its bulbous eyes, six hairy jointed legs, and tentaclelike projections. This plate clearly demonstrates that at times Potter retrieved and re-created her natural history studies in her book illustrations, in this case her 1887 microscopic studies of ground and water beetles (1887; Fig. 4).[26] The illustration of Jeremy struggling to the surface of the water (1906; Fig. 5) contains a skillfully drawn waterlily that adds authenticity and scale to the scene. Potter often drew waterlilies amongst reeds in Esthwaite Lake; these studies reveal her precise knowledge of the shape of the reeds, white flower petals, and yellow center as well as the spongy texture of the green leaves.[27] The three cropped reeds at the far left of the illustration suggest that the waterlilies are part of a larger pond, allowing the viewer to imagine the vastness of "the surface of the water" against which Jeremy pops "like a cork."[28]

Drawings of Jeremy demonstrate Potter's familiarity with frogs, for example, the webbed feet and the positioning of his hands below the water surface. The angle of Jeremy's right leg anticipates a swift kick that will propel him through the water toward the lily leaf.[29] Poking through the water, Jeremy's bulging eyes, reptilian ridged nose, and curving underside establish his authenticity.

In some illustrations, such as the cover drawing of Jeremy casting off on a lily leaf or the picture of him at the doorway of his lily-pond home, Jeremy stands upright and is partially clothed in a suit coat or mackintosh, wearing galoshes on his webbed feet.[30] Potter never used clothing to disguise the animal nature of her characters; rather, she used it to make a point, such as to frustrate the trout who swallows Jeremy but spits him out because of the awful taste of the frog's mackintosh. The clothing, in turn, becomes the character's trademark. Potter never changed the anatomy nor violated the nature of her animal characters and was critical of Kenneth Grahame because in Mr. Toad of *The Wind in the Willows* (1908), he created "A mistake to fly in the face of nature—A frog may wear galoshes; but I don't hold with toads having beards or wigs!''[31] When the accuracy of her drawings for Jeremy was challenged, Potter put her model in a jam jar and brought it to Warne's office to prove that the storybook frog's yellowish-green coloring was true to nature. Potter insisted on accuracy because she wanted her book illustrations also to serve as nature lessons for children.

With royalties from book sales and a small legacy from an aunt, Potter, unlike most single Victorian women, gained some degree of independence from her authoritarian parents. She purchased land in the Lake District, the first being Hill Top Farm. It was there that she retreated to work following the death in 1905 of her fiancé, Norman Warne of Frederick Warne and Company. She settled permanently in the Lake District town of Sawrey upon her marriage in 1913 (at age 44) to local solicitor William Heelis, who helped her acquire and protect her Lake District properties.

After her marriage Potter wrote only an occasional story. She conformed to some of the traditional expectations for women in becoming—as she referred to herself—Mrs. William Heelis. In her later years, she expanded her interests into breeding livestock and conservation and so remained a woman ahead of her time. On her death, Potter bequeathed 4,000 Lake District acres to the National Trust to preserve the natural habitat that inspired many of her best tales.

In 1967 the quality of her naturalist studies was finally recognized when mycologist W. P. K. Findlay used 59 of Potter's watercolors to illustrate his natural history, *Wayside and Woodland Fungi*.[22] Although she had wished during her lifetime for such recognition by the scientific community, through her children's tales Beatrix Potter in fact became a naturalist artist. Thus, she fulfilled her own desire for ''drawing, painting, modeling, the irresistible desire to copy any beautiful object which strikes the eye. Why cannot one be content to look at it? I cannot rest, I must draw.''[33]

NOTES

1. A complex portrait of Potter as a naturalist emerges from the growing scholarship on the artist. In *The Art of Beatrix Potter* (London:

Frederick Warne, 1972), Leslie Linder traces Potter's development as a naturalist during the 1880s and 1890s. The section headings include "Gardens, Plant Studies and Still Life," "Microscopic Work and Drawings of Fungi," and "Animal Studies." (All the books cited in these notes were published by Frederick Warne, unless indicated otherwise.) The catalogue *Beatrix Potter: The V & A Collection* by Anne Stevenson Hobbs and Joyce Irene Whalley (London: Victoria and Albert Museum and Warne, 1985) similarly devotes several sections to Potter's natural history studies. Margaret Lane's biography, *The Magic Years of Beatrix Potter* (1978), offers pointed discussion of Potter's illustrations and writing, particularly as her career progressed and her writing declined, and Judy Taylor focuses on Potter as a countrywoman and conservationist in *Beatrix Potter: Artist, Storyteller, and Countrywoman* (1986). See also Judy Taylor, Joyce Irene Whalley, Anne Stevenson Hobbs, and Elizabeth M. Battrick, *Beatrix Potter 1866–1943: The Artist and Her World* (1987). The crowds attending the 1988 exhibition of "Beatrix Potter: Artist and Storyteller" at London's Tate Gallery and New York's Pierpont Morgan Library attest to the unprecedented popularity of Potter's art.

2. In *Art,* Linder notes that Potter's certificate was "of Second Grade," x. Lane questions exactly what the Art Student's Certificate actually meant during that time period; *Magic Years,* 39–40.

3. On the day of Millais's death (August 13, 1896), Potter, then age 30, recalled in her journal her overwhelming fear of Millais as a child, her growing affection for the artist, and his one compliment; quoted in *The Journal of Beatrix Potter* (1966), 418. From age 15, Potter kept a journal in secret code, which Linder decoded and translated. Although it does not contain anything particularly revelatory, it enriches an understanding of Potter's thoughts and aspirations.

4. Ibid., 54.

5. Ibid., 16.

6. Ibid., 27–28.

7. Lane, *Magic Years,* 57.

8. Potter, *Journal,* 405.

9. Ibid., 414.

10. Lane discussed the appraisal of Potter's art by the scientists of Kew in *Magic Years,* 45–47.

11. The paper was read on April 1, 1897, by George Massee, the same man who received Potter coolly at Kew. Neither Lane nor Taylor comment on the paper's reception. Linder adds that the paper was never published (and is now lost) because Potter asked for its withdrawal, presumably for further research; *Art,* 133. Potter's discovery was later proved correct.

12. Helen Goodman, "Women Illustrators of the Golden Age of American Illustration," *WAJ* (S/S 1987), 14. Goodman discusses six women artists' contributions to American illustration during its Golden Age (1880–1914).

13. See Elaine Showalter, *A Literature of Their Own: British Women Artists From Bronte to Lessing* (Princeton, N.J.: Princeton University, 1977), 20. Although Showalter uses birthdates between 1840 to 1860 to identify the third generation of feminine novelists, she includes Potter, b. 1866, in her Biographical Appendix, 343.

14. Potter, *Journal,* 357. Potter actually made this comment at Lennel in 1894, aware that the encroaching winter would temporarily interrupt her fungus studies. Lane similarly perceives this statement as an expression of her determination to pursue her naturalist art in a different forum following her rejection by Kew; *Magic Years,* 47.

15. In *The History of the Writings of Beatrix Potter* (1971), Linder integrates salient illustrations within his chapters on the history of specific tales, and in *Art* he mentions a few of Potter's plant studies and still lifes associated with her books. However, he does not pursue this important insight or posit that she returned to these studies for her book illustrations. In a section entitled "Background for Books" in *The V & A Collection,* Hobbs and Whalley juxtapose rough drafts of book illustrations with naturalist studies. Desiring accuracy, they placed in this section only those naturalist studies "whose relevance to a particular book was immediately obvious." (72) Thus, they did not include a number of studies whose inclusion would have revealed the extent to which Potter's naturalist artwork informed her book illustrations. Responding to this point in a 1987 correspondence, Hobbs affirmed that many more of Potter's natural history studies are associated with her illustrated books than noted in the 1985 catalogue.

16. See *The Tale of Two Bad Mice* (1904), for example, where the mice Hunca Munca and Tom Thumb raid a doll's house, and *The Tale of Mrs. Tiggy-Winkle* (1905), in which Mrs. Tiggy-Winkle the hedgehog lives in a human house and has a human occupation: she launders other animals' clothing.

17. For more discussion of Potter's artistic technique, see Hobbs's and Whalley's chapters 2–4 in *Beatrix Potter 1866–1943.*

18. Several squirrel sketches and watercolors are included in Linder, *Art,* 154–55.

19. Beatrix Potter, *The Tale of Squirrel Nutkin* (1903), 37.

20. Linder, *Art,* 18. Linder includes many examples of Potter's early naturalist studies in the section "Early Work."

21. For the illustration of Nutkin playing "marbles" with oak apples,

see *Squirrel Nutkin,* 28–29; for ''ninepins'' with fir cones, 42–43. The mushrooms in the former are conspicuously positioned below Nutkin.

22. Linder, *Art,* 144. Linder includes this in the section ''Microscopic Work and Drawings of Fungi.''

23. In *Modern Painters* (5 vols., 1843–60), John Ruskin noted the similarities between the Pre-Raphaelite approach to natural detail and natural history studies. For more discussion of leading Victorian naturalists and the relationship between Pre-Raphaelite art and natural history, see Lynn L. Merrill's ''Natural History'' in Sally Mitchell, ed., *Victorian Britain: An Encyclopedia* (New York: Garland, 1988), 530–32.

24. However, Potter reveals a degree of inconsistency in her rendering of rabbits. Sometimes the rabbits look like stuffed animals, and in an illustration for *Benjamin Bunny* (1904) that shows Peter and Benjamin gathering onions (31), Peter's chubby figure, hand gestures, and upright posture are humanlike. But the illustration in *Peter Rabbit* (1902) that shows Peter lying unclothed outside the rabbit hole (45) reveals Potter's understanding of natural rabbit posture and skill at drawing precise anatomical detail.

25. Beatrix Potter, *The Tale of Mr. Jeremy Fisher* (1906), 28–29.

26. Linder, *Art,* 136–38. Linder includes several microscopic studies of ground and water beetles composed during the 1880s.

27. See, for instance, the watercolor and pen-and-ink illustration, ''Waterlilies: a close-up view of leaves and flowers amongst reeds'' in Hobbs and Whalley, *The V & A Collection,* 31–33.

28. Potter, *Jeremy Fisher,* 46.

29. Linder reproduces ''Sketches of Frogs,'' a pencil study showing frogs in different positions and postures, which is among the drawings Potter recalled for this illustration; *History,* 178.

30. Potter, *Jeremy Fisher,* cover illustration and p. 12. In the latter illustration, the plant life surrounding the doorway lends naturalism to the human home that Jeremy inhabits.

31. Quoted in Linder, *History,* 175.

32. W. P. K. Findlay, *Wayside and Woodland Fungi* (1967). The book was reprinted by Warne in 1978.

33. Potter, *Journal,* 106.

ILLUSTRATORS, BOOKS, AND CHILDREN: AN ILLUSTRATOR'S VIEWPOINT
Celia Berridge

In recent years, there has been a revival of the debate among literary critics and children's book reviewers on the central issue of how to define and evaluate children's literature. The argument has produced some splendid controversy (see *Signal* Nos. 14,[1] 15[2] and 16;[3] and *Children's Literature in Education* 14[4] for example). One crucial strand in the debate has been the relevance or otherwise to the reviewer of children's possible responses. This article is not the place for an account of the historical background, but certainly the argument has rumbled on intermittently ever since Arthur Ransome declared in 1937, "You write not for children but for yourself."

The controversy provoked by this artist-centered approach has encompassed the genre of children's picture books, and some illustrators have become frequent targets for criticism, especially from educationists. Brian Alderson also has concerned himself with "the irrelevance of children to the children's book reviewer"—see his article of that title[5] and his famous catalogue for the 1973 National Book League exhibition, *Looking at Picture Books.*[6] I want to look at this debate from an illustrator's point of view.

It is rare for an individual writer or illustrator to reply to criticism. Charles Keeping[7,8] is an interesting exception. His discussion of his own work is very different from that of, for example, Trevor Stubley.[9] The difference stems partly from the fact that Stubley illustrates other people's texts exclusively,

Reprinted with permission from *Children's Literature in Education,* V. 11, No. 1, 1980, pp. 21–30.

whereas Keeping writes his own picture books, as well as illustrating those of other writers. When an illustrator writes his or her own words, the mental approach to the task of illustrating is subtly different: one assumes the author's stance of addressing oneself to an audience, as well as being involved in the construction of the book, trimming the plot to fit into 32 pages, and so on. The illustrator has total control over the creation of the book, and total responsibility too.

To consider the role of the picture book illustrator in relation to children, I'd like to sidetrack for a moment, turn to educational psychology, and consider by way of analogy Arthur Applebee's model for relationships between writer and reader.[10] In his doctoral thesis, drawing upon the theory of spectator role in children's developing knowledge of the conventions of stories which James Britton had outlined, Applebee suggested a three-part model consisting of: the author or speaker; the discourse or story itself; and the audience or responder. This gives us three relationships: author-discourse; author-responder and responder-discourse. Each of the three elements generates its own conventions or "systems of constructs"; hence, evaluations depend on whose perspective is adopted. This last point is significant. Traditionally, literary criticism has consisted mainly of values, ideologies, and concepts thought to pertain solely to the book itself—or discourse—as if it existed in isolation. In fact the reviewer or critic is in the position of the third relationship: responder-discourse.

I think Applebee's model can be adapted to study the position of the illustrator. When he/she is illuminating someone else's words, the illustrator feels wholly absorbed in the first relationship—in this case, illustrator-discourse. The task is to find images for the words, and the most appropriate medium and technique to realize these images. But if the illustrator is making the whole of a book, words and all, he or she is in an equivalent position to an author engaged in the first and second relationships simultaneously. An author may well be writing *for* himself, but presumably he's not talking *to* himself. The end product is intended to be read by someone else eventually, and this is so for illustrators too. It means that an illustrator *must* be accommodating his/her graphic execution to the child viewer in some way, whether consciously or not. Why else should there be a distinctly different

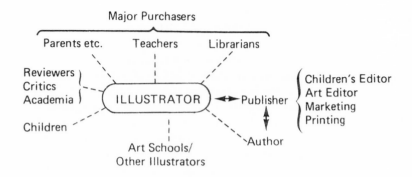

FIGURE 1

style of illustration in children's books? Compare the graphic styles in comics for teenagers with those in comics for five-year-olds; the adaptations *by the artists* are clearly visible.

"An artist, like a writer, is, of course, always entitled to say that he does the work he has it in him to do, and what becomes of it afterwards is not his business," wrote John Rowe Townsend.[11] But he went on to say that it is not possible, nevertheless, for anyone whose work appears on a children's list to work without "a special sense of audience." Yet many picture book illustrators hotly dispute that they do this.

It is at art school that many would-be illustrators first absorb the professional values and attitudes that will color their subsequent working life.

Graphic design courses are an uneasy mixture of Fine Arts values—personal freedom of expression, self-exploration, etc.—supposedly independent aesthetic standards of assessing work, and design objectives of "problem-solving," meeting the client's needs, and fulfilling the brief. Probably the degree of emphasis on Fine Arts values or graphic design practicalities varies from college to college at any given time. But the art student enters a college world in which complex and often contradictory attitudes seem to be held by the teachers, but where, nevertheless, there seems always to be an underlying, unspoken tacit agreement about ways and standards of evaluating artwork.

The student's visual discrimination and taste become more sophisticated, even idiosyncratic; his/her standards of execution become increasingly perfectionist, although some of the ideas acquired at this time may be subsequently modified by experience. And when, as an illustrator, he/she becomes increasingly absorbed into the world of the professionals, there grows the inevitable gap between those who are highly involved inside an expertise and the ordinary public outside. Graphic design students are now trained to be competent in many areas of design, the assumption being that they may find work in anything from record covers to book jackets, TV graphics to book layout or typography, label and package design to toy design. (I wonder how many reviewers realize that a book illustrator may be doing other quite different kinds of work—Nicola Bayley and Alan Baker do advertisements, for instance.)

Illustrating is a craft; it is applied art, and that means, among other things, accepting the restraints imposed by the discipline of doing a picture for someone else, not just for yourself. That ''someone else'' may be an art editor acutely aware of what is likely to prove popular out there in the bookstores. That is not to say that illustrators are expected by the publisher to show their drawings to children as they work! The professional people involved in the business make informed guesses, based on experience, about what is the best, most appropriate presentation of a story. Short of testing every book at proof stage on a representative sample of not less than one thousand children (half boys, half girls; one-third inner city, one-third suburban, one-third rural; using teams of trained interviewers and calculating the results statistically, eliminating any possibility of bias), there is no accurate way to predict whether an individual book is going to prove popular with children or adults. Publishers make guesses; publishing is a gamble. So when a reviewer knocks a book for its probable lack of appeal to children—''. . . is unlikely to interest those inner-city kids it's intended for . . .''—or makes *any* kind of assumption about children's responses to the pictures—''. . . stirring stuff, Matilda thinks—children likewise, who aren't bothered by the sub-Scarry illustrations and forced ideas . . .''[12]—two thoughts spring to my mind: first, how does the reviewer know? and second, how is the illustrator supposed to know?

Consider the picture-book illustrator's working world. In diagram form, I suppose it looks something like Figure 1. Of all these interested parties, the only ones the illustrator will definitely meet are the publisher's children's book editor and art editor and occasionally another illustrator. But until the National Book League recently compiled a list of authors and artists willing to give talks about their work, very few illustrators ever met parents, teachers, librarians, or academics. They worked in happy oblivion.

And what about children? Brian Wildsmith claims never to show his work to his own family. Raymond Briggs summed up the attitude of many illustrators in a recent interview: "I'm not really aware of liking or disliking kids, but in general I do not choose to be with them. This does not affect my work. I write and I draw and then the publisher tells me that it is suitable for children of various ages."[13]

So to a large extent, the illustrator is locked in an isolated dialogue with the words and form of the book. And yet I believe that there is always some consideration of the audience, this ghostly circle of children for whom either the illustrator makes subtle accommodations in style, or towards whose supposed taste the illustrator's style naturally leans.

The business of deciding for what age a book is suitable is less clear than it might seem. For example, Alan Garner's *Red Shift*[14]—although it is written in words and sentences simple enough to be read by my seven-year-old daughter when I showed it to her—has a plot and structure far too complex for her to grasp yet and deals with emotions which will not be part of her experience for some time. I think that one can only guess a book's lower age limit, both in terms of content and technical accessibility. Like adults, children need in their reading some books which are safe, undemanding, and very easy; a lot of books which are just about on their current level of development; and constant encounters with books just that little bit too hard for them, so that mentally they have to stretch out towards them.

Naturally this applies to picture books, and publishers try to build up their children's lists so as to cater to these simultaneous needs. But an illustrator who likes to be innovative and to explore new forms within the picture-book convention is in danger of being accused of using picture books to explore his/her own artistic development. The defence argument (Keeping again!) is that picture-books form part of a child's early art experience as well as book experience, and that being fresh, open-minded, and naturally experimental, children are less likely than adults to have rigid expectations of what should be in a book. Moreover, artists know more about their area than the general public and play a part in developing public taste. It is not an illustrator's job to take note of uninformed criticism, yet, paradoxically, the mass of critics (and purchasers) are amateur, untrained nonartists. So do we give them what they want, or do we stretch them a little?

Here is Jean Renoir discussing his father's disappointment when the public failed to appreciate his work, for Renoir père had had great faith in the good taste and natural discernment of ordinary people:

> Ultimately it is the public which, after a long period of assimilation, renders the final verdict. . . . This tardiness in making people accept the evolution of art, literature, music and even thought, frightened Renoir. . . . This evolution is slowed down by mass media, for example the press, which must provide its readers with material which does not startle them. The artist is obliged, in consequence, to take refuge in an ivory tower among a little band of admirers. Renoir frankly disapproved. "It quickly degenerates into a mutual-admiration society, and you're done for." My father hoped his works would last long enough to be judged by the public at the propitious moment. His hopes have certainly been fulfilled.[15]

Lucky Renoir. Poor illustrator—whose art is strictly for immediate consumption! In today's market, the illustrated picture book is hardly an appropriate arena for artistic pioneers. On the whole, the illustrator produces what both he/she and the publisher think will be popular and sell. The illustrator knows the job is a craft—but the purist critic/reviewer tends to judge the end-product by supposed Fine Arts values, ignoring the functional aspects. So, given the fact that critics are divided anyway on the issue of relevance, how much should an illustrator consider it while working?

So long as the debate remains theoretical, it continues revolving in the same old grooves. One way of moving forward would be to consider the known facts of children's needs and picture preferences—i.e., research carried out so far. Mentioning the relevance of "depth psychology" applied to children's reading, C. S. Hannabuss writes, ". . . there's a need to take psychology into account. You can't leave it out, for instance, in assessing a young child's experience of picture books."[16]

The trouble is, you can't easily use it either. I don't mean the solid background of Piaget, Bruner, the Gibsons and so on. I mean the papers on research into "children's preferences in illustration" and the like. There is often a lack of clarity in thinking among researchers about the purpose of the research; this leads them to draw inferences from the findings that are not applicable in another context. There is often also a carelessness in distinguishing different functions for various kinds of illustrations, so that incompatible pictures are lumped together in the experimental method. You cannot compare unlike with unlike, and you cannot generalize from slipshod findings.

From Rudisill in 1952[17] to Hutt in 1976[18] and Smerdon in 1977[19] the same fault persists: that of generalizing from data obtained in an artificial testing situation because of the need to restrict the variables in the interest of scientific objectivity. The funniest example I can think of is Child, Hansen, and Hornbeck,[20] who studied age and sex differences in children's color preferences by showing children bits of colored paper, then generalized from their findings to recommend, for example, that children's textbooks should have red covers. Many researchers pick stimulus material to represent different graphic styles from widely differing sources, ignoring its precise intended function. For example, Hutt chose three kinds of illustration: a cartoon or representational illustration; some "abstract designs" from a Sunday color magazine intended for adults; and some "realistic pictures," whatever that means. All these were "assessed as roughly comparable," Bloomer[21] acknowledged the different purposes of his stimulus material, then proceeded to ignore this factor.

Not counting reading research, during the last year I have read over forty papers on children's responses to pictures in various kinds of tests. The only ones I could envisage an illustrator finding helpful have been the least "scientific," such as Rump and Southgate's study of children looking at pictures in an exhibition,[22] and the Crago's current study of their daughter and her picture books,[23] a similar exercise to the still unsurpassed account by Dorothy Neal White, *Books Before Five*.[24] There is also an excellent study by Sharon White of children's responses to illustrations depicting characters of various races.[25] What makes these studies useful is that they treat the stimulus material in its real-life context, and the subjects of the experiments—the children—are similarly in their natural settings. We need many more such studies where the research is less esoteric and more applicable to other situations; less concerned with artificial constraints in the name of scientific rigour and more concerned with finding out what children think and feel in normal circumstances. "When you are working in the field, not the laboratory, your obligation is to be as rigorous as the situation will permit," wrote Lionel Elvin.[26]

We need some good research into pictures for children in "transactional modes" to use Harding's phrase—that is, we do need to know more about the effectiveness of illustrations in functional contexts such as reading primers, textbooks, instructional leaflets, and so on, so that they may be better designed in the future. But I wonder whether a so-called objective enquiry is the right approach to discovering those elements in a picture book which affect a child's response. Until some research or study has been documented sensibly, neither critics nor educationists nor psychologists can pronounce on children's picture preferences, in or out of picture books.

Much of the above-mentioned research was carried out with the aim of discovering principles underlying the effectiveness of graphics in learning materials. Even so, it's impossible to extrapolate from all the various findings a prescription for illustrators to follow in either information books or fiction, and I detect a strong urge on the part of the researchers to prescribe. You simply can't vet every book in the country and produce a correct formula: "Who can say what is the right book for the right child? That, thank God, is the child's own adventure."[27] Which brings me back to illustrators and children, because for there to be freedom of choice, there must also be availability.

One of the undercurrents in the relevance debate has been the issue raised by the Children's Rights Group: that many children's books are racist, sexist, or anti-working class by default—that by simply not depicting the despised group, the author reveals his/her bias. Publishers have begun actively seeking stories which are less middle-class largely in response to the economic power of schools and libraries, their main customers. So far, though, illustrators have not been much involved in this. Caldecott and Greenaway in the last century drew children from a largely mythical era some fifty years before their own time, and illustrators have tended to do the same ever since. What a sentimental, escapist bunch we are! Each year, out of well over 250 new picture books, fewer than 20 will be illustrated with recognizably realistic contemporary settings. City settings are even rarer than rural ones. Why has "Mother Goose comes to Cable Street" taken two hundred years to appear?[28]

I suspect it has something to do with artists' heightened perception and greater sensitivity towards visual ugliness, plus conventions about books absorbed as children, mixed with notions about beauty acquired at art school. Artists aren't the only people who find cities ugly places in which to live. There is a wave of romanticism about "the country" everywhere just now. Personally I've always liked cities and town centers. One of my favorite childhood memories is of wet pavements reflecting the lights from shop windows late on a winter afternoon, and this is the kind of visual memory I like to use in my own picture books. I believe that young children are very observant: if they live in towns, they notice all sorts of funny things about buildings and vehicles and those slices of vistas you get looking down a narrow street with tall buildings on either side. Rows of shopfronts, crowded markets, busy docksides and disused ones, crumbling old houses all have their own beauty; and so do modern children dressed in chainstore clothes, doing all the daft things children do. There is no need to idealize it: let's just make the choice available so that those children who live in towns and want to see their kind of life mirrored in a book can do so. If illustrators would only be a little more consciously aware of their child audience, we wouldn't have quite such a gross imbalance in book content. This is one aspect of the relevance debate about which artists should take notice.

In summary, the question of the relevance of children's responses to the evaluation of books must be faced and sorted out by examining the criteria of criticism and by considering the available evidence from both marketing and academic research.

The evidence of research must be carefully scrutinized: findings must be considered in the light of the research method and their appropriateness in a wider context. Shortcomings must be acknowledged, and better research approaches adopted. Experimental research may prove to be more suitable for non-fiction and learning materials than fiction.

Studies of children's responses to fiction must not attempt to straitjacket it in a mistaken pursuit of scientific objectivity. Let's consider the possibility that we can have "communication without necessarily explicit understanding."[29]

Illustrators must stop pretending that they make no concessions towards their child audience and stop being ashamed of it, as though it were some kind of awful weakness that debased one's status as an artist. Whether one sees oneself as an *artist* or as a *craftsman* is probably what causes the confusion.

There should be much more contact between all the various interested parties, with less prejudice all round. Let psychologists visit art schools, critics meet artists, illustrators go into primary schools, publishers meet parents, etc. After all, books are for everybody's children—aren't they?

NOTES

1. J. R. Townsend, "Standards of Criticism," *Signal,* 14 (1974), 91–105.

2. Peter Hunt, "Criticism and Children's Literature, *Signal,* 15 (1974), 117–130.

3. Bob Leeson, "To the Toyland Frontier," *Signal,* 16 (1975), 18–25.

4. N. Tucker, "Looking at Pictures," *Children's Literature in Education,* No. 14 (1974), 37–51.

5. Brian Alderson, "The Irrelevance of Children to the Children's Book Reviewer," *Children's Book News,* 4, No. 1 (1965), 10–11.

6. Brian Alderson, *Looking at Picture Books* (London: National Book League, 1973).

7. Charles Keeping, "Illustration in Children's Books," *Children's Literature in Education,* No. 1 (1970), 41–54.

8. "Charles Keeping—Illustrator," *School Bookshop News,* 8 (1977), 16–18.

9. Trevor Stubley, "Illustrating Children's Books," *Growing Point,* 15 (1976), 2996–3002.

10. Arthur Applebee, "The Spectator Role: Theoretical and Developmental Studies of Ideas About, and Responses to Literature, with Special Reference to Four Age Levels," Ph.D. Thesis, London University, 1974.

11. J. R. Townsend, *Written for Children,* 2nd ed. (London: Kestrel, 1974).

12. Geraldine Carter, "From Sad to Zany," *Guardian,* 29 September 1978, p. 9.

13. Linda Christmas, "Coming Clean with the Snowman," *Guardian,* 7 September 1978, p. 9.

14. Alan Garner, *Red Shift* (London: Collins, 1973).

15. Jean Renoir, *Renoir, My Father* (London: Collins, 1962).

16. C. S. Hannabuss, "Review of *The Cool Web,*" *Signal,* 23 (1977), 88–90.

17. M. Rudisill, "Children's Preferences of Colour Versus Other Qualities in Illustrations," *Elementary School Journal,* 52 (1952), 444–451.

18. C. Hutt, B. Forrest, and J. Newton, "Visual Preferences of Children," *Journal of Child Psychology and Psychiatry,* 17 (1976), 63–68.

19. G. Smerdon, "Children's Preferences in Illustration," *Children's Literature in Education* No. 20 (1977), 17–31.

20. I. Child, J. Hansen, and F. Hornbeck, "Age and Sex Differences in Children's Colour Preferences," *Child Development* 39 (1968), 21–27.

21. Richard Bloomer, "Children's Preferences and Responses as Related to Styles and Themes of Illustration," *Elementary School Journal* 60 (1960), 334–340.

22. E. Rump and V. Southgate, "Variables Affecting Aesthetic Appreciation in Relation to Age," *British Journal of Educational Psychology* 37 (1967), 58–72.

23. M. Crago and H. Crago, *One Child and Her Books,* (in press).

24. Dorothy Neal White, *Books Before Five* (Auckland: New Zealand Council for Educational Research, 1954).

25. Sharon White, "A Study of the Relationship Between Racial Illustrations Accompanying Stories in Basal Readers and Children's Preferences for These Stories," Ed. Diss. SUNY at Buffalo, 1972.

26. Lionel Elvin, *The Place of Commonsense in Educational Thought* (London: Unwin, 1977).

27. Mrs. Miller, *Horn Book* Editorial, quoted by P. Heins in V. Haviland, *Children and Literature: Views and Reviews* (London: Bodley Head, 1973), p. 406.

28. R. Stones and A. Mann, *Mother Goose Comes to Cable Street* (London: Kestrel, 1978).

29. Frank Eyre, *British Children's Books in the Twentieth Century* (London: Longmans, 1971), p. 146.

CODA

A NOTE FOR LIBRARIANS: SOMETHING TO MAKE US ILL
William Studwell

For the sake of simplification, the Library of Congress, in *Cataloging Service Bulletin* 44:21, 24 (Spring 1989), made several significant policy changes affecting descriptive cataloging. The most controversial of these new policies related to rules 2.5C1 and 2.5C2, the notation of illustration in the physical description (300) field.

For most books, the revised rules only allowed for three notations in the 300 field, "ill.," "ill. (some col.)," and "col. ill." If a book entirely or predominantly consisted of a specific type of illustration, for instance, maps in an atlas, rule 2.5C6, which was unchanged, still allowed notation like "chiefly col. maps" or "all maps." But in the majority of cases revised rules 2.5C1 and 2.5C2 applied, creating an overly simplistic and potentially misleading situation.

In a response to LC's shift in this matter, this author wrote a brief essay, "Something to Make Us Ill: LC's New Policy on 'ill.'," which proposed some modifications (*RTSD Newsletter* 14, no. 6:65–66 [1989]). The essay suggested that for those books containing many portraits, music examples, and/or maps, but with text predominating, it should be permissible to use the notations "ports.," "music," and "maps" plus the variants describing the presence of color. In other words, obvious situations of multiple portraits, music examples, and/or maps, should be represented by specific notation rather than the vague, general term "ill." These three types of illustration were singled out because it was felt that they were the most important of the various kinds which appear in books.

But the matter didn't end there. In the very next issue of the same publication, now renamed *ALCTS Newsletter* (possibly due to a certain piece in the previous issue), a response to this author's response was printed. The second article, by a New York City cataloger, partially agreed with the first article but felt that the suggestion offered for portraits, music, and maps should also be extended to facsimiles, genealogical tables, and other types of illustrations. That is, when there were a lot of a specific type of illustration present, it should be notated in the 300 field. This idea, if adopted, would have mostly eliminated the simplification intended by LC in its directive.

Soon after, Ben Tucker, Chief of the Office for Descriptive Cataloging Policy at LC, sent a letter to this author. The February 2, 1990 letter, written in response to the "Something to Make Us Ill" article, stated, among other things, that LC because of pressure would partially rescind the policies spelled out in *Cataloging Service Bulletin* 44. The only change affecting illustration, however, was the allowance once again of the terminology "map," "maps," and their variations indicating color. The policy statements in Tucker's letter were later officially promulgated in a *Cataloging Service Bulletin.*

This entire scenario was reviewed in yet another article by this author, "Much Ado About Maps" (*Western Association of Map Libraries Information Bulletin* 21, no. 3:167 [June 1990]). Several months after that, the present essay was assembled. Yet in spite of all the words and heat produced, LC's 1989 decisions affecting the notation of illustration still remain mostly intact. Those policies are definitely too simplistic and should be modified to provide a clearer picture of the types and extent of illustration in each book.

If the abundance of writings about this issue has not made you a little sick, then the continuance of these "ill." policies by LC should provide a non-ending irritant to keep all of us more than a bit ill.

BIBLIOGRAPHY

THE BEST: A SELECTIVE BIBLIOGRAPHY OF THE HISTORY OF THE ILLUSTRATED BOOK

The books, monographs, articles, studies, reports and, yes, even films and videos on the history of the illustrated book are impressive in number, if not always in quality. By 1991 there were close to 3,000 items, published primarily in the 20th century, which are major contributions to such a history. The amount of material is much greater when one considers ancillary subjects from the development of the codex to paleography and computer books.

Experts, as in all fields, concentrate on a small, relatively easy to circumscribe subject section of the illustrated book. Laypersons and students, to whom this compendium primarily is directed, either become bogged down in the countless books and articles, or, more likely, search about for a single work which covers the topic and, if they wish, points them in the direction of specialization.

The purpose of the following bibliography is to limit, to control. Limit by annotating only books, and control by holding the choices down to a mere 30 titles published in English. Works on individual artists, publishers and printers are not included, although many of these are quite superior for the advanced student.

This list is primarily for the beginner, for the individual who wants an accurate overview of the primary subject areas on the history of the book.

It is an evaluative and descriptive bibliography of only the best—best in terms of coverage, style and scholarship. The designation is determined primarily by the author, although without exception the titles are supported by previous reviews, comments and use as being primary in an overcrowded field.

The number is somewhat arbitrary, but the selection does reflect the needs of students and laypersons seeking a firm grounding.

First are the basic bibliographies in the field. Here, of course, one may turn for detailed analyses of what is available in both broad and narrow subject areas. Again, however, only the basic bibliographies are listed, and most particularly those published in the past decade.

A. BASIC BIBLIOGRAPHIES

Banks, Doris. *Medieval Manuscript Bookmaking: A Bibliographic Guide.* Metuchen, NJ: Scarecrow Press, 1989. 290p.

In two parts, with the second section listing in alphabetical order, but without annotations, 1,044 books and articles on the medieval manuscript. The first half is a seven-part discussion closely tied to the second section, which moves from medieval libraries to particular types of works such as science and technology. While most of this deals with the process of making books rather than with illustration *per se,* it is a basic guide for anyone who has need for a current bibliography on the subject. The first section is a good, popular history of medieval books, and is quite suitable for students and laypersons.

Best, James J. *American Popular Illustration; A Reference Guide.* Westport, CT: Greenwood Press, 1984. 174p.

While not limited to books, this group of bibliographic essays has the advantage of covering the primary illustrators from about 1800 to the present. There are six chapters, with some 2,000 items: historical background; aesthetics of American illustration; a listing of major bibliographies and books on the subject; major illustrators; illustration techniques; and ''the social and artistic context of illustration.'' The scope is limited to the popular press. There is a good index of illustrators, but it is of limited value for subjects. Although useful as a guide to additional readings, its value lies in its emphasis on individual illustrators and in one of three appendices— to collections of illustrated materials in various parts of the United States, and illustrated books liked by illustrators.

Brenni, Vito Joseph. *Book Illustration and Decoration: A Guide to Research,* Westport, CT: Greenwood Press, 1980. 191p.

A bibliography, this lists (without annotations) some 2,000 articles, books, monographs, etc. which are concerned with the techniques and the aesthetics of book illustration. These are in English as well as German, French, Italian, etc. Arrangement is in eleven categories. The chapters are: reference works, book decoration; manuals of illustration and other writings on techniques; history of methods of illustration; history of book illustration from ancient times to the present day; history of book illustration and decoration in the countries of the world; and children's book illustration. The last four sections cover illustration of scientific, medical, music, and geography and history. Individual artists are not included. There is an author and a subject index. Anyone fishing for not only common but out-of-the-way citations may find them here, particularly in the general history of book illustration, which is subdivided by type and by century. The major fault is that the coverage is too diffuse and, in trying to do all, the author offers too many areas of only limited interest to the history of illustration expert.

Marantz, Sylvia and Kenneth Marantz. *The Art of Children's Picture Books; A Selective Reference Guide.* New York: Garland, 1988. 165p.

A 451-item bibliography, this is in six parts covering books, articles and audiovisuals on children's picture books. A seventh section is a description of 15 institutions with large research collections in this area. Each item is annotated briefly. There are artist, title and author-editor-compiler indexes. The problems are obvious: too much is attempted and there is no real focus. Be that as it may, it is a useful bibliography for someone looking for out-of-the way materials.

B.   THE BEST 30 BOOKS ON THE HISTORY OF BOOK ILLUSTRATION

Bader, Barbara. *American Picturebooks from Noah's Ark to the Beat Within.* New York: Macmillan, 1976. 615p.

This is a brief examination and history of American picture-books published since the 1905 *Noah's Ark* by E. B. Smith. The author traces the way picturebooks have changed over almost a century and how they reflect the social aspects of childhood. In addition there are sketches of all the primarily illustrators, in-depth explanations of various techniques, as well as everything from the role of the publisher to the psychologist in the development of the form. There are some 700 illustrations, of which 300 are in color. These are quite good. The author's enthusiasm is sometimes ahead of her sentence construction. But while much of it is a trifle hard to read, it is worth the effort because of the amount of data collected and, here and there, original viewpoints about sometimes lesser known illustrators. As one of the more comprehensive studies of American picturebooks, it deserves a first place in almost any collection and certainly is among the top ten when the collection is limited to children's books.

Benesch, Otto. *Artistic and Intellectual Trends from Rubens to Daumier as Shown in Book Illustration.* Cambridge, MA: Harvard University Press, 1943. 176p.

The "slightly revised text of three lectures which Dr. Otto Benesch, former Chief Curator of the Albertina Museum in Vienna, gave . . . for the friends of the Harvard Library." The three lectures include: "Rubens, Callot and Rembrandt"; "Major and Minor Masters of the Baroque"; and "Reality and Fiction, Eighteenth and Nineteenth Centuries." There are 11 pages of notes and 66 black-and-white illustrations. The theme is sounded in the first line: "The history of the illustrated book constitutes a chapter in the development of the graphic arts to which many lovers and even connoisseurs of prints give less attention than it merits." All major figures are covered in the first and third chapters, but the third may be the more interesting for its notes on minor artists. A basic essay for anyone who wishes to understand the intellectual aspects of book illustration.

Bland, David. *A History of Book Illustration: The Illuminated Manuscript and the Printed Book.* Cleveland, OH: World Publishing Co., 1958. 514p. (2nd rev. ed. Berkeley: University of California Press, 1969).

The best single, popular history of the illustrated book, this has

the advantage of being well written and nicely (if not sumptu-
ously) illustrated. Despite the subtitle, only about one-quarter of
the work is devoted to early illustration and illumination. Most of
the focus, which gives it a particular value, is on illustration from
the advent of printing. Arrangement is by the time period and by
country. Bland gives a nod to the Orient, but most of the emphasis
is on Western illustration. The format, in any of the editions, is
pleasing and the writing style consistently good. While experts
will fault Bland for sometimes skipping over important areas and
artists, the average layperson will be grateful for his ability to
cover so much with such ease. Among the first four or five basic
titles in any collection of this type; and a first for the average
individual with an interest in the subject.

Bliss. Douglas. *History of Wood-Engraving.* New York: Dutton,
1928. 263p.
    A classic, this English history of the art of wood engraving
remains one of the best of its type even though it is over 50 years
old. It offers easy-to-understand information on the development
and techniques of wood engraving from the 15th century through
the early 20th. There are 120 excellent black-and-white illustrations ''from Dürer to Paul Nash.'' Almost all of the examples are
discussed by the author who was, not incidentally, a notable wood
engraver. Based upon his experience and his appreciation of the
problems involved with the use of wood engravings in books,
Bliss is able to offer the layperson a concise, easy to follow
explanation of a major process. The real strength is not so much in
the discussions of well-known artists and engravers, but in the
minor characters and the minor problems; it offers a true history of
the subject. It is still the single best overview for laypersons.

Boston: Museum of Fine Arts. *The Artist and the Book: 1860–
1960 in Western Europe and the United States.* Boston: Museum
of Fine Arts, 1962. 232p. (Reprinted, 1972.)
    A basic title for almost any size or type of collection in this
subject area. This is a catalog, which opens with a typical entry for
Edwin Austin Abbey (1852–1911). There is about a 150-word
biographical sketch. This is about the length of all of the
descriptions of slightly over 100 artists. There are examples of one
to a half-dozen books illustrated by each individual. After a

complete bibliographical description, one finds "references" which offer contemporary comments on the particular book. Sometimes quotes are given. There are full-page and quarter-page black-and-white illustrations throughout this valuable guide to a 1961 exhibition. A five-page, two-column bibliography is as strong on individual artists as books of a more general nature. A key work for reference, this covers most of the major artists for the period as well as their titles.

Cahn, Walter. *Romanesque Bible Illumination.* Ithaca, NY: Cornell University Press, 1982. 304p.

This is a scholarly analysis, in an oversized volume, of the 11th-century illuminated Bible. There are 60 striking color plates and some 200 smaller black-and-white illustrations. The text is interwoven with the plates, and the match is consistent enough so that one usually does not have to turn back or forward to see what the author is discussing. A bonus: the first three chapters (pp. 11–90) give the background and actually are a good general overview of Bible illumination from the beginnings to the 11th century. With Chapter 5 the author turns to his primary subject and considers "themes and variations" as well as "the artists and their patrons." Another bonus: a detailed descriptive catalog, arranged by area or country, of 150 major Bibles. The author has a pleasing style and supports his views with documentation.

Calkins, Robert. *Illuminated Books of the Middle Ages.* Ithaca, NY: Cornell University Press, 1986. 341p.

Concentrating in detail on forms of the illuminated manuscript, with illustrious examples for each, this is the best beginner student guide to the subject. After short summaries of the illuminated manuscript before the insular gospel books (i.e. *The Book of Darrow, The Lindisfarne Gospels* and the *Book of Kells*), the author discusses other types up to the beginning of printing. Each of the nine chapters is divided by form (insular gospel book to the book of hours) and the primary examples of each form are analyzed in considerable detail. The concentration on a few select examples, primarily liturgical and extremely famous, gives this a different scope than DeHamel's history, which casts a wider sect. It offers more detail, more attention to fascinating trends and facts then the other general histories. Following 24 color plates, all unfortunately at the beginning of the book, there are over 150 black and white, usually full-page illustrations closely tied to the text. The annotated notes and the bibliography both serve as excellent sources of additional reading which can be considerable; e.g. the bibliography alone covers from pp. 324 to 334. It's useful for the focus on relatively recent articles.

See, too, Calkins' *Program of Medieval Illumination*. The Franklin D. Murphy Lectures V. (Kansas City, MO: Spenser Museum of Art, 1984. 158p.) Some of this material is found in the aforementioned book.

DeHamel, Christopher. *A History of Illuminated Manuscripts.* Boston: Godine, 1986. 256p.

This is the best carefully illustrated popular work on the illuminated manuscript and can be used by the student in conjunction with Calkins, although for the layperson it would be a first choice, with Calkins second. The expert at Sotheby's in London has an easy style and a thorough knowledge of the subject. The divisions are by types of readers, beginning with missionaries, and ending with "books for collectors." There are numerous, usually full-page illustrations which are closely tied to the text. Two important points: DeHamel offers a discursive bibliography (pp. 245–249) which draws upon all of the basic works, including scholarly and popular. He has judicious short comments to make about most, although not all, of the titles in the bibliography. This makes it a good place to begin a study of the literature. See *The New Yorker* profile of the author by Israel Shenker (May 29, 1989, pp. 47–68).

Gottlieb, Gerald. *Early Children's Books and Their Illustration.* Boston: Godine, 1975. 263p.

A catalog of a 1975 show, this, as many of the Morgan Library catalogs, is really a beautifully illustrated history of the subject. The Morgan's curator of early children's books (Gerald Gottlieb) offers brief introductions to the 34 sections. He has, too, a foreword which parallels an essay by the historian, J. H. Plumb. The introductory section opens with a third-century papyrus fragment and closes with Rackham's 1912 fables. The remainder of the 225 annotated books are found in sections which include everything from "The ABC's" to "Street Cries" and "Courtesy

Books.'' Most of the focus is on printed books, but some manuscripts are described. The book is nicely illustrated, although the color plates seem to be scattered at random. In all there are over 300 carefully produced illustrations—often photographs of the books. The never-to-be-found-again first editions are a fine guide for collectors. Others will profit from the descriptive matter and the detailed notes on reading and reading habits of the young and their parents.

Grabar, Andre. *Early Medieval Painting from the Fourth to the Eleventh Century.* New York: Skira, 1957.

One major section (pp. 89–219) of this general history includes ''book illumination.'' This is written by Carl Nordenfalk, has numerous illustrations and brief explanations. It's particularly useful for a broad overview of early illumination, which is not often covered in a general title.

Hamilton, Sinclair. *Early American Book Illustrators and Wood Engravers, 1670–1870.* Princeton University Library. Princeton: Princeton University Press, 1958. 265p. (Supplement, 1968. 179p.)

These are key works in any study of American illustration and illustrators. Following a 25-page, closely packed discussion of ''Early American book illustration,'' the first volume opens with 1670 and a detailed description of the ''Portrait of Richard Mather,'' our ''earliest portrait print.'' There are 192 items, some quite briefly noted, from here through the 18th century. With the 19th century, the arrangement changes from chronological order to artist and illustrator, opening with Joseph Alexander Adams and closing with John T. Young. ''No illustrator is listed who had not begun working by 1870.'' Under each there is a description of his/her work, or at least books ''illustrated for the most part with woodcuts and wood engravings in the Princeton University Library.'' The 124 black-and-white illustrations are judiciously spread throughout the volume, which concludes with indexes of illustrators and engravers, authors, and titles. The supplement picks up with item No. 1303 and includes some 700 additional works. Several points: each illustrator is given a brief biographical sketch; while the concentration is on books, periodical illustration is included, particularly in the supplement; and there are frequent references to other readings about individuals and illustrations.

Harvey, John. *Victorian Novelists and Their Illustrators.* New York: New York University Press, 1970. 240p.

Published first in England, here is a scholarly explanation of the various relationships among author, publisher, engraver and the public. The author concentrates on the works of Dickens and Thackeray and considers Thackeray's own illustrations as well as the art of Cruikshank and Phiz. The relationship between text and illustration is discussed convincingly, as is the iconography. There are some 80 drawings which make the author's point that the illustrations are such an inextricable part of the novels that it is difficult to imagine reading them without reference to the familiar art. This is one of the best studies of its type.

Hind, Arthur. *An Introduction to a History of Woodcut; with a Detailed Survey of Work Done in the Fifteenth Century.* London: Constable, 1935. 2 vols.

The basic reference work of its type, this is often simply referred to as "Hind." There are two books. The first concentrates on the history and techniques of the woodcut. The first chapter discusses "processes and materials" and the second is a "general historical survey." The origins of the woodcuts from the Netherlands to Italy are considered in the third chapter. The second volume not only includes book illustration but "contemporary single cuts" in England as well as France. There's a concluding chapter on Spain and Portugal. There is a listing by country and chronologically of the major (and many minor) examples of books with woodcuts as illustrations. The catalog gives a massive amount of necessary detail about the books, the printers and the illustrators. There are close to 500 illustrations, numerous references and a detailed bibliography. As a guide to be used by both collectors and librarians, it is without rival. The pleasant bonus is that the work is written with verve and style.

Hofer, Philip. *Baroque Book Illustration: A Short Survey from the Collection in the Department of Graphic Arts, Harvard College Library.* Cambridge, MA: Harvard University Press, 1951. 192p. (Second ed., 1970.)

This is primarily a book of rich illustrations (about 150 pages of the total). The baroque period, up to 1715, is covered in detail.

One may question the merit of some of the examples, but this is not the fault of the compiler; rather it is a matter of judgment on the part of the viewer. Which is to say that this overlooked type of illustration will not appeal to all, or to many in total. The enthusiastic text more than explains Mr. Hofer's interest and is a bid to educate the reluctant reader. The book is divided so that the baroque is first examined in total and then subdivided by variations in numerous countries. The mixture of everything from the classics to gardens is, as noted, marvelously reproduced in the fine illustrations. It is a bit special, but a delight.

See, too, his *Eighteenth Century Book Illustrations.* Los Angeles, William Andrews Clark Memorial Library: University of California, 1956. 50p. (This is a catalog of an exhibit selected by Hofer.)

Hogben, Carol (ed.) and Rowan Watson. *From Manet to Hockney: Modern Artists' Illustrated Books.* London: Victoria and Albert Museum, 1985. 380p.

Virtually every modern important Western book illustrator, from the United States to Russia, is covered in this museum catalog. With illustrations on each page, there are short entries showing examples of the work of 132 artists. The work opens with an excellent essay by Carol Hogben on the artists' books. The development of the modern illustrated work is documented and explained. Emphasis is placed, rightfully, on the pioneer work done by French publishers and artists. What is exciting is the pains the compiler has taken to show how the painters adapt their work to the book page. There is the necessary material, too, on how the V&A has helped to foster and preserve these books. No single work is better than this for an overview of modern book illustrations. What it may lack in detail it makes up with the wide scope and the excellent illustrations.

Ivins, William. *Prints and Visual Communication.* Cambridge, MA: Harvard University Press, 1953. 190p.

Although this is not directly concerned with book illustration, its mission, "to find a pattern of significance in the story of prints," is of concern to anyone interested in the illustrated book. In fact, Ivins' work has become a minor classic of sorts and is required reading for anyone who wants to go beyond a superficial view of illustrations.

After an introductory chapter on "pictorial communication," the author takes the reader chronologically from the woodblock of the fifteenth century to the late nineteenth century and the introduction of photography. The learned, sometimes a bit confusing text by the Emeritus Curator of Prints at the New York Metropolitan Museum of Art is highly personal and equally brilliant. A major drawback for researchers: no bibliography, no footnotes. His tendency to overstate the value of prints and underrate book illustration's numerous forms is a trifle discouraging, but the contribution more than counters the arguments. There are 84 black-and-white plates bunched in various parts of the book.

Note: A brief, quite easy to follow manual by the same author, with black-and-white illustrations on almost every page, covers the history of print (illustration) techniques. Except for short explanations of the illustrations and the processes involved, there is a minimum of text. This is *How Prints Look* (Boston: Beacon Press, 1943), 164p. See, also, his *Notes on Prints* (New York: Metropolitan Museum of Art, 1930) and *The Artist and the 15th Century Printer* (New York: The Tyofiles, 1940), 78p.

Jussim, Estelle. *Visual Communications and the Graphic Arts.* New York: R. R. Bowker, 1974. 364p.

Subtitled "photographic technologies in the nineteenth century," this is a basic study which shows how photography revolutionized the illustration process—both in books and in magazines. Along the way, the author examines individual artists from Frederick Remington to Howard Pyle. She demonstrates how the elimination of the middleperson (i.e. the engraver) influenced the quality and type of illustration. Possibly more important to the understanding of illustration are the chapters which consider such things as "visual information and the graphic arts" and "illustrators and the photographic media." The book is beautifully written and represents an original point of view. There are 121 black-and-white illustrations and a six-page bibliography. Essential for any personal or library collection on the history of illustration.

Kren, Thomas. *Renaissance Painting in Manuscripts, Treasures from the British Library.* New York: Hudson Hills Press, 1983. 200p.

An oversize book, this features 32 gorgeous color plates and black-and-white illustrations on nearly every page. Although appearing to be only for browsing, it is a scholarly work complete with a ten-page bibliography and footnotes for each of the three major sections. Kren writes on "Flemish manuscript illumination," is followed by Mark Evans on "Italian manuscript illumination," and Janet Backhouse concludes with "French manuscript illumination." The period covered is from 1450 to 1560, although the period differs slightly with each author. About a half-dozen to ten glorious books are featured in each part. The book is for both laypersons and scholars.

Madan, Falconer. *Books in Manuscript.* London: K. Paul, Trench, Trübner, 1893. 188p.

DeHamel considers this "still the most readable general account [of the illuminated manuscript]," but the breathless generalizations will leave many current readers less than satisfied. At the same time Madan has a winning style which is by no means dated, and his first four chapters on writing, materials and scribes is an overview of the subject for laypersons. With the fifth chapter he considers illumination, and there is a charming sixth chapter on "the blunders of scribes and their corrections." Famous libraries, famous manuscripts, literary forgeries, cataloging, and public and private records make up the other chapters. There are eight black-and-white plates. As the subtitle suggests, this is "a short introduction to their [i.e. illuminated manuscripts] study and use." As such it is still useful for the layperson with little or no knowledge of the field, as well as for the expert looking for a few odd facts and some rather excellent evaluations.

Major, A. Hyatt. *Prints and People: A Social History of Printed Pictures.* New York: Metropolitan Museum of Art & Graphic Society, 1971. Unpaged, 752 illustrations.

Beginning with the invention of paper and the first 15th-century prints, the curator of prints at the Metropolitan Museum of Art concludes with a Jasper Johns print of 1960. The more than 700 black-and-white illustrations are chronologically arranged and trace not only the artistic development of the print, but the various forms of reproduction. In his evaluation of prints and artists, the author concentrates on how illustration borrowed from and gave to our understanding of our times and self. True, there is little here on book illustration as such, but the comments on the processes and the artists (who often turned to book illustration as well as prints) make this a basic work.

Meyer, Susan E. *A Treasury of Great Children's Book Illustrators.* New York: Abrams, 1983. 272p. (Reprinted, 1990, by Arsdale.)

''Great'' is limited here to thirteen prominent illustrators from Edward Lear to N. C. Wyeth. The primary focus is on Victorians, with a nod to the early 20th century. For each illustrator there are excellent examples of book illustrations as well as essays on his/her life, times and work. The book opens with a sound essay on Victorian illustrators. Throughout there are important contributions on how the new technologies influenced the work of the individual artists. The book, itself, is beautifully illustrated and a delight to look at, as well as to read. The popular approach will appeal to beginners in the field. While the scope is limited, it is among the best of its type.

Pacht, Otto. *Book Illumination in the Middle Ages.* New York: Oxford University Press, 1987. 224p.

This splendid introduction to the development of the illuminated manuscript is highly recommended for all types of libraries. Translated into English from a lecture series by the author in 1967/68, it stresses the close relationship of text and illustration. The fascination is with the clear explanation and the countless examples of various types of illumination for different purposes. There are over 30 excellent color plates and some 200 in black and white, as well as a useful, select bibliography. See, too, the index of manuscripts by place. The organization and approach are somewhat similar to Calkins' and the two should be found on most library shelves.

Pacht's other writings in this area are outstanding: *The Rise of the Pictorial Narrative in Twelfth Century England* (Oxford: Clarendon Press, 1962); *Italian Illuminated Manuscripts from 1400 to 1550.* (Oxford: Clarendon Press, 1948), 51p.; and, with J. J. G. Alexander, *Illuminated Manuscripts in the Bodleian Library* (Oxford: Clarendon Press, 1966).

Pitz, Henry. *200 Years of American Illustration.* New York: Random House, 1977. 436p.

Here is a popular, massive (close to 900 illustrations) coffee-table-type book which does cover, as the title suggests, the history of American illustration. The work includes both magazine and book illustration from the 17th century; but as one moves into the 20th century other media are highlighted—from posters to advertisements. Of primary value to view, not to read. Some data are included about the artists, but too little for more than quick-reference purposes. Introductions by Norman Rockwell and E. Crozier.

Pitz edited or wrote a number of books on illustration, including: *The Practice of Illustration,* 1947; *Illustrating Children's Books: History, Technique, Production,* 1963; *A Treasury of American Book Illustration,* 1947.

Ray, Gordon N. *The Illustrator and the Book in England from 1790 to 1914.* New York: Oxford University Press, 1976. 336p.

While this is a catalog of a show of Ray's collection (at the Pierpont Morgan Library in 1976), it is equally an excellent overview of a major period in book illustration. There are plates and illustrations for virtually all of the 333 items listed and carefully analyzed. Ray's descriptive text is invaluable and offers numerous insights for the period as well as for individual titles, such as the effort of many artists and publishers to turn an indifferently produced book into an art object by the addition of sometimes superficial illustrations and bindings. The tension among illustrator, author and publisher is highlighted in many of the descriptions. See, too: "100 Outstanding Illustrated Books Published in England Between 1790 and 1914," a bibliography with annotations by Thomas V. Lange. This is a superb example of bookmaking in its own right. Among the most important titles in book illustration, and certainly one of the top ten for the period and country covered.

Ray, Gordon N. *The Art of the French Illustrated Book, 1700–1914.* Ithaca, NY: Cornell University Press, 1982. 2 Vols.

A catalog of a show and a companion to *The Illustrator and the Book in England from 1790 to 1914,* this traces the work of both major and minor illustrators. Each of the artists has a separate biography and most of the 450 titles mentioned are extravagantly illustrated. Often, in fact, there are original or draft drawings of the finished illustration to appear in the book. As might be expected, Ray includes information on the techniques employed as well as on the publishing of the particular titles—which includes, need one add, scrupulous and detailed bibliographical data. As an added bonus, there is considerable background information on the social and political life of France for the close to 225 years covered. And Ray, as in his other guide, writes with skill and clarity. For collectors (with a large income and luck) there is a list of the 100 outstanding illustrated books of the period. A required item for any large collection.

Slythe, R. Margaret. *The Art of Illustration, 1750–1900.* London: The Library Association, 1970. 144p.

An excellent layperson's introduction to the various illustration processes from 1750 to 1900, this is in six parts. An introductory chapter surveys the whole period, while a second section discusses the general (and some unusual) processes. The remainder of the volume is neatly divided into the wood cut and the wood engraving; the etching; the engraving; and the lithograph. There are numerous black-and-white illustrations throughout, many of which suffer from lack of clarity. This hardly detracts from the clear and easy-to-follow text, which is one of the best in terms of its easy explanation of some difficult-to-understand processes. A brief bibliography is included. As a manual of illustration techniques, at least for the period covered, this is hard to beat.

Weitenkampf, Frank. *The Illustrated Book.* Cambridge: Harvard University Press, 1938. 314p.

The author, whose love for the subject is as impressive as his ability to pass on the affection to the reader, was one of the first in this century to offer the public a general overview of illustration with due attention to scholarship. The guide, for that reason, still is useful, particularly for beginners. It opens with the advent of printing and the 15th-century wood block illustration. There is nothing on earlier illustration. Three illustrated chapters cover the 15th through the 18th centuries. There are, throughout the book, numerous black-and-white drawings and plates which are clear, but often so reduced as to be only indicative of the book illustration it represents. More than two-thirds of the discussion is about the 19th-century book, with a short chapter on children's works and a nod to the 20th century. "A List of Books," which augments the infrequent footnote references, is keyed to each of the chapters. Most references are to German and French studies. While the work is now dated, it is useful for details not covered in other standard, more recent popular histories.

Weitzmann, Kurt. *Ancient Book Illumination.* Cambridge: Harvard University Press, 1959. 230p.

The debatable premise is that numerous no longer extant Greek papyrus rolls were illustrated and that the iconography and techniques were copied by Romans and Christians and developed in early illuminated manuscripts. As there is a paucity of surviving material, and hardly a single illustration, the whole argument is a brilliant example of deduction. The systematic comparison of the available evidence comes down in favor of the author, although—and this is worth stressing—other authorities take exception to his conclusions and believe that the literary illustration came into its own only with the codex. There are some line drawings and a few plates at the end of the text. These are adequate, if not numerous. By now this work has become famous, and it is about as basic in the field of early illustration as possible.

Weitzmann, Kurt. *Studies in Classical and Byzantine Manuscript Illumination.* Chicago: University of Chicago Press, 1971. 346p.

A collection of Weitzmann's papers and previously published articles, this is arranged in chronological order from the Hellenistic period down to the 15th century and late Byzantine illumination. In addition, there is a bibliography of the author's writings, all of which have been important, if not major contributions to the literature of the illuminated manuscript. Among the topics covered in the illustrated collection: Biblical illustrations, Byzantine illumination during the early Latin period, scenes from *The Odyssey* (from a tablet), and the like. Social, literary and sometimes political history are closely tied to the author's thoughts and deductions about illustration. The influence of the classical on subsequent book illustration dominates the numerous contributions. Written over 30 years, the papers have a great consistency and attention to detail—detail which may puzzle some layreaders, but will be of value to any student of the period and the illuminated manuscript. A basic work, along with all other Weitzmann volumes.

Whalley, Joyce Irene. *A History of Children's Book Illustration.* London: John Murray, 1988. 268p.

This catalog of a show at the Victoria and Albert Museum is an excellent overview of children's illustrations from the 16th century to the present. It is generously illustrated, with examples on almost every page, and 37 of these are in color. The author has a pleasing style and in an intelligent, easy to follow fashion shows the relationship of the books to the social and economic aspects of the periods they reflect. There is much, too, on the illustrators, their techniques and their individual works. While the book is wide in scope, by the time it reaches the 18th century the concentration is primarily on English illustrators. A best of type, and a good item for almost any collection which is concerned with children's illustrated books.

AUTHOR LIST

Baines, John.
Oriental Institute
Puley Lane
Oxford OX1 2LE
England

Berridge, Celia.
Author: *Illustrators, Books and Children: An Illustrator's Viewpoint*

Boime, Albert.
1428 Colby Ave. #2
Los Angeles, CA 90025

Breitenbach, Dr. Edgar.
Author: *The Bibliography of Illustrated Books: Notes with Examples from English Book Illustration of the 18th Century*

Brewer, Daniel.
French Department
University of California
Irvine, CA 92713

Camille, Michael.
Department of Art
University of Chicago
5540 Greenwood Ave.
Chicago, IL 60637

Canham, Stephen.
Department of English
University of Hawaii at Manoa
Honolulu, HI 96822

Cave, Roderick.
Information Studies Programme
Nanyang Technological University
Singapore

Clark, Willine B.
Marlboro College
Marlboro, VT 05344

Conkey, Margaret.
Department of Anthropology
University of California
Berkeley, CA 94720

Dyson, Anthony M.
61, Hampton Road
Teddington
Middlesex, TW11 OLA, UK

Gingerich, Owen.
Harvard-Smithsonian Center for Astrophysics
60 Garden Street
Cambridge, MA 02138

Golden, Catherine.
Department of English
Skidmore College
Saratoga Springs, NY 12866

Harcourt, Glenn.
Department of Art History
University of Southern California
666 Childs Way
Los Angeles, CA 90089-0911

Henry, Dr. Francoise.
Author: *The Lindisfarne Gospels*

Hindman, Sandra.
Department of Art History
Northwestern University
254 Kresge Centennial Hall
1859 Sheridan Road
Evanston, IL 60201

Hofer, Philip.
Author: *The Early Illustrated Book: Highlights from a Lecture for Hofer Collection*
Anne Anninger
Curator of Printing and Graphic Arts
Houghton Library
Harvard University
Cambridge, MA 02138

Holtz, William.
University of Missouri
Columbia College of Arts and Sciences
Department of English
107 Tate Hall
Columbia, MO 65211

Horsfall, Nicholas.
Author: *The Origins of the Illustrated Book*

Lewis, Napthali.
Author: *Papyrus and Ancient Writing*

Life, Alan.
Department of English
University of North Carolina
Chapel Hill, NC 27514

Morris, Sarah P.
Department of Classics
University of California at Los Angeles
Los Angeles, CA 90024

O'Gorman, James F.
Wellesley College
Wellesley, MA 02181

Pantazzi, Sybille
Author: *Author & illustrator: Images in Conformation*
Michael Pantazzi
Associate Curator of European Art
National Gallery of Canada
380 Sussex Drive
P.O. Box 427, Station A
Ottawa, Ontario
K1N 9N4 Canada

Pickering, Samuel F.
English Department
University of Connecticut
Storrs, CT 06268

Seavey, Charles A.
Assistant Professor
University of Arizona
Graduate Library School
1515 East First Street
Tucson, AZ 85719

Studwell, William
Professor
Northern Illinois University
DeKalb, IL 60115-2868

Vaughan, John.
Department of Education
University of Liverpool
P.O. Box 147
Liverpool L69 3BX
England

Widman, Jeffrey P.
26899 Moody Road
Los Altos Hills, CA 94022

Willard, James F.
Author: *Occupations of the Months in Mediaeval Calendars*

INDEX

Ackermann, Rudolph, 341
Aesthetic Movement, 556–557
Aggregation sites, 13, 18
Akrotiri, 90
  architecture of, 90
  frescoes of, 90–91
Aldhelm, letter of, 146–148
Allegory in children's books, 603,
    606, 607, 610
Altamira, 3, 4, 7, 10, 12, 13, 15, 17,
    18, 20
Apianus, Petrus, 288, 294
  "Astronomicum Caesareum,"
    293, 294, 295
Archeological method, 252, 253
Architecture and Egyptian art, 50–
    51
Army (U.S.), 537
  use of illustrations, 520–522
Art, Greek
  and illustration, 65–66
  and literary texts, 66–67
Art in society, in "The Newcomes,"
    468–469, 471, 473
Artist as subordinate to author,
    587–589
Author as subordinate to artist,
    586–587
Author reaction to illustration of his/
    her works, 587–589, 591–
    592, 594–596
Authors and illustrators, rivalry and
    relations between, 585–
    600
Aviary, illustrated medieval, and the
    lay brotherhood, 202–230
Aviary, Latin, 202–230
  extant copies of, 205, 207

illustrations of, 218–222
  cedar, 218–219
  dove, 218
  palm, 218
and Latin Bestiary, 207
prologues of, 203, 208
as a text, 208–217
use of, 220–222

Bamler, Johannes, 258
Bartolozzi, Francesco, 336–338,
    340
Behavior (good and bad) in children's
    illustrations, 624
Behneseh, 29
Bestiary, Latin, 202, 203
  and integrated Aviary text, 207
  use of, 220–222
Bibliographies
  basic, 660–661
  history of book
    illustration, 661–675
Birch, Thomas, Spenser's "The
    Faerie Queene," Kent's
    illustrations for, 379–
    385
Bison, 8, 10, 20
  polychrome, 13
  polychrome, symbolism of, 15
Blake, William
  as an apprentice, 430–431
  education of, 427–429
  as an engraver, 430–431, 435–
    437
  family background, 425, 427
  "God Judging Adam," 448
    and industrial images, 448–
    449, 451

681

ABOUT THE EDITOR

BILL KATZ (Ph.D., Chicago) is Professor, School of Information Science and Policy, at the State University of New York in Albany. He is the author of the standard text on reference services, *Introduction to Reference Services,* now in its sixth edition. Currently he edits *The Reference Librarian* and *The Acquisitions Librarian* and is a former editor of *RQ* and the *Journal of Education for Librarianship.* For Scarecrow Press, he has edited *Reference and Information Services: A Reader for Today* (1982); *Reference and Information Services: A New Reader* (1986); *Reference and Information Services: A Reader for the Nineties* (1991); and from 1971 to 1988, the annual *Library Lit.—the Best of* . . . covering the years 1970 to 1987.